The West

The West

Encounters & Transformations

Volume 1: To 1715

Third Edition

Brian Levack

University of Texas at Austin

Edward Muir

Northwestern University

Meredith Veldman

Louisiana State University

Longman

Boston   Columbus   Indianapolis   New York   San Francisco   Upper Saddle River
Amsterdam   Cape Town   Dubai   London   Madrid   Milan   Munich   Paris   Montréal   Toronto
Delhi   Mexico City   São Paulo   Sydney   Hong Kong   Seoul   Singapore   Taipei   Tokyo

Editorial Director: Craig Campanella
Executive Editor: Jeff Lasser
Editorial Assistant: Amanda Dykstra
Senior Development Editor: Gerald Lombardi
Editor-in-Chief of Development: Rochelle Diogenes
Director of Marketing: Brandy Dawson
Senior Marketing Manager: Maureen E. Prado Roberts
Marketing Assistant: Marissa O'Brien
Senior Managing Editor: Ann Marie McCarthy
Project Managers: Lynn Savino; Debra Wechsler
Senior Manufacturing and Operations Manager for Arts and Sciences: Nick Sklitsis
Operations Specialists: Christina Amato; Sherry Lewis
Senior Art Director: Maria Lange
AV Project Manager: Mirella Signoretto
Manager, Visual Research: Beth Brenzel

Photo Researcher: Francelle Carapetyan
Manager, Rights and Permissions: Zina Arabia
Image Permission Coordinator: Michelina Viscusi
Manager, Cover Visual Research & Permissions: Karen Sanatar
Cover Art: "Marco Polo (1254–1324)." Galleria Nazionale d'Arte Moderna, Rome, Italy/The Bridgeman Art Library
Director of Media: Brian Hyland
Media Editor: Sarah Kinney
Supplements Editor: Emsal Hassan
Full-Service Project Management: Elm Street Publishing Services
Composition: Integra Software Services Pvt. Ltd.
Printer/Binder: Courier/Kendallville
Cover Printer: Coral Graphics Services, Inc.
Text Font: 10/12 Sabon

Credits and acknowledgments borrowed from other sources and reproduced, with permission, in this textbook appear on appropriate page within text (or on page C-1).

Library of Congress Cataloging-in-Publication Data
Levack, Brian P.
  The West : encounters & transformations/Brian Levack, Edward Muir, Meredith Veldman.—3rd ed.
    p. cm.
  "Combined volume."
  Includes bibliographical references and index.
  ISBN-13: 978-0-13-213284-8 (combined vol. : alk. paper)
  ISBN-10: 0-13-213284-2 (combined vol. : alk. paper)
  1. Civilization, Western—History—Textbooks. I. Muir, Edward. II. Veldman, Meredith. III. Title.
CB245.W455 2011
909'.09821—dc22

                                                        2009053898

10 9 8 7 6 5 4 3 2 1

Longman
is an imprint of

www.pearsonhighered.com

ISBN 10:   0-13-213285-0
ISBN 13: 978-0-13-213285-5

à la carte edition
ISBN 10:   0-205-79778-4
ISBN 13: 978-0-205-79778-3

BRIEF CONTENTS

DETAILED CONTENTS

MAPS

PREFACE

We wrote this textbook to answer questions about the identity of the civilization in which we live. Journalists, politicians, and scholars often refer to our civilization, its political ideologies, its economic systems, and its cultures as "Western" without fully considering what that label means and why it might be appropriate. The classification of our civilization as Western has become particularly problematic in the age of globalization. The creation of international markets, the rapid dissemination of ideas on a global scale, and the transmission of popular culture from one country to another often make it difficult to distinguish what is Western from what is not. *The West: Encounters & Transformations* offers students a history of Western civilization in which these issues of Western identity are given prominence. Our goal is neither to idealize nor to indict that civilization, but to describe its main characteristics in different historical periods.

The West: Encounters & Transformations gives careful consideration to two basic questions. The first is, how did the definition of the West change over time? In what ways did its boundaries shift and how did the distinguishing characteristics of its cultures change? The second question is, by what means did the West—and the idea of the West—develop? We argue that the West is the product of a series of cultural encounters that occurred both outside and within its geographical boundaries. We explore these encounters and the transformations they produced by detailing the political, social, religious, and cultural history of the regions that have been, at one time or another, a part of the West.

DEFINING THE WEST

What is the West? How did it come into being? How has it developed throughout history? Many textbooks take for granted which regions or peoples of the globe constitute the West. They treat the history of the West as a somewhat expanded version of European history. While not disputing the centrality of Europe to any definition of the West, we contend that the West is not only a geographical realm with ever-shifting boundaries, but also a cultural realm, an area of cultural influence extending beyond the geographical and political boundaries of Europe. We so strongly believe in this notion that we have written the introductory essay "What Is the West?" to encourage students to think about their understanding of Western civilization and to guide their understanding of each chapter. Many of the features of what we call Western civilization originated in regions that are not geographically part of Europe (such as North Africa and the Middle East), while ever since the fifteenth century various social, ethnic, and political groups from non-European regions (such as North and South America, eastern Russia, Australia, New Zealand, and South Africa) have identified themselves, in one way or another, with the West. Throughout the text, we devote considerable attention to the boundaries of the West and show how borderlines between cultures have been created, especially in eastern and southeastern Europe.

Considered as a geographical and cultural realm, *the West* is a term of recent origin, and the civilization to which it refers did not become clearly defined until the eleventh century, especially during the Crusades, when western European Christians developed a distinct cultural identity. Before that time we can only talk about the powerful forces that created the West, especially the dynamic interaction of the civilizations of western Europe, the Byzantine Empire, and the Muslim world.

Over the centuries Western civilization has acquired many salient characteristics. These include two of the world's great legal systems (civil law and common law), three of the world's monotheistic religions (Judaism, Christianity, and Islam), certain political and social philosophies, forms of political organization (such as the modern bureaucratic state and democracy), methods of scientific inquiry, systems of economic organization (such as industrial capitalism), and distinctive styles of art, architecture, and music. At times one or more of these characteristics has served as a primary source of Western identity: Christianity in the Middle Ages, science and rationalism during the Enlightenment, industrialization in the nineteenth and twentieth centuries, and a defense of individual liberty and democracy in the late twentieth century. These sources of Western identity, however, have always been challenged and contested, both when they were coming into prominence and when they appeared to be most triumphant. Western culture has never been monolithic; even today references to the West imply a wide range of meanings.

CULTURAL ENCOUNTERS

The definition of the West is closely related to the central theme of our book, which is the process of cultural encounters. Throughout *The West: Encounters & Transformations,* we examine the West as a product of a series of cultural encounters both outside the West and within it. We show that the West originated and developed through a continuous process of inclusion and exclusion resulting from a series of encounters among and within different groups. These encounters can be described in a general sense as external, internal, or ideological.

External Encounters

External encounters took place between peoples of different civilizations. Before the emergence of the West as a clearly defined entity, external encounters occurred between such diverse peoples as Greeks and Phoenicians, Macedonians and Egyptians, and Romans and Celts. After the eleventh century, external encounters between Western and non-Western peoples occurred mainly during periods of European exploration, expansion, and imperialism. In the sixteenth and seventeenth centuries, for example, a series of external encounters took place between Europeans on the one hand and Africans, Asians, and the indigenous people of the Americas on the other. Two chapters of *The West: Encounters & Transformations* (Chapters 13 and 18) and a large section of a third (Chapter 24) explore these external encounters in depth and discuss how they affected Western and non-Western civilizations alike.

Internal Encounters

Our discussion of encounters also includes similar interactions between different social groups *within* Western countries. These internal encounters often took place between dominant and subordinate groups, such as between lords and peasants, rulers and subjects, men and women, factory owners and workers, masters and slaves. Encounters between those who were educated and those who were illiterate, which recurred frequently throughout Western history, also fall into this category. Encounters just as often took place between different religious and political groups, such as between Christians and Jews, Catholics and Protestants, and royal absolutists and republicans.

Ideological Encounters

Ideological encounters involve interaction between comprehensive systems of thought, most notably religious doctrines, political philosophies, and scientific theories about the nature of the world. These ideological conflicts usually arose out of internal encounters, when various groups within Western societies subscribed to different theories of government or rival religious faiths. The encounters between Christianity and polytheism in the early Middle Ages, between liberalism and conservatism in the nineteenth century, and between fascism and communism in the twentieth century were ideological encounters. Some ideological encounters had an external dimension, such as when the forces of Islam and Christianity came into conflict during the Crusades and when the Cold War developed between Soviet communism and Western democracy in the second half of the twentieth century.

* * *

The West: Encounters & Transformations illuminates the variety of these encounters and clarifies their effects. By their very nature encounters are interactive, but they have taken different forms: They have been violent or peaceful, coercive or Cooperative. Some have resulted in the imposition of Western ideas on areas outside the geographical boundaries of the West or the perpetuation of the dominant culture within Western societies. More often than not, however, encounters have resulted in a more reciprocal process of exchange in which both Western and non-Western cultures, or the values of both dominant and subordinate groups, have undergone significant transformation. Our book not only identifies these encounters, but also discusses their significance by returning periodically to the issue of Western identity.

COVERAGE

The West: Encounters & Transformations offers both comprehensive coverage of political, social, and culture history and a broader coverage of the West and the world.

Comprehensive Coverage

Our goal throughout the text has been to provide comprehensive coverage of political, social, and cultural history and to include significant coverage of religious and military history as well. Political history defines the basic structure of the book, and some chapters, such as those on Hellenistic civilization, the age of confessional divisions, absolutism and state building, the French Revolution, and the coming of mass politics, include sustained political narratives. Because we understand the West to be a cultural as well as a geographical realm, we give a prominent position to cultural history. Thus, we include rich sections on Hellenistic philosophy and literature, the cultural environment of the Italian Renaissance, the creation of a new political culture at the time of the French Revolution, and the atmosphere of cultural despair and desire that prevailed in Europe after World War I. We also devote special attention to religious history, including the history of Islam as well as that of Christianity and Judaism. Unlike many other textbooks, our coverage of religion continues into the modern period.

The West: Encounters & Transformations also provides extensive coverage of the history of women and gender. Wherever possible the history of women is integrated into the broader social, cultural, and political history of the period. But there are also separate sections on women in our chapters on classical Greece, the Renaissance, the Reformation, the Enlightenment, the Industrial Revolution, World War I, World War II, and the postwar era.

The West and the World

Our book provides broad geographical coverage. Because the West is the product of a series of encounters, the external areas with which the West interacted are of major importance. Three chapters deal specifically with the West and the world.

- Chapter 13, "The West and the World: The Significance of Global Encounters, 1450–1650"
- Chapter 18, "The West and the World: Empire, Trade, and War, 1650–1815"
- Chapter 24, "The West and the World: Cultural Crisis and the New Imperialism, 1870–1914"

These chapters present substantial material on sub-Saharan Africa, Latin America, the Middle East, India, and East Asia. Our text is also distinctive in its coverage of eastern Europe and the Muslim world, areas that have often been considered outside the boundaries of the West. These regions were arenas within which significant cultural encounters took place. Finally, we include material on the United States and Australia, both of which have become part of the West. We recognize that most American college and university students have the opportunity to study American history as a separate subject, but treatment of the United States as a Western nation provides a different perspective from that usually given in courses on American history. For example, this book treats America's revolution as one of four Atlantic revolutions, its national unification in the nineteenth century as part of a broader western European development, its pattern of industrialization as related to that of Britain, and its central role in the Cold War as part of an ideological encounter that was global in scope.

What's New to This Edition?

■ In preparing this edition we have thoroughly revised every chapter to ensure that we include the most recent research in the field and to make it even more accessible to students. Most significantly, we have reduced the length of each chapter by approximately 20 to 25 percent.

■ We have written separate chapters on Hellenistic civilization and the Roman Republic. In the second edition we had included both subjects in the same chapter because Rome was a part of the Hellenistic world and absorbed large doses of Greek culture. Separate chapters, however, allow us not only to devote more space to each topic, but also to clarify the ways in which republican Rome developed a distinctive brand of Hellenism.

■ The discussion of ancient Egypt, which was divided between Chapters 1 and 2 in the second edition, has been consolidated into Chapter 1 for ease of teaching. Discussion of the ancient Hebrews, now in Chapter 2, has been expanded.

■ Instead of including three separate primary source documents in each chapter we have

included two documents that present different and often contradictory positions on the same person, event, or development. These documents, which are followed by questions for discussion, appear in the "Different Voices" feature in each chapter.

■ We have written new "Encounters and Transformations" features in Chapters 2, 5, 6, 11, and 12, and new "Justice in History" features for Chapters 2, 4, 13, and 14.

FEATURES AND PEDAGOGICAL AIDS

In writing this textbook we have endeavored to keep both the student reader and the classroom instructor in mind at all times. The text includes the following features and pedagogical aids, all of which are intended to support the themes of the book.

"What Is the West?"

The West: Encounters & Transformations begins with an essay to engage students in the task of defining the West and to introduce them to the notion of cultural encounters. "What Is the West?" guides students through the text by providing a framework for understanding how the West was shaped. Structured around the six questions of What? When? Where? Who? How? and Why?, this framework encourages students to think about their understanding of Western civilization. The essay serves as a blueprint for using this textbook.

"Encounters and Transformations"

These features, which appear in about half the chapters, illustrate the main theme of the book by identifying specific encounters and showing how they led to significant transformations in the cultures of the West. These features show, for example, how camels

ENCOUNTERS AND TRANSFORMATIONS

**The Introduction of the Table Fork:
The New Sign of Western Civilization**

Sometime in the sixteenth century, western Europeans encountered a new tool that initiated a profound and lasting transformation in Western society: the table fork. Before the table fork, people dined in a way that, to our modern sensibilities, seems disgusting. Members of the upper classes indulged themselves by devouring meat in enormous quantities. Whole rabbits, lambs, and pigs roasted on a spit were placed before diners. A quarter of veal or venison or even an entire roast beef, complete with its head, might be heaved onto the table. Diners used knives to cut off a piece of meat that they then ate with their hands, allowing the juices to drip down their arms. They used the long sleeves of their shirts to wipe meat juices, sweat, and spittle from their mouths and faces. These banquets celebrated the direct physical contact between the body of the dead animal and the bodies of the diners themselves who touched, handled, chewed, and swallowed it.

During the sixteenth century, puritanical reformers who were trying to abolish the cruder aspects of popular culture also promoted new table manners.

THE INTRODUCTION OF THE TABLE FORK
During the late sixteenth century the refinement of manners among the upper classes focused on dining. No innovation was more revolutionary than the spread of the use of the table fork. Pictured here is the travel cutlery, including two table forks, of Queen Elizabeth I.

enabled encounters among nomadic tribes of Arabia, which led to the rapid spread of Islam; how the Mayans' interpretation of Christian symbols transformed European Christianity into a hybrid religion; how the importation of chocolate from the New World to Europe changed Western consumption patterns and the rhythms of the Atlantic economy; and how Picasso's encounter with African art contributed to the transformation of modernism. Each of these essays concludes with questions for discussion.

"Justice in History"

Found in every chapter, this feature presents a historically significant trial or episode in which different notions of justice (or injustice) were debated and resolved. The "Justice in History" features illustrate cultural encounters within communities as they try to determine the fate of individuals from all walks of life.

Many famous trials dealt with conflicts over basic religious, philosophical, or political values, such as those of Socrates, Jesus, Joan of Arc, Martin Luther, Charles I, Galileo, and Adolf Eichmann. Other "Justice in History" features show how judicial institutions, such as the ordeal, the Inquisition, and revolutionary tribunals, handled adversarial situations in different societies. These essays, therefore, illustrate the way in which the basic values of the West have evolved through attempts to resolve disputes and conflict.

Each "Justice in History" feature includes two pedagogical aids. "For Discussion" helps students explore the historical significance of the episode just examined. These questions can be used in classroom discussion or as student essay topics. "Taking It Further" provides the student with a few references that can be consulted in connection with a research project.

JUSTICE IN HISTORY

The _Auto-da-Fé_: The Power of Penance

Performed in Spain and Portugal from the sixteenth to eighteenth centuries, the _auto-da-fé_ merged the judicial processes of the state with the sacramental rituals of the Catholic Church. An _auto_ took place at the end of a judicial investigation conducted by the inquisitors of the Church after the defendants had been found guilty of a sin or crime. The term **auto-da-fé** means "act of faith," and the goal was to persuade or force a person who had been judged guilty to repent and confess. Organized through the cooperation of ecclesiastical and secular authorities, autos-da-fé brought together an assortment of sinners, criminals, and heretics for a vast public rite that dramatized the essential elements of the sacrament of penance: _contrition_, by which the sinner recognized and felt sorry for the sin; _confession_, which required the sinner to admit the sin to a priest; and _satisfaction_ or _punishment_, by which the priest absolved the sinner and enacted some kind of penalty. The auto-da-fé transformed penance, especially confession and satisfaction, into a spectacular affirmation of the faith and a manifestation of divine justice.

The _auto_ symbolically anticipated the Last Judgment. By suffering bodily pain in this life the soul

miters or hats their sin, four devils, and th their necks to tives. The sinr sent their lack escaped arres sion by effigie who had died carried in thei appeared befo zens stripped dressed only i Among them mous _sanbeni_ yellow strip d painted with the unrepenta

The proces platform on w lic penances a their knees, pr and to plead f church. For th announced fro from the pains _auto_. The sent tial procession

"Different Voices"

Each chapter contains a new feature consisting of two primary source documents that present different and often opposing views regarding a particular person, event, or development. An introduction to the documents provides the necessary historical context, identifies the authors of the documents and suggests the different perspectives they take. A set of questions for discussion follows the two documents.

DIFFERENT VOICES WERE THERE REALLY WITCHES?

Even during the height of the witch-hunt the existence of witches was controversial. Most authorities assumed that the devil worked evil on earth and that hunting witches, therefore, was an effective means of defending Christians. These authorities used the church and secular courts to interrogate alleged witches, sometimes supplemented by torture, to obtain confessions and the identities of other confederate witches. These authorities considered the hunting of witches part of their duty to protect the public from harm. Others accepted the reality of witchcraft but doubted the capacity of judges to determine who was a witch. A few doubted the reality of witchcraft altogether.

Johann Weyer (1515?–1588) was a physician who argued that most witches were deluded old women who suffered from depression and need medical help rather than legal punishment. The devil deceived them into thinking they had magical powers, but because Weyer had a strong belief that only God had power over nature, he did not credit the devil or witches with any special powers. No one else during the sixteenth century disputed the reality of the powers of witches as systematically as he. Jean

permission and
and storms, he
them to use th
when the troub
witches are cor
have caused it.
make hail and
deluded and bl
whom they hav
they think that
storms. Not on
godless lives sh
severely. . . .

Our witches
phantasy by th
they have done
pen or caused r
did not take pla
cially under tor
causing many t
them and for ar
them when the
themselves to t

Chapter Review and Questions for Discussion

This edition of *The West* offers three different sets of questions in each chapter.

- Each of the major sections of the chapter begins with the main question that the section addresses. These questions are printed in blue. These section questions appear once again at the end of the chapter under the heading "Chapter Questions."
- At the end of each chapter a set of questions under the heading "Taking It Further" ask the student to think about some

of the more specific issues discussed in the chapter.

- Each Justice in History and Different Voices feature is followed by a set of questions under the heading "For Discussion."

Maps and Illustrations

Artwork is a key component of our book. We recognize that many students often lack a strong familiarity with geography, and so we have taken great care to develop maps that help sharpen their geographic skills. Complementing the book's standard map program, we include maps focusing on areas outside the borders of Western civilization. More than 300 images of fine art and photos tell the story of Western civilization and help students visualize the past: the way people lived, the events that shaped their lives, and how they viewed the world around them.

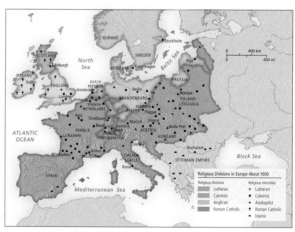

Chronologies

Each chapter includes a varying number of chronologies that list in tabular form the events relating to a particular topic discussed in the text. Chronologies present the sequence of events and can be helpful for purposes of review.

CHRONOLOGY: SPAIN AND THE NETHERLANDS, 1568–1648	
1568	Edict against Morisco culture
1580	King Philip II inherits Portugal and the Portuguese Empire
1584	Assassination of William the Silent
1588	Defeat of the Spanish Armada, failed Spanish invasion of England; the seven northern provinces of the Netherlands becomes a republic
1609	Expulsion of the Moriscos from Spain
1648	Treaty of Westphalia recognizes independence of the Netherlands

Key Terms and Glossary

We have sought to create a work that is accessible to students with little prior knowledge of the basic facts of Western history or geography. Throughout the book we have explained difficult concepts at length. For example, we present in-depth explanations of the concepts of Zoroastrianism, Neoplatonism, Renaissance humanism, the various Protestant denominations of the sixteenth century, capitalism, seventeenth-century absolutism, nineteenth-century liberalism and nationalism, fascism, and modernism. We have identified these concepts as key terms by printing them in bold in the text. Key terms for each chapter are listed at the end of each chapter, and all key terms are listed in alphabetical order, together with their definitions, in the Glossary at the end of the book.

Suggested Readings

An annotated list of suggested readings for all the chapters appears at the end of the book. The items listed there are not scholarly works for the benefit of the instructor, but suggestions for students who wish to explore a topic in greater depth or to write a research paper. References to books or articles relevant to the subject of the "Justice in History" feature appear in each chapter under the heading "Taking it Further."

A Note About Dates and Transliterations

In keeping with current academic practice, *The West: Encounters & Transformations* uses B.C.E. (before the common era) and C.E. (common era) to designate dates. We also follow the most current and widely accepted

English transliterations of Arabic. *Qur'an,* for example, is used for *Koran; Muslim* is used for *Moslem.* Chinese words appearing in the text for the first time are written in pinyin, followed by the older Wade-Giles system in parentheses.

ANCILLARY MATERIALS

The ancillary materials that accompany *The West: Encounters and Transformations,* Third Edition, are designed to reinforce and enliven the richness of the past and inspire students with the excitement of studying the history of Western Civilization.

For Instructors

THE INSTRUCTOR'S RESOURCE CENTER (www.pearsonhighered.com) Text-specific materials, such as the instructor's manual, and the test item file, are available for downloading by adopters.

INSTRUCTOR'S RESOURCE MANUAL/TEST ITEM FILE The Instructor's Manual contains chapter outlines, summaries, key points and vital concepts, and information on audio-visual resources that can be used in developing and preparing lecture presentations. The Test Item File includes 1,200 multiple-choice and essay test questions. **Available on the Instructor's Resource Center: www. pearsonhighered.com/irc/**

MYTEST MyTest is an online test management program. The program allows instructors to select items from the Test Item File in order to create tests. It also allows for online testing. **Available on the Instructor's Resource Center: www.pearsonhighered.com/irc/**

DIGITAL TRANSPARENCY MASTERS AND POWER-POINTS   The Digital Transparency Masters are full-color PDFs containing high-resolution images of all the maps and line art that appear in the text. These files are suitable for both printing to acetate or electronic display. The PowerPoints contain chapter outlines and full-color images of maps and line art. Both are text specific and available for download from the Instructor's Resource Center. **Available on the Instructor's Resource Center: www. pearsonhighered.com/irc/**

For Instructors and Students

MYHISTORYLAB   (www.myhistorylab.com) SAVE TIME. IMPROVE RESULTS. MyHistoryLab is a

dynamic website that provides a wealth of resources geared to meet the diverse teaching and learning needs of today's instructors and students. MyHistoryLab's many accessible tools will encourage students to read their text and help them improve their grade in their course.

Here are some of the features that will help you and your students save time and improve results:

- Pearson eText—Just like the printed text, students can highlight and add their own notes. Students save time and improve results by having access to their book online.
- Gradebook—Students can follow their own progress and instructors can monitor the work of the entire class. Automated grading of quizzes and assignments helps both instructors and students save time and monitor their results throughout the course.

- History Bookshelf—Students may read, download, or print 100 of the most commonly assigned history works like Homer's *The Iliad* or Machiavelli's *The Prince.*
- MySearchLab—This website provides students access to a number of reliable sources for online research, as well as clear guidance on the research and writing process.

COURSESMART TEXTBOOKS ONLINE   www. coursesmart.com. provides students an inexpensive alternative to purchasing the print textbook by subscribing to the same text online. Features include search, online note-taking, a print option and bookmarking.

For Students

Please contact your Pearson Arts and Sciences representative for ordering information.

LIVES AND LEGACIES: BIOGRAPHIES IN WESTERN CIVILIZATION, SECOND EDITION   Extensively revised, *Lives and Legacies* includes brief, focused biographies of 60 individuals whose lives provide insight into the key developments of Western civilization. Each biography includes an introduction, pre-reading questions, and suggestions for additional reading.

Volume One: **ISBN-10: 0205649157 | ISBN-13: 9780205649150**
Volume Two: **ISBN-10: 0205649149 | ISBN-13: 9780205649143**

A variety of Penguin-Putnam texts are available at a discounted prices when bundled with *The West: Encounters & Transformations,* Third Edition. The complete list of titles is available at www.pearsonhighered. com/penguin

THE PRENTICE HALL ATLAS OF WEST-ERN CIVILIZATION, SECOND EDITION Produced in collaboration with Dorling Kindersley, the leader in cartographic publishing, the updated second edition of *The Prentice Hall Atlas of Western Civilization* applies the most innovative carto-graphic techniques to present western civiliza-tion in all of its complexity and diversity. Copies of the atlas can be bundled with *The West: Encounters & Transformations,* Third Edition, for a nominal charge. Contact your Pearson Arts and Sciences sales representative for details. **ISBN-10: 0136042465 | ISBN-13: 9780136042464**

A GUIDE TO YOUR HISTORY COURSE: WHAT EVERY STUDENT NEEDS TO KNOW Written by Vincent A. Clark, this concise, spiral-bound guidebook orients students to the issues and problems they will face in the history classroom. Available at a discount when bundled with *The West: Encoun-ters & Transformations,* Third Edition. **ISBN-10: 0131850873 | ISBN-13: 9780131850873**

A SHORT GUIDE TO WRITING ABOUT HISTORY, SEVENTH EDITION Written by Richard Marius, late of Harvard University, and Melvin E. Page, Eastern Tennessee State University, this engaging and practical text helps students get beyond merely compiling dates and facts. Covering both brief essays and the documented resource paper,

the text explores the writing and researching processes, identifies different modes of historical writing, including argument, and concludes with guidelines for improving style. **ISBN-10: 0205673708 | ISBN-13: 9780205673704**

ACKNOWLEDGMENTS

We wish to thank Michael Maas, whose contri-butions to the second edition have been incor-porated into Chapters 1–8 of this edition. We are also grateful to Priscilla McGeehon, for her support during the production of all three editions of the book; Janet Lanphier, for help-ing us plan the third edition; Gerald Lombardi, for his editorial comments on the first eight chapters; and Charles Cavaliere, who guided us through the long process of preparing the third edition.

We would also like to thank the following friends and colleagues for their valuable advice and suggestions: Gabor Agoston, Catherine Clinton, Catherine Evtuhov, Wojciech Falkowski, Andrzej Kaminski, Adam Kozu-chowski, Christopher Lazarski, David Linden-feld, John McNeill, Suzanne Marchand, John Merriman, James Miller, Daria Nalecz, Karl Roider, and Mark Steinberg. Finally, we wish to thank Graham Nichols for telecommunications assistance and expertise.

Brian Levack grew up in a family of teachers in the New York metropolitan area. From his father, a professor of French history, he acquired a love for studying the past, and he knew from an early age that he too would become a historian. He received his B.A. from Fordham University in 1965 and his Ph.D. from Yale in 1970. In graduate school he became fascinated by the history of the law and the interaction between law and politics, interests that he has maintained throughout his career. In 1969 he joined the history department of the University of Texas at Austin, where he is now the John Green Regents Professor in History. The winner of several teaching awards, Levack teaches a wide variety of courses on British and European history, legal history, and the history of witchcraft. For eight years he served as the chair of his department, a rewarding but challenging assignment that made it difficult for him to devote as much time as he wished to his teaching and scholarship. His books include *The Civil Lawyers in England, 1603–1641: A Political Study* (1973), *The Formation of the British State: England, Scotland and the Union, 1603–1707* (1987), *The Witch-Hunt in Early Modern Europe* (3rd edition, 2006), and *Witch-Hunting in Scotland: Law, Politics, and Religion* (2008).

His study of the development of beliefs about witchcraft in Europe over the course of many centuries gave him the idea of writing a textbook on Western civilization that would illustrate a broader set of encounters between different cultures, societies, and ideologies. While writing the book, Levack and his two sons built a house on property that he and his wife, Nancy, own in the Texas hill country. He found that the two projects presented similar challenges: It was easy to draw up the design, but far more difficult to execute it. When not teaching,

writing, or doing carpentry work, Levack runs along the jogging trails of Austin and has recently discovered the pleasures of scuba diving.

Edward Muir grew up in the foothills of the Wasatch Mountains in Utah, close to the Emigration Trail along which wagon trains of Mormon pioneers and California-bound settlers made their way westward. As a child he loved to explore the broken-down wagons and abandoned household goods left at the side of the trail and from that acquired a fascination with the past. Besides the material remains of the past, he grew up with stories of his Mormon pioneer ancestors and an appreciation for how the past continued to influence the present. During the turbulent 1960s, he became interested in Renaissance Italy as a period and place that had been formative for Western civilization. His biggest challenge is finding the time to explore yet another new corner of Italy and its restaurants.

Muir received his Ph.D. from Rutgers University, where he specialized in the Italian Renaissance and did archival research in Venice and Florence, Italy. He is now the Clarence L. Ver Steeg Professor in the Arts and Sciences at Northwestern University and former chair of the history department. At Northwestern he has won several teaching awards. His books include *Civic Ritual in Renaissance Venice* (1981), *Mad Blood Stirring: Vendetta in Renaissance Italy* (1993 and 1998), *Ritual in Early Modern Europe* (1997 and 2005), and *The Culture Wars of the Late Renaissance: Skeptics, Libertines, and Opera* (2007). His books have also been published in Italian.

Some years ago Muir began to experiment with the use of historical trials in teaching and discovered that students loved them. From that experience he decided to write this textbook, which employs trials as a central feature. He lives beside Lake Michigan in Evanston, Illinois. His twin passions are skiing in the Rocky Mountains and rooting for the Chicago Cubs, who manage every summer to demonstrate that winning isn't everything.

 **Meredith Veldman** grew up in the western suburbs of Chicago, where she learned to love winter and the Cubs—which might explain her preference for all things improbable and impractical. Certainly that preference is what attracted her to the study of history, filled as it is with impractical people doing the most improbable things. Veldman majored in history at Calvin College in Grand Rapids, Michigan, and then earned a Ph.D. in modern European history, with a concentration in nineteenth-and twentieth-century Britain, from Northwestern University in 1988.

As an associate professor of history at Louisiana State University, Veldman teaches courses in nineteenth- and twentieth-century British history and twentieth-century Europe, as well as the second half of "Western Civ." In her many semesters in the Western Civ. classroom, Veldman tried a number of different textbooks but found herself increasingly dissatisfied. She wanted a text that would convey to beginning students at least some of the complexities and ambiguities of historical interpretation, introduce them to the exciting work being done in cultural history, and, most important, tell a good story. The search for this textbook led her to accept the offer made by Levack and Muir to join them in writing *The West: Encounters & Transformations.*

An award-winning teacher, Veldman is also the author of *Fantasy, the Bomb, and the Greening of Britain: Romantic Protest, 1945–1980* (1994). She and her family ride out the hurricanes in Baton Rouge, Louisiana. She remains a Cubs fan and she misses snow.

The West

What Is the West?

Many of the people who influence public opinion—politicians, teachers, clergy, journalists, and television commentators—refer to "Western values," "the West," and "Western civilization." They often use these terms as if they do not require explanation. But what *do* these terms mean? The West has always been an arena within which different cultures, religions, values, and philosophies have interacted; any definition of the West will inevitably arouse controversy.

The definition of the West has always been disputed. Note the difference in the following two poems, the first by Rudyard Kipling (1865–1936), an ardent promoter of European imperialism who wrote "The Ballad of East and West" at the height of the British Empire:

> *OH, East is East, and West is West, and never the twain shall meet,*
> *Till Earth and Sky stand presently at God's great Judgment Seat....*

The second, "East/West Poem," is by a Chinese-American living in Hawaii, Wing Tek Lum (1946–), who expresses the confusion caused by terms that designate both cultural traits and directions around the globe:

> *O*
> *East is East*
> *and*
> *West is West.*
> *but*
> *I never did*
> *understand*
> *why*
> *in Geography class*
> *the East was west*
> *and*
> *the West was east*
> *and that no*
> *one ever*
> *cared*
> *about the difference.*

This textbook cares about the difference. It also shows that East and West have, in contrast to Kipling's view, often "met." These encounters created the idea of the East and the West and helped identify the ever shifting borders between the two.

THE SHIFTING BORDERS OF THE WEST

The most basic definition of the West is of a place. Western civilization is now typically thought to comprise the regions of Europe, the Americas, Australia, and New Zealand. However, this is a contemporary definition of the West. The inclusion of these places in the West is the result of a long history of European expansion through colonization and conquest.

This textbook begins about 10,000 years ago in what is now Iraq; the final chapter returns to discuss the Iraq War, but in the meantime the Mesopotamian region is only occasionally a concern for Western history. The history of the West begins with the domestication of animals, the cultivation of the first crops, and the establishment of long-distance trading networks in the Tigris, Euphrates, and Nile River valleys. Cities, kingdoms, and empires in those valleys gave birth to the first civilizations in the West. By about 500 B.C.E., the civilizations that were the cultural ancestors of the modern West had spread from southwestern Asia and north Africa to include the entire Mediterranean basin—areas influenced by Egyptian, Hebrew, Greek, and Roman thought, art, law, and religion. The resulting Greco-Roman

THE TEMPLE OF HERA AT PAESTUM, ITALY:

Greek colonists in Italy built this temple in the sixth century B.C.E. Greek ideas and artistic styles spread throughout the ancient world, both from Greek colonists, such as those at Paestum, and from other peoples who imitated the Greeks.

culture created the most enduring foundation of the West. By the first century C.E. the Roman Empire drew the map of what historians consider the heartland of the West: most of western and southern Europe, the coastlands of the Mediterranean Sea, and the Middle East.

For many centuries, these ancient foundations defined the borders of the West. During the last century, however, the West came to be less about geography than about culture, identity, and technology. When Japan, an Asian country, accepted human rights and democracy after World War II, did it become part of the West? Most Japanese might not think they have adopted "Western" values, but the thriving capitalism and stable democracy of this traditional Asian country

that was never colonized by a European power complicates the idea of what is the West. Or consider the Republic of South Africa, which the white minority—people descended from European immigrants—ruled until 1994. The oppressive white regime violated human rights, rejected full legal equality for all citizens, and jailed or murdered those who questioned the government. Only when democratic elections open to blacks replaced that government did South Africa fully embrace what the rest of the West would consider Western values. To what degree was South Africa part of the West before and after these developments?

Or how about Russia? Russia long saw itself as a Christian country with cultural, economic,

WHERE IS THE WEST?

The shifting borders of the West have moved many times throughout history, but they have always included the areas shown in this satellite photo. These include Europe, north Africa, and the Middle East.

CHANGING IDENTITIES WITHIN THE WEST

In addition to being a place, the West is the birthplace of Western civilization, a civilization that encompasses a cultural history—a tradition stretching back thousands of years to the ancient world. Over this long period the civilization we now identify as Western gradually took shape. The many characteristics that identify it emerged over this time: forms of governments, economic systems, and methods of scientific inquiry, as well as religions, languages, literature, and art.

Throughout the development of Western civilization, the ways in which people identified themselves changed as well. People in the ancient world had no such idea of the common identity of the West, only of being members of a tribe, citizens of a town, or subjects of an empire. But with the spread of Christianity and Islam between the first and seventh centuries, the notion of a distinct civilization in these "Western" lands subtly changed. People came to identify themselves less as subjects of a particular empire and more as members of a community of faith—whether that community comprised followers of Judaism, Christianity, or Islam. These communities of faith drew lines of inclusion and exclusion that still exist today. Starting about 1,600 years ago, Christian monarchs and clergy began to obliterate polytheism (the worship of many gods) and marginalize Jews. From 1,000 to 500 years ago, Christian authorities fought to expel Muslims from Europe. Europeans developed definitions of the West that did not include Islamic communities, even though Muslims continued to live in Europe, and Europeans traded and interacted with the Muslim world. The Islamic countries themselves erected their own barriers, seeing themselves in opposition to the Christian West, even as they continued to look back to the common cultural origins in the ancient world that they shared with Jews and Christians.

During the Renaissance in the fifteenth century, these ancient cultural origins became an alternative to religious affiliation for thinking

and political ties with the rest of Europe. The Russians have intermittently identified with their Western neighbors, especially during the reign of Peter the Great (1682–1725), but their neighbors were not always sure about the Russians. After the Mongol invasions of the thirteenth and fourteenth centuries much of Russia was isolated from the rest of the West, and during the Cold War from 1949 to 1989 Western democracies considered communist Russia an enemy. When was Russia "Western" and when not?

Thus, when we talk about where the West is, we are almost always talking about the Mediterranean basin and much of Europe (and later, the Americas). But we will also show that countries that border "the West," and even countries far from it, might be considered Western in many aspects as well.

about the identity of the West. From this Renaissance historical perspective Jews, Christians, and Muslims descended from the cultures of the ancient Egyptians, Hebrews, Greeks, and Romans. Despite their differences, the followers of these religions shared a history. In fact, in the late Renaissance a number of Jewish and Christian thinkers imagined the possibility of rediscovering the single universal religion that they thought must have once been practiced in the ancient world. If they could just recapture that religion, they could restore the unity they imagined had once prevailed in the West.

The definition of the West has also changed as a result of European colonialism, which began about 500 years ago. When European powers assembled large overseas empires, they introduced Western languages, religions, technologies, and cultures to many distant places in the world, making Western identity a transportable concept. In some of these colonized areas—such as North America, Argentina, Australia, and New Zealand—the European newcomers so outnumbered the indigenous people that these regions became as much a part of the West as Britain, France, and Spain. In other European colonies, especially on the Asian continent, Western cultures failed to exercise similar levels of influence.

As a result of colonialism Western culture sometimes merged with other cultures, and in the process, both were changed. Brazil, a South American country inhabited by large numbers of indigenous peoples, the descendants of African slaves, and European settlers, epitomizes the complexity of what defines the West. In Brazil, almost everyone speaks a Western language (Portuguese), practices a Western religion (Christianity), and participates in Western political and economic institutions (democracy and capitalism). Yet in Brazil all of these features of Western civilization have become part of a distinctive culture in which indigenous, African, and European elements have been blended. During Carnival, for example, Brazilians dressed in indigenous costumes dance in African rhythms to the accompaniment of music played on European instruments.

MARINER'S COMPASS

The mariner's compass was a navigational device intended for use primarily at sea. The compass originated in China; once adopted by Europeans, it enabled them to embark on long ocean voyages around the world.

WESTERN VALUES

For many people today, the most important definition of the West involves adherence to "Western" values. The values typically identified as Western include democracy, individualism, universal human rights, toleration of religious diversity, ownership of private property, equality before the law, and freedom of inquiry and expression. These values, however, have not always been part of Western civilization. In fact, they describe ideals rather than actual realities; these values are by no means universally accepted throughout the West. Thus, there is nothing inevitable about these values; Western history at various stages exhibited quite different ones. Western societies seldom prized legal or political equality until quite recently. In ancient Rome and throughout most of medieval Europe, the wealthy and the powerful enjoyed more protection under the law than did slaves or the poor. Most medieval Christians were completely convinced of the virtue of making war against Muslims and heretics and curtailing the actions of Jews. Before the end of the eighteenth century, few Westerners questioned the practice of slavery, a social hierarchy of birth that remained powerful in the West through the nineteenth century; in addition, most women were excluded from equal economic and educational opportunities until well into the twentieth century. In many places women still do not have equal opportunities. In the twentieth century, millions of Westerners followed leaders who stifled free inquiry, denied basic human rights to many of their citizens, made terror an instrument of the state, and censored authors, artists, and journalists.

The values that define the West have not only changed over time, they also remain fiercely contested. One of the most divisive political issues today, for example, is that of "gay marriage." Both sides in this debate frame their arguments in terms of "Western values." Supporters of the legalization of same-sex marriages highlight equality and human rights: They demand that all citizens have equal access to the basic legal protections afforded by marriage. Opponents emphasize the centrality of the tradition of monogamous heterosexual marriage to Western legal, moral, and religious codes. What this current debate shows us is that no single understanding of "Western values," or of the West itself, exists. These values have always been contended, disputed, and fought over. In other words, they have a history. This text highlights and examines that history.

ASKING THE RIGHT QUESTIONS

So how can we make sense of the West as a place and an identity, the shifting borders and definitions of the West, and Western civilization in general? In short, what has Western civilization been over the course of its long history—and what is it today?

Answering these questions is the challenge this book addresses. There are no simple answers to any of these questions, but there is a method for finding answers. The method is straightforward. Always ask the *what, when, where, who, how,* and *why* questions of the text.

The "What" Question

What is Western civilization? The answer to this question will vary according to time and place. In fact, for much of the early history covered in this book, "Western civilization" did not exist. Rather, a number of distinctive civilizations emerged in the Middle East, northern Africa, and Europe, each of which contributed to what later became Western civilization. As these cultures developed and intermingled, the idea of Western civilization slowly began to form. Thus, the understanding of Western civilization will change from chapter to chapter. The most extensive change in the place of the West was through the colonial expansion of the European nations between the fifteenth and twentieth centuries. Perhaps the most significant cultural change came with acceptance of the values of scientific inquiry for solving human and philosophical problems, an approach that did not exist before the seventeenth century but became one of the distinguishing characteristics of Western civilization. During the late eighteenth and nineteenth centuries, industrialization became the engine that drove economic development in the West. During the twentieth century, industrialization in both its capitalist and communist forms dramatically gave the West a level of economic prosperity unmatched in the nonindustrialized parts of the world.

The "When" Question

When did the defining characteristics of Western civilization first emerge, and for how long did they prevail? Dates frame and organize the content of each chapter, and numerous short chronologies are offered. These resources make it possible to keep track of what happened when. Dates have no meaning by themselves, but the connections *between* them can be very revealing. For example, dates show that the agricultural revolution that permitted the birth of the first civilizations unfolded over a long span of about 10,000 years—which is more time than was taken by all the other events and developments covered in this textbook. Wars of religion plagued Europe for nearly 200 years before Enlightenment thinkers articulated the ideals of religious toleration. The American Civil War—the war to preserve the union, as President Abraham Lincoln termed it—took place at exactly the same time as wars were being fought for national unity in Germany and Italy. In other words, by paying attention to other contemporaneous wars for national unity, the American experience seems less peculiarly an American event.

By learning *when* things happened, one can identify the major causes and consequences of events and thus see the transformations of Western civilization. For instance, the production of a surplus of food through agriculture and the domestication of animals were prerequisites for the emergence of civilizations. The violent collapse of religious unity after the Protestant Reformation in the sixteenth century led some Europeans to propose the separation of church and state two centuries later. And during the nineteenth century many Western countries—in response to the enormous diversity among their own

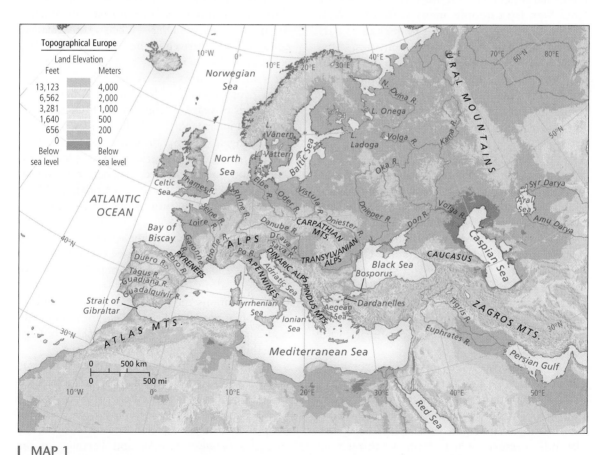

MAP 1

Core Lands of the West

These are the principal geographical features that will appear recurrently throughout this book.

peoples—became preoccupied with maintaining or establishing national unity.

The "Where" Question

Where has Western civilization been located? Geography, of course, does not change very rapidly, but the idea of where the West is does change. By tracing the shifting relationships between the West and other, more distant civilizations with which it interacted, the chapters highlight the changing "where" of the West. The key to understanding the shifting borders of the West is to study how the peoples within the West thought of themselves and how they identified others as "not Western." During the Cold War, for example, many within the West viewed Russia as an enemy rather than as part of the West. In the previous centuries, Australia and North America came to be part of the West because the European conquerors of these regions identified themselves with European cultures and traditions and against non-European values.

The "Who" Question

Who were the people responsible for making Western civilization? Some were anonymous, such as the unknown geniuses who invented the mathematical systems of ancient Mesopotamia. Others are well-known—saints such as Joan of Arc, creative thinkers such as Galileo Galilei, or generals such as Napoleon. Most were ordinary. Humble people, such as the many millions who migrated from Europe to North America or the unfortunate millions who suffered and died in the trenches of World War I, also influenced the course of events.

Perhaps most often this book encounters people who were less the shapers of their own destinies than the subjects of forces that conditioned the kinds of choices they could make, often with unanticipated results. During the eleventh century when farmers throughout Europe began to employ a new kind of plow to till their fields, they were merely trying to do their work more efficiently. They certainly did not recognize that the increase in food they produced would stimulate the enormous population growth that made possible the medieval civilization of thriving cities and magnificent cathedrals. Answering the *who* question requires an evaluation of how much individuals and groups of people were in control of events and how much events controlled them.

The "How" Question

How did Western civilization develop? This is a question about processes—about how things change or stay the same over time. This book identifies and explores these processes in several ways.

First, woven throughout the story is *the theme of encounters and transformations*. What is meant by encounters? When the Spanish *conquistadores* arrived in the Americas some 500 years ago, they came into contact with the cultures of the Caribs, the Aztecs, the Incas, and other peoples who had lived in the Americas for thousands of years. As the Spanish fought, traded with, and intermarried with the natives, each culture changed. The Spanish, for their part, borrowed from the Americas new plants for cultivation and responded to what they considered serious threats to their worldview. Many native Americans, in turn, adopted European religious practices and learned to speak European languages. At the same time, Amerindians were decimated by European diseases, illnesses to which they had never been exposed. The native Americans also witnessed the destruction of their own civilizations and governments at the hands of the colonial powers. Through centuries of interaction and mutual influence, both sides became something other than what they had been.

The European encounter with the Americas is an obvious example of what was, in fact, a continuous process of encounters with other cultures. These encounters often occurred between peoples from different civilizations, such as the struggles between Greeks and Persians in the ancient world or between Europeans and Chinese in the nineteenth century. Other encounters took place among people living in the same civilization. These include interactions between lords and peasants, men and women, Christians and Jews, Catholics and Protestants, factory owners and workers, and capitalists and communists. Western civilization developed and changed, and still does, through a series of external and internal encounters.

Second, *features in the chapters* formulate answers to the question of how Western civilization developed. For example, each chapter contains an essay titled "Justice in History." These essays discuss a trial or some other episode involving questions of justice. Some "Justice in History" essays illustrate how Western civilization was forged in struggles over conflicting values, such as the discussion of the trial of Galileo, which examines the conflict between religious and scientific concepts of truth. Other essays show how efforts to resolve internal cultural, political, and religious tensions helped shape Western ideas about justice, such as the essay on the *auto da fé*, which illustrates how authorities attempted to enforce religious conformity.

Some chapters include another feature as well. The "Encounters and Transformations" features show how encounters between different groups of people, technologies, and ideas were not abstract historical processes, but events that brought people together in a way that transformed history. For example, when the Arabs encountered the camel as an instrument of war, they adopted it for their own purposes. As a result, they were able to conquer their neighbors very quickly and spread Islam far beyond its original home in Arabia.

The "Different Voices" feature in each chapter includes documents from the period that represent contrasting views about a particular issue important at the time. These conflicting voices demonstrate how people debated what mattered to them and in the process formulated what have become Western values. During the Franco-Algerian War of the 1950s and early 1960s, for example, French military officers debated the appropriateness of torture when interrogating Algerian prisoners alleged to be insurgents. The debate about the use of torture against terrorist suspects continues today, revealing one of the unresolved conflicts over the appropriate values of the West.

The "Why" Question

Why did things happen in the way they did in history? This is the hardest question of all, one that engenders the most debate among historians. To take one persistent example, why did Hitler initiate a plan to exterminate the Jews of Europe? Can it be explained by something that happened to him in his childhood? Was he full of self-loathing that he projected onto the Jews? Was it a way of creating an enemy so that he could better unify Germany? Did he really believe that the Jews were the cause of all of Germany's problems? Did he merely act on the deeply seated anti-Semitic tendencies of the German people? Historians still debate the answers to these questions.

Such questions raise issues about human motivation and the role of human agency in historical events. Can historians ever really know what motivated a particular individual in the past, especially when it is so notoriously difficult to understand what motivates other people in the present? Can any individual determine the course of history? The *what, when, where, who,* and *how* questions are much easier to answer; but the *why* question, of course, is the most interesting one, the one that cries out for an answer.

This book does not—and cannot—always offer definitive answers to the *why* question, but it attempts to lay out the most likely possibilities. For example, historians do not really know what disease caused the Black Death in the fourteenth century that killed about one-third of the population in a matter of months. But they can answer many questions about the consequences of that great catastrophe. Why were there so many new universities in the fourteenth and fifteenth centuries? It was because so many priests had died in the Black Death, creating a huge demand for replacements. The answers to the *why* questions are not always obvious, but they are always intriguing; finding the answers is the joy of studying history.

1

The Beginnings of Civilization, 10,000–1150 B.C.E.

■ Defining Civilization, Defining Western Civilization
■ Mesopotamia: Kingdoms, Empires, and Conquests
■ Egypt: The Empire of the Nile

IN 1991 HIKERS TOILING ACROSS A GLACIER IN THE ALPS BETWEEN AUSTRIA AND Italy made a startling discovery: a man's body stuck in the ice. They alerted the police, who soon turned the corpse over to archaeologists. The scientists determined that the middle-aged man had frozen to death about 5,300 years ago. Ötzi the Ice Man (his name comes from the Ötztal Valley where he perished) quickly became an international celebrity. The scientists who examined Ötzi believe that he was a shepherd leading flocks of sheep and goats to mountain pastures when he died. Grains of wheat on his clothing suggested that he lived in a farming community. Copper dust in his hair hinted that Ötzi may also have been a metalworker, perhaps looking for ores during his journey. An arrowhead lodged in his back indicated a violent death, but the circumstances remain mysterious.

Ötzi's gear was state-of-the-art for his time. His possessions showed deep knowledge of the natural world. He wore leather boots insulated with dense grasses chosen for protection against the cold. The pouch around his waist contained stone tools and fire-lighting equipment. The wood selected for his bow offered strength and flexibility. In his light wooden backpack, Ötzi carried containers to hold burning embers and dried meat and seeds to eat on the trail. The arrows in his quiver featured a natural adhesive that tightly bound bone and wooden points to the shafts. The most noteworthy find among Ötzi's possessions was his axe. Its handle was made of wood, but its head was copper, a remarkable innovation at a time when most tools were made of stone. Ötzi was ready for almost anything—except the person who shot him in the back.

Ötzi lived at a transitional moment, at the end of what archaeologists call the **Neolithic Age,** or "New Stone Age," a long period of revolutionary change lasting from about 10,000 to about 3000 B.C.E. in which many thousands of years of human interaction with nature led to food production through agriculture and the domestication of animals. This chapter begins with this most fundamental encounter of all—that between humans and the natural world.

The achievement of food production let humans develop new, settled forms of communities—and then civilization itself. The growth of civilization also depended on constant interaction among communities that lived far apart. Once people were settled in a region, they began trading for commodities that were not available in

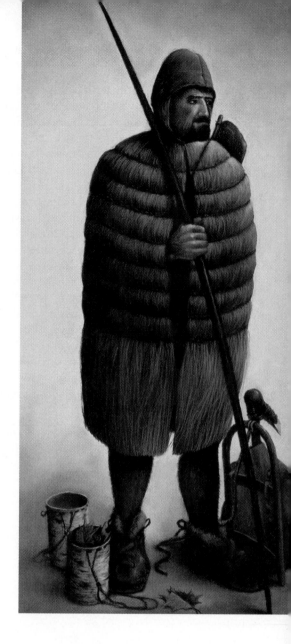

ÖTZI THE ICE MAN
This artist's recreation shows Ötzi in his waterproof poncho carrying his state-of-the-art tools.

their homelands. As trade routes extended over long distances and interactions among diverse peoples proliferated, ideas and technology spread. This chapter focuses on two questions: How did the encounters between early human societies create the world's first civilizations? And, what was the relationship between these civilizations and what would become the "West"?

DEFINING CIVILIZATION, DEFINING WESTERN CIVILIZATION

- What is the link between the food-producing revolution of the Neolithic era and the emergence of civilization?

Anthropologists use the term **culture** to describe all the different ways that humans collectively adjust to their environment, organize their experiences, and transmit their knowledge to future generations. Culture serves as a web of interconnected meanings that enable individuals to understand themselves and their place in the world. Archaeologists define **civilization** as an urban culture with differentiated levels of wealth, occupation, and power. One archaeologist notes that the "complete checklist of civilization" contains "cities, warfare, writing, social hierarchies, [and] advanced arts and crafts."[1] With cities, human populations achieved the critical mass necessary to develop specialized occupations and a level of economic production high enough to sustain complex religious and cultural practices—and to wage war. To record these economic, cultural, and military interactions, writing developed. Social organiza-

tion grew more complex. The labor of most people supported a small group of political, military, and religious leaders. This urban elite controlled not only government and warfare, but also the distribution of food and wealth. They augmented their authority by building monuments to the gods and participating in religious rituals that linked divinity with kingship and military prowess. Thus, in early civilizations four kinds of power—military, economic, political, and religious—converged.

As **Map 1.1** shows, a number of civilizations developed independently of each other across the globe. This chapter focuses on the Mesopotamian and Egyptian civilizations because many of the characteristics of "Western civilization" originated in these areas. The history of "Western civilization" thus begins not in Europe, the core territory of the West today, but in what we usually call the Middle East and what ancient historians

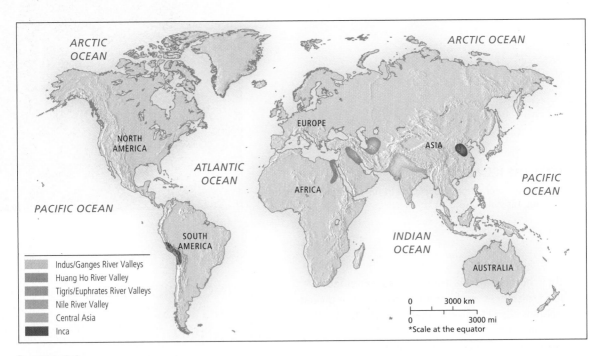

MAP 1.1

The Beginnings of Civilization

Civilizations developed independently in India, China, central Asia, and Peru, as well as in Egypt and southwest Asia. Western civilization, however, is rooted in the civilizations that first emerged in Egypt and southwest Asia.

call the "Near East."* By 2500 B.C.E., when, as we will see, city-states in Mesopotamia formed a flourishing civilization and Egypt's Old Kingdom was well-developed, Europeans still lived only in scattered agricultural communities. Without the critical mass of people and possessions that accompanied city life, early Europeans did not develop the specialized religious, economic, and political classes that characterize a civilization.

Making Civilization Possible: The Food-Producing Revolution

For more than the first 175,000 years of their existence, modern humans, known as **Homo sapiens sapiens** ("most intelligent people"), did not produce food. Between 200,000 and 100,000 years ago, *Homo sapiens sapiens* first appeared in Africa and began to spread to other continents. Scientists refer to this stage of human history as the Paleolithic Age, or Old Stone Age, because people made tools by cracking rocks and using their sharp edges to cut and chop. These early peoples scavenged for wild food and followed migrating herds of animals. They also created beautiful works of art by carving bone and painting on cave walls. By 45,000 years ago, these humans had reached most of Earth's habitable regions.

The end of the last Ice Age about 15,000 years ago ushered in an era of momentous change: the food-producing revolution. As the Earth's climate became warmer, cereal grasses spread over large areas. Hunter-gatherers learned to collect these wild grains and grind them up for food. When people learned that the seeds of wild grasses could be transplanted and grown in new areas, the cultivation of plants was underway.

People also began domesticating pigs, sheep, goats, and cattle, which eventually replaced wild game as the main sources of meat. The first signs of goat domestication occurred about 8900 B.C.E.

in the Zagros Mountains in Southwest Asia. Pigs, which adapt well to human settlements because they eat garbage, were first domesticated around 7000 B.C.E. By around 6500 B.C.E., domestication had become widespread.

Farming and herding were hard work, but the payoff was enormous. Even simple agricultural methods could produce about 50 times more food than hunting and gathering. Thanks to the increased food supply, more newborns survived past infancy. Populations expanded, and so did human settlements. With the mastery of food production, human societies developed the mechanisms not only to feed themselves, but also to produce a surplus, which allowed for economic specialization and fostered the growth of social, political, and religious hierarchies.

The First Food-Producing Communities

The world's first food-producing communities emerged in southwest Asia. People began cultivating food in three separate areas, shown on **Map 1.2**. Archaeologists have named the first area the **Levantine Corridor** (also known as the **Fertile Crescent**)—a 25-mile-wide strip of land that runs from the Jordan River valley of modern Israel and Palestine to the Euphrates River valley in today's Iraq.† The second region was the hilly land north of Mesopotamia at the base of the Zagros Mountains. The third was Anatolia, or what is now Turkey.

The small settlement of Abu Hureyra near the center of the Levantine Corridor illustrates how agriculture developed. Humans first settled here around 9500 B.C.E. They fed themselves primarily by hunting gazelles and gathering wild cereals. But sometime between 8000 and 7700 B.C.E., they began to plant and harvest grains. Eventually they discovered that crop rotation—planting different crops in a field each year—resulted in a much higher yield. By 7000 B.C.E. Abu Hureyra had grown into a farming community, covering nearly 30 acres that sustained a population of about 400.

---

*Terms such as the "Near East," the "Middle East," and the "Far East"—China, Japan, and Korea—betray their Western European origins. For someone in India, say, or Russia or Australia, neither Mesopotamia nor Egypt is located to the "east."

†The term *Levant* refers to the eastern Mediterranean coastal region. "Levant" comes from the French: "the rising [sun]"—in other words, the territory to the east, where the sun rises.

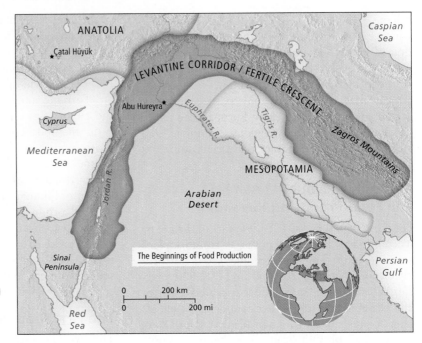

MAP 1.2

The Beginnings of Food Production

This map shows early farming sites where the first known production of food occurred in ancient southwest Asia.

A few generations later, the inhabitants of Abu Hureyra began herding sheep and goats to supplement their meat supply. These domesticated animals became the community's primary source of meat when the gazelle herds were depleted about 6500 B.C.E.

Families in Abu Hureyra lived in small, rectangular dwellings containing several rooms. Archaeological evidence shows that many women in the community developed arthritis in their knees, probably from crouching for hours on end to grind grains. Thus, we assume that while men hunted and harvested, women prepared food. The division of labor along gender lines indicates a growing complexity of social relations within the community.

Similar patterns of agricultural development characterized the early histories of other regions in southwest Asia. By 6000 B.C.E., for example, the Anatolian town of Çatal Hüyük (meaning "Fork Mound") consisted of 32 acres of tightly packed rectangular mud houses that the townspeople rebuilt more than a dozen times as their population expanded. By 6700 B.C.E. about 6,000 people lived in houses built so closely together that residents could only enter their homes by walking along the rooftops and climbing down a ladder set in the smoke hole. Such a set-up, while physically uncomfortable, also strengthened Çatal Hüyük's security from outside attack.

Archaeologists have uncovered about 40 rooms that served as religious shrines. The paintings and engravings on the walls of these rooms focus on the two main concerns of ancient societies: fertility and death. In these scenes, vultures scavenge on human corpses while women give birth to bulls (associated with virility). These shrines also contain statues of goddesses whose exaggerated breasts and buttocks indicate the importance of fertility rites in the villagers' religious rituals.

Only a wealthy community could allow some people to work as artists or priests rather than as farmers, and Çatal Hüyük was wealthy by the standards of its era. Much of its wealth rested on trade in obsidian. This volcanic stone was the most important commodity in the Neolithic Age because it could be used to make sharp-edged tools such as arrowheads, spear points, and sickles for harvesting crops. Çatal Hüyük controlled the obsidian trade from Anatolia to the Levantine

CHRONOLOGY: THE FOUNDATIONS OF CIVILIZATION

150,000 years ago	Modern humans first appear in Africa
45,000 years ago	Modern humans spread through Africa, Asia, and Europe
15,000 years ago	Ice Age ends
11,000 years ago	Food production begins in southwest Asia
9,500–3,000 years ago	Settled villages, domesticated plants and animals, and long-distance trade appear in Mesopotamia, Anatolia, and Egypt

Corridor. With increasing wealth came widening social differences. While most of the burial sites at Çatal Hüyük showed little variation, a few corpses were buried with jewelry and other riches, a practice that indicates the beginning of distinctions between wealthy and poor members of the society.

The long-distance obsidian trade that underlay Çatal Hüyük's wealth also sped up the development of other food-producing communities in the Levantine Corridor, the Zagros Mountains, and Anatolia. These trade networks of the Neolithic Age laid the foundation for the commercial and cultural encounters that fostered the world's first civilization.

Transformations in Europe

In all of these developments, Europe remained far behind. The colder and wetter European climate meant heavier soils that were harder to cultivate than those in the Near East. The food-producing revolution that began in southwest Asia around 8000 B.C.E. did not spread to Europe for another thousand years, when farmers, probably from Anatolia, ventured to northern Greece and the Balkans. Settled agricultural communities had become the norm in southwest Asia by 6000 B.C.E., but not until about 2500 B.C.E. did most of Europe's hunting and gathering cultures give way to small, widely dispersed farming communities. (See **Map 1.3.**)

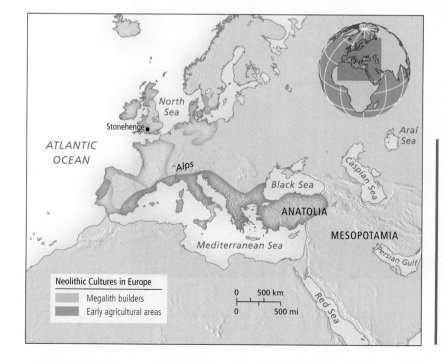

MAP 1.3

Neolithic Cultures in Europe

During the Neolithic period, new cultures developed as most of the peoples of Europe changed their way of life from hunting and gathering to food production. Trade and warfare constructed networks of village communities, but two key components of civilization—writing and cities—did not emerge in these centuries.

As farmers and herders spread across Europe, people adapted to different climates and terrain. A variety of cultures evolved from these differences but most shared the same basic characteristics: Early Europeans farmed a range of crops and herded domesticated animals. They lived in villages, clusters of permanent family farmsteads. Jewelry and other luxury goods left in women's graves might indicate that these village societies granted high status to women, perhaps because these communities traced ancestry through mothers.

Two important technological shifts ushered in significant economic or social change in these early European groups. The first was metallurgy, the art of using fire to shape metals. Knowledge of metallurgy spread slowly across Europe from the Balkans, where people started to mine copper about 4500 B.C.E. Jewelry made from copper and gold became coveted luxury goods. As trade in metals flourished, long-distance trading networks evolved. These networks provided the basis for the meeting and blending of different groups of peoples and different cultural assumptions and ideas.

The introduction of the plow was the second significant technological development for early Europe. The plow, invented in Mesopotamia in the late fifth or early fourth millennium B.C.E., became widely used in Europe around 2600 B.C.E. The use of plows meant that fewer people were needed to cultivate Europe's heavy soils. With more people available to clear forest lands, farming communities expanded and multiplied, as did opportunities for individual initiative and the accumulation of wealth.

As a result of these developments—and as had occurred much earlier in the Near East—the social structure within European villages became more stratified, with growing divisions between the rich and the poor. From the evidence of weaponry buried in graves, we know that the warrior emerged as a dominant figure in these early

STONEHENGE

This megalithic monument in southern England consists of two circles of standing stones with large blocks capping the circles. It was built without the aid of wheeled vehicles or metal tools, and the stones were dragged from many miles away.

European societies. With the growing emphasis on military power, women's status may have declined.

These early Europeans constructed enduring monuments that offer tantalizing glimpses of their cultural practices and religious beliefs. Around 4000 B.C.E. Europeans began building communal tombs with huge stones called **megaliths.** Megaliths were constructed from Scandinavia to Spain and on islands in the western Mediterranean. The best-known megalith construction is Stonehenge in England. People began to build Stonehenge about 3000 B.C.E. as a ring of pits. The first stone circle of "bluestones," hauled all the way from the Welsh hills, was constructed about 2300 B.C.E. Only an advanced level of engineering expertise, combined with a high degree of organization of labor, made such construction possible.

The purpose of these magnificent constructions remains controversial. Some archaeologists argue that Stonehenge was used to measure the movement of stars, the sun, and the planets. Others view it as principally a place for religious ceremonies. Recent excavations suggest a third possibility: Stonehenge may have been a complex devoted to healing ceremonies. All three theories could be correct, for ancient peoples commonly associated healing and astronomical observation with religious belief and practice.

If we recall the "complete checklist" needed for a civilization—"cities, warfare, writing, social hierarchies, [and] advanced arts and crafts"[2]—we can see that by 1600 B.C.E., Europeans had checked off all of these requirements except cities and writing—both crucial for building human civilizations. The rest of this chapter, then, will focus not on Europe, but on the dramatic developments in southwest Asia and Egypt from the sixth millenium B.C.E. on.

MESOPOTAMIA: KINGDOMS, EMPIRES, AND CONQUESTS

■ What changes and continuities characterized Mesopotamian civilization between the emergence of Sumer's city-states and the rise of Hammurabi's Babylonian empire?

Long before the early Europeans living in Britain began to build Stonehenge, the first civilization and the world's first empires emerged on the Mesopotamian floodplain. Standing at the junction of the three continents of Africa, Asia, and Europe, southwest Asia became the meeting place of peoples, technologies, and ideas.

The Sumerian Kingdoms

About 5300 B.C.E. the villages in Sumer in southern Mesopotamia began a dynamic civilization that would flourish for thousands of years. The key to Sumerian civilization was water. Without a regular water supply, villages and cities could not have survived in Sumer. The name *Mesopotamia*, an ancient Greek word, means "the land between the rivers." Nestled between the Tigris and Euphrates Rivers, Sumerian civilization developed as its peoples learned to control the rivers that both enabled and imperiled human settlement.

The Tigris and Euphrates are unpredictable water sources, prone to sudden, powerful, and destructive flooding. Sumerian villagers first built their own levees for flood protection and dug their own small channels to divert floodwaters from the two great rivers to irrigate their dry lands. Then they discovered that by combining the labor force of several villages, they could build and maintain levee systems and irrigation channels on a large scale. Villages merged into cities that became the foundation of Sumerian civilization, as centralized administrations developed to manage the dams, levees, and irrigation canals; to direct the labor needed to maintain and expand the water works; and to distribute the resources that the system produced.

By 2500 B.C.E., about 13 major city-states—perhaps as many as 35 in all—managed the Mesopotamian floodplain in an organized fashion. (See **Map 1.4.**) In Sumer's city-states, the urban center directly controlled the surrounding countryside. Uruk, "the first city in human history,"[3] covered about two square miles and had a population of approximately 50,000 people,

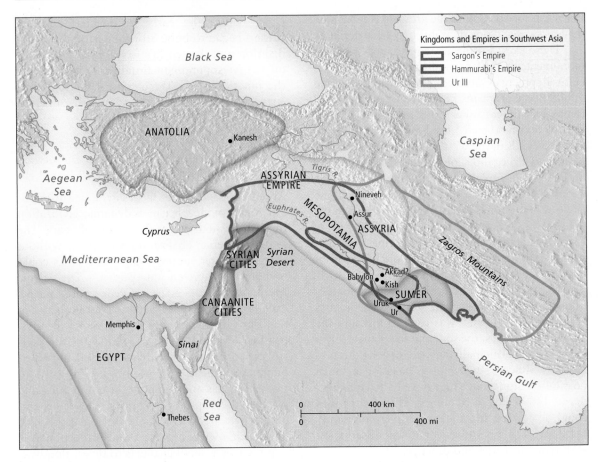

MAP 1.4

Kingdoms and Empires in Southwest Asia

Between 3000 and 1500 B.C.E., the Sumerian city-states, Sargon's Akkadian Empire, and Hammurabi's empire in Babylon emerged in southwest Asia.

including both city-dwellers and the peasants living in small villages in a radius of about ten miles around the city.

Sumer's cities served as economic centers where craft specialists such as potters, toolmakers, and weavers gathered to swap information and trade goods. Long-distance trade, made easier by the introduction of wheeled carts, enabled merchants to bring timber, ores, building stone, and luxury items unavailable in southern Mesopotamia from Anatolia, the Levantine Corridor, Afghanistan, and Iran.

Within each city-state, an elite group of residents regulated economic life. Uruk and the

other Sumerian city-states were **redistributive economies**. In this type of economic system, the central authority (such as the king) controlled the agricultural resources and "redistributed" them to his people (in an unequal fashion!). Archaeologists excavating Uruk have found millions of bevel-rimmed bowls, all the same size and shape—and, as the archaeologist Robert Wenke notes, "surely one of the ugliest ceramic types ever made outside a kindergarten."[4] One theory is that the bowls were ration bowls—containers in which workers received their daily ration of grain. What is certain is that the bowls were mass-produced,

BEVEL-RIMMED BOWLS

These bowls, found in abundance at Uruk, were mass-produced with a mold rather than a wheel. Porous, they cannot hold liquids, but rather were most likely used to carry the laborer's daily wages in grain.

expanded, competition for land increased. Such competition led to warfare, and during warfare, military leaders amassed power and eventually, became kings.

The king's power rested on his military might. Yet to retain the people's loyalty and obedience, a king also needed religious legitimacy. Kingship, then, quickly became a key part of Sumerian religious traditions. Sumerians believed that "kingship descended from heaven," that the king ruled on the god's behalf. According to a Sumerian proverb, "Man is the shadow of god, but the king is god's reflection."[5] To challenge the king was to challenge the gods—never a healthy choice. The royal household and the temple priesthood thus worked together to exploit the labor of their subjects and amass power and wealth. Religious and political life were thoroughly intertwined.

and that only a powerful central authority could organize such mass production.

In the earliest era of Sumerian history, temple priests constituted this central authority. Sumerians believed that their city belonged to a god or goddess: The god owned all the lands and water, and the god's priests, who lived with him (or her) in the temple, administered these resources on the god's behalf. In practice, this meant that the priests collected exorbitant taxes in the forms of goods (grains, livestock, and manufactured products such as textiles) and services (laboring on city building and irrigation projects), and in return provided food rations for the workers from these collections.

As Sumer's city-states expanded, a new form of authority emerged. The ruins of monumental palaces as well as temples testify to the appearance of powerful royal households that joined the temple priesthood in managing the resources of the city-state. Historians theorize that as city-states

Although the Sumerian city-states did not unite politically—and, in fact, frequently fought each other—a number of factors created a single Sumerian culture. First, the kings maintained diplomatic relations with one another and with rulers throughout southwest Asia and Egypt, primarily to protect their trading networks. These trade networks also helped tie the Sumerian cities together and fostered a common Sumerian culture. Second, the city-states shared the same pantheon of gods. The surviving documents reveal that Sumerians in the different city-states sang the same hymns, used the same incantations to protect themselves from evil spirits, and offered their children the same proverbial nuggets of advice and warning. They did so, however, in two different languages—Sumerian, unrelated to any other known language, and Akkadian, a member of the Semitic language family that includes Hebrew and Arabic.

The Akkadian Empire of Sargon the Great

The political independence of the Sumerian city-states ended around 2340 B.C.E. when they were conquered by a warrior who took the name Sargon ("true king") and built a capital city at Agade (or Akkad), the ruins of which may rest under the modern city of Baghdad. With the reign of Sargon (ca. 2340–ca. 2305 B.C.E.), the history of Mesopotamia took a sharp turn. Sargon created the first empire in history. The term **empire** identifies a kingdom or state that controls foreign territories, either on the same continent or overseas. Except for relatively brief periods of fragmentation, imperial rule became the standard form of political statehood in southwest Asia for millennia. Because an empire, by definition, brings together different peoples, it serves as a cauldron of cultural encounters. As we will see, such encounters often transformed not only the conquered peoples, but the conquerors themselves.

Map 1.4 shows that the empire Sargon built embraced a string of territories running far west up the Euphrates River toward the Mediterranean. Sargon was probably the first ruler in history to create a standing army, one that was larger than any yet seen in the Near East. This formidable fighting force certainly helps explain how he conquered so many peoples. To meld these peoples into an empire, however, required not only military power but also innovative organizational skills. The formerly independent Sumerian city rulers became Sargon's governors, required to send a portion of all taxes collected to Akkad. Akkadian became the new administrative language, and a standard measurement and dating system was imposed to make record-keeping more efficient.

Raising the revenues to meet the costs of running this enormous empire was vital. Akkadian monarchs generated revenues in several ways. They, of course, taxed their people. Hence, the Mesopotamian proverb: "There are lords and there are kings, but the real person to fear is the tax collector."[6] They also leased out their vast farmlands and required conquered people to pay regular tribute. In addition, Akkadian kings depended on the revenue generated by commerce. They placed heavy taxes on raw materials imported from foreign lands. In fact, most Akkadian kings made long-distance trade the central objective of their foreign policy. They sent military expeditions as far as Anatolia and Iran to obtain timber, metals, and luxury goods. Akkadian troops protected international trade routes and managed the maritime trade in the Persian Gulf, where merchants brought goods by ship from India and southern Arabia.

Akkadian troops also waged war. Warfare during this era changed with the use of two new military technologies. The **composite bow** boosted the killing power of archers. Multiple layers of wood from different types of trees as well as bone and sinew added to the tensile strength of the bow and so increased the distance an arrow could fly and the speed at which it did so. The second important military innovation was an early form of the chariot, a heavy four-wheeled cart that carried a driver and a spearman. Mounted on fixed wheels (and so incapable of swift turns) and pulled by donkeys (the faster horse did not come into use until the second millennium), the early chariot must have been a slow, clumsy instrument. Yet it proved effective in breaking up enemy infantry formations.

The cities of Mesopotamia prospered under Akkadian rule. Even so, Akkadian rulers could not hold their empire together for reasons that historians do not completely understand. One older explanation is that marauding tribes from the Zagros Mountains infiltrated the kingdom and caused tremendous damage. More recent research suggests that civil war tore apart the empire. Regardless of the cause, Akkadian kings lost control of their lands, and a period of anarchy began about 2250 B.C.E. "Who was king? Who was not king?" lamented a writer during this time of troubles. After approximately a century of chaos, the kingdom finally collapsed. Sargon, however, lived on in the memories and folk tales of the peoples of southwest Asia as the model of the mighty king.

THE SUMERIANS AT WAR

This Sumerian battle wagon, a heavy four-wheeled cart pulled by donkeys, appears on the "Standard of Ur" (ca. 2500 B.C.E.). Excavated in the 1920s, the "Standard" is actually a wooden box, about 8.5 × 20 inches, with an inlaid mosaic of shells, red limestone, and lapis lazuli. One panel of the mosaic depicts a Sumerian war scene, the other a banquet; hence, archaeologists have labeled the panels "War" and "Peace."

The Ur III Dynasty and the Rise of Assyria

With the fall of Akkad, the cities of Sumer regained their independence, but they were soon—and forcibly—reunited under Ur-Nammu (r. ca. 2112–ca. 2095 B.C.E.), king of the Sumerian city of Ur, located far to the south of Akkad. Ur-Nammu established a powerful dynasty that lasted for five generations.

The Ur III dynasty (as it is called) developed an administrative bureaucracy even more elaborate than that of Sargon. Like all bureaucracies, it generated vast amounts of documents—we have more documentary sources for the Ur III era than for any other in ancient southwest Asia. Local elites, who served as the king's governors, administered the empire's 20 provinces. To assure their loyalty, they were often bound to the king by ties of marriage. As governors, these locals controlled the temple estates, maintained the canal system, and acted as the highest judge in the province. Significantly, they did not control the military. Ur III's kings set up a separate military administration and made sure that the generals assigned to each province came from somewhere else. In this way, the king could be sure that the general owed his allegiance to the royal household, not to the local elite. Ur's kings also strengthened their power by assuming the status of gods. Royal officials encouraged the people to give their children names such as "Shulgi is my god" to remind them of the king's divine authority.

Despite their sophisticated bureaucratic apparatus and their claims to divinity, the kings of Ur proved unable to stave off political fragmentation indefinitely. Rebellions increased in size and tempo. About 2000 B.C.E., semi-nomadic peoples known as Amorites began invading Mesopotamia from the steppes to the west and north. The

Amorites seized fortified towns, taking food and supplies and causing widespread destruction. Their invasions destabilized the economy. Peasants fled from the fields, and with no food or revenues, inflation and famine overcame the empire. Ur collapsed, and Mesopotamia shattered again into a scattering of squabbling cities.

Assyria and Babylonia

For a long period, the political unity Sargon forged in Mesopotamia remained elusive, as states and peoples fought each other for control. This period of political fragmentation allowed for an important development: a partial "privatization" of the Mesopotamian economy, as individuals began to trade on their own behalf. Not connected in any way to the temple or the palace and, therefore, outside the redistributive economy, many of these free people grew prosperous. Merchants traveling by land and sea brought textiles, metals, and luxury items such as gold and silver jewelry and gems from lands bordering the Mediterranean and along the Persian Gulf and Red Sea.

Assyrian merchants, for example, developed an elaborate trade network linking the city-state of Assur with Anatolia. (See **Map 1.4.**) In Assur, they loaded up donkey caravans with tin and textiles for an arduous 50-day journey to the southern Anatolian city of Kanesh. (The surviving documentation is so detailed that we know that each donkey carried 150 pounds of tin or 30 textiles weighing about five pounds each.) Once they arrived in Kanesh, the merchants sold the donkeys, exchanged their merchandise for silver and gold, and headed back to Assur. Meanwhile, Assyrian merchants stationed in Kanesh sold the tin and textiles throughout Anatolia. The enterprise was risky—a storm, bandits, or a sick donkey could imperil it—but the profits were huge: 50–100 percent annually. Building on this economic prosperity, Assur (or Assyria) flourished as a powerful city-state until one of the most powerful empire-builders in the history of ancient southwest Asia reduced its power.

By 1780 B.C.E., the kingdom of Babylon had become a mighty empire under Hammurabi (r. 1792–1750 B.C.E.). Hammurabi never entirely conquered Assyria, but he dominated Mesopotamian affairs. Like Ur-Nammu and Sargon, Hammurabi developed a centralized administration to direct irrigation and building projects and to foster commerce throughout his realm. Both his law code (discussed later in this chapter) and his surviving letters to his royal agents reveal that no detail of economic life was too small for Hammurabi's notice. In one letter, for example, he ordered his agent to give "a fallow field that is of good quality and lies near the water, to Sin-imguranni, the seal-cutter."[7] Hammurabi did not, however, reverse the partial "privatization" of the economy that had developed during the era of political fragmentation. Babylonian society contained a prospering private sector of merchants, craftspeople, farmers, and sailors. Hammurabi liked to think of himself as a benevolent ruler, a kind of protective father. He declared, "I held the people of the lands of Sumer and Akkad safely on my lap."[8]

Nevertheless, Hammurabi and his successors imposed heavy taxes on their subjects. These financial demands provoked resentment, and when Hammurabi died, many Babylonian provinces successfully revolted. The loss of revenue weakened the Babylonian imperial government. By 1650, Hammurabi's empire had shrunk to northern Babylon, the territory Hammurabi had inherited when he first became king. Hammurabi's successors remained in control of northern Babylon for another five generations, but by 1400 B.C.E., a new people, the Kassites, ruled the kingdom.

Cultural Continuities: The Transmission of Mesopotamian Cultures

Although the rise and fall of kingdoms and empires punctuated the political history of Mesopotamia between the emergence of Sumerian civilization in 5300 B.C.E. and the collapse of Babylon in 1500 B.C.E., Mesopotamian culture exhibited remarkable continuity. Over these millennia,

Sumerian religious values, architectural styles, literary forms, and other cultural concepts were absorbed, transformed, and passed on by the various peoples they encountered in both commerce and conquest.

THE MESOPOTAMIAN WORLD VIEW: RELIGION

Religion—powerfully influenced by Mesopotamia's volatile climate—played a central role in the Sumerian and, hence, the wider Mesopotamian world view. The Sumerians did not tend to think of their gods as loving or forgiving. Sumerian civilization arose on a floodplain subject to extreme and unpredictable climate conditions, with results ranging from devastating drought to torrential floods. Sumerians knew firsthand the famine and destruction that could result from sudden rainstorms, violent winds, or a flash flood They envisioned each of these natural forces as an unpredictable god who, like a human king or queen, was often unfair and had to be pleased and appeased:

> The sin I have committed I know not;
> The forbidden thing I have done I do not
>   know.
> Some god has turned his rage against me;
> Some goddess has aimed her ire.
> I cry for help but no one takes my hand.[9]

Sumer's religion was **polytheistic**. Sumerians believed that many gods controlled their destinies. In the Sumerian pantheon, the all-powerful king Anu, the father of the gods, ruled the sky. Enlil was master of the wind and guided humans in the proper use of force. Enki governed the Earth and rivers and guided human creativity and inventions. Inanna was the goddess of love, sex, fertility, and warfare. These gods continued to dominate Mesopotamian culture long after Sumer's cities lost their political independence. After Hammurabi conquered most of Mesopotamia, Babylon's city-god Marduk joined the pantheon as a major deity.

Because the priests conducted the sacrifices that appeased the often-angry gods, the priesthood dominated Mesopotamian culture as did the temples in which they served and the gods to whom they sacrificed. In the center of every Sumerian city stood the temple complex, comprising temples to various gods, buildings to house the priests and priestesses, storage facilities for the sacrificial gifts, and looming over it all, the **ziggurat.** As the photograph of the ziggurat of Ur reveals, ziggurats were enormous square or rectangular temples with a striking stair-step design. Ur's ziggurat, built around 2100 B.C.E. by Ur-Nammu, had a 50-foot high base, on which three stairways, each of 100 steps, led to the main gateways. The top of Ur's ziggurat did not survive, but in Ur-Nammu's time, a central staircase would have led upward to a temple.

Ur-Nammu built Ur's ziggurat to house the chief god of the city. The Sumerians believed that one god or goddess protected each city, and that the city should serve as an earthly model of the god's divine home. Towering over the city, the deity's ziggurat reminded all the inhabitants of the omnipresent gods who controlled not only their commerce, but their very destiny.

ZIGGURAT OF UR

Built of mud-brick, the Ziggurat of Ur was the focal point of religious life in the city. This vast temple was built by King Ur-Nammu of the Third Dynasty (2112–2095 B.C.E.) and restored by the British archaeologist, Sir Leonard Woolley, in the 1930s.

THE MESOPOTAMIAN WORLDVIEW: SCIENCE?
Struggling to survive within an often hostile environment, Mesopotamians sought to understand and control their world through the practice of **divination**. To "divine"—to discern or to "read"—the future, a local wise woman or a priest looked for the messages imprinted in the natural world, such as in the entrails of a dead animal or in an unusual natural event. Once a person knew what the future was to hold, he or she could then work to change it. If the omens were bad, for example, a man could seek to appease the god by offering a sacrifice.

Divination and religious sacrifice seem to have little to do with science—and in Western culture in the twenty-first century, "religion" and "science" are often viewed as opposing or at least separate realms. Yet the Mesopotamian practice of divination helped shape a "proto-scientific" attitude toward the world. Much of divination consisted of "if . . . then . . ." equations:

> If a horse attempts to mount a cow, then there will be a decline in the land.
> If a man's chest-hair curls upward, he will become a slave.
> If the gallbladder [of the sacrificial sheep] is stripped of the hepatic duct, the army of the king will suffer thirst during a military campaign.[10]

Such statements seem silly, not scientific. Yet they rest on one of the fundamentals of modern science: close observation of the natural world. Only by observing and recording the *normal* processes of the natural world could Mesopotamians hope to recognize the omens embedded in the *abnormal*. Moreover, in the practice of divination, observation of individual events led to the formulation of a hypothesis of a general pattern—what we call **deduction**, a crucial part of scientific analysis. In their effort to discern rational patterns in the natural world to improve the circumstances of their own lives, Mesopotamians were moving toward the beginnings of a scientific mentality—a crucial aspect of Western civilization.

This proto-scientific understanding is even more evident in the technological, astronomical, and mathematical legacy of ancient Mesopotamia. Sumerians devised the potter's wheel, the wagon, and the chariot. They developed detailed knowledge about the movement of the stars, planets, and the moon, especially as these movements pertained to agricultural cycles, and they made impressive innovations in mathematics. Many Sumerian tablets show multiplication tables, square and cube roots, exponents, and other practical information such as how to calculate compound interest on loans. The Sumerians divided the circle into 360 degrees and developed a counting system based on 60 in multiples of ten—a system we still use to tell time.

THE DEVELOPMENT OF WRITING Perhaps the Sumerians' most important cultural innovation was writing. The Sumerians devised a unique script to record their language. Historians call the symbols that Sumerians pressed onto clay tablets with sharp objects **cuneiform,** or wedge-shaped, writing. The earliest known documents written in this language come from Uruk about 3200 B.C.E. Writing originated because of the demands of record-keeping. By around 4000 B.C.E., officials in Uruk were using small clay tokens of different shapes to represent and record quantities of produce and numbers of livestock. They placed these tokens in clay envelopes, and impressed marks on the outer surface of the envelopes to indicate the contents. By 3100 B.C.E., people stopped using tokens and simply impressed the shapes directly on a flat piece of clay or tablet with a pointed stick or reed.

As commodities and trading became more complex, the number of symbols multiplied. Learning the hundreds of signs required intensive study. The scribes, the people who mastered these signs, became important figures in the royal and religious courts as their work enabled kings and priests to regulate the economic life of their cities. Sumerian cuneiform writing spread, and other peoples of Mesopotamia and southwest Asia began adapting it to record information in their own languages.

CUNEIFORM TEXTS

The cuneiform, or "wedge-shaped" letters, on this clay tablet date from about 3000 B.C.E. The tablet lists what are probably temple offerings under the categories day one, day two, and day three.

THE EPIC OF GILGAMESH   Writing made a literary tradition possible. Sumerians told exciting stories about their gods and heroes. Passed on and adapted through the ages, these stories helped shape ideas about divine action and human response throughout Mesopotamian history.

One of the most popular of these stories concerned the legendary king Gilgamesh of Uruk. Part god and part man, Gilgamesh harasses his subjects. He demands sex from the young women and burdens the young men with construction tasks. The people of Uruk beg the gods to distract this bothersome hero. The gods send the beastly Enkidu to fight Gilgamesh, but after a prolonged wrestling match that ends in a draw, the two become close friends and set off on a series of adventures. The two heroes battle monsters and even outwit the gods. Finally the gods decide that enough is enough and arrange for Enkidu's death. Mourning for his stalwart friend, Gilgamesh sets out to find the secret to living forever. In the end, immortality eludes his

grasp. A mere mortal, Gilgamesh becomes a wiser king, and his subjects benefit from his new wisdom. He realizes that while he must die, his fame may live on, and so he seeks to leave behind him a magnificent city that will live forever in human memory.

The *Epic of Gilgamesh* as we know it was recorded in Akkadian, but it is clear that the stories date from long before the rise of the Akkadian Empire. Recited and read by Mesopotamian peoples for millennia, the Gilgamesh story's influence extended beyond the borders even of the empires of Sargon or Hammurabi. Its themes, plots, and characters reappear in revised form in the literatures of such diverse peoples as the ancient Hebrews (recorded in the Hebrew Bible or Old Testament) and the early Greeks. These peoples, however, reworked the stories in accordance with their own cultural values. As a Sumerian tale, the *Epic of Gilgamesh* demonstrates a Mesopotamian world view in its emphasis on the capriciousness of the gods, the hostility of nature, and the unpredictability of human existence. It offers no hope of heaven, only resignation to life's unpredictability and the chance of finding some sort of reward during one's short time on earth.

LAW AND ORDER   Mesopotamian culture also made a lasting imprint on future societies through another important innovation: the code of law, preserved in written form. Archeologists have so far uncovered three Sumerian law codes, the earliest dating to around 2350 B.C.E. The most famous lawgiver of the ancient world was the Babylonian empire-builder Hammurabi. The **Law Code of Hammurabi**—282 civil, commercial, and criminal laws—is the world's oldest complete surviving compendium of laws. We do not know to what extent these laws were actually implemented. Many scholars argue that the code was a kind of public relations exercise, an effort by Hammurabi both to present a social ideal and to persuade his people (and the gods) to view him as the "King of Justice." (See *Justice in History* in this chapter.)

What is clear is that Hammurabi's laws unveil the social values and everyday concerns of

JUSTICE IN HISTORY

Gods and Kings in Mesopotamian Justice

Mesopotamian kings placed a high priority on ruling their subjects justly. Shamash, the sun god and protector of justice, named two of his children Truth and Fairness. In the preface to his law code, Hammurabi explained the relationship between his rule and divine justice:

> At that time, Anu and Enlil [two of the greatest gods], for the well-being of the people, called me by name, Hammurabi, the pious, god-fearing prince, and appointed me to make justice appear in the land [and] to destroy the evil and wicked, so that the strong might not oppress the weak, [and] to rise like Shamash over the black-headed people [the people of Mesopotamia].[12]

Mesopotamian courts handled cases involving property, inheritance, boundaries, sale, and theft. A special panel of royal judges and officials handled cases involving the death penalty, such as treason, murder, sorcery, theft of temple goods, or adultery. Mesopotamians kept records of trials and legal decisions on clay tablets so that others might learn from them and avoid additional lawsuits.

A lawsuit began when a person brought a dispute before a court. The court consisted of three to six judges chosen from among the town's leading men, such as merchants, scribes, and officials in the town assembly. The judges could speak with authority about the community's principles of justice.

Litigants spoke on their own behalf and presented testimony through witnesses, written documents, or statements made by leading officials. Witnesses took strict oaths to tell the truth in a temple before the statue of a god. Once the parties presented all the evidence, the judges made their decision and pronounced the verdict and punishment.

Sometimes the judges asked the defendants to clear themselves by letting the god in whose

THE LAW CODE OF HAMMURABI

Hammurabi receives the law directly from the sun god, Shamash, on this copy of the Law Code.

Source: Stele of Hammurabi. Hammurabi standing before the sun-god Shamash and 262 laws. Engraved black basalt stele. 1792–1750 BCE, 1st Babylonian Dynasty. Louvre, Paris, France. © Giraudon/Art Resource, NY.

name the oath was taken make the judgment. The accused person would then undergo an ordeal or test in which he or she had to jump into a river and swim a certain distance underwater. Those who survived were considered innocent. Drowning constituted proof of guilt and a just punishment rendered by the gods.

The following account of one such ordeal comes from the city of Mari, about 1770 B.C.E. A queen was accused of casting spells on her husband. The maid forced to undergo the ordeal on her behalf drowned, and we do not know whether the queen received further punishment:

> Concerning Amat-Sakkanim . . . whom the river god overwhelmed. . . . : "We made her undertake her plunge, saying to her, 'Swear that your mistress did not perform any act of sorcery against Yarkab-Addad her lord; that she did not reveal any palace secret nor did another person open the missive of her mistress; that your mistress did not commit a transgression against her lord.' In connection with these oaths they had her take her plunge; the river god overwhelmed her, and she did not come up alive."[13]

This account illustrates the Mesopotamian belief that sometimes only the gods could make decisions about right and wrong. By contrast, the following trial excerpts come from a homicide case in which humans, not gods, made the final judgment. About 1850 B.C.E., three men murdered a temple official named Lu-Inanna. For unknown reasons, they told the victim's wife, Nin-dada, what they had done. King Ur-Ninurta of the city of Isin sent the case to be tried in the city of Nippur, the site of an important court. When the case came to trial, nine accusers asked that the three murderers be executed. They also requested that Nin-dada be put to death because she had not reported the murder to the authorities. The accusers said:

> They who have killed a man are not worthy of life. Those three males and that woman should be killed.

In her defense, two of Nin-dada's supporters pointed out that she had not been involved in the murder and therefore should be released:

> Granted that the husband of Nin-dada, the daughter of Lu-Ninurta, has been killed, but what had the woman done that she should be killed?

The court agreed, on the grounds that Nin-dada was justified in keeping silent because her husband had not provided for her properly:

> A woman whose husband did not support her . . . why should she not remain silent about him? Is it she who killed her husband? The punishment of those who actually killed him should suffice.

In accordance with the decision of the court, the defendants were executed.

This approach to justice—using witnesses, evaluating evidence, and rendering a verdict in a court protected by the king—demonstrated the Mesopotamians' desire for fairness. This court decision became an important precedent that later judges frequently cited.

For Discussion

1. How would a city benefit by letting a panel of royal officials make judgments about life-and-death issues? How would the king benefit?
2. How do these trials demonstrate the interaction of Mesopotamian religious, social, and political beliefs?

Taking It Further

Greengus, Samuel. "Legal and Social Institutions of Ancient Near Mesopotamia," in *Civilizations of the Ancient Near East*, ed. Jack M. Sasson, vol. 1 (Peabody, MA: Hendrickson Publishers, 2001). Describes basic principles of law and administration of justice, with a bibliography of ancient legal texts.

Babylonia's rulers. For example, many of the laws focus on the irrigation system that made Babylonian agriculture possible. One such law reads: "If a man has opened his channel for irrigation and has been negligent and allowed the water to wash away a neighbor's field, he shall pay grain equivalent to the crops of his neighbors"—or be sold as a slave.[11]

Hammurabi's law code buttressed Babylon's social hierarchy by drawing legal distinctions between classes of people. The crimes of aristocrats (called free men) were treated more leniently than were the offenses of common people, while slaves were given no rights at all. If an aristocrat killed a commoner, he or she had to pay a fine, whereas if a commoner killed an aristocrat, he or she was executed. But the code of Hammurabi also emphasized the responsibility of public officials and carefully regulated commercial transactions. If a home was robbed, and city officers failed to find the burglar, then the householder had the right to expect reimbursement for his losses from the city government. If a moneylender suddenly raised interest rates beyond those already agreed on, then he forfeited the entire loan.

Almost one-quarter of Hammurabi's statutes concern family matters. The laws' focus on questions of dowry and inheritance reflect the Mesopotamian view of marriage as first and foremost a business matter. The Sumerian word for *love* literally translates "to measure the earth"—to mark land boundaries and designate who gets what. Hammurabi's laws also highlight the **patriarchal** structure of Mesopotamian family life. In a patriarchal society, the husband/father possesses supreme authority in the family. Hence, Hammurabi's code declared that if a wife had a lover, both she and her lover would be drowned, while a husband was permitted extramarital sex. If a wife neglected her duties at home or failed to produce children, her husband had the right to divorce her. Yet Mesopotamian women, at least those in the "free" class, were not devoid of all rights. If a husband divorced his wife without sufficient cause, then he had to give her back her entire dowry. Unlike in many later societies, a married woman was an independent legal entity: She could appear in court and she could engage in commercial contracts. Some Babylonian women ran businesses, such as small shops and inns.

Many of Hammurabi's laws seem harsh: If a house caved in because of faulty workmanship and the householder died, then the builder was put to death. If a freeman hit another freeman's pregnant daughter and caused her to miscarry, he had to pay ten silver shekels for the unborn child, but if his blow killed the daughter, then his own daughter was executed. Yet through these laws Hammurabi's Code introduced one of the fundamentals of Western jurisprudence: the idea that the punishment must suit the crime (at least in crimes involving social equals). The principle of "an eye for an eye" (rather than a life for an eye) helped shape legal thought in southwest Asia for a millennium. It later influenced the laws of the Hebrews and, thus through the Hebrew Bible (the Christian Old Testament), still molds ideas about justice.

CHRONOLOGY: MESOPOTAMIAN CIVILIZATION

ca. **3000** B.C.E.	Sumerian city-states emerge
ca. **2340** B.C.E.	Sargon unites Sumerian cities into the Akkadian Empire
ca. **2250** B.C.E.	Collapse of the Akkadian empire
ca. **2100** B.C.E.	Ur-Nammu reunites Sumerian cities; empire of "Ur III"
ca. **2000** B.C.E.	Collapse of Ur
ca. **1790** B.C.E.	Hammurabi creates the Babylonian empire
ca. **1400** B.C.E.	Kassites overrun Babylon

EGYPT: THE EMPIRE OF THE NILE

■ What distinctive features characterized Egyptian civilization throughout its long history?

As the civilizations of Mesopotamia rose and fell, another civilization emerged far to the south: Egypt. A long and narrow strip of land in the northeast corner of Africa, Egypt depended for its survival on the Nile, the world's longest river, which flows north into the Mediterranean Sea from one of its points of origin in eastern Africa 4,000 miles away. The northernmost part of Egypt, where the Nile enters the Mediterranean, is a broad and fertile delta. The river flooded annually from mid-July to mid-October, leaving behind rich deposits of silt ideal for planting crops. Unlike in Southwest Asia, the annual floods in Egypt came with clockwork regularity. For the Egyptians, nature was not unpredictable and random in its destruction, but a benevolent force, generous in sharing its riches.

Egypt was also fortunate in another of its physical features: it rested securely between two desert regions that effectively barricaded it from foreign conquest. Whereas Mesopotamia stood at the intersection of three continents, vulnerable to invading armies, Egyptian civilization emerged in a far more easily defended position. Egyptian history, then, is remarkable for its political stability. This stability, combined with the predictability and generosity of the Nile, may explain the confidence and optimism that marked Egyptian culture.

Historians organize the long span of ancient Egyptian history into four main periods: Predynastic and Early Dynastic (10,000–2680 B.C.E.), the Old Kingdom (ca. 2680–2200 B.C.E.), the Middle Kingdom (2040–1720 B.C.E.), and the New Kingdom (1550–1150 B.C.E.). Times of political disruption between the kingdoms are called *intermediate periods*. Despite these periods of disruption, the Egyptians maintained a remarkably stable civilization for thousands of years.

Egypt's Rise to Empire

Like the peoples of Mesopotamia, the Egyptians were originally hunter-gatherers who slowly turned to growing crops and domesticating animals. Small villages, in which people could coordinate their labor most easily, appeared along the banks of the Nile between 5000 and 4000 B.C.E. By 3500 B.C.E., Egyptians could survive comfortably through agriculture and herding. Small towns multiplied along the Nile, and market centers connected by roads emerged as hubs where artisans and merchants exchanged their wares.

Toward the end of the Predynastic period, between 3500 and 3000 B.C.E., trade along the Nile River resulted in a shared culture and way of life. Towns grew into small kingdoms whose rulers constantly warred with one another, attempting to grab more land and extend their power. The big consumed the small, and by 3000 B.C.E., the towns had been absorbed into just two kingdoms: Upper Egypt in the south and Lower Egypt in the north. These two then united, forming what historians term the **Old Kingdom.** (See **Map 1.5.**)

THE KINGS AND THE GODS IN THE OLD KINGDOM
In the new capital city of Memphis, the Egyptian kings became the focal points of religious, social, and political life. While in Mesopotamia, kings were regarded as the gods' representatives on earth, as sort of semi-divine intermediaries, Egyptian kings were acknowledged as divine, gods on earth who ruled Egypt on behalf of the other gods. In the Old Kingdom, Egyptians called their king "the good god." (The label *pharaoh* was not used until the New Kingdom.) Egyptian religious tales emphasized the divinity of the king. In one such story, the god Osiris, ruler of Egypt, was killed and chopped into bits by his evil brother, Seth. Osiris' son, Horus, avenged his father by defeating Seth and reclaiming the Egyptian throne. All Egyptian kings, then, embodied Horus during their reign.

The story of the conflict between Osiris and Seth not only emphasized the divinity of the king, it also stressed the central theme of the

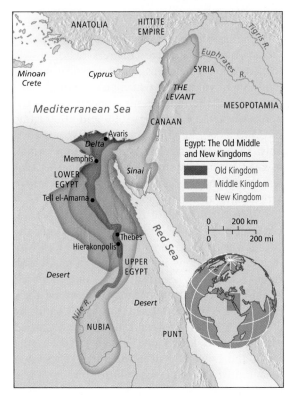

MAP 1.5

Egypt: The Old, Middle, and New Kingdoms

As this map shows, Egyptian power expanded from its base along the Nile delta, first southward along the Nile River, and then, through trade and conquest, into southwest Asia. Egypt's control of mineral resources, especially gold, turquoise, and copper, played an important role in its commercial prosperity. During the New Kingdom, Egyptians converted trading dominance into political control, with the reconquest of Nubia and the extension of Egypt's empire into Canaan and parts of Syria.

Egyptian worldview: the struggle between the forces of chaos and of order. Seth embodied the forces of evil and disorder. In defeating Seth, Horus overcame chaos and restored what the Egyptians called **ma'at** to the world. The word *ma'at* has no English equivalent; in various contexts, it can mean truth, wisdom, justice, or stability. *Ma'at* was the way the gods had made the world—everything in its proper place, everything the way the gods wanted it to be.

The king's essential task was to maintain *ma'at*, to keep things in order and harmony. The king's presence meant that cosmic order reigned and that the kingdom was protected against forces of disorder and destruction.

Like the Mesopotamians, the Egyptians believed in many gods, but in Egypt the gods were not prone to punish men and women without reason. Because the Nile River flooded regularly and predictably, each year leaving behind rich soil deposits, the natural world seemed far less harsh and erratic to the Egyptians. They thus regarded their gods as largely helpful. Ordinary Egyptians tended to pray to minor household gods, such as Tauret, portrayed as a pregnant hippopotamus who protected women during childbirth. Official religion, however, centered on the major state gods, worshiped and housed in monumental temples across the kingdom. The sun god Re was one of the most important Egyptian deities. Re journeyed across the sky every day in a boat, rested at night, and returned in the morning to resume his eternal journey. By endlessly repeating the cycle of rising and setting, the sun symbolized the harmonious order of the universe that Re established. Evil, however, in the form of Apopis, a serpent god whose coils could trap Re's boat like a reed in the Nile, constantly threatened this order. Re's cosmic journey could continue only if *ma'at* was maintained.

THE PYRAMIDS One spectacular feature of Egyptian religion in the Old Kingdom was the construction of pyramids. These elaborate monuments reflected Egyptian emphasis on the afterlife. The earliest pyramids, erected around 2680 B.C.E., were elaborate temples in which priests worshiped statues of the king surrounded by the enormous mud-brick monument. The pyramid contained compartments where the king could dwell in the afterlife in the same luxury he enjoyed during his life on Earth. King Djoser (2668–2649 B.C.E.) built the first pyramid complex, and the world's first monumental stone building, at Saqqara near Memphis. Known today as the Step Pyramid (pictured on p. 31), this structure rests above Djoser's burial place

DJOSER'S STEP PYRAMID

Djoser ascended to the throne of Egypt around 2668 B.C.E. and immediately ordered his vizier Imhotep to oversee the construction of his tomb. Up until this point, Egyptians constructed pyramids out of mud brick, but Imhotep deviated from tradition and chose stone.

and rises high into the air in six steps, which represent a ladder to Heaven.

In the centuries after Djoser's reign, kings continued building pyramids for themselves and smaller ones for their queens, with each tomb becoming more architecturally sophisticated. The walls grew taller and steeper and contained hidden burial chambers and treasure rooms. The Great Pyramid at Giza, built around 2600 B.C.E. by King Khufu (or Cheops), was the largest human-made structure in the ancient world. It consists of more than two million stones that weigh an average of two and a half tons each. Covering 13 acres, it reaches over 480 feet into the sky.

Building the pyramid complexes was a long and costly task. In addition to the architects, painters, sculptors, carpenters, and other specialists employed on the site throughout the year, stone masons supervised the quarrying and transport of the colossal building blocks. Peasants, who were organized into work gangs and paid and fed by the king, provided the heavy labor when the Nile flooded their fields every year. As many as 70,000 workers out of a total population estimated at 1.5 million sweated on the pyramids every day. Entire cities sprang up around pyramid building sites to house the workmen, artisans, and farmers. The construction of elaborate pyramids stopped after 2400 B.C.E., probably because of the expense, but smaller burial structures continued to be built for centuries

THE SOCIAL AND POLITICAL ORDER IN THE OLD KINGDOM The king and the royal family stood at the top of the Old Kingdom's social and political hierarchy. As a god on earth, the king possessed absolute authority. All of Egypt—all the land, every resource, every person—theoretically belonged to the king. Yet royal Egyptians were not free to act in any way they might choose. Maintaining *ma'at* meant following carefully regulated rituals at almost all times. The rules that governed royalty differed from those for commoners. Kings, for example, had many wives and frequently married their daughters and sisters, whereas ordinary Egyptians were monogamous (a man took only one wife) and married outside the family.

Below the royal family stood the nobility, made up of priests, court officials, and provincial governors. Men in these ranks carried out the king's orders. Egypt, like the Mesopotamian empires, was a redistributive economy. The kings' officials collected Egypt's produce and redistributed it throughout the kingdom. The job of keeping records of the kings' possessions and supervising food production fell to the scribes, who were trained in **hieroglyphic** writing. *Hieroglyphs* (literally "sacred carvings") represented both sounds (as in our alphabet) and objects (as in a pictorial system). Learning the hundreds of signs for literary or administrative purposes took years of schooling. It was worth the effort, however, for knowledge of hieroglyphs gave scribes great power. For 3,000 years, these royal bureaucrats kept the machinery of Egyptian government running despite the rise and fall of dynasties.

Ordinary Egyptians fell into three categories: skilled artisans, peasants, and slaves. Craftsmen and skilled workers such as millers and stone masons stood below the nobility on the social ladder. Employed in large workshops owned by the king or nobility, the craftsmen served the privileged classes above them. Below them were the peasants, who not only farmed, but also labored on public works such as temples, roads, and irrigation projects. As in

medieval Europe, these peasants were tied to the land: They could not leave the estates that they farmed for the king or nobility, and if the land was sold, they passed on to the new owner as well. Slaves occupied the bottom of the social ladder. They toiled on monumental building projects as well as within the temples and royal palaces. Slavery, however, was not dominant in the Egyptian economy. Free Egyptians did most of the work.

Free Egyptian women—whether from the nobility or the skilled artisans—possessed clear rights. They could buy and sell property, make contracts, sue in court, and own their own businesses. In a marriage, the husband and wife were regarded as equals. Women dominated certain occupations, such as spinning and weaving, and even worked as doctors.

WHERE IS MA'AT? THE COLLAPSE OF THE OLD KINGDOM Around 2200 B.C.E. the Old Kingdom collapsed, perhaps because terrible droughts lowered the level of the Nile. Famine followed. The king could no longer maintain *ma'at*, and the political order collapsed. For 200 years, anarchy and civil war raged in Egypt during what historians call the First Intermediate Period.

The chaos and disorder of the First Intermediate Period resulted in a significant religious and cultural shift. The optimism that had characterized Egyptian culture gave way to uncertainty and even pessimism as Egyptians wondered how to restore *ma'at* in a world so out of balance:

> Whom can I trust today?
> Hearts are greedy,
> And every man steals his neighbor's goods.[14]

In their quest to make sense out of the chaos, Egyptian writers began to emphasize rewards in the afterlife as recompense for righteous action here on earth. In the Old Kingdom, Egyptians had sought to act justly in accordance with *ma'at* because they were confident that right action would be rewarded in the here and now. In the new climate of turmoil and hunger, however, they found comfort in the idea that although the good suffered in their earthly life, they would be rewarded in the life to come. During this period, the Egyptians developed the concept of a final judgment—the earliest known instance of such an idea in human history. After death, a person's heart would be weighed in the balance against *ma'at*. Those who tipped the scales—those who failed the test—would be consumed by the Devourer, a god with a crocodile's head. But those who passed would live like gods in the afterlife. (See *Different Voices* in this chapter.)

THE MIDDLE KINGDOM   The First Intermediate Period ended when the governors of Thebes, a city in Upper Egypt, set out to reunify the kingdom. In 2040 B.C.E., Mentuhotep II (r. 2060–2010 B.C.E.) established a vigorous new monarchy, initiating the **Middle Kingdom.** (See **Map 1.5.**) He and his successors restored *ma'at* to Egypt: They rebuilt the power of the monarchy, reestablished centralized control, and repaired Egypt's commercial and diplomatic links to southwest Asia. Prosperity and stability returned.

Yet the Middle Kingdom was not a reincarnation of the Old Kingdom. The chaos of the First Intermediate Period modified political ideas and social relations. The king was no longer an omnipotent god. Capable of making mistakes and even of being afraid, the Middle Kingdom monarch appeared in texts as a lonely figure, seeking to serve as a good shepherd to his people. With this new concept of kingship came a slightly altered social order, with the nobility possessing more power and autonomy than in the Old Kingdom.

New developments also marked religion. With the return of *ma'at*—with life on earth more prosperous and stable—Egyptians began to see the final judgment as more of a problem that needed to be solved than as a source of comfort. How could one enjoy life and yet be assured of

living like a god for eternity, rather than being consumed by the Devourer? To be sure that they passed the final judgment, Egyptians had themselves buried with special scarabs. A scarab is a small figure of a dung beetle, but these funeral scarabs featured human heads and carried magic incantations or charms. This powerful magic prevented the heart from testifying against the individual when it was weighed in the final judgment. In other words, it was a kind of false weight, a finger on the scales, a way to deceive the gods and ensure passage to the afterlife.

ENCOUNTERS WITH OTHER CIVILIZATIONS   While Egypt's position between two deserts guaranteed its military security, it did not isolate Egypt from the rest of the ancient world. During both the Old and Middle Kingdoms, Egyptian kings forged an economic network that included trading cities in the Levant, Minoan Crete (see Chapter 2), the southern Red Sea area called Punt, and Mesopotamia. To protect the trade routes along which raw materials and luxury goods were imported, rulers did not hesitate to use force. They also, however, used diplomacy to stimulate trade.

Egyptian interactions with Nubia (modern Sudan) were particularly important. Rich in gold and other natural resources, Nubia also benefited from its location at the nexus of trade routes from central and eastern Africa. Agents of Egyptian rulers, called Keepers of the Gateway of the South, tried to protect this trade by keeping the peace with the warlike Nubian tribes. Slowly, Egyptian monarchs made their presence more permanent. King Mentuhotep II, whose reign marked the start of the Middle Kingdom, not only reunified Egypt but also gained control of Lower Nubia. This expansion of Egyptian control ensured the free flow of Nubian resources northward. Around 1900 B.C.E., King Amenemhet built ten forts at strategic locations where trade routes from the interior of Africa reached the Nile River. These forts reinforced Egyptian access to Nubian gold, ivory, and other natural resources.

DIFFERENT VOICES EXPLAINING EVIL IN ANCIENT TIMES

The gap that separates twenty-first-century Western readers from the inhabitants of ancient Mesopotamia or Egypt is huge, and yet some of their questions sound familiar: Why do the good and the just suffer? Where do we turn for hope when life seems hopeless? The two documents below offer different responses to evil times. The first is an excerpt from a lengthy poem inscribed on four tablets during the Akkadian Empire in Mesopotamia. The Akkadian era was generally prosperous, but as this document shows, daily survival remained difficult for many. The second document comes from the tumultuous intermediate period following the collapse of Egypt's Old Kingdom. The writer may have been king of one of the fragmented states that emerged as the Old Kingdom disintegrated. In The Instructions for Merikare, *he shares with his son the lessons he has learned in a world gone mad.*

I. From Mesopotamia: *I Will Praise the Lord of Wisdom*

I turn around, but it is bad, very bad;
My ill luck increases and I cannot find what is right.
I called to my god, but he did not show his
    face,
I prayed to my goddess, but she did not raise
    her head.
Even the diviner with his divination could not
    make a prediction,
And the interpreter of dreams with his libation
    could not elucidate my case....

What strange conditions everywhere!
When I look behind [me], there is persecution,
    trouble.
Like one who has not made libations to his god,
Nor invoked his goddess when he ate,
Does not make prostrations nor recognize
    [the necessity of] bowing down,
In whose mouth supplication and prayer are
    lacking,
Who has even neglected holy days, and ignored
    festivals...
Like one who has gone crazy and forgotten
    his lord,
Has frivolously sworn a solemn oath by his god,
    [like such a one] do I appear.
For myself, I gave attention to supplication and
    prayer;
My prayer was discretion, sacrifice my rule.
The day for worshipping the god was a joy to
    my heart;
The day of the goddess's procession was profit
    and gain to me.
The king's blessing—that was my joy....
I wish I knew that these things would be pleasing
    to one's god!
What is good for oneself may be offense to
    one's god,
What in one's own heart seems despicable may
    be proper to one's god.
Who can know the will of the gods in heaven?
Who can understand the plans of the underworld
    gods?

Attracted by Egypt's stability and prosperity, peoples from different lands settled in the Nile Valley. They took Egyptian names and assimilated into Egyptian culture. The government settled these immigrants, as well as war captives, throughout the kingdom where they could mix quickly with the local inhabitants. This willingness to accept newcomers into their kingdom lent Egyptian civilization even more vibrancy.

Immigrants from Canaan (modern-day Lebanon, Israel, and parts of Jordan and Syria) played a significant role in Egyptian history toward the end of the Middle Kingdom. Around 1720 B.C.E., centralized state control began to deteriorate (for reasons that remain unclear), and Canaanites began to seize political control over the regions in which they had settled. A century of political decentralization and chaos—the

Where have humans learned the way of a god?
He who was alive yesterday is dead today....
As for me, exhausted, a windstorm is driving
    me on!
Debilitating Disease is let loose upon me;
An Evil Wind has blown [from the] horizon,
Headache has sprung up from the surface of
    the underworld....
Feebleness has overcome my whole body,
An attack of illness has fallen upon my flesh.

II. From Egypt: *The Instruction for Merikare*

Be just that you may prosper upon the earth;
    soothe the weeper, do not oppress the widow;
Do not deprive a man of his father's goods
    nor interfere with high officials in their
    functions.
Beware of punishing unfairly,
    and cause no injury—that will not help you!...
The Conclave of the gods that judges suffering
    Man—
    you know They are not lenient
On that day of judging the poor wretch,
    in that hour of weighing out his life.
    and it is painful when the guilty is a
    wise man.
Do not fill your heart with length of years,
    for They see lifetimes in an hour.
A man lives on after his final mooring,
    and his deeds are heaped beside him.
Existence over There is certainly forever,
    and one who takes it lightly is a fool;
But one who reaches there free of wrong
    doing—

he shall live on like a god,
    wide-striding like the Lords of all eternity.

Sources: I. James B. Pritchard (ed.), *The Ancient Near East: Supplementary Texts and Pictures Relating to the Old Testament*, 597–598. Copyright © 1968 Princeton University Press, 1996 renewed Princeton University Press. Reprinted by permission of Princeton University Press. II. *Ancient Egyptian Literature: An Anthology*. Translated by John L. Foster, 195–196. Copyright © 2001. By permission of the University of Texas Press.

For Discussion

1. What picture of Akkadian religious practice can we draw from the first document?

2. In this excerpt from *I Will Praise the Lord of Wisdom*, the anonymous author files a sort of cosmic complaint. What grievance does he present?

3. In the second excerpt, what advice does the king offer to his son Merikare? What does he want his son to understand?

4. How does *The Instruction for Merikare* demonstrate the new religious concepts that the Egyptians developed in response to the disappearance of political stability and economic prosperity during the First Intermediate Period?

5. Each of these documents reveals timeless existential concerns, but how do they point to the specific historical contexts in which they were written?

Second Intermediate Period—ensued, with even larger groups of Canaanite immigrants settling in Egypt's Delta region:

> Foreigners have become people [i.e. Egyptians] everywhere....
> See now, the land is deprived of kingship
> by a few men who ignore custom.[15]

By approximately 1650 B.C.E., one of these Canaanite groups had established control over the entire northern delta region and forced the Egyptian rulers there to pay them tribute. The era of Hyksos rule had begun. Although *Hyksos* meant "rulers of foreign lands" in Egyptian, the Hyksos dynasty (ca. 1650–1540 B.C.E.) quickly assimilated Egyptian culture. They used Egyptian names and symbols, worshiped Egyptian gods, and employed native Egyptians to staff their bureaucracies and keep their state records—in Egyptian hieroglyphs.

But the Hyksos, and the Canaanite immigrant community from which they emerged, not only absorbed Egyptian ways, they also transformed them. Canaanite immigrants brought with them into Egypt a vital skill: the ability to make bronze. An alloy of copper and tin, **bronze** is much harder and lasts much longer than either copper or tin alone. From about 3500 B.C.E. when people living in northern Syria and Iraq began making bronze, the technology spread slowly throughout southwest Asia. Archaeologists talk about the "Early Bronze Age" (roughly 3500–2000 B.C.E.), the "Middle Bronze Age" (ca. 2000–1550 B.C.E.), and the "Late Bronze Age" (ca. 1500–1100 B.C.E.). It was in the Middle Bronze Age, then, that Canaanite immigrants introduced bronze to Egypt. Bronze meant new possibilities in agricultural, craft production—and war.

In particular, bronze made possible the horse-drawn light chariot. This advanced military technology was already revolutionizing warfare throughout southwest Asia, Anatolia, and Greece when the Hyksos brought it to Egypt. Unlike earlier chariots, the Bronze Age model featured only two wheels fixed to an axle for easier maneuvering. Bronze spokes made the wheels more durable. Two men wearing bronze chain-mail armor rode into battle on each chariot, one driving the horses, the other shooting bronze-tipped arrows at the enemy. Troops of trained charioteers and bowmen easily outmaneuvered the traditional massed infantry forces and inflicted terrible casualties on them from a distance.

Chariot warfare reshaped the economic policies and foreign relations of Egypt, its rivals, and its allies. Imperial systems of governing and revenue collection became more sophisticated and centralized as rulers sought to meet the expenses of training and supplying armies of charioteers by expanding their economic resources. As a result, empires flourished as never before. Archaeologists thus see the period after approximately 1500

B.C.E. as a new era, the "Late Bronze Age," a period of unprecedented imperial stability and international exchange. In Chapter 2, we will examine the international structures of this period in detail. In the section below, we continue the story of Egypt as it reemerged as a great power.

The New Kingdom: The Egyptian Empire in the Late Bronze Age

Egypt's **New Kingdom** began about 1550 B.C.E., when King Ahmose I (r. ca. 1550–ca. 1525 B.C.E.) expelled the Hyksos from Egypt. During the New Kingdom, Egypt's kings first took the title **pharaoh,** which means "great house"—or master of all Egyptians. As **Map 1.5** shows, Ahmose's new dynasty not only reasserted the monarch's authority and rebuilt the power of the central state, it also pushed Egypt's territorial boundaries into Asia as far as the Euphrates River.

BUILDING AN EMPIRE: MILITARY CONQUEST AND TERRITORIAL EXPANSION   A large standing army made the New Kingdom conquests possible. Trained in the new chariot warfare and equipped with the composite bow (long known in Mesopotamia, but introduced into Egypt during the New Kingdom), Egypt's army was a mighty fighting force. One man in every ten in every village was forced into military service. Egyptian officers supplemented these troops with both mercenaries hired abroad and soldiers recruited in conquered regions of Palestine and Syria.

Egyptian attitudes toward non-Egyptians also encouraged the imperial expansion of the New Kingdom. Egyptians divided the world into two groups: themselves (whom they referred to as "The People") and everyone else. Egyptians believed that forces of chaos resided in foreign lands where the pharaoh had not yet imposed his will. Thus, it was the pharaoh's responsibility to crush all foreign peoples and bring order to the world.

In their drive to establish order in the world, Egyptian rulers in the New Kingdom clashed with kingdoms in Anatolia and Mesopotamia. Under the dynamic leadership of Thutmose I (r. 1504–1492 B.C.E.), the armies of

Egypt conquered southern Palestine. A coalition of Syrian cities slowed further advance, but by the end of the reign of the great conqueror, Thutmose III (r. 1458–1425 B.C.E.), Egypt had extended its control over the entire western coast (see **Map 1.5**). Thutmose III led his armies into Canaan 17 times and strengthened the empire's hold on it and Syria. Canaan proved an economic asset, both because of its own natural resources and because it was a vital trading center with ties to Mesopotamia and beyond.

The New Kingdom also regained control over Nubia about 1500 B.C.E. To strengthen their grip on the area, pharaohs encouraged Egyptians to establish communities along the Nile River there. These Egyptian colonies exploited the fertile river lands in Nubia for the benefit of the pharaoh.

KEEPING AN EMPIRE: ADMINISTRATIVE AND DIPLOMATIC INNOVATION The Egyptians amassed a vast empire with military might. They maintained it with administrative skill and diplomatic innovation. In the New Kingdom, the pharaoh's bureaucracy divided Egypt into two major administrative regions: Upper Egypt in the south, governed from the city of Thebes, and Lower Egypt in the north, ruled from the city of Memphis. Regional administrators raised taxes and drafted men to fight in the army and work on the pharaoh's building projects. The chief minister of state, the **vizier**, superintended the administration of the entire kingdom. Every year he decided when to open the canal locks on the Nile to irrigate farmers' fields. He supervised the Egyptian treasury and the warehouses into which produce was paid as taxes.

New Kingdom pharaohs also relied on diplomacy to control their vast realm. They corresponded frequently with their provincial governors, the leaders of their vassal states, and the rulers of other great states. These letters testify that the Egyptian monarchs used trade privileges and political benefits as much as military coercion to control restless subordinates and interact with neighboring realms.

CONTINUITY IN THE NEW KINGDOM During the New Kingdom, many of the characteristics of life under the Old and Middle Kingdom continued unchanged. The basic social hierarchy remained intact, with village-based peasants laboring on the land owned by the royal family, priests of the major temples, and nobility. Both the pharaoh's government and the major temples continued to administer the redistributive economy by collecting taxes in the form of produce and paying the peasants who labored on their building projects and estates from their storehouses. The temple of the god Amun at Karnak, for example, controlled over 100,000 workers.

In the New Kingdom, as in the Old and Middle Kingdoms, monumental architecture remained a focal point of political and religious life. Amenhotep III (r. 1388–1350) constructed both an enormous palace for himself and a gigantic burial temple, with a large open solar court as its sanctuary and two 64-foot high statues of the pharaoh flanking the entryway. Ramesses II (r. 1279–1212 B.C.E.) ornamented his long reign by building the Great Temple at Abu Simbel in Nubia. Four 65-foot high statues of the pharaoh guard the entrance to the temple. The sanctuary penetrates over 200 feet into the mountainside, where four gigantic statues of the four gods sit. Twice a year (on February 21 and October 21), the rising sun shines directly through the entrance and falls right on three of the statues; the fourth, the god of the underworld, remains in the shadows.

Women maintained their position in Egyptian society in the New Kingdom. They had complete equality with men in matters of property, business, and inheritance. Some women held priesthoods. The most powerful, the "God's Wife of Amun," was often a member of the royal family. This priestess had administrative responsibilities as well as the obligation to perform religious rituals.

CHANGE IN THE NEW KINGDOM While there was much continuity between the New Kingdom and its predecessors, at two points in its history the New Kingdom took a new direction. In the

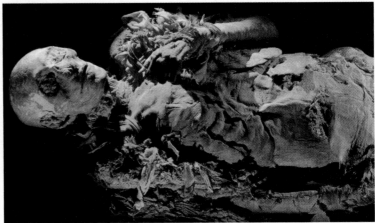

HATSHEPSUT: IMAGE AND REALITY

Although she was a woman, tradition required that Hatshepsut be depicted as a man, as in this statue where she wears the pharaoh's customary beard. In 2007, archaeologists discovered Hatshepsut's mummy. Research revealed that the queen was between ages 45 and 60 when she died, that she had cancer, and that she was quite obese.

Source: Head from an Osiride Statue of Hatshepsut. Egypt, New Kingdom, 18th dynasty, joint reign of Hatshepsu and Thutmose III. Ca. 1473–1458 BCE. From Deir-el- Bahri, Thebes. Limestone, H. 124.5 cm (49 in.). Rogers Fund, 1931 (31.3.157). The Metropolitan Museum of Art, New York, NY, U.S.A. Image © The Metropolitan Museum of Art/Art Resource, NY.

first, Egypt came under the rule of a remarkable woman; in the second, of a religious visionary.

In 1479 B.C.E. the pharaoh Thutmose II (ca. 1491–1479 B.C.E.) died. His son—by a subordinate wife—and successor, Thutmose III, was a child, so Thutmose II's chief wife and half-sister, Hatshepsut, became regent for the child-king. While Hatshepsut at first kept the titles often associated with the pharaoh's wife, such as "God's Wife," within two years she claimed the title of pharaoh. Evidence indicates that women had ruled Egypt on four earlier occasions, but these women may have been only regents and so not recognized as kings. In contrast, Hatshepshut clearly claimed to be, and was acclaimed as, pharaoh.

Because pharaohs had always been men, all of the images of kingly power were male, and the elaborate royal rituals presumed a male ruler. Hatshepsut adapted her image to these expecta-

tions. For example, in most inscriptions she is referred to by masculine titles and pronouns, and most of her statues depict her as a man, complete with a ceremonial beard. On some statues, however, Hatshepsut does appear as a woman, and in some inscriptions she is called "Daughter [rather than Son] of Re."

Hatshepsut ruled for over 20 years. Like most male pharaohs, she waged war when necessary, including a major campaign in Nubia, but most of her reign was peaceful. When she died about 1458 B.C.E., Thutmose III took the throne. Late in his 30-year reign, he ordered that Hatshepsut's name be chiseled off monuments throughout Egypt and all her statues be destroyed. Why he did so is a mystery. Because Thutmose waited so long to try to erase the evidence of Hatshepsut's rule, it seems unlikely that he was angry at her for becoming king. A more convincing explanation is that

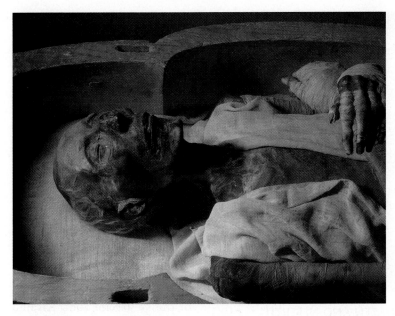

MUMMY OF RAMESSES II

Both a science and an art, mummification preserved the body of King Ramesses II (r. 1279–1213 B.C.E.) for more than 3,000 years. Using a metal hook, embalmers extracted the brains through the nostrils. Sometimes they filled the skull with linen cloth and resin. Through an incision below the ribs, they removed all the organs except for the heart, which represented a person's life and would be examined by the gods on Judgment Day. The embalmers then dried the corpse by packing it with natrum, a natural compound of sodium carbonate and bicarbonate. After adding hairpieces and artificial eyes, the embalmers applied a layer of resin over the face and body, followed by a coat of paint—red for men and yellow for women.

Source: The Art Archive/Egyptian Museum Cairo/Dagli Orti

Thutmose was attempting to fulfill his basic duty as Egypt's king: to maintain *ma'at*. Hatshepsut's reign may have seemed too disorderly, too much of a change from the proper way of doing things. And so, to inform the gods that Egypt had returned to "proper" male kingship, Thutmose III ordered Hatshepsut erased from history.

Thutmose may have regarded the memory of Hatshepsut's reign as a danger to *ma'at*. It was, however, a stable era, in contrast to the second point at which the New Kingdom took a short, sharp change in direction. During the reign of Amenhotep IV (r. 1351–1334 B.C.E.),

Egypt experienced a religious revolution. His father, Amenhotep III (r. 1388–1351 B.C.E.), had emphasized worship of Aten, the solar disc associated with the sun god Re, during his years on the throne. Building on this emphasis, Amenhotep IV, changed his own name to Akhenaten ("one useful to Aten") and declared that Aten was not just the supreme god, but the only god.

Akhenaten attacked the worship of other gods, dismissed priests, closed temples, and appropriated their wealth and lands for himself. He forbade the celebration of ancient public festivals to the other gods and even the mention of their names, which his agents chiseled from monuments and buildings. Full of religious enthusiasm, Akhenaten and his queen, Nefertiti, abandoned the capital of Thebes and built a new city where no temple had ever stood. Because the modern name for this site is Tell el-Amarna, historians refer to this period of religious ferment as the **Amarna Period.**

Because Akhenaten forbade the worship of other gods, some historians have argued that the Egyptians in the Amarna Period were the first people in history to develop **monotheism,** the idea of a single, all-powerful god. Yet this ignores the importance of pharaoh worship in Akhenaten's new religion. Akhenaten insisted that he and Nefertiti be worshiped as gods. Rather than inventing monotheism, then, Akhenaten may have been trying to restore the Old Kingdom conception of the king as a divine being.

Whatever Akhenaten's intentions or personal beliefs, his religious revolution proved

THE SUN GOD BLESSES AKHENATEN AND NEFERTITI

In this panel that once decorated an altar, the Sun God Aten beams his blessing down onto Akhenaten and his wife Nefertiti, as they play with their daughters.

B.C.E.), rebuilt the temples destroyed by Akhenaten's agents and returned the revenue that Akhenaten had appropriated from the priests. Egypt turned back to its traditional religious beliefs and practices, and *ma'at* was restored.

In the twelfth century B.C.E., however, Egypt slipped into a long decline. Drought, poor harvests, and inflation ruined the Egyptian economy, while weak rulers struggled to hold the kingdom together. But as we will see in Chapter 2, domestic developments alone do not explain the collapse of the New Kingdom. Around 1150 B.C.E., the interconnected societies of Anatolia, Mesopotamia, and the eastern Mediterranean coast, as well as Egypt, experienced economic hardship and political fragmentation. The prosperity and stability of the Late Bronze Age abruptly disappeared. In the next chapter we will look closely at the factors that shaped this period of prosperity, the developments that brought it to an end, and the kingdoms that emerged in its aftermath.

short-lived. Because ordinary Egyptians were unwilling to abandon the many traditional gods who played an important role in their daily lives, the priests whose power Akhenaten had undermined succeeded in arousing opposition to the reforms. After Akhenaten's death, the royal court returned to Memphis. The new pharaoh, Tutankhamun (r. 1334–1325

CHRONOLOGY: CIVILIZATION IN EGYPT

ca. 2680	Earliest pyramids built; Old Kingdom emerges
ca. 2200	Collapse of the Old Kingdom; First Intermediate Period Begins
ca. 2040	Mentuhotep II reunites Egypt; Middle Kingdom begins
ca. 1720	Disintegration of the Middle Kingdom; Second Intermediate Period begins
ca. 1650	Hyksos rule begins
ca. 1550	Ahmose I expels the Hyksos; New Kingdom begins
ca. 1480	Hatshepsut rules as female pharaoh
ca. 1351	Amenhotep IV (Akhenaten) attempts a religious revolution
ca. 1150	Collapse of the New Kingdom

CONCLUSION

Civilization and the West

During the millennia covered in this chapter, early Europeans such as Ötzi the Ice Man learned to control and capitalize on nature in many ways—cultivating crops, domesticating animals, and smelting copper. Linked by trade networks, their villages were growing larger and their societies more stratified and specialized. Even so, most of Europe did not make the leap into civilization during the third and second millennia B.C.E., and "the West" did not yet exist. The idea of "Western civilization" as both a geographic and cultural designation emerged much later, with the Greeks (see Chapter 3) who used the term *Europe* to designate the West—and who, like us, were often unclear about the West's actual boundaries.

Yet in areas that we often regard as outside the boundaries of the West, in Iraq and in Egypt, Western civilization had its beginnings. From the ancient Mesopotamian and Egyptian civilizations, the West inherited such crucial components as systems of writing and numeracy, and the core of its legal traditions. These civilizations also left a treasury of religious stories and ideas that, adapted and revised by a small, relatively powerless people called the Hebrews, became the foundational ethic of Western civilization. That development, within the context of the collapse of the International Bronze Age, is one of the main themes of Chapter 2.

KEY TERMS

Neolithic Age	*Homo sapiens sapiens*
culture	Levantine Corridor
civilization	Fertile Crescent
megalith*s*	patriarchy
redistributive	*ma'at*
economies	Old Kingdom
empire	hieroglyph
composite bow	Middle Kingdom
polytheism	bronze
ziggurat	New Kingdom
divination	pharaoh
deduction	vizier
cuneiform	Amarna Period
Law Code of Hammurabi	monotheism

CHAPTER QUESTIONS

1. What is the link between the food-producing revolution of the Neolithic era and the emergence of civilizations? (page 11)

2. What changes and continuities characterized Mesopotamian civilization between the emergence of Sumer's city-states and the rise of Hammurabi's Babylonian empire? (page 17)

3. What distinctive features characterized Egyptian civilization throughout its long history? (page 29)

TAKING IT FURTHER

1. Each of the cultures studied in this chapter developed a distinctive architectural form: the megalith, the ziggurat, and the pyramid. What do they tell us about the societies that built them?

2. Sargon was the first empire builder in history. How did he do it? Why did he do it?

3. How and why did Mesopotamian and Egyptian cultural and religious patterns differ? Which is the more striking, the differences between them or the parallels?

 Practice on MyHistoryLab

2

The Age of Empires: The International Bronze Age and Its Aftermath, ca. 1500–550 B.C.E.

■ The Dynamism of the International Bronze Age ■ Recovery and Rebuilding: Empires and Societies in the Aftermath of the International Bronze Age ■ The Civilization of the Hebrews

In 1984, SCUBA-DIVING ARCHAEOLOGISTS BEGAN TO EXCAVATE THE WRECK OF A merchant ship that sank about 1300 B.C.E. at Uluburun, off the southern coast of Turkey. Its cargo included ostrich eggshells, elephant tusks, and a trumpet carved from a hippopotamus tooth from Egypt, a ton of scented resin from Southwest Asia, and pomegranates packed in finely painted storage jars from the island of Cyprus. The ship's hold also contained 354 flat copper bars, each weighing about 50 pounds, and several bars of tin.

The Uluburun ship's cargo highlights two defining features of the **Late Bronze Age** (1500–1100 B.C.E.). First, the ship carried copper and tin, the metals needed to make bronze, one of the most desired commodities of this era. Because substantial deposits of tin and copper were rarely found in the same region, merchants—such as those who contracted with the Uluburun ship owner—traded over long distances and across political boundaries to obtain both ores. In turn, monarchs devoted military and

diplomatic resources to fostering and protecting this trade, the foundation of much of their prosperity and power. Thus, a second defining feature of the Late Bronze Age was its unprecedented degree of international trade and diplomatic exchange. The Uluburn ship could not have stopped at so many ports and picked up such a diverse cargo had monarchs not worked together to construct a stable international structure. Trade networks, an international diplomatic system, and cultural exchanges made the Late Bronze Age the "International Bronze Age."

The International Bronze Age collapsed suddenly and somewhat mysteriously between (roughly) 1200 and 1100 B.C.E. Like a wrecked cargo ship, once-vibrant cultures sank into a dark age of invasions, migrations, and political fragmentation. In the aftermath of these turbulent events, two of the most powerful empires the world has ever known, the Neo-Assyrian and the Neo-Babylonian, rose to dominate the ancient world. Regarding themselves as the

HOUSE OF THE ADMIRAL

Created about 1500 B.C.E., this lively wall painting is about 22-feet long and a foot and a half high and comes from the so-called House of the Admiral on the island of Thera, midway between Crete and Greece. The scenes of busy maritime activity outside a harbor town provide a glimpse of the international connections that created the "International Bronze Age."

heirs of the Sumerian, Akkadian, and Old Babylonian civilizations examined in Chapter 1, the rulers of these new empires consciously sought to preserve and pass on Mesopotamian traditions. Thus, the continuity of Mesopotamian culture remained unbroken, despite the political tumult of these centuries.

While mighty empires dominated the International Bronze Age and its aftermath, for the history of the West, the most important development of this period occurred on the fringes of empire, amidst a relatively small and powerless people. Called the Israelites or the Hebrews, these people developed the world's first monotheistic religious system and created the ethical framework of Western civilization.

THE DYNAMISM OF THE INTERNATIONAL BRONZE AGE

■ What elements made up the international system of the Late Bronze Age and why did this system suddenly collapse?

Trade in not only tin and copper for the making of bronze but also luxury goods and princess brides, ships and chariots, and even architectural styles and religious ideas created the International Bronze Age—and numerous sources for the historian to study. Rulers used the wealth generated by trade to erect palaces and temples, the remains of which provide archaeo-logical evidence. These rulers also employed numerous scribes who recorded their economic agreements, diplomatic maneuvers, and military accomplishments. Inscribed on clay tablets rather than written on perishable parchment or paper, many of these documents survived across the millennia. In 1887, for example, an Egyptian peasant woman uncovered a collection of over 370 cuneiform tablets, the diplomatic and impe-rial correspondence of the pharaohs from the mid-fourteenth century B.C.E. These **Amarna Let-ters,** as they are called (because they were found at Tell El-Amarna), include correspondence between the pharaoh and rulers of other empires, and communications sent to the pharaoh by the leaders of his vassal states in Canaan. Written in Akkadian (the Mesopotamian language used for international communication), the Amarna Let-ters offer detailed evidence about the interna-tional system of the Late Bronze Age.

Zones of Power within the International Bronze Age

The economic and diplomatic network of the International Bronze Age covered five separate but interconnected zones. **Map 2.1** highlights

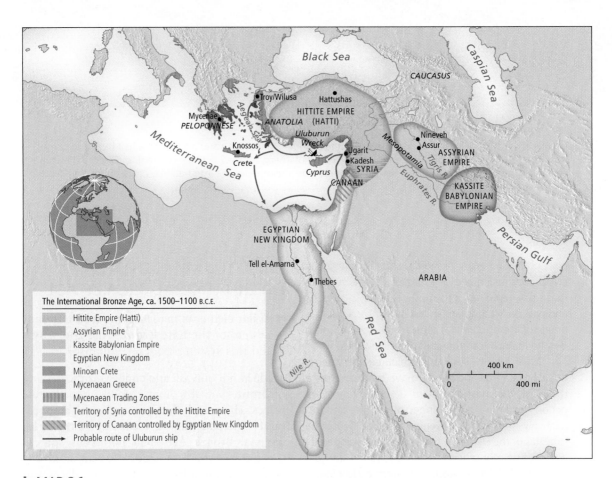

MAP 2.1

The International Bronze Age, ca. 1500–1100 B.C.E.

For 500 years, networks of commerce and diplomacy tied together the distinct cultures of Egypt, Greece, Anatolia, and Southwest Asia.

these zones: to the south, the New Kingdom in Egypt; to the north, the Hittite Empire in Anatolia; to the east, the Assyrian and Babylonian Empires in Mesopotamia; to the west, the eastern Mediterranean kingdoms of the Minoans on Crete and the Mycenaeans on mainland Greece; and finally, several small kingdoms along the Syrian–Canaanite coast.

THE HITTITE KINGDOM OF HATTI In Chapter 1, we explored the history of the first zone of power in the International Bronze Age: New Kingdom Egypt. The second zone of power lay in the rich plateau of Anatolia (modern Turkey). By about 1650 B.C.E., an **Indo-European** people called the Hittites had established control over this region. "Indo-European" is a linguistic term: Armenian, Persian, and a majority of European languages, share similarities in vocabulary and grammar inherited from an Indo-European parent language. Distinguished, then, from the Semitic and other peoples of Southwest Asia by the language they spoke, the Hittites' origins remain obscure. Some scholars argue that they originated in northern India. Others believe that Indo-Europeans traveled from a homeland in the Caucasus to populate not only Anatolia but also modern-day India, Europe, and Iran. Still other scholars contend that Indo-Europeans existed in Anatolia from prehistory on.

Whatever their origins, by 1650 B.C.E. the Hittites had established a prosperous kingdom in central Anatolia called Hatti. The once-prominent idea that the Hittites invented the process of smelting iron and that their power rested on this secret skill has now been debunked. But even without iron, Hittite power gradually expanded from Anatolia into western Mesopotamia and Syria, and by the fourteenth century B.C.E., into Canaan.

This expansion meant that the Hittite Empire and New Kingdom Egypt were soon competing for the same territories. Competition erupted into outright war at a number of points and finally produced an epic yet curiously indecisive military encounter: the Battle of Kadesh of 1274 B.C.E. (See *Encounters and Transformations* in this chapter.) Drained by this battle and

those that succeeded it, Pharaoh Ramesses II and Hittite King Hattusili III turned to a diplomatic solution: They agreed that the Hittites would control northern Syria while Egypt kept its Canaanite territories. This treaty transformed long-term enemies into allies and marked a crucial step in stabilizing international relations.

Imperial expansion brought many diverse peoples under Hittite rule and reshaped Hittite religious practice. The Hittites rightly called their country "the land of a thousand gods." To unify its peoples, the Hittite monarchy transported its subjects' gods to its capital city of Hattushas and built many temples for them. Called the "Great King," the Hittite monarch played the role of chief priest of all the gods worshiped by the many different communities under his control. The new gods were simply added to the Hittite pantheon, regardless of any overlap or duplication of function. Thus, Hittite religion contained numerous Sun Gods, Father Gods, warrior deities, and fertility goddesses, and countless contradictory religious legends.

Just as they embraced new gods, the Hittites adopted other aspects of different cultures—such as architecture, diet, medical practices, and folklore—and transmitted these cultural borrowings to other peoples. The Hittites, then, played an important role in passing ancient Mesopotamian ideas to the Greeks, and thus to what became Western civilization. The Greek myth of Hercules likely resulted from this process. The survival of the *Epic of Gilgamesh* in Hittite archives reveals that the Hittites adopted this Mesopotamian story (see Chapter 1), which they then passed on, via trade and conquest, to the Greeks. Over centuries of cultural transmission and transformation, Gilgamesh, the quintessential Mesopotamian hero, became Hercules. Similarly, Mesopotamian mathematical concepts probably made their way into Greek (and, hence, Western) culture via the Hittites.

Some scholars argue that the Hittites also deserve credit for creating the concept of history. In the Hittite kingdom, official proclamations often contained lengthy introductions that set the decree or treaty in context by reciting the

A GOD OF WAR

This bas-relief of a Hittite warrior god comes from the King's Gate at what was the royal city of Hattusas (Boghazkoy in modern Turkey). The two most important gods in the Hittite state religion were the Storm God (also called the Weather God) and his consort the Sun Goddess. In Hittite myth, the Storm God's rains caused the Sun Goddess to conceive. Paradoxically, this god of life was also a god of war (who displayed his power in thunder and lightning) and may be the figure on this relief—but the Hittite tendency to adopt the gods of the peoples they conquered makes a definite identification difficult.

past events that made it necessary or possible. These historical narratives demonstrate that the Hittites believed human beings could and should learn from history. Hittite kings, for example, were willing to acknowledge the incompetence or sins of past kings (something unthinkable in Egyptian annals in which the god-king could do no wrong), and to link such misbehavior to current misfortunes. Hittite historical accounts show that the Hittites sought to understand the present in terms of the past and saw history as the result of human action as well as divine whim.

KASSITE BABYLON AND ASSYRIA The third zone of power during the International Bronze Age lay in Mesopotamia. Around 1600 B.C.E. people known as Kassites infiltrated Mesopotamia as raiders, soldiers, and laborers. Their language and precise place of origin are unknown, but by 1400 B.C.E. they had gained control of most of southern Mesopotamia. For the next 250 years, Kassite monarchs maintained order and prosperity in Babylonia, establishing the longest ruling dynasty in ancient southwest Asian history.

During these centuries, Babylonia enjoyed a golden age. Kassite kings unified Babylonia's many cities through a highly centralized administration that controlled both urban centers and the countryside. The Kassite kings gained a reputation for fair rule by giving land to individuals of all ranks and by spending lavishly on temples, public buildings, and canals throughout the kingdom. Political stability and economic prosperity enabled Kassite Babylonia to become a renowned center of literature and learning. Seeking to overcome their outsider origins, Kassite kings claimed the Mesopotamian cultural legacy as their own. They ordered their scribes to copy and thus preserve Sumerian and Akkadian works.

Babylonia's chief rival for dominance in the Mesopotamian region during the International Bronze Age lay to the north: Assyria. Around 1360 B.C.E., the Assyrian kingdom began a new phase of expansion that culminated in the reign of the mighty Tukulti-Ninurta I (r. 1244–1208 B.C.E.), who led his armies to victory over Babylonia itself. By the time of Tukulti-Ninurta's death, Assyria controlled all the lands from northern Syria to southern Iraq.

THE MEDITERRANEAN CIVILIZATIONS: MINOAN CRETE AND MYCENAEAN GREECE The fourth zone of power in the International Bronze Age lay to the east, with the Mediterranean civilizations of

Minoan Crete and Mycenean Greece. Although not as large and powerful as Egypt's New Kingdom or the Mesopotamian empires of Kassite Babylon and Assyria, these seafaring civilizations played a vital role in the international system that shaped the Late Bronze Age. They were also the predecessors of ancient Greece.

Minoan civilization emerged about 2600 B.C.E. when small urban communities on the island of Crete began to trade with Egypt and to import copper and tin from the eastern Mediterranean. By 1700 B.C.E., the Minoans had developed a magnificent palace-centered culture. These palaces served as political, economic, and religious centers. Unlike the symmetrical monumental buildings of Mesopotamia and Egypt, Minoan palaces were so sprawling that the Greeks later termed them "labyrinths." Ordinary Minoans lived in houses built around the palace. Some of these palace-centered communities were actually small cities. Knossos, for example, housed approximately 25,000 people.

Minoan prosperity rested on its sea trade and the export of luxury goods—jewelry, painted vases, and delicate figures carved in the deep blue gemstone called lapis lazuli. The Minoans developed a merchant navy that traded with Greece, Egypt, and the coastal communities of the eastern Mediterranean. High-prowed and sturdy, Minoan vessels were well-suited for sailing the Mediterranean Sea.

Although their language was evidently Indo-European, the Minoans learned their pictographic script from the Egyptians. Called "Linear A," Minoan script has yet to be fully deciphered. As a result, what we know about the Minoans comes from art and architecture, rather than texts. The lack of military fortifications around Minoan palaces—in contrast to the strong defenses that ringed other Late Bronze Age centers—and the many images of women on the wall paintings from Minoan palaces have provoked speculation about Minoan social life. Some scholars argued that Minoan society was unusually peace-loving and **matriarchal** (female-dominated). Later discoveries

LEAPING THE BULL

Scholars used to think that this Minoan mural ca. 1500 B.C.E. depicted a sporting event, perhaps similar to the contests staged between animals and men in the Roman Colosseum centuries later. Scientists now tell us that it is impossible to somersault over a charging bull, so perhaps the mural has religious or astrological significance. What is clear is the undeniable Minoan artistry, able to communicate power and grace across the millennia.

A Diplomatic Revolution

To greedy and ambitious rulers, the lands stretching from western Syria down the Canaanite corridor (today's Lebanon, Israel, and Palestine) offered numerous temptations—timberlands, agricultural fields and pasture lands, hills heavy with metals, and port cities with international commercial connections. In the thirteenth century B.C.E., this region became the site of an important encounter between the Hittite and Egyptian empires, one that transformed not only Great Power alignments for the next century, but also diplomacy itself.

During the fourteenth century B.C.E., the Hittite Empire had expanded southward. By the turn of the century, however, Egypt under the New Kingdom had regained enough power to challenge Hittite control of Syria and Canaan. For two decades, the two empires jostled for advantage. Then, Ramesses II (1279–1212 B.C.E.) succeeded to the throne of New Kingdom Egypt. Determined to push the Hittites out of Canaan and Syria, Ramesses spent five years gathering troops for battle. In 1274 B.C.E. he led his army northward. Muwattalli II (ca. 1295–1272) awaited him with a Hittite and mercenary army of 37,000 infantry and 3,500 chariotry. The stage was set for a decisive battle between the two empires.

As the Egyptians under Ramesses drew near to the Syrian city of Kadesh, they captured two supposed deserters from the Hittite army. These men reported that Muwattalli, alarmed by Ramesses' advance, had retreated with his army about 200 miles to the north. Delighted with the news, Ramesses decided to press on to Kadesh with just one division in the hopes of capturing the city before the Hittites moved south again. This decision left the Egyptian army strung out over several miles. Moreover, the "deserters" were actually Muwattalli's spies: Ramesses had fallen into a carefully set trap. The Hittite army launched a surprise attack on Ramesses' poorly situated forces.

Panic-stricken, the Egyptians broke—but then Ramesses himself led a chariot charge. Inspired by the pharaoh's personal bravery (or so Ramesses' account of the battle insisted), his

men rallied. In addition, both Hittite lack of discipline—Hittite soldiers turned to plunder the Egyptian camp rather than press their advance—and the lucky arrival of a force of allied Canaanite charioteers helped swing the day in the Egyptians' favor. Yet Egypt did not win the battle. Muwattalli lost almost all of his chariots, but the next day his infantry withstood Ramesses' attacks. Deciding enough was enough, Ramesses turned around and went home. Once back in Egypt, he boasted of a great victory. Although no such victory had occurred, Ramesses' less-than-accurate version of the battle was inscribed on pillars across the land.

The struggle over Syria and Canaan continued. Over the next several years, Ramesses and his army fought a number of battles against the forces of Muwattalli and his successors. Neither, however, possessed the strength to annihilate the other because the Battle of Kadesh had depleted the resources of both Great Powers. And while they were busy draining each other dry, Assyria was amassing military power and economic strength. This new player could seize control of the entire game if the two seasoned veterans did not switch strategy.

In 1258 B.C.E., Ramesses II and the Hittite king Hattusili III (ca. 1267–1237 B.C.E.) signed an innovative treaty. Ramesses abandoned claims to northern Syria and Hattusili acknowledged Egyptian control over Canaan. Yet the treaty did more than end the fighting. It also created an alliance: The two powers agreed to aid one another in case of invasion or rebellion. The treaty demonstrated that diplomatic ties could serve Great Power interests. This diplomatic innovation survived long after both the Hittite Empire and the New Kingdom had disappeared into history.

For Discussion

Despite Ramesses' grandiose claims to the contrary, Egypt did not win a great victory in the Battle of Kadesh. Why, then, is this battle seen as historically significant?

of weapons collections and the strong evidence for the existence of bull worship—a practice usually linked with patriarchal societies—call these arguments into question. The dominance of female images in the paintings more likely points to an emphasis on fertility, while the lack of defensive fortifications probably indicates that the Minoans possessed a navy strong enough to make them feel secure on their island home.

This security ended abruptly and mysteriously. Minoan prosperity and power disappeared around 1400 B.C.E. Archaeologists do not know whether invaders caused the collapse of Minoan power or whether Minoan Crete was destroyed by a natural disaster, perhaps a tidal wave linked to a volcanic eruption on the nearby island of Thera.

In the wake of the Minoan collapse, the balance of economic power in the eastern Mediterranean shifted to the mainland of Mycenaean Greece. The term *Mycenaean* refers both to the kingdom of Mycenae (located in the Peloponnese, the southern peninsula of mainland Greece) and, more generally, to the culture of Greece during the International Bronze Age. Mycenae dominated the Peloponnese, but did not rule all of Greece. Instead, the Mycenaean kingdoms traded with and warred against each other.

In the century before the Minoan collapse, the Mycenaeans interacted extensively with Minoan Crete and adapted many of its cultural practices, including its palace-centered economy and a script related to Linear A. Called "**Linear B,**" it is the earliest written form of Greek. Unfortunately, the surviving palace records, written on clay tablets, all relate to economic matters—landholding records, lists of broken equipment, inventories of available storage space, and the like. None of the tablets contains a story or religious hymn or battle chronicle.

Although we have no literary record of Mycenaean values or beliefs, the archaeological evidence, particularly Mycenaean burial sites, reveals a prosperous and militaristic culture. Mycenaean merchants extended Minoan commercial routes as far west as Spain and northern Italy. The line between trading and raiding was never very solid, however, and the Mycenaeans earned a well-deserved reputation for piracy.

CITY-STATES AND COASTAL COMMUNITIES: SYRIA AND CANAAN As **Map 2.1** shows, the final zone of power in the International Bronze Age consisted of the regions of Syria and Canaan (or Palestine). The political fragmentation of this region and its key location made it the battleground on which the Hittite, Mesopotamian, and Egyptian empires fought for supremacy. Often reduced to pawns in imperial power plays, the small states of Syria and Canaan nevertheless played an active role in fostering trading relations, shaping diplomatic patterns, and initiating cultural innovation.

The city-state of Ugarit, for example, appears frequently in Late Bronze Age texts. A port city, Ugarit controlled a kingdom of about 2,000 square miles blessed with rich natural resources. The fertile plain offered arable land for grape vines, olive trees, and grains, while the surrounding hill forests provided timber for shipbuilding and construction. Ugarit's greatest asset was a natural harbor that made the city a hub of international trade. Merchant ships, such as the one that sank at Uluburun, sailed to Ugarit from across the Mediterranean, while caravans laden with goods arrived from Mesopotamia, the Hittite lands, and Canaan. People from all these places settled in Ugarit, whose population was estimated at about 6,000–8,000 inhabitants. Perhaps another 25,000 people lived as farmers in about 150 villages in the Ugarit countryside. Its natural resources and strategic location, however, made Ugarit a natural target for acquisitive empires. By the thirteenth century B.C.E., the Hittite emperor chose the occupant of Ugarit's throne.

Ugarit was fairly typical of the city-states of Syria and Canaan during the International Bronze Age. In scattered cities throughout the region, urban culture thrived as a result of the flourishing international trade (and heavy exploitation of the rural agricultural populations). Continued prosperity, however, demanded that Syrian and Canaanite rulers walk a diplomatic tightrope, allying first with this empire and then with that, negotiating for survival in an age of imperial might.

TROY: A CITY OF LEGEND   The five zones of power that we have delineated provide the parameters of the International Bronze Age. Scattered among these zones were small city-states and kingdoms, sometimes swallowed up by one of the large empires, sometimes independent. One of these, the Anatolian city-state of Troy, has captured the popular imagination for 3,000 years, ever since it was immortalized as the site of the Trojan War in Homer's epic poem, the *Iliad,* which recounts the final year of the tragic clash between the Greeks and the Trojans. According to the *Iliad,* the war began when Paris of Troy kidnapped the beautiful Helen, queen of the Greek city-state of Sparta, and ended with the total destruction of Troy.

The *Iliad* was put into written form about 750 B.C.E., yet most scholars agree that it came out of an oral tradition extending back to the Late Bronze Age. The name "Troy" does not appear in Bronze Age documents, but many archaeologists argue that a conflict between Mycenae and a city-state called Wilusa in ancient texts may have sparked the oral tradition that became Homer's story of the war between the Greeks and Trojans—although if so, the point of contention was probably something dull, such as the question of safe passage for merchant ships, rather than the raging passion stirred up by a beautiful queen.

Archaeologists have identified the likely site of Troy/Wilusa on the northwestern Anatolian coast. Excavations there reveal that Troy prospered in the Late Bronze Age. Numerous distinct layers of occupation and construction tell us that generations of inhabitants rebuilt the city time and time again from about 3000 to 1000 B.C.E. Like the Troy of Homer's story, Troy VI (the sixth layer of occupation) was a grand city. It featured monumental gateways and a royal palace compound containing many mansions. But sometime around 1300 B.C.E., the city was destroyed—not by an enemy army, as in the legend of Troy, but probably by an earthquake. Troy's inhabitants rapidly

THE "DEATH MASK OF AGAMEMNON"

This thin gold mask, about eleven inches long, was found at the citadel of Mycenae in the tomb of a ruler who died about 1550 B.C.E. Heinrich Schliemann, whose excavations were the first to show that Troy did exist in history as well as legend, mistakenly jumped to the conclusion that it was the death mask of King Agamemnon, who led the Greek forces during the Trojan War, as told in Homer's *Iliad.*

rebuilt, but this new city (Troy VIIa) was smaller and poorer, not at all like the glorious civilization of Homer's tale.

So is Homer's Troy purely fiction? Perhaps... but perhaps not. We know that around 950 B.C.E. something decimated the city (Tory VIIb3) and left it a pile of rubble. Enemy raids could have caused Troy's final destruction. Possibly the memory of these events fused with earlier tales of the grand civilization of Troy VI and its conflicts with Mycenaean Greeks and eventually took the form of Homer's *Iliad.* Like the *Epic of Gilgamesh,* the *Iliad* is a verbal version of an archaeological site, with many different layers of "occupation."

The Club of the Great Powers

Historians have used the label "the Club of the Great Powers" to describe the international network that shaped the Late Bronze Age. As the word *club* indicates, these Great Powers interacted closely and in so doing, developed concepts and tools of international diplomacy and interchange that survived long after the Great Powers themselves had collapsed.

GREAT POWER RELATIONS AND EXCHANGES Great Power rulers knew who was in their club, who was leveraging for entrance, and who was vulnerable for expulsion. In the beginning of the Late Bronze Age, for example, Assyria was still too small and weak to be a member. By around 1330 B.C.E., however, Assyrian power was expanding and King Assur-Ubalit I decided it was time to join the Great Powers' Club. He sent lavish gifts and a letter to the pharaoh that dared address the Egyptian ruler as an equal: "Up to now, my predecessors had not written: today I write to you."[1] In many ways, Great Power rulers acted as if they all belonged to the same extended (if somewhat dysfunctional) family. They addressed each other as "Brother," exchanged boastful letters, and exchanged gifts to celebrated enthronements, military conquests, and marriages (often to each others' daughters and sisters).

The gift exchanges among the Great Powers were highly formalized. Rulers did not hesitate to correct colleagues who failed to abide by the rules. For example, the Hittite king, Hattusili III, lectured the king of Assyria when he failed to send a suitable gift:

> It is the custom that when kings assume kingship, the kings, his equals in rank, send him appropriate gifts of greeting, clothing befitting kingship, and fine oil for his anointing. But you did not do this today.

Abiding by the rules of gift exchange was more than a matter of reciprocal greed. First, these exchanges signaled that each ruler recognized the legitimacy of the other, and so helped maintain the stability of international relations. Second, the rules of gift-giving were, for Great Power rulers, part of the definition of "civilization," and therefore one of the characteristics that differentiated them from barbarians. To be a member of the Club of Great Powers was to be a part of the civilized world. And third, gift-giving served as a disguised form of trade. One king would send a "gift" to another, and then demand a "gift" of equal value in return. In this way, luxury goods and other items in high demand circulated throughout the International Bronze Age economy. Egypt, for example, was the source of most of the Near Eastern gold supply as well as ivory, ebony, and alabaster.

Gift exchanges were confined to the Great Power kings and their queens, but Great Power rulers also actively fostered and protected trade in its wider forms. Much of their correspondence concerned the safety of caravan routes and shipping lanes. A ruler was responsible for the security of his realm. If bandits attacked a merchant's caravan, the ruler of the region in which the attack occurred was expected to make restitution. Trade was important to Great Power rulers both for the wealth it produced and for the taxes it generated. Moreover, international trade brought together the tin and copper needed to make bronze.

CONQUEST AND CLIENT STATES We saw in Chapter 1 that bronze was the key component of the light chariot, the central military technology of International Bronze Age empires. Because of the expense of maintaining armies of trained charioteers, Great Power rulers were constantly on the lookout for new sources of income. In addition to relying on trade to generate revenue, rulers depended on the spoils they claimed from military conquests and the tribute they collected from client states. War in the International Bronze Age was thus a business venture.

After conquest, most states became vassals or client-states of the conquering Great Power. Client-states provided their Great Power overlord with annual tribute and often with auxiliary troops. The relationship between a client-state and a Great Power was clearcut. A Great Power monarch writing to the ruler of one of his client-states would begin, "My servant." A client king's salutation to his overlord made the relationship even plainer:

> My king, my lord, my sun god, I prostrate myself at the feet of my lord, my sun god, seven times and seven times.[2]

COMMONALITIES AMONG THE GREAT POWER CULTURES   The Egyptian, Hittite, Assyrian, Babylonian, and Minoan-Mycenean societies occupied different agricultural spaces; the fertility of the Nile delta, for example, contrasted with the aridity of most of Anatolia. They also possessed different histories, religions, and customs. Nevertheless, the Great Power societies in the International Bronze Age shared the same basic socioeconomic structures and militaristic values.

Archaeologists and historians use the term **palace system** to describe Late Bronze Age societies. In this system, wealth and power concentrated in the hands of the small ruling elite, who lived separated from the laboring masses in monumental fortified palaces. Sometimes constituting entire cities, these palaces were set apart from the neighborhoods of ordinary people. In Assur, capital city of the Assyrian Empire, for example, all the palaces and temples stood within the walled inner city, far from the areas where the rest of the city's populace lived.

The Minoan palace at Knossos exemplifies the International Bronze Age palace system. The palace occupied three acres. At its center stood a courtyard surrounded by hundreds of rooms that served as living quarters for the political and religious elite, administrative headquarters, and shrines for religious worship. Frescoes (plaster painted while it is still wet) of sea creatures, flowers, acrobats, and scenes of daily life adorned the walls. The residents enjoyed indoor plumbing and running water, comforts that most people in the West would not enjoy until the nineteenth century C.E.

Two distinct social hierarchies delineated International Bronze Age societies: the palace dependents and the free people in the villages. The first group comprised the military officers, religious officials, scribes, craftsmen, and agricultural laborers within the palace system. Paid with rations, in the case of lower ranked laborers and craftsmen, and with royal land grants in the upper ranks, they ensured the continuity of imperial administration and the luxurious lifestyle of the royal family. At Knossos, the palace dependents' rations were stored in warehouses that could hold more than a quarter million gallons of wine or olive oil. The regularity of such rations meant that the palace dependents were probably better off than the free villagers in the countryside. Obliged to pay taxes and to labor on royal building projects for a part of every year, these villagers practiced mixed farming, scraping out a living growing grains, cultivating fruit trees, and grazing sheep and goats. In bad times, they were forced to borrow from wealthier neighbors. If they could not pay back the debt, they were forced into slavery.

At the top of all Bronze Age societies stood the royal family, the members of which lived in luxury beyond the comprehension of most of their subjects—and of most of us today. Thirty royal graves uncovered at Mycenae contain skeletons nearly six feet tall—taller than the average Mycenaean and clear evidence that the kings enjoyed better nutrition than their subjects. The many gold and silver drinking vessels and pieces of jewelry found in the graves further demonstrate the luxury in which not only Mycenaean but all Bronze Age rulers lived.

All Late Bronze Age cultures glorified military conquest and so placed the warrior high on the social scale. Kings personally led annual military campaigns; hence, battle accounts dominate royal chronicles. In Mycenaea, the graves of warriors contain not only their bodies, but also their armor, weapons, and even their chariots. The burial of such prized items indicates the prestige of the warrior class. To be manly was to be a warrior, as this

THE INTERNATIONAL MONUMENTAL STYLE

Many Late Bronze Age kings constructed new capital cities as a way to proclaim their power to their people and to their potential rivals at home and abroad. In constructing these palaces and cities, kings borrowed from each other's cultures to such a degree that a single "international style" in monumental building emerged, as these Hittite and Mycenaean fortress gates illustrate. The entrance gate to the Hittite capital of Hattusas and the gate into the citadel of Mycenae both feature massive stone lions, the symbol of royal strength in many Bronze Age societies.

account of a Hittite ritual for inducting troops into the army makes clear:

> They bring the garments of a woman, a distaff [for spinning cloth] and a mirror, they break an arrow and you speak as follows: "Is not this that you see here garments of a woman? We have them here for [the ceremony of taking] the oath. Whoever breaks these oaths and does evil to the king and the queen and the princes, let these oaths change him from a man into a woman!" ... Let them break the bows, arrows, and clubs in their hands and let them put in their hands distaff and mirror![3]

Crisis and Collapse: The End of the International Bronze Age

The diplomatic, cultural, and economic connections between Egypt, Southwest Asia, Anatolia, and Greece broke between 1200 and 1100 B.C.E. These civilizations plummeted into a dark age marked by invasions, migrations, and the collapse of stable governments. On the Greek mainland, the Greek language and some religious beliefs endured, but the population declined by an estimated 75 percent; the crafts, artistic styles, and architectural traditions of Mycenaean life were forgotten. Drought, famine, and invasion dominate the surviving records. A later text, *The Epic of Erra*, recalled this era as a time of horror:

> Sealand shall not spare Sealand....nor Assyrian Assyrian.
> Nor shall Elamite spare Elamite, nor Kassite Kassite...
> Nor country country, nor city city,
> Nor shall tribe spare tribe, nor man man, nor brother brother, and they shall slay one another.[4]

THE SEA PEOPLES What happened to cause the end of the International Bronze Age? Ancient texts point to raids and invasions by wandering migrants as a key cause. Around 1100 B.C.E., for example, the king of Ugarit warned the king of another Syrian kingdom, "The ships of the enemy have been coming. They have been burning down my villages and have done evil things to the country."[5] Egyptian accounts, which called these invaders the **Sea Peoples,** described their coming in dramatic terms:

> No land could stand before their arms....They desolated its people, and its land was like that which had never come into being. They were coming forward into Egypt, while the flame was prepared for them.[6]

Who were these "Sea Peoples" and were they responsible for the collapse of the International Bronze Age system? Scholars have yet to reach agreement on an answer to this key question. One set of explanations focuses on events in Mycenaean Greece and the Hittite Empire. We know that warfare among the many Mycenaean kingdoms resulted in the breakdown of its palace-centered economic system by about 1150 B.C.E. Searching for the means of survival, many Greeks migrated. Approximately 50 years later, a deadly combination of famine, civil war, and international invasion triggered the collapse of the Hittite imperial government. As in Mycenaea, economic chaos followed and desperate peasants fled.

The fall of the Mycenaean kingdoms and the Hittite Empire contributed to destabilizing migrations throughout the eastern Mediterranean. Displaced groups plundered cities and brought destruction to the entire eastern Mediterranean as they moved southward. By 1170 B.C.E., the Egyptian Empire had lost control of Syria and Canaan, and Ugarit fell. Groups of raiders settled on the Mediterranean coast and extended their power inland. Organized political life in Canaan soon disintegrated.

SYSTEMIC INSTABILITY The story of the Sea Peoples is dramatic and compelling; it does not, however, fully explain the sudden end of the International Bronze Age. A second set of explanations for this collapse focuses on internal instability, the result of a key weakness of the Late Bronze Age palace system: Its exploitation of agricultural laborers produced high levels of indebted servitude. Peasants took out loans to survive, and then, unable to pay their debts, were forced into slavery. Facing enslavement, many peasants fled to mountainous regions or inaccessible marshes, places where they could eke out a living outside the palace system. They became **habiru**. The term *habiru* is often translated as "robber," "bandit," or "mercenary," and many of the habiru were one or all of those things, forced into such a life by the harshness of the socioeconomic order. For Great Power governments, the *habiru* were a constant problem, not only because of the threat of criminality and social disorder, but more fundamentally, because the flight of peasants worsened agricultural labor shortages and so threatened to undercut the entire palace system.

By the twelfth century B.C.E., this key weakness in the palace system helped destroy it. Many areas appear to have suffered from a lengthy drought, which heightened demands on laborers and escalated the numbers of *habiru*. In turn, those left behind found the demands placed on them even more arduous—and so even more peasants fled. Moreover, when bands of Sea Peoples appeared, many *habiru* were more than happy to join them in ransacking the palaces and temples, the symbols of their oppression. While ancient texts tend to portray the Sea Peoples as outside invaders, recent archaeological and historical research demonstrates that many of them were already settled in the lands they attacked— they were, in other words, rebels rather than invaders, and their rebellion helped to destroy the International Bronze Age.

RECOVERY AND REBUILDING: EMPIRES AND SOCIETIES IN THE AFTERMATH OF THE INTERNATIONAL BRONZE AGE

■ What patterns shaped the development of southwest Asian and Mediterranean societies after the collapse of the Late Bronze Age international system?

After the collapse of the International Bronze Age, the peoples of southwest Asia and the Mediterranean gradually rebuilt their world. Three important changes distinguished this new era from what had come before. First, the sophisticated international diplomatic and economic networks of the Late Bronze Age had disappeared, as had principal players in that network. Second, the disruption of Late Bronze Age trade routes resulted in an important metallurgical shift. No longer able to obtain both the tin and the copper necessary to create bronze, people began turning to a resource more plentiful and nearer to hand: iron. Ancient peoples had long been familiar with iron, but unforged iron is not very durable. Sometime after 1200 B.C.E., however, metalsmiths figured out how to smelt iron: By repeatedly heating the metal in a charcoal furnace, and then cold-hammering it, they created carbon steel, a sturdy metal that could outfight bronze. The **Iron Age** was born. By 1000 B.C.E. iron was widely used throughout the Mediterranean region, and by the ninth century B.C.E.,

CHRONOLOGY: THE INTERNATIONAL BRONZE AGE

ca. 1700 B.C.E.	Minoan civilization flourishes on Crete
ca. 1650–1600 B.C.E.	Hittite Kingdom emerges
ca. 1550 B.C.E.	New Kingdom begins in Egypt
ca. 1450 B.C.E.	First palaces built at Mycenae in Greece
ca. 1400 B.C.E.	Kassites gain control of Babylonia
ca. 1360 B.C.E.	Assyria begins period of expansion
ca. 1200–1100 B.C.E.	International Bronze Age ends

throughout Mesopotamia and Egypt. As we will see, iron enabled the kings of Neo-Assyria and Neo-Babylonia to field armies far larger than ever before—and so to rule empires of unprecedented size.

A third change that distinguishes this era from the Late Bronze Age was the use of the domesticated camel for transport and travel. Camels began to appear in Near Eastern artwork and texts around 1100 B.C.E., although they had probably been domesticated centuries before. Because they can travel on little water, camels opened up desert routes to merchants. Rather than having to take roundabout roads that skirted the desert, they could opt for the direct—therefore, quicker and more profitable—route. As the camel trade became a significant factor in ancient economies, the Arab peoples began to play a larger role in southwest Asian cultures, usually as objects of fear. The ability of Arab raiders to plunder a caravan or to sack a city and then to disappear into the desert became legendary.

Before and Between the Empires

In the so-called "Dark Age" between the collapse of the International Bronze Age and the reemergence of Assyria as an imperial power (roughly 1100–950 B.C.E.), the weakening or disappearance of Great Powers allowed smaller kingdoms and city-states in Mesopotamia and the Levantine Corridor to flourish. As we will see later in this chapter, this period of transition saw the Israelite or Hebrew culture emerge in Canaan. **Map 2.2** shows that the Hebrew states of Israel and Judah rested within a network of Iron Age kingdoms and city-states. For over 600 years, these states formed shifting coalitions and alliances with and against each other and eventually the resurgent Assyrian and Babylonian empires as well.

NEW PEOPLES OF THE LAND: THE ARAMEANS Within the kaleidoscope of peoples, tribes, and migrants that surged through Syria and the Levant, the Arameans played a dominant role. Originally semi-nomadic pastoralists from northern Syria, Aramean tribes expanded into Assyrian and

Babylonian territories during the waning years of the Late Bronze Age. Their raids helped weaken these kingdoms and loosen their hold on their empires. During the subsequent Iron Age, Arameans spread throughout the Near East; by the ninth century B.C.E. Aramean tribes dominated the whole of inland Syria and much of the Mesopotamian countryside, where Aramaic became the language of ordinary people.

The most important Aramaean state was Aram-Damascus, centered on the city of Damascus (see **Map 2.2**). Occupied long before the Arameans emerged in the region, Damascus may be the oldest continuously inhabited city in the world. Damascus prospered and grew powerful during the Iron Age in part because of its location as a key trading post along one of the most economically vital "highways" in the ancient world: the camel caravan route from the Arabian desert to the Mediterranean Sea.

NEW PEOPLES OF THE SEA: THE PHOENICIANS Like the Arameans, the Phoenicians entered the historical record in the final centuries of the Late Bronze Age. Egypt's Late Bronze Age empire included Phoenician city-states along the northern Syrian coast (what is now Lebanon). In the tumult that accompanied the collapse of the International Bronze Age, these cities gained their independence. By 1000 B.C.E., the Phoenicians had developed a dynamic maritime civilization, based in eastern Mediterranean port cities such as Byblos, Tyre, and Sidon. By following old Minoan and Mycenaean trade routes, the port cities created a large commercial sphere of influence.

The Phoenicians, however, ventured beyond these old Bronze Age routes, even sailing into the Atlantic Ocean, as **Map 2.3** shows. The most dramatic Phoenician voyage occurred when Pharoah Necho II (610–595) hired a Phoenician crew to circumnavigate the African continent—almost 2000 years before Europeans would do so. Their sailing experience explains why the Phoenicians were probably the first peoples to develop the *bireme*, a ship with two sets of oars that could, therefore, achieve more speed and power when used in battle.

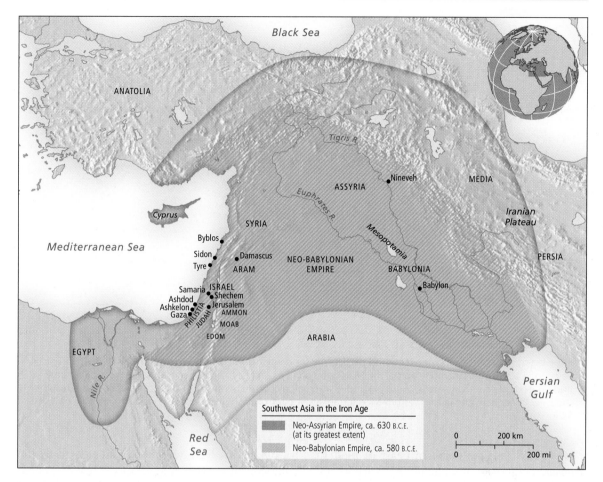

MAP 2.2

Southwest Asia in the Iron Age

The economic and social crisis that accompanied the end of the International Bronze Age brought with it surges of migration, resulting in new peoples settling throughout Southwest Asia and the coalescence of indigenous peoples into new tribal groups. Free (for a time) of Great Power control, Syria and Canaan splintered into small kingdoms and city-states.

When the writers of the Hebrew Bible wanted to demonstrate the fabled wealth of King Solomon, they wrote that he contracted with King Hiram of Tyre for luxury goods and that he imported timber from Byblos. These biblical references to Phoenician city-states highlight Phoenician commercial dominance in the Iron Age. Renowned for their artisanal skills, the Phoenicians traded in weapons, jewelry, woodcraft, and the prized reddish-purple cloth for

which the Phoenicians were named. (The word *Phoenician*, a Greek coinage, translates as "people of the purple cloth.") **Map 2.3** shows that the search for metal ores also motivated much of Phoenician exploration and commerce.

To protect and expand their trade, the Phoenicians established overseas trading posts that grew into self-governing Phoenician colonies. These colonies extended as far as the coast of Spain, but the most important was Carthage

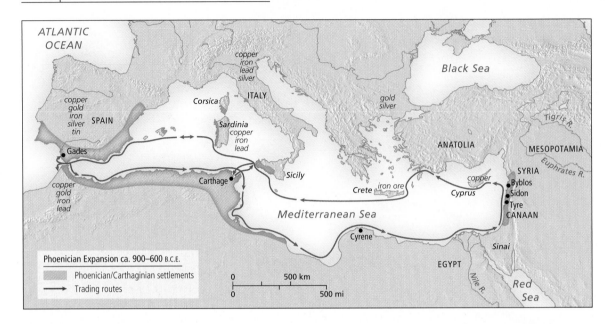

MAP 2.3

Phoenician Expansion, ca. 900–600 B.C.E.

Impelled by the quest for commerce—and particularly for control of the lucrative metals trade—Phoenicians developed a commercial empire across the Mediterranean Sea. Initially, the Phoenician settlements were only trading posts, but in many areas, these expanded into colonial settlements. By 600 B.C.E. Carthage had become the chief Phoenician city in the western Mediterranean. It controlled the resources of north Africa and parts of Spain.

("New City") on the northern coast of modern Tunisia. Because of its magnificent harbor and strategic location, Carthage controlled trade between the eastern and western Mediterranean.

Their economic connections with lands that would later become the center of Western civilization meant that the Phoenicians served as cultural conduits between Near Eastern civilizations and Europe. Through trade and colonization, Phoenicians brought Asian and Egyptian artistic styles, many of them Bronze Age survivals, to western Mediterranean lands. One of the most important of these survivals was the phonetic alphabet. The principle of the phonetic alphabet seems to have been discovered around 1900 B.C.E. by Canaanites working in Egypt. The Canaanites simplified the complex Egyptian hieroglyphic system, keeping fewer than 30 signs, each representing a single consonant. The resulting "Proto-Canaanite"

alphabet evolved into the alphabet used by the Phoenicians, who spread this efficient system of writing throughout the Mediterranean world, where the Greeks and then the Romans adopted it. In this way it became the source of all alphabets and writing in the West.

CANAANITE CULTURES AND CONTINUITIES With the collapse of Egyptian imperial control at the end of the International Bronze Age, Canaan entered a period of instability, with semi-nomadic peoples moving through the region and new states coalescing. **Map 2.2** shows that by around 1000 B.C.E., political power was dispersed among the coastal city-states of the Philistines and the small inland kingdoms of Ammon, Moab, and Edom, as well as Israel and Judah (discussed in the next section).

Many archaeologists argue that the Philistines originated as Aegean "Sea Peoples" who made their way to the Canaanite coast after living for

TABLET AND PARCHMENT; CUNEIFORM AND ALPHABET

This Neo-Assyrian relief from the southwest Palace at Nineveh (ca. 630–620 B.C.E.) shows Assyrian scribes making an inventory of the booty from a military campaign against Babylonia. Significantly, one scribe holds a clay tablet and is writing in Akkadian cuneiform, whereas the second scribe is writing in Aramaic (and therefore in a phonetic alphabet script) on papyrus. By the seventh century B.C.E. both papyrus and parchment were widely used, but few of these fragile documents have survived.

standing stones, obelisks, and special trees. These sacred objects were often located on hilltops (called the "high places" in the Hebrew Bible or Old Testament). The core of Canaanite religious life remained, as it had been for millennia, the quest for fertility, both human and agricultural. The effort to ensure the birth of healthy children and abundant harvests accounts for the sensational features of Canaanite religious practices, such as cultic prostitution, in which the sexual union of the worshipper and priest or priestess reenacted the union of Ba'al and Ashtart, and child sacrifice, in which a couple offered their baby to the gods.

Empire Strikes Back: Neo-Assyrian and Neo-Babylonian Dominance

The independence of the small kingdoms and city-states of southern Anatolia, Syria, and Canaan did not last. Beginning in about 1050 B.C.E., the Assyrian and then the Babylonian imperial regimes began to regain control over their territories, reestablish their commercial power, and reconquer neighboring lands.

NEO-ASSYRIAN IMPERIALISM Even during the worst period of Aramean incursions and economic breakdown, Assyrian rulers never lost control of the Assyrian heartland, the rich agricultural region north and east of the city of Assur. As **Map 2.2** shows, from about 1000 B.C.E. on, Assyria began again to exert control over the lands around this central zone. The reign of Ashurnasirpal II (883–859 B.C.E.) marked a key step in Assyrian imperial resurgence. Ashurnasirpal II campaigned throughout Syria and the Levant, gradually picking off the smaller city-states. He reasserted Assyrian power all the way to the Mediterranean coast, with the Phoenician city-states voluntarily paying tribute and accepting vassal status rather than facing the onslaught of the Assyrian military machine. Reviving and expanding Hittite

some time in Egypt. One of the names of these peoples, the Peleset, may be the origin of the name "Palestine." By 1000 B.C.E. the Philistines inhabited five coastal city-states, each governed by a king. Loosely joined in a confederation, the Philistines became a major Canaanite power.

In contrast to the Philistines, most of the inhabitants of the Iron Age inland kingdoms were, archaeologists believe, indigenous Canaanites. They worshiped variations of the pre-Bronze Age Canaanite gods El and Ba'al and their wives, the fertility goddesses Asherah and Ashtart (Astarte). Iron Age Canaanites also continued the ancient practice of worshiping their gods through non-figural sacred objects, such as

CULTURAL CONTINUITIES: BA'AL ACROSS THE CENTURIES

This 13th-century B.C.E. bronze statuette of the Canaanite god Ba'al comes from Ugarit. The worship of Ba'al was a feature of Canaanite religion throughout both the Bronze and Iron Ages. A gold foil overlay distinguishes the head and face, and silver on the chest, arms, and legs perhaps represents armor.

Source: Réunion des Musées Nationaux/Art Resource, NY

imperial practice, Ashurnasirpal used mass deportations to punish conquered peoples, terrify potential enemies, and supply labor for monumental building projects such as his new, more glorious capital city.

Subsequent Assyrian monarchs extended and consolidated Ashurnasirpal's conquests. During the reign of Tiglath-Pileser III (r. 745–727 B.C.E.), the empire expanded rapidly. Ascending to the throne after four decades of rebellions and epidemics, Tiglath-Pileser reorganized the army and deployed it to quell rebellious subjects,

annex parts of Canaan, and make himself king of Babylon. His achievements ushered in a century of Assyrian dominance—even, for a time, over Egypt. The Neo-Assyrian Empire was the first in history to control the Tigris, Euphrates, and Nile River valleys.

Administering such a large empire posed problems, especially in the realm of communication. Provincial governors ruled on the king's behalf, but if the king's orders took months to arrive, provinces could develop dangerous autonomy. To solve this problem, the Assyrians developed an early version of express mail. They erected road stations at intervals of about 20 to 30 miles (a day's march) along every major route (called "royal roads"). At these stations, the king's messengers would find supplies and fresh horses and mules for their chariots, so that they could travel from one end of the empire to the other in a matter of days.

The Assyrians fielded a standing army that was massive for the age—at least 100,000 men. All Assyrian men were required to serve in the military (although the wealthy could pay for substitutes), but the government also conscripted soldiers from the peoples it conquered. To pay for this army and for royal building projects, the Assyrian state imposed high taxes on its peoples, demanded tribute from its vassal states, and plundered the lands it conquered. Annual military campaigns, therefore, were an economic necessity.

Assyria's military successes rested in part on its innovative approach to fighting. The Assyrians invented mobile battering rams and siege towers to assault enemy cities, and pontoon bridges to transport heavy equipment across rivers. They also created the world's first cavalry unit. Ranks of highly skilled horsemen proved more adept than even the light chariot at breaking an infantry line, and unlike chariot forces, could conduct reconnaissance and fight in mountainous regions.

With its great size and its innovative technologies, the Assyrian army developed a deserved reputation for terror. If a city or region resisted Assyrian control, its inhabitants met with no mercy. The Assyrians tortured, raped,

ASSYRIAN MILITARY INNOVATIONS: THE CAVALRY

Ashurnasirpal II (883–859 B.C.E.) chose what had once been a minor provincial town, Kalhu, as the site of his new capital city. Proclaiming his greatness with monumental architecture, Ashurnasirpal built the Northwest Palace, a magnificent stone structure decorated with massive stone reliefs celebrating the king's triumphs. This photograph of a segment of one of those reliefs shows early Assyrian cavalry tactics. Because saddles and stirrups had not yet been invented, horsemen initially rode in pairs, one to hold the two sets of reins and control the animals, one to fight with bow or spear.

mutilated, and skinned alive their defeated enemies. The survivors of these brutal conquests were then rounded up, forced to march for hundreds of miles, and dumped in strange lands to serve as an Assyrian labor source. By treating resistors and rebels with such cruelty, the Assyrians avoided having to fight very often: News of Assyrian atrocities spread to neighboring areas, which quickly and understandably surrendered to avoid such a fate. Hence, historians have described the Assyrian policy as "calculated frightfulness."[7]

Despite its ferocity, the Neo-Assyrian Empire played a crucial role in preserving and transmitting ancient Mesopotamian culture for future generations. Although the Assyrians ruled over Babylonia during the eighth and seventh centuries B.C.E. and even sacked the city of Babylon during the reign of Sennacherib (704–681 B.C.E.), they also recognized their cultural debt to Babylon and to its Akkadian and Sumerian predecessors. They treasured this cultural legacy and sought to collect and preserve scientific and literary works. During the Neo-Assyrian period, the final editions of the Akkadian creation story (the *Enuma Elish*) and the *Epic of Gilgamesh*—the versions that we know today—were written down.

The most remarkable effort in cultural collecting occurred during the reign of Asshurbanipal (668–627 B.C.E.). A warrior like all Assyrian kings, Asshurbanipal also fancied himself a scholar. At his palace in the city of Nineveh he aimed to build a library that would contain every bit of Mesopotamian literature and learning produced up to his time. In perhaps the first known instance of what librarians call "collection development," Asshurbanipal sent representatives throughout the empire to purchase—or confis-

CHRONOLOGY: THE NEO-ASSYRIAN AND NEO-BABYLONIAN EMPIRES

ca. 1200–1150 B.C.E.	International Bronze Age ends
ca. 1000 B.C.E.	Phoenician civilization develops
883 B.C.E.	Ashurnasirpal II succeeds to the Assyrian throne; rise of the Neo-Assyrian Empire begins
626 B.C.E.	Neo-Babylonian Empire begins with Nabopolassar's reign
612 B.C.E.	Nabopolassar's forces seize Nineveh
605 B.C.E.	Final collapse of Neo-Assyrian Empire
539 B.C.E.	Neo-Babylonian Empire falls to the Persians

cate—tablets and texts. Back in Ninevah scribes copied and catalogued these tablets, and then shelved them in rooms divided by subject area. Classified documents such as spy reports and records of secret state affairs were stored in the deepest, least accessible rooms. Over 30,000 tablets, containing perhaps 10,000 different texts (many of them mere fragments), survive from Asshurbanipal's library.

Mighty as it was, the Assyrian Empire came to a sudden end. In the final decades of the seventh century B.C.E., a series of succession crises and revolts fatally weakened the empire. "Calculated frightfulness" produced such bitter resentment that subject peoples rebelled. The most significant of these rebels was the Babylonian king Nabopolassar in southern Mesopotamia (r. 626–605 B.C.E.). The self-described "son of a nobody," Nabopolassar fought for ten years to free Babylon from Assyrian control. He then took the war into Assyria itself. In 616 B.C.E., after a three-month siege, Nineveh fell to the invaders. The victorious Nabopolassar proclaimed,

> I slaughtered the land of Subartu [Assyria]....The Assyrian, who since distant days had ruled over all the peoples, and with his heavy yoke had brought injury to the people of the Land, his feet from Akkad I turned back, his yoke I threw off.

For some years Assyrians fought on with the assistance of Egyptian forces, but by 605 B.C.E., when Nabopolassar died, the Neo-Assyrian Empire had entirely collapsed.

THE NEO-BABYLONIAN EMPIRE Nabopolassar became the founder of the Neo-Babylonian (or Chaldean) Empire, which lasted until 539 B.C.E. Conflict with Egypt dominated the early years of the empire as the two great powers scrambled to fill the power vacuum left by Assyria's collapse. In the course of this conflict, the brilliant general Nebuchadnezzar II (r. 604–562 B.C.E.) seized Syria, the Phoenician city-states, and the kingdom of Judah. (See **Map 2.2**.)

The Neo-Babylonians continued the Assyrian practice of deporting conquered peoples, both as a weapon of terror and as a means of filling labor shortages. The deported upper classes of conquered peoples often were allowed to live at the royal court, where they were treated well, as long as they accepted Babylonian rule. Most of the deportees, however, lived in villages, where they were required to turn over most of their harvests to their landlords and to pay the temple taxes.

While agricultural laborers endured conditions of extreme exploitation, the Babylonian economy flourished. Neo-Babylonian rulers devoted resources to restoring roads and canals and to expanding the irrigation system. Private trading houses financed commercial expeditions and exchanges, and Babylon became a center of imperial and international trade. Political boundaries and war did not seem to matter. Egyptian merchants, for example, were welcome throughout Babylonian territories, as were their goods, even during periods of warfare between the two empires.

With the wealth acquired from both conquest and trade, Neo-Babylonian kings made their capital city of Babylon into one of the wonders of the ancient world. According to tradition, Nebuchadnezzar built the "Hanging Gardens of Babylon" for a favorite wife who missed her mountainous homeland. Splendid flowers and plants cascaded down the slopes of a terraced hillside that, from a distance, seemed to float in the air. A moat flooded with waters from the Euphrates River surrounded Babylon's eight miles of walls. As the illustrations below show, brightly colored tiles decorated the Ishtar Gate, which opened onto a grand avenue leading to the temple of Marduk, Babylon's greatest god.

In addition to their architectural achievements, the Neo-Babylonians compiled an impressive record in astronomical research and observation. Confident that such research could uncover the will of the gods, Babylonian astronomers recorded the movements of the stars, the planets, and the moon. They kept a continuous log of observations between 747 B.C.E. and 61 C.E., an astonishing achievement. By 500 B.C.E., they had accumulated so much astronomical data that they could perform complex mathematical computations to predict eclipses of the moon and sun. These astronomers' calculations, which Persians and Greeks would later adopt, helped lay the foundation of Western science. The Neo-Babylonians also gave the West the names of

THE ISHTAR GATE

The magnificently tiled Ishtar Gate provided a dramatic entrance to Babylon, capital city of the Neo-Babylonian Empire. Babylonian artists used brightly colored tiles to create complex three-dimensional depictions of animals and warriors. The gate now rests in a museum in Berlin. An artist's reconstruction is also shown.

many constellations, the zodiac, and many mathematical models of astronomical phenomena.

The Neo-Babylonians looked not only to the stars but also to the past to orient themselves in their world. Like the rulers of the Neo-Assyrian Empire, the kings of Babylon regarded themselves as heirs and custodians of a long and valuable cultural tradition. Although Aramaic was now the language of everyday life, Akkadian remained the language of state affairs, and Babylonian kings even sought to revive archaic expressions and script. They also worked to preserve artworks from past generations and to restore ruined temples and palaces. King Nabonidus (555–539 B.C.E.) has been called "the first archeologist" because of his restoration of the holy places of Sumer and Akkad and his interest in collecting and identifying ancient artifacts, which he kept in a museum in his daughter's palace in Ur.

Nabonidus was also a deeply religious man, the son of a priestess to the moon goddess Sin. During his reign, Nabonidus's devotion to Sin alienated many Babylonians, who believed that he jeopardized Babylonian prosperity by neglecting the worship of Marduk. This alienation at least partly explains why in 539 B.C.E., the Neo-Babylonian Empire quickly fell under Persian control. The end of the Neo-Babylonian dynasty, however, did not destroy Babylon's economic networks or cultural traditions. Both continued to flourish under Persian rule, which we will examine in Chapter 3.

THE CIVILIZATION OF THE HEBREWS

■ What political and religious beliefs and institutions gave Hebrew civilization its unique character and account for its important legacy to Western civilization?

One of the most influential civilizations in the West has been that of the Hebrews, a people who originated in Canaan in the tumultuous era at the end of the Late Bronze Age. The history of the Hebrews—or Israelites—took shape within the

context of the events we have examined in this chapter: the International Bronze Age and its collapse, the emergence of several small states in Canaan and Syria, and the resurgence of the Assyrian and Babylonian empires after 1000 B.C.E.

The Early History of the Hebrews

The history of the early Hebrews is one of the most controversial subjects in the study of the ancient Near East. Our primary textual source for this history is the Hebrew Bible, or what Christians call the Old Testament. Drawn from a variety of oral and written sources, and composed many centuries after the events they describe, the Hebrew biblical texts condense a complex process of migration, settlement, and religious development. These texts are not historical narratives, in the sense that twenty-first century readers understand history. Some scholars, in fact, argue that these texts can tell us little about early Hebrew history. They point out that the books that make up the Hebrew Bible were first written down in the seventh and sixth centuries B.C.E., some 400 to 600 years after many of the events that they describe. According to these scholars, the apparent history in these texts is almost entirely fictional, a myth of origins composed to give meaning, solace, and identity to an oppressed people. The majority of scholars, however, argue that although the biblical texts first achieved written form centuries after the events they narrate, these documents were based on oral traditions, some of which go back to the original episodes. The biblical texts, then, are not "history" but when checked against the archaeological evidence, can be used as an important source for uncovering that history.

The people who became the Hebrews first appear in the historical record in Canaan around 1200 B.C.E. at the end of the Late Bronze Age. Archaeological evidence points to a dramatic growth in the numbers of small settlements in the hill country of inland Canaan, on the margins of established urban society. Certain features distinguish these hamlets from others in the area. The houses were grouped in clusters of three or four, with common walls and courtyards. These material remains confirm the portrait of early Israelite culture that we receive from the Hebrew Bible: a largely self-sufficient agricultural society, with a strong emphasis on family and community life.

But from where did these new hill-dwellers come? Many centuries later, the biblical book of Exodus explained that a leader called Moses led them from slavery in Egypt to freedom in Canaan. The archeological and linguistic evidence, however, indicates that these "proto-Israelites" were indigenous Canaanites, most likely a coalescence of semi-nomadic peoples and urban refugees who fled to the hills to escape the economic disarray and political tumult that accompanied the collapse of the International Bronze Age. Yet we need not discard the Exodus narrative entirely. Sea Peoples raided Egypt in the thirteenth century B.C.E. and many of these peoples wound up in Canaan and Syria. One of these groups, then, may have mixed with indigenous Canaanites to form what became the Hebrews; their story, told and retold, may have come to stand for the identity of the entire group.

Israel: From Monarchy to Exile

With the collapse of the Late Bronze Age empires, a power vacuum existed in Canaan. The Philistines and the Israelites competed for advantage. The Philistines controlled the Mediterranean coastal plain in Canaan and pushed relentlessly at the Hebrews living in the inland hills. According to traditions recorded in the Bible, the desperate Hebrews decided that a king would give them stronger leadership. Such a turn to kingship marked a sharp break in Hebrew culture. If historians are correct in locating early Hebrew origins at least in part in the flight of oppressed city-dwellers to the hill country, then much of Hebrew identity was rooted in opposition to centralized political power. In the biblical texts, anti-royalism—resistance to kingship and the corresponding exploitation of the agricultural masses—constitutes a powerful and repeated theme.

THE UNITED MONARCHY According to the biblical record, the Israelites chose Saul to be their first king around 1020 B.C.E. Some 20 years later, a popular warrior named David (ca. 1005–970) succeeded Saul, defeated the Philistines, and built a prosperous, centralized kingdom with Jerusalem, an old Canaanite city, as its capital. (See **Map 2.2.**) David created a royal court complete with a harem; established a census as the basis for tax collection, military conscription, and forced labor; and set up a centralized bureaucracy run by professional soldiers, administrators, and scribes. (See *Justice in History* in this chapter.)

The Bible tells us that David's son Solomon (c. 970–931 B.C.E.) raised Israel to the pinnacle of its power and prosperity. One of Solomon's greatest achievements was the construction of a grand temple in Jerusalem. Built with the technical assistance of Phoenician architects and artisans and the forced labor of Solomon's subjects, the Jerusalem temple became the focal point of Israel's religious worship. Highlighting Solomon's wealth and his wisdom, the biblical text paints a picture of a monarch forging long-distance economic and diplomatic relationships throughout the ancient world. He married foreign princesses to cement diplomatic agreements, controlled the trade routes running from Egypt and Arabia to Syria, and established economic ties with kingdoms as far away as that of Sabaea (Sheba) in Yemen.

Like almost every aspect of early Hebrew history, however, this history of the **United Monarchy** is extremely controversial. No other ancient texts bear witness to the monarchies of David and Solomon, and scholars disagree about the meaning of the archaeological evidence. Three main sets of explanations exist. A minority of scholars contends that David and Solomon never existed at all. A larger group of specialists argues that the biblical story of the United Monarchy blends tenth-century B.C.E. realities and later events. In this view, the historical David and Solomon were relatively poor, rough tribal chieftains of the tenth century (B.C.E.), while the kingly details of the Biblical narrative reflect the conditions of the seventh and sixth centuries B.C.E. The mainstream of historical scholarship, however, insists that the United Monarchy did exist in the tenth century. Extra-biblical textual and archaeological evidence testifies that by the tenth century B.C.E., Canaan was politically divided among small kingdoms—including, it seems likely, the United Monarchy of Israel.

THE DIVIDED MONARCHY   The monarchy built by David and Solomon did not last long. The Bible tells us that after Solomon died, the northern Israelites rebelled. Dissatisfied with Solomon's policies of high taxes and forced labor, they refused to acknowledge the kingship of Solomon's son and broke away to form a separate northern kingdom. They kept the name "Israel" for this northern state, but moved its capital to the city of Shechem (and later, Samaria). Solomon's successors retained the throne in Jerusalem and ruled over the smaller southern kingdom that remained, now called Judah (see **Map 2.2**, pp. 57). Solomon's death thus ushered in the period of the **Divided Monarchy** or the "successor kingdoms."

The fate of the Divided Monarchy became entangled with the rise of the Neo-Assyrian and Neo-Babylonian Empires. Judah, as the smaller and poorer of the two kingdoms, was less attractive to invaders and therefore more politically stable. David's descendants remained on the throne throughout Judah's history and enjoyed relatively strong support from their people. In contrast, Israel experienced a number of revolutions and succession shifts, often a result of the meddling of outside powers. The northern state entered its period of greatest strength around 885 B.C.E., when an army commander named Omri (ca. 885–875 B.C.E.) seized power. Omri's son and successor Ahab (ca. 873–852) built on his father's legacy to make Israel into one of the most formidable powers in Canaan.

INTO EXILE   The emergence of the Neo-Assyrian Empire, however, meant Israel's independence could not last. As we saw earlier in this chapter,

in 744 B.C.E. Tiglath-Pileser III succeeded to the throne and expanded the Assyrian empire. In just over a decade, Israel, like many of the smaller Syrian and Canaanite kingdoms, found itself an Assyrian vassal. And, like so many of the peoples under Assyrian control, the Israelites quickly grew weary of imperial demands. In 722 B.C.E., Israel's King Hoshea (ca. 731–722 B.C.E.) led a rebellion against Assyrian domination. In keeping with their policy of "calculated frightfulness," the Assyrians responded with brutality. The following year they wiped Israel off the map by annexing the territory outright and dividing it into four Assyrian provinces. Nearly 30,000 Israelites were deported to Mesopotamia. Today known as the Lost Ten Tribes of Israel, these deportees eventually forgot their cultural identity in their new homes and disappeared from history. Many of the remaining inhabitants of Israel took refuge in Judah (nearly doubling its population).

Although the destruction of its larger, more powerful northern neighbor increased Judah's regional importance, this small state survived during the age of empires only as an imperial vassal, first, of the Neo-Assyrians, then the Egyptians, Neo-Babylonians, and Persians. Judahite kings who attempted to shrug off vassal status had little success. King Hezekiah (ca. 727–697 B.C.E.), for example, made the mistake of joining a Canaanite–Phoenician coalition against the mighty Assyrian monarch, Sennacherib. When the Assyrian army surrounded Jerusalem, Hezekiah surrendered and pledged his loyalty to his Assyrian overlord. The costs of survival were high: According to Sennacherib,

> Hezekiah himself, overwhelmed by the terror-inspiring splendor of my lordship...sent me in Nineveh, my lordly city,...elephant hides, ivory tusks, ebony-wood, boxwood, all kinds of valuable treasures, as well as his daughters, concubines, male and female musicians. He sent a personal messenger to deliver the tribute and render homage as a slave.[8]

ASSYRIAN TORTURE TACTICS

This Assyrian relief shows Assyrian soldiers impaling prisoners from Judah. In 701 B.C.E. the emperor Sennacherib and his army marched into Judah to put down a rebellion. They besieged the city of Lachish and then brutally tortured its inhabitants. They later besieged Jerusalem, but King Hezekiah's surrender saved the capital city.

Hezekiah's successors were not so fortunate. In 586 B.C.E., when King Zedekiah (ca. 597–586) led another revolt, Babylonian forces burned Jerusalem to the ground and demolished Solomon's temple, the spiritual and political center of Judah. About 20,000 people were deported to Babylon, an event called the **Babylonian Exile.**

Unlike the inhabitants of Israel, however, the Hebrews deported from Judea retained their cultural and religious identity during their years in exile—and some were able to return to Judah. In 538 B.C.E., King Cyrus of Persia, now ruler of the Neo-Babylonian Empire as well, permitted all peoples exiled by the Babylonians to return to their homelands. Two generations later the Judahites finished building a new temple in Jerusalem, called the Second Temple. For the next 500 years this restored temple worship was the center of Hebrew religious life. Historians call the Hebrews who lived after the completion of the Second Temple *Jews* and their religion *Judaism.*

The Hebrew Religious Legacy

Were it not for this religion, Western civilization textbooks would barely mention Israel under the United Monarchy or the successor kingdoms of Israel and Judah. Like Ammon or Moab, Israel and Judah were minor Canaanite states, fairly

CHRONOLOGY: THE KINGDOMS OF THE HEBREWS

ca. 1100 B.C.E.	The International Bronze Age ends
ca. 1020–922 B.C.E.	The United Monarchy under Saul, David, and Solomon
922 B.C.E.	The Divided Monarchy: The Israelite kingdom splits into Judah (southern kingdom) and Israel (northern kingdom)
ca. 800 B.C.E.	The prophetic movement begins
721 B.C.E.	Assyrians destroy Israel
586 B.C.E.	Babylonians defeat Judah and destroy Jerusalem and Solomon's Temple; beginning of "Babylonian Exile"
538 B.C.E.	Cyrus of Persia permits Judahites to return to Palestine and rebuild the Temple

DIFFERENT VOICES HOLY WAR IN THE ANCIENT WORLD

The peoples of the ancient world drew no distinction between religion and politics. No king could rule without the gods' blessing and warfare served not only to expand the king's territory but also to glorify the gods and to demonstrate the divine power that upheld the political and social order. The accounts of "holy war" in these excerpts cannot be read as journalists' reports or historians' reconstructions. They are religious texts that allow us glimpses of the deepest motivations and aspirations of the societies that produced them.

I. The Annals of Assurnasirpal II of Assyria

One of the most famous Assyrian documents, The Annals of Assurnasipal II, *provides detailed year-by-year records of the military campaigns of King Assurnasipal (r. ca. 883–859).*

Assur, my great lord, who called me by name and made great my kingship over the kings of the four quarters [of the world], had made my name exceeding great, and...had commanded me to conquer, to subdue and to rule; trusting in Assur, my lord, I marched by difficult roads over steep mountains with the hosts of my army, and there was none who opposed me....

While I was staying in the land of Kutmuhi, they brought me the word: "The city of Suru of Bit-Halupe has revolted...and Ahia-baba, the son of a nobody...they have set up as king over them." With the help of...the great gods who have made great my kingdom, I mobilized [my] chariots and armies and marched....To the city of Sura of Bit-Halupe I drew near, and the terror of the splendor of Assur, my lord, overwhelmed them. The chief men and the elders of the city, to save their lives, came forth into my presence and embraced my feet, saying: "If it is thy pleasure, slay! If it is thy pleasure, let live! That which thy heart desireth, do!" Ahiababa, the son of nobody...I made captive. In the valor of my heart and with the fury of my weapons I stormed the city. All the rebels they seized and delivered up. My officers I caused to enter into his palace and his temples. His silver, his gold...a great hoard of copper, alabaster, tables with inlay, the women of his palaces, his daughters, the captive rebels together with their possessions, the gods together with their possessions, precious stone from the mountains, his chariots with equipment, his horses...garments of brightly colored wool and garments of linen, goodly oil, cedar, and fine-scented herbs...his wagons, his cattle, his sheep, his heavy spoil, which like the stars of heaven could not be counted, I carried off....I built a pillar over against his city gate, and I flayed all the chief men who had revolted, and I covered the pillar with their skins; some I walled up within the pillar, some I impaled upon the pillar on stakes, and others I bound to stakes round about the pillar;...and I cut off the limbs of the officers, of the royal officers who had rebelled. Ahiababa I took to Nineveh, I flayed him, I spread his skin upon the wall of Nineveh. My power and might I established over the land of Lake....I increased the tribute and taxes and imposed upon them....At that time I fashioned a heroic image of my royal self, my power and my glory I inscribed thereon, in the midst of his palace I set it up. I fashioned memorial steles and inscribed thereon my glory and prowess, and I set them up by his city gate.

insignificant players in the imperial power game. But unlike Ammon and Moab, Israel and Judah possessed and passed on a powerful religious legacy, one that shaped the very heart of Western cultural identity.

EARLY SYNCRETISM Early Hebrew religious practice, like all of early Hebrew history, remains controversial. The existing evidence indicates that as they coalesced as a people in the hill country of Canaan, the proto-Israelites combined Canaanite religious practices with the worship of the god Yahweh (written as "Jehovah" or "the Lord" in English Bibles), a deity likely brought to Canaan by migrants from Midian, a desert region north of the

II. The Book of Numbers: The Israelites' War against Midian

The Old Testament's Book of Numbers (titled in the Hebrew Bible, In the Wilderness), *tells the story of the Israelites after their exodus from Egypt and before their settlement in Canaan. Like the rest of the Pentateuch (the first five books of the Bible), Numbers is likely based on oral traditions first written down about 950* B.C.E. *This early account was then revised, expanded, and edited over subsequent centuries, probably achieving final form in the sixth century* B.C.E.

While Israel dwelt in Shittim the people began to play the harlot with the daughters of Moab. These invited the people to the sacrifices of their gods, and the people ate and bowed down to their gods. So Israel yoked himself to Ba'al of Pe'or. And the anger of the Lord was kindled against Israel. *[The Lord sends a plague.]*...those that died by the plague were twenty-four thousand.

And the Lord said to Moses, "Harass the Midianites and smite them; for they...beguiled you in the matter of Pe'or."...And Moses said to the people, "Arm men from among you for the war, that they may go against Midian, to execute the Lord's vengeance on Midian. You shall send a thousand from each of the tribes of Israel to the war." So there were provided...twelve thousand armed for war. And Moses sent them to the war, a thousand from each tribe, together with Phinehas the son of Eleazar the priest....They warred against Midian, as the Lord commanded Moses, and slew every male....And the people of Israel took captive the women of Midian and their little ones; and they took as booty all their cattle, their flocks, and all their goods. All their cities in the places where they dwelt, and all their encampments, they burned with fire....Then they brought the captives and the booty and the spoil to Moses, and to Eleazar the priest, and to the congregation of the people of Israel, at the camp on the plains of Moab by the Jordan at Jericho.

Moses, and Eleazar the priest, and all the leaders of the congregation, went forth to meet them outside the camp. And Moses was angry....Moses said to them, "Have you let all the women live? Behold, these caused the people of Israel...to act treacherously against the Lord in the matter of Pe'or, and so the plague came among the congregation of the Lord. Now therefore, kill every male among the little ones, and kill every woman who has known man by lying with him. But all the young girls who have not known man by lying with him, keep alive for yourselves."...And Moses and Eleazar the priest received the gold from the commanders...and brought it into the tent of meeting, as a memorial for the people of Israel before the Lord.

Sources: I. D. D. Luckenbill, *Ancient Records of Assyria and Babylonia*, vol. I (Chicago, IL: University of Chicago Press, 1926), 141, 144–145; II. Numbers 25: 1–3, 9, 16–18; Numbers 31: 3–18, 52–54.

For Discussion

1. How does the first excerpt illustrate the Assyrian policy of "calculated frightfulness"?

2. Compare these accounts: What motivated these holy wars? Who received credit and why? What do the differences between these accounts reveal about these different cultures?

Arabian peninsula. Belief in Yahweh became central to Hebrew identity. Nevertheless, the Israelites also continued to worship the god El, the head Canaanite god, his consort Asherah, and the fertility deity Ba'al. By the time of the United Monarchy, **syncretism**—the practice of fusing foreign beliefs to an indigenous system—remolded Israelite religion.

The Israelites now identified early Canaanite shrines to El as places where Yahweh revealed himself to his people. Similarly, the "Ark of the Covenant," a sacred box associated with Yahweh's divine presence and often described as Yahweh's throne, featured two cherubim—winged, semi-divine beings with human heads and the bodies of bulls or lions that frequently

ASTARTE WORSHIP IN JUDAH

Archaeologists uncovered these small statues (called Astarte figurines after the most important Canaanite fertility goddess) in the remains of a number of private houses in what was the kingdom of Judah. Dating from about 800–600 B.C.E., these figurines provide evidence on the continuation of Canaanite religious practices among the Hebrews.

guarded the thrones of gods and kings in Canaanite culture. **Yahwism** (the worship of Yahweh) also adopted Canaanite liturgical practices, such as the celebration of the harvest (Succoth, in later Judaism) and the New Year (Rosh ha-Shanah).

THE PROPHETIC MOVEMENT   In the ninth century B.C.E., Yahwism took a new turn, a revolutionary move of marked significance for Western history. In the years after the formation of the monarchy, the gap between rich and poor widened. The centralization and growth of the state increased the tax burden on peasants, many of whom fell into debt and lost their land. They cried out for justice and a return to what they remembered as a more egalitarian society. From these roots emerged the **prophetic movement,** a call for social justice and religious purity that eventually transformed Yahwism into the world's first monotheistic religion.

The prophet Elijah led the initial movement. He and his followers demanded that Israelites worship *only* Yahweh, and thus called for puri-

fying Yahwism of Canaanite religious beliefs and practices. Speaking on behalf of the down-trodden with words they believed Yahweh had given to them, these social critics condemned the religious and moral corruption of landowners and kings. They linked the worship of Yahweh (and only Yahweh) to a social ideal of community, in which exploitation of the poor was seen as a sin against Yahweh's plan for humanity.

Over the next century, prophets such as Amos, Hosea, Isaiah, and Micah continued to denounce the economic inequalities of Israel and Judah and to call for the worship of only Yahweh. They also began to articulate a vision of religion as a heartfelt spiritual practice resulting in social action, rather than a matter of placating the gods through ritual. In a revolutionary statement, Micah presented Yahweh as rejecting typical religious worship:

With what shall I come before the Lord, and
    bow myself before God on high?...
Will the Lord be pleased with thousands of
    rams, with ten thousands of rivers of oil?

Shall I give my first-born for my transgres-
sion, the fruit of my body for the sin of
my soul?
He has showed you, O man, what is good;
and what does the Lord require of you but to
do justice, and to love kindness,
and to walk humbly with your God?[9]

YAHWEH ALONE: THE EMERGENCE OF MONOTHEISM

The destruction of the northern kingdom of
Israel in 721 B.C.E. persuaded many within
Judah of the truth of the prophets' message.
They concluded that Yahweh had chosen the
Assyrians as his means of punishing Israel for
its sins. A mood of religious reform spread
throughout the southern state. King Hezekiah
sought to purify Judah's religious practice by
destroying the shrines and sacred sites dedicated to Ba'al and Asherah, and by centralizing
the worship of Yahweh in the Temple in
Jerusalem.

Hezekiah's successor, Manasseh (697–642
B.C.E.), tried to reverse his father's reforms and
return to traditional practices, but this counter-
reformation proved short-lived. Manasseh's
successor was assassinated after only two years
on the throne, clearing the way for the boy
king, Josiah (640–609 B.C.E.), during whose
reign the most thorough-going reform of
Hebrew religion occurred. In 622 B.C.E., when
Josiah was 26 years old, workers repairing the
Temple uncovered a scroll called the "Book of
the Law" (an early version of what we know as
Deuteronomy, the fifth book of the Bible),
ostensibly written by Moses and containing the
basic principles by which the Hebrews should
live. Deuteronomy in its earliest written form
dates not from the time of Moses (i.e., 1300s
B.C.E.), but from the 600s (B.C.E.). Inspired by
this supposed "archaeological find," Josiah
implemented a host of reforms, all of them
based on the central theme of Deuteronomy:
the **Covenant** between Yahweh and the
Israelites. According to the terms of this
Covenant, Yahweh designated Israel his chosen
people, and in return, the Israelites were to worship only him and to seek to abide by his law.

Stirred by this religious reformation, one
of Josiah's subjects used the ideal of the
Covenant to reinterpret the Hebrew past by
writing the "Deuteronomistic History," an
early version of the biblical books of Joshua,
Judges, Samuel, and Kings. This history projects the vision of Yahweh as the true God of
Israel back onto the earliest days of the
Hebrew people, and recasts the story of the
Israelites as a struggle between the true followers of Yahweh and those who strayed to worship other gods. In its narrative, the History
emphasized the intertwined concepts of Land
and Law: Yahweh had given his chosen people
the land of Israel, but on the condition that
they worshiped him as his law, spelled out in
Deuteronomy, demanded.

Josiah's religious reformation ended in
609 B.C.E. when Egyptian forces captured and
killed him. Within decades Judah had fallen to
Babylonian conquest, Jerusalem was destroyed,
and the period of the Babylonian Exile had
begun. As they struggled to make sense of these
horrific events, the Hebrew exiles took the final
step toward monotheism. Grappling with the
lessons of their history and the meaning of their
religious faith now that the Temple was
destroyed, they came to a revolutionary understanding of the divine. They came to see Yahweh as unbounded by time and space, not
confined to a temple. The one and only God, he
ruled not only Israel and Judah, but all people
in all places and in all time—and even beyond
time. This idea of the one eternal and transcendent God would have a powerful impact on
Western culture.

The Babylonian Exile also resulted in a number of other important developments in Hebrew
religion. First, the fear of losing their identity as
Hebrews as they lived in a foreign land amid foreign gods led to a new emphasis on religious
purity. Hebrew leaders developed a complex
code of ethical and ritual requirements designed
to reinforce the separate identity of the Hebrew
people. For example, Hebrews could no longer
marry non-Hebrews and they had to observe
strict dietary laws.

This new emphasis on purity resulted in significant but contradictory changes for Hebrew women. On the one hand, they found their religious role more restricted: Childbirth and menstruation made women "unclean" and therefore unfit for public worship. On the other hand, many of the dietary and ritualistic requirements took place within the home, in the family context, and so gave women central responsibility in sustaining Hebrew identity.

A second important religious development during the Babylonian Exile was the compilation of the basic texts of the Hebrew Bible. During this era Hebrew leaders added to Deuteronomy a number of texts written earlier or preserved in oral tradition. Edited and compiled, these texts with Deuteronomy became the **Pentateuch** or the **Torah**—the first five books of the Bible. Exiled Hebrews also produced a second edition of the Deuteronomistic History, one that particularly emphasized the central role of the now-destroyed Temple and its priesthood in the life of the Israelites.

By emphasizing the priesthood and Temple sacrifices, the editors of this later version of the Deuteronomistic History (who probably were themselves priests) tried to make correct religious practice the key to Hebrew faith and identity. This stress on religious ritual, however, ignored the social concerns that the prophets had placed at the heart of Yahweh's law. The period of the Exile, then, saw a continuation of the prophetic movement, as new prophets arose to challenge the priestly emphasis on right ritual and instead demanded social justice. The prophet Ezekiel, for example, depicted Yahweh as a shepherd with a special love for the weakest in his flock:

> I myself will be the shepherd of my sheep...says the Lord God....Behold, I judge between sheep and sheep. Is it not enough for you to feed on the good pasture, that you must tread down with your feet the rest of your pasture; and to drink of clear water, that you must foul the rest with your feet?...Behold, I, I myself will judge between the fat sheep and the lean sheep.[10]

The tension between the prophetic call for social justice, implemented through practical action, and the priestly demand for religious purity, demonstrated through ritual practices, would never be fully reconciled, either in Judaism or in the monotheistic religions of Christianity and Islam, which like Judaism, drew on ancient Hebrew roots.

THE HEBREW LEGACY   From those Hebrew roots grew many characteristic features of Western civilization. The notion of the "chosen people" shaped not only Christian theology but also modern expressions of nationalism. "Manifest destiny"—the idea that the United States had the right and responsibility to extend its political control across the North American continent—is rooted in this ancient Hebrew idea. Western culture also draws on the Hebrew ideal of the Law. In Hebrew tradition, Yahweh's Law stands supreme: Every king, even God's chosen ruler, will be judged on how well he implements God's law and how fairly he treats God's people. This idea provides the seeds of the key Western legal and political principle that no ruler or leader stands beyond the law. The summary of Yahweh's Law found in the Ten Commandments remains for many the foundation of Western ethics, while the Hebrew Bible still provides some of the most powerful and poetic narratives in the Western tradition.

Most important, the belief in an all-powerful, all-encompassing God who transcends space and time, and yet intervenes in human history to take care of his people, has had a powerful influence on Western societies. Seeing the hand of God in history allowed Western cultures to adopt a notion of human history as linear, as meaningful movement through time, rather than an endless repetition or a steady degradation, and so helped make possible the idea of progress. Similarly, the concept of a transcendent God contributed to the Western scientific tradition. Because God transcends rather than permeates the natural world, nature itself is not sacred. Human beings can study it; they can also use it, manipulate it, and transform it.

JUSTICE IN HISTORY

Crime and Punishment in a King's Court

Around 990 B.C.E., "in the spring of the year, the time when kings go forth to battle," Israel's King David sent his troops against the Ammonites. Although a renowned warrior, David stayed behind in Jerusalem. One afternoon he took a walk on his roof after he woke from his nap. (An afternoon siesta was then, like now, common in Mediterranean cultures, and the roof constituted the coolest part of the building.) From his rooftop David saw a woman bathing, "and the woman was very beautiful." When the king discovered that the woman was Bathsheba, wife of Uriah the Hittite* who was serving in the war against Ammon, he ordered her brought to him. In the spare vocabulary of the biblical text, David "took her, and she came to him, and he lay with her." This action set in motion a sequence of events that ultimately divided the Israelite kingdom.

The story of David and Bathsheba is part of the "Court History of David," found in the Old Testament books of II Samuel and I Kings.† Some scholars argue that one of Solomon's officials wrote the first version of the History, which was then combined with other stories and fragments of stories in the seventh century B.C.E. during the reign of King Josiah, and revised again after the Babylonian Exile. Others place the original writer in the seventh century B.C.E. Both sets of scholars, however, acknowledge that the values that propelled Josiah's religious reformation permeate the History and produced a revolutionary idea of social justice.

David, the handsome warrior and popular hero whom the Lord chose to lead his people, sowed the seeds of national tragedy. A few weeks after his sexual encounter with Bathsheba, the king received a message from her: "I am with child." Caught in adultery, David scrambled to cover up his crime. Assuming that Uriah, like most soldiers on leave, would want sex, David ordered Bathsheba's husband home from the battlefield. If Uriah slept with Bathsheba, then everyone would assume he was the baby's father. But the Hittite soldier refused to violate the rules of purity that required a soldier engaged in holy war to abstain from sex. Even when David invited him to dinner and plied him with so much wine that he became drunk, Uriah resisted the temptation to bed his lovely wife.

Frustrated, David sent Uriah back to the battle, along with a message for his commander, Joab: "Set Uriah in the forefront of the hardest fighting, and draw back from him, that he may be struck down and die." Joab obeyed. Uriah and several of Israel's mightiest fighters died in a hard-fought engagement with the Ammonites. Shortly after, David added Bathsheba to his stable of wives. The king thought he had gotten away with murder. But, the Court History tells us, "the thing that David had done displeased Yahweh."

A short time later, Yahweh's prophet, Nathan, arrived at court and told the king a story:

> There were two men in a certain city, the one rich and the other poor. The rich man had very many flocks and herds; but the poor man had nothing but one little ewe lamb, which he had bought. And he brought it up, and it grew up with him and with his children; it used to eat of his morsel, and drink from his cup, and lie in his bosom, and it was like a daughter to him. Now there came a traveler to the rich man, and he was unwilling to take one of his own flock or herd to prepare for the wayfarer who had come to him, but he took the poor man's lamb, and prepared it for the man who had come to him.

---

* "Hittite" here does not refer to the Hittite Empire, which disintegrated over one century earlier, but rather to a small Canaanite kingdom or tribe.
† II Samuel 9–20 and I Kings 1–2 of the Christian Old Testament.

Infuriated by this injustice, David insisted, "As the Lord lives, the man who has done this deserves to die." Nathan replied, "You are the man."

Nathan's parable forced David to see himself as the selfish rich man who stole everything, including life itself, from Uriah. David recognized his crime and confessed, "I have sinned against Yahweh." But his confession did not mean he could evade the consequences of his actions. Nathan warned, "The sword shall never depart from your house.... Thus says Yahweh, 'Behold, I will raise up evil against you out of your own house.' "

David's and Bathsheba's baby boy soon sickened and died. Bathsheba's second son by David, Solomon, inherited his father's throne, but only after the royal household endured a series of tragedies, including incestuous rape, murder, a civil war that forced David to flee his capital city, and the deaths of two more of David's sons (with a third executed by Solomon shortly after he took power). Solomon's reign may have marked the high point of the Hebrew monarchy, but his decision to continue the heavy taxation and forced labor policies of his father meant that resentment against the Davidic royal house festered among the people. This resentment finally burst into rebellion after Solomon's death and divided the kingdom.

By linking these unfolding tragedies to David's crime, the Court History revealed an idea of justice new to the ancient world. Because the kingdom belonged to Yahweh, not to David or any of his sons, Yahweh's law applied to all. Although a mighty king, David was expected to obey the same laws that governed the behavior of an ordinary peasant. His failure to do so shattered his family, weakened his reign, and tarnished his legacy.

This emphasis on actions and consequences highlights a second important feature of the Court History: the importance of human action in a world under Yahweh's control. Although the History contains no miracles, no angels, no points of supernatural intervention in the natural world, the tragedies that unfold do not just happen by chance. Yahweh is in charge. Yet David and his sons are not pawns in a divine chess game. Their choices have consequences. What each person does, matters. Justice, then, is individual as well as social, a working of Yahweh's will for the world in both communal and personal life.

For Discussion

1. How does the idea of kingship and justice revealed in the Court History differ from that of other Bronze and Iron Age monarchies?
2. How does the concept of justice revealed in this story strengthen and/or challenge the values that underlay the prophetic movement?

Taking It Further

Michael Dever, *What Did the Biblical Writers Know and When Did They Know It?* Grand Rapids, MI: Wm. B. Eerdmans Publishing Co., 2002. A clear and engaging introduction to the sources of the books of the Old Testament.

Israel Finkelstein and Neil Asher Silberman. *David and Solomon: In Search of the Bible's Sacred Kings and the Roots of the Western Tradition.* New York: Free Press, 2006. A more radical approach to the historical accuracy of the biblical picture of the United Monarchy than Dever's.

CONCLUSION

International Systems, Ancient Empires, and the Roots of Western Civilization

The International Bronze Age marked an early but crucial phase in the formation of Western civilization. Within a geographical area centered on the eastern Mediterranean but stretching far beyond its shores, a network of political, commercial, and cultural ties emerged among cities and kingdoms that had lived in relative isolation from each other. Long before it was possible to identify what we now call the West, the exchange of commodities, the spread of religious ideas, the growth of common political traditions, the dissemination of scientific and technological techniques, and the borrowing of one language from another created a complex pattern of cultural diffusion over a vast geographical area.

When the international system of the Late Bronze Age collapsed, these elements did not all disappear. The cultural inheritance of the Sumerians and Akkadians passed on to the Neo-Assyrian and Neo-Babylonian Empires, consciously preserved in libraries and literary collections. The diplomatic innovations, most clearly seen in the treaty between Ramesses II and Hatusilli III in 1258 B.C.E., became an important feature of international affairs. The proto-Canaanite alphabet survived, to be passed on to the Western world by the Phoenicians via the Greeks. And most important of all, in the midst of the collapse of Great Powers and the rise of new empires, a small, seemingly insignificant people with a still controversial origin, encountered the divine in ways that continue today to influence, comfort, challenge, and transform peoples of the West and around the world.

KEY TERMS

Late Bronze Age
Amarna Letters
Indo-European

matriarchal
Linear B
palace system

Sea Peoples
habiru
Iron Age
United Monarchy
Divided Monarchy
Babylonian Exile

syncretism
Yahwism
prophetic movement
Covenant
Pentateuch
Torah

CHAPTER REVIEW

1. What elements made up the international system of the Late Bronze Age and why did this system suddenly collapse? (page 43)
2. What patterns shaped the development of southwest Asian and Mediterranean societies after the collapse of the Late Bronze Age international system? (page 55)
3. What political and religious beliefs and institutions gave Hebrew civilization its unique character and account for its important legacy to Western civilization? (page 64)

TAKING IT FURTHER

1. What does the phrase "The Club of the Great Powers" mean? Who were its members? What privileges did "membership" provide? Were there any responsibilities?
2. Consider this argument: "Empires dominated southwest Asia in the millennium from 1500 to 500 B.C.E.—and yet the developments of greatest significance for Western history and culture occurred not in the imperial systems, but in the smaller states, in the areas on the periphery of power." In what ways is this argument accurate? In what ways must it be modified or rejected?
3. Explain this statement: "When the historian turns to the Hebrew Bible for historical evidence, he or she must act like an archeologist on a dig: Each historical layer of the text must be carefully sifted, identified and contextualized."

 Practice on MyHistoryLab

3

Greek Civilization

■ Greece Rebuilds, 1100–479 B.C.E. ■ The Greek Encounter with
the Persian Empire ■ The Classical Age of Greece, 479–336 B.C.E.

IN 480 B.C.E. XERXES, THE GREAT KING OF PERSIA
(R. 485–465 B.C.E.), launched a massive invasion of
Greece by leading 150,000 troops across the Hellespont, the narrow strait known today as the Dard-
anelles that separates Asia from Europe. Xerxes'
intention was to conquer Greece and make it part of
the largest and most powerful empire the world
had ever known. Against all odds 31 Greek city-
states, which had formed an alliance to repel the
invaders, prevailed. In September of that year
the highly maneuverable Athenian navy defeated
the Persian fleet off the coast of the island of
Salamis, forcing Xerxes to withdraw most of his
forces to Anatolia for the winter. At the Battle of
Plataea early the next year the combined Greek
armies, led by Sparta, routed the troops that Xerxes
had left behind. The surviving Persians were driven
out of Greece, never to return.

The victories of the Greeks over the Persian
colossus at Salamis and Plataea mark a milestone in
the history of the West. They gave Greece, most
notably the city-state of Athens, the security within
which it could develop its political institutions as well
as its philosophy, science, literature, and art. The
resulting achievements of Greek civilization, which
continued to interact with those of other states in the
Mediterranean region, became the bedrock of Western civilization.

It would be misleading, however, to celebrate
the Greek victory over Persia as a triumph of the West
over the East. The location of Greece in Europe and
Persia in Asia suggests such a contrast. But as we

have seen, the terms *the West* and *the East* refer to
more than geography; they also designate a constel-
lation of cultural traditions. Some of the political,
religious, and scientific traditions that we identify as
Western can be traced back to the Persian Empire;
many of them were the products of cultural encounters between Greece and Persia.

This chapter will discuss the growth of Greek civilization in the context of its relationship with the Persian Empire and will describe both the Persian and
the Greek role in the making of the West.

GREECE REBUILDS,
1100–479 B.C.E.

■ How did Greek city-states develop their
culture and political institutions during the
Archaic Age?

As we saw in Chapter 2, Greek civilization
entered a period of economic and political
decline at the end of the international Bronze
Age. The years from about 1100 to 750 B.C.E,
known as the Dark Age, were followed by a
period of economic growth at home and
encounters with Phoenicians and Persians
abroad. The revival of Greece during the
Archaic Age, which lasted until 479 B.C.E, set
the stage for Greece's cultural achievements
during its Classical Age.

THE BATTLE OF SALAMIS, 480. B.C.E.

This victory of the Athenian navy over Persia ended a major threat to Greek independence. This nineteenth-century painting of the battle accurately depicts the closeness of naval engagements in ancient times.

During the Dark Age, Greece endured economic, political, and cultural stagnation that contrasted with the wealth and splendor of the Mycenaean states that had flourished during the Bronze Age. Few new settlements were established on the Greek mainland, and urban life disappeared. Maritime trade declined sharply and the economies controlled by the palaces collapsed. Because there was no longer a need for scribes to record inventories, Linear B writing disappeared. A serious decline in agriculture led to a steep decrease in food production and population.

A slow economic recovery began in the Greek world about 850 B.C.E., when the population began to grow and trade became brisker. Because of the harsh living conditions on the mainland during the Dark Age, many Greeks moved to a region called Ionia on the coasts and islands of western Anatolia. Relatively isolated from other Greek communities, these pioneers developed their own dialect of the Greek language. By 800 B.C.E. the Ionian Greeks were regularly interacting with the Phoenicians in the eastern Mediterranean.

Writing and Poetry during the Archaic Age

Between about 750 and 650 B.C.E., fresh ideas poured into Greece from the Near East through contact with the Phoenicians and other peoples. Encounters with Near Eastern poets, merchants, artisans, refugees, doctors, slaves, and spouses brought innovations to Greece. These included new economic practices (such as charging interest on loans), new gods and goddesses (such as Dionysos, the god of wine), and inventions of convenience (such as parasols to provide shade).

The most valuable import from the Phoenicians was the alphabet. As we saw in Chapter 2, the Phoenicians, who had been using an alphabet of 22 letters for at least three centuries, introduced the system to Greece around 750 B.C.E. The adoption of the alphabet, to which the Greeks added vowels, was one of the developments that marked the beginning of the Archaic Age. Because an alphabet records sounds, not words, it can be adjusted easily for any language. Greeks soon recognized the potential of the new system and learned to write and read, first for

business and then for pleasure. They began to record their oral traditions, legends, and songs. At the same time, they began to compose a new literature and write down their laws.

Two of the greatest works of Western literature, the *Iliad* and the *Odyssey*, were soon written down in the new alphabet. A Greek poet named Homer, who probably lived around 750 B.C.E., is credited with composing these poems, but they were not entirely his invention. In writing the poems, Homer drew on oral tales about the legendary Trojan War that wandering poets had been reciting for centuries. The poets had elaborated on the stories so many times that they lost their historical accuracy. Nevertheless, many details in the poems, especially about weapons and armor no longer used in Homer's day, suggest that the earliest versions of the poems were first recited in the Bronze Age and may be loosely based on events of that time.

The *Iliad* and the *Odyssey* were part of a larger body of stories that told how an army of Greek warriors sailed to Troy, a wealthy city on the northwest coast of Anatolia, to recover a beautiful Greek princess, Helen, who had been abducted by a Trojan prince. After ten years of savage fighting, the Greeks finally stormed Troy and won the war, though their greatest fighters had died in battle. When the surviving heroes returned to Greece, they were met with treachery and bloodshed.

Homer's genius lay in his retelling of these old stories. He did not relate the entire saga of the Trojan War because he knew that his audiences were familiar with it. Instead, he selected certain episodes, and in fresh ways he emphasized aspects of human character and emotion in the midst of violent conflict. In the *Iliad*, for example, he describes how the hero Achilles, the mightiest of all the Greeks fighting at Troy, grows angry when his commander in chief, Agamemnon, steals his favorite concubine. In a rage, Achilles withdraws from the battle and returns to fight only to avenge his best friend, who had been killed by Hector, the main Trojan hero. Achilles eventually slays Hector, but does not relinquish his fury until Hector's father,

CHART OF THE DEVELOPMENT OF THE ALPHABET

This chart shows how the first five letters of the Phoenician alphabet developed into the first five letters of the English alphabet.

Priam, the king of Troy, begs him to return his son's corpse for proper burial. Achilles relents and weeps, his humanity restored after so much killing. In Homer's hands, the story of Achilles' anger becomes a profound investigation into human alienation and redemption.

Political Developments during the Archaic Age

Greeks in the Archaic Age also experimented with new forms of social and political life. They developed a new style of community called the **polis** (plural *poleis*), or city-state. A polis was a self-governing community consisting of an urban center with a defensible hilltop, called an **acropolis,** and all the surrounding land farmed by citizens of the polis. Greek cities varied in size from a few square miles to several hundred. All contained similar institutions: an assembly in which the male citizens of the community gathered to discuss and in some instances decide public business; a council of male elders (usually aristocrats) who advised on public matters and in many cities made laws; temples to gods who protected the polis and on whose goodwill the community's prosperity depended; and an open area in the center of town called an **agora,** which served as a market and a place for informal discussions.

Living in a polis provided an extremely strong sense of community. A person could be a citizen of only one polis, and every citizen was expected to place the community's interests above all other concerns. Even the women, who were citizens but not permitted to play a role in public life, felt powerful ties to their polis. While only citizens had full membership in a polis, enjoying the greatest rights and bearing the greatest responsibilities, every city had noncitizens from other communities. Some of these noncitizens had limited rights and obligations, whereas slaves had no rights at all.

THE OLYMPIC GAMES AND GREEK UNITY During the Archaic Age Greeks also began to develop a sense of Greek unity that had been absent during the Dark Age. Athletic contests called panhellenic games, so called because they drew participants from the entire Greek world, became one of the means by which Greeks cultivated this new sense of Greek identity. The panhellenic games became a mainstay of aristocratic Greek culture in the Archaic Age. As many as 150 cities regularly offered aristocratic men the chance to win glory through competition in chariot-racing, discus-throwing, wrestling, footracing, and other field events. Through sports the Greeks found a common culture that allowed them to express their Greek identity and honor the gods at the same time because the games were also religious festivals.

The **Olympic Games,** which originated in 776 B.C.E., carried the most prestige. Every four years Greek athletes from southern Italy to the Black Sea gathered in the sacred grove of Olympia in the central Peloponnese to take part in games dedicated to Zeus, the chief Greek god. The rules required the poleis to call truces to any wars, even if they were in the middle of battle, and allow safe passage to all athletes traveling to Olympia. Records show the naming of champions at Olympia from 776 B.C.E to 217 C.E. The Roman emperor Theodosius I, who was a Christian, abolished the games in 393 C.E. because they involved the worship of Greek gods.

COLONIZATION AND THE SETTLEMENT OF NEW LANDS A population boom during the Archaic Age forced Greeks to emigrate because the rocky soil of the mainland could not provide enough food. From about 750 to 550 B.C.E., cities such as Corinth and Megara on the mainland and Miletos in Ionia established more than 200 colonies around the Mediterranean and Black Seas.

Greek emigrants sailed to foreign shores. Many colonists settled on the Aegean coast north into the Black Sea region, which offered plentiful farmlands. The important settlement at Byzantium controlled access to the agricultural wealth of these Black Sea colonies. Greeks established many new cities in Sicily and southern Italy as well as on the southern coast of France and the eastern coast of Spain. By 600 B.C.E. Greeks had founded colonies in North Africa in the region of modern Libya and on the islands of Cyprus and Crete. Greek merchants also set up a trading community on the Syrian coast and another in the Egyptian delta, with the pharaoh's permission. (See **Map 3.1.**)

Although all Greek colonies maintained formal religious ties with their mother city-states, or *metropoleis*, they were self-governing and independent. Some colonies grew rich and populous enough to establish their own colonies. Because

the Greek colonists seized territory by force and sometimes slaughtered the local inhabitants, relations with the people already living in these lands were often tense.

The Greek adoption of coinage spurred commercial activity. Coinage first replaced barter as a medium of exchange in the kingdom of Lydia in western Anatolia about 630 B.C.E. Minted from precious metals—gold, silver, copper, bronze—and uniform in weight, coins helped people standardize the value of goods, a development that

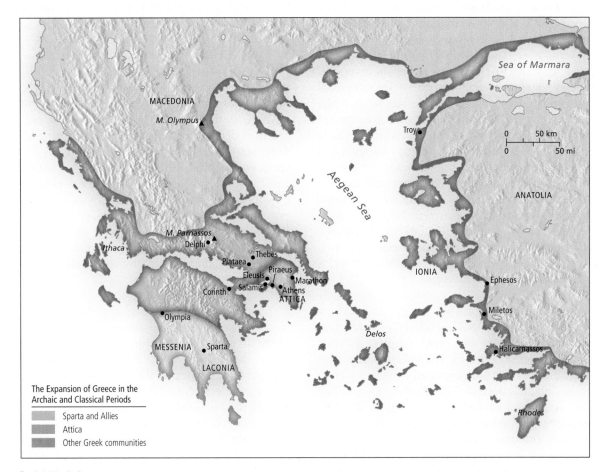

MAP 3.1

The Expansion of Greece in the Archaic and Classical Ages

During the Archaic and Classical Ages, Greek cities spread from Greece to the shores of the Black Sea and as far west as Italy and southern France. This map shows the Greek heartland: the mainland, the islands of the Aegean Sea, and Ionia. Although never unified politically in the Archaic and Classical Ages, the people in these cities spoke Greek, worshiped the same gods, and shared a similar culture.

revolutionized commerce. During the sixth century B.C.E., Greeks living in Ionia and on the Greek mainland began to mint their own coins. Each polis used a distinctive emblem to mark its currency. When Athens became the dominant economic power in the Aegean during the second half of the fifth century B.C.E., Athenian silver coinage became the standard throughout the Greek world and far beyond.

Greek colonization played a critical role in shaping Western civilization by creating wealthy centers of Greek culture in Italy and the western Mediterranean. Sometimes overshadowed in the historical record by city-states of the Greek mainland, such as Athens, Sparta, and Corinth, the impressive new poleis spread Greek civilization, language, literature, religion, and art far beyond Greece itself. The colony of Syracuse in Sicily, for example, grew to be larger than any city in Greece. Greek communities deeply influenced local cultures and made a significant impact on Etruscan and Roman civilization in Italy, as we will see in Chapter 5.

THE HOPLITE REVOLUTION   The new wealth flowing through the Greek world facilitated the introduction of a new type of fighting force known as **hoplites.** These were units of well-armed, well-drilled infantry that entered the battlefield in massed ranks, four to eight deep, in a formation called a **phalanx.** Inspired by military developments in Assyria, Greek city-states came to realize that large infantry units were more effective than individual aristocratic warriors. Hoplite warfare required more soldiers than the aristocracy could provide, so the poleis had to recruit them from among the general population. Because the new recruits had to be wealthy enough to purchase their own armor and swords, hoplites generally came from the middle ranks of society.

In hoplite warfare each man relied for protection on the man to his right, whose shield protected his own sword arm. Cooperation was all-important, for if the line broke, the individual soldier became more vulnerable. Hoplite fighting generated a sense of common purpose that had

political consequences, as hoplites demanded a political voice in the communities for which they fought. Their growing confidence challenged aristocratic families who traditionally controlled community decision-making. Military organization thus contributed to political change.

THE RISE OF THE TYRANTS   In many poleis new political leaders arose to champion the cause of the hoplite citizenry. These political leaders were known as **tyrants,** a word borrowed from the Near East that did not bear the negative connotation of cruel and arbitrary rule that it carries today. Originally the word *tyrant* meant someone who seized power in a polis rather than acquiring it by heredity, election, or some legal process. Tyrants were typically aristocrats, but they found their political support among the hoplites and the poor who felt left out of the political life of the community. Tyrants usually served the interests of the community as a whole, not just the aristocrats. They promoted overseas trade, built harbors, protected farmers, and began public works projects to employ citizen workers and to beautify their cities. They also cultivated alliances with tyrants in other poleis to establish peace and prosperity. Most important, the tyrants' authority enabled a broad range of citizens to participate in government for the first time.

But tyrannies contained a fatal flaw. The power of the tyrant was handed down from father to son, and the successors rarely inherited their fathers' qualities of leadership. As a result, tyrannies often became oppressive and unpopular, especially among the hoplites and poor who had supported the tyrants in the first place. Few tyrannies lasted more than two generations.

The most famous of the early Greek tyrannies arose in the large and immensely wealthy and powerful polis of Corinth in the mid-seventh century B.C.E. For many years an aristocratic family, the Bacchiads, had dominated Corinth. In 657 B.C.E., however, the tyrant Cypselus, who had been born into this family, seized power with popular support. He ruthlessly suppressed his aristocratic rivals but maintained his popularity with the people. Disenchantment, however, set in with the rule of Cypselus's son, Periander, who succeeded his father in 625 B.C.E. Periander's brutal methods of rule, which included the systematic execution or banishment of his political opponents and the murder of his wife, lost him the support of the people. Soon after his succession by a third tyrant, in 585 B.C.E., Corinth replaced the tyranny with an aristocratic form of government.

Contrasting Societies of the Archaic Age

The two most important poleis on the Greek mainland, Sparta and Athens, developed very different political and social systems during the Archaic Age. Both city-states experienced hoplite revolutions, and both resisted the rule of tyrants, but they nonetheless developed in different directions. Sparta became an **oligarchy,** which means government by a few. Athens, on the other hand, developed into a **democracy,** a word meaning rule by the people. Democracy is a form of political organization in which the people share equally in the government of their communities, devise their own political institutions, and select their own leaders.

SPARTA: A MILITARIZED SOCIETY   Cut off from the rest of Greece by mountain ranges to the west and north, Sparta dominated the Peloponnese, the southernmost part of Greece. Until about 700 B.C.E. Spartans lived much like other Greeks except that their hoplites, who called themselves "the Equals," achieved political power without the aid of tyrants. Sparta was formally a monarchy, ruled by two hereditary kings, each from one of the city-state's prominent aristocratic families. The two kings were equal in authority, which meant that one could veto the decisions of the other, except in time of war, when one of the kings was chosen commander in chief. Effective political power in this polis, however, resided in the *gerousia*, a council of 28 elders whom the assembly of Spartan citizens, known as the *damos*, elected for life. The damos, which comprised only hoplites, had little effective power. It elected the members of the gerousia by

acclamation and could only vote to accept or reject policies that this council proposed.

Rapid expansion in the Peloponnese prompted Spartans to develop a highly militarized society, especially after 700 B.C.E., when the Spartans conquered Messenia, a fertile region in the western Peloponnese. To control the Messenians, who vastly outnumbered them, the Spartans reduced the Messenians to the status of **helots** or serfs. Technically free, helots were nevertheless bound to the land and forced to farm it for the Spartans who owned it. If a Spartan master sold the land to another Spartan, the helots stayed with the land. Helots paid half of their produce to their Spartan masters, who could and did kill them with impunity. Controlling the helots through terror became the Spartans' preoccupation.

In Sparta's social hierarchy free subjects stood one level above the helots. They included merchants, manufacturers, and other businessmen who lived in communities throughout Spartan territories. Free subjects paid taxes and served in the army when necessary, but they were not Spartan citizens.

The male and female citizens of Sparta stood at the top of the social pyramid. The greatest responsibility of all Spartan citizens was to fulfill the military needs of the polis. From early childhood, boys trained to become soldiers and girls trained to become the wives and mothers of soldiers. Boys left home at age seven to live in barracks, where they mastered the skills of battle. They were periodically beaten to make them able to endure pain without flinching. Their comrades-in-arms played a more important role in their lives than their own families. Young married Spartan men were not permitted to live with their wives, but had to sneak away from their barracks at night to visit them.

Contempt for pain and hardship, blind obedience to orders, simplicity in word and deed, and courage were the chief Spartan virtues. Cowardice had no place in this society. Before sending their men to war, wives and mothers warned, "Come home with your shield—or on it!" Sparta's armies won a reputation as the most ferocious fighting force in all of Greece.

After its conquest of Messenia, Sparta organized the Peloponnesian League, an informal alliance of most of the other poleis in the Peloponnese, which it dominated. Spartans avoided wars far from home, but they and their allies joined with the Athenians and other Greeks in resisting Persia's aggression against Greece, as we will see shortly.

ATHENS: TOWARD DEMOCRACY Athens, the best known polis of ancient Greece, made an incalculably rich contribution to the political, philosophical, artistic, and literary traditions of Western civilization. The first democracy in the ancient world, Athens developed principles of government that remain alive today. Athens's innovative form of government and the flowering of its intellectual life stemmed directly from its response to tyranny and Persian aggression.

In the eighth and seventh centuries B.C.E., the Athenians settled Attica, the territory surrounding their city, rather than sending colonists abroad. In this way, Athens gained more land—about 1,000 square miles, the size of Rhode Island—and a larger population than any other polis on the Greek mainland. By the beginning of the sixth century, aristocrats controlled most of the wealth of Attica, and many of the Athenian peasants became heavily indebted to them. They risked being sold into slavery abroad if they could not repay their debts.

To forestall civil war between the debt-ridden peasantry and the aristocracy, both segments of the population of Attica agreed to let Solon, an Athenian statesman known for his practical wisdom, reform the political system. In 594 B.C.E. Solon (ca. 650–570 B.C.E.) enacted several reforms that limited the authority of the aristocracy and enabled all male citizens to participate more fully in public life. These reforms created the institutions from which democracy eventually developed. Solon cancelled debts, eliminated debt-slavery, and bought the freedom of Athenians who had been enslaved abroad. Taking advantage of a rise in literacy, Solon directed scribes to record his new laws on wooden panels for the whole community to read. This policy diminished aristocratic control of the interpretation of Athenian law and ensured that the laws would be enforced fairly for all Athenian citizens, regardless of their status.

Solon next organized the population into four political groups based on wealth. Only men in the two richest groups could hold the highest administrative office of *archon* and be elected to the highest court, traditionally a base of aristocratic authority. The third group could hold lower political office. The fourth group, the landless *thetes*, who could not afford hoplite weapons, did not hold any offices in the polis. All four groups, however, were represented in the council or **boule** of

CHRONOLOGY: GREECE REBUILDS	
ca. 1100 B.C.E.	Mycenaean palace states collapse; the Dark Age begins
850 B.C.E.	Greek population begins to grow; trade and settlements increase
776 B.C.E.	Traditional date of first Olympic Games
750–720 B.C.E.	Homer composes the *Iliad* and the *Odyssey*
750 B.C.E.	City-states emerge, overseas colonization begins; Greeks adopt the alphabet from the Phoenicians
700–650 B.C.E.	Hoplite armor and tactics develop; Spartans conquer Messenia
670–500 B.C.E.	Tyrants rule many city-states
600 B.C.E.	Coins are first minted in Lydia in Anatolia; science and philosophy start in Ionia
594 B.C.E.	Solon reforms Athenian Constitution
ca. 560–510 B.C.E.	Peisistratus and sons rule as tyrants in Athens; Sparta dominates Peloponnese
508 B.C.E.	Cleisthenes' democratic reforms unify Attica

400 male citizens (100 from each class), which served as an advisory body for the general assembly of all male citizens. Finally, men of any class could serve on a new court that Solon established. Women, slaves, and foreigners had no voice in government at all.

The changes introduced by Solon did not end social discontent or achieve political stability. Small farmers continued to become impoverished despite his cancellation of agricultural debt; many of them lost their land to their creditors. Solon's political compromises satisfied no one. The aristocracy felt that Solon had given away too much of their power, whereas the merchants, shopkeepers, and artisans who occupied the third political group were unhappy because they had not received more political power. Most of the elected offices remained in the hands of the aristocracy.

Capitalizing on this widespread discontent, a nobleman named Peisistratus (ca. 590–528 B.C.E.) seized power in 561 and ruled Athens as a tyrant from 547 until his death in 528 B.C.E. Like other tyrannies in Greece, Peisistratus's regime initially enjoyed wide support. He alleviated the plight of the small landowners by giving them land that he had seized from aristocrats. He sponsored building works, supported religious festivals, encouraged trade and economic development, and supported the arts. He initiated a vigorous tradition of Athenian intellectual life by inviting artists and poets to come to Athens from all over Greece. His sons, however, abused their power, and jealous aristocrats, assisted by Sparta, toppled the family's rule in 510. Peisistratus's surviving son fled to Persia.

Two years later, the assembly selected a nobleman named Cleisthenes to reorganize Athenian political institutions. By cleverly rearranging the basic political units of Attica into ten artificial tribes, Cleisthenes unified this territory and made Athens the center of all important political activity. Building upon Solon's reforms, he set the basic institutions of democracy in place with a new boule of 500 male citizens, in which each of the tribes chose 50 members by lot. The boule heard proposals from citizens and on this basis made up the agenda for the assembly, which consisted of all adult male citizens. All these male citizens could also hold public office. In this way Cleisthenes broke the power of aristocratic families and set up the lasting, fundamental structures of Athenian democracy.

THE GREEK ENCOUNTER WITH PERSIA

■ How did the Persian Empire bring the peoples of the Near East together in a stable realm, and what elements of Persian religion and government have influenced Western thought?

Persian history began about 1400 B.C.E., when small groups of herdsmen started migrating into western Iran from areas north of the Caspian Sea. Over 500 years these settlers slowly coalesced into two closely related groups, the Medes and the Persians.

By about 900 B.C.E., the Medes had established mastery over all the peoples of the Iranian plateau, including the Persians. In 612 B.C.E., with the assistance of the Babylonians, the Medes conquered the Assyrians. They then pushed into central Anatolia (modern Turkey), Afghanistan, and possibly farther into Central Asia. In the sixth century, under the leadership of Cyrus the Great (r. 550–530 B.C.E.), Persia broke away from Median rule and soon conquered the kingdom of the Medes. Under the guidance of this brilliant monarch and his successors, the Persians acquired a vast empire. They followed a monotheistic religion, Zoroastrianism, and governed their subjects with a combination of tolerance and firmness.

Cyrus the Great and Persian Expansion

After ascending the Persian throne Cyrus (r. ca. 550–530 B.C.E.) embarked on a dazzling 20-year career of conquest. His military genius and organizational skills transformed the small kingdom into a giant multiethnic empire that stretched from India to the Mediterranean Sea. Cyrus's swift victory over the Medes put Persia at the center of the Near East and thrust it into encounters with a diverse array of peoples.

Cyrus, who took the title of Great King, expanded his empire in several stages. In 546 B.C.E. he conquered Anatolia, where he first came into contact with Greeks. After his victories over these Greek cities, he installed loyal Greek rulers. Next he defeated the kingdom of Babylonia in 539 B.C.E., thus gaining control of Mesopotamia. Then he overran Afghanistan and fortified it against the raids of the Scythian nomads who

lived on the steppe lands to the north. These fierce warriors posed a perpetual threat to the settled territories of Persia.

After Cyrus died in 530 B.C.E., his son Cambyses II (r. 529–522 B.C.E.) continued his father's policy of expansion by subduing Egypt and the wealthy Phoenician port cities of the Levant. Control of Phoenician naval resources enabled Persia to extend its empire overseas to Cyprus and the islands of the Aegean. Within barely 30 years, Persia had become the mightiest empire in the world, with territorial possessions spanning Europe, the Near East, and North Africa (see **Map 3.2**).

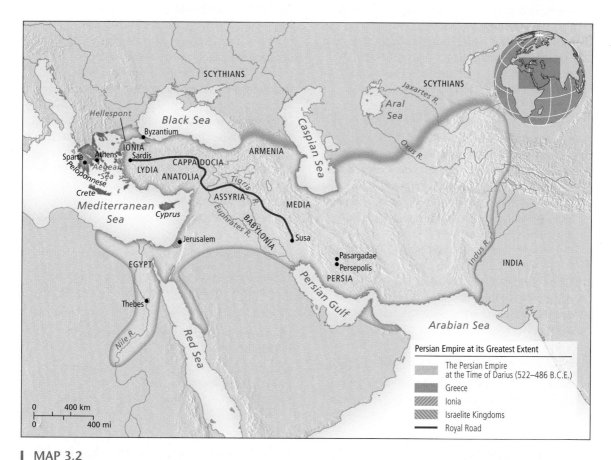

MAP 3.2

The Persian Empire at Its Greatest Extent

The Persian Empire begun by Cyrus about 550 B.C.E. grew to include all of the Middle East as far as India, Egypt, and northern Greece. This multiethnic, multireligious empire governed its many peoples firmly but tolerantly.

DIFFERENT VOICES LIBERTY AND DESPOTISM IN ANCIENT PERSIA

During the Persian Wars (490–479 B.C.E.), Greeks developed an image of Persia as a despotic state that denied its subjects the liberty that Greeks enjoyed in their poleis. The voices of Cyrus the Great King of Persia in the sixth century B.C.E. and the Greek historian Herodotus in the fifth century B.C.E. reveal how misleading those stereotypes could be. On the day of his coronation as king of Babylon in 539 B.C.E., Cyrus issued a proclamation assuring the Babylonian people that he would rule peacefully, repeal the oppressive burdens imposed on them by the tyrant Nabonidus, and restore the images of the Babylonian and Sunmerian gods that Nabonidus had banished from their sanctuaries. Cyrus appeals to Marduk, the Babylonian god, to legitimize his rule. It is misleading to consider this proclamation the "first charter of human rights," a claim based on an inaccurate translation made in 1971. Nonetheless, Cyrus, known as "The Lawgiver." did use this opportunity to guarantee Babylonians freedom of religious worship and end the despotic rule of Babylon's last king.

The Greek historian Herodotus, who grew up in Ionia while it was under Persian control, also challenged the prevailing Greek stereotype of Persian despotism. In this excerpt from The Histories, *Herodotus claimed that Persia had discussed the merits and drawbacks of the three forms of government— monarchy, oligarchy, and democracy—when Darius I (r. 522–486 B.C.E.) succeeded Cyrus as Great King. Darius decided in favor of maintaining monarchical rule, but he reputedly defended his position on the grounds that the king had given Persians their "freedom" and only he could preserve that liberty.*

Cyrus Ends the Despotism of a Babylonian Tyrant

When I went as harbinger of peace i[nt]o Babylon I founded my sovereign residence within the royal palace amid celebration and rejoicing. Marduk, the great lord, bestowed on me as my destiny the great magnanimity of one who loves Babylon, and I every day sought him out in awe. My vast troops marched peaceably in Babylon, and the whole of [Sumer] and Akkad had nothing to fear. I sought the welfare of the city of Babylon and all its sanctuaries. As for the population of Babylon [..., w]ho as if without div[ine intention] had endured a yoke not decreed for them, I soothed their weariness, I freed them from their bonds(?). Marduk, the great lord, rejoiced at [my good] deeds, and he pronounced a sweet blessing over me, the king who fears him,. . . . From [Shuanna] I sent back to their places . . . the gods who lived therein, and made permanent sanctuaries for them. I collected together all of their people and returned them to their settlements, and the gods of the land of Sumer and Akkad which Nabonidus – to the fury of the lord of the gods – had brought into Shuanna, at the command of Marduk, the great lord, I returned them unharmed to their cells, in the sanctuaries that make them happy. May all the gods that I returned to their sanctuaries, every day before Marduk and Nabu, ask for a long life for me, and mention my good deed.

Herodotus Recounts Persia's Rejection of Democracy

Otanes recommended that the management of public affairs should be entrusted to the whole nation. "To me," he said, "it seems advisable,

---

To ensure that they could easily communicate with their subjects, the Great Kings of Persia developed an elaborate system of roads that their Assyrian predecessors had begun to link their provinces. Officials maintained supply stations at regular intervals along these roads. The chief branch of this system, called the Royal Road, stretched between Anatolia and the Persian homeland in Iran. Persian roads not only facilitated the transportation of soldiers and commercial goods from

that we should no longer have a single man to rule over us—the rule of one is neither good nor pleasant.... How indeed is it possible that monarchy should be a well-adjusted thing, when it allows a man to do as he likes without being answerable? Such license is enough to stir strange and unwonted thoughts in the heart of the worthiest of men. Give a person this power, and straightway his manifold good things puff him up with pride ... leading on to deeds of savage violence.... He sets aside the laws of the land, puts men to death without trial, and subjects women to violence. The rule of the many, on the other hand ... is free from all those outrages which a king is wont to commit.... I vote, therefore, that we do away with monarchy, and raise the people to power."

Megabyzus spoke next, and advised the setting up of an oligarchy: "In all that Otanes has said to persuade you to put down monarchy," he observed, "I fully concur; but his recommendation that we should call the people to power seems to me not the best advice. For there is nothing so void of understanding, nothing so full of wantonness, as the unwieldy rabble. It were folly not to be borne, for men, while seeking to escape the wantonness of a tyrant, to give themselves up to the wantonness of a rude unbridled mob.... Let the enemies of the Persians be ruled by democracies; but let us choose out from the citizens a certain number of the worthiest, and put the government into their hands. For thus both we ourselves shall be among the governors, and power being entrusted to the best men, it is likely that the best counsels will prevail in the state." ...

After him Darius came forward, and spoke as follows: "All that Megabyzus said against democracy was well said, I think; but about oligarchy he did not speak advisedly; for take these three forms of government—democracy, oligarchy, and monarchy—and let them each be at their best, I maintain that monarchy far surpasses the other two. What government can possibly be better than that of the very best man in the whole state? ... Contrariwise, in oligarchies, where men vie with each other in the service of the commonwealth, fierce enmities are apt to arise between man and man, each wishing to be leader, and to carry his own measures; whence violent quarrels come, which lead to open strife, often ending in bloodshed. Then monarchy is sure to follow; and this too shows how far that rule surpasses all others....

Lastly, to sum up all in a word, whence, I ask, was it that we got the freedom which we enjoy? Did democracy give it us, or oligarchy, or a monarch? As a single man recovered our freedom for us, my sentence is that we keep to the rule of one.

Source: Herodotus, *The Histories*, trans. by George Rawlinson III. 80-1. (New York: Dutton, London: Dent, 1962) Reprinted by permission of Everyman's Library, Random House UK.

For Discussion

1. Was the edict issued by Cyrus in 539 B.C.E. really a charter of human rights? What practical political considerations might have led him to issue this edict?

2. Did Darius's criticism of democracy and defense of monarchy have any merit, or were they merely rhetorical justifications of Darius's own desire for power?

one part of the empire to another, but they also made possible the flow of ideas and the transmission of cultural traditions.

The key to maintaining power over such a diverse empire lay in the Persian government's treatment of its many ethnic groups. The highly centralized Persian government wielded absolute power, but it rejected the brutal model of the Assyrian and Babylonian imperial system in favor of a more tolerant approach. After conquering

Babylonia Cyrus allowed peoples exiled by the Babylonians, including the Hebrews, to return to their homelands. Subject peoples could worship freely and enjoy local autonomy if they acknowledged the political supremacy of the Great King. (See *Different Voices* in this chapter.)

ZOROASTRIANISM: AN IMPERIAL RELIGION   The Great Kings of Persia and the Persian people followed **Zoroastrianism,** a monotheistic religion that still has followers around the world today. Its founder, the prophet Zarathustra, known more commonly by his Greek name Zoroaster, lived and preached sometime between 1400 and 900 B.C.E. His message spread throughout Iran for many centuries before it became Persia's chief faith.

Persians transmitted Zoroaster's teachings, known collectively as the *Avesta,* through oral tradition until scribes recorded them in the sixth century C.E. According to Zoroaster, Ahura Mazda (Lord Wisdom), the one and only god of all Creation, is the cause of all good things in the universe. He represents wisdom, justice, and proper order among all created things. Another supernatural being, Angra Mainyu (or Ahriman), the spirit of destruction and disorder, opposes Ahura Mazda and threatens his benevolent arrangement of creation. The conflict between good and evil supernatural powers means that Zoroastrianism is a **dualistic** but not a polytheistic religion, because Angra Mainyu does not possess divine status.

In Zoroastrian belief, Ahura Mazda will eventually triumph in this struggle with the forces of evil, leaving all creation to enjoy a blissful eternity. Until then, the cosmic fight between Ahura Mazda's forces of light and Angra Mainyu's forces of darkness gives meaning to human existence and lays the foundation for a profoundly ethical way of life. Ahura Mazda requires humans to contribute to the well-being of the world. Everyone must choose between right and wrong actions.

At the Day of Judgment, sinners who have not listened to Ahura Mazda's instructions, such as those succumbing to the "filth of intoxication," will suffer eternal torment in a deep pit of terrible darkness. Those who have lived ethical lives will live forever in a world purged of evil. In a period of transformation called "the Making Wonderful," the dead will be resurrected, and all will live together in the worship of Ahura Mazda.

The Great Kings of Persia believed themselves to be Ahura Mazda's earthly representatives, responsible for fighting the forces of disorder in their world. Zoroastrianism thus provided an ideological support for the Persian Empire's wars of conquest and rule. The Great Kings lavishly supported the Zoroastrian church, and its priests, called magi, established the faith as the empire's official religion. They built grand temples with sacred fires throughout the empire. Although the Persian Empire tolerated other religions, Zoroastrianism became the official religion that supported the Great Kings.

Zoroastrian beliefs played an important role in shaping the three great Western religions: Judaism, Christianity, and Islam. The Zoroastrian belief that a powerful spirit of evil opposed God contributed to the Jewish belief in Satan, who appears in the later books of the Hebrew Bible as a demon with a distinct personality. Some Jews developed the concept of Satan, later known as the Devil, more

CHRONOLOGY: PERSIA

550 B.C.E.	Cyrus starts the Persian Empire; Zoroastrianism becomes the empire's religion
546 B.C.E.	Persians conquer Asia Minor
539 B.C.E	Persians capture Babylon
525 B.C.E	Persian conquers Egypt
522 B.C.E	Darius I becomes king
490 B.C.E	Greeks stop Persian invasion of Greece at battle of Marathon
480–479 B.C.E	Xerxes' invasion of Greece fails

clearly during the first century B.C.E. when they transformed him into a cosmic force of evil. Early Christianity inherited these ideas. The Christian belief in a final struggle against the Devil, followed by the establishment of the kingdom of God on Earth, also originated in Zoroastrianism. The Zoroastrian idea of a final judgment, followed by an afterlife in Heaven or Hell, became a central concept in Christianity and Islam, although it was later downplayed within Judaism.

Persia under Darius the Great

In 522 B.C.E. Darius, a Persian nobleman related to the royal family, seized the imperial throne by murdering one of the sons of Cyrus the Great. Assuming the status of the new Great King, Darius I inaugurated a new period of territorial expansion and cultural activity that lasted until the Macedonian conqueror Alexander the Great overwhelmed Persia in 330 B.C.E.

Darius controlled an efficient administration. He expanded and improved Persia's roads, set up a postal system, and standardized measures and coinage. He also reorganized Cyrus's system of provincial government, dividing the empire into 20 provinces called satrapies. Each province paid an annual sum to the central government based on its productivity. From the provincial capitals the governors, Persian noblemen called satraps, collected these taxes, gathered military recruits, and oversaw the bureaucracy.

DARIUS THE GREAT GIVING AN AUDIENCE

In this carved panel from the Treasury of the Palace at Persepolis, the Great King Darius I (r. 522–486 B.C.E.) is shown receiving a dignitary. Darius is seated on his throne and holds a staff of office. Subject kings from all over the Persian Empire also came to court to pay their respects and bring tribute.

By 513 B.C.E. Darius had greatly expanded his empire. On his northeastern frontier he annexed parts of India as far as the Indus River. To facilitate commerce he built a canal in Egypt that linked the Mediterranean and Red Seas. His conquests on the northwestern frontier of the Persian Empire, however, had the greatest impact on Western civilization because they brought Persia into direct contact with the Greeks. Eager to conquer Greece, Darius sent troops across the Hellespont to establish military bases in the north of Greece. Such incursions along the Greek frontier were only a small part of Darius's grand imperial strategy, but to the Greeks the growing Persian presence caused profound anxiety. The stage was set for the confrontation between the Persians and the Greeks, a conflict that demonstrated the limits of Persian imperialism.

Around 510 B.C.E Darius conquered the Ionian Greek poleis. The Persians ruled their new subjects with a light hand, but the Ionian Greeks nevertheless revolted in 499 B.C.E. and asked Sparta and Athens for military assistance. The Spartans, who were further away from Ionia, refused, but the Athenians sent an expeditionary force that helped the rebels burn Sardis, a Persian provincial capital. The Persians crushed the rebellion in 494 B.C.E., but they did not forget Athens's intervention in it.

The Persian Wars, 490–479 B.C.E.

In 490 B.C.E., after four years of meticulous planning, a Persian army crossed the Aegean Sea in the ships of their Phoenician subjects. They landed at the beach of Marathon, some 26 miles from Athens. The area around Marathon was the traditional stronghold of the family of Peisistratus, the former Athenian tyrant. The Persians planned to install Peisistratus's son Hippias as the new tyrant of Athens.

To save their city, the Athenians marched to Marathon, and with the aid of troops from a neighboring polis (Spartan reinforcements arrived too late), defeated the Persians. The surprising Greek victory demonstrated that a force of heavily armed hoplites could defeat a more numerous but more lightly armored body of Persian infantry. Pride in this Greek victory also unified Athenians by making it unpopular to advocate a treaty or an alliance with Persia, as many had done before the battle.

After Marathon, Athens embraced even more dramatic reforms. A new political leader, Themistocles (ca. 523–ca. 458 B.C.E.) persuaded his fellow citizens to spend the proceeds from a rich silver mine in Attica on a new navy and port. By 480 B.C.E. Athens possessed nearly 200 warships, called **triremes.** With three banks of oars manned by the poorest citizens of the polis, who were paid to row them, the triremes transformed Athens into a naval powerhouse. The entire male citizen body of Athens, not just the aristocrats and hoplites, could now be called to arms. The Athenian navy embodied Athenian democracy in action in that every male citizen had an obligation to defend his homeland.

Marathon dealt a blow to the Persians' pride that they resolved to avenge, but a major revolt in Egypt and Darius's death in 486 B.C.E. prevented them from invading Greece again for nearly a decade. In 480 B.C.E., Xerxes I, the new Great King, launched a massive invasion of Greece. He brought an overwhelming force of some 150,000 soldiers, a navy of nearly 700 mostly Phoenician vessels, and ample supplies. His troops crossed from Asia into Europe by means of a bridge of boats over the Hellespont, while the navy followed by sea in order to supply the troops. They intended to smash Athens.

Terrified by the size of the Persian army, fewer than 40 of the more than 700 Greek poleis joined the defensive coalition that had formed in anticipation of the invasion. Under the leadership of Sparta, the Greek allies planned to hold back the Persian land force in the north, while the Athenian navy would attack the invaders at sea. Leonidas, the Spartan king, led the coalition. A Greek force under his command stopped the Persians at the pass of Thermopylae until a traitor revealed an alternate path through the mountains that allowed the Persians to attack the Greeks from the rear. On the last day of the battle Leonidas, his entire force of 300 Spartans, and perhaps 1,200 allies died fighting.

LEONIDAS MONUMENT, THERMOPYLAE

This monument celebrating the heroism of Leonidas and the Spartans at the battle of Themopylae in 480 B.C.E. was commissioned in 1955 by King Paul of Greece.

Their sacrifice was not in vain. Thermopylae gave the Athenians precious time to evacuate their city and station their highly maneuverable fleet in the narrow straits of Salamis, just off the Athenian coast. In a stunning display of naval skill, the Athenian triremes defeated the Persian navy in a single day of heavy fighting. Xerxes returned to Persia, although he left a large army in central Greece.

Early in 479 B.C.E. a combined Greek army once again stopped the Persians at the battle of Plataea, north of Attica. In this battle a large contingent of Spartans led the decisive final charge. The surviving Persian troops were driven out of Greece. That same year, the combined Greek naval force again defeated the Persian navy off the Ionian coast. Xerxes gave up the attempt to conquer Greece.

THE CLASSICAL AGE OF GREECE, 479–336 B.C.E.

■ What were the intellectual, social, and political innovations of Greece in the Classical Age?

The defeat of mighty Persia by a handful of Greek cities shocked the Mediterranean world. Xerxes' failure did not seriously weaken Persia, but it greatly strengthened the Greeks' own position in the Mediterranean and enhanced what we would now call their self-image. After the defeat of the Persians, the Greeks exhibited immense confidence in their ability to shape their political institutions and to describe and analyze their society and the world around them. The emboldened Athenians created a powerful empire that made them the dominant power in the Greek world while democratic institutions flourished in the polis. Yet Athens's very success sowed the seeds of its demise. After alienating many of the other Greek poleis, Athens lost the long and bitter Peloponnesian War with Sparta.

The distinguishing feature of the Classical Age was its remarkable creativity, especially in drama, science, history writing, philosophy, and the visual arts. Despite the turmoil of the Persian and Peloponnesian Wars, Greek society remained rigidly hierarchical with strictly defined gender roles and many slaves who did much of the heavy work. The structures of Greek society provided many male citizens with leisure time for debating public affairs in a democratic fashion, attending plays, and speculating about philosophical issues. The numerous Greek gods became the subject of much Greek art. Greeks worshiped these gods in temples in the Classical style, which the Romans and other Western peoples later imitated. None of the Greek cities produced as many creative men as Athens, which makes its experience as an empire and a democracy particularly revealing.

The Rise and Fall of the Athenian Empire

With the Persian threat to Greece nearly eliminated, Athens began a period of rapid imperial expansion. This aggressive foreign policy eventually backfired. It created resentment among the other Greek city-states that led to war and the collapse of the Athenian Empire.

FROM DEFENSIVE ALLIANCE TO EMPIRE   After the battle of Plataea, the Greek defensive alliance set out to evict the Persians from the Ionian coast. The Spartans soon grew disillusioned with this campaign and withdrew their troops, leaving Athenians in charge. In the winter of 478 B.C.E., Athens reorganized the alliance, creating the **Delian League,** named for the small island of Delos where the members of the league met.

Athens contributed approximately 200 warships to continue attacks against the Persians, while the other members supplied either ships or funds to pay for them. The league ultimately gathered a naval force of 300 ships. By 469 B.C.E. it had driven the last Persians from the Aegean.

With the Persians ousted, several poleis tried to leave the league, but the Athenians forced them to remain in it. The Athenians were rapidly turning the Delian League into an Athenian Empire organized for their own benefit. In subsequent decades the Athenians established garrisons in many cities of the league and intervened in their political life by imposing heavy taxes and financial regulations. Several revolts broke out, but no polis in the empire could overcome Athens's might. In 460 B.C.E. Athens sent approximately 4,000 men and 200 warships to assist an Egyptian revolt against Persia, but Persia destroyed the expedition. Sobered by this debacle, the Athenians moved the treasury of the Delian League from Delos to Athens, claiming that they were protecting it from Persian retaliation. In fact, the Athenians spent the league treasury on public buildings in Athens, including the Parthenon. Athens had become indifferent to the original purpose of the league, but the revenues it generated by exploiting the other cities in the league simultaneously enabled democracy to flourish in Athens itself.

DEMOCRACY IN THE AGE OF PERICLES   The chief designer of the Athenian Empire was Pericles (ca. 490–429 B.C.E.), an aristocrat who dominated Athenian politics from 461 B.C.E. until his death. During the so-called "Age of Pericles," Athenian democracy at home and empire abroad reached their peak.

During the Age of Pericles, Athens had about 40,000 male citizens. Only free men over age 18 could participate in the city's political life. Women, foreigners, slaves, and other imperial subjects had no voice in public life.

The representative council of 500 men established by Cleisthenes continued to administer public business. The citizen assembly met every ten days and probably never had more than

WARFARE AT SEA

In the classical world, navies relied on long-rowed vessels with bronze battering rams to attack enemy ships. This painting of a war galley was made about 550 B.C.E. and shows soldiers, oarsmen, and a man at the helm. Athenians perfected the war galley. Their ships could reach a speed of more than nine nautical miles per hour for short distances.

5,000 citizens in attendance, except on the most important occasions. The assembly decided issues of war, peace, and public policy by majority vote. Because men gained political power through debate in the assembly, a politician's rhetorical skills were crucial in convincing voters.

Ten officials called *generals* were elected every year by popular vote to handle high affairs of state and direct Athens's military forces. Generals typically were aristocrats of proven expertise. Pericles, for example, was reelected general almost continually for more than 20 years.

The vast increase in public business required to run the empire multiplied the number of administrators. By the middle of the fifth century, Athens had about 1,500 officials in its bureaucracy. Boards of assessors determined how much money the members of the Delian League had to pay. Legal disputes among cities in the league forced Athens to increase the number of its courts. Because of the constant need for jurors and other officeholders, Pericles began paying wages for public service, the first such policy in history. Jurors were chosen by lot, and trials lasted no more than a day to expedite cases, save money, and prevent jury tampering.

Pericles also gave women a more important role in Athenian society. Before 451 B.C.E. children born to Athenian men and their foreign wives became full citizens. Pericles allowed citizenship only if both parents were Athenian citizens. As a result, Athenian women took pride in giving birth to the polis's only legitimate citizens. Nevertheless, Athenian female citizens could not speak or vote in the assembly, hold public office, or serve on juries.

THE PELOPONNESIAN WAR AND THE COLLAPSE OF ATHENIAN POWER Sparta and its allies felt threatened by growing Athenian power. Between 460 and 431 B.C.E., Athens and a few allies skirmished intermittently with Sparta and the Peloponnesian League it dominated. Full-scale war broke out between the two poleis in 431 B.C.E., dragging on until 404 B.C.E. (see **Map 3.3**). In the

early stages of the conflict, which was called the Peloponnesian War, the Spartans repeatedly invaded Attica in the hope of defeating Athenian forces in open battle.

Thanks to Athens's fortifications, the Athenians endured these invasions. Safe behind their fortifications, they relied on their navy to deliver food and supplies from cities in the Athenian Empire. They also launched attacks against Spartan territory from the sea. Although plague struck the overcrowded city in 430 B.C.E., killing almost one-third of the population including Pericles, the Athenians fought on.

In 421 B.C.E., Sparta and Athens agreed to a 50-year truce, but a mere six years later war broke

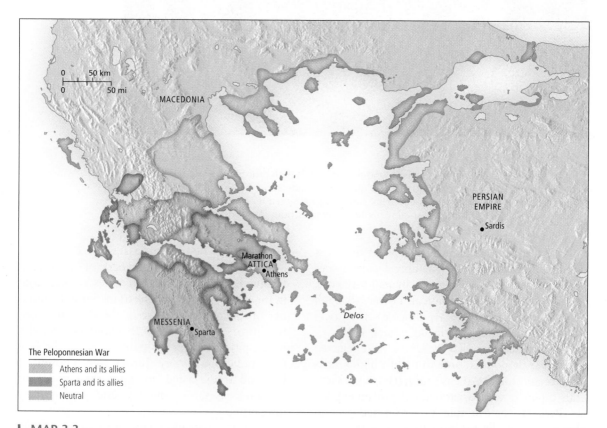

MAP 3.3

The Peloponnesian War

During this long conflict that lasted from 431 to 404 B.C.E., the forces of Athens and its allies struggled with Sparta and its allies for control of mainland Greece. Though Sparta defeated the Athenian Empire, Athens survived as an influential force in Greek social, political, and economic life.

CHRONOLOGY: CLASSICAL GREECE

490 B.C.E.	Battle of Marathon; first Persian invasion stopped
480–479 B.C.E.	Xerxes invades Greece and is defeated
478 B.C.E.	Delian League formed; expansion of Athenian democracy and imperialism
450s B.C.E.	Pericles ascendant in Athens; Herodotus writes his *Investigations* (*Histories*)
477–432 B.C.E.	Parthenon built in Athens; sophists active
431–404 B.C.E.	Peloponnesian War; Thucydides writes his *History*
429 B.C.E.	Death of Pericles; Euripides and Sophocles active
415–413 B.C.E.	Athens's campaign in Sicily fails
405 B.C.E.	Sparta defeats Athens at Aegospotami
399 B.C.E.	Trial and death of Socrates
399–347 B.C.E.	Plato writes *Dialogues* and founds Academy

out again. The reckless policies of Alcibiades (ca. 450–404 B.C.E.), a young Athenian general, started a new round of warfare. A nephew of Pericles, Alcibiades lacked his uncle's wisdom. In 415 B.C.E. he persuaded the Athenians to send an expeditionary force of 5,000 hoplites to invade Sicily and seize the rich resources of the city of Syracuse for the war effort. Just as the fleet was about to sail, Alcibiades' enemies accused him of profaning a religious festival, and he fled to Sparta. After two years of heavy fighting, the Athenian expedition ended in utter disaster. Every Athenian ship was captured, and Athenian soldiers were killed or sold into slavery.

The Peloponnesian War dragged on for another ten years, but Athens never recovered from the catastrophic loss of men and ships in Sicily. At the suggestion of Alcibiades, the Spartans established a permanent military base within sight of Athens, which enabled them to control Attica. When 20,000 slaves in the Athenian silver mines escaped to freedom under the Spartans, Athens lost its main source of revenue. The final blow came when Lysander, the Spartan commander in chief, used money from Persia to build a navy strong enough to challenge Athenian sea power. At the battle of Aegospotami on the Hellespont, Lysander's navy destroyed every Athenian ship. Athens surrendered in 404 B.C.E.

The victorious Spartan forces pulled down Athens's long walls stretching to Piraeus, but they refused to burn the city to the ground as some of its enemies demanded, because Athens had been Sparta's valiant ally in the Persian Wars. Instead, the Spartans set up an oligarchy in place of democracy. Led by the "Thirty Tyrants," a violent and conservative political faction, the oligarchy soon earned the hatred of Athenian citizens. Within a year the Athenians overthrew the tyrants and restored democracy.

Social and Religious Life in the Classical Age

During the Classical Age, the Greek poleis developed a way of life in which gender and social status determined one's position in society and politics. Greek men and women lived very different lives, guided by strict rules of behavior. A hierarchy of gender roles determined a person's access to public space, legal rights, and opportunities to work. In this emphatically patriarchal society, only men held positions of public authority, controlled wealth and inheritance, and participated in political life. Women were restricted to domestic activities that mostly took place out of sight of nonfamily members. At the bottom of society slaves of both genders were completely subject to their masters.

GENDER ROLES Greek women were expected to marry early in puberty, typically to men at least ten years older than they were. Through marriage legal control of women passed from father to husband. In the case of divorce, which only men could initiate, the husband had to return his wife's dowry to her father. Most Greek houses were small and usually divided into two parts. In the brighter front rooms husbands entertained their male friends at dinner and enjoyed social interaction with other males. Wives spent most of their time in the more secluded part of the house, supervising the household slaves if there were any, raising children, dealing with their mothers-in-law, and weaving cloth.

Greek men feared that their wives would commit adultery, which carried the risk of illegitimate offspring and implied that husbands could not control their possessions or access to their homes. Consequently, men strictly controlled women's sexual activity. Because men considered females powerless to resist seduction, respectable women rarely ventured out in public without a chaperone. Whenever possible, slaves went to market and ran errands. To the typical Greek husband, the ideal wife stayed out of public sight and dutifully obeyed him. She was not supposed to mind if he had relations with prostitutes or adolescent boys. Above all, she was expected to produce legitimate children, preferably sons, who would continue the family line and honorably serve the polis.

Women who worked outside the home did so primarily in three capacities: as vendors of farm produce or cloth in the marketplace, as priestesses, and as prostitutes. Female vendors in the marketplace came from the lower classes. Their skills in weaving cloth and making garments, as well as in growing vegetables, enabled them to supplement the family income.

GREEK MALE VIEW OF WOMEN

In male-dominated Greek communities men idealized passive women. This Athenian vase of the fifth century B.C.E. reflects Greek men's view of a properly subordinate woman. In the image, the wife bids goodbye to her young husband, who is going off to war. Her place is at home, tending to chores until his return.

Priestesses served the temples of goddesses such as Hera in Argos and Athena in Athens. In classical Athens, more than 40 publicly sponsored religious cults had female priests. These women gained high prestige in their communities. Greeks believed that some women possessed a special spirituality that made them mediums through whom the gods spoke. Such women served as oracles, as in the temple of Apollo at Delphi. They attracted visitors from all over the Mediterranean world who wanted to discern the gods' wishes or learn what the future might bring.

All Greek cities had prostitutes, but unlike priestesses, their profession was considered shameful. In Athens, most prostitutes were foreign slaves. Some women worked as elite courtesans called **hetairai.** Because Greek men did not think it possible to have intellectual conversations with their spouses, they hired hetairai to accompany them to social gatherings and to discuss politics, philosophy, and the arts. Like ordinary prostitutes, hetairai also were expected to be sexually available for pay.

The most famous of all hetairai was Aspasia, who came to Athens from the Ionian city of Miletus. She became Pericles' companion, and their son gained Athenian citizenship by special vote of the assembly. Aspasia participated fully in the circle of scientists, artists, and intellectuals who surrounded Pericles and made Athens "the school of Greece." According to legend, she taught rhetoric, wrote many of Pericles' speeches, and regularly conversed with the philosopher Socrates.

The Athenian orator Demosthenes famously summed up Greek attitudes toward women with these words: "We have hetairai for the sake of pleasure, regular prostitutes to care for our physical needs, and wives to bear legitimate children and be loyal custodians of our households."[1]

In classical Greece, where men considered women intellectually and emotionally inferior, some men, especially prominent members of society, believed that the best sort of friendship was found in male relationships and took adolescent boys as lovers. In these relationships, which were publicly acknowledged, the older man often assumed the role of mentor to his younger companion. Some poleis institutionalized such relationships. In the city of Thebes, for example, the elite "Sacred Band" of 150 male couples led the city's hoplites into battle during the fourth century B.C.E. These men were considered the best warriors because they would not endure the shame of showing cowardice to their lovers. The Sacred Band could defeat even Spartan warriors.

SLAVERY: THE SOURCE OF GREEK PROSPERITY Slaves had no political, legal, or personal rights. Masters could kill them without serious penalty and could demand sexual favors at any time. Slavery existed in every polis and at every social level. The slave population expanded in the period after 600 B.C.E. as poleis prospered and demands for labor increased.

Most information about Greek slavery comes from Athens, which was the first major slave society that is well documented. Between about 450 and 320 B.C.E., Athens had a total population of perhaps 250,000 people, one-third of whom were enslaved. The proportion of slaves to free people was similar in other poleis. In the Archaic Age the Athenian aristocracy had begun to rely on slave labor to work their large landed estates. Most of these slaves had fallen into bondage for debt, but after Solon made the enslavement of Athenian citizens illegal in 594 B.C.E., the wealthy bought slaves outside Attica. Many slaves were captured during the Persian Wars, but most slaves were either the children of slaves or purchased from the thriving slave trade in non-Greek peoples from around the Aegean.

Slaves performed many tasks. The city of Athens owned public slaves who served as a police force, as executioners, as clerks in court, and in other capacities. Most slaves, however, were privately owned. Some were highly skilled artisans and businessmen who lived apart from their owners but were required to pay them a high percentage of their profits. Most Greek households had male and female slaves who performed menial tasks such as cooking and cleaning. Some rich landowners owned gangs of slaves who worked in the fields. Others rented slaves to the polis to labor in the silver mines, where they were worked to death under hideous conditions.

Slavery did not necessarily last until a person's death. A few slaves were freed by their owners. Others saved enough money from their trades to buy their freedom. Freed slaves could not become citizens. Instead, they lived as resident foreigners in the polis of their former masters and often maintained close ties of loyalty and obligation to them.

Slavery was so widespread in Athens because it was profitable. The Athenian political system evolved to permit and support the exploitation of slaves to benefit the citizen class. The slaves were primarily responsible for the prosperity of Athens and gave the aristocrats the leisure to engage in intellectual pursuits and create the rich culture that became part of the core of Western civilization.

RELIGION AND THE GODS Religion permeated Greek life. Greeks worshiped many gods, whom they asked for favors and advice. Every city kept a calendar of religious observances established for certain days. Festivals marked phases in the

agricultural year, such as the harvest or sowing seasons, and initiation ceremonies marked a person's transition from childhood to adulthood.

Above all, Greeks gave their devotion to the gods who protected their city. For instance, during the annual Panathenaea festival in Athens, the entire population, citizens and noncitizens alike, honored the city's patron goddess Athena with a grand procession and sacrifices. Every fourth year, the celebration was expanded to include athletic and musical competitions. In a joyous parade, the citizens would convey a robe embroidered with mythological scenes to the statue of Athena in her temple, called the Parthenon, or House of the Virgin Goddess, that stood on the Acropolis in the center of the city.

Although every polis had its own set of religious practices, people throughout the Greek world shared ideas about the gods. Like the Greek language, these shared religious beliefs gave Greeks a common identity. They also distinguished them

THE ACROPOLIS AND THE PARTHENON
The Acropolis of Athens, crowned by the Parthenon, the temple to the Greek goddess Athena, the patron of the polis.

from so-called barbarians who worshiped strange gods in ways the Greeks considered uncivilized.

Most Greeks believed that immortal and powerful gods and goddesses were all around them. These deities often embodied natural phenomena such as the sun and moon, but Greeks attributed human personalities and desires to them. Because these divine forces touched every aspect of daily life, human interactions with them were unavoidable and risky, for the gods could be as harmful as they were helpful to humans.

The Greeks believed that the twelve greatest gods lived on Mount Olympus in northern Greece as a large, dysfunctional family. Zeus was the father of some of the gods and king of them all. Hera was his sister and wife. Aphrodite was the goddess of sex and love. This jealous clan also included Apollo, god of the sun, prophecy, and medicine; Poseidon, god of the sea; and Athena, the goddess of wisdom. Greek mythology developed a set of stories about the Olympian gods that have passed into Western literature and art.

In addition to their home on Mount Olympus, the gods also maintained residences in cities. Temples served as the gods' living quarters. Worship at Greek temples consisted of offerings and sacrifices. Outside, in the open air, worshipers offered the gods small gifts, such as a small bouquet of flowers, a pinch of incense, or a small grain cake. On especially important festivals the Greeks sacrificed live animals to their gods on altars in front of the temples. Priests and priestesses supervised these rituals. The god inside the temple supposedly watched the priests prepare the sacrifice, heard the sacrificial animals bleat as their throats were slit, and listened to women howl as blood poured from the beasts. Finally, the god smelled the aroma of burning meat as the victim was cooked over the flames. Satisfied, the god awaited the next sacrifice while the cooked meat was usually distributed to the worshippers.

The Greeks also took pains to discern the future. Religious experts analyzed dreams and predicted the future based on the examination of the internal organs of sacrificed animals. Greeks and non-Greeks alike traveled to consult the priestess of Apollo, the so-called Oracle of Delphi, at a shrine in central Greece. If the god chose to reply to a query, he spoke through the mouth of his oracle, a priestess who would lapse into a trance. Priests recorded and explained the oracle's utterances, which could have more than one interpretation. When King Croesus of Lydia (r. 560–547 B.C.E.) supposedly asked the oracle what would happen if he went to war with the Persians, Apollo told him that "a great kingdom will fall." Croesus never dreamed it would be his own.

Cultural and Intellectual Life in Classical Greece

In the Classical Age, Greeks investigated the natural world and explored the human condition with astonishing freshness and vigor. Their legacy in drama, science, philosophy, and the arts has inspired people for many subsequent centuries. The term *renaissance,* which is applied to several cultural movements in later periods, refers to attempts to recapture the intellectual vitality of the Greek Classical Age and of the Romans, which drew heavily from it.

DRAMA Greek men and women examined their society's values through public dramatic performances. Athenian drama had its origins in an annual festival dedicated to Dionysus, the god of wine, which Peisistratus, the tyrant of Athens, introduced in 535 B.C.E. Plays, which included choral dancing, became part of these festivals, and authors entered their work in competition for a prestigious prize. Dramatic productions soon became a mainstay of Greek life. In their plays, usually set in the mythical past, the playwrights explored issues relevant to contemporary society. Above all, Greeks who attended the plays could expect to be educated and entertained. Fewer than 50 plays of the hundreds that were written during from the Greek classical period have survived, but they count among the most powerful examples of Western literature.

In tragedies Athenian men watched stories about the terrible suffering underlying human society. In many of these plays a fatal personal flaw beyond one's ability to control led to the destruction of an important aristocrat or ruler. With an unflinching gaze, playwrights examined conflicts between violent passion and reason and between the laws of the gods and those of human communities. Their dramas depicted the terrible consequences of vengeance, the brutality of war, and the relationship of the individual to the polis. In the plays of the three great Athenian tragedians—Aeschylus, Sophocles, and Euripides—the audience learned vital lessons through the sufferings of the characters.

Aeschylus (525–456 B.C.E.) believed that the gods were just and that suffering stemmed directly from human error. His most powerful works include a trilogy called the *Oresteia.* These three plays express the notion that a polis can survive only when courts made up of citizens punish criminals, rather than leaving justice to family vendettas.

In the plays of Sophocles (ca. 496–406 B.C.E.), humans are free to act, but they are trapped by their own weaknesses, their history, and the will of the gods. In *Antigone,* a young woman buries her outlaw brother in accordance with divine principles but in defiance of her city's laws against burying rebels, knowing that she will be executed for her brave act. The misguided king who made the law and ordered her death realizes too late that a polis will prosper only if human and divine laws come into proper balance. In *Oedipus the King,* Oedipus unknowingly kills his father and marries his mother. When he learns what he has done, he blinds himself. Although he knows that fate caused his tragedy, he understands that he was the one who committed the immoral acts.

The plays of Euripides (ca. 484–406 B.C.E.) portray humans struggling against their fates. In these works, the gods have no human feeling and are capable of bestial action against humans. Euripides showed remarkable sympathy for women, who often fall victim to war and male deceit in his plays. At the end of *The Trojan Women,* the despairing Trojan queen Hecuba stands amid the smoldering ruins of her vanquished city, lamenting the cruel life as a slave that awaits her: "Lead me, who walked soft-footed once in Troy, lead me a slave where earth falls sheer away by rocky edges, let me drop and die withered away with tears."[2]

In addition to the tragedies, Greeks delighted in irreverent comedies. Performances of comedy probably began in the seventh century B.C.E. as lewd sketches associated with Dionysos, the god of wine and fertility. The playwright Aristophanes of Athens (ca. 450–388 B.C.E.) proved a master at presenting comedy as social commentary. No person, god, or institution escaped his mockery. Although committed to Athenian democracy, Aristophanes had no patience for hypocritical politicians or self-important intellectuals. His comic plays are full of raunchy sex, sarcasm, puns, and allusions to contemporary issues. Audiences howled at the fun, but these plays always carried a thought-provoking message. *The Birds* is an apt example. In this satire, Aristophanes tells the story of two down-on-their-luck Athenians who flee the city looking for peace and quiet. On their trek they have to deal with an endless stream of Athenian bureaucrats and frauds, whom Aristophanes mercilessly skewers. Finally the travelers seize power over the Kingdom of the Birds—and then transform it into a replica of Athens. This satire of Athenian imperialism shows Athenians helpless to avoid their own worst instincts.

SCIENTIFIC THOUGHT Greek science began about 600 B.C.E. in the cities of Ionia, when a handful of men began to ask new questions about the natural world. Living on the border with Near Eastern civilizations, these Greek thinkers encountered the vigorous Babylonian scientific and mathematical traditions that still flourished in the Persian Empire. Carefully observing the natural world and systematically recording data, these men began to reconsider traditional Greek explanations for natural phenomena. They rejected the idea that gods arbitrarily inflicted floods, earthquakes, and other disasters on humanity. Instead, they looked for general principles that could explain each natural phenomenon. To these investigators, the natural world was orderly, knowable through careful inquiry, and therefore ultimately predictable. These scientists inquired about the physical composition of the natural world, tried to formulate the principles that explained why change occurs, and began to think about proving their theories logically.

Thales of Miletus (ca. 625–547 B.C.E.), the first of these investigators, theorized that the Earth was a disk floating on water. When the Earth rocked in the water, he proposed, the motion caused earthquakes. Thales traveled to Egypt to study geometry and established the height of the pyramids by calculating the length of their shadows. Perhaps influenced by Egyptian and Babylonian teachings, he believed that water gave rise to everything else. His greatest success as an astronomer came when he predicted a solar eclipse in 585 B.C.E.

One of Thales' students, Anaximander (ca. 610–547 B.C.E.), wrote a pioneering essay about natural science called *On the Nature of Things*. Anaximander became the first Greek to create a map of the inhabited world. He also argued that the universe was rational and symmetrical. In his view, it consisted of Earth as a flat disk at its center, held in place by the perfect balance of the limitless space around it. Anaximander also believed that change occurred on Earth through tension between opposites, such as hot versus cold and dry versus wet.

A third great thinker from Miletus, Anaximenes (ca. 545–525 B.C.E.), suggested that air is the fundamental substance of the universe. Through different processes, air could become fire, wind, water, earth, or even stone. His conclusions, along with those of Thales and Anaximander, may seem odd and unsatisfactory today, but these men were pioneers in the scientific exploration of the natural world. Their willingness to remove the gods from explanations of natural phenomena, and their effort to defend their theories, established the foundations of modern scientific inquiry and observation.

These Milesian thinkers sparked inquiry in other parts of the Greek world. Heraclitus of Ephesus (ca. 500 B.C.E.) argued that fire, not gods, provided the true origin of the world. Leucippus of Miletus (fifth century B.C.E.) and Democritus of Abdera (ca. 460–370 B.C.E.) proposed that the universe consisted of an endless number of minute particles called atoms that floated everywhere. When the atoms collided or stuck together, they produced the elements of the world

we live in, including life itself. These atomists had no need for gods to explain the natural world.

HISTORY The Western tradition of writing history has its roots in the work of Herodotus (ca. 484–420 B.C.E.), who grew to adulthood in the Ionian city of Halicarnassus. Herodotus sought to find the general causes of human events, not natural phenomena. He called his work *Investigations* (the original Greek meaning of the word *history*), and he attempted to explain the Persian Wars, which he considered the greatest wars ever fought.

Gods appear in Herodotus's narrative but do not play a causal role in events. Instead, Herodotus attempted to show that humans always act in accordance with the general principle of reciprocity; that is, people predictably respond in equal measure to what befalls them. He described reciprocal violence in legends, such as that of the Trojan War, and recounted the conquest of Lydia by Cyrus the Great in the sixth century. He tells how the Greeks became involved in Persian affairs and finally triumphed over Persian aggression.

Herodotus traveled widely and made the description and analysis of foreign cultures an integral part of his "investigations." He frequently visited Athens, where he read portions of his history of the Persian War to appreciative audiences. He also went to Egypt, Babylonia, and other foreign lands, gathering information about local religions and customs. Herodotus relished the differences among cultures, and his narrative brims with vivid descriptions of exotic habits in far-off lands.

Although he considered Greeks superior to other peoples, Herodotus raised basic questions about cultural encounters that still engage us today. Are one culture's customs better than another's? Can we evaluate a foreign culture on its own terms or are we doomed to view the world through our own eyes and experiences?

Western civilization also owes an incalculable debt to Thucydides of Athens (d. ca. 400 B.C.E.). His brilliant *History of the Peloponnesian War* is perhaps the single most influential work of history in the Western tradition because it provides a model for analyzing the causes of human events and the outcomes of individual decisions. In it he combines meticulous attention to detail with a broad moral vision. To Thucydides, the Peloponnesian War was a tragedy. At one time under the leadership of Pericles, Athens epitomized all that was good about a human community. Its culture and political achievement had made it the "school of Greece." Unfortunately Athenians, like all humans, possessed a fatal flaw—the unrelenting desire to possess more. Never satisfied, they followed unprincipled leaders after Pericles' death, embarking on foolhardy adventures that eventually destroyed them.

In Thucydides' analysis, humans, not the gods, are entirely responsible for their own triumphs and defeats. As an analyst of the destructive impact of uncontrolled power on a society, Thucydides has no match. Even more than Herodotus, he set the standard for historical analysis in the West.

PHILOSOPHY The Greeks believed that their communities could prosper only when governed by just political institutions and fair laws. They questioned whether political and moral standards were rooted in nature or whether humans had invented them and preserved them as customs. They wondered whether absolute standards should guide polis life or whether humans are the measure of all things. No one has answered these questions satisfactorily to this day, but one of the legacies of classical Greece is that they were asked.

During the fifth century B.C.E., a group of teachers known as **sophists,** or wise men, traveled throughout the Greek-speaking world. They shared no common doctrines, and they taught everything from mathematics to political theory with the hope of instructing people to lead better lives. The best-known sophist was Protagoras (ca. 485–440 B.C.E.), who questioned the existence of gods and absolute standards of truth. All human institutions, he argued, were created through human custom or law and not through nature. Thus, because truth is relative, a person should be able to defend either side of an argument persuasively.

SYMPOSIUM

At drinking parties called *symposia,* men would gather to enjoy an evening meal, complete with dancing girls, musicians, and wine. After dinner they often discussed serious issues, including philosophy and ethics. This cup, painted in Athens about 480 B.C.E., shows a young man reclining on a couch while a young woman dances for his pleasure.

Socrates (469–399 B.C.E.) challenged the sophists' notion that there were no absolutes to guide human life. He tried to help his fellow Athenians understand the basic moral concepts that governed their lives by relentlessly questioning them. Because Socrates wrote nothing himself, we know of his ideas chiefly through the accounts of his student, Plato (ca. 428–347 B.C.E.), who made his teacher the central figure in his own philosophical essays. (See *Justice in History* in this chapter.)

Plato established a center called the Academy in Athens for teaching and discussion, and earned a towering reputation among Greek philosophers. Like Socrates, he rejected the notion that truth and morality are relative concepts. Plato taught that absolute virtues such as goodness, justice, and beauty do exist, but on a higher level of reality than human existence. He called these eternal, unchanging absolutes **Forms.** In Platonic thought, the Forms constitute reality. Like shadows that provide only an outline of an object, what we experience in daily life merely approximates this reality. Plato's theories about the existence of absolute truths and how humans can discover them continue to shape Western thought. In particular, Platonic theory emphasizes how the senses deceive us and how the truth is often hidden. We can discover truth only through careful, critical questioning rather than through observation of the physical world. As a result, Platonic thought emphasizes the superiority of theory over scientific investigation.

According to Plato, humans can gain knowledge of the Forms because we have souls that are small bits of a larger eternal Soul that enters our bodies at birth, bringing knowledge of the Forms with it. Our individual bits of Soul always seek to return to their source, but they must fight the constraints of the body and physical existence that obstruct their return. Mortals can aid the Soul in its struggle to overcome the material world by using reason to seek knowledge of the Forms. This rational quest for absolutes, Plato argued, is the particular responsibility of the philosophers, but all of us should embark on this search.

In his great political work, *The Republic,* Plato described how people might construct an ideal community based on the principles he had established. In this ideal state, educated men and women called the Guardians would lead the polis because they alone were capable of comprehending the Forms. They would supervise the brave Auxiliaries who defended the city. At the bottom of society were the Workers who produced the basic requirements of life, but were the least capable of abstract thought.

Plato and his student Aristotle (384–322 B.C.E.) were the two greatest thinkers of classical Greece. Aristotle founded his own school in Athens, called the Lyceum. Unlike Plato, Aristotle did not envision the Forms as separate from matter. In his view, form and matter are completely bound together. For this reason, we can acquire knowledge of the Forms by observing the world around us and classifying what we find. Following this theory, Aristotle investigated many subjects, including animal and plant biology, aesthetics, psychology, and physics. His theories regarding mechanics (the study of motion) and his argument that the sun and planets revolve around the Earth acquired great authority among ancient and medieval thinkers and were not effectively challenged until the Scientific Revolution of the late sixteenth and seventeenth centuries.

Aristotle's political ideas were equally influential. Unlike Plato, who described an ideal state, Aristotle analyzed the political communities that actually existed in his day, the Greek poleis. This empirical approach to politics, which paralleled his study of the natural world, led him to conclude that human beings were by nature "political animals" who had a natural tendency to form political communities. By living in such societies they learned about justice, which was essential to the state and was its guiding principle. Aristotle's view that the people themselves, not the gods, established the state was immensely important in the history of Western thought. It has survived in modern democracies, especially in the United States, where the Constitution proclaims that the people themselves established the government and determined how it should be structured.

THE ARTS: SCULPTURE, PAINTING, AND ARCHITECTURE Like philosophers and dramatists during the Classical Age, Greek sculptors, painters, and architects pursued ideal beauty and truth. Classical artists believed the human body was beautiful and was the most appropriate subject of their attention. They also valued the human capacity to represent in art the ideals of beauty, harmony, and proportion found in nature. Greek men celebrated their ability to make rational judgments about what was beautiful and to create art that embodied those judgments.

To create a statue that was an image of physical perfection, sculptors copied the best features of several human models while ignoring their flaws. They strove to depict the muscles, movement, and balance of the human figure in a way

JUSTICE IN HISTORY

The Trial and Execution of Socrates the Questioner

In 399 B.C.E. the people of Athens tried and executed Socrates, their fellow citizen, for three crimes: not believing in Athenian gods, introducing new gods, and corrupting the city's young men. The charges were paradoxical, because Socrates had devoted his life to investigating how to live ethically and morally. Although Socrates could have escaped, he chose to die rather than betray his fundamental beliefs. Socrates wrote nothing down, yet his ideas and the example that he set by his life and death make him one of the most influential figures in the history of Western thought.

Born in Athens in 469 B.C.E., Socrates fought bravely during the Peloponnesian War. Afterward he openly defied the antidemocratic Thirty Tyrants whom the Spartans had installed in Athens. Socrates did not seek a career in politics or business. Instead he spent his time thinking and talking, which earned him a reputation as an eccentric. His friends, however, loved and respected him.

Socrates did not give lectures. Instead, he questioned people who believed they knew the truth. By asking them such questions as "What is justice? Beauty? Courage?" and "What is the best way to lead a good life?" Socrates revealed that they—and most people—did not truly understand their basic assumptions. Socrates did not claim to know the answers, but he did believe in the relentless application of rational argument to elicit answers. This style of questioning, known as the Socratic method, infuriated complacent men because it made them seem foolish. But it delighted people interested in taking a hard look at their most cherished beliefs.

Socrates attracted many followers. His brightest student was the philosopher Plato, to whom Socrates was not only a mentor but a hero. Plato wrote a number of dialogues, or dramatized conversations, in which Socrates appears as a questioner, pursuing the truth about an important topic. Four of Plato's dialogues—*Euthyphro, Apology, Crito,* and *Phaedo*—involve Socrates' trial and death.

The trial began when three citizens named Lycon, Meletus, and Anytus accused Socrates before a jury of 501 men. After hearing the charges, Socrates spoke in his own defense, but instead of showing remorse, he boldly defended his method of questioning. Annoyed by Socrates' stubbornness, the jury convicted him.

Athenian law permitted accusers and defendants to suggest alternative penalties. When the accusers asked for death, Socrates responded with astonishing arrogance. He suggested instead that Athens pay him for making the city a better place. Outraged by this response, the jury chose death by an even wider margin. Socrates accepted their verdict calmly.

While Socrates sat in prison waiting for his execution, a friend named Crito offered to help him escape. Socrates refused to flee. He told Crito that only a man who did not respect the law would break it, and that such a man would indeed be a corrupting influence on the young. Socrates pointed out that he had lived his life as an obedient Athenian citizen and would not break the law now. Human laws may be imperfect, he admitted, but they allow a society to function. Private individuals should never disregard them. To the end he remained a loyal citizen.

On his final day, with his closest friends around him, Socrates drank a cup of poison and died bravely. Plato wrote, "This is the way our dear friend perished. It is fair to say that he was the bravest, the wisest, and the most honorable man of all those we have ever known."[3]

Historians and philosophers have discussed Socrates' case since Plato's time. Were the accusations fair? What precisely was his crime? In the matter of corrupting Athens's youth, there is no doubt that at least two of his most fervent young followers, Alcibiades and Critias, had earned terrible reputations. Alcibiades had betrayed his city in the Peloponnesian War.

CWKPATHC

SOCRATES ON TRIAL

Many sculptors made portraits of Socrates in the centuries after his death. Though Socrates was viewed as a hero who died for his beliefs, this sculptor did nothing to glamorize him. Socrates was famous for the beauty of his thoughts—and the ugliness of his face.

Critias was one of the most violent of the Thirty Tyrants. Many Athenians suspected Socrates of influencing them, even though these men represented everything he opposed.

Charges of impiety were harder to substantiate, but Athenians took them seriously. Socrates always participated in Athenian religious life. But during his defense he admitted that his religious views were not exactly the

same as those of his prosecutors. His claim to have a divine *daimon* or "sign" who sat on his shoulder and gave him advice was eccentric though not actually sacrilegious. Many Athenians thought this daimon was a foreign god rather than Socrates' metaphor for his own mental processes.

The reasons for Socrates' prosecution lie deeper than the official charges indicate. His trial and execution emerged from an anti-intellectual backlash arising from the frustrations of Athens's defeat in the Peloponnesian War and in the Thirty Tyrants' rule. Even though Athenians had restored democracy, deep-seated resentments sealed Socrates' fate. In many societies throughout history, especially democratic ones like that of Athens that grant freedom to explore new ideas, people who fear change and creativity often attack artists, intellectuals, and innovators in times of stress. Athenians resented Socrates because he challenged them to think. He wanted them to live better lives, and they killed him.

For Discussion

1. What does this trial reveal about the nature of Athenian justice?

2. What does this trial tell us about the attitude of Athenians toward philosophy?

3. Was the execution of Socrates a failure or a logical consequence of Athenian democracy?

Taking It Further

Brickhouse, Thomas C., and Nicholas D. Smith. *Socrates on Trial.* 1989. A thorough analysis of Socrates' trial.

Stokes, Michael. *Plato: Apology, with Introduction, Translation, and Commentary.* 1997. The best translation, with important commentary.

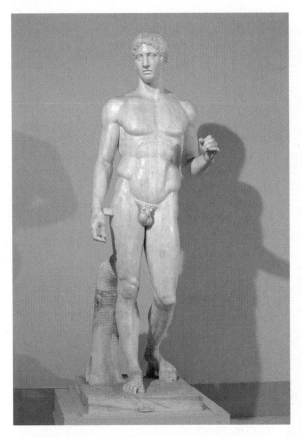

THE MALE NUDE IN GREEK SCULPTURE: POLYCLITUS'S SPEAR-CARRIER

This Roman replica of a bronze statue of a warrior, probably the hero Achilles from the *Iliad,* by the Greek sculptor Polyclitus of Argos, reflects the desire of Greek artists to depict the ideal man. The spear-carrier's anatomy is perfectly proportioned, and his muscles indicate discipline and preparation for battle. He is the perfect male citizen, balanced and controlled yet poised to fight. The original statue has not survived.

that was both lifelike in its imitation of nature and yet idealized in the harmony and symmetry of the torso and limbs. This balance between realism and idealism, as well as the belief that the human male body came closest to perfection and that men embodied the most admirable virtues, explains the proliferation of male statues—many of them nude—throughout the Greek world.

Greek painters explored movement of the human body as well as colors and the optical illusion of depth. The figures that they depicted on vases and walls became increasingly lively and realistic as the Classical Age unfolded. Artists portrayed every sort of activity from religious worship to erotic fun, but regardless of the subject, they shared a similar goal: to create a lifelike depiction of the human figure.

In a similar effort to capture ideals of perfection, Greek architects designed their buildings, especially temples, to be symmetrical and proportional. They used mathematical ratios that they observed in nature to shape their designs. The buildings they created show a grace, balance, and harmony that have inspired architects for more than two millennia.

The temple of the goddess Athena in Athens, called the Parthenon, stood as the greatest triumph of classical Greek architecture. Built on the Acropolis of Athens, the temple symbolized Athens's imperial glory. Using funds appropriated from the Delian League, Athenians built the huge temple between 447 and 432 B.C.E. and dedicated it to the city's divine protector. The architects Ictinus and Callicrates achieved a superb example of structural harmony, perfectly balancing all the building's elements according to mathematical proportions copied from nature. For the Parthenon's sacred inner room, Phidias, a friend of Pericles, sculpted a statue of Athena made of gold and ivory over a wooden core and decorated it with gems and other precious metals. The temple also displayed an elaborate series of carved and brightly painted marble panels depicting the mythology of Athena. The Parthenon remained nearly intact until 1687 C.E., when powder kegs stored inside exploded, causing irreparable damage and leaving the structure much the way it appears today.

CONCLUSION

The Cultural Foundations of the West

Under the leadership of Athens, Greek city states made the most enduring contributions of the ancient world to Western civilization. The influence of Greek philosophy, literature, science, art, and architecture remains evident even today in Europe and the lands Europeans settled. The most distinctive contribution of the Greeks to politics, the theory and practice of democracy, also thrives in many parts of the Western world. None of these political and cultural legacies of Greece, however, has come down through the ages without modification, alteration, and mixture with other non-Greek or nonclassical traditions. Greek culture underwent a process of modification in the Mediterranean lands, especially in Italy and in Asia during the Hellenistic period, as we will see in Chapter 4. The Greco–Roman culture that emerged from that process of cultural encounter and exchange has undergone further adaptation, revival, and modification in Europe during the past two thousand years.

This process of cultural encounters between Greek and non-Greek peoples in the ancient world, becomes even more complicated when we consider the cultural exchanges that took place between Persia and Greece. Many of these encounters occurred as Persians transmitted older Near Eastern traditions of science, mathematics, astronomy, and religion to the Greeks and the people of the western Mediterranean, North Africa, and eventually Europe. An even more durable Persian influence on the West occurred after a Macedonian ruler, Alexander the Great, conquered Greece and then defeated the Persian Empire in the fourth century B.C.E. Alexander promoted Greek culture in the lands he conquered, but he also assumed the powers of the Persian Great King, which were antithetical to the principles of Athenian democracy. Alexander combined a theory of divinely authorized absolute monarchy with a tradition of Persian imperial rule that had a lasting impact on Western civilization. To the complex and sometimes contradictory political and cultural encounters of the Hellenistic age we now turn.

KEY TERMS

polis	helots
acropolis	boule
agora	Zoroastrianism
Olympic games	dualistic
hoplites	triremes
phalanx	Delian League
tyrants	hetairai
oligarchy	sophists
democracy	Forms

CHAPTER QUESTIONS

1. How did Greek city-states develop their culture and political institutions during the Archaic Age? (page 76)
2. How did the Persian Empire bring the peoples of the Middle East together in a stable realm, and what elements of Persian religion and government have influenced Western thought? (page 84)
3. What were the intellectual, social, and political innovations of Greece in the Classical Age? (page 91)

TAKING IT FURTHER

1. Like modern-day Iran, Persia is usually considered part of Asia or the East. What role did ancient Persia play in the development of the West?
2. What were the lasting contributions of Greek civilization to the West?
3. Why did the three great poleis of Greece—Corinth, Athens, and Sparta—follow different paths of political development?
4. What were the differences between Athenian and Spartan women?

✓•⎯[Practice on MyHistoryLab

4

Hellenistic Civilization

- The Impact of Alexander the Great
- Hellenism in the East and West
- Hellenistic Society and Culture
- Hellenistic Philosophy and Science

IN 323 B.C.E. AN UNPRECEDENTED SUCCESSION OF MILITARY VICTORIES BY THE YOUNG Macedonian monarch, Alexander the Great, came to an end. In the space of a mere eleven years Alexander had gained control of all of Greece and conquered the mighty Persian Empire. Slashing through what is today Iran and Afghanistan, he defeated the Indian ruler Poros and reached northwest India. Only then did his soldiers, suffering from fatigue and homesickness, refuse to advance farther. After consulting an omen that told him it was inauspicious to cross the rain-swollen River Beas, Alexander ordered a retreat. At Susa in southwest Iran he married his second and third wives (while still married to his first wife, Roxanna) and made plans for further conquests from India to the Atlantic. But Alexander's apparent ambition to establish a "universal monarchy" covering most of the known world was not to be realized. In June 323 B.C.E. he died, just two months shy of his thirty-third birthday. After his death his empire—the largest the world had ever known—collapsed and was divided into a number of smaller kingdoms, which acquired their own hereditary dynasties and continued the type of monarchical rule that Alexander had exercised.

The conquests of Alexander the Great marked the beginning of the Hellenistic period of Western civilization. Greeks called themselves *Hellenes,* and thus historians use the term **Hellenistic** to describe the complex cosmopolitan civilization, based on that of Greece, that developed in the wake of Alexander's conquests. This civilization offered a rich variety of goods, technologies, and ideas to those who knew

the Greek language. Just as people throughout the world today study English because it is the primary language used in science and technology, global business, and international politics, people in the Hellenistic period used Greek as the common tongue in trade, politics, and intellectual life. Greek culture also became the standard by which civilized people identified themselves. Convinced of their intellectual and cultural superiority over inferior people—an idea promoted by the philosophy of Aristotle, Alexander's tutor—civilized people referred to those who did not speak Greek as **barbarians,** a term derived from the Greeks' description of these people's language as "ba-ba," meaning unintelligible to Greeks.

Hellenistic culture thrived within Alexander's successor kingdoms. It also spread far beyond the lands he conquered, mainly to the western Mediterranean, where it had a profound influence on the civilizations of North Africa and Europe, especially Rome. Romans, Jews, Persians, Celts, Carthaginians, and other peoples all absorbed elements of Greek culture—its philosophy, religion, literature, and art. Hellenism gave a common language of science and learning to diverse peoples speaking different languages and worshiping different gods. Hellenism thus provided a cultural unity to an area stretching from Europe in the west to Afghanistan in the east. Large parts of this cultural realm ultimately became what historians call the West.

The spread of Hellenistic culture over this vast area involved a series of cultural exchanges. Greek culture had great prestige and possessed a powerful intellectual appeal to non-Greek peoples, but it also threatened

CELT AND WIFE

This dramatic statue epitomizes the mixing of cultures in the Hellenistic Age. The statue is a Roman copy in marble of a bronze original made at Pergamum in Anatolia by a Greek sculptor. The artist tells the tragic story of a defeated Celt (Gaul). Rather than be captured alive, he has just killed his wife and is at the precise moment of taking his own life. In typically Hellenistic style, the artist combines anatomical accuracy with psychological agony.

their local, traditional identities. Instead of simply accepting Greek culture, these non-Greek peoples engaged in a process of cultural adaptation and synthesis. In this way Hellenism, which throughout this period remained open to outside influences, absorbed foreign scientific knowledge, religious ideas, and many other elements of culture. These were then transmitted to the greater Hellenistic world. Some of the basic components of Western civilization originated in these cultural encounters between Greek and non-Greek peoples. These include the seven-day week, beliefs in Hell and Judgment Day, the study of astrology and astronomy, and technologies of metallurgy, agriculture, and navigation.

The Hellenistic era and the age of independent Hellenistic kingdoms came to a close in 30 B.C.E., when the Roman ruler Octavian brought an end to the Ptolemaic dynasty, which had ruled Egypt since the death of Alexander. Rome now controlled almost all the states that had been established in the lands that Alexander had conquered. The end of Ptolemaic Egypt therefore marked the end of the Hellenistic age, but it did not put an end to the influence of Hellenism. As we will see in Chapter 5, Rome rose to power during the Hellenistic period and blended Greek culture with its own. The resulting Greco-Roman cultural synthesis, which Rome transmitted to the lands that it controlled, became the bedrock of Western civilization.

THE IMPACT OF ALEXANDER THE GREAT

■ How did the kingdom of Macedon gain control of Greece and large parts of Asia in the fourth century B.C.E., and how did Alexander the Great create an empire in which Greek civilization flourished in the midst of many diverse cultures?

The Hellenistic Age had its roots in Macedon, a kingdom to the north of Greece that was rich in timber, grain, horses, and fighting men. Most Macedonians lived in scattered villages and made a living by engaging in small-scale farming, raiding their neighbors, and trading over short distances. Relentless warfare against wild Thracian and Illyrian tribes to the north and east kept Macedonians constantly ready for battle.

Macedonians spoke a dialect of Greek, but their customs and political organization differed from those of the urbanized Greek communities that lay to their south. Unlike democratic Athens, Macedon had a hereditary monarchy. Cutthroat struggles for ascendancy in the royal family trained Macedonian kings to select the best moment to deliver a lethal blow to an enemy. Maintaining control over their territory was a constant problem for Macedon's kings because independent-minded nobles resented their rule. Only the army of free citizens could legitimize a king's reign. In return for their support, the soldiers demanded the spoils of war.

As a result, Macedonian kings had to wage war continually to obtain that wealth and keep their precarious position on the throne.

The Rise of Macedon under King Philip

Throughout most of the Classical Age of Greece these fierce Macedonian highlanders seemed like savages to the sophisticated Greeks. When cities started to appear in Macedon in the fifth century B.C.E., Macedonian noblemen began to emulate the culture of classical Greece. The members of the Macedonian royal family, for example, claimed the mythical Greek hero Heracles, son of the god Zeus, as their ancestor. This claim won them the right to compete in the Olympic Games, which were open only to Greeks. Macedonian kings also offered Greek playwrights and scholars large sums of money to lure them to their capital city of Pella.

In the political realm, however, Macedon shrewdly avoided involvement in Greek affairs. During the Persian Wars (490 B.C.E. and 480–479 B.C.E.), Macedonian kings pursued a cautious and profitable policy of friendship with the Persian invaders. During the convulsions of the Peloponnesian War (431–404 B.C.E.) and its turbulent aftermath, Macedon refrained from exploiting Athens, Sparta, and the other Greek cities as they bled to exhaustion. The lack of Greek entanglements, however, could not ease the tensions between kings and nobles in Macedon itself. In 399 B.C.E., Macedon slid into 40 years of anarchy. Just as Macedon was on the verge of disintegration, King Philip II (r. 359–336 B.C.E.) transformed the Macedonian kingdom.

A ruthless opportunist with a gift for military organization, the one-eyed Philip consolidated his power by eliminating his rivals, killing many of them in battle. He unified the unruly nobles who controlled different regions of Macedon by demonstrating the advantages of cooperation under his leadership. As Philip led the nobles to victory after victory over hostile frontier tribes and shared his plunder with them and with the common soldiers, the Macedonians embraced his leadership.

Philip created a new army in which the nobles had a special role as cavalry armed with heavy lances. Called the **Companions,** these cavalrymen formed elite regiments bound to their king by oaths of loyalty. Philip reorganized the infantry, or foot soldiers, who were recruited mainly from the rural peasantry, into phalanxes. These Macedonian phalanxes, unlike those of the Greek hoplites, used long lances to hold off the enemy while the cavalry attacked the enemy formations from the rear. This new strategy, which Philip probably learned about when he was a hostage in Thebes, gave his armies an enormous tactical advantage over traditional Greek hoplite formations. After seizing the gold and silver mines of the north Aegean coast of Greece, Philip also had ample funds to hire additional armies of mercenaries to augment his Macedonian troops.

With Macedon firmly under his control, its borders secure, and his army eager for loot, Philip stood poised to strike at Greece. In 349 B.C.E. he seized several cities in northern and central Greece, inaugurating a decade of diplomacy, bribery, and threats as he maneuvered to dominate the rest of the Greek poleis.

Recognizing that Philip represented a threat to Greek liberty, the brilliant Athenian orator Demosthenes (384–322 B.C.E.) organized resistance among the city-states. In 340, when Philip attempted to seize the Bosporus, the narrow water link between the Aegean Sea and Athens's vital Black Sea trade routes, Demosthenes delivered a series of blistering speeches against Philip known as "the Philippics" and assembled an alliance of cities. In 338 B.C.E., however, Philip crushed the allied armies at the Battle of Chaeronea. Philip's 18-year-old son Alexander led the Companions in a cavalry charge that won the day for the Macedonians.

Philip then set up a coalition of Greek cities called the League of Corinth under his leadership. He also stationed Macedonian garrisons at strategic sites in Greece and forbade Greek cities to change their form of government without his approval. For the Greek poleis, the age of independence was over.

Philip next cast his eyes on the Persian Empire. In 337 B.C.E. he cloaked himself in the mantle of Greek culture and announced that he would lead his armies and those of the Greek cities against the Persians. His goal was to avenge Persia's invasion of Greece in the previous century. Philip's shrewd linking of classical Greek civilization with Macedonian military might now became a rallying cry for imperialist expansion under his direction. But as Philip laid plans for his assault on Persia in 336 B.C.E., one of his bodyguards assassinated him at the wedding of one of his daughters. Alexander, the son of Philip and Olympias, the king's bitterly estranged wife whom he had forced into exile the previous year, succeeded Philip as king and continued his father's plans to invade Persia. While Alexander honored his slain father, Olympias hung the sword that the assassin had used to kill him in the temple of Apollo and proceeded to murder Philip's son and daughter and his wife, Cleopatra Eurydice.

The Conquests of Alexander the Great

A man of immense personal charisma and political craftiness, Alexander (r. 336–323 B.C.E.) won the support of his soldiers by demonstrating fearlessness in combat and military genius on the battlefield. He combined a predatory instinct for conquest and glory with utter ruthlessness in the pursuit of power. These traits proved to be the key to his success. By the time of his death, Alexander had won military victories as far east as India, creating a vast empire. His successes made him a legend during his lifetime, and millions of his subjects worshiped him as a god. Historians consider him a pivotal figure in Western civilization because his conquests led to the spread of Hellenistic culture in lands that were to become important components of the West.

After brutally consolidating power in Macedon and Greece following his father's death, Alexander launched an invasion of Persia. With no more than 40,000 infantry and 5,000 cavalry, he crossed the Hellespont and marched into Persian territory in 334 B.C.E. The young Macedonian king won his first great victory over Persian forces at the Battle of the Granicus River, giving him control over Anatolia with its rich Greek coastal cities. He then marched into Syria, where he broke the main Persian army near the town of Issus in 333 B.C.E. Here, just as he had done at Granicus River, Alexander led the

ALEXANDER THE GREAT

Detail of a Roman mosaic depicting Alexander the Great at the Battle of Issus, where he defeated the Persian army in 333 B.C.E. The empire he established by the time of his death in 323 B.C.E. defined the main boundaries of the Hellenistic world.

Darius again on the battlefield at Gaugamela near the Tigris River.

When Alexander entered Babylon in triumph after Gaugamela, he again received an enthusiastic welcome as a liberator. From Babylon his forces ventured southeast to Persepolis, the Persian palace city, which fell in January 330 B.C.E. There Alexander ordered his soldiers to kill all the adult males, enslave the women, loot the palace's vast treasures, and burn it to the ground. The enormous wealth Alexander acquired from Persepolis and other Persian treasure centers paid for all of his military activities for the next seven years and invigorated the entire Macedonian economy. Darius III, the Great King of Persia (r. 335–330 B.C.E.), escaped to the east, but was soon murdered by his own nobles. The once-powerful Persian Empire, which covered one million square miles and had a population of 50 million people, lay in ruins.

Alexander had fulfilled his father's pledge to gain vengeance against Persia, but he had no intention of stopping his march of conquest (see **Map 4.1**). He pushed past the tribesmen of the harsh Afghan mountain ranges to penetrate Central Asia. Then in 327 B.C.E. he entered what is today Pakistan through the Khyber Pass, the narrow route that separates Central Asia from the South Asian subcontinent. At the Battle of the Hydaspes River, Alexander defeated the Indian king Poros, who had assembled a formidable army of 6,000 cavalry, 30,000 infantry, and 200 war elephants. But Alexander's exhausted armies refused to advance farther into India, and he was forced to retreat. The route he chose for his return westward passed through a scorching desert, where many of his soldiers died, and Alexander himself suffered nearly fatal wounds. While recuperating at Babylon in 323 B.C.E., where he had begun to plan more conquests, Alexander succumbed to fever after a drinking bout. He had never lost a battle.

Macedonian cavalry's victorious charge into the teeth of the enemy. From this victory Alexander gained control of the entire eastern coast of the Mediterranean Sea and the Persian naval bases located there.

When Alexander captured the port city of Tyre in 332 B.C.E., Darius panicked and offered the young Macedonian his daughter in marriage and all of his empire west of the Euphrates River in return for peace. Alexander rejected the offer and marched into Egypt, where the inhabitants welcomed him as a liberator from their Persian masters and crowned him as Pharaoh. From Egypt he advanced into Mesopotamia, where he crushed

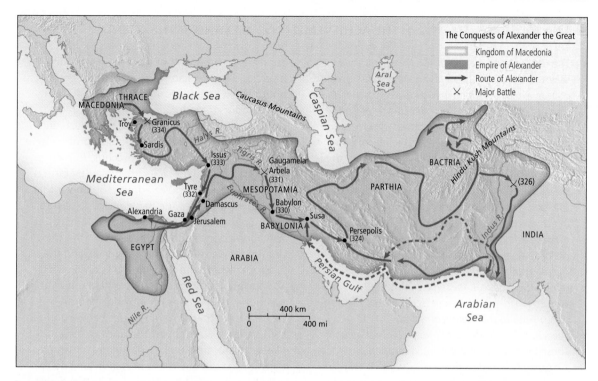

MAP 4.1

The Conquests of Alexander the Great

Alexander led troops from his Macedonian homeland as far east as the Indus Valley. He defeated the Persian Empire and incorporated it into his own empire. This map shows Alexander's march of conquest and the sites of his most important victories.

CHRONOLOGY: ALEXANDER THE GREAT AND THE GREEK EAST

359–336 B.C.E.	Philip II rules Macedon
338 B.C.E.	Philip II conquers Greece (Battle of Chaeronea)
336 B.C.E.	Alexander the Great becomes king of Macedon
334 B.C.E.	Battle of Granicus River
333 B.C.E.	Battle of Issus
331 B.C.E.	Battle of Gaugamela; Alexander founds Alexandria in Egypt
330 B.C.E.	Alexander destroys Persepolis
327 B.C.E.	Alexander reaches India
323 B.C.E.	Alexander dies at Babylon
323–ca. 300 B.C.E.	Successors to Alexander establish kingdoms

DIFFERENT VOICES THE ACHIEVEMENT OF ALEXANDER THE GREAT

The conquests of Alexander the Great lent them-selves to different interpretations that depended to a large extent on whether one focused on the diffu-sion of Greek culture in Asia and Europe or on the brutal methods Alexander employed in subjecting different people to his rule. The Greek biographer Plutarch (ca. 46 C.E.–120 C.E.), writing during the Roman empire, credited Alexander with facilitating the reception of Greek philosophy and culture in the lands that he conquered. In a speech celebrat-ing these achievements Plutarch claimed that Alexander had gained a wider acceptance of Greek philosophy among the people whom he had con-quered than the Greeks themselves had achieved during the Classical Age. One can attribute Plutarch's claim that Alexander promoted the unity of mankind to the rhetorical excesses of his speech. It is unlikely that Plutarch himself actually subscribed to such a noble interpretation of Alexander's relentless quest to establish a universal monarchy. The Jews, who had been conquered by Alexander, understandably had a far less positive view of his legacy. The Jewish author of the biblical book 1 Maccabees, written in the second century B.C.E., saw Alexander's reign as a period of violence and instability.

A Greek Biographer Celebrates the Cultural Achievement of Alexander the Great

But if you consider the effects of Alexander's instruction, you will see that he educated the Hyrcanians to contract marriages, taught the Arachosians to till the soil, and persuaded the Sogdians to support their parents, not to kill them, and the Persians to respect their mothers, not to marry them. Most admirable philosophy, which induced the Indians to worship Greek gods, and the Scythians to bury their dead and not to eat them! We admire the power of Carneades, who caused Clitomachus, formerly called Hashdrubal and a Carthaginian by birth, to adopt Greek ways. We admire the power that persuaded Diogenes the Babylonian, to turn to philosophy. Yet when Alexander was taming Asia, Homer became widely read, and the chil-dren of the Persians, of the Susianians and the Gedrosians sang the tragedies of Euripides and Sophocles. And Socrates was condemned by the sychophants in Athens for introducing new deities, while thanks to Alexander Bactria and the Caucasus worshipped the gods of the Greeks. Plato drew up in writing one ideal constitution but could not persuade anyone to adopt it because of its severity, while Alexander founded over 70 cities among barbarian tribes, sprinkled Greek institutions all over Asia, and so overcame its wild and savage manner of living.... Those who were subdued by Alexander were more fortunate than those who escaped him, for the latter had no one to rescue them from their wretched life, while the victorious Alexander compelled the former to enjoy a better existence. Alexander's victims would not have been civilized if they had not been defeated.... If, therefore, philosophers take the greatest pride in taming and correcting the

In strategic locations through the lands he had conquered, Alexander established cities as garrisons for his troops. More than a dozen of these cities received the name Alexandria in his honor. Thousands of Greeks migrated east to set-tle in the new cities to take advantage of the expanded economic opportunities for trade and farming. These Greek settlers became the cul-tural and political elite of the new cities.

Governing an empire of this size proved to be a difficult challenge. The Macedonian kingdom that Alexander led was geared to seizing land and plun-dering cities. It was another task entirely to create the infrastructure and discipline necessary for rul-ing an immense territory that had little linguistic or cultural unity. Alexander recognized that the only model of rule suitable to such a diverse empire was that which his Persian predecessors had devised: a

fierce and untutored elements of men's character, and if Alexander has been shown to have changed the brutish customs of countless nations, then it would be justifiable to regard him as a very great philosopher. . . .

Believing that he had come as a god-sent governor and mediator of the whole world, he overcame by arms those he could not bring over by persuasion and brought men together from all over the world, mixing together, as it were, in a loving-cup, their lives, customs, marriages, and ways of living. He instructed all men to consider to be their native land and his camp to be their acropolis and their defense, while they should regard as kinsmen all good men, and the wicked as strangers. The difference between Greeks and barbarians was not a matter of cloak or shield, or of a scimitar or Median dress. What distinguished Greekness was excellence, while wickedness was the mark of the barbarian; clothing, food, marriage and the way of life they should all regard as common, being blended together by ties of blood and the bearing of children.

Source: Plutarch, *On the Fortune or Virtue of Alexander*, in Michel Austin (ed.), *The Hellenistic World from Alexander to the Roman Conquest*, 2006, 57–58.

A Jewish Writer Describes the Misery Caused by Alexander the Great

After Alexander son of Philip, the Macedonian, who came from the land of Kittim, had defeated King Darius of the Persians and the Medes, he succeeded him as king; he had already become king of Greece. He fought many battles, conquered strongholds, and put to death the kings of the earth. He advanced to the ends of the earth, and plundered many nations. When the earth became quiet before him, he was exalted, and his heart was lifted up. He gathered a very strong army and ruled over countries, nations, and princes, and they became tributary to him. After this he fell sick and perceived that he was dying. So he summoned his most honored officers, who had been brought up with him from youth, and divided his kingdom among them while he was still alive. And after Alexander had reigned twelve years, he died. Then his officers began to rule, each in his own place. They all put on crowns after his death, and so did their descendants after them for many years; and they caused many evils on the earth.

Source: *1 Maccabees 1–9*.

For Discussion

1. What criteria did Plutarch and the author of 1 Maccabees use to evaluate the achievement of Alexander the Great?

2. Did Alexander bring "civilization" to the lands he conquered?

3. How might the author of I Maccabees have responded to Plutarch's claim that Alexander brought men together from all over the world?

Great King presiding over a hierarchy of nobles who governed Persian territory and some non-Persian provinces, and subject kings who ruled other non-Persian regions.

Necessity thus forced Alexander to bring his Macedonian troops and his new Persian subjects together in an uneasy balance. To that end, he persuaded his army to proclaim him "King of Asia"—that is, the new Great King. With his Companions he simply took over the government of the former Persian Empire from the top. He included a handful of loyal Persians in his administration by making them regional governors or **satraps**, while offering other Persian noblemen minor roles in his regime. These practical steps promised to bring order to the empire. By adopting the elaborate Persian ceremonial role of the Great King, Alexander demonstrated to his foreign subjects that his regime stood for security and continuity of orderly rule.

Alexander's proud Macedonian soldiers, however, ultimately stymied his efforts to achieve this balance. They refused to prostrate themselves before him, as Persian royal ceremony dictated. Alexander may well have thought of himself as a god, but his soldiers refused to worship him. Instead, they saw Alexander's recruitment of 30,000 Persian troops into their army as a threat to the traditional relations between Macedonian soldiers and their king. They also resented the marriages with the daughters of Persian noblemen that Alexander forced on them in order to unite Macedonians and Persians—although no Persian nobles received Greek or Macedonian wives. The Macedonian troops expected to keep all the spoils of victory for themselves. They wanted to be conquerors, not partners in a new government. They failed to understand that men of other cultures within the new empire might be equally loyal to Alexander and thus deserve a share of power and honor. Alexander's charismatic personality held his conquests together, but his death destroyed any dreams of cooperation between Persians and Greeks.

Alexander's adoption of the powers and symbolism of Persian kingship, even though it was unpopular with his Macedonian soldiers, was the product of an encounter between Macedonian and Persian styles of rule. The political culture that emerged from this encounter had a lasting influence on Western civilization. In contrast to the democratic and republican culture that had flourished in classical Athens, Alexander offered a model of royal and imperial rule that gave the king absolute power and identified that power, if not his own person, with that of the gods. Both traditions—democratic republicanism and divine-right absolutism—competed with each other throughout the history of the West. The competition became evident in classical Rome, which began as a republic but was later transformed into an empire in which the ruler had unrivalled power. The tension between the two ideologies persisted throughout the Middle Ages and into the Renaissance, when the Italian state of Florence revived the republican culture of ancient Greece and Rome at the same time that the duke of Milan revived the aspirations of the Roman Empire.

HELLENISM IN THE EAST AND WEST

- What was the relationship between Greeks and non-Greeks in the lands that Alexander conquered and those with whom Greeks came into contact after his death?

The Hellenistic Successor States

Alexander left no adult heir, and the Macedonian nobles who served as his generals fought viciously among themselves to control his conquered territory. Eventually, these generals created a number of kingdoms out of lands Alexander had acquired (see **Map 4.2**). One general, Ptolemy (r. 323–286 B.C.E.), established the Ptolemaic dynasty in Egypt, which lasted until 30 B.C.E. Antigonus "the One-Eyed" (r. 306–301 B.C.E) gained control of the Macedonian homeland, where his descendants established the Antigonid dynasty, which survived until Rome overthrew the last of these monarchs in 167 B.C.E. The largest portion of Alexander's conquests, comprising the bulk of the old Persian Empire, fell to his general Seleucus (r. 312–281 B.C.E.). But the territory controlled by Seleucus' successors constantly shrank, and in the mid-third century B.C.E. the Parthians, a people from northeastern Persia, shook off Seleucid rule and created a vigorous new state in what is today Iran. By 150 B.C.E. the Seleucids ruled only Syria, Palestine, and a small portion of southeastern Anatolia.

Following the example of Macedon itself, the Hellenistic successor states all maintained a

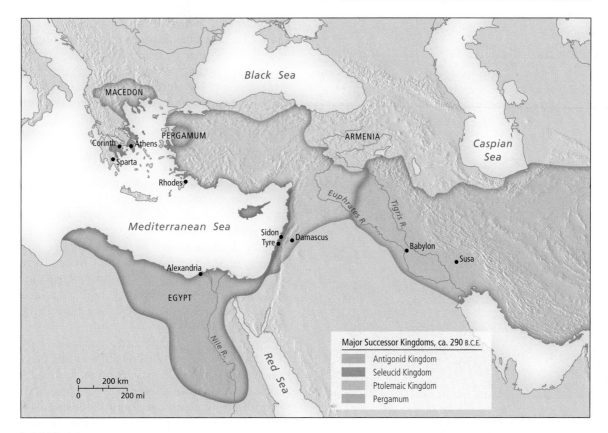

MAP 4.2

Major Successor Kingdoms ca. 290 B.C.E.

After Alexander's death, his generals divided his empire into several kingdoms. This map shows the boundaries of the Antigonid, Seleucid, and Ptolemaic kingdoms about 290 B.C.E. The Antigonids acquired control of the old kingdom of Macedon in 294 B.C.E., although this control was not secured until the reign of Antigonus II (r. 276–239 B.C.E.). The city of Pergamum in Anatolia became a kingdom under Attalus I around 230 B.C.E.

monarchical form of government in which a king ruled the people with the support of the army and highly regimented bureaucracies. The leading administrators and bureaucrats were all Greeks and Macedonians. Indigenous people were not recruited into the ruling elite. Greek was the language of government and the elite in the successor kingdoms. The talented queen Cleopatra VII (r. 51–30 B.C.E.), who was the last descendant of Ptolemy to rule in Egypt, was the first of her line ever to speak Egyptian. Greek-speaking monarchs nonetheless knew that they needed to cultivate the goodwill of their non-Greek-speaking subjects. As one monarch asked in a Hellenistic political dialogue, "How can I accommodate myself to all the different races in my kingdom?" A subject answered: "By adopting the appropriate attitude to each, making justice one's guide."

The king towered over Hellenistic society, holding authority over all his subjects and bearing ultimate responsibility for their welfare. Following the example of Alexander, the Hellenistic monarch earned legitimacy by leading

PTOLEMAIC KING OF EGYPT

This golden ring depicts Ptolemy VI, who ruled Egypt from 176 to 145 B.C.E. Although he and his court spoke only Greek, he is depicted as a pharaoh wearing a double crown, the age-old symbol of Egyptian monarchy. The image on the ring demonstrated the integration of old and new political symbols in Egypt during the Hellenistic Age.

his troops into wars of conquest. The king embodied the entire community that he ruled. He was at once the ruler, father, protector, savior, source of law, and god of all his subjects. His garb reinforced his elevated position—the king arrayed himself in battle gear with a helmet or Macedonian sombrero, a crown, purple robes, a scepter, and a special seal ring. The monarch earned the loyalty of his subjects and glorified his own rule by founding cities, constructing public buildings, and rewarding his inner circle.

Ptolemy II, who ruled in Egypt from 283 to 246 B.C.E., exemplified these notions of Hellenistic kingship. Ptolemy expanded his dominions by conquering parts of Anatolia and Syria from the Seleucids. He also expanded the bureaucracy, refined the tax system, and funded new towns for his soldiers and veterans. With his support, merchants established new posts on the Red Sea, where they traded with merchants from India and other eastern lands. Ptolemy patronized the arts and sciences by building research institutes and libraries. He transformed Egypt's capital city of Alexandria, the port founded by Alexander in Egypt in 331 B.C.E., into the leading center of Greek culture and learning in the Hellenistic world. To reinforce his authority and majesty, Ptolemy II encouraged his subjects to worship him as a god the way earlier Egyptians had worshipped the pharaohs.

This worship of Hellenistic monarchs drew from indigenous traditions throughout the Near East, but in its Hellenistic form it had more political than religious significance. People worshiped their kings as a spontaneous expression of gratitude for the protection and peace that good government provided. For example, when the Antigonid king Demetrius "the Besieger" captured Athens in 308 B.C.E., the pragmatic Athenians sang a song in honor of their new master: "The other gods either do not exist or are far off, either they do not hear, or they do not care; but you are here and we can see you, not in wood and stone but in living truth."[1] Deification legitimized a king's rule and helped secure his subjects' loyalty.

Hellenistic monarchs depended on large professional armies to maintain their authority and defend their territories. These rulers fought wars over much larger territories than those that had led to squabbles among Greek city-states in previous centuries. The conquest of such territories required an increase in the size of field armies. The Athenian hoplites had numbered about 10,000 men in the fifth century B.C.E., but Hellenistic kings routinely mustered

THE ROYAL LIBRARY OF ALEXANDRIA

The cosmopolitan city of Alexandria, the capital of Egypt founded by Alexander in 331 B.C.E., became the leading center of Greek culture in the Hellenistic world. Its famous library, depicted here in a nineteenth-century German engraving, functioned as a major center of scholarship until the first century B.C.E.

armies of between 60,000 and 80,000 men. Many soldiers came from military colonies that the kings established. In return for land, the men of these Greek-speaking colonies had to serve generation after generation in the king's army and police the native, non-Greek populations.

Encounters with Foreign Peoples

During the Hellenistic Age, Greeks encountered many foreign peoples; the effects of these interactions laid some of the foundations of the West. The encounters took place when Greeks explored regions in Africa and Europe where they had not penetrated before; when Hellenistic Babylonians,

Egyptians, Persians, Afghans, and Hebrews resisted or adopted Hellenistic culture; and when Celtic peoples migrated to the boundaries of the Hellenistic world in Europe and Anatolia.

EXPLORING THE HELLENISTIC WORLD A spirit of inquiry—combined with a hunger for trade and profit—drove men to explore and map the unknown world during the Hellenistic Age (see **Map 4.3**). Explorers supported by monarchs ventured into the Caspian, Aral, and Red Seas. By the second century B.C.E., Greeks had established trading posts along the coasts of modern Eritrea and Somalia in East Africa, where merchants bought goods, particularly ivory, transported

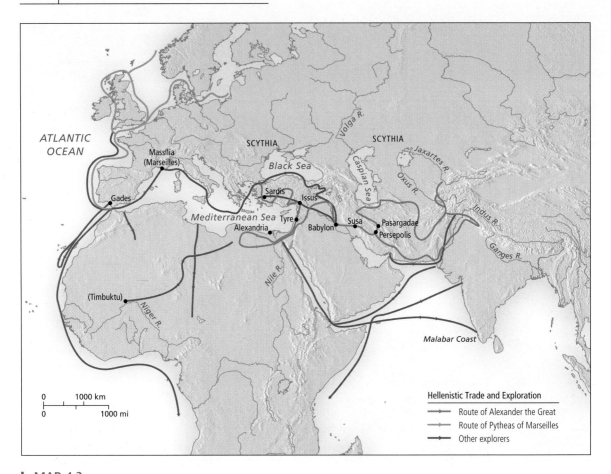

MAP 4.3

Hellenistic Trade and Exploration

During the Hellenistic Age, merchants traveled widely across the breadth of the Mediterranean and throughout the Near East. They sailed into the Persian Gulf and Indian Ocean on commercial ventures. Some explorers sailed along the east and west coasts of Africa as well as Europe's Atlantic coast, reaching Britain and the North Sea.

from the interior of Africa. Hellenistic people also craved pepper, cinnamon, cloves, and other spices and luxury goods from India, but Arab middlemen made direct trade between the Hellenistic world and India nearly impossible. One intrepid navigator named Eudoxus tried to find a sea route to India by sailing around Africa, but he never got farther southwest than the coast of Morocco.

The most ambitious and successful of all Hellenistic explorers was Pytheas of Marseilles (ca. 380–306 B.C.E.). Setting out from the Carthaginian city of Gades (the modern Spanish port of Cadiz) in about 310 B.C.E., he sailed north around Britain and reported the existence of either Iceland or Norway. He may have even reached the Vistula River in Poland by sailing through the Baltic Sea. Throughout his journeys Pytheas contributed much to navigational knowledge by recording astronomical bearings and natural wonders such as the northern lights.

He is the first person known to have reported the midnight sun and polar ice.

As these explorers expanded geographical horizons, Greeks developed a condescending interest in the peoples of the world. Greeks considered themselves culturally superior to non-Greek-speaking peoples who lived beyond the borders of Hellenistic kingdoms, including Jews, Babylonians, Celts, steppe nomads, and sub-Saharan Africans. Greeks considered all of these peoples barbarians. Despite this prejudice, educated men and women throughout the Hellenistic world enjoyed reading accounts in Greek of foreign peoples' customs, myths, natural history, and forms of government.

Knowledge about different peoples often came from non-Greek intellectuals who translated their accounts into Greek. For example, Berosus, a Babylonian priest, wrote a history of his people that also provided Greek readers with extensive astronomical knowledge. Manetho, an Egyptian priest, composed a history of his land. Hecataeus of Abdera, a Greek, wrote a popular history arguing that Egypt was the site of the origin of civilization. Most of what the West believed it knew about India until the Middle Ages derived from the reports of Megasthenes, a Seleucid diplomat who served as ambassador in India. Information about the histories and belief systems of their non-Greek neighbors entertained Greek intellectuals and helped Hellenistic rulers govern their conquered peoples.

RESISTANCE TO HELLENISTIC RULE Despite this curiosity among educated Greeks about foreign customs, barriers of mutual incomprehension, suspicion, and resentment separated Greeks from their subjects. Language was one such barrier. In most kingdoms, administrators conducted official business only in Greek. Few Greek settlers in the cities or even in isolated military colonies bothered to learn the local languages, and only a small percentage of the local populations learned Greek. Many communities ignored their Greek rulers completely. In Mesopotamia and Syria, Aramaic remained the dominant language, not Greek. Some non-Greeks, however, hoped to rise in the service of their Greek masters. They made an effort to learn Greek and assimilate into Hellenistic culture. But their collaboration with Greek rulers alienated them from their own people and divided native societies into those who accepted Hellenistic culture and those who did not.

Many people conquered by the Greeks continued to practice their traditional religions. In Babylonia, age-old patterns of temple worship continued uninfluenced by Greek culture. Stunned by the loss of their empire, some aristocratic Persians found solace in Zoroastrianism, the traditional Persian religion. As we have seen in Chapter 3, Zoroastrianism teaches that the world is in the grip of an eternal struggle between the good forces of light, represented by the divine creator, Ahura Mazda, and the evil forces of darkness, represented by Angra Mainyu, the demonic destroyer. Persian Zoroastrianians considered Alexander to be Angra Mainyu's agent. In the aftermath of the Persian defeat, an important religious text (written in Greek, ironically) predicted that a warrior messiah would soon overthrow the Seleucid kings and restore Persia's true religion and rulers. A book known as the *Dynastic Prophecy* (ca. 300 B.C.E.) expressed similar hopes for Babylonians.

Resentful voices also rang out in Egypt. The *Demotic Chronicle* and *The Oracle of the Potter* (ca. 250 B.C.E.) maintained that the Ptolemies had brought the punishment of the gods to Egypt by displacing the pharaohs and interfering with religious customs. One day, the books assured readers, a mighty king would expel the conquerors. Not coincidentally, rebellions erupted in Egypt about the same time that these works gained popularity.

The Jewish response to Hellenism produced the best-known account of resistance, preserved in the First and Second Book of Maccabees in the Hebrew Bible. (See *Different Voices* in this chapter.) After Alexander's death, first the Ptolemies and then the Seleucids controlled

Jerusalem and Jewish Palestine. The Ptolemaic monarchs at first tolerated Judaism and welcomed the rapid assimilation of Jerusalem's priestly aristocracy into Greek culture. Although traditional Jewish worship at the temple in Jerusalem continued, a gymnasium and other elements of Greek culture first appeared in Jerusalem during the rule of these Hellenized Jewish priests.

In 167 B.C.E., however, the Seleucid king Antiochus IV Epiphanes (r. 175–164 B.C.E.) tried to make the city more Hellenistic. When the Jews resisted, his soldiers put up statues of Greek gods in the Temple, an abomination in Jewish eyes. Initially, Antiochus had intended to advertise his own strength, not to suppress Judaism, but his plan backfired. A family of Jewish priests, the Maccabees, began a religious war of liberation. They drove the armies of Antiochus out of Palestine, purified the Temple in Jerusalem, and established an autonomous Jewish kingdom under their rule. Later, when Jewish writers sought to explain these actions to the Greek-speaking Jews of Alexandria, they described them in terms of resistance to Hellenism. However, the Maccabeans themselves soon adopted many Greek customs and used Greek names, causing deep rifts within Jewish society.

CELTS ON THE FRINGES OF THE HELLENISTIC WORLD In addition to the Greek culture that spread throughout the Mediterranean and Near East, Celtic civilization flourished in Europe during the Hellenistic Age. The Celts, who lived in tribes that were never politically unified on a large scale, shared common dialects, metal- and pottery-making techniques, and agricultural and home-building methods. They were the ancestors of many Europeans today.

Through trade and war, Celts influenced the northern margins of the Hellenistic world from Anatolia to Spain. Trade routes with the Celts from the Mediterranean were established as early as the eighth century B.C.E., but war often interrupted commerce. The military activities of Celtic tribes restricted the expansion of Hellenis-

tic kingdoms, in Macedon and Anatolia, thereby pressuring these kingdoms to strengthen their military capacities.

Archaeologists call the first Celtic civilization in central Europe **Hallstatt culture,** because of excavations of Celtic settlements in Hallstatt, Austria. Around 750 B.C.E., Hallstatt Celts started to spread from their homeland into Italy, the Balkans, Ireland, Spain, and Anatolia, conquering local peoples on the way. These early Celts left no written records, so we know little of their political practices. The luxury goods and weapons they buried in graves, however, indicate a stratified society led by a warrior elite. Hallstatt sites were heavily fortified, suggesting frequent warfare. Men gained status through the competitive exchange of gifts, raiding, and valor in battle. In southern France, Celts encountered Hellenistic civilization at the Greek city of Massilia (modern Marseilles). There they participated in lively trade along the Rhône River for Greek luxury goods, including wine and drinking goblets.

In the mid-fifth century B.C.E. a new phase in Celtic civilization began. It is called **La Tène culture,** which takes its name from a site in modern Switzerland. More weapons were found in La Tène tombs than in the Hallstatt period, possibly indicating intensified warfare. La Tène Celts developed new centers of wealth and power, especially in the valleys of the Rhine and Danube Rivers. They also founded large, fortified settlements in these regions and in present-day France and England.

La Tène craftsmen benefited from new trade routes across the Alps to northern Italy, the home of Etruscan merchants and artisans (see Chapter 5). Etruscans traded bronze statuettes to the Celtic north, and they may have also introduced the two-wheeled fighting chariots found in aristocratic Celtic tombs. Greek styles in art reached the Celts through these Etruscan intermediaries, but Celtic artists developed their own distinctive style of metalwork and sculpture. Many Celtic communities began to use coinage, which they adopted from the Greeks.

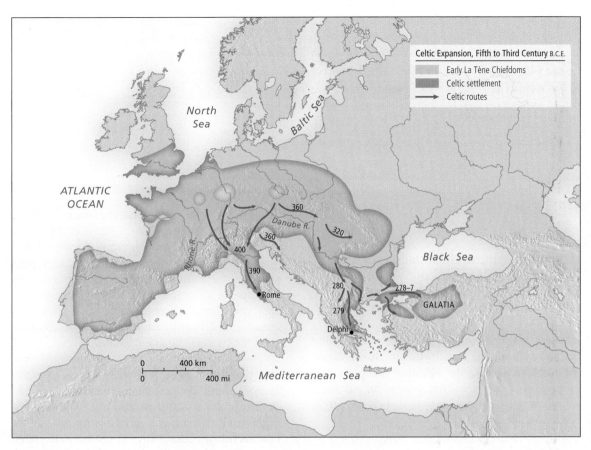

MAP 4.4

Celtic Expansion, Fifth to Third Century B.C.E.

During the Hellenistic Age, Celtic peoples migrated into many parts of Europe and Asia Minor. This map shows their routes.

For about a century relations between the Celtic and Mediterranean peoples centered on trade, but around 400 B.C.E. overpopulation in central Europe caused massive migrations of Celtic tribes. In 387 B.C.E. one migrating group of Celts, called Gauls, sacked the city of Rome. Their invasion had an unexpected effect on Roman military technology: The highly effective Celtic short sword became the standard weapon of the Roman legions.

Hostile migrations lasted until 200 B.C.E. Some Celts traveled to lands that are Slavic today (Slovakia and southern Poland), while others settled in northern Italy, Spain, Britain, and Ireland. Other Celts invaded the Balkans, plundered Greece, and finally settled in Anatolia, where they established a kingdom called Galatia (from the word *Gauls*). Galatian soldiers, known for their bravery and cruelty, became mercenaries in the constant wars among the Hellenistic successor kingdoms. Ultimately, most Celts were absorbed, together with the peoples in the Hellenistic kingdoms in the eastern Mediterranean, into the Roman Empire.

CHRONOLOGY: THE WORLD OF THE CELTS

ca. 750 B.C.E.	Hallstatt Celts start settling in Europe
ca. 450 B.C.E.	La Tène Celts develop centers in Rhine and Danube valleys
ca. 400 B.C.E.	Celts expand from Central Europe
ca. 390–386 B.C.E.	Celts invade Italy and plunder Rome
279 B.C.E.	Celts invade Greece
270s B.C.E.	Celts establish kingdom of Galatia in Anatolia

HELLENISTIC SOCIETY AND CULTURE

■ What were the distinguishing features of Hellenistic society and culture, and what was the result of encounters between Greeks and non-Greeks?

Chronic warfare among monarchs made political unity among the Hellenistic kingdoms impossible. Nevertheless, the social institutions and culture of Greek-speaking people in all these kingdoms gave them a unity that their monarchs could not achieve.

Urban Society

Greek city life defined Hellenistic civilization. Alexander and his successors seized dozens of Greek city-states scattered across the eastern Mediterranean and founded dozens of new cities in all the territories they conquered. Hellenistic cities were much more than garrisons established to enforce the conquerors' power. They continued traditions of learning, art, architecture, and citizen participation in public life that had flourished in the classical poleis. Most important, people in cities throughout the Hellenistic world spoke a standard version of Greek called **Koine** that gave them a sense of common identity.

On the surface, many of the institutions of the classical poleis remained the same: magistrates, councils, and popular assemblies ran the cities' affairs, and some form of democracy or election to office remained the norm in local government. Yet beneath the surface, the poleis had undergone radical changes. Because kings wielded absolute power, once-independent cities such as Athens and Corinth lost their freedom to make peace or wage war. Although they chose their own local governments, these cities now served as the bureaucratic centers that administered their rulers' huge kingdoms.

As we saw in Chapter 3, citizenship in the city-states of classical Greece was a carefully limited commodity that gave people a sense of identity, guaranteed desirable rights and privileges, and demanded certain responsibilities. The territories that any city-state controlled were relatively small, yet even Athens at the height of its empire in the fifth century B.C.E. never considered giving Athenian citizenship to all the people it ruled, even within Attica. In contrast, during the Hellenistic Age, large kingdoms containing many cities were the basic political units. People were both subjects of a king and citizens of their particular cities. To be sure, some philosophers played with the idea of a universal citizenship of all humankind, but there was no notion of a citizenship that all the people in one kingdom would share. Citizenship lost its political force because individual cities had lost their political autonomy. In a sharp break with earlier practice, important men sometimes gained the honor of citizenship in more than one city, which Greeks in the Classical Age would have found inconceivable.

To maintain the illusion of the cities' independence, Hellenistic kings permitted considerable autonomy in local government. Nonetheless, while democracies had developed in Greece during the Archaic and Classical periods to protect the interests of the poor as well as the rich, in the Hellenistic Age the wealthy dominated society and government, and the condition of the poor deteriorated. Rich men appointed or approved by the king controlled all the courts, held all the magistracies, and represented all the cities at the court of the kings, who in return showered these civic leaders with honors and rewards. Through land grants, tax immunities, and other favors, the monarchs developed networks of personal ties that bound civic leaders to them. In return, these urban elites served their king and spent their vast fortunes building magnificent temples, gymnasiums, and other structures for their fellow citizens.

Hellenistic kings and aristocrats turned their cities into showcases of art and design. Distinctive styles of building and ornamentation quickly spread from the east to Carthage, Rome, and other communities in the western Mediterranean. The most distinctive architectural innovations in the cities were vast palace complexes, which were built to accommodate the Hellenistic monarchs and their entourages in the successor kingdoms. Laying out streets on a grid plan became standard in the Mediterranean world, lending a sense of order to urban space. Stone theaters for plays and spectacles, council halls, and roofed colonnades called *stoas* sprang up everywhere, as did public baths with heated pools and gymnasium complexes with sports facilities, libraries, and lecture halls.

Hellenistic cities contained more diverse populations than had classical poleis. Alexandria, Egypt's largest and most cosmopolitan Greek city, boasted large communities of Macedonians, Greeks, Jews, Syrians, and Egyptians. Although these groups lived in different areas of the city and often fought violently with one another, they all participated to varying degrees in Alexandria's culture. For example, Alexandrian Jews who spoke Greek translated the Hebrew Bible into Greek, a version called the **Septuagint,** so

APHRODITE OF MELOS

Aphrodite, the goddess of sexual love, displayed the perfection of the female form. This marble statue of her, which was found on the Greek island of Melos, was sculpted in the middle of the second century B.C.E. Popularly known by her Italian name, Venus di Milo, the goddess is half-nude. She rests on her right foot and seems to step forward toward the viewer. Originally one of her missing arms was probably raised to cover her breasts in a gesture of modesty. Her facial expression is serene. The garment draped loosely around her hips allowed the sculptor to explore the play of thin cloth over her thighs, expressing his delight in movement and physicality. More sedate than other voluptuous representations of Aphrodite from the Hellenistic period, this statue portrays a male vision of a perfect woman, highly sexual but also charmingly modest.

that Jews who had lost their command of Hebrew could understand it. The Septuagint later provided early Christians, many of whom spoke and read Greek, with their knowledge of the Hebrew Bible, which Christians refer to as the Old Testament.

New Opportunities for Women

One measure of the status of women in a society is the level of female infanticide. Greek parents in the Classical Age routinely abandoned unwanted female babies, leaving them to die. Hellenistic families, however, particularly those of the Ptolemaic nobility, raised more baby girls than before. Greek women in Egypt and other Hellenized lands as well as many other Hellenized lands, enjoyed full citizenship and held religious offices. Many owned land and property, paying taxes as men did, but they could only enter into business contracts of minimal value on their own.

Some aristocratic Hellenistic women wielded considerably more power than had been conceivable in the classical Greek period. The wives of Hellenistic kings were models of the new, more powerful Hellenistic woman. Inscriptions praise Hellenistic queens for demonstrating such traditional female virtues as piety and for producing sons. As public benefactors, these women built temples and public works, sponsored charioteers at the Olympic Games, and provided dowries for poor brides. Queens sometimes exerted real authority, supporting and commanding armies. For example, Arsinoë II (r. 276–270 B.C.E.), sister and wife of Ptolemy II, directed the Egyptian armies and navies of the Ptolemaic kingdom in their conquest of Phoenicia and much of the coast of Anatolia. Egyptian sources refer to her as Pharaoh, a royal title usually reserved for men, and she was often identified with the goddess Isis.

To a lesser extent, opportunities for non-aristocratic Greek women also increased during the Hellenistic Age. In Alexandria young women were taught dancing, music, reading and writing, and scholarship and philosophy. Often the daughters of scholars became scholars themselves. We know that non-aristocratic Greek women wrote about astronomy, musical theory, and literature, and many female poets competed for honors. In addition, a few Hellenistic women distinguished themselves as portrait painters, architects, and harpists. Despite these accomplishments, women still had fewer rights and opportunities than men, and they remained under the supervision of their male relatives. In Egypt, a woman could not travel overnight without her husband's permission.

Art and Architecture

Art and architecture during the Hellenistic period changed as Greek civilization was introduced into the successor kingdoms. Artists and architects continued to use classical motifs and themes, but instead of simply imitating classical models, they used them in new ways. This creative development of Greek classicism resulted from both the freedom that artists experienced working in a new environment and from the influences of native cultures. The most notable stylistic innovation of the Hellenistic age was the **baroque** style, which suggested movement rather than repose and often appealed to the emotions.

The baroque style was evident in many of the Hellenistic temple precincts, where the designers created sweeping vistas across carefully planned terraces and grand stairways. Some of the finest examples of Hellenistic baroque architecture have survived in Pergamum, a Greek city on the southern coast of modern Turkey, close to the Aegean Sea. To commemorate the victory of Pergamum over the Celts and the Seleucids, King Attalus I (241–197 B.C.E.) commissioned a series of monuments. The Acropolis in Athens provided the classical model for this work, but the commission of native craftsmen to create these monuments helps to explain their baroque features, most notably their vast scale and their many different focal points, which lead the viewer's eye across the façades of the buildings.

Hellenistic sculptors also took classical Greek forms in new directions. Turning away from representations of ideal perfection, Hellenistic artists delighted in exploring the movement of the human body and varieties of

JUSTICE IN HISTORY

Divine Justice in the Hellenistic World

The widespread belief that personal misfortunes, such as illness, accidents, or destruction of one's property, indicated divine displeasure frequently led people in the Hellenistic world to confess their crimes. These offenses included secular crimes such as theft, slander, bodily injury, sorcery, and adultery, as well as religious crimes such as violating dietary rules, insulting the gods, or entering a sanctuary without cleansing the body or one's clothes. It did not matter whether the person had committed such an offense intentionally. The crucial factor was the sign of the gods' displeasure. When offenders became convinced of their guilt, they often went to the local sanctuary to discover the cause of the gods' anger and learn how they could atone for their misbehavior. Their objective was to receive signs from the gods through oracles or in dreams while they slept.

Inscriptions in the temple of the goddess Demeter at Knidos in Anatolia during the late second and first centuries B.C.E. reveal that the wronged party would sometimes initiate the judicial process by depositing an inscribed stone tablet at a sanctuary. The inscription would identify the alleged culprit and ask the gods to force the offender to come to the sanctuary to confess the crime. One of these inscriptions in a case of slander read: "I dedicate to Demeter and Kore [another goddess, Demeter's daughter] the man who has made imputations against me, [claiming] that I made a poison against my own man; may he come up to the sanctuary of Demeter, with his entire family, burning [with fever] and confessing." Such inscriptions resembled the writing on "curse tablets" that people in the Hellenistic world occasionally inscribed to bring

misfortune on an enemy. The purpose of these "confession inscriptions," however, was not to cause harm to another human being but to call the gods' attention to an act of injustice and to motivate those gods to pressure the guilty party to confess. The confessions were prayers for divine

TEMPLE OF APHRODITE

This temple near Denizli, in modern-day Turkey, built in the first century B.C.E., was the preeminent temple of the goddess Aphrodite in Anatolia. People asking for divine assistance in eliciting confessions to crimes would often enter sanctuaries such as this.

justice that would give the aggrieved party moral satisfaction or possibly revenge.

People suspected of crimes could also appeal to the gods to establish their innocence. When a woman named Tatias heard rumors that she had given her son-in-law a magical potion that had driven him insane, she went to the local sanctuary and "deposited curses in the temple." This public ceremony, which differed from the writing of a malevolent curse in private, was her way of demonstrating to the community that she was innocent. Unfortunately for Tatias, her relatives publicly annulled her curses, leaving her guilty in the eyes of society.

Ideally the only parties involved in this process were the accusers, the confessing criminals, and the gods, but the priests in the sanctuary often played a crucial role in the process. They would receive or perhaps even solicit accusations from the victims of crime, assist in writing the confessions, and interpret the supposed signs of the divine will. In many cases they attempted to show that the afflictions that brought people to the sanctuary in the first place were punishments for their offenses. The priests did not, as historians once believed, inflict corporal punishment, but they did advise those who confessed how they might atone for their transgressions. Sometimes they interrogated an afflicted person who came to the sanctuary to determine the cause of the gods' wrath. Thus, the priests played a role usually assigned to judges in actual trials. The procedures followed in the sanctuaries were not trials in the proper sense of the word because they did not involve the testimony of witnesses or the delivering of verdicts. But the inscriptions often used legal language, which the priests probably suggested, and the procedure served the same purpose as a trial, which was to resolve conflict in society. Like trials, these proceedings involved encounters between the priest serving in a quasi-judicial capacity and the person who came to the sanctuary, as well as between that person and the god who was believed to have spoken through an oracle or a dream.

The involvement of priests in a process that resembled a trial of both secular and religious crimes reveals that Hellenistic societies drew no firm line between the secular and the religious spheres. Crimes that were prosecuted in the secular courts could also be dealt with in religious sanctuaries. Without the assistance of the priests, who controlled access to the sanctuaries and helped formulate the confessions, the process could not have functioned properly. The dedication of appeals and confessions to the gods also shows that the gods in these polytheistic societies were believed to play an active role not only in the resolution of problems of everyday life, but also in the administration of justice.

For Discussion

1. Why might a person in a Hellenistic kingdom go to a local sanctuary and later confess to a religious or secular offense?
2. How did Hellenistic religious beliefs influence prevailing notions of justice?

Taking It Further

Angelos Chaniotis, "Under the Watchful Eyes of the Gods," in S. Colvin (ed.), *The Greco-Roman East: Politics, Culture, Society* (2006). A study based on more than 140 confessions inscribed in stone.

facial expression. Their subjects ranged from alluring love goddesses to drunks and haggard old boxers. Artists enjoyed portraying the play of fabrics across the human body to accentuate the contours of male and female flesh. The statue of Nike of Samothrace, probably carved on the island of Rhodes about 200 B.C.E., depicts this Greek goddess as if she has just landed on the

PERGAMUM ALTAR OF ZEUS

The buildings at Pergamum in northwest Anatolia (present-day Turkey) were constructed in the Hellenistic baroque style. They were based on classical Greek models but had sweeping facades that presented the viewer with multiple focal points. The Altar of Zeus at Pergamum, shown here in a twentieth-century reconstruction, is positioned on a massive stone podium with a 371-foot colonnade (a porch with a line of columns). Like many baroque buildings, the altar was opulently decorated. The two long friezes below the colonnade depict the life of the Greek mythological figure Telephos, son of Heracles, who was believed to be the founder of the city of Pergamum.

bow of a ship, with her wings outstretched and her garment blowing in the wind. Sometimes painted in bright colors, these statues explored human frailty and homeliness as often as they celebrated beauty and lofty emotions. The statue of the Celt and his wife, also carved in Pergamum in the third century B.C.E. (see page 109), conveys not only physical movement, but also the depth of human emotions experienced by the man who is committing suicide.

Literature

Much Hellenistic literature has vanished, but surviving works give a glimpse of creativity and originality that often combined urbanity and scholarship. Hellenistic poets turned to frivolous themes because the repressive political climate discouraged them from questioning authority. Light comedy became immensely popular, especially in the hands of the playwright Menander of Athens (ca. 300 B.C.E.). This clever author delighted audiences with escapist, frothy tales of temporarily frustrated love and happy endings. These plays, known now as New Comedy, developed from the risqué satires of classical Athens. They featured vivid street language and a cast of stock characters: crotchety parents, naive young men, silly young women, clever slaves, and wicked pimps.

Theocritus (ca. 300–ca. 260 B.C.E.), who came from the city of Syracuse in Sicily but wrote in Alexandria, invented a new genre called pastoral

NIKE OF SAMOTHRACE

This statue of Nike, the winged Greek goddess of victory, found on the Greek island of Samothrace, captures the sensation of her flight through the air by portraying her wings outstretched and the wind blowing the folds of her garment. The statue was situated on the sculpture of a bow of a ship, where Nike has just landed.

learning in works ranging from *Collections of Wonders of the World* to his moving love poems, the *Elegies*. His poetry provides the best example of the erudite style known as **Alexandrianism,** which demonstrated a command of meter and language and appealed more to the intellect than to the emotions.

The most accomplished historian of the Hellenistic period was Polybius (ca. 202–120 B.C.E.), a native of the Greek city of Megalopolis. Polybius devoted the latter part of his life to writing a history of Rome's meteoric rise to power within the Mediterranean region. As a work of literature, Polybius's *Histories* cannot compete with those of the great Greek historians Thucydides and Herodotus; his leaden style prevented him from capturing the drama of events. The strength of *Histories* lies in its comprehensive coverage of events in all the countries of the Mediterranean world and its adherence to high standards of accuracy and impartiality, both of which were noticeably absent in the works of his predecessors.

HELLENISTIC PHILOSOPHY AND SCIENCE

■ What did Hellenistic thinkers contribute to philosophy and the scientific investigation of the natural world?

Hellenistic philosophers distinguished between three branches of their discipline: logic or the study of abstract reasoning; ethics, the study of how one should conduct one's life; and physics, the study of the natural world. In the Middle Ages educated people began to refer to physics as natural philosophy; since the eighteenth century they have identified this type of investigation as science. During the Hellenistic period all three branches of philosophy remained anchored in the works of Plato and Aristotle, but philosophy acquired its own distinctive features.

poetry. His verses described idyllic life in the countryside, but his rustic herdsmen reflected the sadness and tensions of city life. Of all the Hellenistic poets, Theocritus has had the most wide-ranging and enduring influence, providing a model for pastoral verse in Rome, Shakespeare's England, and even nineteenth-century Russia. The other great poet of Alexandria, Callimachus (ca. 305–240 B.C.E.), combined playfulness with extraordinary

COMEDY MOSAIC FROM POMPEII

Many brilliant decorative mosaics have survived from the Hellenistic world. Often derived from Greek paintings that have been lost, these scenes give a vivid glimpse into everyday life. This mosaic is based on a scene from a comedy performed in a theater.

Philosophy: The Quest for Peace of Mind

The Hellenistic contribution to philosophy was most striking in the study of ethics. Three of the philosophical groups that emerged during this period—the Epicureans, the Stoics, and the Cynics—shared the common goal of acquiring an inner tranquility or peace of mind. According to Xenocrates (d. 314 B.C.E.), the head of the Platonic Academy in Athens, the purpose of studying philosophy "is to allay what causes disturbance in life." This quest for personal tranquility did not disregard the needs of other people. Its goal was to determine which ways of interacting with other people were right and which were wrong.

The first of these philosophical schools, the **Epicureans**, was founded by Epicurus of Samos (341–271 B.C.E.). Known by its meeting place in Athens, the Garden, this school was open to women and slaves as well as free men. Because Epicurus believed that "the entire world lives in pain," he urged people to gain tranquility through the rational choice of pleasure. The word *epicurean* today denotes a person of discriminating taste who takes pleasure in lavish eating and drinking, but the pleasure Epicurus sought was intellectual, a perfect harmony of body and mind. To achieve this harmony, Epicurus recommended a virtuous and simple life, characterized by plain living and withdrawal from the stressful world of politics and social competition. Epicurus also

ZENO OF CITIUM

Zeno, the Athenian founder of Stoicism, argued that one should submit to the cosmic order, otherwise defined as nature or fate, in one's search for inner peace. Stoicism had considerable influence among Roman politicians and writers.

Source: Dagli Orti/Picture Desk, Inc./Kobal Collection

reassured his students that they should fear neither death nor the gods. There was no reason to fear death because the soul was material; hence, there was no afterlife. Nor was there any reason to fear the gods, who lived happily, far from Earth, unconcerned with human activity. Freed from these fears, humans could find inner peace.

The main rival to Epicureanism was Stoicism, the school established by Zeno of Cition (ca. 335–ca. 263 B.C.E.) at Athens in 300 B.C.E. Taking its name from the Stoa Poikile (the Painted Portico) where Zeno and his successors

taught, Stoicism remained influential well into the time of the Roman Empire. **Stoics** believed that all human beings have an element of divinity in them and therefore participate in one single indissoluble cosmic process. They could find peace of mind by submitting to that cosmic order, which Stoics identified with nature or fate. Thus, the word *stoic* today denotes a person who responds to pain or misfortune without showing emotion. Stoics believed that wise men did not allow the vicissitudes of life to distract them. Rather than calling for withdrawal from the world, like the Epicureans, Stoicism encouraged people to participate actively in public life. Because Stoicism accepted the status quo, many kings and aristocrats embraced it. They wanted to believe that their success formed part of a cosmic, divine plan.

Cynics took a different approach to gaining peace of mind. The word *cynic* today usually refers to a person who sneers at the sincerity of human motives and behavior. But the ancient Cynics, inspired by Antisthenes (ca. 445–360 B.C.E.), a devoted follower of Socrates, taught that the key to happiness was the rejection of all needs and desires. To achieve this goal, Cynics abandoned all possessions to lead a life of rigorous asceticism. Diogenes (ca. 412–324 B.C.E.), the chief representative of this philosophy, made his home in an empty barrel. Cynics showed contempt for the customs and conventions of society, including wealth, social position, and prevailing standards of morality. One prominent Cynic, Crates of Thebes (ca. 328 B.C.E.), caused a public scandal when he did the unthinkable: He took his wife, the philosopher Hipparchia, out for a meal in public instead of leaving her at home, where respectable women belonged. Some Cynics took the example of Diogenes to further extremes by satisfying, rather than denying, their simplest natural needs. Their behavior, which included public masturbation and defecation, gave them their name, which derived from the Greek word for dog. Their rejection of prevailing social values, coupled with their offensive public behavior, explains why their teachings failed to have a lasting impact.

Explaining the Natural World: Scientific Investigation

While Athens remained the hub of philosophy in the Hellenistic Age, the Ptolemaic kings made Alexandria the center of scientific learning. There King Ptolemy I founded the Museum, an institution named after the Muses, goddesses of the arts and knowledge, that sponsored research and lectures on the natural world. Nearby, the royal Library housed hundreds of thousands of texts in an attempt to organize the entire body of knowledge of the world.

In addition to summarizing the work of previous scholars, scientists in Alexandria and throughout the Hellenistic world sought to describe the natural world as it actually was. This emphasis on scientific realism involved the rejection of some of the more speculative notions that had characterized classical Greek science. Theophrastus (ca. 371–287 B.C.E.), a disciple of Aristotle who is often considered the first scientist of the Hellenistic period, rejected

the philosophical view of Aristotle that nature was static rather than dynamic and could be explained in terms of philosophical "first principles." Theophrastus's nine-volume *Enquiries into Plants* led him to the conclusion that plants had not devolved or "degenerated" from animals, as Aristotle had claimed.

In mathematics, Euclid (flourished ca. 300 B.C.E.) produced a masterful synthesis of geometry in his work, *Elements*, which remained the standard geometry textbook until the twentieth century. Euclid demonstrated how one could attain knowledge of a subject by rational methods alone—by mathematical reasoning through the use of deductive proofs and theorems. Equally famous as a mathematician was Archimedes of Syracuse (ca. 287–212 B.C.E.), who calculated the value of *pi* (the ratio of a circle's circumference to its diameter) and measured the diameter of the sun. A sophisticated mechanical engineer, Archimedes reputedly said: "Give me a fulcrum and I will move the world." Archimedes put his scientific knowledge to work in wartime. During the Roman siege of Syracuse in 212 B.C.E., he reportedly built a huge reflecting mirror that focused the bright Sicilian sun on Roman warships, burning holes in their sails.

CHRONOLOGY: HELLENISTIC LITERATURE, SCIENCE, AND PHILOSOPHY

ca. 445–360 B.C.E.	Antisthenes defines the spirit of Cynicism at Athens
390–320 B.C.E.	Heraclides of Pontus notes that some planets orbit the sun
ca. 350 B.C.E.	First books on human anatomy written
310–230 B.C.E.	Aristarchus of Samos proposes heliocentric theory
ca. 310–230 B.C.E.	Pytheas of Marseilles explores coasts of the North Sea
ca. 306 B.C.E.	Epicurus of Samos founds the Epicurean school of philosophy
ca. 300 B.C.E.	Zeno of Cition founds the Stoic school of philosophy at Athens
ca. 295 B.C.E.	Ptolemy I founds Museum and Library in Alexandria in Egypt; Menander of Athens writes New Comedy; Zeno of Cition teaches Stoicism at Athens; Euclid writes *Elements of Geometry*
287–212 B.C.E.	Archimedes of Syracuse calculates the value of *pi*
276–194 B.C.E.	Eratosthenes of Cyrene calculates the Earth's circumference
ca. 190–127 B.C.E.	Hipparchus of Nicaea argues that Earth is the center of the universe
140s B.C.E.	Polybius writes history of Rome's rise to world power

Knowledge of astronomy also advanced during the Hellenistic Age. In their research, Hellenistic investigators borrowed from the long tradition of observation of the heavens that Babylonian and Egyptian scholars had established. This intersection of Greek and Near Eastern astronomical work produced one of the richest new areas of knowledge in the Hellenistic world. For example, Heraclides of Pontus (ca. 388–312 B.C.E.) anticipated a heliocentric (sun-centered) theory of the universe when he observed that the planets Venus and Mercury orbit the sun, not Earth. Aristarchus of Samos (ca. 310–230 B.C.E.) established the idea that the planets revolve around the sun while spinning on their own axes. Eratosthenes of Cyrene (ca. 276–194 B.C.E.) made a calculation of the Earth's circumference that came within 200 miles of the actual figure.

The sun-centered view never won wide acceptance, however, because of fierce opposition from the followers of Aristotle, whose geocentric (Earth-centered) theories had become canonical. To support Aristotle's **cosmology** (a map of the universe), Hipparchus of Nicaea (ca. 190–127 B.C.E.) produced the first catalog of stars and insisted that they encircled the Earth. The geocentric view of the universe prevailed until the sixteenth century C.E., when the Polish astronomer Nicholas Copernicus, who had read the work of Heraclides and Aristarchus, provided mathematical data to support the sun-centered theory (see Chapter 17).

Medical theory and research also flourished in the great Hellenistic cities. Diocles, a Greek doctor of the fourth century B.C.E. who combined theory and practice, wrote the first handbook on human anatomy and invented a spoon-like tool for removing arrowheads from the human body. Doctors during this period believed that both human behavior and health were products of the balance of fluids, called humors, in the body. They argued about whether to categorize the humors as hot, cold, wet, and dry or as blood, phlegm, yellow bile, and black bile. Praxagoras of Cos (late fourth century B.C.E.) argued that the body contained more than a dozen kinds of humors. He also studied the relation of the brain to the spinal cord. Other doctors, such as Herophilus and Erasistratus, who lived in Alexandria in the fourth century B.C.E., systematically dissected human cadavers. They also may have practiced vivisection, operating on living subjects to study their organs. There is some evidence that they conducted experiments on condemned criminals who had not yet been executed, a practice outlawed today. Through dissection, whether of the dead or the living, these physicians learned a great deal about the human nervous system, the structure of the eye, and reproductive physiology.

CONCLUSION

Defining the West in the Hellenistic Age

During the Hellenistic Age the cultural and geographical boundaries of what would later be called the West began to take shape. These boundaries encompassed the regions where Hellenistic culture had a lasting influence. The lands within the empire of Alexander the Great, all of which lay to the east of Greece and Egypt, formed the core of this cultural realm, but the Hellenistic world also extended westward across the Mediterranean, embracing the lands ruled by Carthage from North Africa to Spain. Hellenism also reached the edges of the lands inhabited by the Celts. In all these areas Greek culture interacted with those of the indigenous peoples it penetrated, and the synthesis that resulted from these encounters became one of the main foundations of Western civilization.

As the next chapter shows, the encounter between Greek culture and the culture of non-Greek lands during the Hellenistic period was most creative in Rome, a small republic that eventually conquered the Hellenistic kingdoms and established its own hegemony over the lands that lay both to the west and the east of the Italian peninsula. When the Roman politician and military commander Octavian (later known as Augustus) won control of the Mediterranean world, the Near East, Egypt, and parts of Europe in 31 B.C.E., the Hellenistic era came to an end. This political achievement, and the resulting transformation of the Roman Republic into the Roman Empire at the same time, did not, however, put an end to the influence of Hellenistic culture. By forging a new, more resilient civilization in which Greeks, Romans, and many other peoples intermingled in peace, the Romans created their own version of Hellenism.

KEY TERMS

Hellenistic
barbarians
Companions
satraps
Hallstatt culture
La Tène culture
Koine

Septuagint
baroque
Alexandrianism
Epicureans
Stoics
Cynics
cosmology

CHAPTER QUESTIONS

1. How did the kingdom of Macedon gain control of Greece and large parts of Asia in the fourth century B.C.E., and how did Alexander the Great create an empire in which Greek civilization flourished in the midst of many diverse cultures? (page 110)
2. What was the relationship between Greeks and non-Greeks in the lands that Alexander conquered and those with whom Greeks came into contact after his death? (page 116)
3. What were the distinguishing features of Hellenistic society and culture, and what was the result of encounters between Greeks and non-Greeks? (page 124)
4. What did Hellenistic thinkers contribute to philosophy and the scientific investigation of the natural world? (page 130)

TAKING IT FURTHER

1. What were the main differences between the political institutions of the Hellenistic successor states and those in Greece during the classical age?
2. In what ways did Hellenistic culture modify or change the culture of Greece during the classical age?
3. Why did the Hellenistic successor states fail?

✓•⌐Practice on MyHistoryLab

5

The Roman Republic

- The Nature of the Roman Republic
- The Culture of the Roman Republic
- The End of the Roman Republic
- Roman Territorial Expansion
- Social Life in Republican Rome

In 146 B.C.E. THE ROMAN GENERAL LUCIUS MUMMIUS LED A LARGE MILITARY FORCE into the Greek city of Corinth, about 50 miles west-southwest of Athens. Mummius had just won a victory over the forces of the Achaean League, a confederation of Greek cities. Corinth was the most powerful city in this federation. Recognizing that their cause was hopeless, most Corinthians fled before the Romans reached the city gates, and Mummius entered the city unopposed. The Romans killed the men who remained, enslaved the women and children, plundered the city's treasures, and then burned Corinth to the ground. Thus ended a long chapter in the history of a Greek city known for its international trade, wealth, and the luxury in which many of its residents lived. The cities in the Achaean League came under the direct control of Rome and later became part of the Roman province of Achaea.

The sack of Corinth had a broader significance than the destruction of this once powerful Greek city. It marked the final step in the establishment of Rome as the dominant power in the Mediterranean world. The significance of this event was not lost on contemporaries. The Greek historian Polybius, who had tried to prevent the Achaean League from aligning itself with the kingdom of Macedon against Rome in 171 B.C.E., concluded his narrative of the rise of Rome in the Mediterranean with an account of this final blow to Greek independence. After the destruction of Corinth Rome continued its meteoric rise. within little more than a century, Rome would gain control of the entire Mediterranean world, most of western Europe, and many of the Asian territories that Alexander the Great

had conquered in the fourth century B.C.E. The lands that came under Roman rule would mark the geographical boundaries of what would later become the West. Rome also developed political and cultural traditions that became central to Western identity. These traditions were largely based on those of Greece, but they had a distinctive Roman imprint. The Greco–Roman culture that resulted from this encounter was then transmitted to the many lands that came under Roman rule. Greco–Roman culture, in which Latin, rather than Greek, was the dominant language in politics, diplomacy, commerce, and literature, thus became the most enduring foundation of Western civilization.

This chapter will address the question how this small republic on the Italian peninsula rose to power within the Hellenistic world and thus laid the foundations of the geographical and cultural realm that we call the West.

THE NATURE OF THE ROMAN REPUBLIC

- What type of government did Rome establish when it eliminated kingship, and what social groups competed for power in this state?

From Rome's Capitoline Hill a tourist today can look down on the **Roman Forum** and see a field of broken buildings and monuments. These remains lie at the heart of what was once an

VIEW OF THE FORUM FROM CAPITOLINE HILL
This view of the Forum was taken from the site of the temple of Jupiter, Rome's mightiest god. All victory processions after a successful war would have ended at this temple, where sacrifices were made. Now tourists visit the remains of buildings from which Rome ruled an international empire.

enormous empire extending from northern England to the Black Sea and from Morocco to Mesopotamia. On the western slope of the neighboring Palatine Hill, archaeologists have uncovered hut foundations from Rome's earliest occupants in the tenth century B.C.E. How the Roman Empire emerged from this crude village above a swamp remains one of the most remarkable stories in the history of the West.

During the Hellenistic Age, Rome expanded from a relatively small city-state with a republican form of government into a vast and powerful empire. As it conquered the peoples who ringed the Mediterranean—the Carthaginians, the Celts, and the Hellenistic kingdoms of Alexander's

successors—Rome incorporated these newcomers into the political structure of the Republic (see **Map 5.1**). Trying to govern these sprawling territories with institutions and social traditions suited for a city-state overwhelmed the **Roman Republic** and led to the establishment of a new form of government, the Roman Empire, by the end of the first century B.C.E.

Roman Origins and Etruscan Influences

Interaction with outsiders shaped the story of Rome from its beginning. Resting on low but easily defensible hills covering a few hundred acres above the Tiber River, Rome lies at the intersection of north-south and east-west trade routes that had been used in Italy since the Neolithic Age. Romans used these same routes to develop a thriving commerce with other peoples, many of whom they eventually conquered and absorbed.

Settlements began in Rome about 1000 B.C.E., but we know little about the lives of these first inhabitants. So small was the scale of village life that clusters of huts on the different hills may have constituted entirely different communities. What would one day be the Forum—the place of assembly for judicial and other public business—was a marsh that villagers used as protection and burial grounds.

Control of the Tiber River crossing and trade allowed Rome to grow quickly. Excavated graves

from the eighth century B.C.E. reveal that a wealthy elite had already emerged. Women evidently shared the benefits of increased prosperity. One grave contained a woman buried with her chariot, a symbol of authority and status. During the seventh century Rome's population increased rapidly. Extended families or clans became a force in Roman life. Throughout this early period, according to Roman legend, kings ruled the city.

Historians think that Latin, the Roman language, was only one of at least 140 distinct languages and dialects spoken by Italy's frequently warring communities during the first four centuries of Rome's existence. During this period, Romans developed their military skills to defend themselves against their neighbors. Nevertheless,

RAPE OF THE SABINE WOMEN

In the legendary history of Rome, the first generation of Roman men acquired wives from the Italian tribe of Sabines, who inhabited the region around Rome. When the Sabines refused, the Romans supposedly abducted the Sabine women and then asked them to accept Roman husbands. The legend, which has no factual basis, was enshrined in the literary works of Livy and Plutarch. The word *rape* in this context refers to abduction, not sexual violation. The rape of the Sabine women became a popular subject for artists in the sixteenth and seventeenth centuries. This depiction of the rape was painted by Pietro da Cortona between 1627 and 1629.

the Romans had amicable relations with some neighbors—particularly the Etruscans, who lived northwest of Rome.

In the seventh and sixth centuries B.C.E., Etruscan culture strongly influenced Rome. By 800 B.C.E. Etruscans, whose origins remain unknown although they may have migrated to Italy from Anatolia, were firmly established in Etruria (modern Tuscany), a region in central Italy between the Arno and Tiber rivers. By the sixth century B.C.E. they controlled territory as far south as the Bay of Naples and east to the Adriatic Sea. The Etruscans maintained a loose confederation of independent cities that often fought against other Italian peoples.

Etruscans carried on a lively trade with Greek merchants, exchanging native iron ore and other resources for vases and other luxury goods. Commerce became the conduit through which Etruscans and later Romans absorbed many aspects of Greek culture. The Etruscans, for example, adopted the Greek alphabet and subscribed to many Greek myths, which they later transmitted to the Romans.

During the sixth century B.C.E., the Etruscans ruled Rome. Although the Etruscans and Romans spoke different languages, a common culture deriving from native Italian, Etruscan, and Greek communities gradually evolved, especially in religious practice. The three main gods of Rome—Jupiter, Minerva, and Juno—were first worshiped in Etruria. (The Greek equivalents were Zeus, Athena, and Hera.) Etruscan seers taught Romans how to interpret omens, especially how to learn the will of the gods by examining the entrails of sacrificed animals. Etruscans also gave the Romans a distinctive temple architecture that differed from that of the Greeks. Etruscan and later Roman temples had much deeper porticos, covered porches supported by colonnades.

Establishing the Roman Republic

By about 600 B.C.E. Romans had prospered sufficiently to drain the marsh that became the Forum. They also began to construct temples and public buildings, including the first Senate house,

where the elders met to discuss community affairs. Under the rule of its kings, some of whom were of Etruscan origin, Rome became an important military power in Italy. Only free male inhabitants of the city who could afford their own weapons voted in the citizen assembly, which made public decisions with the advice of the Senate. Poor men could fight but not vote. Thus began the struggle between rich and poor that would plague Roman life for centuries.

About 500 B.C.E., when Rome had become a powerful city with perhaps 35,000 inhabitants, the Romans put an end to kingship and established a **republic,** a state in which political power resides in the people and their representatives rather than in a monarch. According to legend, in 509 B.C.E. Lucius Junus Brutus, a member of the ruling dynastic family, overthrew the tyrannical Etruscan king, Tarquin the Proud.

After the monarchy was abolished, Rome established several new institutions that structured political life for 500 years. An assembly comprising Rome's male citizens, called the Centuriate Assembly, managed the city's legislative, judicial, and administrative affairs. As in the Greek poleis, only men participated in public life. Each year, the assembly elected two chief executives called consuls, who could administer the law but whose decisions could be appealed to the assembly. In time, the assembly also elected additional officers to deal with legal and financial responsibilities. The Senate, comprising about 300 Romans who had held administrative offices, advised the consuls, though the senators had no formal authority. Priests performed religious ceremonies on behalf of the city. Hatred of kings, which became a staple of Roman political thought, prevented any one man from becoming too prominent. A relatively small group of influential families held real power within the political community by monopolizing the main offices and working behind the scenes. As we saw in Chapter 3, this kind of government is known as an oligarchy, or the rule of the few.

To celebrate the end of the monarchy, the people of Rome built a grand new temple to Jupiter on the Capitoline Hill, looking down on the Forum. They also established the community of Vestal Virgins, priestesses who served as care-takers of the sacred fire and hearth in the Temple of Vesta, one of Rome's most ancient religious sites. In such ways the welfare of Rome became a shared public concern.

Tensions between social groups shaped Roman political life during the Republic. At the top of the social hierarchy stood the **patricians,** a wealthy elite who traced their ancestry back to royal Rome. These families claimed to have top-pled the monarchy. Because they monopolized the magistracies and the priesthoods, patricians occu-pied most of the seats in the Senate. Other rich landowners and senators with lesser pedigrees, as well as the prosperous farmers who made up the army's ranks, joined the patricians in resisting the **plebeians,** the general body of Roman citizens. The plebeians generally occupied the lower ranks of Roman society, although some of them man-aged to acquire significant wealth. The plebeians demanded more political rights, such as a fair share of distributed public land and freedom from debt bondage. These efforts of poor Romans to acquire a political voice, called the **Struggle of the Orders,** accelerated during the fifth century B.C.E., when Rome experienced a severe economic recession.

The main weapon that the plebeians had in this struggle was the threat, realized on only three occasions, of literally leaving the city, thereby bringing economic life to a standstill and depriving the army of its soldiers. The first victory in the ple-beians' struggle came in 494 B.C.E., when they won the right to elect two tribunes each year as their spokesmen. Tribunes could veto magistrates' deci-sions and so block arbitrary judicial actions by the patricians. In 471 B.C.E., a new Plebeian Assembly gave plebeians the opportunity to express their political views in a formal setting, although with-out the authority to enact legislation.

In 445 B.C.E., a new law permitted marriage between plebeians and patricians. This enabled wealthy plebeians to marry into patrician families. In 367 B.C.E., politicians agreed that one of each year's two consuls should be a plebeian. The plebeians now were fully integrated into Roman government. Moreover, Romans also limited the amount of public land that could be distributed to any citizen. The new arrangement prevented patri-cians from seizing the lion's share of conquered ter-ritories and enabled poor citizen soldiers to receive captured land. The last concession to the plebeians came in 287 B.C.E., when the decisions of the Ple-beian Assembly became binding on the whole state.

When Polybius chronicled the meteoric rise of Rome to world power, he attributed the success of the Republic to its mixture of the three forms of government identified by Aristotle: monarchy, aristocracy and democracy. In the Roman Repub-lic, two consuls represented monarchy, the Senate aristocracy (those considered most fit to rule), and the assemblies, which included both patricians and plebeians, democracy. According to Polybius, this republican mixture of the three forms of govern-ment was supposed to prevent the evils that threat-ened to emerge from each: despotism from monarchy, oligarchy from aristocracy, and mob-rule from democracy. As it turned out, aristocracy tended to prevail in the Roman Republic because the two consuls were almost always rich senators and because patricians usually had the upper hand in the assemblies. It is true that the plebeians in the assembly could check the power of the patricians, and to that extent the Roman constitution was "balanced." But wealthy plebeians, who repre-sented the "democratic" element in the Roman constitution, joined the patricians to form a new ruling elite. The government of the Roman Repub-lic was therefore not as balanced as Polybius boasted. His description of that government, how-ever, had a lasting impact on the efforts of later Western regimes to establish a form of government in which representatives of "the one," "the few," and "the many" all had a voice.

Roman Law

The conflict between the patricians and the ple-beians during the early Republic resulted in the formulation of a body of law governing rela-tions between individuals (private law) and between individuals and the government (public law). When the Republic was first established, legal disputes were settled by appealing to a body of unwritten customs that were believed

JUSTICE IN HISTORY

A Corrupt Roman Governor Is Convicted of Extortion

Governors sent by the Roman Senate to rule the provinces wielded absolute power, which often corrupted them. One such man was Gaius Verres, who was convicted in 70 B.C.E. in a court in Rome for his flagrant abuse of power while governor of Sicily. The courtroom drama in which Verres was found guilty reveals one of the deepest flaws of the Roman Republic: the unprincipled exploitation of lands under Roman control. It also reveals one of Rome's greatest strengths: the presence of men of high ethical standards who believed in honest government and fair treatment of Roman subjects. The trial and its result reveal republican Rome at its best and worst.

While governor from 73 to 71 B.C.E., Verres had looted Sicily with shocking thoroughness. In his pursuit of gold and Greek art, Verres tortured and sometimes killed Roman citizens. His outraged victims employed the young and ambitious lawyer Marcus Tullius Cicero (106–43 B.C.E.) to prosecute Verres. They could not have chosen a better advocate.

The prosecution of Verres marks the beginning of Cicero's illustrious career as one of the most active politicians and certainly the greatest orator of the Republic. Cicero also stands as one of the most influential political philosophers of Western civilization, one who hated the corruption of political life and opposed tyranny in any form. His many literary works have influenced political thinkers from antiquity to the present.

In the Roman Republic, only senators and equestrians, the two ranks of the Roman aristocracy, between ages 30 and 60 could serve on juries for civil crimes such as those Verres committed. All adult male citizens had the right to bring a case to court, but women had less freedom to do so. After swearing oaths of good faith, accusers would read the charges in the presence of the accused, who in turn agreed to accept the decision of the court.

When a trial actually began, the prosecutor was expected to be present, but the accused could decline to attend. The prosecution and the defense both produced evidence, then cross-examined witnesses. Because a Roman lawyer could discuss any aspect of the defendant's personal or public life, character assassination became an important—and amusing—rhetorical tool.

After deliberating, the jury delivered its verdict and the judge gave the penalty required by law, generally fines or periods of exile. No provisions for appeal existed, but the assembly could grant a pardon by means of a legislative act.

Cicero worked this system to his advantage in his prosecution of Verres. He quashed an attempt to delay the trial until 69 B.C.E., when the president of the court would be a crony of Verres. Then, with a combination of ringing oratory and irrefutable evidence of Verres's crimes, Cicero made his case. The following excerpt from his speech shows Cicero's mastery of persuasive rhetoric:

Judges: At this grave crisis in the history of our country, you have been offered a peculiarly desirable gift....For you have been given a unique chance to make your Senatorial Order less unpopular, and to set right the damaged reputation of these courts. A belief has taken root which is having a fatal effect on our nation—and which to us who are senators, in particular, threatens grave peril. This belief is on everyone's tongue, at Rome and even in foreign countries. It is this: That in these courts, with their present membership, even the worst criminal will never be convicted provided that he has money....And at this very juncture Gaius Verres has been brought to trial. Here is a man whose life and actions the world has already condemned—yet whose enormous fortune, according to his own loudly expressed hopes, has already brought him acquittal! Pronounce a just and scrupulous verdict against Verres and you will keep the good name which ought always to be yours.... I spent fifty days on a careful investigation of the entire island of Sicily; I got to know every document, every wrong suffered either by a community or an individual....

For three long years he so thoroughly despoiled and pillaged the province that its restoration to its previous state is out of the question.... All the property that anyone in Sicily still has for his own today is merely what happened to escape the attention of this avaricious lecher, or survived his glutted appetites.... It was an appalling disgrace for our country.

...In the first stage of the trial, then, my charge is this. I accuse Gaius Verres of committing acts of lechery and brutality against the citizens and allies of Rome, and many crimes against God and man. I claim that he has illegally taken from Sicily sums amounting to forty million sesterces. By the witnesses and documents, public and private, which I am going to cite, I shall convince you that these charges are true.[1]

Cicero's speech was persuasive, and the jury found Verres guilty. Verres went into exile in Marseilles to avoid his sentence, but he did not avoid punishment altogether. Justice—relentless and ironic—caught up with him years later during the civil wars that followed Julius Caesar's death in 44 B.C.E. Mark Antony, who was also a connoisseur of other people's wealth, wanted Verres's art collection for himself and so put Verres's name on a death list to obtain it. The former governor of Sicily was murdered in 43 B.C.E.

In his prosecution of Verres, Cicero delivered more than an indictment of one corrupt man. He revealed some of the deepest flaws of the Roman Republic. The trial inspired short-term reforms, but not until the reign of Emperor Augustus (r. 27 B.C.E.–14 C.E.) did Roman administration of provincial populations become more just.

Source: From *Selected Works: Against Verres 1; Twenty-Three Letters; The Second Philippic Against Antony; On Duties, 111; On Old Age* by Cicero, translated by Michael Grant (Penguin Classics 1960, second revised edition 1971.) Copyright © 1960, 1965, 1971 by Michael Grant. Reproduced by permission of Penguin Books, Ltd.

For Discussion

1. What does the trial of Verres reveal about weaknesses in the Roman Republic?

2. Cicero's speech illustrates his disdain for corruption and tyranny. What are the tensions between personal morality and the requirements of governing a large empire?

Taking It Further

Gruen, Erich S. *The Last Generation of the Roman Republic.* Berkeley: University of California Press, 1974. A magisterial analysis of the republic's decline, with emphasis on legal affairs.

Rawson, Elizabeth. *Cicero: A Portrait.* Ithaca: Cornell University Press, 1975. This book gives a balanced account of Cicero's life.

to have originated in the distant past. When the application of these ancient customs in a specific case was unclear, a body of patricians known as the pontiffs would interpret the law. When plebeians began to participate in the political life of the Republic, they recognized that the patricians might interpret the law in favor of their social class. The assembly therefore demanded that the law be put in writing so that decisions by the pontiffs had to be based on an authoritative and publicly known text. Accordingly, a commission appointed in 451 B.C.E. produced a body of written law known as known as the **Law of the Twelve Tables,** which was inscribed on twelve bronze tablets and posted in the Forum. This legislation, which was supposedly modeled on the Athenian law of Solon, was actually a written summary of existing customary law, not new law being handed down for the first time.

The original text of the Law of the Twelve Tables has not survived, but references in later legal documents provide a fairly good idea of its broad outlines. It covered such matters as the proper protection of women ("Women shall remain under the guardianship [of a man] even when they have reached legal adulthood") and debt bondage ("Unless he pays his debt or someone stands surety for him in court, bind him in a harness, or in chains...."). The value of the text to the plebeians resided not so much in the substance of the law, which was in many respects unfavorable to them, but in the legal procedures it spelled out. With the law now published, citizens discovered how to start a legal proceeding, which in civil cases (those involving property) meant they would bring the charge before a magistrate, who would then appoint a private citizen to examine witnesses and reach a decision. Only in serious criminal cases, such as homicide, would the magistrate take the initiative in prosecuting the case by himself. Because the Roman Republic did not have a large bureaucracy, the Twelve Tables encouraged citizens to settle cases among themselves, even in criminal cases involving serious physical injury.

The Twelve Tables governed civil and criminal disputes among Roman citizens. The frequency of disputes involving noncitizens, especially as Rome acquired distant lands, led to the establishment of another body of law, the *jus gentium* or law of nations. Because this law was based on what was considered to be the law of all civilized people, it was often equated with **natural law**, a system of justice believed to be inherent in nature rather than prescribed by human beings. The *jus gentium* beame, in effect, the first body of international law.

Roman law developed significantly during the later years of the Roman Republic and the empire, and in the sixth century C.E. the Roman emperor Justinian promulgated a massive legal code known as the *Corpus Juris Civilis* (Body of Civil Law). This legal code later became the foundation of the legal systems of most European countries. But Romans never failed to recognize that the Law of the Twelve Tables lay at the core of this comprehensive legal code. Thus, the law written down at the behest of plebeians in the early Roman Republic became the foundation of the legal culture of the West.

ROMAN TERRITORIAL EXPANSION

■ How did the Roman Republic come to dominate the Mediterranean world during the Hellenistic Age?

Under the republic, Rome conquered and incorporated all of Italy, the vast Carthaginian Empire in North Africa, Spain, and many of the Celtic lands to the north and west of Italy (see **Map 5.2**). As a result of these conquests, the Roman state had to change the methods of government established in the fifth century B.C.E.

The Italian Peninsula

The new political and military institutions that developed in Rome enabled the Romans to conquer the entire Italian peninsula by 263 B.C.E. In the process the Romans learned the fundamental lessons necessary for ruling larger territories abroad. Romans began to expand their realm by allying with neighboring cities in Italy. For centuries, Rome and the other Latin-speaking peoples of Latium (the region of central Italy where Rome was situated) had belonged to a loose coalition of cities called the Latin League. Citizens of these cities shared close commercial and legal ties and could intermarry without losing citizenship rights in their native cities. More important, they forged close military alliances with one another.

In 493 B.C.E. Rome led the Latin cities in battle against fierce hill tribes who coveted Latium's rich farmlands. From the success of this venture, Rome learned the value of political alliances with neighbors. Rome and its allies next confronted the Etruscans. In 396 B.C.E. the Romans overcame the Etruscan city of Veii through a combination of military might and shrewd political maneuvering. From this experience, the Romans discovered the uses of careful diplomacy.

CHRONOLOGY: ROME'S RISE TO POWER

ca. 509 B.C.E.	Roman Republic created
508 B.C.E.	Romans sign treaty with Carthage
494 B.C.E.	Tribunes of the Plebeians created
474 B.C.E.	Plebeian Assembly created
451 B.C.E.	Twelve Tables of Law published
387 B.C.E.	Celts sack Rome
287 B.C.E.	Laws of Plebeian Assembly become binding on all Romans
280 B.C.E.	Pyrrhus of Epirus defeated
264–241 B.C.E.	First Punic War
218–201 B.C.E.	Second Punic War
215–167 B.C.E.	Wars with Macedon
149–146 B.C.E.	Third Punic War
148–146 B.C.E.	Macedon and Greece become Roman provinces
67–62 B.C.E.	Pompey establishes Roman control over Anatolia, Syria, and Palestine

A temporary setback to Rome's expansion occurred in 389 B.C.E., when a raiding band of Celts from the north of Italy defeated a Roman army and plundered the city of Rome. Only after a generation did Romans recover from this disaster and reassert their preeminence among their allies. Still, they had learned that tenacity and discipline enabled them to endure even a serious military defeat.

The next major step in Rome's expansion came in 338 B.C.E., when Roman troops suppressed a three-year revolt of its Latin allies, who had come to resent Rome's overlordship. The peace settlement of this **Latin War** set the precedent for Rome's future expansion: Rome gave defeated peoples either partial or full citizenship depending on the treaty it struck with each community. (See *Encounters and Transformations* in this chapter.) The conquered allies were permitted to retain their own customs and were not forced to pay tribute. Rome asked for only two things in return: loyalty and troops. All allied communities had to contribute soldiers to the Roman army in wartime. With the huge new pool of troops, Rome became the strongest power in Italy.

In return for their military service and support of Rome, the newly incorporated citizens, especially wealthy landowners from the allied communities, received a share of the profits of war. They also received the guarantee of Roman protection from internal dissension or outside threats. Those communities not granted full Roman citizenship could hope to earn it if they served Roman interests faithfully. Some communities joined the Roman state willingly. Others, particularly the Samnites of south central Italy, resisted bitterly, but to no avail.

Romans then became embroiled in the affairs of Greek cities of the "toe" and "heel" of the boot-shaped Italian peninsula. Some of these Greek cities invited King Pyrrhus of Epirus (r. 318–275 B.C.E.), a Hellenistic adventurer from the western Balkans, to wage war against Rome on their behalf. Pyrrhus invaded southern Italy with 25,000 men and 20 elephants. Though he defeated Roman armies in two great battles in 280 B.C.E., he lost nearly two-thirds of his own troops and withdrew from Italy. "Another victory like this and I'm finished for good!" he said to a comrade, giving rise to the expression "a Pyrrhic victory," which is a win so costly that it is ruinous. Without Pyrrhus's protection, the Greeks in southern Italy could not withstand Rome's legions, and by 263 B.C.E. Rome ruled all of Italy.

RUINS OF ROMAN THEATER IN AOSTA, ITALY
The Greek city of Aosta in southern Italy, which flourished during the Hellenistic period, fell to Rome in the third century B.C.E. Romans built theaters in many of the cities they conquered.

The Struggle with Carthage

By the third century B.C.E., imperial Carthage dominated the western Mediterranean region. From the capital city of Carthage located on the North African coast near modern Tunis, Carthaginians held rich lands from modern Algeria to Morocco, controlled the natural resources of southern Spain, and dominated the sea lanes of the western Mediterranean. Phoenician traders had founded Carthage in the eighth century B.C.E.,and the city's energetic merchants carried on business with Greeks, Etruscans, Celts, and eventually Romans.

Hellenistic culture influenced Carthage as it did other Mediterranean and Near Eastern cities. During the Classical Age, Carthaginian trade with the Greek cities in Sicily, and probably with Greek artisans in North Africa, introduced many aspects of Greek culture to Carthage. For example, Carthaginians worshiped the Greek goddess of agriculture, Demeter, and her daughter, Kore (also called Persephone), in an elegant temple. By the fourth century B.C.E. the Carthaginian Empire was playing an integral role in the economy of the Hellenistic world by exporting agricultural products, raw materials, metal goods, and pottery.

Rome and Carthage were old acquaintances. At the beginning of the Republic, the two had signed a commercial treaty. More than two centuries of wary respect and increasing trade followed. But in 264 B.C.E., just as Rome established power throughout the Italian peninsula, a war between Greek cities in Sicily drew Rome and Carthage into conflict. When a Carthaginian fleet went to help a Greek city in Sicily, another city, controlled by soldiers of Italian descent, asked Rome for assistance in dislodging the Carthaginians. The Senate refused, but the Plebeian Assembly, eager for the spoils of war, voted to intercede. Rome invaded Sicily, setting off the First Punic War, so called because the word *Punic* comes from the Latin word for *Phoenician*.

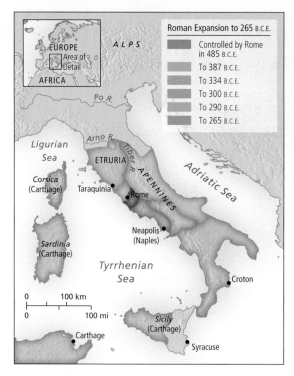

MAP 5.1

Rome's Expansion in Italy

This map shows how Rome gradually acquired control of the entire Italian peninsula by 265 B.C.E.

The First Punic War between Rome and Carthage for control of Sicily lasted from 264 to 241 B.C.E. During this time the Romans, who persisted in the conflict despite costly defeats, learned how to fight at sea, cutting off the Carthaginian supply lines to Sicily. In 241 B.C.E. Carthage signed a treaty in which it agreed to surrender Sicily and the surrounding islands and to pay a war indemnity over the course of a decade. Roman treachery, however, wrecked the agreement. While the Carthaginians struggled to suppress a revolt of mercenary soldiers, Rome seized Corsica and Sardinia, over which Carthage had lost effective control, and demanded larger reparations. Roman bad faith stoked Carthaginian desire for revenge.

War did not resume for another two decades. Under the able leadership of Hamilcar Barca (270–228 B.C.E.), Carthage developed resources in Spain, while Rome campaigned against Celts in north Italy and fierce tribes on the Adriatic coast. During these years trade between Rome and Carthage expanded. The growth of Carthaginian power in Spain, however, led to renewed conflict with Rome. The Second Punic War (218–201 B.C.E.) erupted when Hamilcar's son, Hannibal (247–182 B.C.E.), 25 years old and eager for vengeance, ignored a Roman warning and captured Saguntum, a Spanish town with which Rome had formal ties of friendship. In a daring move, Hannibal then launched a surprise attack on Italy from the north by marching from Spain and crossing the Alps. With an army of nearly 25,000 men and 18 elephants, he crushed the

CHRONOLOGY: IMPERIAL CARTHAGE

ca. 850 B.C.E.	Phoenicians found Carthage
600s B.C.E.	Carthage expands in north Africa, Sardinia, southern Spain, and Sicily
508 B.C.E.	Carthage makes treaty with Rome
500–200 B.C.E.	Conflicts with Greeks in Sicily
264–241 B.C.E.	Carthage fights First Punic War against Rome
218–203 B.C.E.	Hannibal fights in Italy
218–201 B.C.E.	Carthage fights Second Punic War against Rome
202 B.C.E.	Battle of Zama; Hannibal is defeated near Carthage
149–146 B.C.E.	Carthage fights Third Punic War against Rome; end of Carthaginian Empire
146 B.C.E.	Destruction of the city of Carthage

Roman armies sent against him. In the first major battle, at the Trebia River in the Po Valley, 20,000 Romans died. At Lake Trasimene in Etruria in 217 B.C.E., another 25,000 Romans fell. In the same year at Cannae, Rome lost 50,000 men in its worst defeat ever.

Despite these staggering losses, the Romans persevered and eventually defeated the Carthaginian general. They succeeded, first of all, because Hannibal lacked sufficient logistical support from Carthage to capitalize on his early victories to besiege and take the city of Rome. Second, most of Rome's allies in Italy remained loyal. They had often seen Romans prevail in the past and knew that the Romans took fierce revenge on disloyal friends. Thus, the Roman policy of including and protecting allies paid off. A third reason for Hannibal's defeat was the indomitable Roman spirit. Finally, no matter how many times they were defeated, the Romans simply refused to stop fighting.

The turning point in the war came when Roman commanders adopted a new strategy. After incurring so many defeats, the army dared not face Hannibal in open battle. Instead, Quintus Fabius Maximus (d. 202 B.C.E.), the Roman commander in Italy, avoided direct confrontation on the battlefield and used guerilla tactics to pin down Hannibal in Italy, thereby earning the nickname "the Delayer." At the same time Publius Cornelius Scipio, later called Africanus (237–187 B.C.E.), took command of the Roman forces in Spain. Within a few years he defeated the Carthaginian forces there, preventing reinforcements from reaching Hannibal. In 204 B.C.E., Scipio led Roman legions into Africa, forcing Carthage to recall Hannibal from Italy to protect the city.

At the Battle of Zama near Carthage in 202 B.C.E., fortune finally deserted Hannibal. Scipio triumphed, and Hannibal fled into exile. Hannibal had won every battle but his last. Though Scipio did not destroy Carthage, the city lost all of its overseas territories to Rome.

Because the battles against Hannibal had been so costly, many vengeful Romans wanted the total destruction of Carthage. In particular, the statesman Marcus Porcius Cato (234–149 B.C.E.), who ended every public utterance with the demand "Carthage must be destroyed!", goaded Romans to resume war with their old adversary. The Third Punic War (149–146 B.C.E.) resulted in the destruction of Carthage. Survivors were enslaved, and the city was burned to the ground. Its territories became the Roman provinces of Africa.

Roman casualties in the struggle against Carthage resulted in a temporary change in the position of women in Roman society. Roman losses in the Battle of Cannae were so great that according to the historian Livy, "There was not one matron who was not bereaved." The inheritance of the slain soldiers' wealth by widows and children increased the fortunes of many Roman women, some of whom openly displayed their newfound wealth. In 215 B.C.E., to help pay the staggering cost of the war, the government passed the **Oppian Law**, which restricted the amount of gold that any single women or widow could hold and forbade them to wear certain articles of clothing. In 195 B.C.E. a group of wealthier Roman women demonstrated in favor of repealing the Oppian law. The women's participation in these demonstrations—the first of their kind in the West—marked the growing independence of women in the Republic.

The Macedonian Wars

By the end of the Punic Wars, Rome had also become involved in the affairs of the Hellenistic kingdoms of the East. Initially reluctant to take direct control of these regions, Roman leaders gradually assumed responsibility for maintaining order in the region and eventually established absolute control over the entire eastern Mediterranean region.

Rome waged three wars against Macedon between 215 and 167 B.C.E. that resulted in Rome's gaining mastery of Macedon and Greece. The First Macedonian War (215–205 B.C.E.) began when the Macedonian king, Philip V (r. 221–179 B.C.E.), made an alliance with Hannibal after the Roman defeat at the Battle of Cannae. The results

MAP 5.2

Roman Conquest during the Republic

Armies of the Roman Republic conquered the Mediterranean world during the Hellenistic Age, overcoming the Carthaginian Empire, the Hellenistic successor kingdoms, and many Celtic peoples in Spain and Gaul.

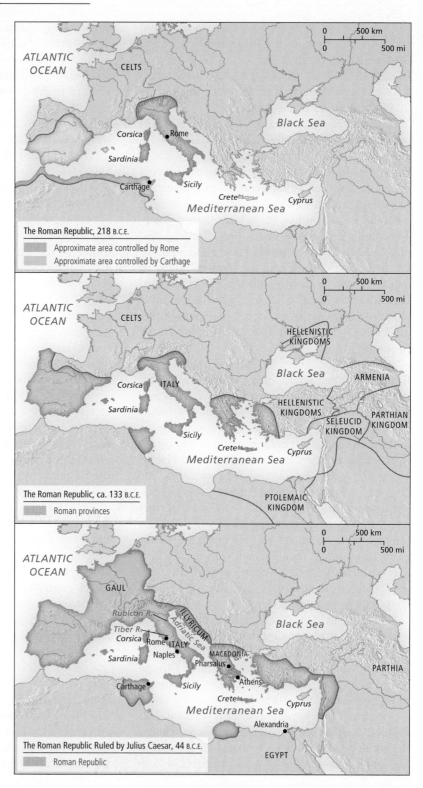

The Roman Republic, 218 B.C.E.

■ Approximate area controlled by Rome
■ Approximate area controlled by Carthage

The Roman Republic, ca. 133 B.C.E.

■ Roman provinces

The Roman Republic Ruled by Julius Caesar, 44 B.C.E.

■ Roman Republic

ENCOUNTERS AND TRANSFORMATIONS

Roman Citizenship

In the early Roman Republic citizenship, as in classical Athens, was a privilege granted to relatively few men. Roman citizens had the full protection of the law and could vote and hold political office. All legitimate male children of Roman citizens acquired the status of their fathers at birth. Neither slaves nor women possessed the rights of citizenship, but freed slaves acquired a limited form of citizenship upon their emancipation, and the sons of freed slaves became citizens.

The nature of Roman citizenship changed as the result of Roman encounters with the inhabitants of the territories in Italy that Rome conquered and absorbed into the Roman state. At the end of the Latin War (340–338 B.C.E.) Rome granted a limited form of citizenship to the former members of the Latin League that had attempted to acquire independence from the Republic. These new citizens acquired rights of property and the right to migrate to a different city within the lands the Republic controlled, but they could not enter into a lawful marriage with full Roman citizens. This form of limited citizenship, known as Latin right, gradually became a legal category that was extended beyond former members of the Latin League.

Citizens of states that were allied with Rome, known as *socii*, could acquire certain legal rights of citizenship in exchange for military service. Dissatisfaction with such arrangements was one of the causes of the Social War of 91–88 B.C.E. During this war the Senate passed a law, known as *Lex Julia,* that granted citizenship to all Italian and *socii* states that were not involved in the war or who would be willing to cease hostilities. Thus, the offer of citizenship became a tool of Roman military and foreign policy. At the end of the war Rome extended full Roman citizenship to all *socii* and those possessing Latin Right.

The *Lex Julia* marked a significant step in establishing the principle that one acquired citizenship by birth in a territory or state. This *lex solis* (law of territory) eventually became the main basis for determining nationality and citizenship in the West, although it has often had to accommodate the *lex sanguinis* (law of blood), in which one acquires citizenship from a parent or other relative. Both principles, for example, have a role in determining citizenship in the United States today. The original form of Roman citizenship as a privilege granted to certain individuals, continued to determine the status of "freemen" in European cities until the nineteenth century, but the basis of Western nationality that prevails today has deep roots in the Roman law of citizenship passed in the first century B.C.E.

For Discussion

1. How did military and diplomatic needs change the Roman law of citizenship?

2. To what extent does the definition of American citizenship today reflect the Roman inheritance?

of the conflict were inconclusive. Rome entered a second war with Macedon (201–196 B.C.E.) because Philip and the Seleucid king Antiochus III of Syria (r. 223–187 B.C.E.) had agreed to split the eastern Mediterranean between them. The poleis of Greece begged Rome for help, and Rome responded by ordering Philip to cease meddling in Greek affairs. Philip refused, and Roman forces easily defeated him with the support of Greek cities. In 196 B.C.E. the Roman general Titus Quinctius Flamininus declared the cities of Greece free and withdrew his forces.

These cities were not truly free, however. Rome installed oligarchic governments, on whose support the Romans could rely. These unpopular regimes reflected the class distinctions of Rome itself. When Antiochus III sent an army to free Greece from Roman control, Rome defeated him in 189 B.C.E. Rome imposed heavy reparations but took no territory, preferring to protect the newly freed Greek cities of Anatolia and Greece from a distance.

Rome's policy of control from a distance changed after a third war with Macedon (172–167 B.C.E.), when a new Macedonian king tried to supplant Rome as protector of Greece. After a smashing victory, Rome divided Macedon into four separate republics and forbade marriage and trade among them. Roman troops ruthlessly stamped out all opposition, destroying 70 cities and selling 150,000 people into slavery. The same fate awaited the Achaean cities that turned against Rome, most notably Corinth, whose destruction at the hands of the Roman general Mummius was described at the beginning of this chapter.

THE CULTURE OF THE ROMAN REPUBLIC

■ How did the Roman encounter with Greek culture in the Hellenistic world lead to the forging of a durable Greco–Roman cultural synthesis?

During five centuries of republican rule, Rome created a new cultural synthesis by mixing elements of its own culture with that of Greece. The resulting synthesis, which Rome later disseminated throughout its empire, became a major foundation of Western identity. Much of the Greek culture that Rome assimilated and modified originated in the Hellenistic period, and the main impetus of this cultural exchange was Roman territorial expansion within the Hellenistic world.

The Encounter between Hellenistic and Roman Culture

Romans had interacted with Greek culture for centuries, first indirectly through Etruscan intermediaries, and then through direct contact with Greek communities in southern Italy and Sicily. During the second century B.C.E., when Rome acquired the eastern Mediterranean through its wars with Macedon and the Seleucids, Hellenism's intellectual influence on Rome accelerated. In addition to fine statues and paintings, Greek ideas about literature, art, philosophy, and rhetoric poured into Rome after the Macedonian wars.

This Hellenistic legacy challenged many Roman assumptions about the world. But there was a paradox in how Roman patricians reacted to Hellenism. Many noblemen in Rome felt threatened by the novelty of Hellenistic ideas. They preferred to maintain their conservative traditions of public life and thought. They wanted to preserve the image of a strong and independent Roman culture, untainted by foreign influences. Thus, during the second century B.C.E., Romans occasionally tried to expel Greek philosophers from Rome because they worried that Greek ideas might undermine traditional Roman values. Yet many Roman aristocrats also admired the sophistication of Greek political thought, art, and literature and wished to participate in the Hellenistic community.

Consequently many members of the Roman elite learned Greek, but refused to speak it while on official business in the East. While Latin remained the language spoken in the Senate house, senators hired Greek tutors to instruct their sons at home in philosophy, literature, history, and rhetoric, and Greek intellectuals found a warm welcome from Rome's upper class. Cato the Censor, the senator who had insisted that Rome destroy Carthage, embodied the paradox of maintaining public distance from Greek culture while privately cherishing it. He cultivated an appearance of forthrightness and honesty, traditional Roman values that he claimed were threatened by Greek culture. He publicly denounced Greek oratory as unmanly, while drawing upon his deep knowledge of Greek rhetoric and literature to write his speeches praising Roman culture.

CIRCULAR TEMPLE

This circular temple from the city of Rome near the Tiber River dates to the late second century B.C.E. It is the earliest surviving marble temple in Rome. The plan of the temple and the original marble of the columns and much of the rest of the building came from Greece.

Before their exposure to the Hellenistic world in the second century B.C.E., Romans had little interest in literature. Their writing consisted mainly of inscriptions of laws and treaties on bronze plaques hung from the outer walls of public buildings. Families kept records of the funeral eulogies of their ancestors, while priests maintained simple lists of events and religious festivals. By about 240 B.C.E., Livius Andronicus, a former Greek slave, began to translate Greek dramas into Latin. In 220 B.C.E., a Roman senator, Quintus Fabius Pictor, wrote a history of Rome in Greek—the first major Roman prose work.

Hellenistic culture also had a major impact on Roman drama. Two Roman playwrights, Plautus (ca. 250–184 B.C.E.) and Terence (ca. 190–159 B.C.E.), took their inspiration from Hellenistic New Comedy and injected humor and wit into Roman literature. Their surviving works, which were always set in the Greek world, offer entertaining glimpses into the pitfalls of everyday life while also reinforcing the patrician values of the rulers of Rome's vast new domains.

Art and Architecture

The massive infusion of Hellenistic art to Rome following the Macedonian wars inevitably affected public taste. The most prestigious works of art decorated public shrines and spaces throughout the city. Many others went to private collectors, including Gaius Verres, the corrupt governor of Sicily who plundered the artistic treasures of that province when he was governor between 73 and 71 B.C.E. (See *Justice in History* in this chapter.) Ironically Cicero, who prosecuted Verres, was himself an avid collector of Greek art. The mania for Greek art became so intense that Greek artists soon moved to Rome to enjoy the patronage of wealthy Romans.

In Rome these artists often produced copies of Greek originals. In many cases only these Roman copies have survived. If it had not been for the Greek artists in Rome, therefore, many treasures of Greek art would have been lost to posterity. The encounter between Greece and Rome was not, however, limited to the imitation of Greek works. In portrait sculpture, for example, a realistic style developed in Rome that unflinchingly depicted all the wrinkles of experience on a person's face. In this way the venerable Roman tradition of making ancestral masks merged with Greek art.

The development of Roman architecture during the Republic tells a similar story. The early Roman works of architecture were essentially copies of Greek originals, complete with the three orders of Doric, Ionic, and Corinthian capitals on the columns. The main contributions that Romans made to architecture were structural, as in the construction of arches, vaults, and domes, rather than in artistic design. In the first century B.C.E., however, the magnificent temple of Fortune at Praeneste, a town near Rome, combined Italian and Hellenistic concepts in a genuinely Greco–Roman style. By the end of the Republic, Romans had gained enough confidence to adopt the intellectual heritage of Greece and use it to serve their own ends without fear of seeming "too Greek."

Philosophy and Religion

Many educated Romans found Greek philosophy attractive. The theory of matter advanced by the Hellenistic philosopher Epicurus, whose ethical philosophy we discussed in Chapter 4,

REPUBLICAN PORTRAIT OF CICERO

This portrait of Cicero captures his uncompromising personality. The style of depicting every wrinkle conforms both to Hellenistic interest in psychological portraiture and traditional Roman directness. In the republican period this type of portraiture was enormously popular.

Source: Dagli Orti/Picture Desk, Inc./Kobal Collection

gained wide acceptance among Romans. Epicurus believed that everything has a natural cause: that "nothing comes from nothing." Romans learned about Epicurus's theories of matter and the infinity of the universe from the poem, *On the Nature of the Universe*, by the Roman poet Lucretius (d. ca. 51 B.C.E.), who wrote in Latin. The Hellenistic ethical philosophy that held the greatest appeal to Romans, however, was Stoicism, because it encouraged an active public life. Stoic emphasis on mastering human difficulties appealed to patrician

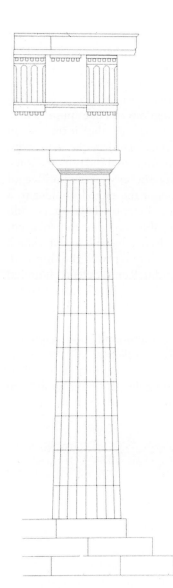

ROMAN AND GREEK DORIC ORDER

The Roman Doric capital on a column of the Theater of Marcellus on the left was not as simple as the Greek Doric order, shown here on the Parthenon. The Doric order was the simplest of the three orders, the Ionic and Corinthian being more highly decorated. In the classical revival of the eighteenth century C.E., the Doric order connoted seriousness of purpose, and in the United States it symbolized republican virtue.

Romans' sense of duty and dignity. Cicero, in particular, combined Stoic ideas in a personal yet fully Roman way. He stressed moral behavior in political life while urging the attainment of a broad education. Cicero's high-minded devotion to the Republic won him the enmity of unscrupulous politicians. He was murdered in 43 B.C.E. after making public speeches accusing

Marc Antony of being a threat to republican freedom.

The encounter between Roman and Hellenistic religion provides a striking example of the Greco–Roman cultural synthesis. Contact with Greek civilization during the Hellenistic period led to the development of a closer correspondence between many Roman and Greek gods. Thus, the powerful Roman god Jupiter acquired many of the characteristics of the Greek god Zeus. The Roman god of war Mars resembled the Greek god Ares, and the Roman goddess of hunting, Diana, acquired many of the attributes of Artemis. But the mythical personalities and activities of Roman gods were never the same as those of their Greek counterparts. Jupiter, for example, was not as sexually voracious as Zeus, while the Roman goddess Venus combined many of the features of the Greek goddess Aphrodite with those of the Etruscan deity Turan. All in all, Roman gods were much better behaved and more dignified than the group that Homer bequeathed to the Greeks.

Romans also recognized the local gods of the territories they conquered and absorbed.

A decision by the Roman Senate to import the image of the foreign nature goddess Cybele to Rome in 204 B.C.E. illustrates the ease with which Rome acquired new deities. The cult of Cybele, known as the Great Mother, flourished in the Hellenistic kingdom of Pergamum, where devotees worshiped her in the form of an ancient and holy rock. During the war with Hannibal, the Senate imported the rock to Rome to inspire and unify the city. A committee of leading citizens brought the sacred boulder to a new temple on the Palatine Hill amid wild rejoicing. When the ship carrying the rock got stuck in the Tiber River, legend has it that a noble lady, Claudia Quinta, towed the ship with her sash. Not only did Rome defeat Hannibal soon after the arrival of Cybele's sacred stone, but the move cemented Roman relations with Pergamum.

The recognition of imported gods resulted in a proliferation of Roman deities. In 27 B.C.E the government constructed a new temple, the Pantheon (literally a "temple of all the gods") to honor the hundreds of gods that the people

TABLE 5.1

ROMAN GODS AND THEIR GREEK COUNTERPARTS

Roman god	Greek god	Association
Apollo	Apollo	the sun, prophecy, medicine
Bacchus	Dionysos	wine, agriculture, festivity
Ceres	Demeter	plants, maternal love
Diana	Artemis	hunting, the moon, fertility
Jupiter	Zeus	light, the sky
Juno	Hera	women
Mars	Ares	war
Mercury	Hermes	trade
Minerva	Athena	wisdom
Neptune	Poseidon	the sea
Victoria	Nike	victory
Pan	Pan	herds, forests
Proserpina	Persephone or Kore	fertility
Pluto	Hades	the underworld and the dead
Venus	Aphrodite	love, sex, beauty

STATUE OF CYBELE, THE GREAT MOTHER

Romans worshiped the Great Mother (*Magna Mater*) after her cult was introduced in Rome during the Second Punic War against Hannibal. People had worshiped this goddess throughout the eastern Mediterranean since remote antiquity. This statue represents her majestic power.

recognized. With so many different gods, the Republic developed a policy of tolerating a wide variety of religious practices. This leniency, however, had its limits. The governing class viewed with suspicion any religious practice that was not conducted publicly, threatened public order, or challenged conventional standards of morality. In 186 B.C.E. the consuls received reports that a new cult of the god Dionysos, whom the Romans called Bacchus, had spread from Erturia to Rome, conducting nocturnal orgies. The members of this cult were allegedly engaging in "the promiscuous intercourse of free-born men and women" and "debaucheries of every kind." They also were accused of "poison and secret murders" that went undetected because the "loud shouting and the noise of drums and cymbals" drowned out the cries of the victims. The government responded to these reports, which were almost certainly exaggerated, by demanding the arrest of the participants, declaring that no religious ceremonies should take place in private, and forbidding such assemblies in the future.

Rhetoric

The Roman passion for oratory, exemplified in the speeches of Cicero, also reflected the Roman adoption of a Greek tradition. As we saw in Chapter 3, Athenians developed the art of oratory to a high level. Romans had great admiration for this Greek tradition and imitated Athenian oratorical style. To some extent, Romans suffered from an inferiority complex regarding their oratorical skills. The great Roman rhetorician Quintilian (35–100 C.E.) admitted that Romans orators could never be as elegant or as subtle as the Greeks, but he argued that they could be "blunter" and "weightier." By emphasizing the power of persuasive speech, employed mainly in politics and law, Romans developed a style of oratory that was more effective, if not as sophisticated, as that of Greece. (See *Justice in History* in this chapter.)

As in many other areas of culture, the Roman achievement in oratory proved to be more durable than that of the Greeks, mainly because Romans developed a tradition of rhetorical instruction that had a lasting influence on Western education. Learning how to give classical orations became a skill once again during the Renaissance of the fifteenth and sixteenth centuries, especially in Italy, which revived the Greco–Roman culture that had flourished in the Roman Republic. Educators in Renaissance Europe, as in ancient Rome, placed a premium on one's ability to inspire citizens to political or military action. Rhetoric, the art of persuasion, became more important, at least for members of the educated elite, than the attainment of philosophical wisdom. Thus, the knowledge of and training in rhetoric became one of the cultural legacies that the Roman Republic bequeathed to the West.

SOCIAL LIFE IN REPUBLICAN ROME

■ How was Roman society structured, and what relationships existed within the Roman family?

Under the Republic a few influential families dominated political life, sometimes making decisions about war and peace from which they could win wealth and prestige. The Roman Republic remained strong because these ruling families took pains to limit the power any one man or extended political family could attain.

Patrons and Clients

The ruling families of Rome established political networks that extended their influence throughout Roman society. These relationships depended on the traditional Roman institution of **patrons and clients.** By exercising influence on behalf of a social subordinate, a powerful man (the patron) would bind that man (the client) to him in anticipation of gaining future support. In this way complex webs of personal interdependency influenced the entire Roman social system. The patron-client system operated at every level of society. It was customary for a man of influence to receive his clients at his home the first thing in the morning. In a modest household the discussion between patron and client might involve everyday business such as shipping fish, arranging a marriage, or making a loan. But in the mansion of a Roman patrician a patron might be more interested in forging a political alliance. When several patron-client groups joined forces, they became significant political factions under the leadership of one powerful patron.

Pyramids of Wealth and Power

Like its political organization, Rome's social organization demonstrated a well-defined hierarchy. By the first century B.C.E. a new, elite class of political leaders had emerged in Rome, composed of both the original patrician families and wealthy plebeians who had attained membership in the Senate through their service in various public offices. The men of this leadership class dominated the Senate and formed the inner circle of government. From their ranks came most of the consuls. They set foreign and domestic policy, led armies to war, held the main magistracies, and siphoned off the lion's share of the Republic's resources.

Beneath this elite group came the equestrian class. Equestrians normally abstained from public office but were often tied to political leaders by personal obligation. They were primarily well-to-do businessmen who prospered from the financial opportunities that Rome's territorial expansion provided. For example, during the Republic, equestrian businessmen could bid on contracts to collect taxes from the provinces. The man awarded such a contract had few restraints on the methods by which he raised the revenue. After paying the treasury the amount agreed upon in the contract, he could keep any surplus as profit. Many equestrians accumulated fortunes in this way.

Next in rank came the large body of citizens who were known as plebeians. As we have seen, this group had acquired political representation and influence, but the Plebeian Assembly had gradually come under the control of politicians who were the clients of patrician patrons. These wealthy plebeian politicians, who had become members of a new ruling elite, had little interest in the condition of other plebeians, who now had no direct means to express their political will. Army service kept many plebeians who had small farms away from their land for long periods of time. Consequently, many plebeian farmers went bankrupt. Rich investors seized this opportunity to create huge estates by grabbing the bankrupt farms and replacing the free farmers with slaves. Sometimes impoverished plebeians became dependent tenant farmers on land they had once owned themselves. As a result, these plebeians increasingly turned to leaders who promised to protect them and give them land.

Rome's Italian allies had even fewer rights than the plebeians, despite their service in the Roman armies. Although millions of allies inhabited lands controlled by Rome, only a privileged few of the local elites received Roman citizenship. The rest could only hope for the goodwill of Roman officials.

At the bottom of the Roman hierarchy were slaves. By the first century B.C.E., about two million slaves captured in war or born in captivity lived in Italy and Sicily, amounting to about one-third of the population. Like Greeks, Romans considered slaves to be pieces of property, "talking tools," whom their owners could exploit at will. Freed slaves owed legal obligations to their former masters and were their clients. The brutal inequities of this system led to violence. The slave gangs who farmed vast estates in Sicily revolted first. In 135 B.C.E. they began an ill-fated struggle for freedom that lasted three years and involved more than 200,000 slaves.

Thirty years later another unsuccessful outburst began in southern Italy and Sicily because slave owners refused to comply with a senatorial decree to release any slaves who once had been free allies of Rome. 30,000 slaves took up arms between 104 and 101 B.C.E. The most destructive revolt occurred in Italy from 73 to 71 B.C.E. An army of more than 100,000 slaves led by the Thracian gladiator Spartacus (gladiators were slaves who fought for public entertainment) battled eight Roman legions, totaling about 50,000 men, before being crushed by the superior Roman military organization.

The Roman Family

A Roman *familia* typically included not just the husband, wife, and unmarried children, but also their slaves and often freedmen and others who were dependent on the household. Legitimate marriages required the agreement of both husband and wife. Women usually married at puberty, as had been the practice in classical Athens, and men did so in their twenties. In most families only two or three children survived infancy. It was fairly common and socially acceptable for men to live with unmarried women (concubines) before they were married or after their wives had died, but not while they were married. Married men seeking extramarital sex generally turned to their slaves or engaged the services of prostitutes, a practice that was legal in republican Rome.

The Roman family mirrored the patterns of authority and dependency found in the political arena. Just as a patron commanded the support of his clients regardless of their status in public life, so the male head of the household directed the destiny of all his subordinates within the *familia*. A man ruled his *familia* with full authority over the purse strings and all of his descendants until he died. The head of the family, the *paterfamilias*, theoretically held power of life and death over his wife, children, and slaves, though few men exercised such power. In practice, women and grown children often enjoyed considerable independence, and patrician women often influenced political life, though always from behind the scenes.

Upper-class Romans placed great value on the continuity of the family name, family traditions,

and control of family property through the generations. For these reasons they often adopted
males, even of adult age, to be heirs, especially if
they had no legitimate sons of their own. Legitimate offspring always took the name of their
father, and in case of divorce, which could be easily obtained, continued to live with him. Illegitimate offspring stayed with their mother.

With few exceptions Roman women remained
legally dependent on a male relative. In the most
common form of marriage, a wife remained under
the formal control of the *paterfamilias* to whom
she belonged before her marriage—in most cases,
her father. In practice this meant that she retained
control of her own property and the inheritance
she had received from her father. A husband in this
sort of marriage would have to be careful to avoid
angering his wife's father or brothers, and so he
might treat his wife more justly. Another, older
form of marriage brought the wife under the full
control of her husband after the wedding. She had
to worship the family gods of her husband's household and accept his ancestors as her own. If her
husband died, one of his male relatives became her
legal protector.

Slaves could not achieve the stability of family life through the generations that free Romans
desired. Former female slaves (freedwomen)
remained tied to their former masters with bonds
of dependency and obligation. Roman law did
not recognize marriage between slaves. Some
Roman handbooks, explaining how to use slaves
to maximum advantage, advocated letting slaves
establish conjugal arrangements. Owners could,
however, shatter such unions by selling either of
the enslaved partners or their offspring.

THE END OF THE ROMAN REPUBLIC

■ Why did the Roman Republic end?

The inequalities of wealth and power in Roman
society eventually destroyed the Republic. The
rapid acquisition of territories and the enormous
wealth that the Roman elite accumulated from
overseas conquest heightened those differences.
Those who profited the most from imperial
rule—politicians, governors, generals, and
businessmen—fiercely resisted reformers' efforts
to achieve a more equitable distribution of
resources. The ruling elite sought personal glory
and political advantage even if it came at the
Republic's expense. Their quest for political
prominence through military adventure, coupled
with flaws in Rome's political institutions, eventually overwhelmed the republican constitution
and brought about a revolution—a decisive, fundamental change in the political system.

The Gracchi

During the second century B.C.E., more and more
citizen farmers in Italy lost their farms to powerful landholders, who replaced them with gangs
of slaves. Some members of the political elite
feared the danger inherent in these developments. If citizen farmers could no longer meet
the property requirements for military service
and pay for their own weapons, as they were
required to do, Rome would lose its supply of
recruits for its legions.

Two young brothers, Tiberius and Gaius
Gracchus, attempted reforms. Although their
mother was a patrician (the daughter of Scipio
Africanus), she had married a wealthy plebeian.
Thus, the brothers were legally plebeian, and they
sought influence through the tribunate, an office
limited to plebeians. As a tribune, Tiberius
Gracchus (162–133 B.C.E.) convinced the Plebeian Assembly to pass a bill limiting the amount
of public land that one man could possess. Excess
land from wealthy landholders was to be redistributed in small lots to poor citizens. While the
land redistribution was in progress, conservative
senators ignited a firestorm of opposition to
Tiberius Gracchus. He responded by running for
a second term as a tribune, which was a break
with precedent. Fearing revolution, a clique of
senators in 133 B.C.E. clubbed Tiberius to death.
Land redistribution did not cease, but a terrible
precedent of public violence had been set.

A decade later, when Tiberius's brother Gaius Gracchus became a tribune in 123 B.C.E., he turned his attention to the problem of extortion in the provinces. With no checks on their authority, many corrupt governors who came from the ranks of the Senate forced provincials to give them money, valuable goods, and crops. Gaius Gracchus attempted to stop these abuses. To dilute the power of these corrupt provincial administrators and to win the political support of equestrians in Rome, he permitted equestrian tax collectors to operate in the provinces and to serve on juries that tried extortion cases. Gaius also tried to speed up land redistribution. But when he attempted to give citizenship to Rome's Italian allies to prevent Romans from confiscating their land, he lost the support of the Roman people, who did not wish to share the benefits of citizenship with non-Romans. In 121 B.C.E. Gaius committed suicide rather than allow himself to be murdered by a mob sent by his brother's senatorial foes.

The ruthless suppression of the Gracchus brothers and their supporters lit the fuse of political and social revolution in Rome. By attempting to effect change through the Plebeian Assembly, the Gracchus brothers unwittingly paved the way for less scrupulous politicians to seek power by falsely claiming to represent the interests of the poor. Their violent deaths signaled the end of political consensus among the oligarchy. Rivalry among the elite combined with the desperation of the poor was an explosive blend, with the army as the potentially decisive factor. If an unscrupulous politician were to join forces with poverty-stricken soldiers, the Republic would be in peril.

Gaius Marius (157–86 B.C.E.) became the first Roman general to use the army for political ends. He rose to power when the angry Roman poor made him their champion. Despite his equestrian origins, this experienced general won the consulship in 107 B.C.E. A special law of the Plebeian Assembly put him in command of the legions fighting King Jugurtha of Numidia in North Africa; and he brought the war to a quick and successful conclusion. Then he crushed Germanic tribes seeking to invade Italy.

In organizing his armies Marius made radical changes. He eliminated the property requirement for enlistment, thereby opening the ranks to the poorest citizens in the countryside and in Rome. These soldiers swore an oath of loyalty to their commander in chief, who in return promised them farms after a victorious campaign. Marius's reforms put generals in the middle of the long-running political struggle between the Senate and the Plebeian Assembly, the two institutions authorized to allocate lands won in war.

Marius achieved great personal power, but he did not use it against the institutions of the Republic. When he left Italy because of his unpopularity among the elite, the Roman Republic lurched ahead to its next major crisis: a revolt of the Italian allies.

War in Italy and Abroad

In 90 B.C.E. Rome's loyal allies in Italy could no longer endure being treated as inferiors when it came to distribution of land and booty. They launched a revolt against Rome known as the **Social War** (from the Latin word *socii*, which means "allies"). The confederation of allies demanded not independence but participation in the Roman Republic. They wanted full citizenship rights because they had been partners in Rome's wars and thus felt entitled to share in the fruits of victory. The allies lost the war, but soon afterward Rome granted citizenship to all Italians. These new citizens tilted the political scales away from the wealthy in Rome toward the population of Italy in general.

The Social War in Italy was followed by wars abroad. The patrician Lucius Cornelius Sulla (138–78 B.C.E.), consul in 88 B.C.E., was setting out with an army to put down a serious provincial revolt in Anatolia when the Plebeian Assembly turned command of his troops over to Marius, whose military reforms had aided the poor. In response, Sulla marched from southern Italy to Rome and placed his own supporters in positions of authority in the Senate, the Plebeian Assembly, and the magistracies.

DIFFERENT VOICES THE CATILINE CONSPIRACY

In 63 B.C.E. Lucius Sergius Catilina, known in English as Catiline, staged a conspiracy to bring down the government of the Roman Republic. Catiline was a member of a patrician family whose fortunes had declined. He had a distinguished military career, but the Senate dismissed him on trumped up charges of debauchery in 71 B.C.E. The conspiracy originated after he failed to become consul once again in 64 B.C.E. The conspirators planned to murder a large number of senators and assassinate Cicero, who was serving as consul that year. That plot failed. Catiline was killed in a battle with republican forces, and four co-conspirators were executed.

The account of the conspiracy by the Roman historian Sallust (ca. 86–35 B.C.E.) involves an analysis of the social and moral decline that proved fertile ground for Catiline in plotting to overthrow the government. Cicero was more concerned with exposing Catiline's bad character. In his first oration denouncing Catiline, Cicero attacked the man for his perfidy.

A Roman Historian's Analysis of the Catiline Conspiracy

At this period the empire of Rome appears to me to have been in an extremely deplorable condition; for though every nation, from the rising to the setting of the sun, lay in subjection to her arms, and though peace and prosperity, which mankind think the greatest blessings, were hers in abundance, there yet were found, among her citizens, men who were bent, with obstinate determination, to plunge themselves and their country into ruin; for, notwithstanding the two decrees of the senate, not one individual, out of so vast a number was induced by the offer of reward to give information of the conspiracy; nor was there a single deserter from the camp of Catiline. So strong a spirit of disaffection had, like a pestilence, pervaded the minds of most of the citizens.

Nor was this disaffected spirit confined to those who were actually concerned in the conspiracy; for the whole of the common

people, from a desire of change, favored the projects of Catiline. This they seemed to do in accordance with their general character; for, in every state, they that are poor envy those of a better class, and endeavor to exalt the factious; they dislike the established condition of things, and long for something new; they are discontented with their own circumstances, and desire a general alteration; they can support themselves amidst revolt and sedition, without anxiety, since poverty does not easily suffer loss.

As for the populace of the city, they had become disaffected from various causes. In the first place, such as everywhere took the lead in crime and profligacy, with others who had squandered their fortunes in dissipation, and, in a word, all whom vice and villainy had driven from their homes, had flocked to Rome as a general receptacle of impurity. In the next place, many, who thought of the success of Sulla, when they had seen some raised from common soldiers into senators, and others so enriched as to live in regal luxury and pomp, hoped, each for himself, similar results from victory, if they should once take up arms. In addition to this, the youth, who, in the country, had earned a scanty livelihood by manual labor, tempted by public and private largesses, had preferred idleness in the city to unwelcome toil in the field. To these and all others of similar character, public disorders would furnish subsistence. It is not at all surprising, therefore, that men in distress, of dissolute principles and extravagant expectations, should have consulted the interest of the state no further than as it was subservient to their own. Besides, those whose parents, by the victory of Sulla, had been proscribed, whose property had been confiscated, and whose civil rights had been curtailed, looked forward to the event of a war with precisely the same feelings.

All those, too, who were of any party opposed to that of the senate, were desirous rather that the state should be embroiled, than that they

CICERO ATTACKS CATILINE

In this nineteenth-century representation of a session of the Roman Senate, Cicero gives one of his orations against Catiline, who is sitting alone to the right. From a fresco in Palazzo Madama, Rome, house of the Italian Senate.

themselves should be out of power. This was an evil, which, after many years, had returned upon the community to the extent to which it now prevailed.

Source: Gaius Sallustius Crispus, *Conspiracy of Catiline*, Translated by J. S. Watson. New York: Harper & Brothers.1867.

Cicero, First Oration against Catiline

When, O Catiline, do you mean to cease abusing our patience? How long is that madness of yours still to mock us? When is there to be an end of that unbridled audacity of yours, swaggering about as it does now? Do not the nightly guards placed on the Palatine Hill—do not the watches posted throughout the city—does not the alarm of the people, and the union of all good men—does not the precaution taken of assembling the senate in this most defensible place—do not the looks and countenances of this venerable body here present, have any effect upon you? Do you not feel that your plans are detected? Do you not see that your conspiracy is already arrested and rendered powerless by the knowledge which every one here possesses of it? What is there that you did last night, what the night before—where is it that you were—who was

there that you summoned to meet you—what design was there which was adopted by you, with which you think that any one of us is unacquainted?

Shame on the age and on its principles! The senate is aware of these things; the consul sees them; and yet this man lives. Lives! aye, he comes even into the senate. He takes a part in the public deliberations; he is watching and marking down and checking off for slaughter every individual among us. And we, gallant men that we are, think that we are doing our duty to the Republic if we keep out of the way of his frenzied attacks.

You ought, O Catiline, long ago to have been led to execution by command of the consul. That destruction which you have been long plotting against us ought to have already fallen on your own head.

Source: *The World's Famous Orations,* 1906.

For Discussion

1. On what grounds did Sallust and Cicero condemn Catiline's conspiracy?
2. If Catiline had the support of the various groups of Romans that Sallust identified, why did his conspiracy fail?

Only a year later, however, while Sulla was still in Anatolia, Marius and the other consul, Cinna, won back political control of Rome. They declared Sulla an outlaw and killed many of his supporters in what became known as the Marian massacres. When Sulla returned to Italy in 82 B.C.E., at the head of a triumphant and loyal army, he seized Rome after a battle in which about 60,000 Roman soldiers died. He then murdered 3,000 of his political opponents. The Senate named Sulla dictator in 81 B.C.E., thereby giving him complete power. With the support of the Senate, whose authority he hoped to restore, Sulla restricted the power of tribunes to propose legislation because they had caused so much political instability for 50 years. After restoring the peace and the institutions of the state, and after becoming consul in 80 B.C.E, Sulla surprised many people by resigning the following year. Like Marius, Sulla was unwilling to destroy the Republic's institutions for the sake of his own ambition. It was enough for him to have restored peace and the pre-eminence of the Senate. Nevertheless, he had set a precedent for using armies in political rivalries. In the next 50 years the Senate conspicuously failed to restrain generals backed by their armies, thereby contributing to the collapse of the Republic.

The First Triumvirate

Three men provoked the Roman Republic's final downward spiral: Pompey (Gnaeus Pompeius, 106–48 B.C.E.), Marcus Licinius Crassus (ca. 115–53 B.C.E.), and Gaius Julius Caesar (100–44 B.C.E.). Pompey, the general who suppressed a revolt in Spain, and Crassus, the wealthiest man in Rome who had been one of Sulla's lieutenants, joined forces to crush the slave revolt of Spartacus in 71 B.C.E. Backed by their armies, they then became consuls for 70 B.C.E., even though Pompey was legally too young and had not yet held the prerequisite junior offices.

During their consulships, Pompey and Crassus made modest changes to Sulla's reforms. They permitted the tribunes to propose laws again and let equestrians serve on juries. After their year in office they retired without making further demands. Pompey continued his military career. In 67 B.C.E. he received a special command to clear pirates from the Mediterranean to protect Roman trade. The following year Pompey crushed the ongoing rebellion in Anatolia and reorganized the Near East, creating new provinces and more client kingdoms subservient to Rome.

When Pompey returned to Rome, he asked the Senate to grant land to his victorious troops. The Senate, jealous of his success and afraid of the power he would gain as the patron of so many veteran troops, refused. To gain land for his soldiers and have his political arrangements in the Near East ratified, Pompey made an alliance with two men even more ambitious than he: his old ally Crassus and Gaius Julius Caesar, the ambitious descendant of an ancient but poor patrician family. The three formed an informal alliance known as

CHRONOLOGY: SOCIAL CONFLICT IN ROME AND ITALY	
133 B.C.E.	Tiberius Gracchus initiates reforms
123–122 B.C.E.	Gaius Gracchus initiates reforms
107 B.C.E.	Marius's first consulship
104–100 B.C.E.	Marius holds consecutive consulships
90–88 B.C.E.	Rome fights "Social War" with Italian allies
88 B.C.E.	Sulla takes Rome
82–80 B.C.E.	Sulla serves as dictator
73–71 B.C.E.	Spartacus's slave revolt
70 B.C.E.	Cicero prosecutes Verres in court

the **First Triumvirate.** No man or institution could oppose their combined influence. Caesar obtained the consulship in 59 B.C.E., despite the objections of many senators. By using illegal means that would return to haunt him, he directed the Senate to ratify Pompey's arrangements in the Near East and grant land to his troops. He resolved the financial problems of Crassus's clients, the equestrian tax collectors, at public expense.

As a reward for his efforts, the perpetually debt-ridden Caesar arranged to receive the governorship of the Po Valley and Illyricum for five years after his consulship ended. Later he extended that term for ten years. During this time, he planned to enrich himself at the expense of the provincials. As he set out for his governorship, however, he was given command of Transalpine Gaul (northwest of the Alps), where the German chieftain Ariovistus threatened Roman security.

This change enabled Caesar to operate militarily in all of Gaul—and ultimately to conquer it.

Julius Caesar and the End of the Republic

Caesar's determination to conquer Gaul lay in his pursuit of personal political power. He knew that he could win glory, wealth, and prestige in Rome by conquering new lands, and to that end he promptly began a war (58–50 B.C.E.) against the Celtic tribes of Transalpine Gaul. A military genius, Caesar chronicled his ruthless tactics and victories in his *Commentaries on the Gallic War,* as famous today for its vigorous Latin as for its unflinching glimpse of Roman conquest, which resulted in the death or enslavement of about one million Celts. In eight years Caesar conquered the area of modern France, Belgium, and the

VERCINGETORIX SURRENDERS TO CAESAR

The Gallic chieftain Vercingetorix, who raised an army of Gallic tribes against Roman legions under Julius Caesar's command, was trapped in the stronghold of Alesia, near modern Dijon, in 52 B.C.E. Reinforcements failed to break the siege, and Vercingetorix was forced to surrender. Five years later he was publicly beheaded. This scene of Verncingetorix throwing down his weapons was painted by L. Royer in 1899.

Rhineland, turning these territories into Roman provinces. He even briefly invaded Britain. His intrusion into Celtic lands led to their eventual Romanization. The French language developed from the Latin spoken by Roman conquerors, as did the other "Romance" languages: Spanish, Italian, Portuguese, and Romanian.

Meanwhile, the other members of the triumvirate, Crassus and Pompey, also sought military glory. The wealthy Crassus failed to conquer the Parthians, the successors to the Persian Empire. In 53 B.C.E. the Parthians destroyed Crassus's army in Syria, killing Crassus himself and capturing the military insignia (metal eagles on staffs, called standards) that each legion proudly carried into battle. Pompey assumed the governorship of Spain, but stayed in Rome while subordinates fought Spain's Celtic inhabitants.

In Rome, a group of senators grew fearful of Caesar's power, ambitions, and arrogance. They appealed to Pompey for assistance, and he brought the armies loyal to him to the aid of the Senate against Caesar. The Senate then asked Caesar to lay down his command in Gaul and return to Rome. Caesar knew that if he complied with this request he would be indicted on charges of improper conduct or corruption as soon as he returned to Rome. Facing certain conviction, he refused to return for a trial. In 49 B.C.E. he left Gaul and marched south with his loyal troops against the forces of the Senate in Rome. Recognizing the magnitude of his gamble ("The die is cast!" he said when he crossed the Rubicon River, the legal boundary between Gaul and the territory of Roman under the direct control of the consuls), he deliberately plunged Rome into civil war. Because of his victories in

COIN FROM THE LATE ROMAN REPUBLIC

The front of this silver coin depicts the god Janus (after whom the month of January is named), who looked in two directions. The reverse depicts a Roman galley.

Gaul and his generosity to the people of Rome, Caesar could pose as the people's champion while seeking absolute power for himself. Intimidated by Caesar's forces and public support, Pompey withdrew to Greece, but Caesar overtook and defeated him there at Pharsalus in 48 B.C.E. When Pompey fled to Egypt, high officials in the Ptolemaic court murdered him to win Caesar's favor.

It took Caesar more than two years to complete his victory over Pompey's supporters and return to Italy in 45 B.C.E. Back in Rome, Caesar had himself proclaimed dictator for life and assumed complete control over the government, flagrantly disregarding the traditions of the Republic. Because he did not live to fully implement his plan, Caesar's long-term goals for the Roman state remain unclear, but he probably intended to establish some version of Hellenistic monarchy.

Once in power, Caesar permanently ended the autonomy of the Senate. He enlarged this body from 600 (its size at the time of Sulla) to 900 men, and then filled it with his supporters. He also established military colonies in Spain, North Africa, and Gaul to provide land for his veterans and to secure those territories. He adjusted the chaotic republican calendar by adding one day every fourth year, creating a year of 365.25 days. The resulting "Julian" calendar lasted in western Europe until the sixteenth century C.E. Caesar regularized gold coinage and urban administration and planned a vast public library. At his death, plans for a major campaign against Parthia were underway, suggesting that conquest would have remained a basic feature of his rule.

Caesar seriously miscalculated by assuming he could win over his enemies by showing them clemency and by making administrative changes that disregarded republican precedent. These changes earned Caesar the hatred of traditionalist senators who failed to recognize that the Republic was dead. On March 15, 44 B.C.E., a group of resentful and envious senators led by the idealistic Marcus Junius Brutus (85–42 B.C.E,) stabbed Caesar to death at a Senate meet-

ing. The assassins claimed that they wanted to restore the Republic, but they had only unleashed another civil war.

Marcus Antonius (Mark Antony), who had been Caesar's right-hand man, stepped forward to oppose the conspirators. He was soon joined by Gaius Julius Caesar Octavianus, (63 B.C.E.–14 C.E.), Caesar's grandnephew and legal heir, who became known as Octavian. Though Octavian was only 19, he gained control of some of Caesar's legions and compelled the Senate to name him consul. Marcus Lepidus, commander of Caesar's cavalry, joined Mark Antony and Octavian to form the **Second Triumvirate** in 43 B.C.E. The new trio coerced the Senate into granting them power to rule Rome legally. By ruling without the active participation of the consuls and the Senate, the Second Triumvirate maintained Rome as a Republic in name only.

At the Battle of Philippi, a town in Macedonia, in 42 B.C.E., forces of the Second Triumvirate crushed the army of Brutus and the senators who had assassinated Caesar. But soon Antony, Octavian, and Lepidus began to struggle among themselves for absolute authority. Lepidus, who had taken control of Spain and North Africa, was forced out of office in 36 B.C.E.; Antony and Octavian agreed to separate the spheres of influence. Octavian took Italy and Rome's western provinces, while Antony took the eastern provinces.

In Egypt, Antony joined forces with Cleopatra VII, the last Ptolemaic monarch to rule there. Both stood to gain from this alliance: Antony secured control of the resources of Egypt while Cleopatra got territory and influence. In response to this alliance, Octavian launched a vicious propaganda campaign. Posing as the conservative protector of Roman tradition, he accused Antony of surrendering Roman values and territory to an evil foreign seductress. The inevitable war broke out in 31 B.C.E. At the Battle of Actium in Greece, Octavian's troops and fleet defeated Antony and Cleopatra's land and naval forces. The couple fled to Alexandria, in Egypt, where they committed suicide a year later.

As we saw in Chapter 4, the Battle of Actium effectively marked the end of the Hellenistic age, which had begun with the creation of successor kingdoms after the death of Alexander the Great in 323 B.C.E. The battle also marked the end of the Roman Republic. Although Octavian, who was given the title Augustus by the Senate in 27 B.C.E., would preserve the forms of the Republic, he acquired effective absolute power in both Rome and the vast empire that Rome controlled. The transition from Republic to Empire also raised the question, which frequently recurred in the history of the West, whether republican political institutions were compatible with imperial power. The history of Athens and Rome suggests that they were not.

CONCLUSION

The Roman Republic and the West

The Roman Republic made four great contributions to the geographical and cultural area that would later be identified as the West. The first was the institution of republican government. Although Rome made many changes in its political institutions over the course of more than 500 years, it bequeathed to the West a model of a government that mixed features of the three forms of government identified by Aristotle and analyzed by Polybius: monarchy, aristocracy, and democracy. The Roman Republic served as a model of government for political communities in the West for the next two thousand years. Not least among them was the United States of America, which became a republic in the late eighteenth century when it declared its independence from Great Britain. By vesting executive power in a president rather than a monarch, just as Rome had given executive power to consuls, and by dividing the legislature into a Senate and a House of Representatives, the new American republic drew inspiration from the history of the Roman Republic. The most important difference between the institutions of the two republics was that the aristocratic Roman Senate played a much greater role than its American counterpart in the government of the republic. Although in theory the Roman Senate was mainly an advisory body that had little formal power, its influence over the consuls and other magistrates was considerable.

Second, the Roman Republic transmitted to the West the ideal of **civic virtue**, the belief that the success of a republic depended on its citizens' possession of personal traits that contributed to the common good. These virtues included *gravitas* (which meant dignity, seriousness, and duty), piety, and justice. Aristotle had emphasized the importance of civic virtue in his claim that citizenship consisted in political duties rather than political rights. There was little discussion of civic virtue in the Hellenistic monarchies, but a revival and development of the concept took place in the Roman Republic. During the late years of the Republic, moral philosophers and historians blamed the loss of Roman liberty on the perceived loss of civic virtue. The idea of civic virtue modelled on that of republican Rome profoundly influenced the history of the West, especially during the Renaissance in the fifteenth and sixteenth centuries, the Enlightenment in the eighteenth century, and the early years of the United States in the late eighteenth and early nineteenth centuries.

The third legacy that Rome bequeathed to the West was its legal system. Based originally upon the Law of the Twelve Tables, and developed gradually through judicial interpretation and eventual codification in the late imperial period, Roman law became the basis of most Western legal systems. Roman law systems in the West were rivalled only by those that followed the English system of common law. Many of the legal traditions associated with both English and Roman law, however, including the participation of citizens in the legal process, originated in the Roman Republic.

The fourth and arguably the most important legacy of Rome to the West was Greco–Roman culture. This distinctive Roman version of Hellenism represented a creative synthesis of Greek and Roman culture. In art and philosophy Roman culture was largely derivative of that of Greece, but in architecture and literature it represented a creative adaptation of the cultures that Romans encountered. Greco Roman culture also preserved a large body of Greek art and philosophy, much of which has survived only through Roman imitations and translations. Credit for the successful transmission of Greco–Roman culture to subsequent generations can be attributed to the long period of peace, the *pax romana*, that prevailed from 31 B.C.E. to 180 C.E. To that period of Roman world dominance, the Roman Empire, we now turn.

KEY TERMS

Roman Forum	*Corpus Juris Civilis*
Roman Republic	Latin War
republic	Oppian Law
patricians	patrons and clients
plebeians	Social War
Struggle of the Orders	First Triumvirate
Law of the Twelve Tables	Second Triumvirate
jus gentium	civic virtue
natural law	

CHAPTER QUESTIONS

1. What type of government did Rome establish when it eliminated kingship, and what social groups competed for power in this state? (page 136)
2. How did the Roman Republic come to dominate the Mediterranean world during the Hellenistic Age? (page 143)
3. How did the Roman encounter with Greek culture in the Hellenistic world lead to the forging of a durable Greco–Roman cultural synthesis? (page 150)
4. How was Roman society structured, and what relationships existed within the Roman family? (page 156)
5. Why did the Roman Republic end? (page 158)

TAKING IT FURTHER

1. The Roman Republic rose to power during the Hellenistic period. In what sense were its political institutions and culture Hellenistic?
2. To what extent did Roman territorial expansion lead to the fall of the Roman Republic?
3. How did Romans model their society on that of classical and Hellenistic Greece? How did they modify or reject that cultural inheritance?
4. Compare the political institutions of the Roman Republic with those of the United States of America in the late eighteenth century.

✓• Practice on MyHistoryLab

Enclosing the West: The Early Roman Empire and Its Neighbors, 31 B.C.E.–235 C.E.

■ The Imperial Center ■ Life in the Roman Provinces: Assimilation, Resistance, and Romanization ■ The Frontier and Beyond
■ Society and Culture in the Imperial Age

IN 155 C.E., AELIUS ARISTIDES, AN ARISTOCRATIC GREEK WRITER WHO HELD ROMAN citizenship, visited Rome, where he gave a public oration in honor of the imperial capital. His words reveal what the Roman Empire meant to a wealthy, educated man from Rome's eastern provinces. According to Aristides, the trait "most worthy of consideration and admiration" in the Roman system was that "everywhere you have made citizens all those who are the more accomplished, noble and powerful people." A man might live thousands of miles from the city of Rome, and yet "neither does the sea nor a great expanse of intervening land keep one from being a citizen.... [Rome] has never refused anyone. But just as the earth's ground supports all men, so it too receives men from every land." Aristides' vision points to the key of the Romans' success—a willingness to assimilate their subjects into Rome's political and social life. Aristides believed that by transforming "non-Romans" into Romans, Rome's imperial expansion brought civilization to the world.

Aristides' praise demonstrates Rome's success in creating a sense of common purpose among its citizens. During its first 250 years of existence, the empire brought cultural unity and political stability to an area stretching from the Atlantic Ocean to the Persian Gulf. The imperial regime brought peace to the Mediterranean world for more than two centuries. Historians call this era the **Pax Romana**, the Roman Peace. But for the slaves whose labor fueled the economy and the small farmers whose taxes supported the state, Roman rule could mean oppression and impoverishment.

This chapter analyzes the Roman Empire as three concentric circles of power—the imperial center, the provinces, and the frontiers and beyond. In the imperial center stood not only the emperor but also the Roman Senate, the chief legal and administrative institutions, and the city of Rome itself, an important model of the Roman way of life. In the second circle, provincial populations struggled with the challenges posed by the imposition of Roman rule, and in the process, helped construct a new imperial culture. The outermost circle of the empire, its frontier zones and the lands beyond, included Romans living within

A HARBOR TOWN
This first-century fresco, found in a Roman villa near Pompeii, offers us a glimpse of the lively seafaring trade that helped maintain the Roman Empire.

the empire's borders and the peoples who lived on the other side, but interacted with Rome through trade and warfare. By exploring what it meant to be a Roman in each of these circles, this chapter seeks to answer a key question: How did the encounters between the Romans and the peoples they conquered transform the Mediterranean world and create a Roman imperial culture?

THE IMPERIAL CENTER

■ How did the Roman imperial system develop, and what roles did the emperor, Senate, army, and city of Rome play in this process?

After civil wars destroyed the Roman Republic, a new political system emerged. Rome's form of

government changed from a republic, in which members of an oligarchy competed for power, to an empire, in which one man, the emperor, held absolute power for life. Roman culture was now anchored by an imperial system based on force (see **Map 6.1**).

Imperial Authority: Augustus and After

As we saw in Chapter 5, Julius Caesar's heir, Octavian (63 B.C.E.–14 C.E.), wrenched the state from the spiral of civil war and claimed that he had restored normal life to the Republic. In fact, Octavian destroyed the Republic while pretending to preserve it. In his own eyes, and those of a people weary of war, Octavian was the savior of *republican* Rome. Yet behind a façade of restored republican tradition, Octavian created a Roman version of a Hellenistic monarchy. By neutralizing

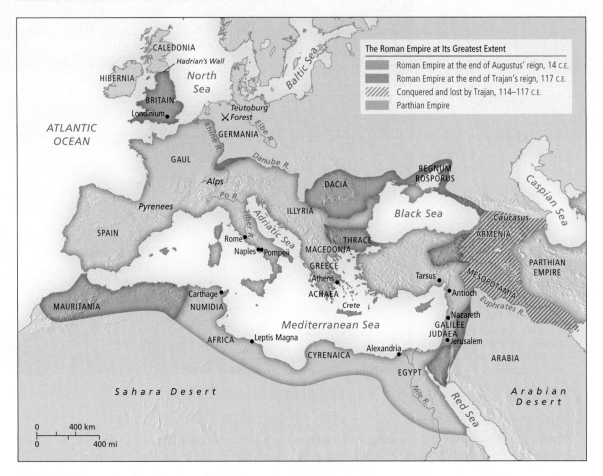

MAP 6.1

The Roman Empire at Its Greatest Extent

The Roman Empire reached its greatest extent during the reign of Trajan (r. 98–117). Stretching from the north of Britain to the Euphrates River, the empire brought together hundreds of distinct ethnic groups.

his political enemies in the Roman Senate, vanquishing his military rivals, and establishing an iron grip on every mechanism of power, Octavian succeeded where Julius Caesar and other republican politicians had failed: He achieved total mastery of the political arena at Rome. No one successfully challenged his authority.

To mask his tyranny, Octavian never wore a crown and modestly referred to himself as *Princeps*, or First Citizen. His position in Rome was all-powerful yet unobtrusive. In 27 B.C.E., as he boasted in the official account of his

reign, he "transferred the Republic from his power into that of the Senate and the Roman people." This abdication was a sham and few people were fooled. Following Octavian's instructions, the Senate showered honors on him, including the name "Augustus" (which is how we will refer to him throughout the rest of this chapter). *Augustus* means "the revered" and implied an exalted, godlike authority. (It became the title of all subsequent emperors.) Augustus "accepted" the Senate's plea to remain consul and agreed to control the frontier

AUGUSTUS: A COMMANDING PRESENCE

This statue of Augustus dating to 19 B.C.E. depicts him as a warrior making a gesture of command. His face is ageless, the carving on his armor celebrates peace and prosperity, and his posture is balanced and forceful.

provinces where the most troops were stationed, including Spain, Gaul, Germany, and Syria. The senators rejoiced, calling Augustus "sole savior of the entire empire."

In 23 B.C.E. Augustus renounced the consulship and was voted the powers of tribune for life. A tribune's power gave Augustus the right to conduct business in the Senate and veto legislation. It also conferred immunity from arrest and punishment. He could now legally interfere in all political and military affairs in the provinces. Augustus personally controlled Egypt, the richest province, as successor to the pharaohs, and soldiers swore an oath of allegiance to him. Other

generals led legions into battle, but always in his name. Other magistrates officially administered the state, but no one was chosen without his approval.

THE PROBLEM OF SUCCESSION Like a Hellenistic monarch, Augustus hoped to pass power down through his family. When he died, his stepson Tiberius (r. 14–37 C.E.) took control of the empire without opposition. Officially Rome remained a republic, but in fact a hereditary monarchy was now in place. For more than half a century, every ruler came from Augustus's extended family—the **Julio–Claudian dynasty.** Some senators muttered about restoring the Republic, but this remained an idle—and dangerous—dream. Neither the army nor the people would have supported a Senate-led republican rebellion.

Hereditary monarchy promised to stave off the instability that accompanied open competition for power. But such open competition, and such instability, returned to Rome after the last of Augustus's line, Nero, committed suicide in the face of rebellion in 68. He left no heir, and four men claimed power over the next year, as Roman armies competed to put their commanders on the throne. This "Year of the Four Emperors" revealed that Rome was more of a military dictatorship than a hereditary monarchy: Whoever held the loyalty of the armies controlled Rome, as the history of the next two centuries made clear.

The general Titus Flavius Vespasianus, or Vespasian (r. 69–79), emerged as the victor from the "Year of the Four Emperors." The **Flavian dynasty** that he established lasted just 25 years, until the death of his last son, Domitian (r. 81–96). A conscientious and able monarch, Domitian nevertheless ruled with an openly autocratic style. He created a reign of terror among Rome's elite until a group of senators murdered him.

To avoid another succession crisis, the Senate cooperated with the army in choosing a new emperor, the elderly senator Nerva (r. 96–98). They hoped that this respected man who had no sons would ensure orderly government, and so he did. Under pressure from the military, Nerva adopted the general Trajan (r. 98–117) as his son and heir. He thus inaugurated the era historians call the **Antonine Age**. For almost a century (96–180), Rome enjoyed competent rule because Nerva's practice of adopting highly qualified successors continued. After Trajan adopted Hadrian (r. 117–138), Hadrian in turn adopted Antoninus Pius (r. 138–161), and Antoninus adopted Marcus Aurelius (r. 161–180) as his successor. The Roman historian Tacitus (ca. 55–120) praised these emperors for establishing "the rare happiness of times, when we may think what we please, and express what we think."

This time of peace ended with another imperial murder. Unlike his immediate predecessors, Marcus Aurelius had a son. So he abandoned the custom of picking a qualified successor, and instead was followed to the throne by his incompetent, cruel, and eventually insane son, Commodus (r. 180–192). Conspirators within the imperial palace arranged to have Commodus strangled in 192, triggering another civil war.

A senator from North Africa, Septimius Severus, emerged victorious from this conflict and assumed the imperial throne (r. 193–211). Septimius Severus exemplified the ascent of provincial aristocrats to the highest levels of the empire. The **Severan dynasty** lasted until 235. Septimius Severus was popular with the army—he raised its pay for the first time in more than 100 years. But when the last emperor of his dynasty, Severus Alexander (r. 222–235), attempted to bribe the German tribes instead of fighting them, his own troops killed him because they wanted the cash for themselves. Again, the murder of an emperor provoked civil war. Fifty years of political and economic crises followed the end of the Severan dynasty. As we will see in Chapter 7, the imperial structure that emerged after this time of crisis differed significantly from the Augustan model.

CHRONOLOGY: DYNASTIES OF ROME

27 B.C.E.–68 C.E.	Julio–Claudian dynasty
69–96	Flavian dynasty
96–192	Antonine dynasty
193–235	Severan dynasty

THE EMPEROR'S ROLE: THE NATURE OF IMPERIAL POWER Under the Augustan imperial system, the emperor had four main responsibilities. First, he protected and expanded imperial territory. Only the emperor determined foreign policy, made treaties with other nations, and waged war, whether to protect the empire from its enemies or expand the empire with aggressive campaigns of conquest.

Second, the emperor administered justice and provided good government. In theory all citizens could appeal directly to him for justice. The emperor and his staff also responded to questions on points of law and administration from provincial governors and other officials who ruled in the emperor's name. Emperors provided emergency relief after natural disasters, looked after the roads and infrastructure of the empire, and financed public works in many provincial cities. During his long reign Augustus—the wealthiest individual in the empire—used his personal fortune to pay his soldiers, erect public buildings, and sponsor public spectacles such as gladiatorial contests.

The emperor's third responsibility stemmed from his religious role. As *Pontifex Maximus*, or High Priest, the emperor supervised the public worship of the gods of Rome, particularly Jupiter. Emperors and subjects alike believed that to fulfill Rome's destiny to rule the world, they needed to make regular sacrifices to the gods.

Finally, the emperor became a symbol of unity for the peoples of the empire. Inevitably, the emperor seemed more than human, even worthy of worship, for he was the guarantor of peace, prosperity, and victory for Rome, and had more power than any other living person.

Worship of the emperor began with Augustus. He was reluctant to call himself a god because Roman tradition opposed such an idea, but he permitted his spirit to be worshiped as a sort of *paterfamilias* or head of a universal family of peoples of the empire. He also referred to himself as the "son of a god"—in this case Julius Caesar, whom the Senate had declared divine. After Augustus, imperial worship became more pronounced, although few emperors, such as Domitian, emphasized their divinity during their lifetimes. Most were content to be worshiped after death. On his deathbed, Vespasian managed to joke, "I guess I'm becoming a god now."

In Rome's eastern provinces such as Egypt, where people for thousands of years had considered their kings divine, the worship of the emperor spread quickly. Each city's official calendar marked the emperor's day of accession to the throne. Soon, cities across the empire worshiped the emperor on special occasions through games, speeches, sacrifices, and public feasts. This cult of the emperor provided a common focus of allegiance for the empire's diverse peoples. Although most people would never see their ruler, he was in their prayers every day.

He was also in their public spaces. Emperors built and restored roads, temples, harbors, aqueducts, and fortifications. These public works demonstrated the emperor's unparalleled patronage and concern for the public welfare. In turn, local aristocrats emulated his generosity by financing lavish building projects in their own cities.

Other elements of material culture also made the imperial presence real for the emperor's subjects. Coins, for example, provided a glimpse of the emperor's face and a phrase that characterized some aspect of his reign. Slogans such as "Restorer of the World," "Concord with the Gods," and "The Best Ruler—Sustenance for Italy" brought the ruler's message into every person's pocket. Statues of the emperor served a similar purpose. (One statue in Carthage in North Africa had a removable head, so that when a new emperor ascended the throne, the town leaders could save money by replacing only the head instead of the whole statue.)

Emperors also used military victories to celebrate their reigns. In the Republic, conquest had brought wealth and glory to generals. In the new imperial system, only the emperor could take credit for victory. Imperial propaganda described the emperor as eternally triumphant.

The City of Rome

The city of Rome stood as a monument to the authority of the emperor. Augustus boasted that he had found Rome built of brick and left it made of marble. Though an exaggeration, this claim reveals the effect of monarchy on Rome's urban fabric. Every emperor wanted to leave his mark on the city as a testimony to his generosity and power. As Rome grew, it became the model for cities throughout the empire. Its public spaces and buildings provided a stage for imperial rule (see **Map 6.2**).

The center of political and public life in Rome was the Roman Forum, a field filled with imposing buildings that housed the treasury and records office, law courts, and the Senate House. Roman law, inscribed on gleaming bronze tablets and placed on the outer walls of these buildings, testified to the principles of justice and order that formed the framework of the Roman state. Basilicas, colonnaded halls in which Romans conducted public business ranging from finance to trials, crowded against the sides of the Forum.

Because public and religious life was intertwined, the Forum also contained temples of the gods who controlled Rome's destiny. Statues to the goddesses Victory and Concord stood in the Senate, while the huge marble temple of Jupiter "Best and Greatest," Rome's chief god, looked down on the Forum from the Capitoline Hill.

The Forum highlighted the emperor's power. Emperors built triumphal arches there. After a victorious military campaign, emperors and their troops paraded through the Forum on the Sacred Way, passed under the arches, and finished at the temple of Jupiter. Delighted crowds watched

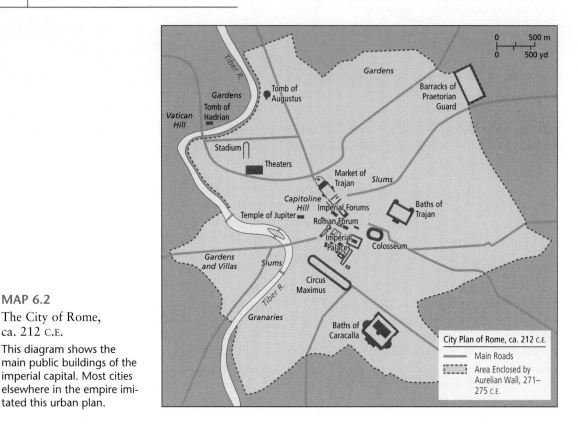

MAP 6.2

The City of Rome, ca. 212 C.E.

This diagram shows the main public buildings of the imperial capital. Most cities elsewhere in the empire imitated this urban plan.

defeated kings pass by in chains and marveled at floats piled with loot and slaves carrying paintings depicting the war.

The might of the emperor was on display throughout the city. Emperors spent gigantic sums on stadiums and additional forums. Trajan's Forum included libraries of Greek and Latin texts, an enormous basilica, a multistoried marketplace, and a marble column 125-feet high on which was carved the story of his conquest of Dacia (modern Romania) in 101–106. The huge arena called the Colosseum, built by Vespasian and his son Titus (r. 79–81), provided a spot in the heart of the city where 50,000 spectators could cheer the slaughter of men and animals Emperors also built and maintained luxurious public baths. Eleven aqueducts provided Rome with 300 million gallons of water every day for these baths, the city's many fountains, and those houses that had indoor plumbing.

To erect their monumental buildings, the Romans developed new architectural techniques. They were the first to build extensively in concrete (and may have invented it), which allowed them to develop new methods of construction such as the vault. The Pantheon, built by Hadrian in 126, is the largest ancient roofed building still standing today. With a diameter of 142 feet, its dome has no interior supports.

Emperors built their palaces on the Palatine Hill, which looked down on the Forum, and mansions covered nearby hills. Wealthy citizens lived in luxury that would not be equaled in the West for centuries. In contrast, the impoverished majority of Rome's inhabitants lived in filthy slums in the valleys between Rome's seven hills or along the Tiber River, where they crowded into apartment buildings up to six stories high. Lacking solid foundations, apartment buildings often collapsed and could become firetraps. (It is

THE PANTHEON

Reconstructed during the reign of Hadrian between 118 and 126 C.E., the Pantheon demonstrates Roman engineering skills and the sophisticated trade and transportation network that helped hold the Empire together. The Pantheon's interior dome, the largest in the world until the erection of the Cathedral of Florence in 1436, was made out of layers of concrete of varying thicknesses with no interior supports. The Pantheon's outside porch rests on 18 massive granite columns, each 39 feet tall and weighing 60 tons. Quarried in Egypt, these pillars were floated on barges up the Nile to Alexandria, where they were loaded onto ships bound for the Roman port of Ostia, and then barged up the Tiber to Rome. The name "pantheon" means "temple to all the gods," an apt name for a building that served as a temple to all of Rome's gods until it was converted into a Christian church in the seventh century.

not a surprise that Augustus established the first professional fire department in Western history.)

The Agents of Control

The emperor stood at the heart of the empire, but the imperial center included other agents of control, the most important of which were the Roman Senate and the army.

THE ROMAN SENATE: FROM AUTONOMY TO ADMINIS-TRATION The Empire retained most of the basic machinery of government inherited from the Republic—but it operated in conformity with the emperor's wishes. The emperor, not the Senate, now controlled military, financial, and diplomatic policy. Free political debate was silenced. Because he wanted to avoid the competition for power that had destroyed the Republic, Augustus eliminated his opponents and filled the Senate with loyal supporters. Nevertheless, to maintain the illusion that he had saved rather than destroyed the Republic and because senators as a class were the wealthiest, most influential men in Rome, Augustus took pains to show respect for the Senate.

Deprived of its autonomy, the Senate became an administrative arm of imperial rule. Senators served as provincial governors, army commanders, judges, and financial officers. They managed the water and grain supplies of the city of Rome, and some of them served on the emperor's advisory council. Senators learned to serve the empire faithfully, even if they disliked the emperor personally.

Emperors often brought able new men into the Senate from the provinces. This practice gave provincial elites a stake in the imperial enterprise. By the end of the third century more than half of Rome's 600 or so senators came from outside Italy.

While the emperor's relationship with the Senate was of primary importance, other social ranks were also prominent in imperial administration. Many members of the equestrian class served in government positions. Emperors also employed freedmen and even slaves on their administrative staffs and benefited from their loyalty and competence.

THE ROMAN ARMY AND THE POWER OF THE EMPEROR The Roman army was another crucial component of imperial rule. The army could make or depose an emperor—something that every ruler understood. Without the army's support, Augustus would never have succeeded in remaking the Republican regime into his imperial system.

Augustus created a highly efficient professional army that served as the bulwark of the empire for nearly 250 years. His first step was to reduce the army from 60 legions to between 25 and 30 legions, so that the legionary troops now totaled 150,000 citizens. To solidify their loyalty, Augustus established regular terms of service and ample retirement benefits for veterans and their families.

Soldiers drawn from subject peoples who were not citizens served as **auxiliary** troops. After completing their years of service, auxiliaries received Roman citizenship—an important incentive for recruitment. The combined legions and auxiliaries brought the military strength of the Roman army to 300,000 men.

Legionaries enlisted for 20 years of active service (with another five in reserve), but only about half survived to retirement. Short life

expectancy rather than death in battle kept the survival figure low, although regular rations and medical care may have helped soldiers live longer than civilians. A soldier with special skills, such as literacy, could rise through the ranks and become an officer. For those who survived their service, Augustus established military colonies in Italy and the provinces. He rewarded more than 100,000 veterans with land. Later emperors continued this practice.

The imperial army epitomized Roman imperial values. It maintained a high degree of organization, discipline, and training—characteristics on which Romans prided themselves. To the Romans, strict military discipline distinguished their soldiers from disorganized barbarians. Military punishments were ferocious. For example, if a soldier fell asleep during sentry duty, his barrack mates were required to beat him to death. But tight discipline and vigorous training produced effective fighters. To keep in fighting shape, troops constantly drilled in weaponry, camp building, and battle formations. A Roman soldier was expected to march 20 miles in four hours—while carrying his 40-pound pack and swimming across rivers encountered along the way.

LIFE IN THE ROMAN PROVINCES: ASSIMILATION, RESISTANCE, AND ROMANIZATION

■ How did provincial peoples assimilate to or resist Roman rule?

Beyond the city of Rome and the imperial center lay the second concentric circle of power, the Roman Empire's provinces. In these regions some people assimilated readily to Roman ways, while others resisted. Unlike the Greeks of the Classical Age, Romans in the imperial era were willing to assimilate the peoples they conquered into Rome's political and cultural life. Formal grants of Roman citizenship gave many people the legal rights and privileges of being Roman.

The Army: A Romanizing Force

The army played an important role in **Romanization**, the process of educating subject peoples in Roman cultural and political practices. Provincial recruits learned Roman ways during their service. Latin, the language of command and army administration, provided another common bond to men whose mother tongues reflected the empire's ethnic diversity.

Each of the legions with a contingent of auxiliary troops was stationed as a permanent garrison in a province with an elaborate logistical infrastructure to provide weapons, food, and housing. Camp architecture and fortifications, as well as weapons, armor, and tactics, followed the same conventions across the empire, thus reinforcing the army's role as a Romanizing force. Generals and staff officers often had postings in different provinces during their careers and so developed a sense of shared enterprise.

Retired Roman soldiers who settled in the provinces also served as a Romanizing force. Until the end of the second century C.E., soldiers could not legally marry during their military service, but many men reared families anyway with local women. Sons born to such unions frequently followed their fathers into the army. At retirement, most soldiers stayed near the bases in which they had been stationed. Many towns arose full of former military personnel and their friends, families, and small businesses. These towns helped transmit Roman culture and values to provincial peoples.

Occupation, Administration, and Commerce

Romanization was neither quick nor unopposed. Revolts against Roman authority often followed soon after a subject people's initial defeat, while freedom was still a living memory. Roman force, however, usually—but not always—proved overwhelming.

One such uprising occurred in Britain. After the conquest of Britain in 43 C.E., several British kingdoms supplied troops to the Roman army in return for protection and a degree of autonomy. But in 60 the Emperor Nero annexed one such kingdom, the Iceni. Emboldened by their new dominance, the Roman agents abused Queen Boudicca and raped her daughters. The queen then led the Iceni into open rebellion. With the aid of neighboring tribes who also resented the Romans, Boudicca destroyed a legion and leveled several cities. Resistance, however, ended quickly in 61 after Roman forces routed Boudicca's troops, and the queen took her own life. The Britons, like other peoples before and after them, learned that resistance to Rome was futile.

The tension between Roman armies and provincial populations never entirely disappeared, but gradually the conquered peoples became Romanized. They adopted Roman customs, and provincial elites began to enter Roman politics. Romanization transformed the provinces from occupied zones where shattered communities obeyed foreign masters to well-integrated territories in which Roman culture flourished, and the population came to think of themselves as Romans.

The Romanization of conquered peoples coincided with the absorption of conquered territories into the Roman provincial system. A governor ruled each province: He and a small staff administered justice, supervised tax collection, and orchestrated the flow of goods back to Rome. This structure of government created an administrative-military class that drew its members from the senatorial and the equestrian orders. In the service of the emperor, these men climbed the ladder of success through appointments in different provinces. Gnaeus Julius Agricola (40–93) is an apt example. The father-in-law of the historian, Tacitus, Agricola had a brilliant military career, yet as governor of Britain, he co-opted the defeated elites into the Roman way of life. (See *Different Voices* in this chapter.)

Transport and commercial networks connected the provinces to Rome. Soldiers marched on the 40,000 miles of paved roads crisscrossing the empire, but because transporting goods by land remained more expensive than moving them by water, rivers and the Mediterranean were the primary arteries of trade. With pirates quelled by Roman fleets, shipping flourished. Improved harbors, ports, and canals further encouraged long-distance trade.

The Cities

The Roman way of life manifested itself most noticeably in cities. Provincial cities became "little Romes." They served the empire by funneling wealth from its massive hinterland into imperial coffers. As centers for tax collection and law courts, cities were where the imperial administrators interacted with provincial aristocrats, who dominated the local population. More than 1,000 cities eventually dotted the imperial map (see **Map 6.3**).

In the West where urban traditions were largely absent, the Romans created new cities, such as Lugdunum (Lyons) in France and Eburacum (York) in Britain. These new urban centers imitated the city of Rome in their physical and architectural layout. All of them had a forum in their center, flanked by a council house (modeled on the Roman Senate), basilicas, and temples. The cities provided all the amenities and requirements of Roman urban life, such as bathhouses, brothels, arenas for gladiatorial combat and wild beast hunts, and slave markets. Main streets in the towns led to the Roman road system.

Such cities were an important Romanizing force. Local elites started to speak Latin, identify local gods with Roman gods, adopt Roman architecture and styles of art, and enjoy the Roman way of life. Often these elites also received the reward of Roman citizenship. Some even entered the Roman Senate.

Common patterns characterized urban life throughout the empire. Women held no

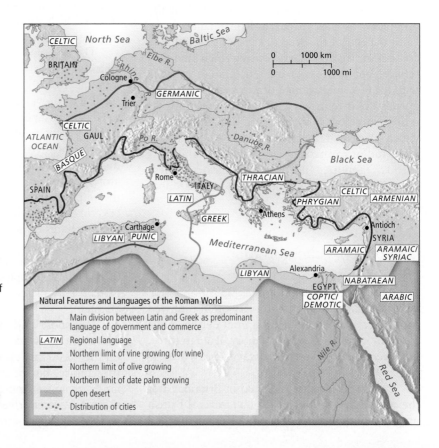

MAP 6.3

Languages and Agriculture in the Roman Empire

The 50 million inhabitants of the Roman Empire spoke many different languages, but the two most dominant were Greek in the east and Latin in the west. Another important division was that between the wine-drinking regions in the south and the beer-drinking territories in the north.

LITTLE ROMES

Built in the early third century C.E., the amphitheater at the Tunisian town of El-Djem (the ancient city of Thysdrus) was one of the largest in the empire. Like the Colosseum in Rome, which it imitated, this arena sat thousands of spectators at gladiatorial fights and other entertainments.

Source: Dagli Orti/Picture Desk, Inc./Kobal Collection

administrative office and had no role in public decision making, although wealthy women sometimes presided as priestesses in civic religious observances. The male citizens of each city voted on local issues and elected town officials. A city council modeled on the Roman Senate presided over each city's affairs. A handful of the community's wealthiest men served in the city council or as magistrates and priests. The councils managed the grain supply, arranged for army recruitment, supervised the marketplaces, administered justice in local law courts, and most important of all, collected taxes for the central government. In imitation of the emperor, councilors paid out of their own pockets for the upkeep of public works,

aqueducts, and baths, and funded religious festivals and public amusements.

The Countryside

As Roman culture came to predominate in urban centers, the division between city and countryside widened. Provincial urban elites benefited from efficient and orderly government. In contrast, rural inhabitants, who formed most of the empire's population, faced economic exploitation and threats to their ways of life.

Despite the growth of trade, the Roman Empire was an agrarian state, and peasants performed the agricultural labor that drove the empire's economy. Some peasants rented their lands from landlords to whom they owed payment in the form of produce, money, or labor. If they failed to pay the rent, they could be punished or enslaved. Other peasants owned small farms sufficient to maintain their families, perhaps with the assistance of seasonal wage laborers or a few slaves. These landowning peasants faced the threat that a more powerful landowner might seize their fields by force. When this happened, peasants had little hope of getting their land back. The imperial system favored the wealthy and worked to the disadvantage of the rural poor. Rabbi Hanina ben Hama, who lived in Palestine about 240, stated bluntly that the empire established cities "to impose upon the people forced labor, extortion and oppression." Famine and natural disasters also posed a constant threat. A bad harvest could mean that peasants would have to sell their land or starve.

Despite these hardships, the peasantry managed to produce enough food to maintain the imperial system, especially the army. Indeed, agricultural productivity during this era was remarkable, considering the low yields of farms, the difficulty and expense of transportation, and the rudimentary technology. Some historians estimate that Europe did not see a comparable level of agricultural productivity again until the seventeenth century.

Food staples in the Mediterranean region included olives, grains, beans, and wine. Pasta had not yet appeared in Italy, and the tomato was unknown in Europe before the sixteenth century, when it was imported from the Americas. Wheat, often cooked in water to make porridge, was the Roman staple. Only the wealthy could afford to eat meat often. Most people relied on cheese, beans, and vegetables such as cabbage, garlic, and onions to supplement their wheat rations. The Romans did not have sugar, but most Romans seemed to enjoy sweets: They ate quantities of dates and honey.

Terrain, climate, and local farming customs determined the type of agriculture practiced. In Sicily and parts of southern Italy, chain gangs of slaves working on vast estates planted and harvested the crops. Migrant workers labored in the olive groves and wheat fields of Spain and North Africa, while seasonal movement of grazing animals predominated in the hilly regions of Italy and the Balkans.

Law, Citizenship, and Romanization

In the early empire, Roman law set Romans apart from the bulk of the population who followed their own laws. For example, Jews lived according to Jewish law or Athenians by Athenian law, as long as they paid their taxes to the emperor and did not cause trouble. If a Jew or an Athenian held Roman citizenship, however, he could also enjoy the rights and benefits of Roman law in addition to being the citizen of his native city. A Roman citizen possessed legally defined rights, including the guarantee of freedom from enslavement. Male citizens had the right to compete for public magistracies, vote in public assemblies, serve in the legions, and make an appeal in a criminal trial.

The peace and prosperity of the first and second centuries encouraged the spread of Roman citizenship and the dominance of Roman law. No matter where they lived, Roman citizens took pride in their legal tradition and rights of citizenship. Roman law thus helped erode local loyalties and traditions and so furthered Romanization.

Then, in 212, Emperor Caracalla (r. 211–217) issued what became known as the **Antonine Decree**, which granted citizenship to virtually all free men and women within the empire, perhaps to increase the tax base. Legal uniformity further strengthened provincial loyalty to Rome.

Roman law made three important contributions to Western legal practices. First, the Romans created a standard feature of Western legal systems: the distinction between civil and criminal law. In Rome, civil law dealt with all aspects of family life, property and inheritance, slavery, and citizenship. It thus defined relations among different classes of Roman society and enabled courts to judge disputes among citizens. Criminal law addressed theft, homicide, sexual crimes, treason, and offenses against the government.

Second, Roman law influenced Western traditions of legal codification and interpretation. By

CHRONOLOGY: POLITICAL AND MILITARY EVENTS

31 B.C.E.	Octavian defeats Mark Antony and controls Mediterranean world
27 B.C.E.	Octavian given the title Augustus
9 CA.E.	Varus and three legions are defeated; Romans abandon Germany
ca. 30 C.E.	Jesus executed in Palestine
63	Revolt of Boudicca crushed in Britain
66–70	Jewish Revolt; Temple and Jerusalem destroyed
69	"Year of the Four Emperors"
101–106	Trajan conquers Dacia
115–116	Trajan conquers Mesopotamia; Rome reaches greatest extent
122–128	Hadrian's Wall built in Britain
132–135	Hadrian crushes Jewish revolt in Judaea
168	Marcus Aurelius defeats the Marcomanni
212	Antonine Decree grants Roman citizenship to all free inhabitants of the empire
235	Fifty years of political turmoil begin

the second century C.E., professional jurists (legal experts) directed imperial legal affairs under the supervision of the emperor. Combining legal scholarship, teaching, and administrative careers, jurists such as Ulpian (d. 228) collected and analyzed earlier laws and judges' opinions. The jurists wrote hundreds of commentaries that shaped the interpretation of Roman law for centuries, were passed on to the lawyers of medieval Europe, and still influence legal traditions. One such interpretative tradition is that under the principle of what the Romans called "equity," or fairness, judges should consider the spirit or intent rather than simply the letter of the law. According to Ulpian, "Law is the art of the good and the fair." On the basis of equity, Roman jurists argued that an accuser bears the burden of proof. A defendant does not have to prove he or she is innocent. Rather, he or she must be proven guilty.

Third, the Roman concept of "the law of nature" influenced Western ideas of justice. This concept stemmed in part from Stoicism (see Chapter 4), with its ideal of an underlying order to all things. From this ideal came the idea that certain principles of justice are part of nature itself, and thus that human laws should conform to natural law. Building on this Roman concept, later thinkers insisted that all human beings have inalienable rights and should be treated equally under the law.

Equality under the law did not, however, exist in the Roman imperial age. Roman citizens had more rights than noncitizens, but not all Roman citizens had the same rights. In the first century C.E. laws began to reflect the differences in wealth that divided citizens. By the third century, law, especially criminal law, distinguished between the wealthy upper class, generally called *honestiores* or "better people," and the poor, called *humiliores* or "humbler people." For example, *honestiores* could not be tortured to force them to give evidence, and if they were convicted of a capital crime, they received a quick death by sword. The "humbler people" received gruesome punishments, such as being burned alive or being thrown to wild animals in the arena.

As the legal distinctions between better and humbler peoples illustrates, Roman law shifted to mirror the new hierarchies of imperial Rome. Control of the law, which had rested with citizen assemblies and magistrates during the Republic, now lay with the emperor. The idea that the emperor's wishes had the force of law was widely accepted by the early third century.

DIFFERENT VOICES ROMAN RULE: BANE OR BLESSING?

In his epic poem, the Aeneid, *the poet Virgil (70–19 B.C.E.) provided Rome with a founding myth that identified the central features of Roman imperial pride:*

> Other men will shape molten bronze with greater artistry;...others will plead cases with more skill,...and will predict the rising constellations. You, Roman, do not fail to govern all people with your supreme authority. *These* will be your skills: to establish law and order within a framework of peace, to be merciful to those who submit, to crush in war those who are arrogant.

As this quotation shows, Roman cultural identity centered on the belief that Romans had a genius for governing and therefore that the spread of Roman rule brought unparalleled benefits not only to Rome, but to those Rome conquered. Yet thoughtful Romans were aware that many peoples experienced Roman rule as oppressive. In the selections that follow, we see the struggles of one such Roman, the great historian Tacitus (ca. 55–120), to acknowledge the complex implications of the "Pax Romana." In addition to writing history, Tacitus climbed the political ranks, becoming consul under Nerva (r. 96–98) and governor of Asia about 112. Despite his political successes, Tacitus was a pessimist. He believed that the transformation from republic to empire had weakened Rome's moral character. Perhaps it is not surprising, then, that he was able to put himself in the position of not only the conqueror, but also the conquered. In the following excerpts, he gives us the voices of both.

A. *In this section of his* Histories, *Tacitus describes the aftermath of a failed revolt in Gaul in 70. The*

Roman general who has just suppressed the revolt addresses the defeated rebels:

> Tyranny and war always existed in Gaul until you yielded to our authority. And we, although we have been provoked many times, have imposed upon you by right of conquest only this one demand: that you pay the costs of keeping peace here. For peace among different peoples cannot be maintained without troops, and troops cannot be maintained without pay, and pay cannot be found without taxation. In other respects, we are equals. You yourselves often command our legions and govern this and other provinces. You are in no respect excluded or shut out. Although you live far from Rome, you enjoy as much as we do the benefits of praiseworthy emperors; on the other hand, the cruel emperors threaten most those closest to them.... Perhaps you expect a milder type of government if Tutor and Classicus [leaders of the defeated revolt] assume power? Perhaps you think that they can equip armies to repel the Germans and the Britons for less tribute than you now pay us? But if the Romans are driven out—God forbid—what situation could exist except wars among all these races? The structure of our Empire has been consolidated by 800 years of good fortune and strict organization, and it cannot be torn apart without destroying those who tear it apart. And you especially will run the greatest risk, for you have gold and natural resources, which are the chief causes of war. Therefore love and cherish peace and the city of Rome which you and I, conquered and conqueror, hold with equal rights.

THE FRONTIER AND BEYOND

■ How did Romans interact with peoples living beyond the imperial borders?

In Virgil's *Aeneid*, Jupiter promises Rome "imperial rule without limit." But by the time of

Hadrian's reign (117–138), the limits of the empire were clear. The third concentric circle of the Roman world consisted of the frontier—the outermost regions of the empire and the non-Roman world beyond. For the Romans, the lines drawn between the Roman Empire and the non-Roman world symbolized a cultural division

B. *In 77 C.E. Tacitus married the daughter of Gnaeus Julius Agricola (40–93), a Roman general and administrator. Between 78 and 85, Agricola served as governor of Roman Britain and consolidated Roman rule over northern England and southern Scotland (which the Romans called Caledonia). In this excerpt from Tacitus's biography of his father-in-law, a chief named Calgacus attempts to rally the British against the Romans:*

Up until this day, we who live in this last strip of land and last home of liberty have been protected by our very remoteness.... Beyond us, there are no tribes, nothing except waves and rocks and, more dangerous than these, the Romans, whose oppression you have in vain tried to escape by obedience and submission. Plunderers of the world they are, and now that there is no more territory left to occupy their hands which have already laid the world waste, they are scouring the seas. If the enemy is rich, they are greedy; if the enemy is poor, they are power-hungry. Neither east nor west has been able to sate them. Alone of all men they covet rich nations and poor nations with equal passion. They rob, they slaughter, they plunder—and they call it "empire." Where they make a waste-land, they call it "peace."

C. *In this section, Tacitus describes Agricola's policies of occupation.*

For, to accustom to rest and repose through the charms of luxury a population scattered and barbarous and therefore inclined to war, Agricola gave private encouragement and public aid to the building of temples, courts of justice and dwelling houses, praising the energetic and reproving the indolent. Thus an honourable rivalry took the place of compulsion. He likewise provided a liberal education for the sons of the chiefs, and showed such a preference for the natural powers of the Britons over the industry of the Gauls that they who lately disdained the tongue of Rome now coveted its eloquence. Hence, too, a liking sprang up for our style of dress and the toga became fashionable. Step by step they were led to things which dispose to vice, the lounge, the bath, the elegant banquet. All this in their ignorance they called civilization, when it was but a part of their servitude.

For Discussion

1. How do Selections B and C illustrate the process of Romanization?

2. In two of the excerpts presented, Tacitus, like other ancient historians, quotes what he thought *might have been said*. How believable are these speeches? What sort of conclusions can we draw from them?

3. Tacitus used his historical writings to criticize many of the features of the Roman Empire. If history is written to promote a political objective, is it invalid?

Sources: A. Tacitus, *Histories*, 4.74; quoted in JoAnn Shelton, *As the Romans Did: A Sourcebook in Roman Social History* (Oxford: Oxford University Press, 1998), p. 288. B. Tacitus, *A Biography of Agricola*, 29–31; quoted in Shelton, p. 287. 3. C. Tacitus, *A Biography of Agricola*, 21; from the *Complete Works of Tacitus,* edited by Moses Hadas, translated by Alfred John Church and William Jackson Brodribb (New York: The Modern Library, 1942).

between civilization and barbarism. Romans used this distinction to define their place in the world and to justify their conquests.

Like the generals of the Republic and the Hellenistic kings, Augustus set out to conquer as much land as possible to win glory and to demonstrate his power. He solidified Rome's control over Gaul and added large parts the Danube River basin to the empire. His successors continued to add new lands to the empire. Britain was conquered in 43, and by 117 Trajan had annexed modern Romania, Mesopotamia, and parts of Arabia. At this point, the empire reached its greatest extent.

After Trajan, emperors turned their attention from conquest to consolidation. Trajan's successor, Hadrian, abandoned Mesopotamia and reorganized Rome's frontier with a series of fortifications, including the wall that still crosses the north of Britain and bears his name. His successors continued to fortify both the borders of the empire. By the early third century, regularly spaced military bases and fortresses dotted the empire's northern border while fleets patrolled the Rhine and Danube. In the East, another line of defenses extended from the Black Sea to the Nile. In North Africa, fortifications indicated the limits of cultivable land along the Sahara.

Rome and the Parthian Empire

One of Rome's most formidable rivals was the Parthian (or Persian) Empire. Stretching from the Euphrates River to Pakistan, Parthia replaced the successor states of Alexander the Great in the mid-third century B.C.E. (see Chapter 4). The Parthian Empire was a powerful state that combined elements of Persian and Hellenistic culture. It survived until 224, when

HADRIAN'S WALL

Hadrian's massive fortification epitomizes the second-century-C.E. military concept of the fortified frontier. Stretched across northern Britain, it separated the Roman provinces to its south from the "barbarians" to the north.

another Persian dynasty, the Sasanian, overthrew the last Parthian king.

The Romans knew the Parthians as fierce warriors. Parthia's specially bred battle horses, famous as far away as China, made heavily armed Parthian cavalrymen and archers worthy opponents of Rome's legions. Augustus—and most of the Roman emperors after him—shifted between war and diplomacy with Parthia. Trajan's conquest of Armenia and the Parthian provinces of Mesopotamia in 115–116 could not be sustained because they overextended Rome's resources.

The rivalry between Parthia and Rome, however, did not prevent commercial and technological exchanges. Romans prized Parthian steel and leather, and learned Parthian techniques of irrigation. In turn, Roman engineers and masons constructed roads and dams in Persia. Caravan routes that brought goods from India to Rome crossed Parthian territory. Most important, the Romans adopted the use of heavily armed cavalry from Parthia. By the fourth century, these units constituted the core of Roman military might.

Roman Encounters with Germanic Peoples

The peoples living north of the Rhine and Danube Rivers, not the Parthians, posed the greatest threat to Rome. Called "Germans" by the Romans, these peoples never used that term or thought of themselves as one group. Numbering in the millions, most of them spoke their own dialects and did not understand the language of other tribes. Led by aristocratic warriors, they often fought among themselves.

In the early years of Augustus's reign, Roman legions conquered large portions of "Germania" between the Rhine and Elbe Rivers. A revolt in 9 C.E. drove out the Romans, however, and Roman civilization never took root in the interior of northern Europe east of the Rhine. (See *Encounters and*

Transformations in this chapter.) The Rhine and Danube Rivers became the boundary between Rome and its northern enemies. Most of Rome's legions were stationed along this key dividing line.

Tribes along the northern border sometimes fragmented into pro- and anti-Roman factions and occasionally formed loose confederations to invade the empire. For example, the *Marcomanni*, meaning "men of the borderlands," constituted one of these hostile confederations during the reign of Marcus Aurelius (161–180). Seeking booty, this confederation attacked the empire with more than 100,000 men.

During long periods of peace, the people on either side of the border interacted with one another through military service and trade. Germanic aristocrats developed a taste for Mediterranean luxuries, including wine and jewelry. Some lived in villas in imitation of Roman aristocrats. Germanic men served in the Roman army as auxiliary troops. Discharged after the standard 25 years of service, many of these men returned to their homes with Roman money in their purses, a smattering of Latin, and knowledge of the riches and power of the empire.

By 200, the weight of different peoples pressing on Rome's northern borders began to crack the imperial defenses. With the end of the Severan dynasty in 235, the empire entered 50 years of disasters. Invading groups from north of the Rhine and Danube Rivers pushed as far south as central Italy in search of plunder. The Romans ultimately repelled the invaders and restored the empire's security, but as we will see in the next chapter, the restored empire differed radically from the system Augustus inaugurated.

Economic Encounters across Continents

The Roman Empire was part of an almost global economic web. One Roman account

ENCOUNTERS AND TRANSFORMATIONS

The Battle of Teutoburg Forest

In September of 9 C.E., the Roman commander in Germania, Publius Quinctilius Varus, received word of an uprising some miles from his army's camp. The report came from Arminius, chief of one of the largest and most powerful German tribes. Arminius had fought for years in the Roman army as an auxiliary commander. His service to Rome earned him Roman citizenship and the rank of equestrian. Thus, when Arminius warned Varus of the rebellion, Varus believed him.

Already heading toward winter camp, Varus detoured into unfamiliar territory to quell the rebellion. After marching for hours, the troops at the head of the two-mile-long column of 18,000 men found themselves on a narrow track between a wooded hill and a bog. Here Arminius and his men, hidden amid the trees, attacked. The Romans were trapped. Packed so tightly that they could not lift their shields or fling their javelins, the soldiers could hardly defend themselves. Within hours, Arminius and his German troops annihilated three legions, along with six auxiliary infantry cohorts and three auxiliary cavalry units. Varus himself committed suicide.

Caesar's conquest of Gaul in 51 B.C.E. had launched Rome on its collision course with the tribes of Germania. Under Augustus, clashes between Roman forces in Gaul and Germanic tribes across the Rhine were commonplace. Augustus decided that the security of Gaul demanded the conquest of Germania. This conquest, however, proved elusive. By 7 C.E., when Augustus appointed Varus provincial governor of the Rhineland, Roman forces had fought in Germania for 20 years. Yet most of Germania east of the Rhine remained outside Roman control.

The impact of Varus's defeat was immense. Romans had come to view their army as unbeatable, particularly against "barbarians" such as the Germans. In panic after Arminius's victory, Roman troops abandoned camps and fortresses that they had built beyond the Rhine. Most of these were never rebuilt. Except for punitive expeditions to avenge Varus's defeat, Roman soldiers did not return deep into Germania. Thus, the Battle of Teutoburg Forest, as the encounter between Varus's legions and Arminius's followers came to be known, transformed Roman imperial expectations and established the empire's boundaries in western Europe.

In 17 Augustus's successor Tiberius (r. 14–37) abandoned any effort to expand the empire across the Rhine. The Rhine River became an important cultural and political dividing line between the Roman and Germanic worlds. To the west and south of this line, Roman rule meant that people drank wine, followed Roman law, and spoke Latin—and eventually, the "Romance" (from "Roman") languages that derive from Latin. East of the Rhine, however, beer-drinking Germany followed a different cultural direction.

Yet Rome influenced that direction. In the decades *before* Varus's defeat, Germanic societies changed as they responded to the imposition of Roman rule over Gaul and the Rhineland. Inter-tribal exchanges and alliances increased—thus enabling these societies to coordinate a surprise attack on three of Rome's finest legions. Germanic societies also grew more hierarchical and militaristic, with mounted warriors gaining in wealth, power, and status. Arminius's victory accentuated these developments. Thus, the Battle of Teutoburg Forest not only halted the expansion of the Roman Empire in western Europe, it also accelerated the transformation of Germanic society that previous Germanic-Roman encounters had already begun.

For Discussion

How were Arminius and his troops able to defeat the better armed and larger Roman army? Why was this defeat so significant?

from the first century C.E., *Voyage Around the Red Sea* (author unknown), describes a vast commercial network. Trade routes linked the Mediterranean basin, the East African coast, the Persian Gulf, and the Red Sea with southeast Asia and China.

ENCOUNTERS WITH CHINA Chinese documents from the first century C.E. mention ambassadors sent to Rome who reached as far as the Persian Gulf, and in 166, Roman merchants who claimed they were ambassadors from Emperor Marcus Aurelius went to China, but the two empires never established formal ties.

Silk, not diplomatic links, bound Rome and China together. Superior to wool and linen in texture and in its ability to retain colored dyes, silk was one of the most desired commodities in Roman society. The Chinese possessed a monopoly on silk production (until the sixth century C.E., when Western monks finally succeeded in smuggling the eggs of silkworms and the seeds of mulberry trees out of China).

In the Republican era, silk was so rare that even the wealthiest Romans could afford only small pieces, which they tended to wear as brooches. Then, during the age of Augustus, Romans learned to use the monsoon winds to travel from ports on the Red Sea coast of Egypt across the Indian Ocean to the west coast of India, a journey that took about 40 days. In India, merchants exchanged glass, gold, wine, copper, and other items for silk. By the time this trade occurred, the price of the silk would have multiplied several times, as payments were made to each middleman along the 5,000-mile "Silk Road" that ran from northern China across the sweltering deserts, towering mountains, and treacherous salt flats of central Asia and down through modern Afghanistan to the Indian coast. (See **Map 6.4**.) Yet silk was so precious that a successful journey guaranteed a Roman merchant a profit 100 times larger than his original investment.

Roman demand for silk, spices (especially pepper), and other luxury items from the Far East produced a trade imbalance. As early as the first century C.E., the Roman statesman and natural scientist Pliny the Elder (23–79) griped, "And by the lowest reckoning India, China, and the Arabian Peninsula take from our Empire many thousands of pounds of gold every year—that is the sum which our luxuries and our women cost us." Many historians view the drain of hard currency to the East to pay for luxury goods as a key economic weakness of the empire.

ENCOUNTERS WITH AFRICA Coins found in the interior of Africa suggest that the Romans may have had commercial dealings with peoples there. To the Romans, however, "Africa" was one of their provinces bordering the Mediterranean Sea—the region we know as North Africa today—not the vast continent that lay to the south, beyond the Sahara Desert. Only in the European Middle Ages would the name *Africa* come to stand for the entire continent.

The Romans knew little about sub-Saharan Africa. In 146 B.C.E., the Roman general Scipio Aemilianus sent the historian Polybius on an expedition down the west coast of Africa, which got as far as Senegal and a place Scipio called Crocodile River. In the first century C.E., a Roman military expedition that marched south from a base in North Africa in pursuit of some raiders may have reached Chad. One hundred years later, an intrepid Roman officer named Julius Maternus traveled south for four months, reaching a place "where the rhinoceroses gather." He emerged in the Sudan, where he found the Nile and returned home.

The Romans used the word *Aethiopians* ("the People with Burned Faces") to refer to the peoples who lived south of the Sahara. Most of their knowledge of these peoples came from the Egyptians, who regularly traded for ivory, gold, and slaves with peoples living in what the Egyptians called Nubia (in modern Sudan), where sophisticated and powerful kingdoms had existed for centuries.

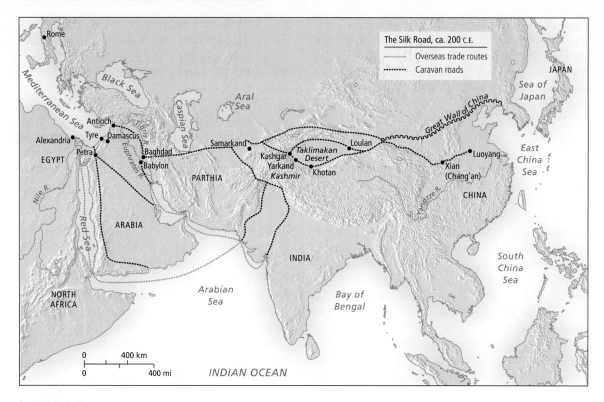

MAP 6.4

The Silk Road

The first-century C.E. development of sea routes to supplement the overland parts of the journey greatly strengthened this cross-continental trading network.

SOCIETY AND CULTURE IN THE IMPERIAL AGE

■ What was the social and cultural response to the emergence and consolidation of the empire?

The central theme of Roman politics after Augustus—the illusion of continuity masking fundamental change—also characterized imperial society and culture. The basic social structure of the Republic survived the shift to empire, but important changes occurred. While writers and poets praised Rome's greatness, they also explored the ambivalence of life under stable but autocratic rule. The spread of religious cults promising salvation hinted that many people under Roman rule found life less than stable and looked outside the political sphere for safety.

Upper and Lower Classes

In the Roman Empire, aristocrats remained at the top of the social pyramid, enjoying the greatest wealth, power, and prestige. Three social groups, or orders, possessed aristocratic status. The first order, the senators of Rome, occupied the top of the social pyramid. The rank of senator was not hereditary, but Augustus encouraged the sons of senators to follow in their fathers' footsteps and hold the offices that gave entry into the Senate. He also offered financial incentives to senators to have children and perpetuate their family line. Despite these efforts, most of the oldest Roman senatorial families had died out by the end of the first century C.E.; new families from Rome and the provinces took their place. All senators, and their descendants for three generations, had the right to wear a broad purple stripe on their togas.

Below the rank of senators stood the larger order of equestrians. Many equestrians continued to follow business careers as they had during the Republic, but the expansion of the empire gave them new opportunities for public service. Equestrians staffed many of the posts in the diplomatic, fiscal, and military services, and some entered the Senate.

The third aristocratic order were the curiales, members of local elites who served in the councils of every provincial city. Like senators and equestrians, they were expected to be wealthy, and of respectable birth and good moral character. Yet many sons of wealthy freedmen became city councilors.

These three aristocratic orders represented only about 1 percent of the empire's population. Below them came the common people—Rome's poor but free underclass of citizens. Although excluded from political life, commoners received benefits from imperial rule. In the city of Rome, adult male citizens received a daily allotment of free grain, olive oil, and pork. Ordinary Romans also received a steady diet of free entertainment, such as gladiatorial combats in the Colosseum and chariot races in the Circus Maximus. The satirist Juvenal (ca. 55–140) described life in the city of Rome as a matter of "bread and circuses": free food and free entertainment.

Ordinary urban Romans needed bread and circuses to compensate not only for their loss of political power, but also for their poor living conditions. Crowded into slums with little light or ventilation, the poor lived in misery. Disease kept birth rates and life expectancies low. Probably more than a quarter of all infants died within their first five years, and a third of those who

survived were dead by age 10. The average life expectancy for Roman men was 45 years and the average for women 34.

Poor people lived in similarly wretched conditions in every Roman city, but without the daily distributions of grain. Most rural Romans were farmers, who provided most of the troops in the Roman army.

Slaves and Freedmen

Slavery was a fact of life in every ancient society. When Augustus took control of Rome, slaves constituted 35–40 percent of the population of Italy. These millions of slaves held the lowest status in a society in which social and legal status meant everything. Ancient slavery was not based on race or skin color. Most slaves had been captured in war. Others, born of a slave mother, were enslaved from birth.

Ownership of slaves reflected a person's status. The emperor and wealthy aristocrats owned tens of thousands of slaves who labored on their estates throughout the empire. Artisans, teachers, shopkeepers, and freedmen might own a slave or two. Because slaves could earn money, even some slaves owned slaves.

Slaves used for domestic service or in commerce and crafts were the lucky ones. Many male slaves worked on plantations, or "latifundia," as part of slave gangs. They often labored in chains and slept in underground prisons. The male slaves sent to work in the mines, some of whom were convicts, experienced even worse conditions. Female slaves were spared the horrors of working in the fields and mines, but they were valued far less than male slaves.

Violence lay at the heart of the institution of slavery. Masters could physically or sexually abuse slaves with impunity. A slave's testimony in court was valid only if extracted by torture. In the face of such brutality, slaves had few options. They could try to escape, but if caught, they were branded on the forehead. No slave revolt succeeded in imperial or republican Rome.

Slaves, however, might obtain their freedom through manumission. Through this carefully regulated legal procedure, a master granted freedom to a slave as a reward for faithful service, good behavior, or even out of affection. Of course, manumission also worked to the best interests of the owner: The hope of freedom kept slaves docile. Moreover, Roman law established limits to manumission. No more than 100 slaves could be freed at the death of an owner, and the slave had to be at least 30 years old and the owner at least 25.

Former slaves made up only about 5 percent of Rome's population, but their enterprise and ambition made the freedmen an important class. Many worked in business or as skilled laborers, teachers, and doctors. A freedman had only partial citizen rights, but his or her children became full Roman citizens, who could freely marry other citizens.

Slavery remained a part of Mediterranean economic and social life until the early Middle Ages, but in the second century C.E., the economic role of slaves diminished. As emperors concentrated on consolidating rather than expanding the empire, the supply of slaves from warfare dwindled and their cost rose. Slave owning may have become less economically viable.

Women in the Roman Empire

Women in the senatorial and equestrian ranks possessed more freedom than was usual in the ancient world, in part because of a gradual shift in marriage customs. By 250, the form of marriage by which a woman passed from the control of her father to that of her husband had nearly died out. Instead, a married woman legally remained under the control of her father or guardian. Because their husbands no longer controlled their dowries, this legal change gave women more freedom. Some women used this freedom to move into the public sphere, taking part in banquets, attending gladiatorial battles at the Colosseum and races at the Circus Maximus, and presiding over literary salons. Women owned property, made investments, and became

LIVES OF LUXURY
A woman pours perfume in this wall painting from around 20 B.C.E. Only the wealthy could afford perfume and paintings.

public benefactors. Many high-ranking women were educated in the liberal arts and lived cultivated lives. Their portraits—carved in stone or painted on walls—reveal a restrained elegance. The portraits of wives and daughters of emperors even appeared on coins.

As these coins suggest, at the highest level of society, some women possessed political power, though expressed behind the scenes. Livia (58 B.C.E.–29 C.E.), married to Augustus for 52 years, wielded enormous political influence during his and her son Tiberius's reigns. The Emperor Hadrian may have received his throne in part because of the influence of his cousin Trajan's wife, Plotina (d. 121). At her funeral, Hadrian admitted, "She often made requests of me, and I never once refused her."

Most women, of course, were not immortalized in stone or coin and had no political power. We have scanty evidence about the lives of nonaristocratic women in the Roman Empire. We do, however, know of women moneylenders, shopkeepers, and investors. Some women became doctors or artists. Most women probably married and gave birth to three or four children.

Although literary evidence demonstrates that many aristocratic Roman men cherished their daughters, female infanticide remained common. The expected ratio of female to male births is 105 to 100. In second-century C.E. Rome, however, the rate was 100 to 131. Unwanted babies—not only girls but also the sick and malformed, and some born outside marriage—were left by the roadside to die or to be reared by strangers.

Literature and Empire

The prosperity and stability of the Roman Empire allowed the literary arts to flourish. Wealthy patrons, including the emperor, sponsored publications and provided an audience for new works. Yet imperial rule also limited free expression. Roman writers confronted the tensions of living in a society that had exchanged freedom for stability.

The career of the philosopher Seneca (ca. 4 B.C.E.–65 C.E.) illustrates the constraints facing writers in the imperial era. Seneca intended his writings to give advice to rulers. Influenced by Stoicism (see Chapter 4), he acknowledged how hard it was to live a moral life. Seneca's integrity and rhetorical brilliance earned him the unenviable task of being Nero's tutor when the emperor was still an impressionable twelve-year-old. For eight years Seneca guided Nero, and the empire enjoyed good government. As Nero matured, however, he found other, less decent advisers. Appalled by his student's descent into corruption, Seneca was accused of plotting to kill Nero. To avoid execution, he killed himself.

HISTORY-WRITING IN AN AGE OF AUTOCRACY The work of the historian Livy (59 B.C.E.–12 C.E.) illustrates the fine line writers in this autocratic society walked. In his history Livy presented Rome's rise to world mastery as a series of moral and patriotic lessons. He showed how Rome's military and moral strength catapulted it to world power. Although proud of Rome's greatness, Livy believed that with power came decadence. He did not gloss over the ruthlessness with which Augustus waged the civil war that destroyed the Republic, nor did he veil his criticism of what he perceived as Rome's moral and political decline. Livy's open criticism displeased Augustus, yet the emperor did not punish the historian, perhaps because Livy also expressed the hope that Augustus would restore Rome's glory.

The historian Tacitus (ca. 55–ca. 120) belonged to a later generation. While Livy experienced the tumultuous transition from republic to empire, Tacitus lived and wrote when the imperial system was firmly in place. Although his own career flourished under both the tyrannical Domitian and the just Trajan, Tacitus hated political oppression. He never abandoned his love for the best of Roman ideals. In the *Agricola*, his biography of his father-in-law, Tacitus affirmed that good men could serve their country honorably, even under bad rulers such as Nero. The *Agricola* thus inadvertently revealed an important accomplishment of Augustus's imperial system: It had tamed Rome's aristocrats, transforming them into an efficient governing class.

IMPERIAL POETRY Poets, too, had to adapt to life in an autocracy. The tragic career of Ovid (43 B.C.E.–17 C.E.) demonstrated the risks of offending an emperor. Ovid's love poems had made him the darling of Rome. But his lighthearted descriptions of Roman sexual life violated Augustus's efforts to restore traditional family values, while his book *Metamorphoses*, with its themes of change and impermanence in Greek and Roman mythology, indirectly challenged the ideal of a stable state under Augustus's leadership. In 8 C.E., Ovid's erotic poem, "The Art of Love," along with a sexual scandal involving Augustus's granddaughter, earned him the hostility of the emperor. Augustus exiled Ovid to a village on the Black Sea where the poet remained for the rest of his life.

Horace (65–8 B.C.E.), son of a wealthy freedman, escaped Ovid's fate by avoiding political and sexual entanglements and maintaining close ties to Augustus. His poetry on public themes praised the emperor for bringing peace and the hope of a moral life to the world. Throughout his work, Horace urged appreciation of life's temporary joys. In his most famous verse, he sings,

> Be wise, taste the wine, and since our time is brief, be moderate in your aspirations. Even as we speak, greedy life slips away from us. Grasp each day (*carpe diem*) and do not pin your hopes on tomorrow.

Virgil also earned Augustus's favor. At Augustus's request Virgil composed the *Aeneid*, an epic poem that legitimized and celebrated the emperor's reign. The *Aeneid* tells the story of Aeneas, a Trojan prince who founds the city of Rome. Through a series of cinematic "flash-forwards," Virgil presented the entire history of the Roman people as culminating in the reign of Augustus. Yet Virgil was not just an imperial propagandist as the ending of the *Aeneid* shows. Tempted by his love for the Carthaginian queen Dido to abandon his mission of founding Rome, Aeneas overcomes his personal desire to fulfill his mission: He abandons Dido who commits suicide. At the end of the poem, Aeneas stands victorious—but he has sacrificed everything. Virgil makes his readers wonder about the costs of public service.

Juvenal also exposed the weaknesses of the imperial age. One of the most quotable of Roman poets, Juvenal's satires mocked overeducated women, duplicitous Greeks, and boring provincials. His favorite target, however, was daily life in Rome. His descriptions of the city's noise, smells, flimsy housing, crowded streets, and pervasive criminality emphasized the wide gap in lifestyles between privileged and ordinary folk, and so highlighted the corruption of republican ideals.

Science in the Roman Empire

The Hellenistic scientific tradition (see Chapter 4) flourished under Roman rule. Using the division of spheres into units of 60 first developed by the Sumerians and perfected by the Babylonians, Claudius Ptolemy (ca. 90–170) codified the Hellenistic theory that the sun revolves around the earth. Western astronomers used Ptolemy's maps of the heavens for nearly 1,500 years, while his *Geography* remained the basis of cartography until the sixteenth century.

Roman medicine shaped Western practices for more than 1500 years. The physician Galen (131–201) sought to make medicine a science. He insisted on the importance of dissection for understanding the body and stressed the need for experimentation. For most of his career, Galen worked in Rome, but he served for four years as physician to the gladiators in Pergamum in Anatolia, where he was able to study firsthand the impact of trauma on the human body.

Galen's main influence on Western medicine, however, was negative. Like Hippocrates before him (see Chapter 3), Galen believed that an imbalance in the body's four "humors," or basic bodily fluids (blood, black bile, yellow bile, and phlegm), produced disease. Too much blood, for example, meant fever. To restore the balance, Galen taught, the physician should restore the balance by applying leeches or cutting open a vein, and thereby draining the patient of "excess" blood. A strong purgative or emetic to induce vomiting or diarrhea could drain "excess" bile. Bloodletting and purging, and the humoral theory on which they were based, remained central in Western medical practice into the early nineteenth century. Unfortunately, these treatments weakened or killed innumerable patients.

Religious Life

Because the imperial regime made no effort to regulate religion, people throughout the empire freely worshiped many gods and maintained their traditional rituals. Nevertheless, this era witnessed significant religious change, including the transformation of Judaism and the emergence of Christianity.

POLYTHEISM IN THE EMPIRE Syncretism, the practice of equating gods and fusing their cults, was a common feature of imperial religious life and helped unify the empire. The Romans often identified foreign gods with their own deities. Romans did not care that other peoples might worship Jupiter, Juno, or any other Roman god in different ways or give the gods different attributes.

Each city in the empire had its own gods, but some religious cults transcended their places of origin. Feeling lost in the sprawl of the empire's cities, slaves, freedmen, and the urban poor turned to religions that offered both community and salvation. Religions that promised victory over death or liberation from the abuses and pain of daily existence spread across the empire.

The goddess Isis, for example, who originated in Egypt, offered freedom from fate to her many followers. Her story revolved around the death and resurrection of her husband, Osiris (also called Serapis). Her worshipers believed that they, too, would experience life after death. Moreover, Isis—often depicted holding her baby son, Horus—represented the universal mother and so promised compassionate nurture. In *The Golden Ass,* the Roman writer Apuleius (ca. 125–170) described the goddess's protective power. Full of eroticism and magic, the story tells of Lucius, a young Romeo, who turns into a donkey after he is caught spying on a gorgeous witch. Lucius stumbles through misadventures until Isis restores him to human form. Lucius thanks her for caring "for the troubles of miserable humans with a sweet mother's love" and becomes her priest.

Another religion that promised salvation to its initiates was that of Mithras, a sun god. According to his followers, Mithras was killed by his enemies on December 21, the winter solstice, and rose from the dead on December 25. By worshipping Mithras, his followers believed they too could achieve life after death. Limited to men,

MUMMY WRAPPING FROM EGYPT

A painted linen cloth, wrapped around a mummy in an Egyptian burial during the second century C.E., shows the Egyptian god Osiris (on the left) and the jackal-headed god Anubis (on the right). Between them is the dead man, dressed in Roman clothing. His portrait has been carefully painted and added separately. The wrapping and portrait demonstrate the continuity of ancient Egyptian religion during Roman imperial rule.

worship of Mithras took place in underground chambers in which small groups celebrated a ceremonial meal that evoked Mithras's memory, recited lessons about the journey of the soul after death, and sacrificed to the god. Because this religion stressed courage and duty, it particularly attracted soldiers.

Worship of the Unconquered Sun (Sol Invictus) also spread throughout the empire.

MITHRAS SLAYS THE BULL

Designed around 200 C.E., a wall painting from a shrine at Marino, south of Rome, shows the god Mithras in the sacred act of sacrificing a bull. Limited to men only, the worship of Mithras occurred throughout the empire. Scholars are unsure of the symbolic meaning of the dog, scorpion, and snake shown in this painting.

Originating in Syria, this deity was associated with Helios-Apollo, the Greco–Roman sun god, and with Mithras. When Elagabalus, the high priest of the Syrian sun god (El-Gabal), became Roman emperor (r. 218–222), he built a huge temple dedicated to his god in Rome, and designated December 25, the birth and resurrection day of Mithras, as a special day of worship to the deity. Within 50 years, the Unconquered Sun became the chief god of official worship.

THE ORIGINS OF RABBINIC JUDAISM Roman rule reshaped Judaism and the history of the Jewish people. In 37 B.C.E., the Roman Senate appointed Herod the Great (37–4 B.C.E.), a Roman ally from southern Palestine, as "King of the Jews." Despite this grand title, Herod ruled at the Romans' behest. Most Jews never regarded him as their rightful king. After Herod's death, his kingdom was divided among his three sons, but in 6 C.E., Augustus annexed the largest and most important of these kingdoms: Judea. The annexation of Judea meant that the Romans now directly controlled the city of Jerusalem, the spiritual center of Jewish life. (See **Map 6.5**.) Inept governors and heavy taxation caused Judea's economy to decline, famines and banditry became common, and a divide opened up among the Jews. The landed elite benefited from Roman rule. Ordinary Jews, however, viewed their leaders as collaborators with a godless power. They followed the scribes and rabbis ("my master" in Hebrew), men of learning who devoted their lives to copying religious texts and interpreting the scriptures and had little stake in Roman rule.

Sixty years of Roman mismanagement and the Jewish desire for independence led to revolt in Judea in 66. Jews formed their own government, appointed regional military commanders,

outside Palestine, but after the Romans ransacked Judea, the **Diaspora** ("dispersion of population") characterized Jewish life. Jerusalem ceased to be the focus of Judaism's religious ceremony, although not of Jewish religious thought and hope. Animal sacrifice centered in the Temple disappeared. The rabbi replaced the priest as religious instructor and community guide. Trained in the Jewish law, rabbis interpreted and taught the Torah and settled disputes. Synagogues developed into centers where Jews celebrated the Sabbath and prayed together.

The **Mishnah** emerged from this era. A collection of opinions, decisions, and homilies from both oral tradition and texts written to explain the Jewish law, the Mishnah was completed around 220. Each of the Mishnah's 63 books deals with a particular aspect of law, from ritual purity to crime. Among the moral principles the Mishnah stresses, saving life was paramount. To save a life, any person could break any Jewish religious law, except those forbidding idolatry, adultery, incest, or murder. Saving one life symbolized saving humanity.

THE EMERGENCE OF CHRISTIANITY   Over a century before the Mishnah was compiled, the new religion of Christianity grew from Jewish roots. Beginning around 28 C.E., Jesus of Nazareth (ca. 4 B.C.E.–ca. 30 C.E.), a Jew from Galilee in northern Palestine, traveled through Palestine with a band of followers, urging men and women to join together in God's Kingdom before the imminent end of this world. (See Map 6.5.) Jesus' followers believed him to be the messiah, an important figure in Jewish prophetic writings. In Jewish belief, the messiah's coming would inaugurate a new age of blessing for God's people.

Sometime between 30 and 33 C.E., Jesus entered Jerusalem to preach his message. Roman authorities convicted him as a revolutionary and crucified him—the usual capital punishment for noncitizens in the empire. Jesus' followers, however, insisted that he rose from the dead and ascended into heaven, and that his spirit remained on earth and guided

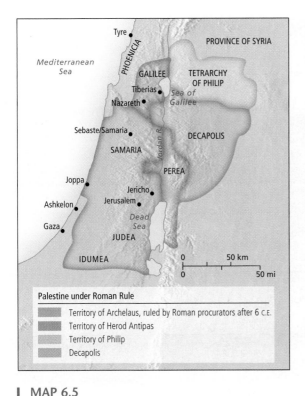

MAP 6.5

Palestine under Roman Rule

Herod the Great (73 B.C.E.–4 B.C.E.) ruled Palestine as a client king of Rome. After he died, three of his sons inherited his kingdom—but under Roman oversight. Archelaus was crowned king of Judea, Samaria, and Idumea; Herod Antipas became the ethnarch (client ruler, slightly below a king in status) of Perea and Galilee; and Philip became tetrarch (client ruler, slightly below an ethnarch in status) of the territories east of the Jordan River. In 6 C.E., the Romans deposed Archelaus and assumed direct rule over Judea. Jesus lived and ministered for most of his life in Galilee and thus under the rule of Herod Antipas, but he died in Judea, which the Romans governed without intermediary.

abolished debt, and issued their own coinage. Internal divisions, however, weakened the rebellion. Imperial forces captured Jerusalem in 70, destroyed the Temple, and enslaved an estimated two million people.

Yet Judaism and the Jews survived. A new kind of religious life developed. Since the sixth century B.C.E., communities of Jews had lived

ARCH OF TITUS

This triumphal arch built at the end of the first century C.E. honored the recently deceased Titus for crushing the Jewish revolt of 66–70 C.E. Marble reliefs inside the arch represent the loot from the Temple of Jerusalem carried in the triumphal parade. Soldiers display the Great Menorah, one of the holiest symbols of Judaism.

their lives. Eventually called "Christians" (from the Greek word *Christ,* meaning "messiah" or "anointed one"), these men and women expected that Jesus would soon return and launch a new age of righteousness. They shared their possessions in common and—in a shocking violation of Roman and Jewish emphasis on family life—downplayed family and social ties. As the decades passed without Jesus's return, however, they focused on building their communities and preserving their distinctive faith.

But what defined this faith? Jesus' first followers were Jews who regarded him as a rabbi, a prophet, and eventually the messiah—all Jewish religious concepts. But as Christianity spread to non-Jews, and as Christians adjusted their expectations of Jesus' return, diverse and often clashing understandings of Jesus emerged.

In this process of religious debate and development, the work and teaching of Paul of Tarsus (d. ca. 65) were crucial. An educated Jew, Paul traveled throughout Anatolia and Greece, founding and developing Christian communities. Even more important, he wrote letters, or Epistles, that circulated among these communities. Written in the 50s, these letters taught that Jesus was not only the Jewish messiah, but also the Son of God who died on the cross as part of the divine plan. In Paul's letters, Jesus' brutal death became a loving sacrifice: By enduring the punishment that sinful men and women deserved, the sinless Son of God gave his followers eternal life in heaven after they died on earth.

Paul's version of Jesus' teaching became the foundation of **orthodox** Christianity. *Orthodox* means "right belief," and from the mid-third century on, Christians who promoted beliefs about Jesus that differed from those defined as orthodox faced the charge of **heresy**. *Heresy* literally translates as "choice." A heretic was someone who chose to believe wrong things. But in the 200 years after Jesus' death, orthodox Christianity did not yet exist, and neither did the **New Testament** (the collection of texts that, together with the Old Testament or Hebrew Bible, comprise the Christian Bible). Because Jesus himself wrote nothing, different groups with different ideas could each claim to be his true followers.

CHRIST AS THE GOOD SHEPHERD

Carved in the second century c.e., this statue depicts Jesus as a good shepherd, a frequent motif in early Christian art. An image drawn from both the Hebrew Bible and Greek representations of the god Apollo, the Good Shepherd illustrates the blending of Greek and Hebrew ideas in Christianity.

While Paul, for example, taught that non-Jewish Christian men did not need to be circumcised (a key Jewish initiation rite) and that non-Jews need not follow Jewish dietary restrictions, others of Jesus' followers insisted that all Christians had to abide by all Jewish laws. Still other early Christians, called Marcionites, rejected not only Jewish laws and customs, but also the Jewish Scriptures and even the Jewish God. In their view, Jesus was not the Jewish messiah, but rather the chosen messenger of a loving God who came to earth to save people from the vengeful God of the Jews.

An even more divisive issue than the relationship of Christians to Judaism was the question of Jesus' divinity. "Adoptionist" Christians saw Jesus as fully human, a man that God adopted to be his special son and to carry out his mission, while "docetic" Christians argued that Jesus only appeared to possess a material body but was in fact divine and not human at all. A third group of Christians believed Jesus was fully God and fully human. In 325 (see Chapter 7), this third view became orthodox doctrine, but in the first and second centuries, the Christian understanding of Jesus was far from set.

The question of Christianity's relationship with the material world also remained open in these centuries, as the emergence of **Gnostic** versions of Christianity illustrates. Gnostic beliefs varied widely (and not all Gnostics embraced Christianity), but in general Gnosticism taught that that men and women are really spiritual beings who belong to God's realm, the world of the good, the world of the spirit. In contrast, the material world (including the human body) is not God's creation, but a fundamentally evil prison in which human spirits are trapped. In the Gnostic view, few humans recognize or *know* these truths. *Gnostic* comes from the Greek word *gnosis*, for knowledge, and Gnosticism taught that only a few men and women possess the secret knowledge that will allow them to escape from the evil of this world and return to their rightful spiritual home. In Gnostic

Christianity, then, Jesus is a kind of cosmic riddler who came not to save the world, but to save his few from the world. Gnosticism tended to promote disengagement from worldly affairs and detachment from physical needs and desires. While the solidification of orthodoxy in the third century meant that Gnostic Christians were labeled heretics, the question of the proper Christian attitude toward worldly concerns and bodily desires divides believers even today.

CHRISTIANITY WITHIN THE ROMAN WORLD Christianity drew many of its first converts from the urban "middle classes"—merchants, artisans, business owners—but it also appealed to socially marginalized groups, such as women, noncitizens, and slaves. Indeed, Jesus' message was revolutionary in the way it overturned boundaries of class, gender, and ethnicity. After Jesus' death, Paul encouraged a communal life in which all followers of Jesus were equal in the eyes of God. As he wrote to a small Christian community in Galatia in Anatolia, "For in Christ Jesus…there is no longer Jew or Greek, there is no longer slave or free, there is no longer male or female; for all of you are one in Christ Jesus."

Many of Christianity's core concepts, such as its ideas about personal salvation, the equality of individual men and women before God, and the redemption of humanity from sin, distinguished it from the empire's polytheistic faiths. Most strikingly, Christianity firmly rejected the existence of multiple gods and sought to convince followers of other religions that they stood in error. This conversionist impulse (called *proselytizing*), in addition to Christians' withdrawal from the public life of Roman culture, earned them suspicion—and sometimes death.

Until the mid-third century, persecutions of Christians tended to be local affairs, sparked by the hostility of a city magistrate or provincial governor. In 64, however, Emperor Nero blamed Christians for a fire that consumed central Rome. (Popular legend blamed him, equally

JUSTICE IN HISTORY

The Trial of Jesus in Historical Perspective

In 30 C.E. imperial authorities in Jerusalem in the Roman province of Judea tried and executed a Jewish teacher known as Jesus of Nazareth. Although an insignificant event at the time, the trial of Jesus and its interpretation has had a profound impact on Western civilization.

Information about Jesus' trial comes from the New Testament books of Matthew, Mark, Luke, and John. These narratives, called the Gospels, were written 30–60 years after Jesus' death. They relate that during three years of teaching and miracles in Galilee and Judea, Jesus earned the resentment of the Jewish religious leadership by disregarding aspects of Jewish religious law. According to the Gospels, when Jesus entered the Temple precinct in Jerusalem, he angered the Jewish elites by denouncing their hypocrisy and overturning the tables of money changers. The priests then conspired to kill him. They paid one of Jesus' followers to reveal his whereabouts. Soldiers arrested Jesus on the night either before or of the Passover feast and brought him to the house of Caiaphas, the Jewish High Priest. There Jesus either had a private hearing before the High Priest and his father-in-law (according to the Gospel of John) or a trial before the Sanhedrin, the highest Jewish court. According to the Gospels of Matthew, Mark, and Luke, the Sanhedrin found Jesus guilty of blasphemy for claiming to be the messiah, the Son of God.

Lacking the authority under Roman rule to put Jesus to death, the Jewish leaders brought him before Pontius Pilate, the Roman governor, and demanded that he execute Jesus. Pilate hesitated, but the priests persuaded him by insisting that Jesus threatened the emperor's authority by claiming to be king of the Jews. Pilate's soldiers crucified Jesus, but according to the Gospels, the blame for Jesus' death lay with the Jews who demanded his execution. In all four Gospels, Jewish crowds in Jerusalem cry out, "Crucify him!" to a reluctant Pilate.

The Gospel accounts of Jesus' arrest, trial, and crucifixion pose problems for historians. Parts of these narratives conflict with what scholars understand about the conduct of trials by Jewish authorities and Roman administrators. For example, the historical evidence that we have indicates that the Sanhedrin did not hold trials at night. It did not meet in the house of the high priest, nor convene on a feast day or the night before a feast.

Far more important than these issues, however, is the question of the crime of blasphemy. In first-century Judaism, the messiah was expected to be a kingly figure—but not God. If Jesus did identify himself as the messiah, he would not have been guilty of blasphemy. Some scholars, however, point out that the Jewish leaders would have regarded Jesus' claim to sit in God's presence (and thus to share in God's rule) as blasphemous.

Jesus' blasphemy remains unclear, but there is little debate about the importance of Jesus' confrontation with the Jewish elites in the Temple. Jesus committed a dangerous act by denouncing the priests in Jerusalem. These men, especially the High Priest himself, owed their power to the Roman overlords and were responsible for maintaining order. Many Jews in the Temple elite saw Jesus as an agitator who threatened their authority. According to Matthew, Mark, and Luke, the Temple guards, not Roman soldiers, arrested Jesus and brought him before the Sanhedrin. The Romans had appointed all 71 members of the court, including Caiaphas, who led it. These men knew that if they could not control Jesus, the Romans would replace them. The court could not execute Jesus, but it could send him before Roman magistrates on a charge that the Romans would prosecute—stirring up rebellion.

Jesus' popularity with the common people and the disturbance in the Temple precinct would have aroused Roman suspicion. Moreover, if Jesus had claimed to be the messiah, he was guilty of insurrection from a Roman standpoint, for the term had royal connotations, and no one within the empire could be called a king without the emperor's permission. Roman officials usually responded to real or imagined threats to the political order by crucifixion. In the eyes of Pontius Pilate, a cautious magistrate, Jesus was a threat to public order, and so deserved execution. Pilate would not have been reluctant to kill him.

Why, then, do the Gospels tend to shift the blame for Jesus' death from Pilate to the Jewish community? The Gospels began to be written down amid growing hostility and suspicion between Jews and Christians. Moreover, after Roman armies destroyed the Temple in the Jewish rebellion of 66–70, Christians wanted to disassociate themselves from Jews. They hoped to persuade Roman authorities to think of them not as rebels, but as followers of a lawful religion. Such concerns may have shaped the Gospel writers' tendencies to emphasize the role of Jewish leaders instead of Pilate in Jesus' death.

The Gospels also relate that before he died, Jesus predicted the destruction of the Temple. Many early Christians came to believe that the fall of the Temple and the savage repression of the Jewish rebellion were divine punishment for the Jews who had caused Jesus' death. These interpretations of Jesus' trial and execution, and of the destruction of the Jewish community in

Palestine, helped poison Christian–Jewish relations for two millennia. From the first century through the twentieth, important segments of the Christian community blamed "the Jews" for Jesus' crucifixion.

For Discussion

1. What does Jesus' trial show about Roman methods of provincial administration—and about the limitations of these methods? Who had power in Judea?
2. In Christian theology, Jesus died for the sins of the world. In theological terms, then, all sinners—all human beings—bear responsibility for his death. Why does it matter if the Gospels blame Jesus' crucifixion on Jews instead of Romans?

Taking it Further

Crossan, John Dominic. *Who Killed Jesus: Exposing the Roots of Anti-Semitism in the Gospel Story of the Death of Jesus.* San Francisco: HarperSanFrancisco,1997. An engaging investigation.

Johnson, Luke Timothy, John Dominic Crossan, and Werner H. Kelber. *The Jesus Controversy.* London: Trinity Press International/Continuum, 1999. Three experts discuss the problems of finding who Jesus "really was."

Sherwin-White, A. N. *Roman Society and Roman Law in the New Testament.* 1963; Eugene, OR: Wipf and Stock Publishers, 2004. A leading historian puts the New Testament in its Roman context.

wrongly.) Hundreds of Christians died in the arena before cheering crowds.

Christians called those who died rather than renounce their beliefs **martyrs,** or witnesses for

their faith. The early Christian leader Tertullian (ca. 160–240) chided his Roman persecutors, "We multiply whenever we are mown down by you; the blood of Christians is [like] seed." But in 235 (the end date of this chapter), Christianity remained a minority movement within the Roman Empire.

CONCLUSION

Rome Shapes the West

The map of the Roman Empire outlined the heart of the regions included in the West today. Rome was the means by which cultural and political ideas developed in Mediterranean societies and spread into Europe. This quilt of lands and peoples was acquired mostly by conquest. An autocratic government stitched the pieces together. Although Roman authorities permitted no dissent, they allowed provincial peoples to become Roman. Being Roman meant that one had specific legal rights of citizenship, not that one belonged to a particular race or ethnic group. Thus, in addition to conquering the empire and patrolling its borders, the Roman army brought a version of Roman society to subject peoples. By imitating Roman styles of architecture and urban life, the cities, too, spread Roman civilization. Moreover, the elites of these cities helped funnel the resources of the countryside into the emperor's coffers, and so sustained the imperial system.

Rome's civilization, including its legal system, its development of cities, and its literary and artistic legacy, became the basis of much of Western civilization. The legal precedents Roman jurists established remain valid in much of Europe. Latin and Greek literature of the early Roman Empire has entertained, instructed, and inspired Western readers for nearly 2,000 years. Until recently all educated people in the West could read Latin, and many could read Greek. Many of our public buildings and memorial sculptures adhere to Roman models. The Roman Empire was the most important and influential model of an imperial system for Europeans until modern times. Of equal importance, the monotheism and ethical teachings of Judaism and Christianity have shaped Western culture.

KEY TERMS

Pax Romana	Diaspora
Julio-Claudian dynasty	Mishnah
Flavian dynasty	orthodox
Antonine Age	heresy
Severan dynasty	New Testament
auxiliary	Gnostic
Romanization	martyr
Antonine Decree	

CHAPTER QUESTIONS

1. How did the Roman imperial system develop, and what roles did the emperor, Senate, army, and Rome itself play in this development? (page 169)
2. How did provincial peoples assimilate to or resist Roman rule? (page 176)
3. How did Romans interact with peoples living beyond the imperial borders? (page 182)
4. What was the social and cultural response to the emergence and consolidation of empire? (page 188)

TAKING IT FURTHER

1. Evaluate this argument: "Behind a carefully crafted façade of restored Republican tradition, Octavian created a Roman version of a Hellenistic monarchy, like those of Alexander the Great's successors in the eastern Mediterranean." What are the characteristics of a Hellenistic monarchy? Which of these characteristics did the Augustan system of imperial rule share? Why did Augustus seek to maintain the "façade of restored Republican tradition"?
2. How did the relationship between the Jewish population of Palestine and the Roman imperial government in the first century C.E. shape the early history of Christianity?

✓• Practice on MyHistoryLab

Late Antiquity: The Age of New Boundaries, 250–600

- Crisis and Recovery in the Third Century ■ Toward a Christian Empire
- New Christian Communities and Identities ■ The Breakup of the Roman Empire

THE EVENTS OF THE LAST WEEK OF AUGUST IN 410 STUNNED THE ROMAN WORLD. A small army of landless warriors—no more than a few thousand men—led by their king, Alaric, forced their way into the city of Rome and plundered it for three days. For more than a year, Alaric had been threatening the city in an attempt to extort gold and land for his people. When his attempts at extortion failed, he attacked the city directly. Because Alaric's followers, the Visigoths, were Christian, they spared Rome's churches and took care not to violate the nuns. But that left plenty of loot—gold, silver, and silk—for them to cart away, and they did not hesitate to plunder the tombs of pagan emperors, including the Mausoleum of Augustus.

For these warriors and their families, who had first invaded the Roman Empire from their homelands in southern Russia 30 years earlier, pillaging the most opulent city in the Mediterranean world was a profitable interlude in a long struggle to secure a permanent home. For the Romans, however, the looting of Rome was an unfathomable disaster. They could scarcely believe that their capital city, the gleaming symbol of world rule, had fallen to an army of people they considered barbarian thugs. "If Rome is sacked, what can be safe?" lamented the Christian theologian Jerome when he heard the news in far-off Jerusalem.

His remark captured the outrage and astonishment felt by Roman citizens everywhere, Christian and non-Christian alike, who believed that their empire was divinely protected and would last forever.

How did the Visigoths manage to sack Rome? The answer is rooted in the radical and debilitating transformations of the Roman Empire during late antiquity, the period between about 250 and 600, which bridged the classical world and the Middle Ages. **Late antiquity** can be divided into three stages. The first stage consisted of the half-century crisis from 235 to 284 of near-fatal civil war, foreign invasion, and economic crisis. During the second stage Rome experienced nearly 100 years of political reform and economic revival that stabilized it during the fourth century. Yet during the fifth century, the third stage of late antiquity, the political unity of the Mediterranean world ended. The Roman Empire collapsed in the West, and new Germanic kingdoms developed in Italy, Gaul, Britain, Spain, and North Africa. In contrast, the Roman Empire in the East, centered on its new capital city of Constantinople (modern Istanbul) managed to survive and prosper. Until their empire fell to the Turks 1,000 years later in 1453, the inhabitants of this eastern realm considered themselves Romans. In both Constantinople (where Roman political administration was maintained) and the new

THE TETRARCHS

To depict their solidarity and readiness for war, the tetrarchs or co-emperors are presented as soldiers in military uniform, holding their swords with one hand and clasping their colleague's shoulder with the other. Each pair of figures shows one junior emperor and one senior emperor, who has more worry lines in his forehead as a sign of his greater responsibilities.

kingdoms of the West (where it was not), Rome's cultural legacy continued in the Greek and Latin languages and some forms of Roman law.

During late antiquity Christianity emerged as the dominant religion throughout the Empire. From there it spread beyond the imperial borders, bringing new notions of civilization to the peoples of northern Europe, north Africa, and the Middle East. Henceforth, Western civilization was for most people a Christian civilization, and the borders that separated peoples were not just political ones, as in the ancient world, but religious ones. The encounter between the Roman Empire and Christianity raised this question: How did their

mutual interactions transform both the culture of the empire and the practice of Christianity?

CRISIS AND RECOVERY IN THE THIRD CENTURY

■ How did the Roman Empire successfully reorganize following the instability of the third century?

Between 235 and 284, the Roman Empire staggered from political and economic turmoil. The institutions of the army and the office of the emperor, which had made the Roman Empire the dominant power in the Mediterranean, seemed incapable of standing up to new threats. Generals competed for the throne, chronic civil war shook the empire's very foundation, and invaders hungry for land and plunder broke through the weakened imperial borders. However, by the end of the third century, the Emperor Diocletian arrested the disintegration with drastic administrative and social reforms.

The Breakdown of the Imperial Government

After the assassination of Emperor Severus Alexander in 235, military coup followed military coup as ruthless generals with nicknames like "Sword-in-Hand" competed for the throne. In the latter half of the third century, not one of more than four dozen emperors and would-be emperors died a natural death. Most emperors held power for only a few months. Preoccupied with merely staying alive and on the throne, they neglected the empire's borders, leaving them vulnerable to attack.

This had dire consequences. Invaders attacked both eastern and western provinces. To the Romans' deep shame, Emperor Valerian was captured in battle by the Great King of Persia in 260. War bands from across the Rhine River reached as far south as Italy, forcing the Emperor Aurelian to build a great wall around the city of Rome in 270. Other cities across the empire constructed similar defenses. As a consequence of the political turmoil in the empire, the seat of power shifted from Rome to provincial cities. Unlike their predecessors, the soldier-emperors of this era, who came mostly from frontier provinces, had little time to cultivate the support of the Roman Senate. Instead, they held court in cities close to the embattled frontiers. Towns far from Rome, such as York in Britain or Trier in Gaul, had long functioned as military bases and supply distribution centers. Now they served as imperial capitals whenever the emperor

SUBJUGATION OF VALERIAN

Persian kings built their tombs in a cliff six miles north of Persepolis, the old Persian royal center. Here at Naqsh-i Rustam, a carving depicts the Great King Shapur I (239–272) on horseback holding the arm of his prisoner, the Roman emperor Valerian. The previous Roman emperor, Philip (known as "the Arab"), kneels in supplication.

resided there. Some cities and provinces took advantage of the weakened government to try to break away from Roman control.

The Restoration of the Imperial Government

Near the end of the third century, Emperor Diocletian (r. 284–305) rescued the empire from its chaotic condition. Drawing on his brilliant organizational talents, he launched a succession of military, administrative, and economic reforms that had far-reaching consequences. Not since the reign of Augustus three centuries earlier had the Roman Empire been so transformed.

After ruling alone for two years, Diocletian recognized that the enormous responsibilities of imperial government overburdened a single

THE WALLS OF ROME

The Emperor Aurelian built a twelve-mile circuit of walls around Rome in the 270s to protect the city from Germanic invaders. Twenty-feet high and twelve-feet thick, the walls had 18 major gates. That Rome should need protective walls would have been unthinkable during the early empire.

emperor. So he divided the administration of the empire into two parts. In 286 he chose a co-ruler, Maximian, to govern the western half of the empire from Rome, while he continued to rule in the east. Then, in 293, Diocletian and Maximian further subdivided the empire by appointing two junior-level emperors. Each of these four co-emperors maintained a separate administrative system and his own army.

Through this system of shared government called the **tetrarchy** or rule of four, Diocletian hoped not only to make the imperial government more efficient, but also to put an end to the bloody cycle of imperial assassinations. Although he had gained the throne by murdering his predecessor, he knew that the empire's survival depended on a reliable succession strategy. To that end, Diocletian dictated that the junior emperors were to step into the senior emperors' places when the seniors retired. Then these new senior emperors were to select two new talented and reliable men to be junior emperors and become their eventual replacements. As supreme power was handed down from capable ruler to capable ruler, the constant cycle of assassinations and civil wars would be broken. Diocletian further subdivided the empire into almost 100 provinces. By focusing the responsibilities of provincial governors on smaller regions, Diocletian encouraged more efficient administration. He grouped these provinces into dioceses, each administered by a vicar who supervised the provincial governors. When Christianity later became legal in the Empire, it borrowed the diocese as its principal administrative unit.

To restore Roman military power, Diocletian reorganized the Roman army, raising its total size to about 400,000 men for all of the empire, an increase of 50,000 soldiers, making it a huge army for its time. To protect the empire from invaders, he stationed most of these troops along the borders and built new military roads. Forces of heavily armed cavalry could race to trouble spots if enemies broke through the frontiers. Diocletian also sought to reduce the army's involvement in political affairs. Although he was a soldier himself, he recognized that the army had played a disruptive role in earlier decades by constantly engaging in civil wars. He created many new legions led by commanders who were loyal to him, but he reduced the size of each legion to limit its commander's power and to increase its maneuverability. With these military reforms in place, Diocletian was able to secure the empire's borders and suppress revolts (see **Map 7.1**).

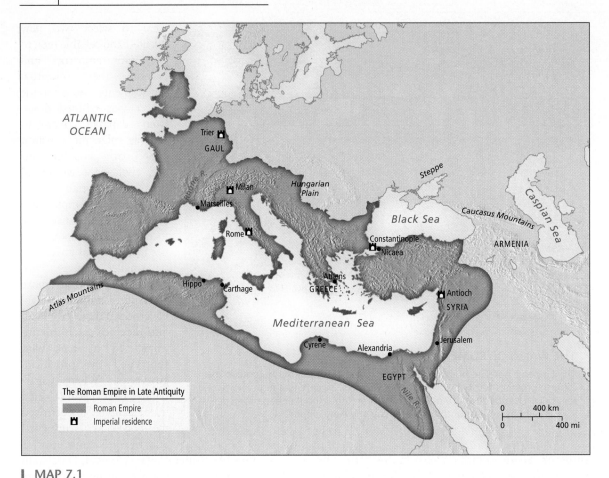

MAP 7.1

The Roman Empire in Late Antiquity

Following the reforms of Diocletian, the Roman Empire enjoyed a century of stable government, with the same borders as in earlier centuries.

Maintaining the expanded civilian and military apparatus created by the tetrarchy, especially in an era of rampant inflation, created new challenges. Diocletian had to make full use of the empire's financial resources and promote economic reforms. To halt the declining value of money, he attempted to freeze wages and prices by imperial decree. He also increased taxes and endeavored to make tax collection more effective by instituting a regular—and deeply resented—census to register all taxpayers. Although senators, army officers, and other influential citizens continued to be undertaxed or not taxed at all, the new

tax system generated enough revenues to fund the enormous machinery of government.

The greatest tax burden fell on those least able to pay it: the peasants. The law required these agricultural workers to remain where the census registered them. Sons were supposed to follow their fathers. This attempt to maintain the agricultural tax base was successful, but it lessened social mobility, and the gap between rich and poor continued to grow. Many poor peasants turned to a few rich and powerful men for protection against the ruthless imperial tax collectors. In return, these peasants granted ownership of their farms to these wealthy patrons. The peasants, called *coloni*, continued to work the land but they gave up their freedom for security.

Diocletian's attempts to strengthen the empire led to religious persecution. He believed that failure to worship the traditional Roman gods had angered the deities and brought hardship to the empire. (See *Justice in History* in this chapter.) In 303, he and his junior emperor Galerius initiated an attack on Christians in the eastern part of the empire, which was under their rule. In what is now known as the **Great Persecution**, Diocletian and Galerius forbade Christians to assemble for worship and ordered the destruction of all churches and sacred books. Several thousand women and men refused to cooperate and were executed.

TOWARD A CHRISTIAN EMPIRE

- How did Christianity become the dominant religion in the Roman Empire, and how did it affect Roman society?

Diocletian left the eastern provinces of the empire, at least, stronger militarily, administratively, and economically than they had been for nearly a century. His attempt to eradicate Christianity, however, was a failure. In the fourth century Christians developed from a persecuted minority to the dominant force in the empire.

Constantine: The First Christian Emperor

In 305, Diocletian stepped down from the imperial throne and insisted that his co-emperor in the West, Maximian, retire too. Only one year later, the troops stationed in Britain proclaimed Constantine (ca. 280–337) a co-emperor. The 20-something-year-old general set out to assert sole rule over the Roman Empire. In 312 he smashed the army of his rival co-emperor in the West at the Battle of the Milvian Bridge over the Tiber River at Rome. Twelve years later he defeated the last tetrarch

ruling in the East. Constantine then rejoined the western and eastern halves of the empire together with himself as absolute ruler. Thus, both the divided rule of the empire and the system of succession through co-emperors that Diocletian implemented came to an end.

THE COLOSSUS OF CONSTANTINE
These fragments are all that remain of the colossal statue of the Emperor Constantine, which stood 40-feet high in the apse of the Basilica of Maxentius in the Roman Forum. The co-emperor Maxentius began the basilica in 307 to glorify himself with a gigantic statue. After Constantine defeated Maxentius at the Battle of the Milvian Bridge in 312, Constantine had the head replaced or recarved with his own facial image. The emperor's head with its disproportionately large eyes that look toward heaven perhaps symbolized the Christian emphasis on the world to come over the transcience of human life.

In other ways, however, Constantine continued along Diocletian's reformist path. Under Constantine the empire's eastern and western sectors retained separate administrations. He retained Diocletian's emphasis on a large field army and heavily armored cavalry. The imperial bureaucracy and army remained immense, so taxes remained high. Under Diocletian coins had been losing their value, which contributed to the rampant inflation of prices and made the burden of taxes on the poor ever harder to sustain. To remedy the situation, Constantine reformed the coinage system. He recognized that the existing coins had become so debased they were effectively worthless, so he created a new gold coin—the *solidus,* which had a fixed gold content. The solidus stabilized the economy by restoring the value of currency. The new coin ended the inflationary spiral that had contributed so much to the political and social turmoil of the third century. It remained the standard coin in the Mediterranean world for 800 years.

Unlike Diocletian, Constantine embraced the new religion of Christianity. Most emperors had associated themselves with a divine protector. Constantine had chosen the sun god Apollo as his first divine companion. But the night before the pivotal battle at the Milvian Bridge in 312, Constantine experienced a vision of the cross upon which Jesus had been crucified. After triumphing in battle, Constantine interpreted his vision as a sign from the Christian God who brought him the victory.

Because monotheistic Christianity repudiated rival gods and alternative forms of worship, Constantine's conversion led to the eventual triumph of Christianity throughout the empire. Constantine did not order his subjects to accept Christianity or forbid polytheist worship. He did, however, encourage widespread and public practice of his new faith. Before Constantine, Christian worship had often been conducted in the privacy of homes, but he lavished funds on church buildings. He obtained the gold for his new solidus coinage by looting the treasures that had been stored for centuries in polytheist temples. Now encouraged by the emperor, Christianity quickly gained strength and became a potent challenge to traditional modes of religious expression.

To create an entirely Christian new Rome, Constantine founded a second capital city, Constantinople, the "City of Constantine," on the site of the Greek city Byzantium in 324. Constantine's choice of location revealed a shrewd eye for strategy. The city lay at the juncture of two military roads that linked Europe and Asia and controlled communications between the Mediterranean and the Black Seas. From this strategic spot the emperor monitored the vast resources of the empire's eastern provinces. Like Diocletian, Constantine recognized that the wealth and power of the empire lay in the East.

Constantine's capital became a strongly fortified city. In response to the threat of attack by pirates, the emperor Theodosius II erected massive defensive walls around the city in 413. In future centuries these fortifications would protect the city—and indeed, the empire—from ruin on many occasions. With a new Senate formed on the model of that of the city of Rome, a steady supply of grain from Egypt to feed the capital's inhabitants, and plenty of opportunities for trade, Constantinople attracted people from all over the empire. The city rapidly grew in size, reaching perhaps several hundred thousand inhabitants by the early sixth century.

The Spread of Christianity

Before the fourth century Christianity had grown through missionaries who established congregations in most cities of the empire. After Constantine, successive emperors encouraged Christianity, which mushroomed throughout the empire through the spread of bishops who became local figures of great prestige. With imperial support, church leaders Christianized the look of cities by building churches and attacking polytheist temples.

THE RISE OF THE BISHOPS   Part of the success of Christianity was due to the sophistication of its internal organization. In the early centuries of Christianity a distinction developed between the laity—the ordinary worshipers—and the priests, who led the worship, administered the sacraments, and acted as pastors for the laity. In imitation of the Roman urban administration, Christians developed their own administrative hierarchy. Just as an imperial official directed each city's political affairs with a staff of assistants, so each city's Christian community came to be led by a chief pastor, called a bishop, who in turn had a staff of subordinate priests and deacons. Just as a provincial governor controlled the political affairs of all of the cities and rural regions in his province, so the bishop of the main city of a province held authority over the other bishops and priests in the province. This main or head bishop came to be called a *metropolitan* (because he resided in the chief city, the metropolis, of the province) in the East, an *archbishop* in the West. This hierarchy of metropolitans/archbishops, bishops, priests, and deacons linked the scattered communities of believers together into what emerged as the Christian Church.

With this administrative structure, the Church grew quickly, and bishops became important authorities in their cities. A bishop supervised the religious life of his *see* or diocese, a unit based on Diocletian's administrative reforms. A diocese comprised not only the city itself, but also its surrounding villages and agricultural regions. Such supervision involved explaining Christian principles and teaching the Bible. Bishops soon became far more than religious teachers. As the Church grew wealthy from the massive donations of emperors such as Constantine and the humbler offerings of pious women and men throughout the empire, bishops used these resources to help the poor. The bishops cared for the general welfare of orphans, widows, sick people, prisoners, and travelers. When famine struck southern Gaul in the fifth century, for example, the bishop of Lyons sent so much food from his church estates that grain barges jammed the Rhône and Saône Rivers and carts full of grain clogged the roads going south.

Constantine permitted bishops to act as judges in civil actions, which made them agents of the imperial government. This policy soon entangled them in secular politics because litigants could choose to be tried before a bishop rather than a civil judge. The decisions of a bishop had the same legal authority as those rendered by civil judges. Using the rhetorical skills they had learned in Roman schools, bishops were also the advocates for their cities before provincial governors or the imperial court. In many ways they usurped the role of the traditional urban aristocracy. For example, when the people of Antioch in Syria rioted and smashed a statue of the emperor, the local bishop, not a local aristocrat, intervened to prevent imperial troops from massacring the city's people.

In the West, Rome became the most important see. Like all bishops, the bishop of Rome came to be called the "pope"—the papa or father of his flock. In his case the title stuck and eventually referred only to him. By the mid-fifth century the emperor formally recognized the pope's claim to have preeminence over other bishops. Two factors explain why the office of the bishop of Rome evolved into the **papacy**. First, together with Jerusalem, Rome was a site of powerful symbolic importance to Christians because the Apostle Peter, considered the first among Jesus's disciples, and Paul of Tarsus, the traveling teacher who took a leading role in spreading Christianity beyond its Jewish origins, died as martyrs in Rome. Second, early Christians considered Peter to have been the first bishop of Rome who passed on his authority to all subsequent popes in what is called the doctrine of the Petrine Succession.

Popes claimed to be the chief bishops of the Christian world. They insisted that their spiritual authority took precedence over that of rival bishops in other important cities, especially Constantinople. The bishops (called patriarchs) of Constantinople often quarreled bitterly with the pope over matters of faith and politics. The tensions among these bishops led to divisions between the eastern and western parts of the empire that have lasted until the present day.

Through the authority of the bishops, the Church began functioning almost as an administrative arm of the government, although it still had its own internal organization. Indeed, when

Roman rule collapsed in western Europe in the fifth century, the Church stepped in to fill the vacuum of public leadership.

CHRISTIANITY AND THE CITY OF ROME Christianity transformed the appearance of Roman cities. Constantine set an example of public and private spending on churches, hospitals, and monastic communities that conformed to Christian values. One of the great churches that Constantine built in Rome was called "Saint Paul Outside the Walls." This imposing structure marked the supposed burial spot of Paul of Tarsus. Constantine also financed the construction of another grand church on the presumed site of Peter's martyrdom and burial, in an obscure cemetery on what was called the Vatican hill, just outside Rome's wall. St. Peter's Basilica was an imposing structure, with five aisles punctuated with marble columns. Its altar rested over Peter's grave. (Today the papal basilica of St. Peter stands on that same spot, in the heart of the Vatican, the city-state of the pope.) The construction of these churches signaled that Jesus's apostles Peter and Paul had replaced Rome's mythical founders Romulus and Remus as the city's sacred patrons. With the construction of Christian churches, spending and construction on traditional buildings such as temples, bathhouses, and public entertainment facilities such as the circuses declined. At the prompting of Rome's bishops, other public buildings, such as the large basilicas used for public business, including legal trials, were turned into churches.

With the proliferation of new Christian churches in Rome and other cities came new religious festivals and rituals, such as the anniversaries

CENTRAL NAVE OF SANTA MARIA MAGGIORE

The church of Santa Maria Maggiore, dedicated to Mary, the mother of Jesus, was built in Rome in the 430s. Like other late antique churches, Santa Maria Maggiore followed the plan of a Roman public building, a basilica, but added an altar in the semicircular apse at one end. Mosaics on the walls above the columns depicted stories from the Bible. They decorated the church and provided lessons for illiterate worshipers.

of the martyrdom of saints. Sometimes a Christian holiday (holy day) competed with a non-Christian holiday. For example, Rome's churchmen designated December 25 as the birthday of Christ to challenge the popular festival of the Unconquered Sun, which fell on the same day. By the early sixth century, the Church had filled the calendar with days devoted to Christian ceremonies. Christmas and Easter (which commemorates Jesus's resurrection) and days for commemorating specific martyrs supplanted traditional Roman holidays. These festivals thus changed the patterns of urban community life throughout the empire. Not all of the traditional Roman holidays disappeared, however. Those that Christians considered harmless continued to be observed as civic holidays. These included New Year's Day, the accession days of the emperors, and the days that celebrated the founding of Rome and Constantinople.

One additional development in the Christian shaping of time was the use of the letters A.D. as a dating convention. A.D. stands for *anno domini*, or "in the year of our Lord," referring to the year of Jesus's birth. The convention began in 531, when a monk in Rome established a simple system for determining the date of Easter every year. He began his calendar with the birth of Jesus in the year one (zero was unknown in Europe at this time) and started counting from there. Although he was probably a few years off in his determination of the year of Jesus's birth, his system came into general use by the tenth century. In many modern secular societies where belief in Christianity is not universal, the abbreviation A.D. has been replaced by C.E.—meaning "in the Common Era"—to designate years.

OLD GODS UNDER ATTACK   Before Christianity became the dominant religion in the Roman Empire, people prayed to gods of all sorts. Different deities met different needs, and the worship of one did not preclude worship of another. To Christians, this diverse range of religious expression was intolerable. They labeled all polytheistic worship with the derogatory term **pagan** from the Latin word *paganus*, which

meant "hillbilly," a reflection of the urban bias of early Christianity and the failure of Christianity to spread among country people.

After converting to Christianity in 312, Constantine ordered the end of the persecution of Christians. Although Christianity did not become the "official" religion of the empire for nearly a century, tolerance for non-Christian beliefs and practices began to fade. In the fourth century, imperial laws forbade sacrificing animals on the altars outside the old gods' temples. State funding for polytheistic worship gradually stopped. Instead of temples, emperors built churches with money collected from the taxpayers. Bishops and monks, often in collusion with local administrators, led attacks on polytheist shrines and holy places.

Because polytheism was not a single, organized religion, it offered no systematic opposition to government-supported attacks, but there were influential opponents to the Christianization of the empire. In sharp contrast to the pious Christian court at Constantinople, the conservative aristocracy of the city of Rome clung hard to the old gods. In 384, their spokesman begged the emperor for tolerance. Quintus Aurelius Symmachus argued that Rome's greatness had resulted from the observance of ancient rites. His pleas fell on deaf ears. Emperor Theodosius I (r. 379–395) and his grandson Theodosius II (r. 402–450) forbade all forms of polytheistic worship, and non-Christian practice lost the protection of the law. By the mid-fifth century, the aristocracy of the city of Rome had accepted Christianity. (See *Justice in History* in this chapter.)

Many less influential people also struggled to maintain ancient forms of worship, but the pace of conversion accelerated in the fifth and sixth centuries. Emperor Justinian (r. 527–565) sponsored programs of forced conversion in the countryside of Anatolia, where many of his subjects still followed ancient ways. Eradicating polytheism in the Roman Empire meant far more than substituting one religion for another. In the pre-Christian world, polytheism lay at the heart of every community, influencing every activity, every habit of social life. To replace

FEMALE PRIEST

This foot-high ivory panel shows a female priest making a sacrifice at an altar to an unnamed god or goddess. *Symmachorum* means "of the family of the Symmachi," an aristocratic Roman clan in which some members defended the old gods in the face of Christianity. Unlike the polytheist cults of Late Antiquity, orthodox Christians did not allow women to serve as priests.

the worship of the old gods required a true revolution in social and intellectual life. Completing that revolution became the challenge of the new Christian communities.

NEW CHRISTIAN COMMUNITIES AND IDENTITIES

■ How did Christianity transform communities, religious experience, and intellectual traditions inside and outside the empire?

Christianity solidified community loyalties and allegiances by providing a shared belief system and new opportunities for participation in religious culture. Yet Christianity also opened up new divisions and gave rise to new hostilities over conflicting interpretations of the doctrines of the faith. Because Christians spoke Greek, Latin, Coptic, Syriac, Armenian, and other languages, different religious interpretations and rituals sometimes took hold among different language groups, creating distinct communities.

The Creation of New Communities

Christianity fostered the growth of large-scale communities of faith by providing a well-defined set of beliefs and values. These basic beliefs and values had to be integrated with daily life and older ways of thinking. Thus, Christianity required followers to study and interpret the Bible. It also demanded allegiance to one God and a complex set of doctrines.

CHRISTIAN DOCTRINE AND HERESY Despite the institutionalization of the Church through the office of bishops, the theological controversies that had shaped Christianity from its very start continued and new controversies emerged. Councils of bishops met frequently to try to resolve doctrinal differences and produce statements of the faith that all parties could accept.

The persistent question was who was or is Jesus? Was he a man, God, or some combination of both? Like Jews, the followers of Christ believe that one God created and governs Heaven and Earth. If Jesus were just a man, as the adoptionist Christians discussed in Chapter 6 thought, then monotheism is preserved. If Jesus were a man that God adopted to be his special son and to carry out his mission, then Jesus was no different in his nature from any other man and could be subject to sin and error. If, however, Jesus were God who only appeared to possess the body of a man, as the docetic Christians believed, then other problems arose. For example, if Christ were entirely divine, then who did he pray to? This emphasis on Jesus's divinity made his death on the cross and his resurrection irrelevant, for God could not suffer and die. It also severed the links between Jesus and his human followers by emphasizing that Jesus was entirely "transcendent" or "other," entirely beyond human comprehension or human limitations.

A group of theologians developed the doctrine of the Trinity during the second and third centuries as an answer to these persistent questions about the nature of Jesus. They argued that the one God was to be understood as existing in three distinct "persons," each fully and absolutely God—God the Father, God the Son, and God the Holy Spirit—the Holy Trinity. This solution, however, did not entirely resolve the controversies. Church leaders continued to argue about the precise relation of the three persons within the Trinity. Were the Son and the Holy Spirit of the same essence as the Father? Were they equally divine? Did the Father exist before the Son?

These questions about the nature of the Trinity just continued the adoptionist-docetic debate in a different form, which came to be called the Arian and Athanasian dispute. The **Arians** followed Arius of Alexandria (ca. 250–336), a priest steeped in Greek philosophy. Arians asserted that God the Father created Jesus, so Jesus could not be equal to or of the same essence as God the Father. Arians argued that the Trinitarian idea that Jesus was both fully divine and fully human was illogical. The Athanasians, followers of Bishop Athanasius of Alexandria (293–373), were horrified by what they saw as the Arians' attempt to degrade Jesus's divinity. They argued that Christian truths were beyond human logic and that Jesus was fully God, equal to and of the same substance as God the Father, yet also fully human.

The Arian-Athanasian dispute resulted in perhaps the most influential of the many church meetings held in late antiquity: the Council of Nicaea. As the first general council, Nicaea signaled the beginning of an empire-wide Church. In 325, Emperor Constantine summoned the quarrelling bishops to Nicaea, a town near Constantinople, to reach a decision about the relationship among the divine members of the Holy Trinity. The bishops produced the Nicene Creed, which is still recited in Christian worship today. The creed, in agreement with Athanasian belief, states that God the Son (Jesus Christ) is identical in nature and essence to God the Father. In 451 the Council of Chalcedon reinforced the Nicene Creed. The assembled bishops agreed that Jesus was both fully human and fully divine, and that these two natures were entirely distinct though united. Their position became the interpretation accepted to this day by Orthodox, Catholic, and Protestant Christians.

COMMUNITIES OF FAITH AND LANGUAGE   The doctrinal differences between Christian groups helped cement different communal and even ethnic identities in late antiquity. Three geographic zones of Christians emerged that held different interpretations of Christian doctrine, each a testament to the remarkable variety of Christian cultures.

A central zone based in Constantinople and including North Africa, the Balkans, and much of western Europe contained Christians called **Chalcedonians,** or orthodox. (In the Latin-speaking western provinces, they were also called Catholics.) These believers followed the decision of the Council of Chalcedon that defined Christ's divine and human natures as equal but entirely distinct. Christ was both God and man at the same time, but his divine and human natures did not mix. In late antiquity, the emperors in Constantinople and the popes in Rome—as well as most of the population of the Roman Empire—were Chalcedonian Christians.

Although the Christians in this first zone agreed on fundamental matters of doctrine, they differed culturally by producing Bibles, delivering sermons, and conducting religious ceremonies in their native languages—Latin in the western part

THE VIENNA GENESIS

The Greek text written in silver ink at the top of the page tells the story of Susanna at the Well from the book of Genesis in the Bible. Though the illustration at the bottom of the page tells a biblical story, certain details reflect conditions in late antiquity, such as fortified cities and the growing importance of camels in travel and commerce. The seated, semi-nude female in the lower left is derived from polytheist religion. She personifies the stream from which the more modestly dressed Susanna gathers water.

Thus, church-based Latin served as a powerful unifying and stabilizing influence. The Latin language combined with Christianity to spur the development of **Latin Christendom**—the many peoples and kingdoms in western Europe united by their common religion and shared language of worship and intellectual life.

In the eastern provinces of the Roman Empire, Christianity had a different voice. There a Greek-based Church developed. Greek was the language of imperial rule and common culture in that region, and Greek became the language of the Eastern Christian Church. In addition to the New Testament, which had been originally written in Greek, eastern Christians used a Greek version of the Hebrew Bible (the Old Testament) called the Septuagint, which Greek-speaking Jews had prepared in Alexandria in the second century B.C.E. for their own community. The Septuagint combined with the Greek New Testament to become the authoritative Christian Bible throughout most of Rome's eastern provinces.

of the central zone; mostly Greek (but also Syriac, Armenian, and Coptic) in the eastern part of the central zone. About 410, the monk Jerome finished a new Latin translation of the Bible that replaced earlier Latin versions. This translation, called the **Vulgate,** became the standard Bible in European churches until the sixteenth century.

The Western Church's use of Latin kept the door open for the transmission of all Latin texts into a world defined by Christianity. This ensured the survival of Roman legal, scientific, and literary traditions, even after Roman rule had evaporated in western Europe. Latin also forged a common bond among different political communities of the empire's western sector, where it served as an international language among ruling elites, even though they spoke different languages in their daily lives.

In a second zone in the eastern Mediterranean and beyond were Anti-Chalcedonians, usually known by the derogatory term of **Monophysites** (literally "one nature"). They did not accept the teaching of the Council of Chalcedon about the combination of the divine and the human in Christ as being "in two natures." Instead, they believed that Christ had one nature in which the human evolved into the divine. In Christ, human nature "dissolved like a drop of honey in the sea." He had a human body and a human "living principle," but the divine took over his thinking. Three anti-Chalcedonian communities had developed by the end of late antiquity—in Armenia in the Caucasus mountain region of eastern Anatolia; in Egypt, among the native Egyptian speakers, called Copts; and among the inhabitants of Syria who spoke Syriac. A vast literature of biblical interpretation, sermons, commentaries, and church documents was gradually created in the languages of each of these communities

In addition to the Chalcedonian and anti-Chalcedonian regions in late antiquity, a third zone of Christians consisted of the Arians. As described earlier, Arians believed that Jesus was not equal to or of the same substance as God the Father because God had created Jesus. Arians saw themselves as more rigidly monotheistic than Chalcedonian Christians, whose belief in the Trinity they regarded as bordering on polytheism. Most of the people who followed Arian Christianity were the Goths and other Germanic settlers who converted to Christianity in the fourth century, when they still lived north of the Danube River and in southern Russia. When they invaded the Roman Empire in the fifth century, they seized political control of Rome's western provinces. While the Goths were still north of the Danube, a missionary named Ulfila devised a Gothic alphabet and used it to translate the Bible from Greek into Gothic, an early version of German. A Christian Gothic culture thrived in the western zone despite its minority status.

In these three zones, variations of the Christian faith expressed in different languages formed the seedbed of ethnic communities, some of which still flourish, such as the Armenians, Copts, and Greek-speaking Orthodox Christians. Yet the spread of Christianity weakened other local groupings. As language-based Christian communities spread inside and outside the empire, many local dialects and languages disappeared. Only the languages in which Christianity found textual expression survived.

THE MONASTIC MOVEMENT Near the end of the third century, a new Christian spiritual movement took root in the Roman Empire. Known today as **asceticism,** this movement called for Christians to subordinate their physical needs and desires to a quest for spiritual union with God. Asceticism both challenged the emerging connection between the political and Christian authorities and rejected the growing wealth of the Church.

The life of an Egyptian Christian, Antony, provided a model for future ascetics. Around 280 he sold all his property and walked away from his crowded village near the Nile into the desert in search of a higher spirituality. A few decades later, Athanasius, the Bishop of Alexandria who had argued against the Arians, composed a biography, the *Life of Antony,* telling how Antony overcame all the temptations the Devil could conjure up, from voluptuous naked women to opportunities for power and fame. Vividly describing the struggle between asceticism ("the discipline") and the lures of everyday life ("the household"), Athanasius's work became one of the most influential books in Western literature. It inspired thousands of men and women to imitate Antony by rejecting the ties of the household and material world. Asceticism appealed to those who desired an alternative to political and especially family life with its coercive parental authority, marriage, sexuality, and children. These all distracted from the contemplation of God.

Ascetic discipline required harsh and often violent treatment of the body. The first ascetics, called anchorites (meaning "withdrawal") or hermits (meaning "of the desert"), lived alone in the most inaccessible and uncomfortable places they could find, such as a cave, a hole in the ground, or on top of a pillar. In addition to praying constantly in their struggle to overcome the Devil and empty themselves of human desires so that God could enter and work through them, these men and women starved and whipped themselves, rejecting every comfort, including human companionship.

Over time, however, many Egyptian ascetics began to construct communities for themselves. The result was the **monastic movement.** Because these communities, called monasteries, often grew to hold 1,000 or more members, they required organization and guidance. Leaders emerged to provide clear instructions for regulating monastic life and offer spiritual guidance to the members of the monasteries. (The male inhabitants of monasteries were called monks, or solitary men. Women were called nuns.)

Drawing from the ideas of these earlier monastic rules written in Greek, Benedict of Nursia (ca. 480–547) wrote a Latin *Rule* that became the foundation of monasticism in western Europe. Benedict built a monastery on Monte Cassino near Naples in 529. While he emphasized voluntary poverty and a life devoted to prayer, he placed more stress on labor. Fearing that the Devil could tempt an idle monk, Benedict wanted his monks to keep busy. He therefore ordered that all monks perform physical labor for parts of every day when they were not sleeping or praying.

In the western Roman Empire, monasticism played a central role in preserving classical learning and thus allowing its integration into Christian culture in later centuries. Much of the credit for preserving the classical intellectual tradition lay with the monasteries founded by Benedict. These monks, called the Benedictine order, established monasteries throughout western Europe, modeled on Benedict's original monastery of Monte Cassino. Benedict himself was wary of classical teaching, but he wanted the monks and nuns under his supervision to be able to read religious books. At least basic education in literacy had to become part of monastic life. The Benedictine definition of "manual labor" expanded to include copying ancient manuscripts, which supplied the libraries in the monasteries and preserved Latin literature.

MONASTICISM AND WOMEN The monastic movement opened new avenues for female spirituality and offered an alternative to marriage and childbearing. By joining monastic communities and leaving the routines of daily life behind, women could escape the obligations of the male-dominated society. As Christian monasticism spread, ascetic women began to create communities of their own. They lived as celibate sisterhoods of nuns, dedicated to spiritual quest and service to God.

The wives or daughters of wealthy and powerful families were typically the founders of female monastic communities. Such women wielded an authority and influence that would not have been available to them otherwise. For example, Melania the Younger (383–439), the daughter of a wealthy Roman senatorial family, decided to sell her vast estates and spend the proceeds in religious pursuits. When the Roman Senate objected to the breaking up of Melania's family estates, she appealed to the empress, who interceded with the legal authorities to enable her to dispose of her property. (Melania's slaves also objected because they did not want to be sold separately to raise cash for her religious projects, but she ignored them.) Melania spent her fortune building monasteries in the Holy Land of Palestine. Most women could not afford to make such dramatic gestures, but they could imitate Melania's accomplishment on a modest scale.

Despite the piety of women such as Melania, an increasingly negative view of women emerged in the writings of late antique churchmen. Christian writers branded women as disobedient, sexually promiscuous, innately sinful, and naturally inferior to men. They interpreted Genesis, the first book of the Bible, to mean that women bore a special curse. In their reading of the Genesis account, Eve, the first woman, seduced Adam, the first man. For this reason late antique Christians blamed Eve—and women collectively—for humanity's expulsion from the Garden of Eden and for all the woes human beings had suffered since. Yet Christians also believed that God would save the souls of women as well as men, and they honored Mary for her role in bringing Jesus, and therefore salvation, into the world. (See *Different Voices* in this chapter.)

JEWS IN A CHRISTIAN WORLD Until Christianity became the official religion of the Roman Empire, Jews had been simply one among hundreds of religious and ethnic groups who lived under Roman rule. Although polytheist Romans considered Jews eccentric because they worshiped only one god and refused to make statues of him, they still respected the Jewish people's faith. Before the fourth century, Jews had enjoyed full citizenship rights and practiced all professions and belonged to all levels of society.

Christianity slowly erased all this. As we saw in Chapter 6, relations between Christians and Jews grew more hostile after the Jewish rebellion and the destruction of Jerusalem by the Roman army in 70. Christian theology mirrored this growing hostility. Christians taught that the Diaspora (the dispersion of Jews around the world after Jerusalem's destruction) was God's way of punishing the Jews for failing to accept Jesus as their messiah and for crucifying Jesus Christ.

Beginning in the fourth century, Roman laws began to discriminate against Jews, forbidding them to marry Christians, own Christian slaves, or accept converts to Judaism. With the support of Christian imperial officials, Church leaders sometimes forced entire communities of Jews to convert to Christianity on pain of death. Although organized resistance among scattered Jewish communities was impossible, many Jews refused to accept the deepening oppression. Their resistance ranged from acts of violence against Jews who had converted to Christianity to armed revolt against Roman authorities.

Individual Jewish communities continued to administer their own affairs under the leadership of rabbis—men who served as teachers and interpreters of Jewish law. We saw in Chapter 6 that the Mishnah, the final codification of Jewish oral law, was completed by the end of the third century. Rabbis incorporated the Mishnah into the **Talmud,** which included commentaries on the law, ethics, and Jewish history. The influential Jerusalem Talmud was compiled about 400, the Babylonian Talmud a century later. Rabbis and their courts now dominated Jewish communities. These learned men established academies of legal study in Roman Palestine and Persian Babylonia, where their interpretations guided everyday Jewish life.

In rabbinic Judaism women continued to play an important role in the household, especially since Judaism emphasized the importance of moral behavior and religious practice rather than dogma. As a result, as wives and mothers, Jewish women had a more positive role in the practice of their religion than women did in Christianity, which considered married women and men morally inferior to celibate nuns and monks. Some Jewish women served as leaders of synagogues in late antiquity, but in public life as opposed to private life, rabbinic Judaism subordinated women. For example, Jewish women did not receive an education at the Jewish academies. Excluded from the formal process of interpreting holy texts, Jewish women did not acquire highly prized religious knowledge.

GREEK ZODIAC IN A SYNAGOGUE

In late antiquity, Jews living in Palestine sometimes decorated their synagogues with mosaic floors depicting the zodiac. Although these mosaics appeared in synagogues and often contained Hebrew writing, the scenes and style of the mosaics were typical of Greek and Roman art. This blending demonstrates that members of the Jewish congregation also participated in the general non-Jewish culture of the province.

DIFFERENT VOICES CHRISTIAN ATTITUDES TOWARD SEXUALITY, CONTRACEPTION, AND ABORTION

Churchmen were hostile to sexuality and considered celibacy the superior way for Christians to live. There were numerous reasons for this hostility, but most of all Christians expected Christ to return at any moment, which made any pursuit except for spiritual purification seem irrelevant. In addition, one of the attractions of early Christianity was liberation from coercive family ties, which distracted believers from their higher obligations to God. Yet as time passed and Christ did not return, churchmen began to recognize the necessity for Christians to produce children for the faith to grow. The result was a double ethic that exalted celibacy and yet placed special obligations on those who were married to bear children. The excerpts below illustrate this double ethic. The first document, attributed to Saint Patrick from the mid-fifth century, shows how an Irish woman's decision to live a celibate life subjected her to persecution from non-Christians who thought her obligation was to bear children. The second comes from a sermon by Caesarius, bishop of Arles from 502 to 542.

A. And there was also a blessed lady of native Irish birth and high rank, very beautiful and grown up, whom I baptized; and a few days later she found some reason to come to us and indicated that she had received a message from an angel of god, and the angel had urged her too to become a virgin of Christ and to draw near to God. Thanks be to God....she most commendably and enthusiastically took up that same course that all virgins of God also do—not with their fathers' consent; no, they endure persecution and their own parents' unfair reproaches, and yet their number grows larger and larger....But it is the women kept in slavery who suffer especially; they even have to endure constant threats and terrorization.

B. No woman should take drugs for purposes of abortion, nor should she kill her children that have been conceived or are already born. If anyone does this, she should know that before Christ's tribunal she will have to plead her case in the presence of those she has killed. Moreover, women should not take diabolical draughts with the purpose of not being able to conceive children. A woman who does this ought to realize that she will be guilty of as many murders as the number of children she might have borne. I would like to know whether a woman of nobility who takes deadly drugs to prevent conception wants her maids or tenants to do so. Just as every woman wants slaves born for her so that they may serve her, so she herself should nurse all the children she conceives, or entrust them to others for rearing. Otherwise, she may refuse to conceive children or, what is more serious, be willing to kill souls which might have been good Christians. Now, with what kind of a conscience does she desire slaves to be born of her servants, when she herself refuses to bear children who might become Christians?

For Discussion

1. What do these documents reveal about Christian views about women?

2. How do Caesarius's reasons for opposing contraception and abortion differ from the arguments of those who oppose these practices today?

Source: *Readings in Late Antiquity: A Sourcebook*, ed. By Michael Maas (2000), 222–223, 230–231, published by Routledge. Copyright © 2000 by Michael Maas. Reproduced by permission of Taylor & Francis Books UK (www.tandf.co.uk and www.eBookstore.tandf.co.uk).

Instead, men expected them to conform to submissive roles as daughters, wives, and mothers, much as women in other religious communities were expected to do.

Access to Holiness: Christian Pilgrimage

In late antiquity, Christians began to make religious journeys, or **pilgrimages,** to visit sacred places, especially those housing holy objects, known as **relics.** Christians believed these relics were inherently holy because they were physical objects associated with saints and martyrs or with Jesus himself. The most highly valued relics were bones from the venerated person. Christians believed that merely by touching something of a holy person, one could share in that holiness, which could cure them of an illness, heighten their spiritual awareness, or help them achieve eternal life.

The mortal remains of Christian martyrs provided the first relics for pilgrims, but after persecution of Christians ceased in 312, believers began to venerate the bodies of great bishops and ascetic monks and nuns. From the fourth century onward, Christians regularly dug up skeletons of saints, chopped them up, and distributed the pieces to churches. The more important the holy person, the fiercer the competition for the bones and other objects associated with him or her. Churches in the largest cities of the empire, such as Rome, Constantinople, Alexandria, and Jerusalem, acquired fine collections. Residents of Constantinople believed that the Virgin Mary's robe, kept in a church inside the city, drove away enemies when it was carried in procession along the battlements.

Emperors and important bishops acquired the greatest and most powerful relics of all—those that had reportedly touched Jesus himself. These included the crown of thorns he wore when crucified, the cross on which he died, and the nails that fastened him to the wood. Relics reminded Christians that the martyrdom of his

followers symbolically repeated Jesus's own death. Hence, they constructed church altars, where followers celebrated the Eucharist (the rite in which bread and wine are offered as Jesus's body and blood in memory of his death) over the graves or relics of martyrs.

Traveling to touch a relic was the primary motive for a pilgrimage. Palestine became a frequent destination of Christian pilgrims because it contained the most sacred sites and relics associated with events described in the Bible and particularly with Jesus's life and death. Between the fourth and seventh centuries, thousands of earnest Christian pilgrims flocked to Palestine to visit holy sites and pray for divine assistance and forgiveness for their sins. Helena, the mother of Emperor Constantine, made pilgrimage fashionable. In the early fourth century, she visited Jerusalem, where she reportedly found remnants of the cross on which Jesus was crucified, and identified many of the sites pertaining to Jesus's life. Inspired by his mother's journey, Constantine funded the construction of lavish shrines and monasteries at these sites and guest houses for pilgrims. Practically overnight Palestine was transformed from a provincial backwater to the spiritual focus of the Christian world. Religious men and women—rich and poor, old and young, sick and healthy—streamed to Palestine and Jerusalem.

Palestine did not have a monopoly on holy places, however. Pilgrims traveled to places throughout the Roman world wherever saints had lived and died and where their relics rested. Pilgrimages contributed to the growth of a Christian view of the world in three ways. First, because pilgrimage was a holy enterprise, Christian communities gave hospitality and lodging to religious travelers. This fostered a shared sense of Christian community among people from many lands. Second, Christians envisioned a Christian "map" dominated by spiritually significant places. Travel guides that explained this "spiritual geography" became popular among pilgrims. Most of all, pilgrims who returned home, enriched in their faith and perhaps cured in mind or spirit, inspired their home communities with news of a growing Christian world directly linked to the biblical lands they heard about in church.

Christian Intellectual Life

During the first three centuries after Jesus's death, when Christians were marginalized and at times persecuted, many church leaders criticized classical learning. Churchmen argued that the learning of pagan intellectuals was false wisdom, that it distracted Christians from what was truly important—contemplation of Jesus Christ and the eternal salvation he offered—and therefore that it corrupted young Christians. Tertullian (ca. 160–240), for example, argued for the separation of Christianity from the learning and culture of the non-Christian world: "What has Athens to do with Jerusalem? What is there in common between the philosopher and the Christian?" Christians like Tertullian mistrusted the human intellect and stressed the need to focus on the divine revelation of the Christian Scriptures.

After Constantine's conversion, influential voices in the Church began to answer these questions. To them, classical learning no longer seemed as threatening as it had before. Many church leaders now came from the empire's urban elite, where they had absorbed classical learning. Christian officials grudgingly approved secular education because they recognized that the traditional curriculum was useful for administering the Church and for the law. Training in classical rhetoric, grammar, and literature became an integral part of upper-class Christian life. By the fifth century, traditional schooling for Christians was accepted as a useful if risky enterprise. As Basil the Great (ca. 330–379), bishop of Caesarea in Cappadocia (in modern Turkey), explained to young men about to embark on their studies, classical learning had both benefits and dangers. Although pagan learning, he advised, had some spiritual value, the charm of words could poison the Christian's heart.

Augustine of Hippo (354–430) most fully took up the challenge of classical learning to Christianity. By examining the most troubling philosophical and historical questions in light of the scriptures, Augustine became the most influential Church Father among Latin-speaking Christians. The **Church Fathers** were writers from both the Greek and Latin-speaking worlds who sought to reconcile Christianity with classical learning.

Born to parents of modest means, Augustine attended traditional Roman schools as a youth, an education that made him thoroughly familiar with the classics and prepared him for a high position in public life. After his conversion to Christianity, Augustine became the influential bishop of the city of Hippo Regius in North Africa. He recounted his spiritual experiences and conversion in the *Confessions* (397), an autobiography written in his middle age. Drawing on the ideas of the Greek philosopher Plato and on Christian scriptures, Augustine in the *Confessions* meditated on the meaning of life, especially on sin and redemption. Augustine showed that intellect alone was incapable of bringing about the spiritual growth that he desired. God needed to intervene. For his spiritual conversion to be complete, Augustine believed he had to cleanse himself of the desires of the flesh, which led him to renounce sexuality completely. Using his episcopal office as a platform from which to defend Christianity from polytheist philosophers and to define all aspects of the Christian life, Augustine displayed a sincere respect for Roman cultural and intellectual accomplishments—especially rhetoric and history. But he always believed Christianity was superior. For Augustine, the most dangerous enemy of all true Christians was "antiquity, mother of all evils"—the source of false beliefs.

In his book *The City of God,* completed in 423, Augustine developed a new interpretation of history. Augustine's historical theory disconnected Christian ideas of human destiny from the fate of the Roman Empire. In his view, the empire was just one among many that had existed and that would exist before Jesus's return. According to Augustine, the only dates humanity should view as spiritually significant were Jesus's time on Earth and the End of Days sometime in the future. Only God knew the significance of all events in between.

Augustine's theory proved timely. Within a few years of his death, the Vandals seized North Africa and the Roman Empire lost control of all of its provinces in western Europe. Augustine thus gave Roman Christians a new perspective with which to view this loss: Rome had contributed to world civilization and to the growth of the Christian Church, but now Christianity would grow on its own without the support of Roman emperors.

After the collapse of the Roman Empire in the western provinces, the challenge for Christian thinkers came less from reconciling Christianity with the power of classical learning than from keeping classical learning alive at all. Outside the monasteries traditional schooling in the classics survived only as long as cities could afford to pay for teachers. In most of the towns of the western provinces of the empire, schools gradually disappeared during the fifth century as a result of the Germanic invasions. In the eastern provinces they survived until the seventh century then faded away.

NEOPLATONISM AND CHRISTIANITY Greek and Roman philosophy remained influential in the late antique period. One branch of this tradition, called **Neoplatonism,** is associated with the thought of Plotinus (205–270), a non-Christian philosopher. His teachings greatly influenced Christianity, an example of how classical and Christian thought intertwined in late antiquity. Plotinus, who taught in Rome, traced his intellectual roots primarily to the works of Plato (ca. 429–327 B.C.E.). He also drew ideas from Aristotle (384–322 B.C.E.), Stoic philosophers (third century B.C.E.), and their followers.

Plotinus argued that all things that exist, whether intangible ideas or tangible matter, originate in a single force called the One. Humans could reunite their souls with the One by overcoming their passions and physical desires that were governed by the body. Many Neoplatonists believed that by gaining the help of the gods through magical rites and studying divine revelations, the human soul could reconnect with the One and realize its fullest potential. Neoplatonism had many similarities to Gnosticism, which was discussed in Chapter 6 and which also guided some early Christians. The Gnostics, however, emphasized magic in a way that the sober, philosophical Neoplatonists such as Plotinus thought was the work of "imbeciles."

Neoplatonism appealed to many Christians. For them, the One was God, and the Bible provided the divine revelations that could lead to the salvation of the human soul and reunification with God. Gregory of Nyssa (331–395) in the

CHRONOLOGY: CHRISTIANITY, POLYTHEISM, AND JUDAISM

ca. 280	Antony goes into the Egyptian desert
303	Great Persecution of Christians
312	Constantine converts to Christianity
325	Council of Nicaea writes the Nicene Creed
391	Roman law forbids polytheist worship
396–430	Augustine is Bishop of Hippo
ca. 400	Jerusalem Talmud completed
410	Jerome completes Latin translation of Bible (Vulgate)
451	Council of Chalcedon
ca. 500	Babylonian Talmud finished
529	Academy in Athens closed; non-Christians forbidden to teach; Benedict founds monastery at Monte Cassino in Italy
534	Benedict writes *Rule* for monastic life

Greek East and Augustine in the Latin West were only two of the many churchmen who incorporated Neoplatonism into their own works in the later fourth century. After Christian and non-Christian Neoplatonists argued over whether the identity of "the One" could be equated with the Christian God, the Emperor Justinian closed Plato's Academy in Athens in 529 and forbade non-Christians to teach philosophy.

Nevertheless, Neoplatonic thought helped shape the Christian doctrine of the immortality of the human soul. It also reinforced the ascetic ideal practiced by monks and nuns. Thus, contempt for the material, temporal world and the physical body took deep root in Christian culture.

THE BREAKUP OF THE ROMAN EMPIRE

■ How and why did the Roman Empire in the West disintegrate?

During the fifth century, the Roman Empire split into two parts: the Latin-speaking provinces in western Europe, and the largely Greek- and Syriac-speaking provinces in the East. As the Roman government lost control of its western domains, independent Germanic kingdoms emerged. The eastern provinces remained under the control of the Roman emperor, whose capital city was not Rome, but Constantinople. The definitive split of the Roman Empire marked the end of late antiquity. In future centuries the legacy of the Roman Empire survived in the West through Latin culture and Latin Christianity. In the East it survived as a political reality until its final collapse 1,000 years later in 1453.

The Fall of Rome's Western Provinces

Why Roman rule remained strong in the eastern Mediterranean while collapsing in western Europe is one of the most hotly debated subjects in history. Most Christians of the time attributed the collapse of Roman rule to God's anger at the stubborn persistence of polytheist worship. Polytheists, for their part, blamed Christians for destroying the temples of the gods who had protected Rome in the past. In later centuries, the explanations varied. Edward Gibbon, an eighteenth-century writer whose *Decline and Fall of the Roman Empire* has influenced all historians of Rome and remains one of the most widely read history books of all time, criticized the Catholic Church for diverting able men away from public service and into religious life. Other historians attributed Rome's collapse in the West to enormous waves of savage barbarian invasions. The reason the Romans lost their western provinces is, however, more complicated and less dramatic than any of these one-dimensional explanations.

LOSS OF IMPERIAL POWER IN THE WEST The end of Roman rule in western Europe came in a haphazard and gradual fashion as the cumulative result of unwise decisions, weak leadership, and military failure. During the first century, the Romans established the northern limits of their empire in Europe along the Rhine and Danube Rivers. From that time forward, Roman generals and emperors withstood invasions of many different northern tribes looking for plunder and new lands. The Roman legions maintained a relatively stable northern frontier through diplomacy as well as military might. Since the time of Augustus, Roman emperors had permitted newcomers to settle on Roman lands. Until the fourth century, the empire had always been able to absorb the settlers.

In the fourth century, the sudden appearance in southern Russia of the Huns, a fierce nomadic people from central Asia, set in motion events that helped bring about the collapse of Roman rule in western Europe. Unlike the settled farmers who lived in Europe, the Huns were nomads who herded their flocks over the plains (or *steppes*) that stretched from southern Russia to central Asia. Able to travel vast distances quickly on their rugged horses, the highly mobile Huns overran adversaries from settled agricultural communities. The Huns also earned a reputation for ferocity. Living under the specter of starvation, they lusted after the great riches and easy lifestyles they observed in the urbanized empires of Rome and Persia.

In 376, in what is now south Russia, an army of Huns drove a group of Visigoths from their farmlands. The Visigoth refugees gained permission from the Roman Emperor Valens to cross the Danube and settle in the Balkans in return for supplying troops to the Roman army. In the past, Roman rulers had frequently made this sort of arrangement. The Roman officials in charge of this resettlement, however, exploited the refugees by charging them exorbitant fees for food and supplies. In 378 the Visigoths revolted. At the Battle of Adrianople in Thrace they killed Valens and destroyed an entire Roman army.

The Visigoths' successful rebellion wounded the empire, but not fatally. Rome's response to the disaster, however, sowed the seeds for a loss of imperial power in the west. Necessity forced the new emperor, Theodosius the Great, to permit Visigothic soldiers to serve in the Roman army under their own Visigothic commanders. But allowing independent military forces of dubious loyalty to operate freely within the empire was a terrible mistake. The consequences of Theodosius's decision became all too clear in the mid-390s when Alaric, the new Visigothic king, began to plunder Roman cities in the Balkans and Greece. As discussed at the beginning of this chapter, in 401 Alaric and his troops sacked Rome for three days. Senators and citizens could only watch as the Visigoths rampaged through their streets.

The Visigoths' sack of Rome not only dealt a psychological blow to the empire's inhabitants, it also led indirectly to the loss of many of Rome's western provinces. To fight Alaric, Rome's armies withdrew from the empire's northwestern defenses, leaving the frontier in Britain and along the Rhine vulnerable. In Britain, Rome abandoned its control entirely after an ambitious general, styling himself Constantine III, led Britain's last legions across the English Channel in 407 in an unsuccessful attempt to grab the imperial throne. This left Britain defenseless, vulnerable to groups of Germanic tribesmen known as the Saxons already settled on British soil.

Elsewhere the chaos spread. Although the invading bands were small, the imperial government in the West no longer possessed the administrative capacity to marshal its military resources and push the invaders out. In December 406, the Rhine River froze, enabling migrating Germanic tribes to enter the empire with little opposition. Small bands of these marauding tribes roamed through Gaul, while the Vandals and their allies raided their way through Spain. In 429 the Vandals crossed to North Africa, where they soon established an independent kingdom. By 450 the Visigoths had formed a kingdom of their own in Gaul and Spain.

Overwhelming numbers of savage tribesmen did not invade the empire. In fact, their numbers were puny. For example, only 40,000 Vandals controlled North Africa, which had a population of several million Romans. And although the Germans plundered and pillaged, they could not hold on to imperial lands and settle there without the active cooperation of Roman administrators who thought they could bargain with the tribesmen. Once they put down roots, however, the Germanic invaders consolidated their strength and established their rule. By then, Roman authorities lacked both the organization and the strength to expel them.

Even though most of the western provinces had fallen to invaders by 450, the Romans held on to Italy for a while longer. The city of Rome remained the home of the Senate, while the emperor of the western provinces resided in Ravenna, a town on Italy's northeast coast. Warlords, however, held the real power in Italy, although they were formally subordinate to the emperor. These soldiers were usually not Romans by birth, but they adopted Roman culture and fought for Rome. In 476 one of these warlords, a Germanic general named Odovacar, deposed the last emperor in the west, a boy named Romulus Augustulus, and named himself king of Italy. For many historians the year 476 used to symbolize the end of the Roman Empire in the west. In fact,

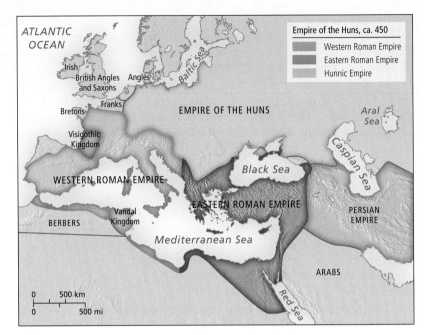

MAP 7.2

Empire of the Huns

During late antiquity, the Huns established a powerful empire based in the Hungarian plain. These fierce horsemen terrified the settled peoples of the Roman world, but their empire broke up within a generation.

however, 476 is a date of little significance. The Romans' control of their western provinces had slipped away decades earlier (see **Map 7.2**).

CULTURAL ENCOUNTERS AFTER THE END OF ROMAN RULE   By the mid-fifth century, when most fighting between Germanic invaders and Romans had ended, the two sides, as rulers and ruled, began an era of intense encounters. In Britain the Germanic invaders were polytheists who snuffed out the Christians. Yet legends hint at a fierce resistance against the invaders. The stories about King Arthur that have captivated English-speaking audiences since the Middle Ages are based on memories of valiant resistance to the Saxon invaders in the mid-fifth century.

In Gaul, North Africa, Italy, and Spain, the new settlers followed Arian Christianity. The Roman inhabitants, on the other hand, followed Chalcedonian (Catholic) Christianity and thus saw the invaders as heretics. Although this religious difference caused friction between the two peoples, it also worked to their mutual advantage. Roman law forbade marriage with Arian Christians, so the conquerors remained a distinctive minority in their new domains. This enabled them to maintain a separate Arian clergy and separate churches.

Of all the former empire's western provinces, Italy prospered the most under Germanic rule, particularly under the long reign of Theodoric the Ostrogoth (r. 493–526). Theodoric murdered Odovacar, the German warrior who had deposed the last Roman emperor in the West, to obtain the throne of Italy. In politics, Theodoric sought to create mutual respect between Ostrogoths and Romans by maintaining two separate administrations—one for his Ostrogoths, the other for the Romans—so that both communities could manage their own affairs under his supervision. He also included aristocratic Romans among his closest advisers and most trusted administrators. Even in his religious policies Theodoric pursued mutual tolerance. As an Arian Christian, he supported the separate Arian clergy, but he also maintained excellent ties with the pope, leader of the Roman Christians. Theodoric united Visigothic kingdoms in Gaul with his own in Italy, ultimately wielding great influence throughout western Europe. Italy prospered under his rule, and the communities of Ostrogoths and Romans lived together amicably.

CHRONOLOGY: ROMAN EMPIRE, EAST AND WEST

235–284	Crisis in Roman government
284	Diocletian begins imperial reforms
293	Tetrarchy established
312	Constantine wins control of western empire
324	Constantinople founded
378	Battle of Adrianople; Visigoths invade empire
406	Vandals and other tribes cross the Rhine
410	Romans withdraw from Britain; Visigoths plunder Rome
418	Visigoths settle in Gaul
429–439	Vandals take North Africa
476	Romulus Augustulus, last western emperor, deposed
493–526	Theodoric the Ostrogoth rules Italy

Although Theodoric had paid formal homage to the emperor in Constantinople, during his rule the western provinces' links to the Roman Empire in the East began to weaken. Most of the invaders, including Theodoric's Ostrogoths, continued their traditional practice of pledging obedience to a local chieftain. This tradition began to erode loyalty to the far-off Roman emperor in Constantinople. By pledging themselves to a Germanic king, men gained a place in the "tribe" of their new chieftain.

Roman culture did not abruptly end with the last vestiges of Roman rule. It remained a vital presence in most regions, but it took different forms in the lands now ruled by Germanic leaders. In Britain, Roman culture perhaps fared the worst and little of it survived into later ages. There the Germanic language of the Saxon invaders and their Anglo allies took hold and began developing into the English spoken today. In Gaul, Italy, and Spain, the Germanic settlers quickly learned Latin. Over time these Latin-based "Romance" (based on the Roman speech) languages grew into the early versions of French, Italian, Catalan, Spanish, and Portuguese. Latin continued as the language of literacy, and the settlers borrowed heavily from Roman literary forms. Writing in Latin, they produced histories of their tribal kingdoms in imitation of Roman

historians. They also developed law codes composed in Latin influenced by Roman models.

The Survival of Rome's Eastern Provinces

Despite the profound alterations wrought by Christianity and Rome's loss of the western provinces, the Roman Empire endured in the eastern Mediterranean without interruption. Constantinople, the imperial city founded by Constantine in 324, became the center of a remodeled empire that merged Christian and Roman characteristics. Historians call the remodeled Roman Empire in the East the **Byzantine Empire,** after Byzantium, the original Greek name of Constantinople.

CHRISTIANITY AND LAW UNDER JUSTINIAN The most important amalgamation of Christian and Roman traditions took place during the reign of the Emperor Justinian (r. 527–565). Born in the Balkans, Justinian was the last emperor in Constantinople to speak Latin as his native language. He combined a powerful intellect, an unshakable Christian faith, and a driving ambition to reform the empire. He defied convention by marrying Theodora, a strong-willed former actress, and included her in imperial decision making once he became emperor.

Justinian inaugurated changes that high-lighted his role as a Christian emperor. First, he emphasized the position of the emperor at the center of society in explicitly Christian terms. He was the first emperor to use the title "Beloved of Christ," and he amplified the emperor's role in Church affairs. Justinian considered it his duty as emperor to impose uniform religious belief throughout the empire by enforcing the decrees of the Council of Chalcedon as he interpreted them. In the East this meant stamping out the sur-vivals of polytheist worship and struggling to find a common ground with the anti-Chalcedonians. After Justinian reconquered some of the western domains of the empire, he had to deal with the Arian Vandals and Ostrogoths living there. In the East Justinian suppressed polytheism, but he never reached an agreement with the anti-Chal-cedonian communities in Syria and Egypt. After the armies of Islam conquered these regions in the following century, the Christian churches there fell out of imperial control (see Chapter 8). In the West the bishops of North Africa and Italy resented Justinian's attempts to determine doc-trine. As a result, a bitter division arose between Christian churches in the eastern and western Mediterranean over the rights of bishops to resist imperial authority on religious matters.

Justinian attempted to create a Christian society by using Roman law coupled with mili-tary force. Unlike rulers of Rome's early empire, who permitted subject peoples to maintain their own customary laws, Justinian suppressed local laws throughout his realm. He envisioned all of his subjects obeying only Roman law—law that he defined and that God approved. (Justinian was sure that if God did not approve of his leg-islative changes, God would not allow him to continue as emperor.)

Thus, in his God-given mission as emperor-legislator, Justinian reformed Roman law. To simplify the vast body of civil law, he ordered his lawyers to sort through all the laws that had accumulated over the centuries and deter-mine which of them should still be enforced.

DIPTYCH OF A CONSUL

This ivory panel celebrates a Roman consul at Con-stantinople in the sixth century. In his right hand he holds the *mappa*, a ceremonial cloth that symbolizes his office. Behind him stand personifications of Rome (on his left) and Constantinople (on his right). Such panels were given as gifts when consuls took office. This one demonstrates Roman traditions continuing in the new world of Byzantium.

Justinian's codification of the law, which was completed in 534, and associated legal texts are now collectively called the *Corpus Juris Civilis*. The body of Roman law passed down to later generations primarily through this compilation. At the end of the eleventh century, scholars in Italy discovered manuscripts of Justinian's legal works in church libraries, and interest in Roman law revived. Thus, the *Corpus Juris Civilis* became a pillar of Latin-speaking European civilization.

RECONQUERING PROVINCES IN THE WEST   Once he had reorganized the empire's legal system, Justinian turned his attention to Rome's fallen western provinces. He wanted to reestablish imperial control over these territories, now ruled by Germanic kings. Once the empire was restored to its former glory, Justinian's plan was to impose his version of Christian orthodoxy upon the Arian Vandals and Ostrogoths in his western domains. He would also force them to live under his version of Roman law and government.

In 533, Justinian sent a fleet of 10,000 men and 5,000 cavalry under the command of his general Belisarius to attack the Vandal kingdom in North Africa. It fell quickly, and within a year Belisarius celebrated a triumph in Constantinople. Encouraged by this easy victory, Justinian set his sights on Italy, where the Ostrogothic ruling family was embroiled in political infighting. This time Justinian underestimated his opponents. The Ostrogoths, who had won the support of the Roman population in Italy, mounted a fierce resistance to Belisarius's invasion in 537. Justinian failed to support Belisarius with adequate funds and soldiers. Bitter fighting dragged on for two decades. Justinian's armies eventually wrestled Italy back under imperial control, but the protracted reconquest had disastrous consequences. The years of fighting devastated Italy, and the financial burden drained the empire's resources. (See **Map 7.3**.)

One of the reasons Justinian's reconquest of Italy took decades was the visitation of a lethal plague that struck the empire in 542 and migrated swiftly to Italy, North Africa, and Gaul. The first onslaught took the lives of about 250,000 people, half the population of Constantinople. An estimated one-third of the empire's inhabitants died. With the population devastated, Justinian's army could not recruit the soldiers it needed to fight on several fronts.

The plague also weakened the economy. In many provinces, farms lay deserted and city populations shriveled. Commercial ties between the eastern and western Mediterranean declined. In the western provinces, economies became more "local" and self-sufficient.

THE STRUGGLE WITH PERSIA   Although Justinian's greatest military successes were in the western Mediterranean, his most dangerous enemy was the Persian Empire (formerly Parthia) on his eastern flank. This huge, multiethnic empire, under the rule of the Sasanian dynasty (ca. 220–633), had been Rome's main rival throughout late antiquity. The tension stemmed chiefly from competition over Armenia, which was a rich source of troops, and Syria, which possessed enormous wealth. Though wars between Romans and Persians were frequent, neither side could win permanent superiority over the other.

Justinian fought several brutal wars with Persia. He gave top priority to this struggle by supplying it with more than half of his troops, led by his best generals. He also provided more financial resources to the struggle in the East than to the wars of reconquest in the West. Chosroes I (r. 531–579), the aggressive and ambitious Great King of Persia, proved a worthy adversary for Justinian. Chosroes repeatedly invaded the Byzantine Empire, causing great damage. In 540, for example, he sacked Antioch, the wealthiest city in Syria. Because war with Persia was extraordinarily expensive, Justinian bought peace by paying thousands of pounds of gold to the Persian monarch. Even this cost less than continuing to fight every year.

By the time of Justinian's death, the two empires had established an uneasy coexistence, but the basic animosity between them remained unresolved. For the next half century, Justinian's successors engaged in intermittent warfare with the Persians. By fighting expensive wars on the western and eastern flanks of his empire, Justinian hastened the disintegration of Roman imperial rule outside the eastern provinces. The overextension of resources ensured that

Two Martyrdoms: Culture and Religion on Trial

Between the reigns of Diocletian (r. 284–305) and Justinian (r. 527–565), Christians went from being a religious minority persecuted by the imperial government to a majority that persecuted non-Christians with the Roman government's backing. One thing did not change during this period, however. Whether polytheist or Christian, emperors used force to compel their subjects to believe and worship in prescribed ways, hoping to keep the empire in the gods' good graces. To ensure religious conformity, emperors used the Roman judicial system. A comparison of the trials of a Christian soldier named Julius in 303, and Phocas, an aristocrat in Constantinople accused of paganism in 529 and 545, illustrates the objectives and methods of the Roman government's religious prosecution.

In 303 officials brought a veteran soldier named Julius before the prefect Maximus. The following excerpt comes from a description of the trial:

"Who is this?" asked Maximus.

One of the staff replied: "This is a Christian who will not obey the laws."

"What is your name?" asked the prefect.

"Julius," was the reply.

"Well, what say you, Julius?" asked the prefect. "Are these allegations true?"

"Yes, they are," said Julius. "I am indeed a Christian. I do not deny that I am precisely what I am."

"You are surely aware," said the prefect, "of the emperors' edicts which order you to sacrifice to the gods?"

"I am aware of them," answered Julius. "I am indeed a Christian and cannot do what you want; for I must not lose sight of my living and true God." ...

"If you think it a sin," answered the prefect Maximus, "let me take the blame. I am the one who is forcing you, so that you may not give impression of having consented voluntarily. Afterwards you can go home in peace, you will pick up your ten-year bonus, and no one will ever trouble you again.... If you do not respect the imperial decrees and offer sacrifice, I am going to cut your head off."

"That is a good plan," answered Julius, "Only I beg...that you execute your plan and pass sentence on me so that my prayers may be answered....I have chosen death for now so that I might live with the saints forever." The prefect Maximus then delivered the sentence as follows: "Whereas Julius has refused to obey the imperial edicts, he is sentenced to death."[1]

After Constantine's conversion to Christianity in 312, Christian officials began to attack polytheism with the government's support. The Emperor Justinian launched three major persecutions of polytheists. In the first episode of persecution in 528–529, one year after Justinian ascended to the throne, a handful of government officials were charged with worshiping pagan gods.

One of these men was Phocas the Patrician, an aristocratic lawyer with an illustrious career in the emperor's service. After serving at court, he was sent to Antioch to rebuild the city after a ruinous earthquake in 527. He was arrested during that first episode of persecution. Cleared of charges of practicing paganism in 529, Phocas continued to enjoy Justinian's trust and earn further promotions. In 532 he served for a year as Praetorian Prefect, the emperor's most powerful official with responsibility for administering the empire. Phocas raised revenue for the construction of the new Cathedral of Holy Wisdom in Constantinople and spent his personal funds in supporting smaller churches and ransoming hostages captured by Byzantium's enemies. Justinian next made him a judge and sent him on a mission to investigate the murder of a bishop. Part of Justinian's confidence in Phocas came from the fact he was deeply learned and competent. Phocas and other victims had a deep commitment to traditional Roman culture. But that very commitment led to their downfall. Their "paganism" was not the furtive worship of old gods like Zeus or Apollo. Rather, Phocas was considered a pagan because he was loyal to classical philosophy, literature, and rhetoric, without any Christian overlay or interpretation.

Then, in 545–546, during the second wave of persecution, despite his publicly recognized activities in support of the church and his faithful service to Justinian, Phocas was arrested again, one of many doctors, teachers, and government officials suddenly charged with paganism. Constantinople endured a time of terror. Officials accused of worshiping the old gods in secret were driven from public office, had their property confiscated by the emperor, and were executed. In a panic, some of the accused took their own lives. Phocas was one of them. Rather than undergo the humiliation of public execution, he committed suicide. The furious emperor ordered that Phocas's body be buried in a ditch like an animal, without prayer or ceremony of any sort.

Phocas thus missed the third purge of 562, when polytheists were arrested throughout the empire, paraded in public, imprisoned, tried, and sentenced. Zealous crowds threw thousands of non-Christian books into bonfires.

The official reason for persecuting Christians such as Julius was relatively simple: Christians broke the law by refusing to make sacrifices to the Roman gods. But why did Christian governments also later use such a heavy hand in persecuting polytheists? Men like Phocas who were attacked as pagans were highly educated in the traditional learning of the Greco–Roman world. Indeed, it was this learning that was really on trial. For Justinian, this sort of classical learning had no place in a Christian empire.

For Discussion

Why did both polytheist and Christian governments of Rome persecute adherents of nonofficial religions?

JUSTINIAN
This mid-sixth-century ivory panel depicts the Emperor Justinian in a standard pose of Roman emperors. The panel sends the message that Justinian rules the world with the approval and support of God.

Taking It Further

Helgeland, John. *Christians in the Military: The Early Experience.* 1985, 64–65. An introduction to the persecutions of Christians in the Roman army and their depiction in Christian literature.

Maas, Michael. *John Lydus and the Roman Past: Antiquarianism and Politics in the Age of Justinian.* 1992. This book explains how Justinian's policies about religion also involved an encounter with the empire's classical heritage.

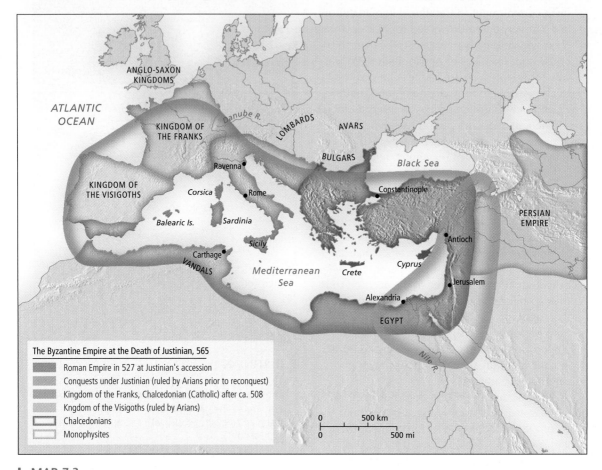

MAP 7.3

The Byzantine Empire at the Death of Justinian, 565

When Justinian died in 565, Italy, North Africa, and part of Spain that had been lost in the fifth century had been restored, temporarily, to imperial rule. Under the dynamic Sasanian dynasty, the Persian Empire fought many wars with the Romans. Neither empire had an advantage because they were roughly the same size and possessed equivalent resources of wealth and manpower.

Constantinople could not maintain control of the western Mediterranean. When new invaders descended on Italy and the Balkans in the late sixth century, the empire did not have the strength to resist them. In the seventh century the remaining Roman provinces in North Africa, Egypt, and Syria were lost. Nevertheless, in what remained of the Roman Empire, Justinian succeeded in creating a Christian–Roman society, united under one God, one emperor, and one law.

CONCLUSION

The Age of New Boundaries

During late antiquity the transformation of the Roman world into new political configurations with new boundaries helped create a new conception of the West. Henceforth, the West was closely associated with the legacy of Roman civilization filtered through the lens of Christianity. The most lasting development of the period came from the encounter between the civilization of the Roman Empire and Christianity, which before the fourth century had been the faith of a persecuted minority. As Christianity became the dominant religion throughout the Roman Empire, it was itself transformed, not the least through the attempts to reconcile Christian revelation with classical learning. Christian thinkers assimilated much of classical culture, and with the support of the Roman emperors, Christianity became the official religion. During this process of assimilation, Christians disagreed among themselves over how they explained the divinity of Jesus Christ, and these disagreements led to distinctive strains of Christian belief.

The Roman Empire itself was irreparably split into two parts, which became the foundations for two distinctive Christian civilizations. After Roman rule in the West collapsed, Germanic rulers established new kingdoms in the old Roman provinces. Some of these kingdoms spoke Romance languages derived from Latin, and all of them used Latin for religious worship, learning, and the law. From the western provinces of the Roman Empire during late antiquity, Latin civilization spread to parts of central, eastern, and northern Europe that had never been part of the Roman Empire. In the eastern Mediterranean, the Roman Empire survived as the Byzantine Empire (discussed in the next Chapter 8) and became the home of Orthodox Christianity. In Byzantium, Greek remained the dominant tongue of daily life, learning, and Christian worship.

When Islam emerged as a powerful religious and political entity at the end of the late antique period, as we will discuss in the next Chapter 8, classical learning and Roman institutions also influenced its adherents. But the Muslim and Christian empires became enemies, a tendency that created the most lasting divisions among the peoples who had once been citizens of the Roman Empire.

KEY TERMS

late antiquity
tetrarchy
Great Persecution
papacy
pagan
Arians
Chalcedonians
Vulgate
Latin Christendom
Monophysites
asceticism
monastic movement
Talmud
pilgrimages
relics
Church Fathers
Neoplatonism
Byzantine Empire
Corpus Juris Civilis

CHAPTER QUESTIONS

1. How did the Roman Empire reorganize after the instability of the third century? (page 203)
2. How did Christianity become the dominant religion in the Roman Empire, and how did that affect Roman society? (page 207)
3. How did Christianity transform communities, religious experience, and intellectual traditions inside and outside the empire? (page 212)
4. How and why did the Roman Empire in the West disintegrate? (page 222)

TAKING IT FURTHER

1. Besides the Bible what were the significant influences on early Christianity?
2. What were the differences between Roman and Germanic ideas of rulership in late antiquity?
3. Why did the Roman Empire survive in the East and not the West in late antiquity?

✔•▢ Practice on MyHistoryLab

Medieval Empires and Borderlands: Byzantium and Islam

■ Byzantium: The Survival of the Roman Empire
■ The New World of Islam

In 860 FIERCE RUS TRIBESMEN ABOARD A FLEET OF SLEEK SHIPS WITH PROWS SHAPED LIKE DRAGONS' HEADS RAIDED the Byzantine villages along the shores of the Black Sea and then advanced to the gates of Constantinople, ready for pillage and rape. Panic gripped the inhabitants of the city. The Patriarch of Constantinople called on the people to repent of their sins to avoid God's wrath, and when the Rus unexpectedly departed, the people of Constantinople interpreted it as an act of divine intervention.

Strategically located where the Black Sea meets the Sea of Marmara, Constantinople was the shining capital of the Byzantine Empire—and the largest and richest city in the world. Its Greek-speaking inhabitants considered the Rus savages, prone to the worst kinds of violence. Like so many other barbarian peoples, the Rus who were Vikings living in what is now Ukraine and Russia could not speak Greek, were not Christians, and did not recognize the authority of the Byzantine emperor, which the Greeks believed came directly from God. The leaders of Constantinople tried to keep these barbarians under control by signing treaties, which stipulated that no more than 50 Rus could enter the city at one time and they all had to leave by autumn. In exchange for civilized behavior, the Rus received free baths, food, provisions for a

month, and equipment for their return to their homeland. By the ninth century the Rus had established a regular pattern. Each spring after spending the winters along the river valleys of the north collecting tribute from the Slavic tribes, the Rus set off in their boats, risking dangerous rapids and waterfalls on the Dnieper River and ambush from hostile tribes, to reach the Black Sea and the splendid emporium of the world, Constantinople, which they called simply the "Great City."

Accustomed to winter treks, grubby villages, and constant danger, they were dazzled by the sight of the Great City, with its half million inhabitants and twelve miles of fortifications. The gilded cupolas of its churches, the marble palaces of the aristocrats and emperor, and the cavernous wharves and warehouses of its merchants amazed these tribesmen. The people of Constantinople were equally astonished—and frightened—by the sun-worn, fur-clad Rus.

The Rus came to Constantinople to trade. The merchants of Constantinople traded Byzantine and Chinese silks, Persian glass, Arabic silver coins (highly prized by the Rus), and Indian spices for honey, wax, slaves, and musty bales of furs from Scandinavia and what is now northern Russia. Despite their sense of superiority, the Byzantines needed the barbarians. In

THE CATHEDRAL OF HOLY WISDOM (HAGHIA SOPHIA)

When Justinian entered his newly completed cathedral of Holy Wisdom (Haghia Sophia) in Constantinople in 537, he boasted, "Solomon, I have outdone you!" He meant that his church was bigger and more splendid than the Jerusalem Temple built by the biblical King Solomon. For centuries, Haghia Sophia was the largest building in Europe. In 1453 the church became a mosque.

Source: Dagli Orti/Picture Desk, Inc./Kobal Collection

the merchant stalls of Constantinople, traders from many cultures met, haggled, and came to know something of one another. None perhaps were more unlike the other than the rough Rus and the refined Byzantines, but their mutual desires for profit kept them in a persistent, if tentative, embrace. These repeated interactions among diverse peoples who traded, competed, and fought with one another offer clues for understanding the medieval world, also known as the Middle Ages.

The term *Middle Ages* refers to the period between the ancient and modern civilizations from about the fifth to fifteenth centuries. Medieval culture rested on the foundations of three great civilizations: the Greek Christianity of Byzantium;

the Arabic-speaking Islamic caliphates of the Middle East, North Africa, and Spain; and the Latin Christian kingdoms of western and northern Europe. The dynamic interactions among these three civilizations, distinguished by religion and language, lay at the heart of medieval culture. From the seventh to the eleventh centuries, the most energetic and creative of these three civilizations was the Islamic world, whose armies threatened both Byzantium and the Latin Christian kingdoms. In the century after the death of its founder, the prophet Muhammad, in 632, Islam's followers burst from their home in Arabia to conquer an empire stretching from Spain to central Asia. Especially during the tenth and eleventh centuries, this Islamic empire produced important philosophical and scientific work, and supported a thriving economy.

The most distinctive feature of the medieval period was that all these civilizations rested on monotheistic religions that shared basic beliefs about God. All struggled to eliminate polytheism either by persuasion or force. However, because each of these medieval civilizations defined itself as an exclusive community of faith, cultural boundaries developed between them that are still visible today. This chapter examines two of these civilizations, Byzantium and Islam. Chapter 9 discusses the Latin Christian kingdoms. The most important question raised by the two civilizations discussed here is this: How did their different versions of monotheism sustain them as empires?

BYZANTIUM: THE SURVIVAL OF THE ROMAN EMPIRE

■ How did the Roman Empire's eastern provinces evolve into the Byzantine Empire?

In late antiquity Constantinople and Rome had symbolized the two halves of the Roman Empire. Once joined in a common Christian culture, eastern and western Christians gradually grew apart, so that by the late ninth century, they began to constitute separate civilizations, one Byzantine and the other Latin. There were still cultural exchanges between them as merchants, pilgrims, and scholars crossed back and forth, but the two civilizations had ceased to understand one another. They held different opinions about religious matters, such as the dating of Easter, the rituals of the liturgy, the role of images in worship, and the extent of the authority of the bishop in Rome, the pope. They also spoke different languages. In the East, Greek was the language of most of the population, and Latin had been largely forgotten by the end of the sixth century. In the West, Latin or local dialects of it prevailed. Except in southern Italy and Sicily, few Westerners knew Greek.

Eastern Europe became an unstable borderland on the flanks of Byzantium inhabited by polytheist farmers and nomads. Rival missionaries practicing Greek and Latin forms of Christianity competed there for converts and allies. Greek missionaries were the most successful in converting the Slavic peoples to Orthodox Christianity, a faith that survived among the Slavs even after the collapse of Byzantium itself.

An Embattled Empire

After the reign of Emperor Justinian (r. 527–565), the Byzantine Empire was gradually reduced to a regional power struggling for survival against many enemies. In the west the Byzantines faced the Germanic kingdom of the Lombards who eroded the imperial rule over Italy that Justinian had reestablished. The threats in the Balkans came from nomadic tribes from the Eurasian steppes, such as the Avars, Slavs, and Bulgars, who permanently settled there within the empire. These peoples became the ancestors of some of the current inhabitants of the region, such as modern Bulgarians, Croats, and Serbs. To the east the Byzantines confronted their old rival, the Persian Empire. Defeating Persia in a series of wars from 603 to 629 took such a huge toll that Byzantium was too exhausted to resist a new threat out of the Arabian peninsula from the armies of Islam. The encounters between these diverse enemies and Byzantium were usually hostile, and their encirclement of Byzantium forced Byzantine administration and military policy to change and adapt.

The Byzantine emperors after Justinian tried to hold on to the western provinces by reorganizing the administration of North Africa and Italy into two new units called *exarchates*—the Exarchate of Carthage (which also administered southern Spain) and the Exarchate of Ravenna. Because of their long distance from Constantinople and the immediate press of the local problems they confronted, the two exarchates were somewhat independent from the rest of the Byzantine Empire. The exarchs (or governors) held both civilian and military authority in these territories—a break from Roman practice, which had kept these two spheres separate. This joint command signaled the gravity of the problems the exarchs faced.

This administrative overhaul did not save Byzantium's western territories. Southern Spain fell to the Visigoths in the 630s, and Muslim armies took Carthage in 698. In 751 the Lombards captured Ravenna and put an end to the exarchate, although Byzantine rule survived in southern Italy until the eleventh century.

The Byzantine hold on eastern Europe also proved fragile. In much of the Balkan peninsula from the late sixth through ninth centuries, Byzantine weakness created a power vacuum that made the settled inhabitants who were Christians and still considered themselves subjects of the Roman Empire vulnerable to polytheist invaders. Like so many others before and after them, raiders and migrants poured out of the Eurasian steppes, a band of grasslands that spread some 5,000 miles from what is now Hungary and Ukraine in Europe into central Asia. Nomads could easily cross the grasslands on horseback. Interactions with the Avars, Slavs, Bulgars, and Rus contributed to the contraction of Byzantine territory and influence.

The nomadic Avars, who suddenly appeared in the sixth century on the plains of present-day Hungary from the steppes north of the Black Sea, had a bone-chilling reputation for ferocity. From Hungary they raided central Europe and the Balkans. These tenacious warriors dominated the region until the early ninth century and threatened Byzantium and the new kingdoms taking shape in Italy, Germany, and France.

The Avars created an empire by forcing conquered peoples to serve in their armies. Some of these peoples were Slavs. Between about 400 and 600, Slavic societies had formed from a blend of many cultures and ethnic groups. The Slavic communities that developed in eastern Europe between the Baltic Sea and the Balkans lay outside Byzantium's borders. Their Avar conquerors ruled by brute force, and most Slavs could not win back their independence. However, a few Slavic communities managed to overthrow Avar rule. In the second half of the sixth century, bands of Slavs began to migrate south across the Danube River into the Balkans. Collaborating with marauding Avars, the Slavs settled in sparsely populated frontier lands in what is now Croatia and Serbia. As the Slavs pushed south, many Byzantines abandoned their cities to the invaders. By 600, Slavic and Avar groups had seized most Byzantine lands from the Danube to Greece.

By the ninth century, these tribes began to convert to one or another form of Christianity, and the patterns of those conversions have had lasting consequences. The tribes in eastern Europe were fragmented politically, which mirrored the intricate distribution of ethnic and linguistic groups. State-building was especially complicated because much of the region had never been under Roman rule and lacked the legacies of Roman cities, institutions, and law that made the survival of Byzantium possible and the Germanic kingdoms of western Europe viable. Conversion patterns exacerbated eastern European fragmentation because the religious dividing line between those who adhered to Roman Catholicism and those who followed Orthodox Christianity cut directly through the region. Religion, like ethnicity and language, became a source of disunity rather than cohesion.

Fast on the heels of the Avars and Slavs from the steppes came the nomadic peoples called the Bulgars, who established rule over the largely Slavic inhabitants of the Balkans by the eighth century. The Bulgars destroyed the surviving old Roman cities there, expelled what Christians remained, and attacked the Byzantine Empire. In 811, after annihilating a Byzantine army, the Bulgarian khan (the head of a confederation of clans) Krum (r. 803–814) lined the skull of the slain Byzantine emperor with silver and turned it into a drinking cup. With this symbolic act of debasement, the Bulgarians gained a fierce reputation as enemies of Christianity and Byzantium.

In 865, however, Khan Boris I (r. 852–889) accepted the Orthodox Christianity of his former enemies in Byzantium. His conversion illustrates the politics of the period. During the ninth century Christianity began to acquire a powerful allure among the polytheistic tribes. Their acceptance of Christianity opened the possibility for diplomatic ties and alliances with the Christian powers. For Boris, therefore, conversion was a way to ward off Byzantine hostility and make peace. For four years, Boris negotiated with Rome, Constantinople, and German missionaries, all of whom sought to convert the Bulgars. In the end, Boris got what he wanted—a Bulgarian Orthodox Church that recognized the ultimate authority of the patriarch of Constantinople but was essentially autonomous.

The autonomy of the Bulgarian Church was further guaranteed later in the ninth century by the adoption of a Slavic liturgy rather than a Latin or Greek liturgy. This was made possible by the missionary work in neighboring Moravia of Cyril (ca. 826–869) and his brother Methodius (815–885), who had invented an alphabet to write the Slavic language. They translated a Greek church liturgy into a version of the Slavic language now known as Old Church Slavonic. The acceptance of the Slavonic liturgy gradually led the ethnically and linguistically mixed peoples of Bulgaria to identify with Slavic culture and language. From a string of monasteries established by the Bulgarians, the Old Church Slavonic liturgy spread among the Serbs, the Romanians, and eventually the Russians, creating cultural ties among these widespread peoples that have survived to the present.

As we saw at the beginning of this chapter, Byzantium also faced assault from the northern Rus. The Rus established a headquarters at Kiev on the Dnieper River and extended their domination over the local Slav tribes. From among the merchant-warriors of the Rus arose the forebears of the princes of Kiev, who by the end of the tenth century ruled a vast steppe and forest domain through a loose collective of subject principalities. The term *Rus* (later *Russian*) came to be applied to all the lands the princes of Kiev ruled.

Kievan Rus reached its zenith under Vladimir the Great (r. 978–1015) and his son Iaroslav the Wise (r. 1019–1054). A ruthless fighter, Vladimir consolidated into a single state the provinces of Kiev and Novgorod, a city in the far north that had grown rich from the fur trade. Born a polytheist, Vladimir had seven wives and took part in human sacrifices. However, when offered a military alliance with Byzantium in 987, he abandoned his wives, married the Byzantine emperor's sister, and converted to Orthodox Christianity. He then forced the inhabitants of Kiev and Novgorod to be baptized and cast their idols into the rivers. The Byzantine Church established administrative control over the Rus Church by appointing an Orthodox archbishop for Kiev. The liturgy was in Old Church Slavonic, which provided a written language and the stimulus for the literature, art, and music at the foundations of Russian culture. Iaroslav employed scribes to translate Greek religious books into Old Slavonic and founded new churches and monasteries across the Kievan state (see **Map 8.1**). The religious and political connection between the Rus and Byzantium shaped Russian history and limited the eastward spread of Latin Christianity (Roman Catholicism).

Byzantine Civilization

In addition to assaults from so many directions, the Byzantine Empire faced turmoil from within. The loss of territories caused economic suffering, and religious controversies at times alienated the population from the government. But despite terrible losses, Byzantium endured. Three institutions held the empire together: the emperor, who set policies and safeguarded his subjects' welfare; the army, which defended the frontiers; and the Orthodox Church, which provided spiritual guidance.

IMPERIAL ADMINISTRATION AND ECONOMY   Based at Constantinople, the emperor stood at the center of Byzantine society. His authority reached to every corner of the empire. This supreme ruler governed with the assistance of a large bureaucracy that he tightly controlled. In this hierarchical bureaucracy, elaborate titles and different clothing indicated different ranks. Only the emperor or members of his family, for example, could wear the color purple, a symbol of royalty.

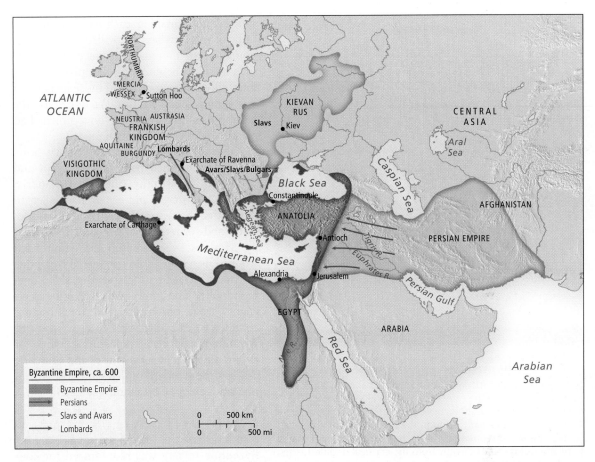

MAP 8.1

The Byzantine Empire, ca. 600

By 600 the Byzantine Empire consisted of Anatolia, Greece, part of the Balkans, Syria, Egypt, and some territories in North Africa and Spain. Until the rise of Islam, the Persian Empire remained Byzantium's greatest enemy.

High dignitaries wore silk garments of distinctive colors encrusted with jewels. The higher the official, the more gems he was permitted to display. Bureaucrats and courtiers (members of the emperor's personal retinue) lined up in elaborate processions in order of their importance, as indicated by the color of their clothing and shoes. Through these ceremonies the emperor displayed the government to the people. Such processions were not just political propaganda. They made the constitution of the empire evident through the hierarchic order of the procession. They also indicated the politics of the court as favored courtiers moved to a higher-ranked position in the procession, and those out of favor moved to a lower-ranked place or disappeared from the procession altogether.

Men fortunate or talented enough to obtain an office in the imperial government acquired wealth and influence. For this reason leading provincial families sent their sons to Constantinople to obtain positions in the bureaucracy. Through this method of recruitment, Constantinople remained in close touch with the outlying

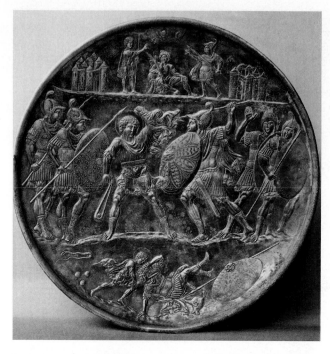

KING DAVID PLATE

Nine silver plates made in Constantinople about 630 illustrate scenes from the career of the biblical King David. The largest plate (about 20 inches in diameter) shows David battling the giant Goliath. Though the subject matter is biblical, the style of representing clothing, human bodies, and spatial relationships comes directly from the classical tradition. The subject connected Byzantium's struggles with Persia to the Bible's heroic king.

Source: Byzantine, early seventh century. Dish: David and Goliath. Silver, Syrian workmanship. D. 19 1/2 in. Found in Karavas, near Kyrenia, Cyprus, 1902. The Metropolitan Museum of Art, Gift of J. Pierpont Morgan, 1917

spurred a flourishing cash-based economy. Official monopolies controlled the production and distribution of specific commodities such as silk. These monopolies protected the interests of the emperor and those he favored by stifling competition. As long as the monopolies flourished, the government had a source of revenue through taxation.

By the end of the seventh century, however, when the rich provinces of Egypt and Syria and the wealthy cities of Alexandria, Antioch, Carthage, and others had fallen to the Arabs, the Byzantine economy stumbled. Thousands of refugees from lands conquered by Muslims streamed into the empire and strained its resources. In conquered Byzantine provinces, Muslim rulers set up their own monopolies and prevented Byzantine merchants from participating in long-distance commerce. Cut off from foreign markets, Byzantines stopped manufacturing goods for export and building new houses and churches. By 750, the standard of living in most Byzantine cities except Constantinople had fallen.

THE MILITARY SYSTEM OF THE THEMES In response to the many external threats, Byzantine society was reorganized for constant war. Emperors relied on their armies to protect Constantinople, the nerve center of the shrinking Byzantine state, and to defend the borders against invaders. By about 650 in Anatolia, which became the empire's main source of recruits for the army, emperors abandoned the late Roman system of relying on the provincial governors to protect the frontiers. To replace the old provinces, emperors created four military districts called *themes*. Each of the themes had its own army and administration commanded by a general chosen by the emperor. The themes' armies developed strong local identities and prided themselves on their military skills, a legacy the Byzantine Empire had inherited from the Roman legions. These military forces kept the empire from collapsing despite devastating losses to Islamic armies throughout the seventh century.

regions of the empire. This system gave provincial families a stake in the success of the empire and the provinces a voice in the capital. However, it was also vulnerable to corruption. Many men obtained their positions by bribing court officials. Other officeholders owed their jobs to family influence rather than talent. But even a corrupt system can be an effective form of government because official corruption made loyalty to the emperor more rewarding than opposition to him.

From his position at the head of this elaborate hierarchy, the emperor also controlled Byzantium's economy. The stable imperial coinage

By 750 the themes had developed considerable autonomy from Constantinople and were the basis of further reorganization of the agricultural economy and procedures for recruitment. Soldiers and sailors who were once paid in cash from the emperor's tax revenues now were granted land on which to support themselves. Fighting men had to provide their own weapons from their income as farmers, and the theme system enabled the parts of the empire to function without direct support from the imperial treasury. The theme system created defensive flexibility for the empire. While it could no longer launch large-scale offensive conquests, Byzantium could at least attempt to defend its borders.

Over time the four original themes were subdivided and new ones added in other regions until by the end of the eleventh century, there were 38 themes. The military strength of the empire came to depend on the theme system in which free, tax-paying soldier-farmers lived in villages under the supervision of a military commander who was also civil administrator. These soldier-farmers usually fought in their own districts, which meant they were defending their homes and families. As a a result they provided a formidable bulwark against invaders.

The Byzantine borders were especially harassed by Muslim enemies, but from the first thrust of Muslim armies against Byzantium's frontier in the seventh century until its fall to the Turks in 1453, Constantinople held on. While the Persian Empire fell to Arab armies by the 630s, Byzantium survived. That fact is perhaps the most important measure of the success of Byzantium's military reorganization.

One of the lasting cultural fruits of these conflicts was legends of great heroes. These legends began as stories recited in verse to entertain Byzantine aristocrats whose ancestors had fought the Arabs. Several of these oral legends were eventually refashioned into popular epic poems. One such poem, *Digenes Akritas*, described the heroic feats of soldiers during the late eighth century on the eastern frontier of the empire, where Byzantines and Arabs both fought and cooperated. The father of the hero of the poem was an Arab commander who abducted the daughter of a Byzantine general, married her, and converted to Christianity. The son of this mixed marriage was Digenes ("two-blooded"), a man of two peoples and two religions, who became a border fighter (an "akritas"). This greatest Byzantine hero, who lived between two cultures, was the poetic embodiment of the engagement between Byzantium and Islam. The legends surrounding *Digenes Akritas* had a profound influence on Greek literature. Later writers retold its stories again and again.

THE CHURCH AND RELIGIOUS LIFE   Constantinople boasted so many churches and sacred relics that by 600 the Byzantines had begun to think of it as a holy city, protected by God and under the special care of the Virgin Mary. Churchmen taught that Constantinople was a "New Jerusalem" that would be at the center of events at the end of days when God would bring history to an end and judge humanity.

One of the institutional pillars of the Orthodox Church in Byzantium was the clergy. They were organized hierarchically like the imperial bureaucracy. The patriarch, or chief bishop, of Constantinople headed several thousand clergymen in the capital and directed church affairs throughout the empire. Emperors generally controlled the appointment of patriarchs, and often the two worked closely together. The patriarch helped impose religious unity throughout the empire by controlling the network of bishops based in cities near and far. Each city's bishop supervised the veneration of the saints' relics housed in its churches. (Byzantines believed that sacred relics protected their communities, just as their polytheistic ancestors believed the gods had provided protection in the pre-Christian past.) Because bishops usually came from the city's elite, they were influential local leaders, responsible for administering many public policies, not just religious ones.

Monasteries, played a significant role in the empire's life. Men and women went to separate monasteries to live a spiritual life, praying for their own salvation and that of others. People who needed help, such as orphans, the elderly, battered wives, widows, and the physically and mentally ill, found refuge in monasteries. Monks and nuns distributed food and clothing to the poor. Donors gave lavishly to fund these activities, and many monasteries grew wealthy through these gifts.

During the seventh and eighth centuries, Christian instruction under the supervision of the Church replaced the traditional Roman educational system. Pious Christians developed a suspicion of classical learning, with its references to ancient gods and to customs the Church condemned. Those few Byzantines who learned how to read did so by studying the Bible, not the classics of Greek antiquity. As a result of this general decline in learning, the Church monopolized culture and thought. Knowledge of classical literature, history, and science disappeared except in Constantinople, and even there the academic community was tiny.

ICONS AND THE ICONOCLASTIC CONTROVERSY   The Orthodox Church created unity of faith and culture, but that unity was broken in the eighth century by controversy within the church itself. As enemies tore at the borders of the empire, Byzantines wondered why God was punishing them. Their answer was that somehow they were angering God. Convinced that only appeasing God could save them, Emperor Leo III (r. 717–741) took action. To make Byzantium a completely Christian empire, he forcibly converted communities of Jews. His most important move, however, was to challenge the use of **icons,** the images of Christ and saints found everywhere in Byzantine worship.

Centuries before, the first Christians had refused to make images of Christ and other holy individuals. They had two reasons for banning such representations. First, the Hebrew Bible forbids creating representations of God, and they considered this prohibition still in effect for Christians. Second, they thought that Christians might start to worship their images the way that polytheists worshiped statues in their temples. "When images are put up, the customs of the

pagans do the rest," wrote one church leader in the fourth century.

Despite such warnings, many Christians responded aesthetically to the beautiful polytheist statues and images that filled their cities. Christian sculptors and painters started to create a distinctive Christian art that combined religious images with the styles and techniques of classical art. After Constantine put an end to the persecutions of Christians, this new art flourished. Artists routinely portrayed Christ and the saints in churches. During the sixth and seventh centuries, Byzantines used religious images with greater zeal than ever before. By 600, for example, the emperor placed a large image of Christ above the Bronze Gate, the main entrance to the imperial palace in Constantinople. Smaller icons became intensely popular in churches, homes, and monasteries.

Byzantine theologians defended icons as doorways through which the divine presence could make itself accessible to believers. Churchmen cautioned that God or saints do not actually reside within the icons, and so believers should not worship the images themselves. Rather, they should consider icons as openings to a spiritual world, enabling believers to encounter a holy presence. Thus, Byzantines treated icons with love and respect. Monks and nuns were particularly zealous in their veneration of icons.

However, by the eighth century, some Byzantine theologians thought icon veneration had gone too far and sought to revive the early Christian prohibitions against religious images. They advised Emperor Leo that icon veneration should be halted because uneducated believers confused the image of the icon with what it represented and worshiped icons as polytheists worshiped idols. When a volcanic eruption destroyed the island of Santorini in the Aegean, Leo concluded that these advisors were correct and that God was angered by icon veneration. In 726 Leo ordered the destruction of holy images (except for crucifixes) throughout the empire, but public resistance forced him to move carefully. For example, when he ordered workers to remove the image of Christ from the Bronze Gate at the imperial palace, the people of Constantinople rioted. Four years later, Leo renewed the general prohibition. The destruction of icons, known as **iconoclasm** (image breaking), divided Byzantine society until 842.

The veneration of icons was such a vital part of popular religious life that Leo found it difficult to enforce iconoclasm outside Constantinople. Revolts broke out in Greece and southern Italy when imperial messengers sought to destroy images. The iconoclastic controversy also affected international politics. Outraged by the emperor's prohibition of icons, which he considered heresy, Pope Gregory III, the dominant religious figure in the West, excommunicated Leo. In retaliation Leo deprived the papacy of religious authority over southern Italy, Sicily, and the Balkan coast of the Adriatic Sea, authority the popes had exercised since the fourth century. The popes never forgave the emperor because with the loss of religious authority came the loss of the principal source of papal revenues. This conflict contributed to a growing rift between Greek Orthodox and Latin Christianity. In the future instead of relying on the Byzantine emperors for military protection, the Roman popes turned north to the Franks. The Iconoclastic Controversy created a lasting shift that allied the Roman pope with the kingdoms of western Europe.

After years of turmoil, two Byzantine empresses who were influenced by monks and who sympathized with their subjects' religious convictions restored icons to churches. In 787, the Empress Irene called a general church council that reversed Leo's condemnation of icons. After Irene was deposed in 802 iconoclasm revived, but in 843 the Empress Theodora introduced a religious ceremony for commemorating images, which Orthodox Christians still celebrate annually. The iconoclastic controversy may have widened the gap between Greek Orthodoxy and Latin Christianity, but its resolution created even greater religious unity within the Byzantine world. A common religious culture also provided solace and a spiritual connection to Byzantium for many Christians who found themselves in the former Byzantine territories that Islamic rulers had conquered.

The Macedonian Renaissance

Byzantium's losses to external enemies were reversed during the Macedonian dynasty (867–1056), the term for a line of emperors from the Balkans that lasted six generations. Before the Macedonians, instability characterized the Byzantine imperial system because when an emperor died, powerful families struggled over who would become the new emperor. But after Basil I (r. 867–886), the first Macedonian, murdered his way to the

BYZANTINE ICONOCLASM

In this ninth-century Byzantine manuscript, the figure with a pole is shown whiting out an image of Christ.

throne, his family retained power by naming emperors' sons as co-emperors and encouraging the principle of dynastic succession.

Under the Macedonian emperors, Byzantine armies and fleets fought Muslims on several fronts. In the east the Byzantines pushed into Syria and Palestine almost to Jerusalem. A large part of the Mesopotamian river valley fell into their hands. They annexed the kingdom of Georgia and part of Armenia. In the Mediterranean the Byzantines retook the islands of Crete and Cyprus and kept the Muslims from southern Italy, although they were unable to prevent the conquest of Sicily, which became a center of Muslim culture.

The economy of Constantinople thrived. Home to more than half a million people by the tenth century, the city became a great marketplace where traders exchanged goods from as far away as China and the British Isles. It was also a center for the production of luxury goods, especially the highly-prized silk cloth and brocades traded throughout Europe, Asia, and North Africa. Aristocratic families, the Church, and monasteries became immensely rich, and embellished the city with magnificent buildings, mosaics, and icons, creating the **Macedonian Renaissance.**

The Macedonian dynasty released creative energies by restoring the religious unity that the iconoclastic controversy had compromised. The most original work was religious, embodied in sermons, theological scholarship, and especially hymns, but thanks to generous imperial patronage, Constantinople also became a center for philosophical study and the writing of history for the first time since the seventh century. The accumulation and study of ancient Greek manuscripts created an important cultural link between the ancient and medieval worlds.

The Patriarch Photius (ca. 810–ca. 893) was one of the most eminent scholars in the history of Byzantium. Photius maintained a huge library, which became a center for the study of ancient Greek literature. He wrote important works, including the *Library,* an encyclopedic compendium of classical and Byzantine writers both

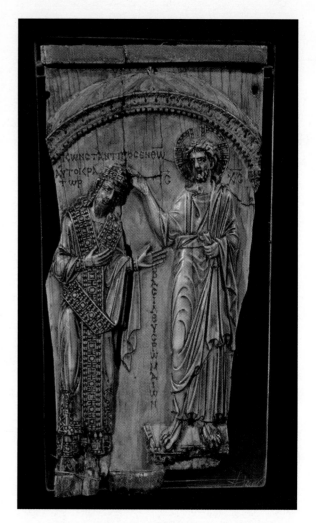

THE BYZANTINE PORTRAIT

This ivory plaque shows the Emperor Constantine VII Porphyrogenetus (r. 913–959) being crowned by Christ. It was probably made in 944 to commemorate Porphyrogenetus' becoming the sole ruler of the empire. Under the emperor's left hand the inscription reads, "Emperor of the Romans."

religious and secular. Photius's summaries and analyses of these writers have remained especially vital because many of these books have subsequently been lost. Photius was also deeply involved in church politics and was twice deposed from office because of political intrigue in Constantinople. His selection as patriarch by Emperor

Michael III in 858 while still a layman met with strong opposition from the Roman pope. A bitter critic of the Latin Christians—Photius and the pope each excommunicated the other—Photius is often blamed for widening the gap between the two main branches of Christianity.

Under the Macedonian dynasty elaborate court ceremonies magnified the quasi-sacred office of the emperor. The historian Emperor Constantine VII Porphyrogenetus (r. 912–959) wrote the *Book of Ceremonies,* which became a model for royal ceremony in kingdoms from Spain to Russia. The *Book of Ceremonies* disseminated Byzantine concepts of rulership, which suggested that the emperor, like Christ, had two natures. One of these natures was human and fallible, but the other was derived from God, which gave the properly consecrated ruler divine authority over his subjects. Hence, Byzantine emperors were anointed with holy oil in a ceremony that was similar to the ordination of priests. The divine authority of monarchs represented by the emperor's or king's anointment became a central feature of political thought during the Middle Ages.

Even under the Macedonians, Byzantium remained under the threat of invasions. The empire's success in meeting these threats depended on two factors—the political stability guaranteed by the Macedonian dynasty, and the organization and recruitment of the army through the military districts of the themes. In the early eleventh century, however, the dynasty weakened and the army deteriorated.

When Emperor Basil II (r. 976–1025) died, Byzantine power and prosperity were at their peak, but he left no direct male heirs. His nieces and their husbands ruled until 1056, largely because Byzantines believed that the peace and prosperity of the empire depended on the dynasty. Basil's successors, however, were not strong leaders. Administration of the empire was highly centralized, with a tangled bureaucracy that supervised everything from diplomatic ceremony to the training of artisans. Without energetic leadership, the Byzantine bureaucracy degenerated into routine and failed to respond to new challenges.

The early Macedonian emperors' success in checking invasions had been largely the result of Byzantium's superior military capacities, guaranteed by the systematic organization of the army in the themes and the strength of the economy. As discussed earlier, the success of the themes depended on a system in which free, tax-paying soldier-farmers fought in their own districts, defending their homes and families. However, by the eleventh century deteriorating economic conditions threatened the independence of these soldier-farmers. Every time a crop failed or drought or famine struck, starving soldier-farmers in the themes were forced to surrender their land and their independence to one of the aristocrats

CHRONOLOGY: THE BYZANTINE EMPIRE

527–565	Reign of Justinian I
630s	Loss of Spain to Visigoths
636	Arabs take Syria from Byzantium
642	Muslims take Egypt
698	Muslims conquer Carthage
716–718	Muslims besiege Constantinople
726–842	Iconoclasm controversy
740	Byzantines defeat Arabs
751	Lombards conquer Ravenna and end the Exarchate of Italy
ca. 810–ca. 893	Life of Photius, patriarch of Constantinople
867–1056	Macedonian dynasty

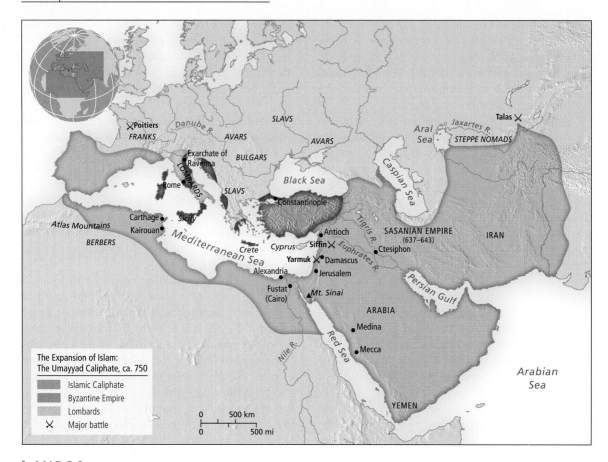

MAP 8.2

The Expansion of Islam: The Umayyad Caliphate, ca. 750

By about 750 the Umayyad caliphate had reached its greatest extent. It provided political unity to territories stretching from central Asia to Spain. Islam became the dominant religion in this vast empire.

who offered them food. As these great landowners acquired more land, the small farmers who were the backbone of the army began to disappear or lose their freedom. Because only free landholders could perform military service, the concentration of land in the hands of a few was disastrous for the army. Qualified soldiers with the land to support them became rare.

The late Macedonian emperors lacked the will to prevent this trend, and the army increasingly depended on foreign mercenaries. These emperors found themselves in a bind. Their income largely depended on their monopoly over industry and trade, but that control meant that land was the only profitable alternative form of investment for aristocrats. Opening up the economy might have hurt their own incomes, and so the emperors failed to do what was necessary to protect the empire. The situation was bleak, and over succeeding centuries, enemies ate away at Byzantium until its final collapse in 1453.

THE NEW WORLD OF ISLAM

■ How did Islam develop in Arabia, and how did its followers create a vast empire so quickly?

The Muslim armies that battered Byzantium created a new civilization that transformed the Mediterranean world and created an empire that stretched from Spain to central Asia (see **Map 8.2**). Today there are more than one billion Muslims around the globe. This growing faith has left an indelible stamp not only on the West, but also on the rest of the world.

Islam originated in the early seventh century among the inhabitants of the Arabian peninsula. Arabs were tribal people. Many of them were nomads herding camels, goats, and sheep. (See *Encounters and Transformations* in this chapter.) In south Arabia, other Arabs farmed, lived in towns, and developed extensive commercial networks. Each tribe claimed descent from a common male ancestor. Tribal chiefs led by their own personal prestige and by the common consent of the tribesmen. Arab tribes, however, performed many of the functions of a state, which included protecting the lives and property of their members.

The Rise of Islam

Islam is based on the Qur'an and the sayings of the prophet Muhammad (ca. 570–632). Muhammad was born to the powerful Hashimite clan of the Quraysh tribe in the cosmopolitan and wealthy west Arabian trading city of Mecca. Mecca was the site of the Ka'aba, a sacred stone where polytheist Arabs worshiped many gods. As a young man Muhammad married a widowed businesswoman, Khadija, and worked as a caravan merchant, earning a reputation as a skilled arbitrator of disputes among tribes.

At about age 40, Muhammad reported that while he was meditating in solitude an angel

THE KA'ABA IN MECCA

In pre-Islamic times, Arabs worshiped a large, black stone at the Ka'aba shrine in the center of Mecca. When Muhammad established Islam in Mecca in 629, he rejected the polytheist past and transformed the Ka'aba into the holiest place in the Islamic world, revered as the House of God. Muslims from all over the world make pilgrimages to the Ka'aba. These journeys foster a shared religious identity among them, no matter where their homelands lie.

ENCOUNTERS AND TRANSFORMATIONS

Ships of the Desert: Camels from Morocco to Central Asia

A remarkable thing happened when the Arab followers of the dynamic new religion of Islam encountered the humble camel, which had been the beast of burden in Arabia and the Near East for at least 2,000 years. The ancient caravan trade that transported goods on the backs of camels brought the Arabs into contact with a vast stretch of the world from Spain to China. In the exchanges that took place along the caravan routes, Islamic religious ideas were widely disseminated, and Arab merchants enriched Muslim cities. The camel also helped make Arab armies formidable in battle, which meant that Islam spread rapidly through conquest.

As the desert dwellers knew, camels were highly efficient for transporting people and goods, especially in arid regions, because of their bodies' capacity to conserve water. Able to drink as much as 28 gallons at a time, camels can last nine days without water and travel great distances. The fat in their humps allows them to survive for even longer without food. Camels are more efficient as pack animals than carts pulled by oxen or mules because they can traverse roadless rough terrain and cross rivers without bridges. They require fewer people to manage them on a journey than do wheeled vehicles.

Arabs developed the "North Arabian saddle," which enabled a rider to grasp the camel's reins

THE CAMEL CARAVAN
This photograph shows a string of camels crossing sand dunes in the desert, carrying heavy loads, just as camel caravans would have in antiquity.

with one hand while slashing downward at enemy troops with a sword in his other hand. Warriors on camels could attack infantry with speed and force. Camel-breeding Arab tribesmen, empowered by their new military technology, seized control of the lucrative spice trade routes and became an economic, military, and political force by exploiting and guarding the wealth of the caravans.

After Muhammad established his community in Mecca in 630, Islam literally "took off" on camelback. Tribesmen-warriors on camels spread Islam first throughout Arabia and the Middle East, and then to central Asia and across North Africa into Spain. Camels played a significant role in the expanding Islamic economy because they made long-distance trade extremely profitable. The transformations the camel brought were most evident in areas where the famous Roman roads had been a primary conduit of land trade. Thousands of miles of roads connected the provinces of the Roman Empire and let troops march easily from one front to another. However, the camels of Arabia changed that. Because these "ships of the desert" did not need paved roads, caravan routes did not have to stick to the Roman road systems, and merchants bypassed them altogether. New trade routes across the desert and other harsh terrains well suited to camels quickly developed from Morocco to central Asia, and paved roads started to disappear. Because camels could easily walk on narrow paths, the broad streets and wide markets suited to carts and wagons that typified Greek and Roman cities also fell out of use. Bazaars with narrow, winding lanes appropriate to camel traffic replaced them. Carts and wheeled vehicles all but vanished in these lands. There were also cultural consequences. In particular, caravan traffic linked China more closely to the Middle East and brought Chinese goods and ideas to the West.

For Discussion

How might the history of the West have differed had not camel caravans replaced the system of Roman roads?

appeared before him, saying, "Muhammad, I am Gabriel and you are the Messenger of God. Recite!" According to Muhammad's account the angel gave him a message to convey to the people of Mecca. Muhammad's message was a call to all Arabs to worship the one true God (the god of Abraham) and to warn of the fires of hell if people failed to answer that call. Muhammad continued to recite his revelations for the rest of his life. They were written down as the Qur'an (meaning "recitation"), the holy book of Islam. Though Muhammad won followers among friends and family, the people of Mecca initially rejected his monotheist message.

In 622, Muhammad and his followers moved from Mecca to Medina, 200 miles to the north, where feuding tribes had invited him to settle their disputes. Muhammad's emigration to Medina, known as the *Hijra,* is the starting date of the Muslim calendar. The event marks a turning point in the development of Islam. For the first time Muhammad and his followers lived as an independent community. Accepted by his disciples as the prophet of God, Muhammad strictly regulated the internal affairs of his new community and its relations with outsiders, creating a society that was political as well as religious. At the center of this Islamic community lay the **mosque,** the place where his followers gathered to pray and hear Muhammad recite the Qur'an.

Initially, Muhammad enjoyed good relations with the Jews who controlled the markets in Medina. He and his followers even abided by Jewish rituals, such as turning toward Jerusalem while praying. But as his influence among the Arab tribes grew, he became involved in disputes with the Jewish tribes who refused to accept him as a prophet. Alienated from the Jews, Muhammad changed the direction of prayer to Mecca, expelled some Jewish tribes from Medina, and massacred the men and enslaved the women and children of others. With Jewish opposition eliminated and control of Medina secured, Muhammad led an army against Mecca, which surrendered in 630.

Using force and negotiation, Muhammad drew many Arab tribes into his new religious community. His authority rested both on his ability as a military leader who raided caravans and defeated enemy tribes and on his reputation as a prophet. By the time he died, he had unified most of Arabia under Islam.

MUHAMMAD'S TEACHINGS Islam teaches that Allah (which means "God" in Arabic) revealed his message to Muhammad, the last in a line of prophets that included Abraham, Moses, and David, all pivotal biblical figures in the Jewish tradition, who transmitted divine instruction to humanity. Muslims also revere Jesus Christ as a prophet, but not as the son of God. Thus, Islam shares some of the beliefs of Judaism and Christianity.

Muhammad taught his followers basic principles that eventually came to be called the five **Pillars of Islam.** *Islam* means "submission," and by performing these acts of faith, Muslims ("those who submit to God") demonstrate obedience to the will of God. First, all Muslims must acknowledge that there is only one God and that Muhammad is his prophet. Second, they must state this belief in prayer five times a day. On Fridays, the noon prayers must be recited in the company of other believers if possible. Muslims may say their prayers anywhere. Third, Muslims must fast between sunrise and sunset during Ramadan, the ninth month of the Muslim calendar. Fourth, Muslims must donate money and food to the needy. Islam expects its followers to be kind to one another, especially to orphans and widows, and to work for the good of the entire Islamic community. Fifth, Muslims must make a

pilgrimage to Mecca at least once in their lives if it is possible. As the focus of prayer and pilgrimage, Mecca quickly became the center of the Muslim world. The Qur'an affirmed Mecca's special role in Islam:

> Announce the Pilgrimage to the people. They will come to you on foot and riding along distant roads on lean and slender beasts, in order to reach the place of advantage (the Ka'aba) for them, and to pronounce the name of God on appointed days over cattle he has given them as food; then eat the food and feed the needy and the poor. (Qur'an 22:26)

With the spread of Islam to Persia, Asia, and parts of Europe in the seventh and eighth centuries, Muslims from different lands encountered one another in Mecca, developing a shared Islamic identity.

While the Qur'an contains many examples of proper behavior for the community to follow, Muslims also looked to Muhammad's example as a guide. Muhammad taught his followers to struggle for the good of the Muslim community. This struggle is called *jihad*. Islam teaches that the duty of *jihad* should be fulfilled by the heart, the tongue, the hand, and the sword. The *jihad* of the heart consists of a spiritual purification by battling the Devil and avoiding temptations to do evil. *Jihad* of the tongue requires believers to propagate the faith and of the hand to correct moral wrongs. *Jihad* of the sword is to wage holy war against unbelievers and enemies of Islam who can avoid attack by converting or paying special taxes, called the *jizya*. (See *Different Voices* in this chapter.) Most modern Muslim scholars understand *jihad* as waging war with one's inner self, the *jihad* of the heart, but some have revived the concept of *jihad* of the sword to support military struggle.

THE SUCCESSION CRISIS AFTER MUHAMMAD: SUNNIS AND SHI'ITES Muhammad had demonstrated a talent for leadership during his lifetime, but he did not designate his successor. His death in 632

DIFFERENT VOICES CHRISTIAN AND MUSLIM JUSTIFICATIONS FOR HOLY WAR

Augustine of Hippo on Just War

Augustine of Hippo (d. 430) was perhaps the most influential early Christian theologian. Early Christian thought was strongly pacifist as the New Testament clearly commands: "I say unto you, that you resist not evil: but if anyone strike you on the right cheek, turn to him the left also." (Luke 6:29) In contrast, Augustine developed a justification for Christian violence. Although he quoted biblical examples, his argument derives from the ancient Roman conception of just war. His case is a good example of the blending of biblical and Roman ideas characteristic of early Christianity.

[The] account of the wars of Moses will not excite surprise or abhorrence, for in wars carried on by divine command, he showed not ferocity but obedience; and God, in giving the command, acted not in cruelty, but in righteous retribution, giving to all what they deserved, and warning those who needed warning. What is the evil in war? Is it the death of some who will soon die in any case, that others may live in peaceful subjection? This is mere cowardly dislike, not any religious feeling. The real evils in war are love of violence, revengeful cruelty, fierce and implacable enmity, wild resistance, and the lust of power, and such like; and it is generally to punish these things, when force is required to inflict the punishment, that, in obedience to God or some lawful authority, good men undertake wars, when they find themselves in such a position as regards to conduct of human affairs, that right conduct requires them to act, or to make others act, in this way."

The Qur'an on Religious War

The sacred book of Islam, the Qur'an, consists of the prophet Mohammed's recitations of his visions of Allah. These excerpts about war and the relations of Muslims with other faiths have the status in Islam of the direct words of God.

Sura 2

190. You shall fight in the cause of god against those who attack you, but do not aggress. God does not love the aggressors.

191. You may kill those who wage war against you, and you may evict them whence they evicted you, for oppression is worse than murder. Do not fight them at the sacred mosque, unless they attack you therein. If they attack you, you may kill them. This is the just retribution for such disbelievers.

Sura 3

113. They are not all the same; among the followers of the scripture [that is, Jews and Christians as well as Muslims], there are those who are righteous. They recite God's revelations through the night, and they fall prostrate.

Sura 5

13. Also those who said, "We are Christians," we took their covenant. But they disregarded some of the commandments given to them. Consequently, we condemned them to animosity and hatred among themselves, until the day of resurrection. God will then inform them of everything they had done.

Sura 60

9. God enjoins you only from befriending those who fight you because of religion, evict you from your homes, and band together with others to banish you. You shall not befriend them. Those who befriend them are the transgressors.

Source: S. J. Allen and Emilie Amt, eds. *The Crusades: A Reader.* 2003, 7, 10–13. Copyright © 2003 by S. J. Allen and Emilie Amt. Reprinted with permission of the publisher, the University of Toronto Press.

For Discussion

1. What makes war acceptable for a Christian or a Muslim?

2. How do Augustine's justifications for war compare with those of the Qur'an?

3. How does the Qur'an distinguish between Islam and Christianity?

therefore caused a crisis. Would the Islamic community stay united under a single new leader? After many deliberations, Muslim elders chose the prophet's father-in-law, Abu Bakr, to lead them. Abu Bakr (r. 632–634) became the first caliph, or successor to Muhammad. The Islamic government that evolved under his leadership, the **caliphate,** combined religious and political responsibilities.

Most Muslims supported Abu Bakr, but a minority opposed him. One group claimed that Muhammad's son-in-law and cousin, Ali, should have become the first caliph. Other Arab tribes rejected Islam itself. They claimed their membership in the Islamic community had been valid only when Muhammad was alive. Abu Bakr crushed them in a struggle called the Wars of Apostasy (a word meaning "renunciation of a previous faith"). By the time he died in 634, Abu Bakr had brought most of Arabia back under his control, but disputes between his followers and those of Ali led to a permanent split within Islam between the minority Shi'ites, who followed Ali, and the majority Sunnis, who followed Abu Bakr. While the Shi'ites and Sunnis both considered the caliphate a hereditary office restricted to members of Muhammad's Hashimite clan of the Quraysh tribe, the Shi'ites believed that only direct descendants of Muhammad through his daughter Fatima and son-in-law Ali should rule the Islamic community. The Sunnis, in contrast, devised a more flexible theory of succession that allowed them later to accept even non-Arab caliphs.

During the wars among Muslims after the death of Muhammad, Abu Bakr created a highly trained Muslim army eager to spread the faith. Under the leadership of the second caliph, Umar (r. 634–644), Muslim forces invaded the rich territories of the Byzantine and Persian Empires. They seized Syria in 636. The next year they crushed the main Persian army, weakened from a long war with Byzantium, and captured the Persian capital, Ctesiphon. Within a decade Islamic troops had conquered Egypt and all of Persia as far east as India. Meanwhile, Muslim fleets, manned by Egyptian and Syrian sailors, seized

Cyprus, raided in the eastern Mediterranean. Muslim armies were racing across North Africa when civil war broke out among the Arabs in 655 and temporarily halted their advance.

Two groups struggled to control the caliphate during this six-year civil war. On one side were Muhammad's son-in-law Ali, who had become caliph in 656, and his supporters, the Shi'ites. On the other side, was the wealthy Umayyad family, who opposed him and whose supporters were Sunnis. (See *Justice in History* in this chapter.) In 661 the Umayyads arranged Ali's assassination and took control of the caliphate, establishing a new dynasty, the Ummayads, that would last until 750. The Umayyads made Damascus in Syria their new capital city, which shifted Islamic power away from Mecca. The Shi'ites continued to oppose the Umayyads, but they remained a minority except in Persia and Iraq.

The Umayyad Caliphate

The Umayyad dynasty produced brilliant administrators and generals. At the end of the civil war, these talented leaders consolidated their control of conquered territories and established peace in the empire. Then they resumed wars of conquest, and in less than a century, built an empire that reached from Spain to central Asia.

THE "HOUSE OF WAR" As we saw in Chapter 6, the Romans distinguished themselves from uncivilized "barbarians" who had not yet come under Roman rule. In a similar fashion, Muslims viewed the world as consisting of two parts: the "House of Islam," which contained the territories they controlled, and the "House of War," which included all non-Muslim lands, which they hoped to conquer. By 700, Muslim armies had conquered North Africa as far as the Atlantic Ocean.

In 711, the Umayyads invaded Spain and easily overthrew the Arian Christian Visigothic kingdom. From Spain they attacked France, but in 732, Charles Martel "the Hammer," leading a Frankish army, stopped their advance at the

JUSTICE IN HISTORY

"Judgment Belongs to God Alone": Arbitration at Siffin

On a spring day in 657, two Muslim armies confronted each other at Siffin, a village on the Euphrates River in Mesopotamia. Men who had been long-time rivals, the Caliph Ali (r. 656–661) and Muawiya, the governor of Syria, commanded the armies. Their rivalry stemmed from Muawiya's refusal to accept Ali's authority as caliph. The Battle of Siffin became a defining moment in the development of the Islamic state. Basic Islamic ideas about divine judgment were put to the test, leading to passionate debate about how God makes his judgment known to Muslims.

Ali had taken power after the assassination of Caliph Uthman, in 656. The murder went unpunished, but many people considered Ali responsible because as caliph he appointed officials known to have taken part in the murder and because he had never disavowed the crime. Uthman belonged to the influential Umayyad clan, and his supporters and family felt obliged to avenge his death. Chief among Ali's opponents was Muawiya, a leading Umayyad, who had a strong army and powerful support in Syria.

Muawiya's and Ali's quarrel also involved tensions within the Muslim community. The earliest converts to Islam and their descendants believed that their association with Muhammad entitled them to greater status than the many new non-Arab converts to Islam, most of whom supported Ali, enjoyed. The early converts supported Muawiya as did tribal leaders who opposed the caliph's growing authority.

The newer converts to Islam also had complaints. In their view, the earliest Muslims, including the Umayyad clan, enjoyed unfair privileges in the Islamic community even though all Muslims were supposed to be equals.

When Ali and Muawiya confronted each other at Siffin, they hesitated to fight because many of their soldiers recoiled from shedding the blood of other Muslims. As one of Ali's followers said,

It is one of the worst wrongs and most terrible trials that we should be sent against our own people and they against us. . . . Yet, if we do not assist our community and act faithfully toward our leader, we deny our faith, and if we do that, we abandon our honor and extinguish our fire.[1]

So for three months, the armies only skirmished.

Finally, in July 657, real fighting broke out. Ali encouraged his men with these words: "Be steadfast! May God's spirit descend on you, and may God make you firm with conviction so that he who is put to flight knows that he displeases his God. . . . ."

The battle came to a sudden halt when Muawiya's soldiers held up pages of the Qur'an on the ends of their spears and appealed for arbitration. Ali's men demanded that their leader settle his differences with Muawiya peacefully through arbitration.

Arab tribes frequently used third-party arbitrators to mediate their conflicts. Muhammad himself had been a skilled mediator before Islam was revealed to him. However, the arbitration between Ali and Muawiya failed, and the two men and their armies separated without having reached an agreement. For the next four years, Ali continued to rule as caliph, but his authority declined because many Arabs interpreted his willingness to go to arbitration as a sign of the weakness of his cause.

In contrast, Muawiya's power grew. He claimed the caliphate for himself and began to make deals with the tribal leaders. In 661 the Ummayyads arranged Ali's assassination, and Muawiya became caliph.

That the arbitration at Siffin occurred at all had lasting consequences. A small but influential faction of Ali's followers argued that God was the only true arbitrator. They believed that Ali should have refused arbitration and submitted to God's judgment through battle. These

THE QUR'AN

Muslim artists devised elaborate Arabic scripts to enhance the beauty of the Qur'an, the holiest text of their faith. This page of the Qur'an, dating to the Umayyad caliphate, is written in the elegant and highly decorative Kufic script.

Source: Courtesy of the Freer Gallery of Art, Smithsonian Institution, Washington, D.C.: Purchase, F1930.60r

Muslims wanted to fight Muawiya to find out what God wanted. This splinter group became known as the Kharijites or "secessionists" because they seceded from Ali's followers. The Kharijites expressed their view of justice in the phrase "Judgment belongs to God alone."

The Kharijites also maintained that Ali was not only wrong to accept human arbitration, but that he and his supporters had thereby committed an unpardonable sin and should no longer be considered Muslims. The Kharijites claimed that they were the only true Muslims. Although their numbers were small, they established independent communities within the Islamic Empire until they disappeared from the historical record in the tenth century.

Other Muslims who disagreed with the Kharijites proclaimed that neither the Kharijites nor any other human being could know whether sinners were still Muslims in the eyes of God. In their opinion, believers would discover God's judgment on these matters only at the End of Days, when God will judge all humanity.

For Discussion

During this early Islamic Empire, how did different beliefs about how God makes his judgment known influence the Islamic sense of the forms human justice should take?

Taking It Further

W. M. Watt. *The Formative Period of Islamic Thought.* 1973. This account discusses the formation of sects and political groups in early Islamic history.

Battle of Poitiers. After this defeat, the Umayyad armies retreated to their territories in Spain.

Umayyad caliphs also attempted to conquer the Christian kingdom of Nubia south of Egypt to obtain its gold and spread Islam. The Nubians repelled several Muslim invasions, however, and a peace treaty was signed between the Umayyad caliphate and Nubian kingdoms. This treaty was without parallel because the Nubians belonged to the "House of War." But what the Arabs failed to achieve through conquest, they gradually gained through immigration. By the fourteenth century Muslim emigrants had Islamized Nubia. While struggling with the Nubians, Umayyad armies also attacked Byzantine territories, sometimes reaching as far as Constantinople, which they besieged but were never able to capture.

Umayyad armies moved eastward with equal speed and success. They reached modern Pakistan and India and captured the caravan city of Samarkand in central Asia, which was a hub on the trade route to China. In 751, just after the murder of the last Umayyad caliph, Muslim armies defeated Chinese troops at the Battle of Talas in central Asia. One consequence of this encounter between Arabs and Chinese was the introduction of paper from China into the Islamic world, from which it gradually spread to Christian Europe.

Like the Battle of Poitiers, which marked the limit of the Umayyads' expansion into western Europe, the Battle of Talas established the limit of Muslim military conquests into central Asia. For the next four centuries, these borders would define the Islamic world.

GOVERNING THE ISLAMIC EMPIRE The Umayyads developed a highly centralized regime that changed the political character of the Muslim community. The first Umayyad caliph, Muawiya (r. 661–680), established a hereditary monarchy to ensure orderly succession of power. This was a major change in the caliphate. Unlike the first four caliphs, who ruled by virtue of their prestige (as did Arab tribal chiefs) and more importantly by the consent of the community, the Umayyads made the caliphate an authoritarian institution.

Because of this, some soldiers protested that the Umayyads had turned "God's servants into slaves," corrupted the faith, and seized the property of God. A second civil war broke out (683–692) between these protestors and the Umayyads, but the Umayyads emerged victorious.

To control their vast empire, Umayyad rulers had to create a new administrative system that both borrowed from and supplanted Byzantine and Persian institutions. The Umayyads designed new provinces that replaced old Byzantine and Persian administrative units. The Umayyads also created a professional bureaucracy based in Damascus to meet their expanding financial needs and ensure that the taxes collected in the provinces reached the central treasury. Most of the administrators had served the Byzantine or Persian Empires and were non-Muslims, although many converted to Islam. These officials provided administrative continuity between the conquered empires and the caliphate.

After the Umayyads made Arabic the official language of their empire, it gradually replaced the languages of the conquered peoples. Only in Persia (now Iran) did Persian, which later evolved into modern Farsi, survive as a widely spoken language, and even there Arabic was the language of government. In the Umayyad caliphate, Arabic functioned as Latin had done in the Roman Empire: It provided a common language for diverse subject peoples. By 800 Arabic had become the essential language of administration and international commerce from Spain to central Asia.

The rapid expansion of Islam created problems for Umayyad rulers eager to consolidate their power. Arab armies had conquered enormous territories, but Arabs were only a small minority among the huge non-Muslim majority. The Umayyads established garrison cities to hold down local populations. Just as Greek colonists followed in the footsteps of Alexander the Great in the fourth century B.C.E., many Arab settlers from the Arabian peninsula migrated to newly conquered lands. They established themselves first in the garrison towns where government officials were based and then in major cities, such as Alexandria, Jerusalem, and Antioch. Some immigrants came from nomadic tribes that adopted a settled way of life for the first time. Others were farmers from the highlands of Yemen, who brought sophisticated irrigation systems and agricultural techniques to their new homes.

Arabs also founded new cities. In Egypt they built Fustat, which would later become Cairo. In North Africa, they established Kairouan in Tunisia. In Mesopotamia they created Basra, an important port on the Persian Gulf and Kufa on the Euphrates River. Though built on a smaller scale than the major urban centers of the Roman and Persian Empires, most new Arab cities drew from Hellenistic town planning. They had a square shape, walls with gates on all four sides, towers, and a central plaza. In the heart of these cities, Umayyad caliphs built a mosque to emphasize the central role of Islam in community life and to celebrate their own authority. The magnificent mosques in Damascus, Jerusalem, and other cities were intended to surpass the grand Christian churches in prestige.

Patterns of daily activity also changed under Muslim rule. With Islam now dominating public life, cities ceased to celebrate Greco–Roman culture. Theaters fell out of use because there was no Arabic tradition of publicly performed drama and comedy. The exercise fields, sports buildings, libraries, schools, and gymnasiums surviving from the Classical Age were also abandoned or adapted for other purposes. Revenues once earmarked for gymnasiums and public buildings now went to local mosques. These centers of Islamic urban culture replaced the forums and agoras of the Roman and Greek world as the chief public space for men. Mosque

THE DOME OF THE ROCK IN JERUSALEM

The Dome of the Rock, an eight-sided building with a gilded dome, dominates Jerusalem's skyline. Completed in 692 on the Temple Mount (the site of the Jewish Temple destroyed by the Romans in 69 C.E.), the building encloses a rock projecting from the floor. During the sixteenth century, the story began to circulate that when Muhammad ascended to heaven, his winged horse took one leap from Mecca to the rock and then sprang skyward.

schools provided education for the community. Muslims gathered at mosques for public festivals and, of course, for religious worship. In their capacity as administrative centers, mosques provided courtrooms, assembly halls, and treasuries for the community. Judges, tax collectors, bureaucrats, and emissaries from the caliph conducted their affairs in the mosque precinct.

During the Umayyad caliphate, most Muslims were farmers and artisans who lived in prosperous villages. Many of these small communities stood on the vast estates of rich landowners who controlled the workers' labor. The caliphate also sponsored huge land reclamation projects on the edges of the desert in Syria and Mesopotamia. Officials of the imperial government drew revenues directly from the villages that sprang up in these new farmlands.

BECOMING MUSLIMS   Islam sharply defined the differences between Muslims and their non-Muslim subjects. Muslim conquerors understood themselves as a community of faith. Only those who converted to Islam could fully participate in the Islamic community. Their ethnicity did not matter. The Qur'an states that "there is no compulsion in religion," meaning that monotheists (Jews, Christians, and Zoroastrians) cannot be forced to convert to Islam. These monotheists were required to accept Islamic political authority, pay a special tax, and accept other restrictions. But polytheists could not be tolerated and had the choice of conversion to Islam or death.

Under the Umayyads, 10 percent of the total population in the caliphate were Muslim. Most of the first converts had probably been Christians, Jews, and Zoroastrians who willingly accepted Islam. Other converts were slaves in the households of their Muslim owners whose willingness to convert is less easy to determine. Still others were villagers who migrated to garrison cities and converted to share in the spoils of conquest—and avoid the taxes non-Muslims had to pay. Their eagerness to convert so threatened the tax base that some Muslim officials refused to acknowledge their conversion and sent them back to their villages.

Conversion to Islam increased as Muslim armies fought their way across North Africa. In the huge area that stretches from Egypt to the Atlantic Ocean, the Muslims conquered many polytheist ethnic groups whom the Arab conquerors collectively called Berbers. Faced with the choice of conversion or death, many Berbers joined the victorious Muslim armies. Islam unified the Berber populations and brought them into a wider Islamic world. With the aid of these additional troops, Islamic power spread even more quickly across North Africa and into Spain.

PEOPLES OF THE BOOK   How do empires govern subject peoples? Do subjects have the same privileges and obligations as their rulers? Can they freely enter into the society of their masters? Previous chapters showed how the Egyptians, Assyrians, Persians, Hellenistic Greeks, and Romans answered these questions. Though their solutions differed, none of these great empires considered the religions of their subjects when deciding their place in society.

By distinguishing their subjects on religious, not ethnic grounds, the Umayyad caliphate took a different approach to governing their subject peoples. Jews, Christians, and Zoroastrians constituted the main religions among conquered peoples. Islamic law called them "Peoples of the Book" because each of these religious communities had a sacred book and they lived as *dhimmis*, non-Muslims protected by the Muslim state. They had lower status than Muslims, but they were free to practice their religion although they could not make converts. Islamic law forbade their persecution or forcible conversion. For this reason, large communities of Jews, Christians, and Zoroastrians lived peacefully under Muslim rule.

Several Christian communities, separated by old controversies about doctrinal issues, coexisted within the Islamic Empire because the caliphate was indifferent to which Christian doctrine they followed. Followers of the Chalcedonian Orthodox church changed the language of prayer from Greek to Syriac and then to

Arabic. Though these Christians had no direct political ties with Constantinople, they followed the Byzantine emperors' Chalcedonian Orthodoxy (see Chapter 7). Thus, their church was called the Melkite, or Royal, church. The Melkite church is still the largest Christian community in the Middle East today. Anti-Chalcedonian (Monophysite) Christians formed the Jacobite Church in the late sixth century. The Jacobite Bible and prayers are in Syriac. The Nestorian church, comprising Christians who emphasized Jesus's humanity rather than the combination of his humanity and divinity, also flourished under Muslim rule. Nestorian missionaries established communities in India, central Asia, and China. The variety of Christian communities in the caliphate was greater than in Byzantium and the Latin Christian kingdoms where laws enforced conformity to the dogmas of one particular Church, Orthodox or Catholic.

Jewish communities also flourished throughout Umayyad lands, notably in southern Spain and Mesopotamia. Jews found their subordinate but protected status under Islam preferable to the open persecution they suffered in many Christian kingdoms. In Persia, Zoroastrian communities fared less well under Islamic rule. As they were slowly forced into remote regions, their numbers dwindled. In the tenth century, many Zoroastrians migrated to India, where they are known today as Farsis, a word that means "Persians."

COMMERCIAL ENCOUNTERS To strengthen their rule, the Umayyads transformed the economic system of the empire. From the time of their first conquests, Muslim rulers derived revenues primarily from the huge amounts of gold and silver taken in war, taxes, and contributions Muslims made to support widows and orphans. To increase their revenues, Umayyad rulers introduced a land tax for Muslim landowners, in imitation of Byzantine and Persian taxation. Even the proud Arab tribesmen, for whom paying taxes was humiliating because it implied subordination, had to pay taxes, though less than non-Muslims paid. With land tax revenues, the Umayyads could afford a standing professional army. This further reduced the fighting role of Arab tribes, enabling caliphs to cement their authority more firmly.

The peace the empire brought led to the rapid expansion of long-distance trade. Although merchants could travel safely from Morocco to central Asia and earn great profits, such expeditions were expensive. The Qur'an approved of mercantile trading, and Islamic law permitted letters of credit, loans, and other financial instruments that made commerce over huge distances possible long before Christian Europe had such sophisticated commercial tools.

Umayyad rulers further stimulated international commerce by creating a new currency that imitated Persian and Byzantine coinage. The Persian silver *drahm* (a word derived from the Greek *drachma*) inspired the Umayyad *dirham,* which became the standard coin throughout the caliphate by the 780s. Muslim merchants, and businessmen as far away as western Europe, Scandinavia, and Russia, paid for goods with silver dirhams. For gold coinage the Umayyads minted the *dinar* (a word derived from a Roman coin, the *denarius*). Like the dirham, the dinar also became a standard coin in the caliphate and distant lands. Merchants could depend on the value of this currency wherever they did business.

Umayyad caliphs also encouraged maritime trade. Alexandria in Egypt became the chief Mediterranean port for Arab commercial shipping. The Umayyads maintained peace in the Persian Gulf and the Indian Ocean. Arab merchants sailed to India and the city of Guangzhou in southern China, following the sea routes Persian navigators had established. Arab traders also sailed down the coast of East Africa to obtain slaves and natural resources such as ivory and gold from the interior. In later centuries Muslim navigators reached Malaysia, Indochina, Indonesia, and the Philippines.

The Abbasid Caliphate

After the last Umayyad caliph died in a battle in 750, the Abbasid clan, who were descendants of Muhammad's uncle, seized the caliphate and tried to exterminate the Umayyad family. The only Umayyad to escape, Abd al-Rahman I (r. 756–788), fled to Spain where he founded what would later become the caliphate of Córdoba.

The Abbasid caliphate (750–945) quickly altered the character of the Muslim world. In 762–763, the Abbasids built a new capital in Baghdad where they were exposed to the ceremonial and administrative traditions of Persia, which helped expand the intellectual horizons of the caliphs, their courtiers, and bureaucrats.

The Abbasid caliphs expanded their control over society, but they were far from despots. The caliph was first and foremost an emir—that is, the commander of a professional army. He was also responsible for internal security, which meant suppressing rebellions, supervising officials, and making sure taxes were honestly collected. But he did not interfere with other public institutions, such as mosques, hospitals, and schools. The principal exception was the office of market inspector, through which the caliph guaranteed fair business practices. In this commitment to the integrity of markets and trade, the Islamic caliphate was more advanced than either Byzantium, where privileged monopolies dominated the economy, or the Latin states of Europe, where a market economy hardly existed.

The period of Abbasid greatness lasted about a century (754–861), and its literature reflects its eclectic nature. The famous *Arabian Nights,* stories written down for the caliph Harun al-Rashid (r. 786–809), were based on Hellenistic, Jewish, Indian, and Arab legends. The *Arabian Nights* and the rich tradition of Arabic poetry, which often recounted tales of thwarted love, in turn influenced the western Christian poetry of romantic love. Harun al-Rashid began the grand project of translating into Arabic the literature of ancient Greece and texts from Syria, India, and Persia.

Philosophical and scientific inquiry thrived under Caliph al-Mamun (r. 813–833), who had an astronomical observatory built in Baghdad and appreciated the work of al-Kindi (d. ca. 870), the first outstanding Islamic philosopher. Al-Kindi grappled with questions specific to Islam but also with the works of Aristotle and problems in astrology, medicine, optics, arithmetic, cooking, and metallurgy—which made him well-known outside the Islamic world. The work of Arabic translators in the ninth and tenth centuries created a crucial cultural link between the ancient and medieval worlds. The Muslims supplied Arabic translations of ancient Greek and Syriac texts to a later generation of Jews and Christians in Spain, who translated them into Latin. These second- and third-hand Latin translations of ancient philosophy and science became the core of the university curriculum in western Europe during the twelfth century.

Abbasid political power ended in 945 when a clan of rough tribesmen from northwest Persia seized Baghdad. The Abbasid caliphs remained in office as religious and ceremonial figureheads, but despite occasional attempts to reinvigorate the caliphate, its power as a ruling institution was over. However, the caliphate remained a vital symbol of Islamic unity and survived as formal institution until 1924.

Islamic Civilization in Europe

During the eighth and ninth centuries, the Muslim armies chipped away at Christian territories in Europe. Unlike their fellow Muslims in the Middle East and North Africa, most of the Muslims in Europe conducted themselves more as raiders than conquerors. They plundered and pillaged but did not stay long or attempt a mass conversion of Christians to Islam. These raids, however, made urban life impossible, and many Mediterranean cities almost disappeared. To survive, populations fled into the countryside, where families could live off the land and find protection with one of the local lords who built castles for defense.

The significant exceptions to the pattern of raiding were in Sicily and Spain. Between 828 and 965, Muslim armies conquered Sicily. Arab farmers and merchants migrated there from North Africa, and Islam spread among the general population although most Sicilians remained Christian. In Spain, Muslim conquests in the early eighth century brought the peninsula into the orbit of Islam except for small Christian states in the extreme north.

Sicily and Spain became the principal borderlands through which Arabic learning and science filtered into Catholic Europe. These borderlands became zones of intense cultural interaction, where several languages were spoken and where Christians and Jews were allowed to observe their own faiths. Although small, Muslim Sicily and Spain were among the most dynamic places in Europe during the eighth to early eleventh centuries. No Christian city in western Europe could rival Córdoba, capital of Muslim Spain, in size and prosperity. Even within the Muslim world, only Baghdad could compare to it. A German nun visiting Córdoba during the tenth century thought the city embodied "the majesty and adornment of the world, the wondrous capital...radiating in affluence of all earthly blessings."[2]

The caliphate of Córdoba became the most important intellectual capital in western Europe, renowned for the learning of its Muslim and Jewish scholars. Córdoba's fame derived from the extensive authority and magnificent building projects encouraged by the Caliph Abd al-Rahman III (r. 912–961) and his three successors. With an ethnically mixed population of more than 100,000, Córdoba boasted 700 mosques, 3,000 public baths, 5,000 silk looms, and 70 libraries. The caliph's library housed more than 400,000 volumes. The streets of the city were paved and illuminated at night, the best houses enjoyed indoor plumbing, and the rich had country villas as vacation retreats. (Rome did not erect streetlamps for another 1,000 years.) Besides the great mosque, which was one of the most famous religious monuments in Islam, the architectural centerpiece of the city was Madinat az-Zahra, a 400-room palace that Abd al-Rahman III built for his favorite concubine, Zahra. Adorned with marble and semiprecious stones from Constantinople, the palace took 20 years to build and housed 13,000 household servants in addition to the diplomats and courtiers who attended the caliph.

GREAT MOSQUE OF CÓRDOBA
The great mosque of Córdoba was one of the wonders of the world during the tenth century. Because Islam prohibited the depiction of the human body, mosques were embellished with geometrical forms and quotations from the Qur'an. The repetition of multiple arches creates an intricate pattern that changes as the viewer moves about in the space.

The influence of the golden age of Córdoba in the tenth century can be found in the legacy of the poets, scientists, physicians, astronomers, and architects who thrived under the caliphs' patronage. Despite tensions between Muslims and Jews, many of the intellectuals in the caliphs' court were Arabized Jews. Typical of the many non-Muslims who served Arab rulers, Hasdai ibn Shaprut (915–970), who was probably a Jew, became famous for his medical skills, in particular his antidotes for poisons. In the caliphs' court the demand for his cures was strong, because several princes had fallen victim to conspiracies hatched in the palace harem or had been poisoned by their lovers. The trust that Hasdai gained from his medical skills led the caliph to appoint him to deal with sensitive customs and diplomatic disputes. Both Muslim and Christian rulers considered Jews such as Hasdai politically neutral, making them prized as diplomatic envoys. The Jew Samuel ibn Nagrela (993–1055) became vizier (chief minister) of the neighboring Muslim kingdom of Granada. An able Hebrew poet, biblical commentator, and philosopher, he

also commanded Muslim armies. Nagrela's career reflected the value Muslims placed on learning and talent.

During the early eleventh century, succession disputes led to the murder of several caliphs, and the caliphate of Córdoba splintered into small states. The disunity of Muslim Spain provided opportunities for the stubborn little Christian states of the north to push against the frontiers of their opulent Muslim neighbors. The kingdom of Navarre under Sancho III (r. 1004–1035) was the first to achieve dramatic success against the Muslims. After his death his conquests were

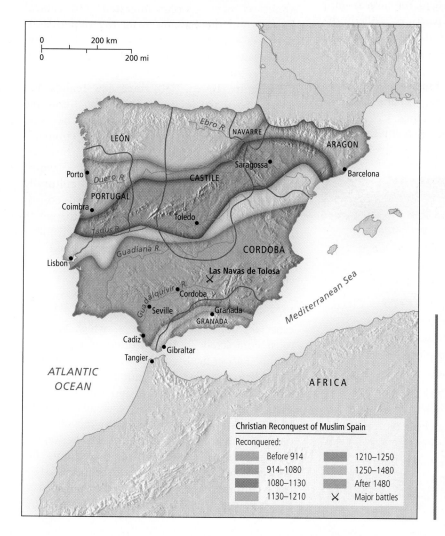

MAP 8.3

Christian Reconquest of Muslim Spain

The Spanish Reconquest refers to the numerous military campaigns by the Christian kingdoms of northern Spain to capture the Muslim-controlled cities and kingdoms of southern Spain. This long, intermittent struggle began with the capture of Toledo in 1085 and lasted until Muslim Granada fell to Christian armies in 1492.

divided into the kingdoms of Navarre, Aragon, and Castile. During the reign of Alfonso VI (r. 1065–1109), Castile became the dominant military power in Spain. Forcing Muslims to pay him tribute and helped by French knights eager for plunder and French monks ardent for converts, Alfonso launched a campaign known as the **Spanish Reconquest** that led to the capture of the city of Toledo in 1085. The center of Spanish Christianity before the Muslim conquests, Toledo provided Alfonso with a glorious prize that made him famous throughout Christian Europe (see **Map 8.3**).

The loss of Toledo so shocked the Muslim states in Spain that they asked for help from a sect of North African warriors called the Almoravids. The Almoravids defeated Alfonso VI and temporarily halted the Spanish Reconquest in 1086. But in 1212 at the Battle of Las Navas de Tolosa, the Christian kingdoms united to defeat the Muslims. Within two generations most Spanish Muslim cities, including Córdoba in 1236, fell to Christian armies. A few remnants of Muslim power hung on in Spain until 1492.

CHRONOLOGY: THE NEW WORLD OF ISLAM

ca. 570	Muhammad born in Mecca
622	Muhammad flees to Medina (the *Hijra*)
632	Muhammad dies in Medina
633–651	Muslims conquer Persia
640–642	Muslims conquer Egypt
661	Caliph Ali is assassinated
661–750	Umayyad caliphate
703–1060	Arab conquest of Sicily
713	Muslims overrun most of Spain
750–945	Abbasid caliphate
756–1031	Umayyad caliphate of Córdoba
ca. 870	Death of al-Kindi
1085	Christian capture of Toledo from Muslims
1212	Battle of Las Navas de Tolosa

CONCLUSION

Three Cultural Realms

The death of the Byzantine Emperor Justinian I in 565 marked the last time one imperial ruler would control most of the territory from Spain to Syria. The Persian Empire still menaced Byzantium's eastern frontier, and except for Italy and some coastal areas of Spain, Germanic kings ruled western Europe. During the next two centuries, western Europe, the Mediterranean world, and the Middle East as far as India and central Asia were reconfigured politically and culturally. Part of that reconfiguration came about as new peoples migrated into central Europe and the Balkans from the steppe frontiers. As threatening as they were, these new arrivals were eventually absorbed into the civilizations of the West through conversions to Christianity. By ca. 750, three new realms had come into sharp focus: the Christian Byzantine Empire based at Constantinople; the vast Umayyad caliphate created by Muhammad's Islamic followers; and, as Chapter 9 examines, Latin Christendom in western Europe, which was fragmented politically but united culturally by Christianity. Each of these regions was constituted as a community of religious faith, which had, at best, a limited toleration of other faiths. The cultural foundations they established and the divisions that emerged among them still shape the West today.

These three cultural realms of the West each borrowed from the heritage of ancient Rome, especially its network of cities, which survived most completely in the Mediterranean and the Middle East in the Byzantine and Islamic Empires. The religious traditions of antiquity, especially the emphasis on monotheism in Judaism, influenced each of the three realms. They each adapted parts of Roman law and reshaped it to suit changing needs and new cultural influences. The heritage of Rome remained strongest in Byzantium. But between the sixth and eleventh centuries, these three cultural realms came to be distinguished by the language that dominated intellectual and religious life and by the forms of monotheism each practiced. In Byzantium the Greek language and Orthodox Christianity with its elaborate ceremonies defined the culture. By the end of the Umayyad caliphate in 750, the Arabic language and many Islamic beliefs and practices were becoming standard over a wide area. In western Europe, many languages were spoken, but Latin became the universal language of the Church and government.

The end of the Umayyad caliphate saw the limit of Muslim expansion in western Europe and central Asia. After that the Byzantine Empire struggled for survival. In Chapter 9 we will see how the kingdom of the Franks arrested Muslim incursions into western Europe. However, the very survival of many western European kingdoms was put to the test during the ninth and tenth centuries by yet more invasions and migrations from the Eurasian steppes and Scandinavia. By the end of the eleventh century, Latin Christianity had gathered sufficient cohesion and military strength to launch a vast counterstroke against Islam in the form of the Crusades.

KEY TERMS

icons
iconoclasm
Macedonian
   Renaissance

mosque
Pillars of Islam
caliphate
Spanish Reconquest

CHAPTER QUESTIONS

1. How did the Roman Empire's eastern provinces evolve into the Byzantine Empire? (page 234)
2. How did Islam develop in Arabia, and how did its followers create a vast empire so quickly? (page 243)

TAKING IT FURTHER

1. How did the Byzantine Empire manage to hold off so many enemies for so long?
2. Why did Islam split between Sunni and Shi'ites?
3. Should Muslim countries be considered part of the West?

✓—[Practice] on **MyHistoryLab**

9

Medieval Empires and Borderlands: The Latin West

■ The Birth of Latin Christendom   ■ The Carolingians
■ Invasions and Recovery in the Latin West
■ The West in the East: The Crusades

ONE GRAY DAY IN CENTRAL GERMANY IN 740, AN ENGLISH MONK named Boniface swung his axe at an enormous oak tree. This was the sacred Oak of Thor, where German men and women had prayed for centuries to one of their mightiest gods. Some local Christians cheered and applauded the monk. But an angry crowd of men and women gathered as well, cursing Boniface for attacking their sacred tree. Then something extraordinary occurred. Though Boniface had only taken one small chop, the entire tree came crashing down, split neatly into four parts. Boniface's biographer, a monk named Willibald, explained the strange event as God's judgment against "pagan" worshipers. In Willibald's account of the incident, the hostile crowd was so impressed by the miracle that they immediately embraced Christianity. As the news spread, more and more Germans converted, and Boniface's fame grew. According to Willibald, "The sound of Boniface's name was heard through the greater part of Europe. From the land of Britain, a great host of monks came to him—readers, and writers, and men trained in other skills."[1]

Boniface played a leading role in spreading Christianity among the peoples of northern Europe. The Christian missionaries who traveled to lands far beyond the Mediterranean world brought Latin books and established monasteries. Through Christianity and the literacy disseminated from these monastic centers, the monks established cultural ties among the new Germanic converts to Roman learning. Historians refer to the Christianized Germanic kingdoms on the continent and Britain as Latin Christendom because they celebrated the Christian **liturgy** in Latin and accepted the authority of the pope in Rome. Even though they no longer celebrate the liturgy in Latin as they did in the Middle Ages, Roman Catholics today continue to revere the pope and the traditions of medieval Latin Christianity.

As discussed in Chapter 8, Latin Christianity and Orthodox Christianity gradually grew apart during the Middle Ages, primarily over theological differences and disputes about who held the ultimate authority in the Church. For most Christians, however, the crucial differences were over liturgy and language. The liturgy consists of the forms of worship—prayers, chants, and rituals. In the Middle Ages there was a great deal of variety in the Christian liturgy, and a number of languages were used, but followers of the Roman church gradually came to identify themselves with the Latin liturgy and the Latin language. As a result, the diverse peoples of medieval western Europe began to be called the "Latin people."

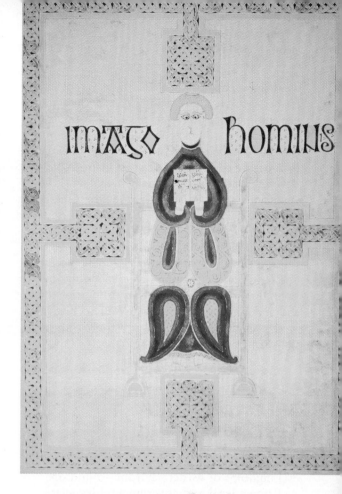

THE IMAGE OF A MAN (*IMAGO HOMINIS*)

In this eighth-century manuscript, the image of a man symbolizes the Evangelist Matthew. The other three evangelists, Mark, Luke, and John, were symbolized by a lion, bull, and eagle, all fixed signs of the zodiac, created by ancient polytheist astronomers. The adaptation of Christianity to pagan symbolism conveyed the message that Christianity represented the fulfillment of ancient wisdom.

The Latin Christendom that came to dominate western Europe joined the Greek Orthodox and Arabic Muslim civilizations that constituted the three pillars of the West during the Middle Ages. Recurrently pressing across the frontiers of the Greek Orthodox and Latin Christian civilizations were wave after wave of barbarian peoples coming from the Eurasian steppes and Scandinavia. The Avars, Slavs, Rus, and Bulgars who threatened Byzantium became Orthodox Christians. The raiders and invaders who entered the western half of the Roman Empire—the Germanic tribes, the Magyars, and the Vikings—eventually became Latin Christians. Their conversions took place through missionary efforts and military expeditions that forced the conquered to convert. By the end of the eleventh century few polytheists could still be found in Europe. With the exception of the Muslim pockets in Spain and Sicily and isolated communities of Jews, Christianity had become the dominant faith.

In this crucial phase in forming Western civilization from about 350–1100, new political formations in western Europe made possible greater political cohesion that brought together ethnically and linguistically diverse peoples under obedience to an emperor or king. As in Byzantium and the Islamic caliphates, the empires and kingdoms of the Latin West enforced or encouraged uniformity of religion, spread a common language among the ruling elite, and instituted systematic principles for governing. The Carolingian Empire, which lasted from 800 to 843 and controlled much of western Europe, reestablished the Roman Empire in the West for the first time in more than 300 years and sponsored a revival of interest in Roman antiquity called the Carolingian Renaissance. The Carolingian Empire's collapse was followed by a period of anarchy as Europe faced further incursions of hostile invaders. During the eleventh century, however, the Latin West recovered in dramatic fashion. By the end of the century the Latin kingdoms were strong enough to engage in a massive counterassault against Islam, in part in defense of fellow Christians in Byzantium. These campaigns against Islam, known as the Crusades, produced a series of wars in the Middle East and North Africa that continued throughout the Middle Ages. But the ideals of the crusaders lasted well into modern times, long after the active fighting ceased. The transformations in this period raised this question: How did Latin Christianity help strengthen the new kingdoms of the Latin West so that they were eventually able to deal effectively with both barbarian invaders and Muslim rivals?

THE BIRTH OF LATIN CHRISTENDOM

■ How did Latin Christendom—the new kingdoms of western Europe—build on Rome's legal and governmental legacies and how did Christianity spread in these new kingdoms?

By the time the Roman Empire collapsed in the West during the fifth century, numerous Germanic tribes had settled in the lands of the former empire. These tribes became the nucleus for the new Latin Christian kingdoms that emerged by 750 (see **Map 9.1**).

Germanic Kingdoms on Roman Foundations

The new Germanic kingdoms of Latin Christendom created a new kind of society. They borrowed from Roman law while establishing government institutions, but they also relied on their own traditional methods of rule. Three elements helped unify these kingdoms. First, in the Germanic kingdoms personal loyalty rather than

legal rights unified society. Kinship obligations to a particular clan of blood relatives rather than citizenship, as in the Roman Empire, defined a person's place in society and his or her relationship to rulers. Second, Christianity became the dominant religion in the kingdoms. The common faith linked rulers with their subjects. And third, Latin served as the language of worship, learning, and diplomacy in these kingdoms. German kingdoms based on Roman foundations appeared in Anglo-Saxon England, Frankish Gaul, Visigothic Spain, and Lombard Italy.

ANGLO-SAXON ENGLAND Roman civilization collapsed more completely in Britain during the fifth century than it did on the European continent, largely because of Britain's long distance from Rome and the small number of Romans who had settled there. About 400, the Roman economic and administrative infrastructure of Britain fell apart, and the last Roman legions left the island to fight on the continent. Raiders from the coast of the North Sea called Angles and Saxons (historians referred to them as Anglo-Saxons) took advantage of Britain's weakened defenses and launched invasions. They began to probe the island's southeast coast, pillaging the small villages they found there and establishing permanent settlements of their own.

Because the small bands of Anglo-Saxon settlers fought as often among themselves as they did against the Roman Britons, the island remained fragmented politically during the first few centuries of the invaders' rule. But by 750, three warring kingdoms managed to seize enough land to coalesce and dominate Britain: Mercia, Wessex, and Northumbria.

FRANKISH GAUL Across the English Channel from Britain lay the Roman province of Gaul. From the third to the seventh century the kingdom of the Franks, centered in Gaul, produced the largest and most powerful kingdom in western Europe. One family among the Franks, called the Merovingians, gradually gained preeminence. A crafty Merovingian war chief named Childeric ruled a powerful band of

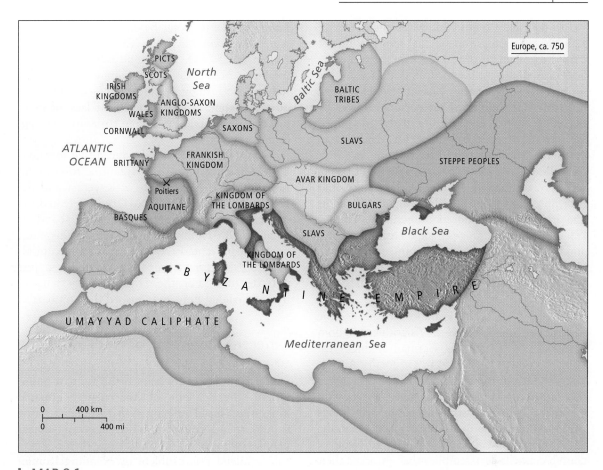

MAP 9.1

Europe, ca. 750

By about 750 the kingdom of the Franks had become the dominant power in western Europe. The Umayyad caliphate controlled Spain, and the Lombard kingdom governed most of Italy. The Byzantine Empire held power in Greece, as well as its core lands in Asia Minor.

Franks from about 460 until his death in 481. With the support of his loyal soldiers, Childeric laid the foundation for the Merovingian kingdom. His energetic and ruthless son Clovis (r. 481–511) made the Franks one of the leading powers in the western provinces of the old Roman Empire. Clovis aggressively expanded his father's power base through the conquest of northern Gaul and neighboring territories. He murdered many of his relatives and other Frankish chieftains whom he considered rivals. In 486 Clovis overcame the last Roman stronghold in northern Gaul.

Around 500 the polytheist Clovis converted to Latin Christianity. About 3,000 warriors, the core of his army, joined their king in this change to the new faith. Clovis had a practical reason to convert. He intended to attack the Visigothic kingdom in southern Gaul. The Visigoths followed Arian Christianity, but their subjects, the Roman inhabitants of the region, were Latin Christians. By converting to Latin Christianity, Clovis won the support of many of the Visigoths' subjects. With their help, he crushed the Visigothic king Alaric II in 507. Clovis now controlled almost all of Gaul as far as Spain.

In the eighth century, however, the Merovingian kings became so ineffectual that real power passed to the man in charge of the royal household called the "Mayor of the Palace." One of these mayors, Charles Martel "the Hammer" (r. 719–741), established his personal power by regaining control over regions that had slipped away from Merovingian rule and by defeating an invading Muslim army at Poitiers in 732. Martel's son, Pepin the Short (r. 741–768), succeeded his father as Mayor of the Palace, but dethroned the last of the Merovingian monarchs and in 751 made himself king of the Franks. Pepin relied on the pope to legitimatize his coup, and in exchange the Franks guaranteed the pope's safety. Thus, began the vital alliance between the Frankish monarchy and the popes in Rome.

VISIGOTHIC SPAIN   The Franks were never able to conquer Spain, where a Visigothic kingdom emerged. As in all the Germanic kingdoms, religion unified the kingdom. Originally Arians, Visigoth kings converted to Latin Christianity in the late sixth century, and Visigothic Spain became a Latin Christian kingdom. The kings began to imitate the Byzantine emperors with the use of elaborate court ceremonies and frequent church councils as assemblies that enforced their will. Thus, the key to their success was the ability to employ the spiritual authority of the Church to enhance the secular authority of the king. However, the autocratic instincts of the Visigoth kings alienated many of the substantial landowners who were easily lured by the promises of Muslim invaders to treat them more favorably.

In 711 invading armies of Muslims from North Africa vanquished the last Visigothic king. As a result, most of Spain became part of the Umayyad caliphate. Many Christians from the upper classes converted to Islam to preserve their property and offices. Some survivors of the Visigoth kingdoms held on in the northwest of Spain, where they managed to keep Christianity alive.

LOMBARD ITALY   Between 568 and 774, a Germanic people known as the Lombards controlled most of northern and central Italy. They were called *Langobardi,* or "Long Beards," from which the name *Lombard* derives. The Lombard king, Alboin (r. ca. 565–572), took advantage of the weakness of the Byzantine Empire and invaded Italy in 569. Alboin's army contained soldiers of different ethnic backgrounds. That lack of unity made it impossible for Alboin to build a strong, lasting kingdom.

The Lombard kings also faced two formidable external enemies—the Byzantine forces who remained in the Exarchate of Ravenna and the Franks. In 751 the Lombards' ruler defeated the Exarchate, leading to the Byzantine abandonment of Ravenna. Internal political disputes, however, prevented the Lombards from capitalizing on their victory over the Byzantines. Just two decades later the Frankish king Charlemagne invaded Italy and crushed the Lombards.

Different Kingdoms, Shared Traditions

With the exception of England, where Anglo-Saxon invaders overwhelmed the Roman population, the leaders of the new Germanic kingdoms faced a common problem: How should the Germanic minority govern subject peoples who vastly outnumbered them? These rulers solved this problem by blending Roman and Germanic traditions. For example, kings served as administrators of the civil order in the style of the Roman emperor, issuing laws and managing a bureaucracy. They also served as war leaders in the Germanic tradition, leading their men into battle in search of glory and loot. As the Germanic kings defined new roles for themselves, they discovered that Christianity could bind all their subjects together into one community of believers. The merging of Roman and Germanic traditions could also be traced in the law, which eventually erased the distinctions between Romans and Germans, and in the ability of women to own property, a right far more common among the Romans than the Germans.

CIVIL AUTHORITY: THE ROMAN LEGACY   In imitation of Roman practice, the monarchs of Latin Christendom designated themselves the source of all law and believed that they ruled with God's approval. Kings controlled all appointments to civil, military, and religious office. Accompanied by troops and administrative assistants, they also traveled throughout their lands to dispense justice, collect taxes, and enforce royal authority.

Frankish Gaul provides an apt example of how these monarchs adopted preexisting Roman institutions. When Clovis conquered the Visigoths in Gaul, he inherited the nearly intact Roman infrastructure and administrative system that had survived the collapse of Roman imperial authority. Merovingian kings (as well as Visigoth rulers in Spain and Lombards in Italy) found it useful to maintain parts of the preexisting system and kept the officials who ran them. For instance, Frankish kings relied on the bishops and counts in each region to deal with local problems. Because Roman aristocrats were literate and had experience in Roman administration on the local level, they often served as counts. Based in cities, these officials presided in local law courts, collected revenues, and raised troops for the king's army. Most bishops also stemmed from the Roman aristocracy. In addition to performing their religious responsibilities, bishops aided their king by providing for the poor, ransoming hostages who had been captured by enemy warriors from other kingdoms, and bringing social and legal injustices to the monarch's attention. Finally, the kings used dukes, most of whom were Franks, to serve as local military commanders, which made them important patrons of the community. Thus, the civil and religious administration tended to remain the responsibility of the Roman counts and bishops, but military command fell to the Frankish dukes.

WAR LEADERS AND WERGILD: THE GERMANIC LEGACY The kingdoms of Latin Christendom developed from war bands led by Germanic chieftains. By rewarding brave warriors with land and loot taken in war, as well as with revenues skimmed from subject peoples, chieftains created political communities of loyal men and their families, called **clans** or **kin groups.** Though these followers sometimes came from diverse backgrounds, they all owed military service to the clan chiefs. Because leadership in Germanic society was hereditary, networks of loyalty and kinship expanded through the generations. The various political communities gradually evolved into distinct ethnic groups led by a king. These ethnic groups, such as the Lombards and the Franks, developed a sense of shared history, kinship, and culture.

Kinship-based clans stood as the most basic unit of Germanic society. The clan consisted of all the households and blood relations loyal to the clan chief, a warrior who protected them and spoke on their behalf before the king on matters of justice. Clan chieftains in turn swore oaths of loyalty to their kings and agreed to fight for him in wars against other kingdoms. The clan leaders formed an aristocracy among the Germanic peoples. Like the Roman elites before them, the royal house and the clan-based aristocracy consisted of rich men and women who controlled huge estates. The new Germanic aristocrats intermarried with the preexisting Roman elites of wealthy landholders, thus maintaining control of most of the land. These people stood at the very top of the social order, winning the loyalty of their followers by giving gifts and parcels of land. Under the weight of this new upper class, the majority of the population, the ordinary farmers and artisans, slipped into a deepening dependence. Most peasants could not enter into legal transactions in their own name, and they had few protections and privileges under the law. Even so, they were better off than the slaves who toiled at society's very lowest depths. Valued simply as property, these men, women, and children had virtually no rights in the eyes of the law.

Though this social hierarchy showed some similarities to societies in earlier Roman times, the new kingdoms' various social groups were defined by law in a fundamentally different way. Unlike Roman law, which defined people by citizenship rights and obligations, the laws of the new kingdoms defined people by their **wergild.** A Germanic concept, *wergild* referred to what an individual was worth in case he or she suffered some grievance at the hands of another. If someone injured or murdered someone else, wergild was the amount of compensation in gold that the wrongdoer's family had to pay to the victim's family.

In the wergild system, every person had a price that depended on social status and perceived usefulness to the community. For example, among the Lombards service to the king increased a free man's worth—his wergild was higher than that of a peasant. In the Frankish kingdom, if a freeborn woman of childbearing age was murdered, the killer's family had to pay 600 pieces of gold. Noble women and men had higher wergild than peasants, while slaves and women past childbearing age were worth very little.

UNITY THROUGH LAW AND CHRISTIANITY Within the kingdoms of Latin Christendom, rulers tried to achieve unity by merging Germanic and Roman legal principles and by accepting the influence of the Church. Religious diversity among the peoples in their kingdoms made this unity difficult to establish. As discussed in Chapter 7, many of the tribes that invaded the Roman Empire during the fifth century practiced Arian Christianity. They kept themselves apart from the Latin Christians by force of law. For example, they declared marriage between Arian and Latin Christians illegal.

These barriers began to collapse when Germanic kings converted to the Latin Christianity of their Roman subjects. Some converted for reasons of personal belief or because their wives were Latin Christians. Others decided to become Latin Christians to gain wider political support. For instance, when Clovis converted about 500, laws against intermarriage between Arians and Latin Christians in Gaul disappeared. More and more Franks and Romans began to marry one another, blending the two formerly separate communities into one and reinforcing the strength of the Latin Church. By 750 most of the western European kingdoms had officially become Latin Christian, though substantial pockets of polytheist practice survived and communities of Jews were allowed to practice their faith.

Germanic kings adopted Latin Christianity, but they had no intention of abandoning their own Germanic law, which differed from Roman law on many issues, especially relating to the family and property. Instead, they offered their Roman subjects the opportunity to live under the Germanic law that governed the king. Clovis's *Law Code* or *Salic Law,* published sometime between 508 and 511, illustrated this development. The *Law Code* applied to Franks and to any other non-Roman peoples in his realm who chose to live according to Frankish law. Because the Romans dwelling in the Frankish kingdom technically still followed the laws of Byzantium, Clovis did not presume to legislate for them. Romans could follow their own law if they wished, or they could follow his laws and become Franks. By 750, however, most Romans had chosen to abandon their legal identity as Romans and live according to Frankish law, and the distinction between Roman and Frank lost all meaning. A similar process occurred in the other Germanic kingdoms. This unification of peoples under one law happened without protest, a sign that various groups had blended politically, religiously, and culturally.

WOMEN AND PROPERTY Roman law influenced more than just local administration in Latin Christendom. It also prompted Germanic rulers to reconsider the question of a woman's right to inherit land. In the Roman Empire, women had inherited land without difficulty. Indeed, perhaps as much as 25 percent of the land in the entire empire had been owned by women. In many Germanic societies, however, men could inherit land and property far more easily than women. Attitudes about female inheritance began to shift when the Germanic settlers established their homes in previously Roman provinces—and began to marry Roman women who owned property.

By comparing the law codes of the new kingdoms over time, historians have detected the impact of Roman customs on Germanic inheritance laws. By the late eighth century, women in Frankish Gaul, Visigothic Spain, and Lombard

Italy could inherit land, though often under the restriction that they had to eventually pass it on to their sons. Despite these limitations, the new laws transformed women's lives. A woman who received an inheritance of land could live more independently, support herself if her husband died, and have a say in the community's decisions.

The Spread of Latin Christianity in the New Kingdoms of Western Europe

As Latin Christianity spread as the official religion through the new kingdoms, churchmen decided that they had a moral responsibility to convert all the people of these kingdoms and beyond. They sent out missionaries to explain the religion to nonbelievers and challenge the worship of polytheist gods.

Meanwhile, bishops based in cities directed people's spiritual lives, instilling the moral and social conventions of Christianity through sermons delivered in church. Monks such as Boniface, who introduced this chapter, traveled from their home monasteries in Ireland, England, and Gaul to spread the faith to Germanic tribes east of the Rhine. Monasteries became centers of intellectual life, and monks replaced urban aristocrats as the keepers of books and learning.

THE GROWTH OF THE PAPACY In theory, the Byzantine emperors still had political authority over the city of Rome and its surrounding lands during this violent time. However, strapped for cash and troops, these distant rulers proved unequal to the task of defending the city from internal or external threats. In the resulting power vacuum, the popes stepped in to manage local affairs and became, in effect, princes who ruled over a significant part of Italy.

Gregory the Great (r. 590–604) stands out as the most powerful of these popes. The pragmatic Gregory wrote repeatedly to Constantinople, pleading for military assistance that never came. Without any relief from the Byzantines, Gregory had to look elsewhere for help. Through clever diplomacy, Gregory successfully cultivated the good will of the Christian communities of western Europe by offering religious sanction to the authority of friendly kings. He negotiated skillfully with his Lombard and Frankish neighbors to gain their support and establish the authority of the Roman church. He encouraged Christian missionaries to spread the faith in England and Germany. In addition, he took steps

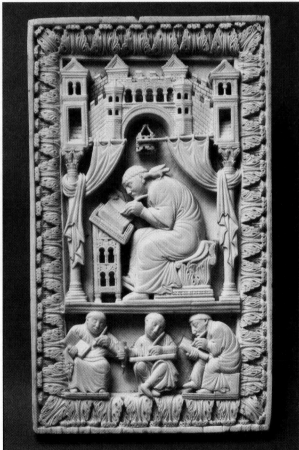

POPE GREGORY THE GREAT AND THREE SCRIBES
In this tenth-century ivory depicting the influential sixth-century Pope Gregory, writing symbolizes his power and influence. During early Middle Ages, the church alone kept literacy and writing alive in the West.

Source: St. Gregory writing with scribes, Carolingian, Franco-German School, c. 850–875 (ivory). Kunsthistorisches Museum, Vienna, Austria/Bridgeman Art Library

to train educated clergymen for future generations, in this way securing Christianity's position in western Europe.

Gregory set the stage for a dramatic increase in papal power. As his successors' authority expanded over the next few centuries, relations between Rome and the Byzantine emperors slowly soured, especially during the Iconoclastic Controversy discussed in Chapter 8. By the early eighth century the popes abandoned the fiction that they were still subject to the Byzantines and sought protection from the Frankish kings.

CONVERTING THE IRISH   Though the Romans had conquered most of Britain during the imperial period, they never attempted to bring Ireland into their empire. Thus, the island off Britain's west coast had had only minimal contact with Christianity. Little is known of how Christianity came to Ireland. There were probably missionaries who traveled with traders from the Roman Empire, but the earliest firm date is 431 when Palladius was supposedly sent to administer to those in Ireland who were already Christians. The figure of Patrick (d. ca. 492 or 493) dominates the subsequent missionary history of Ireland, largely because his later biographers improbably gave him credit for converting all the Irish to Christianity. A ninth-century record describes Patrick's capture from a Roman villa in Britain by Irish raiders, who sold him into slavery in Ireland. He managed to escape and return to Britain, where he was ordained into the priesthood and sent back to Ireland as a missionary. A great deal of confusion exists regarding Patrick's life; some scholars argue that the traditional story of Patrick actually merges the experiences of the two missionaries Palladius and Patrick. Nevertheless, by the end of the fifth century, Christianity had a firm foothold in Ireland.

But Ireland was still an entirely rural place. Elsewhere in the West, Christianity spread out into the countryside from cities, with bishops administering the local church from their city cathedrals. Ireland, however, lacked cities in which to build churches and housing for bishops. No one living in Ireland knew Latin, Greek, or any of the other languages into which the Bible had been translated.

And no schools existed where churchmen might teach the Gospel to new converts.

Irish churchmen found solutions to these problems in monasteries, places where priests could receive training and men and women from the surrounding homesteads and hamlets could learn to read Latin and absorb the basics of Christian education. The Irish scholars produced by these monasteries gained a high reputation for their learning across western Europe. They produced magnificently illustrated manuscripts in their libraries. These books brought Irish art to all the lands where Irish missionaries traveled.

THE BOOK OF KELLS

The Book of Kells consists of an ornately illustrated manuscript produced by Irish monks about 800 C.E. The book contains the four gospels of the New Testament in Latin and is one of the masterpieces of early medieval art. This highly decorated page shows two Greek letters, Chi and Rho, the first two letters of Christ in Greek.

Source: The Board of Trinity College, Dublin, Ireland

CONVERTING THE ANGLO-SAXONS Irish missionaries established new monasteries in England and on the European continent. Columba (521–597), for instance, founded one on the island of Iona, off Scotland's western coast. From this thriving community missionaries began to bring Christianity to the peoples of Scotland. The offshoot monastery of Lindisfarne in northern England also became a dynamic center of learning and missionary activity. During the seventh century, missionaries based there carried Christianity to many other parts of England. They also began converting the people of Frisia on the North Sea, in the area of the modern Netherlands.

Pope Gregory the Great (r. 590–604) understood that the first step in creating new Christian communities was to convert as many people as possible to the faith. Deep learning about the religion could come later. To that end he instructed missionaries to permit local variations in worship and to accommodate harmless vestiges of pre-Christian worship practices. "Don't tear down their temples," Gregory advised, "put a cross on the roofs!"

Following Gregory's pragmatic suggestion, missionaries in England accepted certain Anglo-Saxon calendar conventions that stemmed from polytheist worship. For example, in the Anglo-Saxon calendar, the weekdays took their names from old gods: Tuesday derived from Tiw, a war god; Wednesday from Woden, king of the gods; Thursday from Thor, god of thunder; and Friday from Freya, goddess of agriculture. Anglo-Saxon deities eventually found their way into the Christian calendar as well. Eostre, for example, a goddess whose festival came in April, gave her name to the Christian holiday Easter.

Despite their common commitment to Latin Christianity, the Irish and Roman monks working throughout England disagreed strongly about proper Christian practice. For instance, they argued over how to perform baptism, the ritual of anointing someone with water to admit him or her into the Christian community. They bickered about how monks should shave the tops of their heads to show their religious vocation, and they squabbled about the correct means of calculating the date of Easter. These disputes threatened to create deep divisions among England's Christians. The overall conflict finally found resolution in 664 in the Anglo-Saxon kingdom of Northumbria, where monastic life flourished. At a council of monks and royal advisers called the Synod of Whitby, the Northumbrian monarch commanded that the Roman rather than Irish version of Christianity would prevail in his kingdom. His decision eventually was accepted throughout England.

MONASTIC INTELLECTUAL LIFE The missionaries from Rome were members of the vigorous monastic movement initiated by Benedict of Nursia (ca. 480–547) from his monastery at Monte Cassino in Italy (see Chapter 7). These monks followed Benedict's *Rule,* a guidebook for the management of monastic life and spirituality. In the *Rule,* Benedict had written that individual monks should live temperate lives devoted to spiritual contemplation, communal prayer, and manual labor. So that their contemplations might not depart from the path of truth, Benedict had encouraged monks to seek guidance in the Bible, in the writings of the renowned theologians, and in works of spiritual edification. For Benedict, contemplative reading constituted a fundamental part of monastic life. Thus, monks had to be literate in Latin. They needed training in the Latin classics, which required books.

Medieval monasteries set aside at least two rooms—the **scriptorium** and the library—to meet the growing demand for books. In the scriptorium, scribes laboriously copied Latin and Greek manuscripts as an act of religious devotion. Monastery libraries were small in comparison with the public libraries of classical Rome, but the volumes were cherished and carefully protected. Because books were precious possessions, these libraries set forth strict rules for their use. Some librarians chained books to tables to prevent theft. Others pronounced a curse against anyone who failed to return a borrowed book. Nevertheless, librarians also generously lent books to other monasteries to copy.

CHRONOLOGY: THE BIRTH OF LATIN CHRISTENDOM

481–511	Clovis reigns; Frankish kingdom divided at his death
529	Benedict founds monastery at Monte Cassino
568	Lombards invade Italy
587	Visigothic king of Spain converts to Latin Christianity; Columbanus travels to Gaul from Ireland
ca. 700	Lombards accept Latin Christianity
732	Charles Martel defeats Muslims at Poitiers
751	Pepin overthrows last Merovingian king; Exarchate of Ravenna falls to Lombards

Monks preferred to read texts with a Christian message, so these books were the most frequently copied. In many monasteries, however, monks preserved non-Christian texts as well. By doing so, they helped to keep knowledge of Latin and classical learning alive. Indeed, many of the surviving works by authors of the Classical Age were copied and passed on by monks in the sixth and seventh centuries. Without the monasteries and scriptoria, knowledge today of the literature of the classical world would be greatly reduced.

Monks did far more than merely copy ancient texts, however. Some wrote original books of their own. At the English monastery at Jarrow, for example, Bede (d. 735) became the most distinguished scholar in eighth-century Europe. He wrote many books, including the *History of the English Church and People*. This work provided an invaluable source of information about the early Anglo-Saxon kingdoms.

Monks carried books with them when they embarked on missionary journeys. They also acquired new books during their travels. For instance, Benedict Biscop, the founder of the monasteries of Wearmouth (674) and Jarrow (682) in England, made six trips to Italy. Each time he brought back crates of books on all subjects, including works written by classical authors whom monks studied with interest. Other Anglo-Saxon missionaries transported this literary heritage to the monasteries they founded in Germany during the eighth century. As monks avidly read, copied, wrote, and transported books of all sorts, knowledge and intellectual discourse flourished in the monasteries.

Monks shared their expanding knowledge with Christians outside the monastery walls. They established schools at monasteries where boys (and, in some places, girls) could learn to read and write. In Italy some public schools survived from antiquity, but elsewhere most of the very few literate people who lived between 550 and 750 gained their education at monastery schools. The men trained in these schools played an important role in society as officials and bureaucrats. Their skills in reading and writing were necessary for keeping records and writing business and diplomatic letters.

THE CAROLINGIANS

■ How did the Carolingian Empire contribute to establishing a distinctive western European culture?

Among the successor kingdoms to the Roman Empire in the West, discussed in the previous section, none was more powerful militarily than the Merovingian kingdom of the Franks. The Merovingian dynasty, however, was plagued by factions, royal assassinations, and do-nothing kings. When Pepin the Short deposed the last of the Merovingian kings in 751, he made himself king of the Franks and inaugurated the Carolingian dynasty.

Both the weak Merovingians and the strong Carolingians illustrated how the problem of succession from one king to another could destabilize early medieval monarchies. The kingdom was considered the private property of the royal family, and according to Frankish custom, a father was obliged to divide his estates among all his legitimate sons. As a result, whenever a king of the Franks died, the kingdom was divided up. When Pepin died in 768, the kingdom was divided between his sons, Charlemagne and Carloman. When Carloman died suddenly in 771, Charlemagne ignored the inheritance rights of Carloman's sons and may even have had them killed, making himself the sole ruler of the Franks.

The Leadership of Charlemagne

Charlemagne's (r. 768–814) ruthlessness with his own nephews epitomized the leadership that made him the mightiest ruler in western Europe and gave him the nickname of Charles the Great. An unusually tall and imposing figure, Charlemagne was a superb athlete and swimmer, a lover of jokes and high living, but also a deeply pious Christian. One of his court poets labeled him "The King Father of Europe." No monarch in European history has enjoyed such posthumous fame.

During his reign, Charlemagne engaged in almost constant warfare, especially against polytheistic Germanic tribes that he compelled to accept Christianity after their defeat. He went to war 18 times against the Saxons, whose forced conversion only encouraged subsequent rebellions. Three factors explain Charlemagne's persistent warfare. He believed he had an obligation to spread Christianity. He also needed to protect his borders from incursions by hostile tribes. Perhaps most important, however, was his need to satisfy his followers, especially the members of the aristocracy, by providing them with opportunities for plunder and new lands. As a result of his many wars, Charlemagne established a network of subservient kingdoms that owed tribute to him (see **Map 9.2**).

The extraordinary expansion of the Carolingian Empire represented a significant departure from the small, loosely governed kingdoms that had prevailed after the Roman Empire's collapse.

Charlemagne's empire covered all of western Europe except for southern Italy, Spain, and the British Isles. His military ambitions brought the Franks into direct confrontation with other cultures—the polytheistic German, Scandinavian, and Slavic tribes, the Orthodox Christians of Byzantium, and the Muslims in Spain. These confrontations were usually hostile and violent, characterized as they were by the imposition of Frankish rule and Latin Christian faith.

CORONATION OF CHARLEMAGNE AS EMPEROR   On Christmas Day 800 in front of a large crowd at St. Peter's Basilica in Rome, Pope Leo III (r. 795–816) presided over a ceremony in which Charlemagne was crowned emperor. Historians have debated exactly what happened, but according to the most widely accepted account, the assembled throng acclaimed Charlemagne emperor, and the pope prostrated himself before the new emperor in a public demonstration of submission. Charlemagne's biographer Einhard later stated that the coronation came as a surprise to the king. Certainly there were dangers in accepting the imperial crown because the coronation was certain to antagonize Byzantium, where there already was a Roman emperor. To the Byzantines, Charlemagne was nothing more than a barbarian usurper of the imperial crown. In their minds the pope had no right to crown anyone emperor. Instead of reuniting the eastern and western halves of the ancient Roman Empire, the coronation of Charlemagne drove them further apart. Nevertheless, Charlemagne became the first Roman emperor in the West since the fifth century.

The coronation exemplified two of the most prominent characteristics of the Carolingians. The first was the conscious imitation of the ancient Roman Empire, especially the Christian empire of Constantine. Charlemagne conquered much of the former territory of the western Roman Empire, and the churches built during his reign were modeled after the fourth- and fifth-century basilicas of Rome. The second characteristic of Carolingian rule was the obligation of the Frankish kings to protect

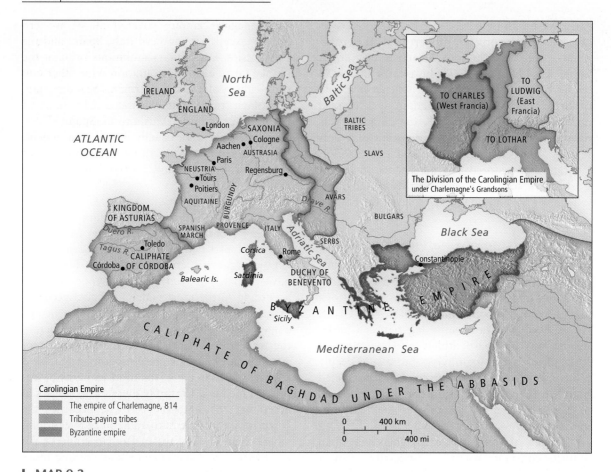

MAP 9.2

Carolingian Empire

Charlemagne's conquests were the greatest military achievement of the Early Middle Ages. The Carolingian armies successfully reunified all western European territories of the ancient Roman Empire except for southern Italy, Spain, and Britain. However, the empire was fragile due to Frankish inheritance laws that required all legitimate sons to inherit lands from their father. By the time of Charlemagne's grandsons the empire began to fragment.

the Roman popes, an obligation that began under Charlemagne's father Pepin. In exchange for Frankish protection, the popes offered the Carolingian monarchs the legitimacy of divine sanction.

CAROLINGIAN RULERSHIP   Even under the discerning and strong rulership of Charlemagne, the Carolingian Empire never enjoyed the assets that had united the ancient Roman Empire for so

many centuries. The Carolingians lacked a standing army and navy, professional civil servants, properly maintained roads, regular communications, and a money economy—a stark contrast with Byzantium and the Muslim caliphates, which could also boast splendid capital cities of Constantinople, Damascus, Baghdad, and Córdoba. However, Charlemagne governed very effectively without a capital, spending much of his time ruling from the saddle.

Such a system of government depended more on personal than institutional forms of rule. Personal loyalty to the Carolingian monarch, expressed in an oath of allegiance, provided the strongest bonds unifying the realm, but betrayals were frequent. The Carolingian system required a monarch with outstanding personal abilities and unflagging energy, such as Charlemagne possessed, but a weak monarch threatened the collapse of the entire empire. Until the reign of Charlemagne, royal commands had been delivered orally, and there were few written records of what decisions had been made. Charlemagne's decrees (called "capitularies") gradually came to be written out. The capitularies began to strengthen and institutionalize governmental procedures. In addition, Charlemagne's leading adviser, Alcuin, insisted that all official communications be stated in the appropriate Latin form, which would help prevent falsification because only the members of Charlemagne's court were well enough educated to know these proper forms.

One of the weaknesses of the previous Merovingian dynasty had been the decentralization of power, as local dukes appropriated royal resources and public functions for themselves. To combat this weakness, Charlemagne followed his father's lead in reorganizing government around territorial units called **counties,** each administered by a count. The counts were rewarded with lands from the king and sent to areas where they had no family ties to serve as a combined provincial governor, judge, military commander, and representative of the king. Traveling circuit inspectors reviewed the counts' activities on a regular basis and remedied abuses of office. On the frontiers of their sprawling kingdom, the Franks established special territories called **marches,** which were ruled by margraves with extended powers necessary to defend vulnerable borders.

In many respects, however, the Church provided the most vital foundations for the Carolingian system of rulership. As discussed in Chapter 7, during the last years of the ancient Roman Empire the administration of the Church was organized around the office of the bishop.

By the late seventh century this system had almost completely collapsed, as many bishoprics were left vacant or were occupied by royal favorites and relatives who lacked qualifications for church office. Because Carolingian monarchs considered themselves responsible for the welfare of Christianity, they took charge of the appointment of bishops and reorganized church administration into a strict hierarchy of archbishops who supervised bishops who, in turn, supervised parish priests. Pepin and Charlemagne also revitalized the monasteries and endowed new ones, which provided the royal court with trained personnel—scribes, advisers, and spiritual assistants. Most laymen of the time were illiterate, so monks and priests wrote the emperor's letters for him, kept government records, composed histories, and promoted education—all essential for Carolingian rule.

THE CAROLINGIAN RENAISSANCE In addition to organizing an efficient political administration, Charlemagne sought to make the royal court an intellectual center. He gathered around him prominent scholars from throughout the realm and other countries. Under Charlemagne's patronage, these scholars were responsible for the flowering of culture that is called the Carolingian Renaissance.

The **Carolingian Renaissance** ("rebirth") was one of a series of revivals of interest in ancient Greek and Latin literature. Charlemagne understood that both governmental efficiency and the propagation of the Christian faith required the intensive study of Latin, which was the language of the law, learning, and the Church. The Latin of everyday speech had evolved considerably since antiquity. During Charlemagne's time, spoken Latin had already been transformed into early versions of the Romance languages of Spanish, Italian, Portuguese, and French. Distressed that the poor Latin of many clergymen meant they misunderstood the Bible, Charlemagne ordered that all prospective priests undergo a rigorous education and recommended the liberal application of physical punishment if a pupil was slow in his lessons. The lack of properly educated teachers, however, ensured that the Carolingian reforms did not penetrate very far into the lower levels of the clergy, who taught by rote the rudiments of Christianity to the illiterate peasants.

Charlemagne's patronage was crucial for the Carolingian Renaissance, which took place in the monasteries and the imperial court. Many of the heads of the monastic scriptoria wrote literary works of their own, including poetry and theology. The Carolingian scholars developed a beautiful new style of handwriting called the Carolingian minuscule, in which each letter was carefully and clearly formed. Texts collected by Carolingian librarians provided the foundation for the laws of the Church (called **canon law**) and codified the liturgy, which consisted of the prayers offered, texts read, and chants sung on each day of the year.

The man most fully responsible for the Carolingian Renaissance was the English poet and cleric Alcuin of York (ca. 732–804), whom Charlemagne invited to head the palace school in Aachen. Charlemagne himself joined his sons, his friends, and his friends' sons as a student, but Charlemagne struggled as a student. Despite many years of practice he still could not learn to form letters. Nevertheless, under Alcuin's guidance the court became a lively center of discussion and exchange of knowledge. They debated issues such as the existence of Hell, the meaning of solar eclipses, and the nature of the Holy Trinity. After 15 years at court, Alcuin became the abbot of the monastery of St. Martin at Tours, where he expanded the library and produced a number of works on education, theology, and philosophy.

A brilliant young monk named Einhard (ca. 770–840), who studied in the palace school, quickly became a trusted friend and adviser to Charlemagne. Based on 23 years of service to Charlemagne and research in royal documents, Einhard wrote the *Life of Charlemagne* (830–833), which describes Charlemagne's family, foreign policy, conquests, administration, and personal attributes. In Einhard's vivid Latin prose, Charlemagne comes alive as a great leader, a lover of hunting and fighting, who unlike his rough companions possessed a towering sense of responsibility for the welfare of his subjects and the salvation of their souls. In Einhard's biography, Charlemagne appears as an idealist, the first Christian prince in medieval Europe to imagine that his role was not just to acquire more possessions but to better humankind.

Charlemagne's rule and reputation have had lasting significance for western Europe. Around 776 an Anglo-Saxon monk referred to the vast new kingdom of the Franks as the Kingdom of Europe, reviving the Roman geographical term *Europa*. Thanks to the Carolingians, Europe became more than a geographical expression. It became the geographical center of a new Christian civilization that supplanted the Roman civilization of the Mediterranean and transformed the culture of the West.

The Division of Western Europe

None of Charlemagne's successors possessed his personal skills, and without a permanent institutional basis for administration, the empire was vulnerable to fragmentation and disorder. When Charlemagne died in 814, the imperial crown passed to his only surviving son, Louis the Pious (r. 814–840). Louis's most serious problem was dividing the empire among his own three sons, as required by Frankish inheritance laws. Disputes among Louis's sons led to civil war, even before the death of their father; while they were fighting, the administration of the empire was neglected.

After years of fighting, the three sons—Charles the Bald (d. 877), Lothair (d. 855), and Louis the German (d. 876)—negotiated the Treaty

CHRONOLOGY: THE CAROLINGIAN DYNASTY	
751	Pepin the Short deposes last Merovingian king
800	Charlemagne crowned emperor in Rome
843	Treaty of Verdun divides Frankish kingdom
987	Death of the last Carolingian king

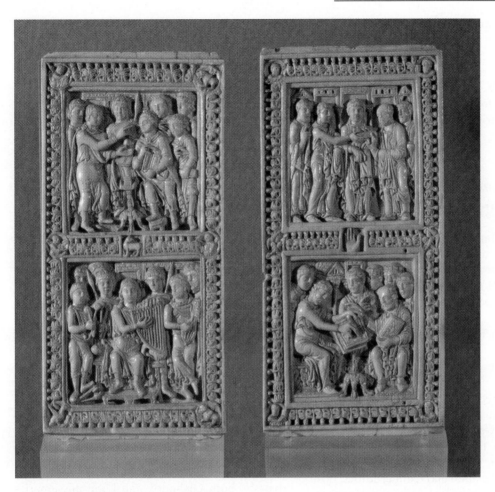

CAROLINGIAN RENAISSANCE ART
This exquisitely carved book cover for the Psalter of Dagulf was made for Pope Hadrian (d. 795) in the workshops of Charlemagne's palace. In the upper left side panel, King David orders the psalms be written down. In the lower left he sings them. In the upper right the pope orders Saint Jerome to edit the psalms for inclusion in the Bible, which he does in the lower right.

of Verdun, which divided the Carolingian Empire. Charles the Bald received the western part of the territories, the kingdom of West Francia. Louis the German received the eastern portion, the kingdom of East Francia. Lothair obtained the imperial title as well as the central portion of the kingdom, the "Middle Kingdom," which extended from Rome to the North Sea (see Map 9.2). In succeeding generations, the laws of inheritance created further fragmentation of these

kingdoms, and during the ninth and tenth centuries the descendants of Charlemagne died out or lost control of their lands. By 987 none were left.

The Carolingian Empire lasted only a few generations. Carolingian military power, however, had been formidable, providing within the Frankish lands an unusual period of security from hostile enemies, measured by the fact that few settlements were fortified. After the empire's collapse, virtually every surviving community in western

Europe required fortifications, represented by castles and town walls. Post-Carolingian Europe became fragmented as local aristocrats stepped into the vacuum created by the demise of the Carolingians—and it became vulnerable, as a new wave of raiders from the steppes and the North plundered and carved out land for themselves.

INVASIONS AND RECOVERY IN THE LATIN WEST

- After the collapse of the Carolingian Empire, how did the western kingdoms consolidate in the core of the European continent and how did Latin Christianity spread to its periphery?

Despite Charlemagne's campaigns of conquest and conversion, the spread of Christianity throughout western Europe remained uneven and incomplete. By 900, Latin Christianity was limited to a few regions that constituted the heartland of western Europe—the Frankish lands, Italy, parts of Germany that had been under Carolingian rule, the British Isles, and a fringe in Spain. Moreover, the heartland was vulnerable because during the ninth and tenth centuries, hostile polytheistic tribes raided deep into the tightly packed Christian core of western Europe (see **Map 9.3**). Despite these attacks Christianity survived, and the polytheist tribes eventually accepted the Christian faith. These conversions were not always the consequence of Christian victories in battle, as had often been the case during late antiquity and the Carolingian period. More frequently they resulted from organized missionary efforts by monks and bishops.

The Polytheist Invaders of the Latin West

Some of the raiders during the eighth to eleventh centuries plundered what they could from the Christian settlements of the West and returned home. Others seized lands, settled down, and established new principalities. The two groups who took advantage of the weakness of the Latin West most often during this period were the Magyars and Vikings.

The original homeland of the Magyars, later known as the Hungarians, was in the central Asian steppes. Gradually driven by other nomads to the western edge of the steppes, the Magyars crossed en masse in 896 into the middle of the Danube River basin, occupying sparsely settled lands that were easily conquered. Mounted raiding parties of Magyars ranged far into western Europe. Between 898 and 920 they sacked settlements in the prosperous Po River valley of Italy and then descended on the remnant kingdoms of the Carolingian Empire. Wherever they went they plundered for booty and took slaves for domestic service or sale. The kings of western and central Europe were powerless against these fierce raiders, who were unstoppable until 955 when the Saxon king Otto I destroyed a band of marauders on their way home with booty. After 955, Magyar raiding subsided.

The definitive end of Magyar forays, however, may have had less to do with Otto's victory than with the consolidation of the Hungarian plain into its own kingdom under the Árpád dynasty. Both Orthodox and Latin missionaries vied to convert the Magyars, but because of western political alliances they accepted Latin Christianity. On Christmas Day 1000, the Árpád king Stephen I (r. 997–1038) received the insignia of royalty directly from the pope and was crowned king. To help convert his people, King Stephen laid out a network of bishoprics and lavishly endowed monasteries.

The most devastating of the eighth- to eleventh-century invaders of western European settlements were the Vikings, also called Norsemen or Northmen. During this period, Danish, Norwegian, and Swedish Viking warriors sailed on long-distance raiding expeditions from their homes in Scandinavia. Every spring the long Viking dragon ships sailed forth, each carrying 50–100 warriors avid for loot. Propelled by a

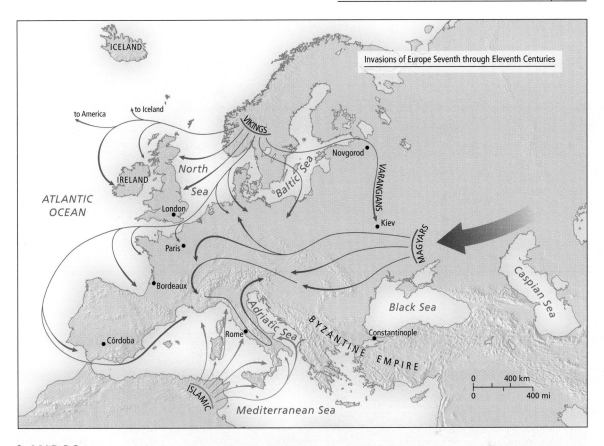

MAP 9.3

Invasions of Europe, Seventh Through Eleventh Centuries

After the division of the Carolingian empire, Britain and northern France, in particular, came under severe pressure from invading Viking bands from Scandinavia. The Varangians were a Viking tribe that invaded Kievan Rus and the territories of the Novgorod. From the east came the Magyars, who eventually settled in the vast Hungarian plain. From the south there were persistent raids and conquests from various Islamic states, some of which established a rich Muslim civilization in Europe. (For these, see Chapter 8.)

single square sail or by oarsmen when the winds failed or were blowing in the wrong direction, Viking ships were unmatched for seaworthiness and regularly sailed into the wild seas of the North Atlantic. The shallow-draft vessels could also be rowed up the lazy rivers of Europe to plunder monasteries and villages far into the interior.

Historians continue to debate the causes for the enormous Viking onslaught. Higher annual temperatures in the North may have stimulated a spurt in population that encouraged raiding and

eventually emigration. But the primary motive seems to have been an insatiable thirst for silver, which was deemed the essential standard of social distinction in Scandinavian society. As a result, monasteries and cathedrals with their silver liturgical vessels were especially prized sources of plunder for Viking raiding parties. In 793, for example, Vikings pillaged the great English monastery at Lindisfarne for its silver—and largely destroyed it in the process.

By the middle of the ninth century, the Vikings began to maintain winter quarters in

VIKING SHIP

This reconstructed Viking ship, discovered at Oseberg, Norway, dates from ca. 800. It would have been propelled by a single square sail or rowed by oarsmen. Horses and warriors crowded into the ship. The tiller was mounted on the starboard side toward the stern. Stern-mounted rudders, which gave the helmsman much greater control of the direction of the ship, were gradually introduced during the twelfth century.

the British Isles and on the shores of the Carolingian kingdoms—locations that enabled them to house and feed ever-larger raiding parties. These raiders soon became invading armies that took land and settled their families on it. As a result, the Vikings moved from disruptive pillaging to permanent occupation, which created a lasting mark on Europe. Amid the ruins of the Carolingian Empire, Viking settlements on the Seine River formed the beginnings of the duchy of Normandy ("Northman land"), whose soldiers in the eleventh century would conquer England, Sicily, and much of southern Italy.

The most long-lasting influence of the Vikings outside Scandinavia was in the British Isles and North Atlantic. In 865 a great Viking army conquered large parts of northeastern England, creating a loosely organized network of territories known as the Danelaw. The Danish and Norse conquests in the British Isles left deep cultural residues in local dialects, geographical names, personal names, social structure, and literature. The most enduring example in Old English, the earliest form of spoken and written English, remains the epic of *Beowulf*, which recounts the exploits of a great Scandinavian adventurer in combat with the monster Grendel, Grendel's mother, and a fiery dragon.

In the North Atlantic, Vikings undertook long voyages into the unknown across cold rough seas. Beginning about 870, settlers poured into unsettled Iceland. Using Iceland as a base, they ventured farther and established new colonies in Greenland. In Iceland the adventures of these Viking warriors, explorers, and settlers were celebrated in poetry and sagas. The sagas of Erik the Red and the Greenlanders recount hazardous voyages to the coasts of Canada. These Europeans arrived in North America 500 years before Christopher Columbus. In 930 the fiercely independent Icelanders founded a national parliament, the *althing*, an institution at which disputes were adjudicated through legal procedures rather than combat.

After the mid-ninth century, the kings of Scandinavia (Norway, Denmark, and Sweden) began to assert control over the bands of raiders who had constituted the vanguard of the Viking invasions. By the end of the tenth century, the great age of Viking raiding by small parties ended. The Scandinavian kings established firm hold over the settled population and converted to Christianity, bringing their subjects with them into the new faith. Hence, the descendants of the Viking raiders settled down to become peaceable farmers and shepherds.

The Rulers in the Latin West

As a consequence of the disintegration of the Carolingian order and the subsequent invasions, people during the ninth and tenth centuries began to seek protection from local warlords who assumed responsibilities once invested in royal authorities. Some of these warlords became the founders of what would become the kingdoms of the Latin West. They provided protection and a modicum of order in a period of anarchy caused by weak or failed governments.

LORDS AND VASSALS The society of warlords derived from Germanic military traditions in which a great chief attracted followers who fought alongside him. The relationship was voluntary and egalitarian. By the eighth century, however, the chief had become a **lord** who dominated others, and his dependents were known as **vassals.**

The bond of loyalty between lord and vassal was formalized by an oath. In the Carolingian period the vassal proved his loyalty to the lord by performing an act of homage, which made the vassal the "man" of the lord. The act of homage was a ritual in which the kneeling vassal placed his clasped hands between the hands of the lord and made a verbal declaration of intent, usually something such as, "Sir, I become your man." In return for the vassal's homage or fealty, as it came to be called, the lord swore to protect the vassal. The oath established a personal relationship in which the lord reciprocated the vassal's loyalty and willingness to obey the lord with protection and in some cases with a land grant called a **fief.** Lords frequently called on their vassals for military assistance to resist invaders or to fight with other lords. The fief supplied the vassal with an income to cover the expenses of armor and weapons and of raising and feeding horses, all of which were necessary to be an effective mounted soldier, known by the twelfth century as a **knight.** Historians called this connection between lord-vassal relations and the holding of a fief **feudalism.** The privileges for lords and vassals and their hold on fiefs lasted for many centuries, well into the eighteenth century in some parts of Europe. The long persistence of feudalism was one of the most important themes in the history of the West.

During the ninth and tenth centuries, after the collapse of public authority during the invasions

Revealing the Truth: Oaths and Ordeals

No participant in a lawsuit or criminal trial today would dream of entering the courtroom without an accompanying pile of documents to prove the case. In modern society we trust written over oral evidence because we are aware of how easily our memories can be distorted. In an early medieval court, however, the participants usually arrived with nothing more than their own sworn testimony and personal reputations to support their cause. Papers alleging to prove one thing or another meant little in a largely illiterate society. Unable to read and perhaps aware that the few who could read might deceive them, most people trusted what they had personally seen and heard. Count Berthold of Hamm expressed the opinion of many when, after being presented with documents opposing his claim to a piece of land, he "laughed at the documents, saying that since anyone's pen could write what they liked, he ought not to lose his rights over it."

To settle disputes, medieval courts put much more faith in confession or in eyewitness testimony than in documents. In 1124 Pope Calixtus II pronounced that "we put greater faith in the oral testimony of living witnesses than in the written word."

Under normal trial procedures, a man would give his oath that what he was saying was true. If he was an established and respected member of the community, he would also have a number of "oath-witnesses" testify for his reliability, although not to the truth or falsehood of his evidence. The court would also hear from witnesses in the case. This system worked well enough when two local men, known in the community, were at odds. But what happened when there was a trial involving a person who had a bad reputation, was a known liar, or was a stranger? What would happen in a case with no witnesses?

In these instances, medieval courts sometimes turned to trial by ordeal—subjecting the accused to a painful test—to settle the matter. The judicial ordeal was used only as a last resort, as a German law code of 1220 declared: "It is not right to use the ordeal in any case, except that the truth may be known in no other way." The wide range of situations and people handed over to the ordeal makes clear that in the eyes of the medieval courts, the ordeal was a fallback method when all else failed to reveal the truth.

There were several types of trial by ordeal. The most common was trial by fire. The accused would plunge his or her arm into a cauldron of boiling water to retrieve a coin or a jewel, or alternately would pick up a red-hot iron and walk nine paces. A variation of this method was to walk over hot coals or red-hot plowshares. After the accused suffered this ordeal, his or her hand or foot would be bound for three days and then examined. If the wound was healing "cleanly," meaning without infection, the accused was declared innocent. If not, he or she was adjudged guilty. Another common form of the ordeal was immersion in cold water, or "swimming," made famous in later centuries by its use in witch trials. The accused would be thrown into a river or lake. If the water "rejected" her and she floated, then she was guilty. If the water "embraced" her and she sank, then she was innocent. The obvious complication that a sinking person, even though innocent, may have also been a drowning person did not seem to deter use of trial by water.

The ordeal was especially widespread in judging crimes such as heresy and adultery and in assigning paternity. In 1218, Inga of Varteig carried the hot iron to prove that her son, born out of wedlock, was the son of deceased King Hakon III, which if true would change the line of succession in Norway. The ordeal was also used to decide much more pedestrian matters. In 1090, Gautier of Meigné claimed a plot of land from the monks of Saint Auban at Angers, arguing that he had traded a horse in return for the property. He too carried a hot iron to prove his claim.

The belief that an ordeal could effectively reveal guilt or innocence in a judicial matter was based on the widespread conviction that God constantly and actively intervened in earthly affairs and that his judgment could be seen immediately. To focus God's attention on a specific issue, the participants performed the ordeal in a ritual manner. A priest was usually present to invoke God's power and to bless the implements employed in the ordeal. In one typical formula, the priest asked God "to bless and sanctify this fiery iron, which is used in the just examination of doubtful issues." Priests would also inform the accused, "If you are innocent of this charge...you may confidently receive this iron in your hand and the Lord, the just judge, will free you." The ritual element of the judicial ordeal emphasized the judgment of God over the judgment of men.

During the eleventh and twelfth centuries, the use of the ordeal waned. The recovery of Roman law, the rise of literacy and written documents in society at large, and a greater confidence in the power of courts to settle disputes all contributed to the gradual replacement of the ordeal with the jury trial or the use of torture to elicit a confession from the accused. In England the common law began to entrust the determination of the truth to a jury of peers who listened to and evaluated all the testimony. The jury system valued the opinions of members of the community over the reliability of the ordeal to reveal God's judgment. These changes mark a shift in medieval society toward a growing belief in the power of secular society to organize and police itself, leaving divine justice to the afterlife. But the most crucial shift came from within the Church itself, which felt its spiritual mission compromised by the involvement of priests in supervising ordeals. In 1215 the Fourth Lateran Council forbade priests from participating, and their absence made it impossible for the ordeal to continue as a formal legal procedure.

For Discussion

1. Why was someone's reputation in the community so significant for determining the truth in a medieval trial? How do reputations play a role in trials today?

TRIAL BY ORDEAL
This fifteenth-century painting by Dieric Bouts (ca. 1415–1475), was commissioned by the city of Louvain in 1468 for a large project on the theme of the Last Judgment.

2. What do oaths and the trial by ordeal reveal about the relationship between human and divine justice during the Middle Ages?

Taking it Further
Bartlett, Robert. *Trial by Fire and Water: The Medieval Judicial Ordeal.* 1986. Associates the spread of the trial by ordeal with the expansion of Christianity. The best study of the ordeal.
van Caenegen, R. C. *An Historical Introduction to Private Law.* 1992. A basic narrative from late antiquity to the nineteenth century that traces the evolution of early medieval trial procedures.

and the dissolution of the Carolingian Empire, the lords often became the only effective rulers in a particular locality. Lords came to exercise many of the powers of a king, such as adjudicating disputes over property or inheritance and punishing thieves and murderers. (See *Justice in History* in this chapter.)

The mixture of personal lord-vassal obligations, property rights conveyed by the fief, and legal jurisdiction over communities caused endless complications. The king's vassals were also lords of their own vassals, who in turn were lords over lesser vassals down to the level of simple knight. In theory such a system created a hierarchy of authority that descended down from the king, but reality was never that simple. In France, for example, many of the great lords possessed as much land as the king, which made it very difficult for the king to force them to enact his will. Many vassals held different fiefs from different lords, which created a confusion of loyalties, especially when two lords of the same vassal went to war against one another.

Women could inherit fiefs and own property of their own, although they could not perform military services. They often managed royal and aristocratic property when men were absent or dead, decided how property would be divided up among heirs, and functioned as lords when receiving the homage of male vassals. The lineage and accomplishments of prominent ladies enhanced their husbands' social prestige. A number of aristocratic families traced their descent from the female line, if it was more prestigious than the male line, and named their children after the wife's illustrious ancestors.

Lord-vassal relationships infiltrated many medieval social institutions and practices. Because most vassals owed military service to their lords, medieval armies were at least partially composed of vassal-knights who were obliged to fight for their lord for a certain number of days (often 40) per year. Vassals were required to provide their lord with other kinds of support as well. When summoned, they had to appear at the lord's court to offer advice or sit in judgment of other vassals who were their peers. When the lord traveled, his vassal was required to provide food and shelter in the vassal's castle, sometimes for a large entourage of family and retainers who accompanied the lord. Vassals were obliged to pay their lord certain fees on special occasions, such as the marriage of the lord's daughter. If the lord was captured in battle, his vassals had to pay the ransom.

THE WESTERN EUROPEAN KINGDOMS AFTER THE CAROLINGIANS At a time when the bonds of loyalty and support between lords and vassals were the only form of protection from invaders and marauders, lordship was a stronger social institution than the vague obligations all subjects owed to their kings. To rule effectively, a king was obliged to be a strong lord, in effect to become the lord of all the other lords, who in turn would discipline their own vassals. Achieving this difficult goal took several steps. First, the king had to establish a firm hand over his own lands, the royal domain. With the domain supplying food, materiel, and fighting men, the king could attempt the second step—establishing control over lords who lived outside the royal domain. To hold sway over these independent-minded lords, kings sometimes employed force but frequently offered lucrative rewards by giving out royal prerogatives to loyal lords. These prerogatives included the rights to receive fines in courts of law, to collect taxes, and to perform other governmental functions. As a result, some medieval kingdoms, such as France and England, began to combine in the hands of the same people the personal authority of lordship with the legal authority of the king, creating feudal kingship.

The final step in the process of establishing royal authority was to emphasize the sacred character of kingship. With the assistance of the clergy, kings emulated the great Christian emperors of Rome, Constantine and Justinian. Medieval kings became quasi-priests who received obedience from their subjects because commoners believed kings represented the majesty of God on Earth. The institution of sacred kingship gave kings an additional weapon for persuading the nobles to recognize the king's superiority over them.

Under the influence of ancient Roman ideas of rulership, some kings began to envision their kingdoms as something grander than private property. As the Germanic king and later emperor Conrad II (r. 1024–1039) put it, "If the king is dead the kingdom remains, just as the ship remains even if the helmsman falls overboard."[2] The idea slowly began to take hold that the kingdom had an eternal existence separate from the mortal person of the king and that it was superior to its component parts—its provinces, tribes, lords, families, bishoprics, and cities. This profound idea reached its fullest theoretical expression many centuries later. Promoting the sacred and eternal character of kingship required monarchs to patronize priests, monks, writers, and artists who could formulate and express these ideas.

EAST FRANCIA: THE GERMAN EMPIRE The kingdoms of East and West Francia, which arose out of the remnants of the Carolingian Empire, produced kings who attempted to expand the power of the monarchy and enhance the idea of kingship. East Francia largely consisted of Germanic tribes, each governed by a Frankish official called a duke. After 919 the dukes of Saxony were elected the kings of East Francia, establishing the foundations for the Saxon dynasty. With few lands of their own, the Saxon kings maintained their power by acquiring other duchies and controlling appointments to high church offices, which went to family members or loyal followers. The greatest of the Saxon kings, Otto I the Great (936–973), combined deep Christian piety with formidable military ability. More than any other tenth-century king, he supported the foundation of missionary bishoprics in polytheist Slavic and Scandinavian lands, thereby pushing the boundaries of Christianity beyond what they had been under Charlemagne. The pope crowned Otto emperor in 962, reviving the Roman Empire in the West, as Charlemagne had done earlier. Otto and his successors in the Saxon dynasty attempted to rule a more restricted version of the western empire than had Charlemagne. By the 1030s the Saxon kingdom had become the German Empire, consisting of most of the Germanic duchies, north-central Italy, and Burgundy. In later centuries these regions collectively came to be called the Holy Roman Empire.

As had been the case under Charlemagne, effective rulership in the new German Empire included the patronage of learned men and women who enhanced the reputation of the monarch. Otto and his able brother Bruno, the archbishop of Cologne, initiated a cultural revival, the **Ottonian Renaissance**, which centered on the imperial court. Learned Irish and English monks, Greek philosophers from Byzantium, and Italian scholars found positions there. Among the many intellectuals patronized by Otto, the most notable was Liutprand of Cremona (ca. 920–972), a vivid writer whose unabashed histories reflected the passions of the troubled times. For example, his history of contemporary Europe vilified his enemies and was aptly titled *Revenge*.

WEST FRANCIA: FRANCE Like East Francia, West Francia included many groups with separate ethnic and linguistic identities, but the kingdom had been Christianized much longer because it had been part of the Roman Empire. Thus, West Francia, although highly fragmented, possessed the potential for greater unity by using fully established Christianity to champion the authority of the king.

Strengthening the monarchy became the crucial goal of the Capetian dynasty, which succeeded the last of the Carolingian kings. Hugh Capet (r. 987–996) was elevated as king of West Francia in an elaborate coronation ceremony in which the prayers of the archbishop of Reims offered divine sanction to the new dynasty. The involvement of the archbishop established an important precedent for the French monarchy: Thereafter, the monarchy and the church hierarchy were closely entwined. From this mutually beneficial relationship, the king received ecclesiastical and spiritual support while the upper clergy gained royal protection and patronage. The term *France* at first applied only to Capet's feudal domain, a small but rich region around Paris, but through the persistence of the Capetians, West Francia became so unified that the name France came to refer to the entire kingdom.

The Capetians were especially successful in soliciting homage and services from the great lords of the land—despite some initial resistance. Hugh and his successors distinguished themselves by emphasizing that unlike other lords, kings were appointed by God. Shortly after his own coronation, Hugh had his son crowned—a strategy that ensured the succession of the Capetian family. Hugh's son, Robert II, the Pious (r. 996–1031), was apparently the first to perform the "king's touch": curing certain skin diseases with the power of his touch. The royal coronation cult and the king's touch established the reputation of French kings as miracle workers.

ANGLO-SAXON ENGLAND Anglo-Saxon England had never been part of the Carolingian Empire, but because it was Christian, England shared in the culture of the Latin West. England suffered extensive damage at the hands of the Vikings. After England was almost overwhelmed by a Danish invasion during the winter of 878–879, Alfred the Great (r. 871–899) finally defeated the Danes as spring approached. As king of only Wessex (not of all England), Alfred consolidated his authority and issued a new law code. Alfred's successors cooperated with the nobility more effectively than the monarchs in either East or West Francia and built a broad base of support in the local units of government, the hundreds and shires. The Anglo-Saxon monarchy also enjoyed the support of the Church, which provided it with skilled servants and spiritual authorization.

During the late ninth and tenth centuries, Anglo-Saxon England experienced a cultural revival under royal patronage. King Alfred proclaimed that the Viking invasions had been God's punishment for the neglect of learning, without which God's will could not be known. Alfred accordingly promoted the study of Latin. He also desired that all men of wealth learn to read the language of the English people. Under Alfred a highly sophisticated literature appeared in Old English. This literature included poems, sermons,

commentaries on the Bible, and translations of important Latin works. The masterpiece of this era was a history called the *Anglo-Saxon Chronicle*. It was begun during Alfred's reign but maintained over several generations.

During the late tenth and early eleventh centuries, England was weakened by another series of Viking raids and a succession of feeble kings. In 1066 William, the duke of Normandy and a descendant of Vikings who had settled in the north of France, defeated King Harold, the last Anglo-Saxon king. William seized the English throne. William the Conqueror opened a new era in which English affairs became deeply intertwined with those of the duchy of Normandy and the kingdom of France.

The Conversion of the Last Polytheists

As the core of the Latin West became politically stronger and economically more prosperous during the tenth and eleventh centuries, Christians made concerted attempts to convert the invaders, especially the polytheistic tribes in northern and eastern Europe. Through conversion, Latin Christianity dominated northern Europe up to the Kievan Rus border where Orthodox Christianity adopted from Byzantium triumphed.

Among the polytheistic tribes in Scandinavia, the Baltic Sea region, and parts of eastern Europe, the first Christian conversions usually took place when a king or chieftain accepted Christianity. His subjects were expected to follow. Teaching Christian principles and forms of worship required much more time and effort, of course. Missionary monks usually arrived after a king's conversion, but these monks tended to take a tolerant attitude about variations in the liturgy. Because most Christians were isolated from one another, new converts tended to practice their own local forms of worship and belief. Missionaries and Christian princes discovered that the most effective way to combat this localizing tendency was to found new bishoprics. Especially among the formerly polytheist tribes in northern and eastern Europe, the foundation of bishoprics created cultural centers of considerable prestige

CHRISTIAN CHURCH IMITATES POLYTHEIST TEMPLE

The stave church was a type of wooden church built in northern Europe during the Middle Ages. Most of the surviving examples in Scandinavia are generally assumed to be modeled on polytheist temples. The Borgund church in Norway pictured here dates from about 1150.

that attracted members of the upper classes. Those educated under the supervision of these new bishops became influential servants to the ruling families, further enhancing the stature of Christian culture.

Christian conversion especially benefited women through the abandonment of polygamous marriages, common among the polytheist peoples. As a result, aristocratic women played an important role in helping convert their peoples to Christianity. That role gave them a lasting influence in the churches of the newly converted lands, both as founders and patrons of convents and as writers on religious subjects. By the end of the fourteenth century organized polytheistic worship had disappeared in Scandinavia.

From the middle of the tenth century, a line of newly established Catholic bishoprics ensured that the Poles, Bohemians (Czechs), and Magyars (Hungarians) looked to the West and the pope for their cultural models and religious leadership. Poland, especially, favored Latin Christianity, an association that helped create strong political and cultural ties to western Europe. The Poles inhabited a flat plain of forested land with small clearings for farming. First exposed to missionaries tied to Saint Methodius, Poland resisted Christianity until Prince Mieszko (ca. 960–992) created the most powerful of the Slav states and accepted Latin Christianity in 966 in an attempt to build political alliances with Christian princes. Mieszko formally subordinated his country to the Roman pope with the Donation of Poland (ca. 991). Thus, began Poland's long and special relationship with the papacy. At Mieszko's death, the territory of Poland approximated what it is today.

CHRONOLOGY: THE WESTERN EUROPEAN KINGDOMS EMERGE

843–911	Carolingian dynasty in East Francia
843–987	Carolingian dynasty in West Francia
919–1024	Saxon or Ottonian dynasty
955	Otto I defeats Magyars
962	Otto crowned emperor in Rome
987–1328	Capetian dynasty in France
1066	William the Conqueror defeats last Anglo-Saxon king

THE WEST IN THE EAST: THE CRUSADES

■ **What were the causes and consequences of the Crusades?**

On a chilly November day in 1095 in a bare field outside Clermont, France, Pope Urban II (r. 1088–1099) delivered a landmark sermon to the assembled French clergy and laypeople eager to hear the pope. In stirring words Urban recalled that Muslims in the East were persecuting Christians and that the holy places in Palestine had been ransacked. He called upon the knights "to take up the cross" to defend their fellow Christians in distress.

Urban's appeal for a crusade was stunningly successful. When he finished speaking, the crowd chanted back, "God wills it." The news of Urban's call for a holy war in the East spread like wildfire. All across France and the western part of the German Empire knights prepared for the journey to Jerusalem. Unexpectedly and probably contrary to the pope's intentions, the poor and dispossessed also became enthused about an armed pilgrimage to the Holy Land. The zealous Peter the Hermit (ca. 1050–1115) preached the Crusade among the poor and homeless and gathered a huge unequipped, undisciplined army, which left for Jerusalem well in advance of the knights. Most of the Peter's People's Crusade starved or were enslaved long before they arrived in Constantinople. The Byzantine emperor was unwilling to feed the few who did arrive and

shipped them off to Turkish territory where the Turkish army annihilated nearly all of them.

Urban's call for a crusade gave powerful religious sanction to the western Christian military expeditions against Islam. From 1095 until well into the thirteenth century, recurrent, large-scale crusading operations attempted to take, retake, and protect Christian Jerusalem (see **Map 9.4**), while the idea of going on a crusade lasted long after the thirteenth century into modern times. (See *Different Voices* in this chapter.)

The Origins of Holy War

The original impulse for the **Crusades** was the threat that Muslim armies posed to Christian peoples, pilgrims, and holy places in the eastern Mediterranean. By the middle of the eleventh century the Seljuk Turks, who had converted to Islam, were putting pressure on the Byzantine empire. In 1071, after the Seljuks defeated the Byzantine army at Manzikert, all of Asia Minor lay open to Muslim occupation. Pope Urban's appeal for a crusade in 1095 came in response to a request for military assistance from the Byzantine emperor Alexius Comnenus, who probably thought he would get yet another band of Western mercenaries to help him reconquer Byzantine territory lost to the Seljuks. Instead, he got something utterly unprecedented—a massive volunteer army of perhaps 100,000 soldiers devoted less to cooperating with their Byzantine Christian brethren than to wresting Jerusalem from Muslim hands.

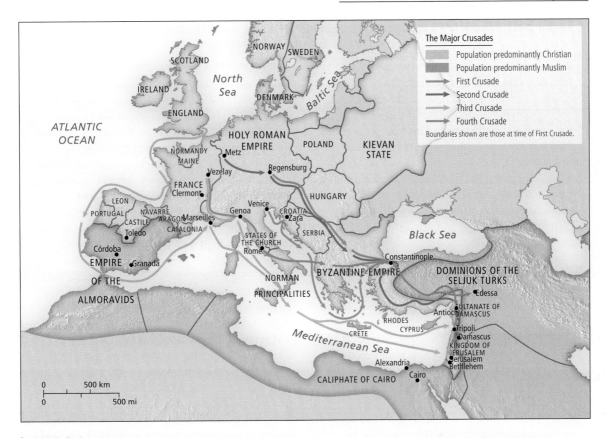

MAP 9.4

The Major Crusades

During the first three Crusades, Christian armies and fleets from western Europe attacked Muslim strongholds and fortresses in the Middle East in an attempt to capture and hold Jerusalem. The Fourth Crusade never arrived in the Middle East, as it was diverted to besiege Constantinople.

Pope Urban made a special offer in his famous sermon at Clermont to remit all penance for sin for those who went on the Crusade. Moreover, a penitential pilgrimage to a holy site such as Jerusalem provided a sinner with a pardon for capital crimes such as murder. Urban's offer muddled the long-standing difference between a pilgrim and a crusader. Until this point, a pilgrim was always unarmed, while a crusader carried weapons and was willing not just to defend other pilgrims from attack, but to launch an assault on those he considered heathens. The innovation of the Crusades was to create the idea of armed pilgrims who received special rewards from the Church. The merger of

a spiritual calling and military action was strongest in the knightly orders—Templars, Hospitallers, and Teutonic Knights. The men who joined these orders were soldiers who took monastic vows of poverty, chastity, and obedience. But rather than isolating themselves to pray in a monastery, they went forth, sword in hand, to conquer for Christ. These knightly orders exercised considerable political influence in Europe and amassed great wealth.

In the minds of crusader-knights, greed probably jostled with fervent piety. Growing population pressures and the spread of primogeniture (passing landed estates on to the eldest male heir) left younger sons with little to antici-

DIFFERENT VOICES CHRISTIAN AND MUSLIM JUSTIFICATIONS FOR HOLY WAR AGAINST THE OTHER

Both Christians and Muslims were convinced that God was on their side during the Crusades. However, leaders on both sides had to find a way to convince people about the justness of their cause and the necessity to take up arms. The problem was to find a way to persuade people to risk their lives and fortunes on behalf of co-religionists and the abstract idea of holy war. Robert the Monk recorded what Pope Urban said to the assembly at the Council of Clermont in 1095. He addressed the crowd as the "race of Franks, race from across the mountains, race beloved and chosen by God." He went on to describe the situation in Jerusalem. Pope Urban's appeal relied a great deal on the idea that the enemy was racially different.

After the First Crusade the gravest threat to the Christians in the Holy Land came from Damascus, Syria, an important Muslim city inland from the crusader states established in what is now Lebanon.

After the Second Crusade (1147–1149) failed to conquer Damascus, an anonymous Muslim author called on all Muslims to resist another Christian attack. In this appeal he calls for a defensive jihad on behalf of fellow Muslims. The passage begins with a quotation from Abu Hamid Al Ghazali (1058–1128), a prominent Muslim scholar, about a Muslim's obligations to take up arms.

I. Pope Urban II Calls for the Crusades

From the confines of Jerusalem and from the city of Constantinople a grievous report has gone forth and has repeatedly been brought to our ears; namely, that a race from the kingdom of the Persians, an accursed race, a race wholly alienated from God, "a generation that set not their heart aright, and whose spirit was not steadfast with God," has violently invaded the lands of those Christians and has depopulated them by pillage and fire. They have led away a part of the captives into their own country, and a part they have killed by cruel tortures. They have either destroyed the churches of God or appropriated them for the rites of their own religion. They destroy the altars, after having defiled them with their uncleanness....

Let hatred therefore depart from among you, let your quarrels end, let wars cease, and let all dissensions and controversies slumber. Enter upon the road to the Holy Sepulcher; wrest that land from the wicked race, and subject it to yourselves. That land which, as the Scripture says, "floweth with milk and honey" was given by God unto the power of the children of Israel. Jerusalem is the center of the earth; the land is fruitful above all others, like another paradise of delights. This spot the Redeemer of mankind has made illustrious by his advent, has beautified by his sojourn, has consecrated by his passion, has redeemed by his death, has glorified by his burial.

pate at home and much to hope for by seeking their fortunes in the Crusades. Nevertheless, crusaders testified to the sense of community they enjoyed by participating in "the common enterprise of all Christians." Fulcher of Chartres recalled the unity displayed by crusaders from so many different countries: "Who has ever heard of speakers of so many languages in one army....If a Breton or a German wished to ask me something, I was utterly without words to reply. But although we were divided by language,

we seemed to be like brothers in the love of God and like near neighbors of one mind." The exhilarating experience of brotherhood in the love of God motivated many crusaders.

Crusading Warfare

The First Crusade (1095–1099) was strikingly successful, but it was as much the result of Muslim weakness as Christian strength. Two factors depleted Arab Muslims' ability to resist the

This royal city, however, situated at the center of the earth, is now held captive by the enemies of Christ and is subjected, by those who do not know God, to the worship of the heathen. She seeks, therefore, and desires to be liberated and ceases not to implore you to come to her aid.... Accordingly, undertake this journey eagerly for the remission of your sins, with the assurance of the reward of imperishable glory in the kingdom of heaven.

Source: From *Readings in European History* vol. 1, ed. James Harvey Robinson (Boston: Ginn 1904).

II. A Muslim Appeal for Jihad against the Crusaders

All Muslims who were free, responsible for their acts and capable of bearing arms must march against (the unbelievers) until they form a force large enough to smite them. This war is to glorify the Word of God and to make His religion victorious over its enemies.... If the enemy attacks a town (in Syria) that is incapable of self-defense, all the towns in Syria must raise an army that could drive him back.... If, however, the soldiers in Syria are insufficient for the task, the inhabitants of the nearer surrounding countries have the duty to assist them, while those of the more remote lands are free from this obligation.

Apply yourself to carry out the precept of jihad! Help one another in order to protect your religion and your brothers! Seize this opportunity and march forth against the unbelievers, for it does not require too great an effort and God has prepared you for it!... Commit jihad to make combat in your soul before committing jihad against your enemies because your souls are worse enemies for you than your foes. Turn your soul away from disobedience to its creator so that you would achieve the much desired victory.... Forsake the sins that you insist on committing and then begin to do good deeds.... Fight for God as He deserves it!

Source: From *Islam from the Prophet Muhammad to the Capture of Constantinople*, ed. and trans. by Bernard Lewis, Vol. II *Religion and Society* (1987). By permission of Oxford University Press. Copyright © 1974 by Bernard Lewis.

For Discussion

1. Both sides see holy war as defensive. Are there differences in how the Christians and Muslims justify holy war?

2. What is more important in these appeals to war, serving God or defending co-religionists?

3. Since the Crusades, appeals for holy war have been a recurrent feature of relations between Muslims and Christians. How would you argue against the idea of holy war?

crusaders. First, the Arab states that controlled access to Jerusalem were already weakened from fighting the Seljuk Turks. Second, Muslims were divided internally. Theological divisions between Sunni and Shi'ite Muslims prevented the Muslim caliphs from uniting against the Christians.

In 1099, after a little more than a month's siege, the crusaders scaled the walls of Jerusalem and took possession of the city, which was also holy to Muslims and Jews and largely inhabited by them. The triumph of the First Crusade led to the establishment of the Latin principalities, which were devoted to maintaining a Western foothold in the Holy Land. The Latin principalities included all of the territory in contemporary Lebanon, Israel, and Palestine.

The subsequent crusades never achieved the success of the first. In 1144 Muslims captured the northernmost Latin principality, the county of Edessa—a warning to Westerners of the fragility of a defensive system that relied

Too in se aef ouerr et eftes vous vn cheoual blauncs · al ge eier eur ao auenn
lesaur et uerreis et il uiue en Ecreture · et se combar · ees oiß sunt auſtcome

JESUS CHRIST LEADING THE CRUSADERS

The rider on the white horse is Jesus, who holds the Gospels in his right hand and the sword of righteousness in his teeth. The crusading knights bearing banners and shields emblazoned with the cross follow him. The figure in the upper left-hand corner represents St. John the Evangelist, whose writings were understood to prophesy the Crusades. This manuscript illumination dates from ca. 1310–1325.

on a few scattered fortresses strung along a thin strip of coastline. In response to the loss of Edessa, Christians launched the Second Crusade (1147–1149). This ambitious offensive on several fronts failed in the East where the crusaders gained little ground. In the West, however, it was a great success because northern European crusaders helped the King of Portugal retake Lisbon from the Muslims. In 1187, the sultan of Egypt and Syria, Saladin (1137–1193), recaptured Jerusalem for Islam.

In response to this dispiriting loss, the Third Crusade (1189–1192) assembled the most spectacular army of European chivalry ever seen, led by Europe's three most powerful kings: German emperor Frederick Barbarossa, Philip Augustus of France, and Richard the Lion-Heart of England. Yet the Third Crusade's results were far from spectacular: After Frederick drowned wading in a river en route and Philip went home, Richard the Lion-Heart negotiated a truce with Saladin.

KRAK DES CHEVALIERS
This crusader castle survives in northern Syria in what was once the County of Edessa, a Latin Christian principality constructed to defend the Holy Land. The word *krak* derives from an Arabic word meaning "strong fort."

Source: Dagli Orti/Picture Desk, Inc./Kobal Collection

In 1199, Pope Innocent III called for the Fourth Crusade with the goal of recapturing Jerusalem. However, the Frankish knights and Venetian fleet diverted to intervene in a disputed imperial succession in Byzantium. Rather than fighting Muslims, Christian knights fought fellow Christians. In 1204 they besieged and captured Constantinople. The Westerners then divided the Byzantine Empire, set up a Latin regime that lasted until 1261, and neglected their oaths to reconquer Jerusalem. The Fourth Crusade dangerously weakened the Byzantine Empire by making it a prize for Western adventurers. None of the subsequent Crusades achieved lasting success in the Middle East. (See *Encounters and Transformations* in this chapter.)

The Significance of the Crusades

Despite the capture of Jerusalem during the First Crusade, the crusaders could not maintain control of the city. For more than two centuries, they wasted enormous efforts on what proved to be a futile enterprise. Neither did any of the Latin principalities in the Middle East survive for more than two centuries. The crusaders who resided in these principalities were obliged to learn how to live and trade with their Muslim neighbors, but few of them learned Arabic or took seriously Muslim learning. The strongest Islamic cultural and intellectual influences on Christian Europe came through Sicily and Spain rather than via returning crusaders.

ENCOUNTERS AND TRANSFORMATIONS

Legends of the Borderlands: Roland and El Cid

From the eighth to the fifteenth centuries, Muslim and Latin Christian armies grappled with one another in the borderlands between their two civilizations in the Iberian peninsula, the territory now called Spain. The borderlands, however, were more than just places of conflict. During times of peace, Christians and Muslims traded with and even married one another, and in the confused loyalties typical of the times, soldiers and generals from both faiths frequently switched sides. These borderland clashes produced legends of great heroes, which once refashioned into epic poems created a lasting memory of Muslim and Christian animosity.

The Song of Roland, an Old French epic poem that dates from around 1100, tells a story about the Battle of Roncesvalles, which took place in 779. The actual historical battle had been a minor skirmish between Charlemagne's armies and some local inhabitants in Spain who were not Muslims at all, but *The Song of Roland* transformed this sordid episode into a great epic of Christian-Muslim conflict. In the climax of the poem, the Christian hero Roland, seeking renown for his valor, rejected his companion Oliver's advice to blow a horn to alert Charlemagne of a Muslim attack. The battle was hopeless; when the horn was finally sounded it was too late to save Roland or Oliver. Roland's recklessness made him the model of a brave Christian knight.

In the subsequent Spanish border wars, the most renowned soldier was Rodrigo Díaz de Vivar (ca. 1043–1099), known to history as El Cid (from the Arabic word for "lord"). He is remembered in legend as a heroic knight fighting for the Christian Reconquest of the peninsula, but the real story of El Cid was much more self-serving. El Cid repeatedly switched allegiances to the Muslims. Even when a major Muslim invasion from North Africa threatened the very existence of Christian Spain, El Cid did not come to the rescue and instead undertook a private adventure to carve out a kingdom for himself in Muslim Valencia.

Soon after El Cid's death and despite his inconstant loyalty to Castile and Christianity, he was elevated to the status of the great hero of Christian Spain. The popularity of the twelfth-century epic poem, *The Poem of My Cid,* transformed this cruel, vindictive, and utterly self-interested man into a model of Christian virtue and self-sacrificing loyalty.

THE DEATH OF ROLAND
No legend from the borderlands between Christianity and Islam had a greater influence on European Christian society than that of Roland.

The medieval borderlands created legends of heroism and epic struggles that often stretched the truth. The borderlands were a wild frontier, not unlike the American frontier, into which desperate men fled to hide or to make opportunities for themselves. However, the lasting significance of the violent encounters that took place in these borderlands was not the nasty realities but the heroic models they produced. Poetry transformed reality into a higher truth that emphasized courage and faithfulness. Because these poems were memorized and recited in the vernacular languages of Old French and Castilian (now Spanish), they became a model of aristocratic values in medieval society and over the centuries a source for a national literary culture. Thus, becoming French or Spanish meant, in some respects, rejecting Islam, which has created a lasting anti-Muslim strain in western European culture.

For Discussion

How did transforming the accounts of battles between Christian and Muslims into heroic poems change how these events would be remembered among Christians?

The most important immediate consequence of the Crusades was not the tenuous Western possession of the Holy Land, but the expansion of trade and economic contacts the expeditions facilitated. No one profited more from the Crusades than the Italian cities that provided transportation and supplies to the crusading armies. The Crusades helped transform Genoa, Pisa, and Venice from small ports of regional significance into hubs of international trade. Genoa and Venice established their own colonial outposts in the eastern Mediterranean, and both vied to monopolize the rich commerce of Byzantium. The new trade controlled by these cities included luxury goods such as silk, Persian carpets, medicine, and spices—all expensive, exotic consumer goods found in the bazaars of the Middle East. Profits from this trade helped galvanize the economy of western Europe, leading to an era of exuberant economic growth during the twelfth and thirteenth centuries.

The crusading ideal survived long after Europeans quit going on actual Crusades. When Columbus sailed west in 1492, he imagined he was engaged in a kind of Crusade to spread

CHRONOLOGY: THE CRUSADES

1071	Battle of Manzikert; Seljuk Turks defeat the Byzantine emperor
1095	Council of Clermont; Urban II calls First Crusade
1095–1099	First Crusade
1099	Christians capture Jerusalem
1147–1149	Second Crusade
1189–1192	Third Crusade, led by Emperor Frederick Barbarossa (who drowned), King Philip II of France, and King Richard the Lion-Heart of England
1202–1204	Fourth Crusade, culminates in capture of Constantinople by Western crusaders

Christianity. Even as late as the twentieth century, some Latin American countries continued to collect a tax to finance crusades.

CONCLUSION

An Emerging Unity in the Latin West

The most lasting legacy of the Early Middle Ages was the distinction between western and eastern Europe, established by the patterns of conversion to Christianity. Slavs in eastern Europe, such as the Poles, who were converted to Latin Christianity looked to Rome as a source for inspiration and eventually considered themselves part of the West. Those who converted to Orthodox Christianity, such as the Bulgarians and Russians, remained Europeans certainly but came to see themselves as culturally distinct from their Western counterparts. The southern border of Christian Europe was defined by the presence of the Islamic caliphates, which, despite recurrent border wars with Christian kingdoms, greatly contributed to the cultural vitality of the West during this period.

During this same period, however, a tentative unity began to emerge among western European Christians, just as Byzantium fell into decline and Islam divided among competing caliphates. That ephemeral unity was born in the hero worship of Charlemagne and the resurrection of the Roman Empire in the West, symbolized by his coronation in Rome. The collapse of the Carolingian Empire created the basis for the European kingdoms that dominated the political order of Europe for most of the subsequent millennium. These new kingdoms were each quite distinctive, and yet they shared a heritage from ancient Rome and the Carolingians that emphasized the power of the law on the one hand and the intimate relationship between royal and ecclesiastical authority on the other. The most distinguishing mark of western Europe became the practice of Latin Christianity, a distinctive form of Christianity identifiable by the use of the Latin language and the celebration of the church liturgy in Latin.

In the wake of the Carolingian Empire, a system of personal loyalties associated with lordship and vassalage came to dominate the military and political life of Latin Christendom. All medieval kings were obliged to build their monarchies on the social foundations of lordship, which provided cohesion in kingdoms that lacked bureaucracies and sufficient numbers of trained officials. In addition to the lords and vassals, the Latin kingdoms relied on the support of the Church to provide unity and often to provide the services of local government. By the end of the eleventh century, emerging western Europe had recovered sufficiently from the many destructive invaders and had built new political and ecclesiastical institutions that enabled it to assert itself on a broader stage.

KEY TERMS

liturgy	canon law
clans	lord
kin groups	vassals
wergild	fief
scriptorium	knight
counties	feudalism
marches	Ottonian Renaissance
Carolingian Renaissance	Crusades

CHAPTER QUESTIONS

1. How did Latin Christendom—the new kingdoms of western Europe—build on Rome's legal and governmental legacies and how did Christianity spread in these new kingdoms? (page 264)
2. How did the Carolingian Empire contribute to establishing a distinctive western European culture? (page 272)

3. After the collapse of the Carolingian Empire, how did the western kingdoms consolidate in the core of the European continent and how did Latin Christianity spread to its periphery? (page 278)
4. What were the causes and consequences of the Crusades? (page 288)

TAKING IT FURTHER

1. Why were the kingdoms of Latin Christendom usually so weak?
2. How did the Carolingian Empire rise above those weaknesses? Why did it eventually fall prey to them?
3. Was military conflict between Christians and Muslims inevitable in the Crusades?

✓● Practice on MyHistoryLab

10

Medieval Civilization: The Rise of Western Europe

■ Two Worlds: Manors and Cities ■ The Consolidation of Roman Catholicism ■ Strengthening the Center of the West ■ Medieval Culture: The Search for Understanding

FRANCIS OF ASSISI (CA. 1182–1226) WAS THE SON OF A PROSPEROUS MERCHANT in a modest-sized town in central Italy. As a young man of 20, Francis joined the Assisi forces in a war with the nearby town of Perugia. Taken prisoner, he spent nearly a year in captivity. After his release he became seriously ill, the first of many painful illnesses that afflicted him throughout his life. During a journey to join another army, he had the first of his many visions or dreams that led him to give up fighting and to convert to a life of spirituality and service to others. Initially he searched about for what to do. He went on a pilgrimage to Rome as a beggar and, although lepers personally disgusted, him he gave them alms and kissed their hands as an act of charity and humility. Then, according to his earliest biographer, while praying in the dilapidated chapel of San Damiano outside the gates of Assisi, he received a direct command from the crucifix above the altar: "Go Francis, and repair my house which, as you see, is nearly in ruins."

At first, Francis understood this command literally and began to repair churches and chapels. To raise money he took some of the best cloth from his father's shop and rode off to a nearby town where he sold the cloth and the horse. Angered by the theft of cloth, his father denounced him to the town's authorities. When Francis refused the summons to court, his father had him brought to the bishop of Assisi for interrogation. Before his father could

explain the situation to the bishop, Francis "without a word stripped off his clothing even removing his pants and gave them back to his father." Stark naked, Francis announced that he was switching his obedience from his earthly to his heavenly father. The astonished bishop gave him a cloak, but Francis renounced all family ties and worldly goods to live a life of complete poverty. Henceforth, he seemed to understand the command to "repair my house" as a metaphor for the entire Church, which he intended to serve in a new way.

Dressed in rags, Francis went about town begging for food, preaching repentance in the streets, and ministering to outcasts and lepers. Without training as a priest or license as a preacher, Francis at first seemed like a devout eccentric or even a dangerous heretic, but his rigorous imitation of Jesus began to attract like-minded followers. In 1210 Francis and twelve of his ragged brothers showed up in the opulent papal court of Pope Innocent III to request approval for a new religious order. A less discerning man than Innocent would have sent the strange band packing or thrown them in prison as a danger to established society, but Innocent was impressed by Francis's sincerity and his willingness to profess obedience to the pope. Innocent's provisional approval of the Franciscans was a brilliant stroke, in that it gave the papacy a way to manage the widespread enthusiasm for a life of spirituality and purity.

ST. FRANCIS RENOUNCES HIS WORLDLY GOODS

St. Francis stripped off all his clothing in the town square and renounced his worldly possessions, a spiritual act signifying his rejection of the material world. Francis's angry father, the figure in left center, has to be restrained to prevent him from striking his son with his clenched fist.

Source: Assisi, Upper Church of S. Francesco. Giotto and pupils, "St. Francis Renouncing his Earthly Possessions." Fresco c. 1295–1330. © Canali Photobank, Capriolo, Italy

The life of Francis of Assisi and the religious order he founded, the Friars Minor (Lesser Brothers), known as the Franciscans, epitomized the strengths and tensions of medieval Europe. Francis was a product of the newly prosperous towns of Europe, which began to grow at an unprecedented rate after about 1050. In the streets of towns such as Assisi that thrived on profits from the international cloth trade, the extremes of wealth and poverty were always on display. Rich merchants such as Francis's father lived in splendid comfort and financed an urban building boom that had not been seen in the West for more than a 1,000 years. The most lasting manifestations of that building boom were the vast new cathedrals, the pride of every medieval city. At the same time wretchedly poor people, many of them immigrants from the overpopulated countryside—starving and homeless—lined the steps into the great churches begging for alms. Francis abhorred the immorality of this contrast between

wealth and poverty. His reaction was to reject all forms of wealth, to give away all his possessions, and to disdain money as poison. He and his followers devoted themselves to the poor and abandoned. They became traveling street preachers who relied entirely on the charity of others for food and shelter. Francis's rejection of the material world was not just a protest against the materialist values of his times. It was a total denial of the self, or to put it in modern terms, a rejection of all forms of egotism and pride, combined with a revolutionary commitment to equality.

The late eleventh through thirteenth centuries were revolutionary in other ways. Based on the efforts of the knights who fought in the Crusades, the European merchants, and the great theologians of the Church, the Catholic West began to assert itself militarily, economically, and intellectually both in Byzantium and against the Muslim world. As a result, western Europeans more sharply distinguished themselves from the Orthodox and Muslim worlds. The West became more exclusively Latin and Catholic.

Internal developments within Europe made possible this consolidation of a distinctive Western identity and projection of Western power outside Europe. The agricultural revolution that began in the eleventh century stimulated population growth and urbanization. Fed by more productive farms, the expanding cities began to produce industrial goods, such as woolen cloth, that could be sold abroad in exchange for luxury goods from the Middle East and Asia. A number of vigorous kings created political stability in the West by consolidating their authority through financial and judicial bureaucracies. The most effective of these kings used a variety of strategies to force the most dangerous element in society, the landed aristocrats, to serve the royal interest. At the same time, the West experienced a period of creative ferment unequaled since antiquity. The Roman Catholic Church played a central role in encouraging intellectual and artistic activity, but there was also a flourishing literature in the vernacular languages such as French, German, and Italian. All these developments led to this question: How did western European civilization mature during the eleventh through thirteenth centuries?

TWO WORLDS: MANORS AND CITIES

■ How was medieval western European economy and society organized around manors and cities?

After the end of the destructive Magyar and Viking invasions of the ninth and tenth centuries, the population of western Europe recovered dramatically. Technological innovations created the **agricultural revolution** that increased the supply of food. With more food available, people were better nourished than they had been in more than 500 years, and the population began to grow. In the seventh century all of Europe was home to only 14 million inhabitants. By 1300 the population had exploded to 74 million. From the seventh to the fourteenth centuries, then, the population grew many times over, perhaps as much as 500 percent.

The Medieval Agricultural Revolution

In the year 1000, the vast majority of people lived in small villages or isolated farmsteads. Peasants literally scratched out a living from a small area of cleared land around the village by employing a light scratch plow that barely turned over the soil. The farms produced mostly grain, which was consumed as bread, porridge, and ale or beer. Vegetables were rare; meat and fish, uncommon. Over the course of the century, the productivity of the land was greatly enhanced by a number of innovations that came into widespread use.

TECHNOLOGICAL INNOVATIONS The invention of new labor-saving devices ushered in the agricultural revolution. Farmers used water and windmills to grind grain, but others gradually adapted them to a wide variety of tasks, including turning saws to mill timber. In addition to these mechanical devices, the power of animals began to be used more efficiently. Metal horseshoes (until then, horses' hooves had been bound in cloth) gave horses better footing and traction. Perhaps even more important was the introduction of a new type of horse and ox collar. Older collars put pressure on the throat, which tended to choke the animal. The new collars transferred the pressure to the shoulders. With enhanced animal pulling power, farmers could plow the damp, heavy clay soils of northern Europe much more efficiently.

The centerpiece of the agricultural revolution was the heavy plow, called the *carruca*. It cut deeply and lifted the soil, aerating it and bringing minerals to the surface vital for plant growth. The *carruca*, however, required six or eight horses or oxen to pull it, and no single peasant family in the eleventh century could afford that many draft animals. Farmers had to pool their animals to create plow teams, a practice that required mutual planning and cooperation.

The introduction of the three-field system supplied the final piece in the agricultural revolution. In the three-field system farmers planted one field in the fall with grain and one in the spring with beans, peas, or lentils. The third field lay fallow. They harvested both fall and spring plantings in the summer, after which all the fields shifted. The

A HEAVY *CARRUCA* PLOW

At the center of the two-wheeled plow is a sturdy timber from which the coulter projects just in front of the plowshare, which is hidden by the earth.

three-field system produced extraordinary advantages: the amount of land under cultivation increased; beans planted in the spring rotation returned nitrogen to the soil; and the crop rotation combined with animal manure reduced soil exhaustion from excessive grain planting.

The agricultural revolution had a significant effect on society. First, villagers learned to cooperate—by pooling draft animals for plow teams, redesigning and elongating their fields to accommodate the new plow, coordinating the three-field rotation of crops, and timing the harvest schedule. To accomplish these cooperative ventures, they created village councils and developed habits of collective decision making that were essential for stable community life. Second, the system produced not only more food, but better food. Beans and other vegetables grown in the spring planting were rich in proteins.

MANORS AND PEASANTS   The medieval agricultural economy bound landlords and peasants together in a unit of management called the **manor.** The lord of the manor usually owned his own large house or stone castle and served as the presiding judge of the villagers in the manor court.

The peasants who worked the land of manors fell into three categories: serfs, freeholders, and cottagers. Lords did not own **serfs,** who were not slaves, but lords tied their serfs to the manor, which they could not leave. Serfs had certain legal rights denied slaves, such as the right to a certain portion of what they produced, but the lord's will was law. Freeholders worked as independent farmers, owned their land outright, and did not have to answer to a lord. At the bottom of rural peasant society struggled numerous impoverished cottagers who had no rights to the land and farmed small, less desirable plots, often as squatters.

No matter what their official status, each family worked the land together with all family members performing tasks suitable to their abilities, strength, and age. The rigors of medieval farm labor did not permit a fastidious division of labor between women and men. Women did not usually drive the heavy plow, but they toiled at other physically demanding tasks. During the critical harvest times, women and children worked alongside men from dawn to dusk. Young girls typically worked as gleaners, picking up the stalks and kernels that the male harvesters dropped or left behind, and girls took responsibility for weeding and cleaning the fields.

THE GREAT MIGRATIONS AND THE HUNGER FOR LAND   After the eleventh century most peasant families were considerably better off than their ancestors had been before the new technological innovations. Due to the agricultural revolution, nutritional levels improved so that famines

TWELFTH-CENTURY MANOR MADE POSSIBLE BY THE HEAVY PLOW
Aerial photograph of the manor of West Whelpington North (England), which was settled in the twelfth century, but whose inhabitants died out during the Black Death of the fourteenth century (see Chapter 11). Outlines of the individual families' farm gardens can be seen in the left center. On the lower right are the ridges and furrows of the elongated fields required by the use of the heavy plow.

decreased, and a "baby boom" led to dramatic population growth.

The effect of the baby boom meant that the amount of land available to farm was insufficient to support the expanding population of the manors. As more and more young people entered the workforce, they either sought opportunities in the cities or searched for land of their own. Both options meant that many young people and whole families had to migrate. The modern phenomenon of mass immigration is hardly new.

Where did all these people go? Migrants seeking to clear new lands for agriculture moved in three directions: Germans into lands of the Slavic tribes to the east, Scandinavians to the far north and the North Atlantic islands, and

Christian Spaniards to the south into previously Muslim territories on the Iberian peninsula, slowly creating the outlines of what would become modern Spain. Between 1100 and 1300, these migrants brought as much as 40 percent more land under cultivation in Europe. The vibrant civilization discussed in the rest of this chapter was the direct consequence of the European demographic success.

The Growth of Cities

All across Europe during the twelfth and thirteenth centuries cities exploded in size. Exact population figures are difficult to determine, and by our own modern standards most of these cities were modest in size—numbering in the tens of thousands rather than hundreds of thousands—but there is ample evidence of stunning growth. Between 1160 and 1300 Ghent expanded its city walls five times to accommodate all its inhabitants. During the thirteenth century the population of Florence grew by an estimated 640 percent.

THE CHALLENGE OF FREE CITIES The newly thriving cities proved troublesome for the lords, bishops, and kings who had legal authority over them. As the population grew and urban merchants, such as Francis of Assisi's father, became increasingly rich, the cities in which they lived enjoyed even greater resources in people and money than those available to the rural lords. In many places the citizens of the new enlarged towns attempted to rid themselves of their lords to establish self-rule or, at least, substantial autonomy for their city. In the cities of north-central Italy, for example, townsmen formed sworn defensive associations called **communes** (from *communis* meaning "shared"), which quickly became the effective government of the towns. The communes evolved into city-states, which seized control of the surrounding countryside. Perhaps as many as 100 or more cities in north-central Italy formed communes after 1070.

The Italian communes created the institutions and culture of self-rule. They were not fully democratic, but, nevertheless, in many of them a significant percentage of the male population, including artisans, could vote for public officials, hold office themselves, and have a voice in important decisions such as going to war or raising new taxes. They also emphasized the civic responsibilities of citizens to protect the weakest members of the community, to beautify the city with public buildings and monuments, and to defend it by serving in the militia and paying taxes. These cities created vital community institutions, some of which survive to this day. In the wake of the Crusades several north Italian communes, especially Venice, Genoa, and Pisa,

A MEDIEVAL TOWN

Painted on the wall of the city council chambers in Siena, Italy, this fresco from 1338–1339 depicts how a well-governed medieval town should look. Workers repair buildings, merchants bring goods into the bustling city, and the streets are so safe that young women dance in the streets on their way to a wedding.

became ports of international significance. Sailors from these cities had transported the crusading knights to the Holy Land, Egypt, Syria, and Byzantium. Even after the crusader kingdoms collapsed, these cities kept footholds in the eastern Mediterranean, some of which evolved into colonies. Through these trading cities western Europe became integrated into the international luxury trade, which they carried out with ships crisscrossing the Mediterranean Sea.

THE ECONOMIC BOOM YEARS   The cities of the medieval West thrived on an economic base of unprecedented prosperity. What made possible the twelfth- and thirteenth-century economic boom? Four related factors explain the thriving medieval economy. We have already touched on the first two reasons: the agricultural revolution of the eleventh century, which enabled population growth; and the expansion of cities, which both facilitated the commercial boom and allowed city dwellers to be the primary beneficiaries of it.

The other two reasons were just as important: advances in transportation networks and the creation of new business techniques. Trade in grain, woolen cloth, and other bulk goods depended on the use of relatively cheap water transportation for hauling goods. Where there were neither seaports nor navigable rivers, drovers hauled goods cross-country by pack train, a very expensive enterprise. In Europe there were no land transportation routes or pack animals that rivaled the efficiency of the camel in the deserts of North Africa and the steppes of Asia. To address the problem and to facilitate transportation and trade, governments and local lords built new roads and bridges and repaired old Roman roads that had been neglected for 1,000 years.

The most lucrative trade was the international commerce in luxury goods. Because these goods were lightweight and high-priced, they could sustain the cost of long-distance transportation across land. Italian merchants virtually monopolized the European luxury trade. Camel caravans transported raw silk from China and Turkestan across Asia. Merchants sold the silk at trading posts on the shores of the Black Sea and in Constantinople to Italian merchants who shipped the goods across the Mediterranean, had the raw silk woven into cloth, and then earned enormous profits selling the shimmering fabrics to the ladies and gentlemen of the European aristocracy. Though small in quantity, the silk trade was of great value to international commerce because silk was so highly prized. One ounce of fine Chinese black silk sold on the London market for as much as a highly skilled mason would earn in a week's labor. Even the bulk commodities the Italians brought from the East were valuable enough to sustain the high transportation costs. Known by the generic term "spices," these included hundreds of exotic items: True spices such as pepper, sugar, cloves, nutmeg, ginger, saffron, mace, and cinnamon enhanced the otherwise bland cuisine; for dyeing cloth, blue came from indigo and red from madder root; for fixing the dyes the Genoese imported alum; and for pain relievers were medicinal herbs including opiates. The profits from spices generated much of the capital in European financial markets.

Long-distance trade necessitated the creation of new business techniques. For example, the expansion of trade and new markets required a moneyed economy. Coins had almost disappeared in the West for nearly 400 years during the Early Middle Ages, when most people lived self-sufficiently on manors and bartered for what they could not produce for themselves. The few coins that circulated came from Byzantium or the Muslim caliphates. By the thirteenth century, Venice and Florence minted their own gold coins, which became the medium for exchange across much of Europe.

Merchants who engaged in long-distance trade invented the essential business tools of capitalism during this period. They created business partnerships, uniform accounting practices, merchants' courts to enforce contracts and resolve disputes, letters of credit (used like modern bankers' checks), bank deposits and loans, and insurance policies. The Italian cities established primary schools to train merchants' sons to write business letters and keep accounts—a sign of the growing professional character of business. Two centuries earlier an international merchant had been an itinerant peddler who led pack trains over dusty and muddy tracks to customers in small villages and castles. But by the end of the thirteenth century an international merchant could stay at home behind a desk, writing letters to business partners and ship captains and enjoying the profits from his labors in the bustling atmosphere of a thriving city.

At the center of the European market were the Champagne fairs in France, where merchants from northern and southern Europe met every summer to bargain and haggle (see **Map 10.1**). The Italians exchanged their silk and spices for English raw

wool, Dutch woolen cloth, German furs and linens, and Spanish leather. From the Champagne fairs, prosperity spread into previously wild parts of Europe. Cities along the German rivers and the Baltic coast thrived through the trade of raw materials such as timber and iron, livestock, salt fish, and hides. The most prominent of the north German towns was Lübeck, which became the center of the Hanseatic League, a loose trade association of cities in Germany and the Baltic coast. Never achieving the level of a unified government, the league nonetheless provided its members mutual

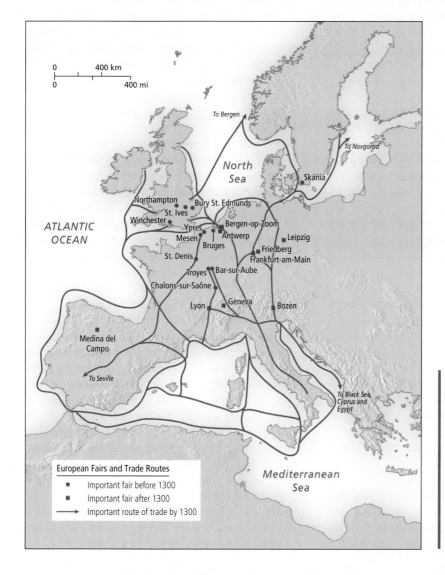

MAP 10.1

European Fairs and Trade Routes

Trade routes crisscrossed the Mediterranean Sea and hugged the Atlantic Ocean, North Sea, and Baltic Sea coastlines. Land routes converged in central France at the Champagne fairs. Other trade routes led to the large market cities in Germany and Flanders.

security and trading monopolies—necessary because of the weakness of the German imperial government.

Urban civilization, one of the major achievements of the Middle Ages, thrived from the commerce of the economic boom. From urban civilization came other achievements. All the cities built large new cathedrals to flaunt their accumulated wealth and to honor God. New educational institutions, especially universities, trained the sons of the urban, commercial elite in the professions. However, the merchants who commanded the urban economy were not necessarily society's heroes. The populace at large viewed them with deep ambivalence, despite the immeasurable ways in which they enriched society. Churchmen worried about the morality of making profits. Church councils condemned usury—the lending of money for interest—even though papal finances depended on it. Theologians promulgated the idea of a "just price," the idea that there should be a fixed price for any particular commodity. The just price was anathema to hardheaded merchants who were committed to the laws of supply and demand. Part of the ambivalence toward trade and merchants came from the inequities created in all market-based economies—the rewards of the market were unevenly distributed, both socially and geographically, as St. Francis's protest demonstrated. The prosperous merchants symbolized disturbing social changes, but they were also the dynamic force that made possible the intellectual and artistic flowering of the High Middle Ages.

THE CONSOLIDATION OF ROMAN CATHOLICISM

■ How did the Catholic Church consolidate its hold over the Latin West?

The late eleventh through thirteenth centuries witnessed one of the greatest periods of religious vitality in the history of Roman Catholicism. Manifest by the Crusades (discussed in Chapter 9), the rise of new religious orders, remarkable intellectual creativity, and the final triumph over the surviving polytheistic tribes of northern and eastern Europe, the religious vitality of the era was due in no small part to the effective leadership of a series of able popes. They gave the Church the benefits of the most advanced, centralized government in Europe.

The Task of Church Reform

As the bishops of the Church accepted many of the administrative responsibilities that in the ancient world had been performed by secular authorities, their spiritual mission sometimes suffered. They became overly involved in the business of the world. In addition, over the centuries wealthy and pious people had made large donations of land to the Church, making many monasteries, in particular, immensely wealthy. Such wealth tempted the less pious to corruption, and the Roman popes were unlikely to eliminate the temptations from which they benefited. Even those popes who wanted to were slow to assemble the administrative machinery necessary to enforce their will across the unruly lands of Roman Catholicism. The impulse for reform derived in many respects from the material success of the Church and the monasteries.

The slow but determined progress of the popes from the eleventh to thirteenth centuries to enforce moral reform is the most remarkable achievement of the medieval papacy. The movement for reform, however, did not begin with the popes. It came out of the monasteries. Monks thought the best way to clean up corruption in the Church would be to improve the morals of individuals. If men and women conducted themselves with a sense of moral responsibility, the whole institution of the Church could be purified. Monks and nuns, who set an example for the rest of the Church, provided the model for self-improvement for society at large. The most influential of the reform-minded monasteries was **Cluny** in Burgundy, established in 910. Cluny itself sustained the reform movement through more than 1,500 Cluniac monasteries throughout Europe.

From the very beginning Cluny was exceptional for several reasons. First, its aristocratic founder offered the monastery as a gift to the pope. As a result, the pope directed the activities of the Cluny monastery from Rome and kept it independent from local political pressures, which so often caused corruption. The Rome connection positioned Cluniacs to assist in reforming the papacy itself. Second, the various abbots who headed Cluny over the years closely coordinated reform activities of the various monasteries in the Cluniac system. Some of these abbots were men of exceptional ability and learning who had a European-wide reputation for their moral stature. Third, Cluny regulated the life of monks much more closely than did other monasteries, so the monks there were models of devotion. To the Cluniacs moral purity required complete renunciation of the benefits of the material world and a commitment to spiritual experiences. The elegantly simple liturgy in which the monks themselves sung the text of the mass and other prayers symbolized Cluniac purity. The beauty of the music enhanced the spiritual experience, and its simplicity clarified rather than obscured the meaning of the words. Because of these attractive traits, the Cluniac liturgy spread to the far corners of Europe.

The success of Cluny and other reformed monasteries provided the base from which reform ideas spread beyond the isolated world of monks to the rest of the Church. The first candidates for reform were parish priests and bishops. Called the *secular clergy* (in Latin *saeculum,* meaning "secular") because they lived in the secular world, they differed from the regular clergy (in Latin *regula,* those who followed a "rule") who lived in monasteries apart from the world. The lives of many secular clergy differed little from their lay neighbors. (*Laypeople* or *the laity* referred to all Christians who had not taken religious vows to become a priest, monk, or nun.) In contrast to celibate monks, who were sexually chaste, many priests kept concubines or were married and tried to bequeath church property to their children. In contrast to the Orthodox Church, in which priests were allowed to marry, the Catholic Church had repeatedly forbidden married priests, but the prohibitions had been ineffective until Cluniac reform stressed the ideal of the sexually pure priest. During the eleventh century bishops, church councils, and reformist popes began to insist on a celibate clergy.

The clerical reform movement also tried to eliminate the corrupt practices of simony and lay investiture. **Simony** was the practice of buying and selling church offices. **Lay investiture** took place when aristocrats, kings, or emperors installed churchmen and gave them their symbols of office ("invested" them). Through this practice, powerful lords controlled the clergy and usurped the property of the Church. In exchange for protecting the Church, these laymen conceived of church offices as a form of vassalage and expected to name their own candidates as priests and bishops. The reformers saw as sinful any form of lay authority over the Church—whether the authority was that of the local lord or the emperor himself. As a result of this controversy, the most troublesome issue of the eleventh century became establishing the boundaries between temporal and spiritual authorities.

THE POPE BECOMES A MONARCH Religious reform required unity within the Church. The most important step in building unity was to define what it meant to be a Catholic. In the Middle Ages, Roman Catholicism identified itself in two ways. First, the Church insisted on conformity in rites. Rites consisted of the forms of public worship called the liturgy, which included certain prescribed prayers and chants, usually in Latin. Uniform rites meant that Catholics could hear the Mass celebrated in essentially the same way everywhere from Poland to Portugal, Iceland to Croatia. Conformity of worship created a cultural unity that transcended differences in language and ethnicity. When Catholics from far-flung locales encountered one another, they shared something meaningful to them all because of the uniformity of rites. The second thing that defined a Catholic was obedience to the pope. Ritual uniformity and obedience to the pope were closely interrelated because both the ritual and the pope were Roman. There were many bishops in Christianity, but as one monk put it, "Rome is...the head of the world."

Beginning in the late eleventh century the task of the popes became to make this theoretical assertion of obedience real—in short, to make the papacy a religious monarchy. Among the reformers who gathered in Rome was Hildebrand (ca. 1020–1085), one of the most remarkable figures in the history of the Church, a man beloved as saintly by his admirers and considered an ambitious, self-serving megalomaniac by many others. From 1055 to 1073 during the pontificates of some four popes, Hildebrand became the power behind the throne, helping enact wide-ranging reforms that enforced uniformity of worship and establishing the rules for electing new popes by the college of cardinals. In 1073 the cardinals elected Hildebrand himself pope, and he took the name Gregory VII (r. 1073–1085).

Gregory's greatness lay in his leadership over the internal reform of the Church. Every year he held a Church council in Rome where he decreed against simony and married priests. Gregory centralized authority over the Church itself by sending out papal legates, representatives who delivered orders to local bishops. He attempted to free the Church from external influence by asserting the superiority of the pope over all other authorities. Gregory's theory of papal supremacy led him into direct conflict with the German emperor, Henry IV (r. 1056–1106). The issue was lay investiture. During the eighth and ninth centuries weak popes relied on the Carolingian kings and emperors to name suitable candidates for ecclesiastical offices in order to keep them out of the hands of local aristocrats. At stake was not only power and authority, but also the income from the enormous amount of property controlled by the Church, which the emperor was in the best position to protect. During the eleventh century, Gregory VII and other reform-minded popes sought to regain control of this property. Without the ability to name his own candidates as bishops, Gregory recognized that his whole campaign for church reform would falter. When Pope Gregory tried to negotiate with the emperor over the appointment of the bishop of Milan,

Henry resisted and commanded Gregory to resign the papacy in a letter with the notorious salutation, "Henry, King not by usurpation, but by the pious ordination of God to Hildebrand now not Pope but false monk."

Gregory struck back in an escalating confrontation now known as the **Investiture Controversy.** He deposed Henry from the imperial throne and excommunicated him. **Excommunication** prohibited the sinner from participating in the sacraments and forbade any social contact whatsoever with the surrounding community. People caught talking to an excommunicated person or writing a letter or even offering a drink of water could themselves be excommunicated. Excommunication was a form of social death, a dire punishment indeed, especially if the excommunicated person were a king. Both sides marshaled arguments from Scripture and history, but the excommunication was effective. Henry's friends started to abandon him, rebellion broke out in Germany, and the most powerful German lords called for a meeting to elect a new emperor. Backed into a corner, Henry plotted a clever counterstroke.

Early in the winter of 1077 Pope Gregory set out to cross the Alps to meet with the German lords. When Gregory reached the Alpine passes, however, he learned that Emperor Henry was on his way to Italy. In fear of what the emperor would do, Gregory retreated to the castle of Canossa, where he expected to be attacked. Henry surprised Gregory, however, by arriving not with an army, but as a supplicant asking the pope to hear his confession. As a priest Gregory could hardly refuse to hear the confession of a penitent sinner, but he nevertheless attempted to humiliate Henry by making him wait for three days, kneeling in the snow outside the castle. Henry's presentation of himself as a penitent sinner posed a dilemma for Gregory. The German lords were waiting for Gregory to appear in his capacity as the chief justice of Christendom to judge Henry, but Henry himself was asking the pope to act in his capacity as priest to grant absolution for sin. The priest in Gregory won out over the judge, and he absolved Henry.

Even after the deaths of Gregory and Henry, the Investiture Controversy continued to poison relations between the popes and emperors until the Concordat of Worms in 1122 resolved the issue in a formal treaty. The emperor retained the right to nominate high churchmen, but in a concession to the papacy, the emperor lost the ceremonial privileges of investiture that conveyed spiritual authority. Without the ceremony of investiture, no bishop could exercise his office. By refusing to invest unsuitable nominees, the popes had the last word. Gregory VII's vision of papal supremacy over all kings and emperors persevered.

HOW THE POPES RULED The most lasting accomplishment of the popes during the twelfth and thirteenth centuries derived less from dramatic confrontations with emperors than from the humdrum routine of the law. Beginning with Gregory VII, the papacy became the supreme court of the Catholic world by claiming authority over a vast range of issues. To justify these claims, Gregory and his assistants conducted massive research among old laws and treatises. These were organized into a body of legal texts called canon law.

Canon law came to encompass many kinds of cases, including all those involving the clergy, disputes about church property, and donations to the Church. The law of the Church also touched on many of the most vital concerns of the laity including annulling marriages, legitimating bastards, prosecuting bigamy, protecting widows and orphans, and resolving inheritance disputes. Most of the cases originated in the courts of the bishops, but the bishops' decisions could be appealed to the pope and cardinals sitting together in the papal consistory. The consistory could make exceptions from the letter of the law, called dispensations, giving it considerable power over kings and aristocrats who wanted to marry a cousin, divorce a wife, legitimate a bastard, or annul a will. By the middle of the twelfth century, Rome was awash with legal business. The functions of the canon law courts became so important that those elected popes were no longer monks but trained canon lawyers, men very capable in the ways of the world.

The pope also presided over the **curia,** the administrative bureaucracy of the Church.

The cardinals in the curia served as ministers in the papal administration and visited foreign princes and cities as ambassadors or legates. Because large amounts of revenue were flowing into the coffers of the Church, the curia functioned as a bank. Rome became the financial capital of the West.

In addition to its legal, administrative, and financial authority, the papacy also made use of two powerful spiritual weapons against the disobedient. Any Christian who refused to repent of a sin could be excommunicated, as the Emperor Henry IV had been. The second spiritual weapon was the **interdict,** the suspension of the sacraments in a locality or kingdom whose ruler had defied the pope. During an interdict the churches closed their doors, creating panic among the faithful who could not baptize their children or bury their dead. The interdict, which encouraged a public outcry, could be a very effective weapon for undermining the political support of any monarch who ran afoul of the pope.

THE PINNACLE OF THE MEDIEVAL PAPACY: POPE INNOCENT III The most capable of the medieval popes was Innocent III (r. 1198–1216). To him, the pope was the overlord of the entire world. He recognized the right of kings to rule over the secular sphere, but he considered it his duty to prevent and punish sin, a duty that gave him wide latitude to meddle in the affairs of kings and princes.

Innocent's first task was to provide the papacy with a strong territorial base of support so that the popes could act with the same freedom as kings and princes. Historians consider Innocent the founder of the Papal State in central Italy, an independent state that lasted until 1870 and survives today in a tiny fragment as Vatican City.

Innocent's second goal was keeping alive the crusading ideal. He called the Fourth Crusade, which went awry when the crusaders attacked Constantinople instead of conquering Jerusalem. He also expanded the definition of crusading by calling for a crusade to eliminate heresy within Christian Europe. Innocent was deeply concerned about the spread of new heresies, which attracted enormous numbers of converts, especially in the growing cities of southern Europe. By crusading against Christian heretics—the Cathars and Waldensians (see the following discussion)—Innocent authorized the use of military methods to enforce uniformity of belief.

The third objective was to assert the authority of the papacy over political affairs. Innocent managed the election of Emperor Frederick II. He also assumed the right to veto imperial elections. He excommunicated King Philip II of France to force him to take back an unwanted wife. And Innocent placed England under the interdict to compel King John to cede his kingdom to the

papacy and receive it back as a fief, a transaction that made the king of England the vassal of the pope. Using whatever means necessary, he made papal vassals of the rulers of Aragon, Bulgaria, Denmark, Hungary, Poland, Portugal, and Serbia. Through the use of the feudal law of vassalage, Innocent brought the papacy to its closest approximation of a universal Christian monarchy (see **Map 10.2**).

Innocent's fourth and greatest accomplishment was to codify the rites of the liturgy and to define the dogmas of the faith. This monumental task was the achievement of the Fourth Lateran Council, held in Rome in 1215. This council, attended by more than 400 bishops, 800 abbots,

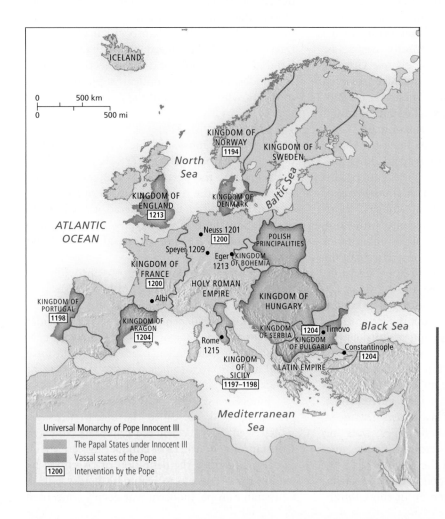

MAP 10.2

Universal Monarchy of Pope Innocent III

Besides his direct control of the Papal States in central Italy, Pope Innocent III made vassals of many of the kings of Catholic Europe. These feudal ties provided a legal foundation for his claim to be the highest authority in Christian Europe.

and the ambassadors of the monarchs of Catholic Europe, issued decrees that reinforced the celebration of the sacraments as the centerpiece of Christian life. They included rules to educate the clergy, define their qualifications, and govern elections of bishops. The council condemned heretical beliefs, and it called for yet another crusade. The council became the guidepost that has since governed many aspects of Catholic practice, especially with regard to the sacraments. It did more than any other council to fulfill the goal of uniformity of rites in Catholicism.

THE TROUBLED LEGACY OF THE PAPAL MONARCHY Innocent was an astute, intelligent man who in single-minded fashion pursued the greater good of the Church as he saw it. No one succeeded better than he in preserving the unity of the Catholic world in an era of chaos. His policies, however, were less successful in the hands of his less able successors. Their blunders undermined the pope's spiritual mission. Innocent's successors went beyond defending the Papal State and embroiled all Italy in a series of bloody civil wars between the Guelfs, who supported the popes, and the Ghibellines, who opposed them. The pope's position as a monarch superior to all others collapsed under the weight of immense folly during the pontificate of Boniface VIII (r. 1294–1303). His claims to absolute authority combined with breathtaking vanity and ineptitude corroded the achievements of Innocent III.

In 1302 Boniface promulgated the most extreme theoretical assertion of papal superiority over lay rulers. The papal bull, *Unam Sanctum*, decreed that "it is absolutely necessary for salvation that every human creature be subject to the Roman pontiff." Behind the statement was a specific dispute with King Philip IV of France (r. 1285–1314), who was attempting to try a French bishop for treason. The larger issue behind the dispute was similar to the Investiture Controversy of the eleventh century, but this time no one paid much attention to the pope. The loss of papal moral authority had taken its toll. In the heat of the confrontation, King Philip accused Pope Boniface of heresy, one of the few sins of which he was not guilty, and sent his agents to arrest the pope who died shortly after. With Boniface the papal monarchy died as well.

THE RELIGIOUS OUTCASTS: CATHARS AND WALDENSIANS In its efforts to defend the faith, the Church during the first half of the thirteenth century began to authorize bishops and other clerics to conduct inquisitions (formal inquiries) into specific instances of heresy or perceived heresy. The so-called heretics tended to be faithful people who sought personal purity in religion. During the thirteenth and early fourteenth centuries, inquisitions and systematic persecutions targeted the Cathars and Waldensians, who at first had lived peacefully with their Catholic neighbors and shared many of the same beliefs with them.

The name *Cathar* derives from the Greek word for purity. The Cathars were especially strong in northern Italy and southern France. Heavily concentrated around the French town of Albi, the Cathars were also known as Albigensians. They departed from Catholic doctrine, which held that God created the Earth, because they believed that an evil force had created all matter. To purify themselves, an elite few—known as "perfects"—rejected their own bodies as corrupt matter, refused to marry and procreate, and in extreme cases gradually starved themselves. These purified perfects provided a dramatic contrast to the more worldly Catholic clergy. For many, Catharism became a form of protest against the wealth and power of the Church. By the 1150s the Cathars had

CHRONOLOGY: THE PAPAL MONARCHY

1073–1085	Reign of Pope Gregory VII
1075–1122	The Investiture Controversy
1198–1216	Reign of Pope Innocent III
1215	Fourth Lateran Council
1294–1303	Reign of Pope Boniface VIII

organized their own churches, performed their own rituals, and even elected their own bishops. Where they became deeply rooted, as in the south of France, they practiced their faith openly until Pope Innocent III authorized a crusade against them.

The Waldensians were the followers of Peter Waldo (d. ca. 1184), a merchant of Lyons, France, who like Francis of Assisi had abandoned all his possessions and taken a vow of poverty. Desiring to imitate the life of Jesus and live in simple purity, the Waldensians preached and translated the Gospels into their own language so that laypeople who did not know Latin could understand them. At first the Waldensians' seemed similar to the Franciscans, but because of the Waldensians' failure to obtain licenses to preach as the Franciscans had done, they came to be depicted by Church authorities as heretics. In response, the Waldensians created an alternative church that became widespread in southern France, Rhineland Germany, and northern Italy.

Catholic authorities, who were often the objects of strong criticisms from the Cathars and Waldensians, grew ever more hostile to them. Bishops declared heretics liable to the same legal penalties as those guilty of treason, which authorized the political authorities to proceed against them. In 1208 Pope Innocent III called the Albigensian Crusade, the first of several holy wars launched against heretics in the south of France. The king of France was only too happy to fight the Albigensian Crusade because he saw it as a means of expanding royal power in a region of France where his authority was weak. To eradicate the remaining Cathars and Waldensians, several kings and popes initiated inquisitions. By the middle of the thirteenth century, Catholic authorities had either converted or exterminated the Cathars except for a few isolated pockets in the mountains. Inquisitorial campaigns nearly wiped out the Waldensians, but scattered groups have managed to survive to this day, mostly by retreating to the relative safety of

the high Alps and later to the Americas. (See *Justice in History* in this chapter.)

Discovering God in the World

Even before the First Crusade, Catholic Europe began to experience an unprecedented spiritual awakening. The eleventh-century papal campaign to reform the morals of the clergy helped make priests both more respectable and better educated. A better-educated clergy in turn educated the laity more effectively. In large numbers Catholic Christians began to internalize the teachings of the Church. The most devout were drawn to dedicating their lives to religion. In England, for example, the number of monks increased tenfold from the late eleventh century to 1200. The newly expanding cities built loyalty and encouraged peaceable behavior through the veneration of civic patron saints. The most vital indication of spiritual renewal was the success of new religious orders, which satisfied a widespread yearning to discover the hand of God in the world.

THE PATRON SAINTS Saints are holy people whose moral perfection gives them a special relationship with the sacred. Ordinary Christians venerated saints to gain access to supernatural powers, protection, and intercession with God.

The relationship between Christian believers and the saints was profoundly intimate and intertwined with many aspects of life: Parents named their children after saints who became special protectors; every church dedicated itself to a saint; every town and city adopted a patron saint. And even entire peoples cherished a patron saint. For example, the Irish adopted Saint Patrick, who supposedly brought Christianity to the island.

A city gained protection from a patron saint by obtaining the saint's relics, the corpse or skeleton or part of the skeleton or some object associated with the saint. These relics, verified by miracles, served as contacts between Earth and Heaven. The belief in the miraculous powers of relics created an enormous demand for them in the thriving medieval cities. But because the remains of the martyrs and early saints of the church were spread across the Middle East and Mediterranean from Jerusalem to Rome, someone had first to discover the saint's relics and then transfer them to new homes in the churches of the growing western and northern European cities. Relics were bought or stolen, and there was ample room for fraud in passing off unauthentic bones to gullible buyers. During the Crusades the supply of relics greatly increased because the knights had access to the tombs of early Christian saints and martyrs.

During the twelfth and thirteenth centuries public veneration of saints began to undergo a subtle shift away from the cults of the local patron saints toward more universal figures such as Jesus and the Virgin Mary. The patron saints had functioned almost like the family deities of antiquity who served the particular needs of individuals and communities, but the papal monarchy encouraged uniformity throughout Catholicism.

Christians had always honored the Virgin Mary, but beginning in the twelfth century her immense popularity provided Catholics with a positive female image that contradicted the traditional misogyny and mistrust associated with Eve. Clerics and monks had long depicted

MOSAICS IN THE BASILICA OF ST. MARK IN VENICE

Pilgrims learned of Venice's intimate association with its patron St. Mark from the magnificent mosaics that adorned the basilica's ceilings and walls. This scene shows a miracle that occurred after St. Mark's body was lost during a fire in the basilica. After the leaders of Venice spent days in prayer, shown on the left, St. Mark opened a door in a column shown at the far right to reveal the place where his body was hidden. In between these two scenes, those who witnessed the miracle turn to one another in amazement. The leaders of Venice derived considerable prestige and political authority from their veneration of St. Mark.

women as deceitful and lustful in luring men to their moral ruin. In contrast, the veneration of the Virgin Mary promoted the image of a loving mother who would intervene with her son on behalf of sinners at the Last Judgment. Theologians still taught that the woman Eve had brought sin into the world, but the woman Mary offered help in escaping the consequences of sin.

The popularity of Mary was evident everywhere. The burgeoning cities of Europe dedicated most of the new cathedrals to her. Mary became a model with whom women could identify, presenting a positive image of femininity. In images of her suckling the Christ child, she became the perfect embodiment of the virtue of charity, the willingness to give without any expectation of reward. In contrast to the early Christian saints who were predominantly martyrs and missionaries, during the twelfth and thirteenth centuries saints exhibited sanctity more through nurturing others, especially by feeding the poor and healing the sick. Women embodied the capacity to nurture, and many more women became saints during this period than during the entire first millennium of Christianity. In 1100 fewer than 10 percent of all the saints were female. By 1300 the percentage had increased to 24 percent. During the fifteenth century about 30 percent were women.

THE TWO MARYS: THE MOTHER OF GOD AND THE REPENTANT PROSTITUTE

Medieval thinking about women began with the fundamental dichotomy between Eve, the symbol of women as they are, and Mary, the ideal to which all women strived. Eve brought sin and sex into the world through her disobedience to God. Mary, the Virgin Mother, kept her body inviolate. Into the gap between the two natures of women emerged Mary Magdalene, a repentant prostitute whose veneration reached a pinnacle in the twelfth century. In contrast to the perpetually virginal ideal of Mary, the mother of Christ, Magdalene offered the possibility of redemption to all women.

THE NEW RELIGIOUS ORDERS   By the eleventh century many men attracted to the religious life found the traditional orders too lax in their discipline and too worldly. In 1098 a small group of Benedictine monks removed themselves to an isolated wasteland to establish the Cistercian Order. The Cistercians practiced a very strict discipline. They ate only enough to stay alive. Each monk possessed only one robe. Unlike other orders, such as the Cluniacs, which required monks to attend frequent and lengthy services, the Cistercians spent more time in private prayer

and manual labor. Their churches were bare of all decoration. Under the brilliant leadership of Bernard of Clairvaux (1090–1153), the Cistercians grew rapidly, as many men disillusioned with the sinful and materialistic society around them joined the new order. Bernard's asceticism led him to seek refuge from the affairs of the world, but he was also a religious reformer and activist, engaged with the important issues of his time. He even helped settle a disputed papal election and called for a crusade.

The Cistercians established their new monasteries in isolated, uninhabited places where they cleared forests and worked the land so that they could live in complete isolation from the troubled affairs of the world. Their hard work had an ironic result. By bringing new lands under the plow and by employing the latest technological innovations, such as water mills, many of the Cistercian monasteries produced more than was needed for the monks, and the sale of excess produce made the Cistercians rich. The economic success of the Cistercians helped them expand even more rapidly, especially into places previously untouched by monasticism in northeastern Europe. The rapid Cistercian push beyond the frontiers of Latin Europe helped disseminate the culture of Catholic Christianity through educating the local elites and attracting them to join the Cistercians. By recruiting lay brothers, known as *converses*, the Cistercians made important connections with the peasants.

More than a century after the foundation of the Cistercians in France, the Spaniard Dominic and the Italian Francis formulated a new kind of religious order composed of mendicant **friars.** From the very beginning the friars wanted to distinguish themselves from monks. As the opening of this chapter indicated, instead of working in a monastery to feed themselves as did the Cistercians, friars ("brothers") wandered from city to city and throughout the countryside begging for alms (*mendicare* means "to beg"; hence, *mendicant friars*). Unlike monks who remained in a cloister, friars tried to help ordinary laypeople with their problems by preaching and administering to the sick and poor.

The Spaniard Dominic (1170–1221) founded the Dominican Order to convert Muslims and Jews and to combat heresy among Christians against whom he began his preaching mission while traveling through southern France. The ever-perceptive Pope Innocent III recognized Dominic's talents while he was visiting Rome and gave his new order provisional approval. Dominic believed the task of conversion could be achieved through persuasion and argument. To hone the Dominicans' persuasive skills, they created the first multigrade, comprehensive educational system. It connected schools located in individual friaries with more advanced regional schools that offered specialized training in languages, philosophy, and especially theology. Most Dominican friars never studied at a university but enjoyed, nevertheless, a highly sophisticated education that made them exceptionally influential in European intellectual life. Famed for their preaching skills, Dominicans were equally successful in exciting the illiterate masses and debating sophisticated opponents.

The Franciscan Order enjoyed a similar success. Francis of Assisi (1182–1226), whose story opened this chapter, deeply influenced Clare of Assisi (1194–1253), who founded a parallel order for women, the Poor Clares. Like the Franciscans, she and her followers enjoyed the "privilege of perfect poverty," which forbade the ownership of any property even by the community itself.

Both the Dominican and Franciscan Orders spread rapidly. Whereas the successful Cistercians had founded 500 new houses in their first century, the Franciscans established more than 1,400 in their first 100 years. Liberated from the obligation to live in a monastery, the mendicant friars traveled wherever the pope ordered them, making them effective agents of the papal monarchy. They preached crusades. They pacified the poor. They converted heretics and non-Christians through their inspiring preaching revivals. Even more effectively than the Cistercians before them, they established Catholic colonies along the frontiers of the West and beyond. They became missionary scouts looking for opportunities to disseminate Christian culture. In 1254 the Great Khan in Mongolia sponsored a debate on the principal religions of the world. There, many thousands of miles from Catholic Europe, was a Franciscan friar

JUSTICE IN HISTORY

Inquiring into Heresy: The Inquisition in Montaillou

In 1208 Pope Innocent III issued a call for a crusade against the Cathars or Albigensians. Fighting on behalf of French King Philip II, Simon de Montfort decisively defeated the pro-Cathar barons of southern France at Muret in 1213. Catharism retreated to the mountains, where a clandestine network of adherents kept the faith alive. The obliteration of these stubborn remnants required methods more subtle than the blunt instrument of a crusade. It required the techniques of inquisitors adept at interrogation and investigation.

Against the Cathar underground, the inquisition conducted its business through a combination of denunciations, exhaustive interrogations of witnesses and suspects, and confessions. Because its avowed purpose was to root out doctrinal error and to reconcile heretics to the Church, eliciting confessions was the preferred technique. But confessed heretics could not receive absolution until they informed on their friends and associates.

One of the last and most extensively documented inquisition cases against Catharism took place in Montaillou, a village in the Pyrenees Mountains, near the border of modern France and Spain. The Montaillou inquisition began in 1308, a century after the launch of the Albigensian Crusade and long after the heyday of Catharism.

However, the detailed records of the Montaillou inquisitors provide a revealing glimpse into Catharism and its suppression as well as the procedures of the inquisition. The first to investigate Montaillou was Geoffrey d'Ablis, the inquisitor of Carcassone. In 1308 he had every resident over age 12 seized and imprisoned. After the investigation, the villagers suffered the full range of inquisitorial penalties for their Cathar faith. The inquisitor's court sentenced some to life in prison, others to be burned at the stake. It forced many of those who were allowed to return to Montaillou to wear a yellow cross, the symbol of a heretic, sewn to the outside of their garments.

Unfortunately for these survivors, the most fearsome inquisitor of the age, Jacques Fournier, who was later elected Pope Benedict XII, investigated Montaillou again from 1318 to 1325. Known as an efficient, rigorous opponent of heresy, Fournier forced virtually all the surviving adults in Montaillou to appear before his tribunal. When the scrupulous Fournier took up a case, his inquiries were notoriously lengthy and rigorous. Both witnesses and defendants spoke of his tenacity, skill, and close attention to detail in conducting interrogations. If Fournier and his assistants could not uncover evidence through interrogation and confession, they did not hesitate to employ informers and spies to obtain the necessary information. When Pierre Maury, a shepherd the inquisitors sought for many years, returned to the village for a visit, an old friend received him with caution: "When we saw you again we felt both joy and fear. Joy, because it was a long time since we had seen you. Fear, because I was afraid lest the Inquisition had captured you up there: if they had they would have made you confess everything and come back among us as a spy in order to bring about my capture."[1]

Fournier's success in Montaillou depended on his ability to play local factions against each other by encouraging members of one clan to denounce the members of another. Fournier's persistence even turned family members against one another. The clearest example of this convoluted play of local alliances and animosities, family ties, religious belief, and self-interest is the case of Montaillou's wealthiest family, the Clergues.

Bernard Clergue was the count's local representative, which made him a kind of sheriff; his brother Pierre was the parish priest. Together they represented both the secular and religious arms of the inquisition in Montaillou. In his youth, Pierre had Cathar sympathies, and he allegedly kept a heretical book or calendar in his home. Nevertheless, at some time before 1308, he and Bernard betrayed the local Cathars to

BURNING OF THE HERETICAL BOOKS OF THE CATHARS

In this fifteenth-century painting, St. Dominic, the figure with a halo on the left, gives a Catholic book to a Cathar priest dressed in blue. The Cathars attempt to burn the book, which miraculously floats unharmed above the flames.

the inquisition. In the proceedings that followed, they had the power to either protect or expose their neighbors and family members. When the inquisition summoned one of his relatives, Bernard warned her to "say you fell off the ladder in your house; pretend you have broken bones everywhere. Otherwise it's prison for you."[2] Pierre relentlessly used his influence for his own and his family's benefit. A notorious womanizer, Pierre frightened women into sleeping with him by threatening to denounce them to the inquisition. Those he personally testified against were primarily from other prominent Montaillou families who represented a challenge to the Clergues' power. As one resident bitterly testified, "The priest himself cause[s] many inhabitants of Montaillou to be summoned by the Lord Inquisitor of Carcassone. It is high time the people of the priest's house were thrust as deep in prison as the other inhabitants of Montaillou."[3]

Despite the Clergues' attempted misuse of the inquisitorial investigation for their own purposes, the inquisitor Fournier persevered according to his own standards of evidence. In 1320 he finally had Pierre Clergue arrested as a heretic. The sly priest died in prison.

For Discussion

1. How did the methods of the inquisition help create outcasts from Catholic society? How did these methods help consolidate Catholic identity?
2. The primary function of the inquisition was to investigate what people believed. What do you think the inquisitors thought justice to be?

Taking It Further

Lambert, Malcolm. *The Cathars.* 1998. The best place to investigate the Cathar movement in the full sweep of its troubled history.

Le Roy Ladurie, Emmanuel. *Montaillou: The Promised Land of Error.* Translated by Barbara Bray. 1978. The best-selling and fascinating account of life in a Cathar village based on the records of Fournier's inquisition.

Moore, R. I. *The Formation of a Persecuting Society: Power and Deviance in Western Europe, 950–1250.* 1987. Places the harassment of heretics in the broader context of medieval persecutions.

ready to debate the learned men representing Islam, Buddhism, and Confucianism.

THE FLOWERING OF RELIGIOUS SENSIBILITIES During the twelfth and thirteenth centuries the widespread enthusiasm for religion exalted spiritual creativity. Experimentation pushed Christian piety in new directions, not just for aristocratic men, who dominated the Church hierarchy and the monasteries, but for women and laypeople from all social levels.

Catholic worship concentrated on the celebration of the Eucharist. The **Eucharist,** which was the crucial ritual moment during the Mass, celebrated Jesus's last meal with his apostles. The Eucharistic rite consecrated bread and wine as the body and blood of Christ. After the consecration, the celebrating priest distributed to the congregation the bread, called the host. Drinking from the chalice of wine, however, was a special privilege of the priesthood. More than anything else, belief in the miraculous change from bread to flesh and wine to blood, along with the sacrament of baptism, distinguished Christian believers from others. The Fourth Lateran Council in 1215 obligated all Christians to partake of the Eucharist at least once a year at Easter.

As simple as it was as a ritual observance, belief in the Eucharistic miracle presented a vexing and complex theological problem—why the host still looked, tasted, and smelled like bread rather than flesh, and why the blood in the chalice still seemed to be wine rather than blood. After the Fourth Lateran Council, Catholics solved this problem with the doctrine of **transubstantiation.** The doctrine rested on a distinction between the outward appearances (the "accidents" in theological terms) of the object, which the five senses could perceive, and the substance of an object, which they could not. When the priest spoke the words of consecration during the Mass, the bread and wine changed into the flesh and blood of Christ in substance ("transubstantiated"), but not in outward appearances. Thus, the substance of the Eucharist literally became God's body, but the senses of taste, smell, and sight perceived it as bread and wine.

Veneration of the Eucharist enabled the faithful to identify with Christ because believers considered the consecrated Eucharistic wafer to be Christ himself. By eating the host, they had literally ingested Christ, making his body part of their bodies. Eucharistic veneration became enormously popular in the thirteenth century and the climax of dazzling ritual performance. Priests enhanced the effect of the miracle by dramatically elevating the host at the moment of consecration, holding it in upraised hands. Altar screens had special peepholes so that many people could adore the host at the elevation, and the faithful would rush from altar to altar or church to church to witness a succession of host elevations.

Many Christians became attracted to mysticism, the attempt to achieve union of the self with God. To the mystic, complete understanding of the divine was spiritual, not intellectual, an understanding best achieved through asceticism, the repudiation of material and bodily comforts. Both men and women became mystics, but women concentrated on the more extreme forms of asceticism. For example, some women allowed themselves to be walled up in dark chambers to achieve perfect seclusion from the world and avoid distractions from their mystical pursuits. Others had themselves whipped, wore painful scratching clothing, starved themselves, or claimed to survive with the Eucharist as their only food. Female mystics, such as Juliana of Norwich (1342 to ca. 1416), envisioned a holy family in which God the Father was almighty, but the Mother was all wisdom. Some female mystics believed that Christ had a female body because he was the perfect nurturer, and they ecstatically contemplated spiritual union with him.

Mystics, however, were exceptional people. Most Christians contented themselves with the sacraments, especially baptism, penance, and the Eucharist; perhaps a pilgrimage to a saint's

CHRONOLOGY: MEDIEVAL RELIGIOUS DEVELOPMENTS

1098	Founding of Cistercian Order
1208–1213	Albigensian Crusade
1215	Fourth Lateran Council promulgates dogma of transubstantiation
1226	Death of Francis of Assisi
1221	Death of Dominic

shrine; and a final attempt at salvation by making a pious gift to the Church on their deathbed.

STRENGTHENING THE CENTER OF THE WEST

■ How did the western European monarchies strengthen themselves?

During the twelfth and thirteenth centuries, the kingdoms of Catholic western Europe became the supreme political and economic powers in the Christian world, eclipsing Byzantium—an achievement that made them potent rivals to the Islamic states. One reason was stronger political unity. These kingdoms laid the foundations of the modern nation-states, which remain to this day the dominant forms of government around the globe. What happened in France and England during the twelfth and thirteenth centuries, therefore, represents one of the most important and lasting contributions of the West to world history.

The Monarchies of Western Europe

During the High Middle Ages, France and England began to exhibit the fundamental characteristics of unified kingdoms. Stable borders, permanent bureaucracies, sovereignty, and the rule of law were the foundations on which they became the most powerful kingdoms in Europe during the twelfth and thirteenth centuries (see **Map 10.3**).

The kings of France achieved unity through military conquests and shrewd administrative reforms. In the turbulent Middle Ages, dynastic continuity was a key ingredient in building loyalty and avoiding chaos. From Philip I (r. 1060–1108) to Philip IV (r. 1285–1314), France enjoyed not only a succession of extremely effective kings but a consistent policy that guaranteed the borders, built a bureaucracy, expanded the idea of royal sovereignty, and enforced the rule of law. By securing complete military and judicial control of the royal domain, the Ile-de-France, these kings provided the dynasty with a dependable income from the region's abundant farms and the thriving trade of Paris. To administer the domain and lands newly acquired by conquest, the French monarchy introduced new royal officials, the *baillis,* who were paid professionals, some trained in Roman law. Directly responsible to the king, they had full administrative, judicial, and military powers in their districts. The *baillis* laid the foundation for a bureaucracy that centralized French government. Louis IX (r. 1226–1270), who was canonized St. Louis in 1297 for his exemplary piety and justice, introduced a system of judicial appeals that expanded royal justice and investigated the honesty of the *baillis*. Philip IV, the Fair (r. 1285–1314), greatly expanded the king's authority and also managed to bring the Church under his personal control, making the French clergy largely exempt from papal supervision. To pay for his frequent wars, Philip expelled the Jews after stripping them of their lands and

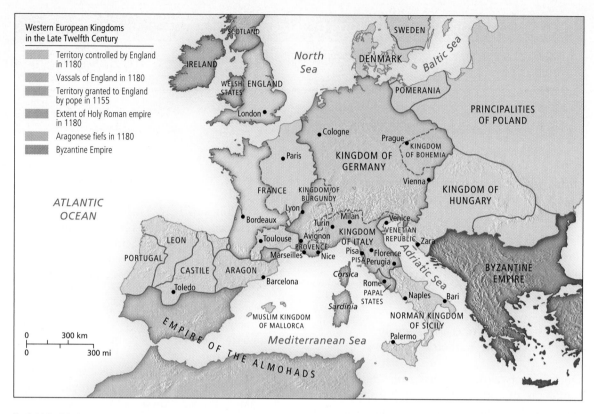

MAP 10.3

Western European Kingdoms in the Late Twelfth Century

The kings of England occupied Ireland as well as much of western France. France itself was consolidated around the Ile-de-France, the area around Paris. The kingdoms of Germany, Bohemia, Burgundy, and Italy were ruled by the German emperors.

goods and then turned against the rich Order of the Knights Templar, a crusader order that had amassed a fortune as the papal banker and creditor of Philip. He confiscated the Templars' lands and tortured the knights to extort confessions to various crimes in a campaign to discredit them. (See *Different Voices* in this chapter.) Philip was perhaps most effective in finding new ways to increase taxation. Under Philip, royal revenues grew tenfold from what they had been in the saintly reign of Louis IX.

England was even better unified than France. When the Duke of Normandy, William I the Conqueror (r. 1066–1087), seized England in 1066, he claimed the crown and all the land for

himself. The new king kept about one-fifth of the land under his personal rule and parceled out the rest to the loyal nobles, monasteries, and the churches. This policy ensured that every land holder in England held his property as a fief, directly or indirectly, from the king, a principle of lordship enforced by an oath of loyalty to the crown required of all vassals. About 180 great lords from among the Norman aristocracy held land directly the king, and hundreds of lesser nobles were vassals of these great lords. William accomplished what other kings only dreamed about: He had truly made himself the lord of all lords. William's hierarchy of nobles transformed the nature of the English monarchy, giving the Norman kings far greater authority over England than any of the earlier Anglo-Saxon kings had enjoyed.

Building on the legacy of the conquest, King Henry II (r. 1154–1189) reformed the judiciary. His use of sheriffs to enforce the royal will produced the legends of Robin Hood, the bandit who resisted the nasty sheriff of Nottingham on behalf of the poor. But in reality the sheriffs probably did more good than harm in protecting the weak against the powerful. In attempting to reduce the jurisdiction of the nobles, Henry made it possible for almost anyone to obtain a writ that moved a case to a royal court. Henry introduced a system of itinerant **circuit court** judges who visited every shire in the land four times a year. When this judge arrived, the sheriff assembled a group of men familiar with local affairs to report the major crimes that had been committed since the judge's last visit. These assemblies were the origins of the **grand jury** system, which persists to this day as the means for indicting someone for a crime. To resolve disputes over the possession of land, sheriffs collected a group of twelve local men who testified under oath about the claims of the disputants, and the judge made his decision based on their testimony. These assemblies began **trial by jury.** Judges later extended to criminal cases trial by jury, which remains the basis for rendering legal verdicts in common-law countries, including Britain, the United States, and Canada.

Henry also subjected priests alleged to have committed crimes to the jurisdiction of the royal courts. The king wanted to apply a principle of universal justice to everyone in the realm, a principle fiercely opposed by Thomas Becket, the archbishop of Canterbury. Becket insisted the Church must be free of interference from secular authorities. When four knights—believing they were acting on the king's wishes—murdered Becket before the altar of the Canterbury cathedral, the public was outraged and blocked Henry's plan to subject the Church to royal justice. The Church soon canonized Becket, revered as England's most famous saint.

The royal authority Henry asserted foundered under King John (r. 1199–1216), who lost to King Philip II of France the duchy of Normandy, which had been one of the foundations of English royal power since William the Conqueror. The barons of England grew tired of John's requests to pay for wars he lost. In 1215 English barons forced John to sign **Magna Carta** ("great charter," in reference to its size), in which the king pledged to respect the traditional feudal privileges of the nobility, towns, and clergy. Contrary to widespread belief, Magna Carta had nothing to do with asserting the liberty of the common people or guaranteeing universal rights. It addressed only the privileges of a select few rather than the rights of the many. Subsequent kings, however, swore to uphold it, thereby accepting the fundamental principle that even the king must respect the law. After Magna Carta the lord of all lords became less so. King Edward I (r. 1272–1307) began to call the **English Parliament** (from the French "talking together") in order to raise sums of money for his foreign wars. The English Parliament differed from similar assemblies on the Continent. It usually included representatives of the "commons," which consisted of townsmen and prosperous farmers who lacked titles of nobility, but whom the king summoned because he needed their money. As a result, a broader spectrum of the population joined parliament than in most other medieval kingdoms.

To the east the Holy Roman Empire suffered from the division between its principal component parts in Germany and northern Italy. Germany itself was an ill-defined region, subdivided by deep ethnic diversity and powerful dukes who ruled their lands with a spirit of fierce independence. As a result, emperors could not rule Germany directly, but only by demanding homage from the dukes who became imperial vassals. These feudal bonds were fragile substitutes for the kinds of monarchic institutions that evolved in France and England. The emperor's best asset was the force of his personality and his willingness to engage in a perpetual show of force to prevent rebellion. In northern Italy, the other part of the emperor's dominion, he did not even enjoy these extensive ties of vassalage and could rely

DIFFERENT VOICES THE TRIAL OF THE KNIGHTS TEMPLAR

The Knights Templar had been one of the most successful crusading orders, but after the end of the Crusades, their popularity declined. Nevertheless, they retained extensive properties given to finance their crusading expeditions. Deeply indebted to the Knights and in need of cash to finance his wars against England, King Philip IV of France seized upon rumors about a secret Templar initiation rite to justify arresting the prominent French Templars and confiscating their properties. Some Templars confessed under torture but later reversed themselves. The documents below describe the alleged secret rites of the Templars and summarize the testimony of some of those arrested. This notorious case not only illustrates how a ruthless king financed his kingdom, but how unsubstantiated rumors of homosexual practices could be used to destroy personal reputations and the order itself. The Crown burned many Templars at the stake, dissolved their order, and seized their property.

Royal Order for the Arrests of the Templars (September 14, 1307)

Some time ago indeed, we received insistent reports from very reliable people that brothers of the Order of the knights of the Temple, wolves in sheep's clothing, in the habit of a religious order vilely insulting our religious faith, are again crucifying our Lord Jesus Christ in these days, He who was crucified for the redemption of the human race. But they are causing Him greater injuries than those He received on the Cross. When they enter the Order and make their profession, they are confronted with His image, and their miserable or rather pitiful blindness makes them deny Him three times and spit in His face three times. Afterwards, they remove the clothes they wore in the secular world, and naked in the presence of the Visitor or his deputy, who receives their profession, they are kissed by him first on the lower part of the dorsal spine, secondly on the navel and finally on the mouth, in accordance with the profane rite of their Order but to the disgrace of the dignity of the human race.... By the vow of their profession they are unequivocally bound to accept the request of another to perform the vice of that horrible, dreadful intercourse, and this is why the wrath of God has fallen on these sons of infidelity.

---

only on vague legal rights granted by the imperial title and his ability to keep an army on the scene.

The century between the election of Frederick I (r. 1152–1190), known as Barbarossa or "redbeard," and the death of his grandson Frederick II (r. 1212–1250) represented the great age of the Holy Roman Empire, a period of relative stability preceded and followed by disastrous phases of anarchy and civil war. In the case of both of these emperors, lofty ambitions contrasted with the flimsy base of support and the failure to sustain judicial reforms, which prevented the centralization that took place in France and England. After Frederick II's death, his successors lost their hold on both Italy and Germany.

During the twelfth and thirteenth centuries, Spain and Poland, both of which would later become major European powers, were broken into small, weak principalities.

MEDIEVAL CULTURE: THE SEARCH FOR UNDERSTANDING

■ **What made western European culture distinctive?**

Medieval intellectuals vastly expanded the range of Western culture. The most important cultural encounters came when thinkers read the books of ancient philosophers and faced challenging ideas that did not fit easily into their view of the world. The greatest medieval

Deposition of Templar, Geoffrey of Charney (October 21, 1307)

He said on oath that after he had been received and the mantle placed on his shoulders, there was brought to him a certain cross bearing the image of Jesus Christ, and the said receptor told him not to believe in the one whose image was portrayed there since he was a false prophet and was not God. And then the said receptor made him deny Jesus Christ three times, but he claimed to have done this only with his tongue and not with his heart.

Asked whether he had spat on the said image, he swore that he could not remember and believed that this was due to the fact that they were acting in haste.

Examined about the kiss, he swore on oath that he kissed the receiving master on the navel, and he heard it said . . . to the brothers present at a chapter he was holding, that it was better to have sex between brothers of the Order than to assuage their lust with women, but he claimed never to have done this or even to have been asked.

Deposition of James of Molay, Grand Master (October 24, 1307)

Asked if, when he vowed chastity, anything was said to him about homosexual practices with the brothers, he said on oath that this was not the case and that he had never done this.

Source: Malcolm Barber and Keith Bate (eds.), *The Templars* (Manchester and New York: Manchester University Press, 2002), 245, 251, 253. Reprinted by permission.

For Discussion

1. Historians now consider the charges against the Templars fabrications. Why would these particular kinds of accusations rather than others be fabricated to destroy the Templars?

2. Which allegation seem worse, the denial of Christ or homosexual practices? Under torture, why might defendants confess they had denied Christ, but not admit to homosexual practices?

thinkers attempted to reconcile the reason of the ancients and the faith of the Christians by creating new philosophical systems. Lawyers began to look back to ancient Roman law for guidance about how to settle disputes, adjudicate crimes, and create governmental institutions. Muslim influences reinvigorated the Christian understanding of the sciences. Themes found in Persian love poetry found their way into the Christian notion of courtly love. Catholic western Europe experienced a cultural flowering through the spread of education, the growing power of Latin learning, and the invention of the university. Distinctively western forms developed in literature, music, drama, and above all the Romanesque and Gothic architecture of Europe's great cathedrals.

Revival of Learning

Some simple statistics reveal the magnitude of the educational revolution in medieval western Europe. In 1050 less than one percent of the population of Latin Christian Europe could read, and most of these literate people were priests who knew just enough Latin to recite the offices of the liturgy. Four hundred years later, as much as 40 percent of men living in cities were literate. Europeans embraced learning on a massive scale. How did this come about?

In 1050 only monasteries and cathedral schools provided an education. The curriculum was very basic, usually only reading and writing. Monastic education trained monks to read the books available in their libraries as an aid to contemplating the mysteries of the next world. In contrast, the cathedral schools, which trained members of the ecclesiastical hierarchy, emphasized the practical skills of rational analysis that would help future priests, bishops, and royal advisers solve the problems of this world.

By 1100 the number of cathedral schools had grown significantly and the curriculum expanded to include the study of the ancient Roman masters, Cicero and Virgil, who became models for clear Latin composition. These schools met the demand for trained officials from various sources—the thriving cities, the growing church bureaucracy, and the infant bureaucracies of the western kingdoms.

SCHOLASTICISM: A CHRISTIAN PHILOSOPHY   In the cathedral schools the growing need for training in logic led to the development of scholasticism. **Scholasticism** refers to the use of logic learned from Aristotle to interpret the meaning of the Bible and the writings of the Church Fathers, who formulated Christian theology in its first centuries. The principal method of teaching and learning in the cathedral schools was the lecture. In the classroom the lecturer recited a short passage in Latin, presented the comments of other authorities on it, and drew his own conclusions. He then moved on to another brief passage and repeated the process. In addition to listening to lectures, students engaged in disputations in which they presented oral arguments for or against a particular thesis, a process called dialectical reasoning. The lecturers evaluated student disputants on their ability to investigate through logic the truth of a thesis. Disputations required several skills—verbal facility, a prodigious memory to produce apt citations on the spot, and the ability to think quickly. The process we know today as debate originated with these medieval disputations. Lectures and disputations became the core activities of the scholastics, who considered all subjects, however sacred, as appropriate for reasoned examination.

None of the scholastic teachers was more influential than the acerbic, witty, and daring Peter Abelard (1079–1142). Students from all over Europe flocked to hear Abelard's lectures at the cathedral school of Paris. Abelard's clever criticisms of the ideas of other thinkers delighted students. In *Sic et Non* ("Yes" and "No"), Abelard boldly examined some of the foundations of Christian truth. Employing the dialectical reasoning of a disputation, he presented both sides of 150 theological problems discussed by the Church Fathers. He left the conclusions open in order to challenge his students and readers to think further, but his intention was to point out how apparent disagreements among the experts masked a deeper level of agreement about Christian truth.

UNIVERSITIES: ORGANIZING LEARNING   From the cathedral schools arose the first universities. The University of Paris evolved from the cathedral school where Abelard once taught. Initially the universities were little more than guilds (trade associations), organized by either students or teachers to protect their interests. As members of a guild, students bargained with their professors, as would other tradesmen, over costs and established minimum standards of instruction. The guild of the law students at Bologna received a charter in 1158, which probably made it the first university. Some of the early universities were professional schools, such as the medical faculty at Salerno, but true to their origins as cathedral schools, most emphasized theology over other subjects.

The medieval universities formulated the basic educational practices still in place today. They established a curriculum, examined students, conferred degrees, and conducted graduation ceremonies. Students and teachers wore distinctive robes, which are still worn at graduation ceremonies. Teachers were clergymen—that is, they "professed" religion, hence, the title of *professor* for a university instructor. In their first years students pursued the liberal arts curriculum, which consisted of the *trivium* (grammar, rhetoric, and logic) and the *quadrivium* (arithmetic, geometry, astronomy, and music). Arts and sciences faculties and distribution requirements in modern universities are vestiges of the medieval liberal arts curriculum.

Medieval universities did not admit women because the Church barred women from the priesthood and most university students trained to become priests. (Women did not attend universities in significant numbers until the nineteenth century.) The few women who did receive advanced educations relied on a parent or a private tutor, such as Abelard who tutored the young Heloise. But tutoring had its own dangers. The relationship of Abelard and Heloise resulted in a love affair, a pregnancy, and Abelard's castration at the hands of Heloise's relatives.

THE ANCIENTS: RENAISSANCE OF THE TWELFTH CENTURY   The scholastics' integration of Greek philosophy with Christian theology represented a key facet of the **Twelfth-Century Renaissance,** a revival of interest in the ancients comparable in importance to the Carolingian Renaissance of the ninth century and the Italian Renaissance of the fifteenth. Between about 1140 and 1260, new Latin translations of the Greek classics arrived from Sicily and Spain, where Christians had close contacts with Muslims and Jews. Muslim philosophers translated into Arabic the Greek philosophical and scientific classics, which were readily available in the Middle East and North Africa. Jewish scholars who knew both languages then translated these Arabic versions into Latin. Later a few Catholic scholars traveled to Byzantium, where they learned enough Greek to make even better translations from the originals.

As they encountered the philosophy of the ancients, Muslim, Jewish, and Christian thinkers faced profoundly disturbing problems. The philosophical methods of reasoning found in Greek works, especially those by Aristotle, were difficult to reconcile with the principles of faith revealed in the Qur'an of Islam and the Hebrew and Christian Bibles. Religious thinkers recognized the superiority of Greek thought and worried that the power of philosophical reasoning undermined religious truth. As men of faith they challenged themselves to demonstrate that philosophy did not, if properly understood, contradict religious teaching. Some of them went even further to employ philosophical reasoning to demonstrate the truth of religion. They always faced opposition within their own religious faiths, however, especially from people who thought philosophical reason was an impediment to religious faith.

The most perceptive Muslim thinker to confront the questions raised by Greek philosophy was Averroës (1126–1198), who rose to become the chief judge of Córdoba and an adviser to the caliph. In *The Incoherence of the Incoherence* (1179–1180), Averroës argued that the aim of philosophy was to explain the true, inner meaning of religious revelations. This inner meaning, however, was not to be disclosed to the unlettered masses, who had to be told only the simple, literal stories and metaphors of Scripture. Although lively and persuasive, Averroës's defense of philosophy failed to stimulate additional philosophical speculation within Islam. Once far superior to that of the Latin Christian world, Islamic philosophy and science declined as Muslim thinkers turned to mysticism and rote learning over rational debate. In fact, Averroës received a more sympathetic hearing among Jews and Catholics than among Muslims.

Within Judaism, Moses Maimonides (1135–1204)—a contemporary of Averroës, also from Córdoba—was the most prominent thinker. His most important work in religious philosophy, *The Guide for the Perplexed* (ca. 1191), synthesized Greek philosophy, science, and Judaism. Widely read in Arabic, Hebrew, and Latin versions, the book stimulated both Jewish and Christian philosophy.

For medieval Catholic philosophers, one of the most difficult tasks was reconciling the biblical account of the divine creation with Aristotle's teaching that the universe was eternal. Even in this early clash between science and religion, creationism was the sticking point. Thomas Aquinas (1225–1274), whose philosophy is called **Thomism,** most effectively resolved the apparent conflict between faith and philosophy. A Dominican friar, Aquinas spent most of his career developing a school system for the Dominicans in Italy, but he also spent two short periods teaching at the University of Paris.

Aquinas avoided distracting controversies and academic disputes to concentrate on his two great summaries of human knowledge—the *Summary of the Catholic Faith Against the Gentiles* (1261) and the *Summary of Theology* (1265–1274). In both of these massive scholastic works, reason fully confirmed Christian faith. Encyclopedias of knowledge, both books rigorously examined whole fields through dialectical reasoning.

Building on the works of Averroës, Aquinas solved the problem of reconciling philosophy and religion by drawing a distinction between *natural truth* and *revealed truth*. For Aquinas, natural truth meant the kinds of things anyone can know through the operation of human reason. Revealed truth referred to the things that one can know only through revelation, such as the doctrines of the Trinity and the incarnation of Christ. Aquinas argued that these two kinds of truths could not possibly contradict one another because both came from God. Apparent contradictions could be accommodated by an understanding of a higher truth. On the issue of Creation, for example, Aquinas argued that Aristotle's understanding of the eternal universe was inferior to the higher revealed truth of the Bible that God created the universe in seven days.

The most influential of the scholastic thinkers, Aquinas asserted that to achieve religious truth one should start with faith and then use reason to reach conclusions. He was the first to understand theology systematically in this way, and in doing so he raised a storm of opposition among Christians threatened by the difficulty of philosophical thinking. The theological faculties in universities at first prohibited Aquinas's writings. Nevertheless, his method remains crucial for Catholic theology to this day.

Just as scholastic theologians looked to ancient Greek philosophy as a guide to reason, jurists revived ancient Roman law, especially at the universities of Bologna and Pavia in Italy. In the law faculties, students learned the legal work of the Emperor Justinian—the text of the *Corpus Juris Civilis*, together with the commentaries on it. The systematic approach of Roman law provided a way to make the legal system less arbitrary for judges, lawyers, bureaucrats, and advisers to kings and popes. Laws had long consisted of a contradictory mess of municipal regulations, Germanic customs, and feudal precepts. Under Roman law, judges had to justify their verdicts according to prescribed standards of evidence and procedure. The revival of Roman law in the twelfth century made possible the legal system that still guides most of continental Europe.

Courtly Love

In addition to the developments in philosophy, theology, and the law, the Twelfth-Century Renaissance included a remarkable literary output of romances in the vernacular languages, the tongues spoken in everyday life. Poets called **troubadours** wrote romances—poems of love, meant to be sung to music—which reflected an entirely new sensibility about the relationships between men and women. Their literary movement is called **courtly love** or chivalry. The troubadours composed their poems in Provençal, one of the languages of southern France, and the princely courts of southern France provided the first audience. These graciously elegant poems show influences from Arabic love poetry and from Muslim mystical literature in which the soul, depicted as feminine, seeks her masculine God/lover. The troubadours secularized this theme of religious union by portraying the ennobling possibilities of the love between a woman and a man. In so doing, they popularized the idea of romantic love, one of the most powerful concepts in all of Western history, an ideal that still dominates popular culture to this day.

The ideal male depicted in courtly love poems was the knight-errant, a warrior who roamed in search of adventure. He was poor and free of ties to home and family, a man who lived a life of perfect freedom, but whose virtue led him to do the right thing. Knights took vows in the name of ladies, revealing that the courtly love ideal included a heavy dose of erotic desire. Besides self-denial, the most persistent chivalric fantasy was the motif of the young hero who liberates a virgin, either from a dragon or from a rioting mob of peasants.

The courtly love poems of the troubadours idealized women. The male troubadours, such as Chrétien de Troyes (1135–1183), placed women on a pedestal and treated men as the "love vassals" of beloved women to whom they owed loyalty and service. Female troubadours, such as Marie de France (dates unknown), did not place women on a pedestal but idealized emotionally honest and open relationships between lovers. From southern France, courtly love spread to Germany and elsewhere throughout Europe.

The Center of Medieval Culture: The Great Cathedrals

When tourists visit European cities today, they usually want to see the cathedrals. Mostly built between 1050 and 1300, these imposing structures symbolize the soaring ambitions and imaginations of their largely unknown builders. During the great medieval building boom, cities built hundreds of new cathedrals and thousands of other churches, sparing no expense and reflecting the latest experimental techniques in architectural engineering and artistic fashion. These buildings became multimedia centers for the arts—incorporating architecture, sculpture, stained glass, and painting and providing a setting for the performance of music and drama. The medieval cathedrals took decades, sometimes centuries, to build at great cost and sacrifice.

The **Romanesque** style of cathedral-building spread throughout western Europe during the eleventh century and the first half of the twelfth century because the master masons who understood sophisticated stone construction techniques traveled from one building site to another, bringing with them a uniform style. The principal innovation of the Romanesque was the arched stone roofs, which were more aesthetically pleasing and less vulnerable to fire than the flat roofs they replaced. The rounded arches of these stone roofs, called barrel vaults, looked like the inside of a barrel. Romanesque churches employed transepts, which fashioned the church into the shape of a cross if viewed from above, the vantage point of God. The high stone vaults of Romanesque churches and cathedrals required the support of massive stone pillars and thick walls. As a result, windows were small slits that imitated the slit windows of castles.

The religious experience of worshiping in a Romanesque cathedral had an intimate, almost familiar quality to it. In such a building, God

FLYING BUTTRESSES OF CHARTRES CATHEDRAL

The flying buttress did more than hold up the thin walls of Gothic cathedrals. The buttress created an almost lacelike appearance on the outside of the building, magnifying the sense of mystery evoked by the style.

ROMANESQUE CATHEDRAL ARCHITECTURE
The rounded arches, the massive columns, the barrel vaults in the ceilings, and the small windows were characteristic of the Romanesque style. Compare the massiveness of this interior with the Gothic style of the Abbey Church of St. Denis in the next illustration.

Source: Dagli Orti/Picture Desk, Inc./Kobal Collection

GOTHIC VAULTS
The delicately ribbed ceiling vaults and vast expanses of stained glass in the Abbey Church of St. Denis, France, contrast with the heavy barrel vaults of the Romanesque Cathedral in Vezelay.

became a fellow townsman, an associate in the grand new project of making cities habitable and comfortable.

During the late twelfth and thirteenth centuries, the **Gothic** style replaced the Romanesque. The innovation of this style was the ribbed vault and pointed arches, which superseded the barrel vault of the Romanesque. These narrow pointed arches drew the viewer's eye upward toward God and gave the building the appearance of weightlessness that symbolized the Christian's uplifting reach for heaven. The neighborly solidity of the Romanesque style disappeared for a mystical appreciation of God's utter otherness, the supreme divinity far

above mortal men and women. The Gothic style also introduced the innovation of the flying buttress, an arched construction on the outside of the walls that redistributed the weight of the roof. This innovation allowed for thin walls pierced by windows much bigger than possible with Romanesque construction techniques.

The result was stunning. The stonework of a Gothic cathedral became a skeleton to support massive expanses of stained glass, transforming the interior spaces into a mystical haven from the outside world. At different times of the day, the multicolored windows converted sunlight into an ever-changing light show that offered sparkling hints of the secret truths of God's Creation. The light that passed through these windows symbolized the light of God. The windows themselves contained scenes that were an encyclopedia of medieval knowledge and lore. In addition to Bible stories and the lives of saints, these windows depicted common people at their trades, animals, plants, and natural wonders. Stained-glass windows celebrated not only the promise of salvation, but all the wonders of God's creation. They drew worshipers out of the busy cities in which they lived and worked toward the perfect realm of the divine.

In France, Germany, Italy, Spain, and England, cities made enormous financial sacrifices to construct new Gothic cathedrals during the economic boom years of the thirteenth century. Because costs were so high, many cathedrals, such as the one in Siena, Italy, remained unfinished, but even the incomplete ones became vital symbols of local identity.

CONCLUSION

Asserting Western Culture

During the twelfth and thirteenth centuries, western Europe matured into its own self-confident identity. Less a semi-barbarian backwater than it had been even in the time of Charlemagne, western Europe cultivated modes of thought that revealed an almost limitless capacity for creative renewal and critical self-examination. That capacity, first evident during the Twelfth-Century Renaissance, especially in scholasticism, is what has most distinguished the West ever since. These critical methods repeatedly caused alarm among some believers. However, this tendency to question basic assumptions is among the greatest achievements of Western civilization. The western European university system, which was based on teaching methods of critical inquiry, differed from the educational institutions in other cultures, such as

Byzantium or Islam, that were devoted to passing on received knowledge. This distinctive critical spirit connects the cultures of the ancient, medieval, and modern West.

KEY TERMS

agricultural revolution	circuit court
manor	grand jury
serfs	trial by jury
communes	Magna Carta
Cluny	English Parliament
simony	scholasticism
lay investiture	Twelfth-Century
Investiture Controversy	Renaissance
excommunication	Thomism
curia	troubadours
interdict	courtly love
friars	Romanesque
Eucharist	Gothic
transubstantiation	

CHAPTER QUESTIONS

1. How was medieval western European economy and society organized around manors and cities? (page 300)
2. How did the Catholic Church consolidate its hold over the Latin West? (page 306)
3. How did the western European monarchies strengthen themselves? (page 319)
4. What made western European culture distinctive? (page 322)

TAKING IT FURTHER

1. What was the role of theology and philosophy in allowing the West to assert itself more forcefully?
2. Why was kingship the most effective form of political organization in the Middle Ages?
3. By the end of the thirteenth century what distinguished Christian from Muslim culture?

✓━[Practice on MyHistoryLab

The Medieval West in Crisis

■ A Time of Death ■ A Cold Wind from the East ■ Economic Depression
and Social Turmoil ■ An Age of Warfare ■ A Troubled Church
and the Demand for Religious Comfort ■ The Culture of Loss

THE FOURTEENTH CENTURY DAWNED WITH A CHILL. IN 1303 AND THEN again during 1306–1307, the Baltic Sea froze over. No one had ever heard of that happening before, and the freezings foretold worse disasters. The cold spread beyond its normal winter season, arriving earlier in the autumn and staying later into the summer. Then it started to rain and did not let up. The Caspian Sea began to rise, flooding villages along its shores. In the summer of 1314 all across Europe, crops rotted in sodden fields. The meager harvest came late, precipitating a surge in prices for farm produce and forcing King Edward II of England to impose price controls. But capping prices did not grow more food.

In 1315 the situation got worse. In England during that year, the price of wheat rose 800 percent. Preachers compared the ceaseless rains to the great flood in the Bible, and floods did come, overwhelming dikes in the Netherlands and England, washing away entire towns in Germany, turning fields into lakes in France. Everywhere crops failed.

Things got much worse. Torrential rains fell again in 1316, and for the third straight year the crops failed, creating the most severe famine in recorded European history. The effects were most dramatic in the far north. In Scandinavia agriculture almost disappeared, in Iceland peasants abandoned farming and turned to fishing and herding sheep, and in Greenland the European settlers began to die out. Already malnourished, the people of Europe became susceptible to disease and famine. Desperate people resorted to desperate options. They ate cats, rats, insects, reptiles, animal dung, and tree leaves. Stories spread that some ate

their own children. In Poland the starving were said to cut down criminals from the gallows for food.

By the 1340s, nearly all of Europe west of Poland was gripped by a seemingly endless cycle of disease and famine. Then came the deadliest epidemic in European history, the Black Death, which killed at least one-third of the total population. The economy collapsed. Trade disappeared. Industry shriveled. Hopeless peasants and urban workers revolted against their masters, demanding relief for their families. Neither state nor church could provide it. The two great medieval kingdoms of France and England became locked in a struggle that depleted royal treasuries and wasted the aristocracy in a series of clashes that historians call the Hundred Years' War. The popes left the dangerous streets of Rome for Avignon, France, where they were obliged to extort money to survive. After the pope returned to Rome, a group of French cardinals refused to go and elected a second pope, leading to the Great Schism when Europe was divided by allegiances to two different popes.

During the twelfth and thirteenth centuries the West had asserted itself against Islam through the Crusades and spread Catholic Christianity to the far corners of Europe. During the fourteenth and early fifteenth centuries, however, the West drew into itself due to war, epidemics, and conflicts with the Mongol and Ottoman Empires. As an additional shock, the Byzantine Empire, once the bastion of Orthodox Christianity, fell to the Muslim armies of the Ottomans. This chapter explores these encounters with death and turmoil, and asks this question: How did the death and

THE OTTOMAN SULTAN

In 1478 the Venetian painter, Gentile Bellini, went to Constantinople to paint the portrait of Sultan Mehmet II, who had conquered the Byzantine Empire. Hence, encounters between the Christian Europe and the Turks became one of the most important themes in the history of West.

turmoil of fourteenth- and fifthteenth-century Europe transform the identity of the West?

A TIME OF DEATH

■ **What caused the deaths of so many Europeans?**

The magnitude of Europe's demographic crisis is evident from the raw numbers. In 1300 the population of Europe was about 74 million—roughly 15 percent of its current population. Population size can be an elementary measure of the success of an economy to keep people alive, and by this measure Europe had been very successful up to about 1300. It had approximately doubled its population over the previous 300 years. After the 1340s, however, Europe's ability to sustain its population evaporated. Population fell to just 52 million. The demographic crisis of the fourteenth century was the greatest natural disaster in Western civilization since the epidemics of antiquity. How did it happen?

Famine

Widespread famine, caused by a crisis in agricultural production, began during the decade of 1310–1320. The agricultural revolution of the eleventh century had made available more food and more nutritious food, triggering the growth of the population during the Middle Ages. During the twelfth and thirteenth centuries, vast tracks of virgin forests were cleared for farming, especially in eastern Europe. After all the good bottomland was cleared, farmers moved to clear the more marginal land on hills and mountainsides. These clearings created soil erosion that contributed to the devastating floods of the 1310s. Thus, human actions facilitated the ecological catastrophe. By the fourteenth century no more virgin land was available for clearing, which meant that a still-growing population tried to survive on a fixed amount of farming land. Because of the limitations of medieval agriculture, the ability of farmers to produce food could not keep up with unchecked population growth. The propensity for famine was especially acute in heavily populated western Europe. In eastern Europe the lower population and better balance between agriculture, animal husbandry, and fishing meant the population remained better fed and less susceptible to famine and disease.

At the same time there was probably a change in climate, known as the "Little Ice Age." The mean annual temperatures dropped just enough to make it impossible to grow crops in the more northerly parts of Europe and at high elevations such as the Alps. Before the fourteenth century, for example, grapes were grown in England to produce wine, but with the decline in temperatures, the grape vineyards ceased to produce. Growing grapes in England became possible again only with global warming in the twenty-first century. The result of the Little Ice Age was twofold. First, there was less land available for cultivation as it became impossible to grow crops in marginal areas. Second, a harsher climate shortened the growing season, which meant that even where crops could still grow, they were less abundant.

The imbalance between food production and population set off a dreadful cycle of famine and disease. Insufficient food resulted in either malnutrition or starvation. Those who suffered from prolonged malnutrition were particularly susceptible to epidemic diseases, such as typhus, cholera, and dysentery. By 1300, children of the poor faced the probability of extreme hunger once or twice during the course of their childhood. In Pistoia, Italy, priests kept the *Book of the Dead*, which recorded the pattern: famine in 1313, famine in 1328–1329, famine and epidemic in 1339–1340 that killed one-quarter of the population, famine in 1346, famine and epidemic in 1347, and then the killing hammer blow—the Black Death in 1348 (see **Map 11.1**).

The Black Death

Following on the heels of the Great Famine, the **Black Death** arrived in Europe in the spring of 1348 with brutal force. In the lovely hilltop city of Siena, Italy, all industry stopped, carters refused to bring produce and cooking oil in from the countryside, and on June 2 the daily records of the city council and civil courts abruptly ended, as if the city fathers and judges had all died or rushed home in panic. A local chronicler, Agnolo di Tura, wrote down his memories of those terrible days:

> Father abandoned child, wife husband, one brother another; for this illness seemed to strike through the breath and sight. And so they died. And none could be found to bury the dead for money or friendship. Members of a household brought their dead to a ditch as best they could, without priest, without divine offices. Nor did the [death] bell sound. And in many places in Siena great pits were dug and piled deep with the multitude of dead....And I, Agnolo di Tura, called the Fat, buried my five children with my own hands. And there were also those who were so sparsely covered with earth that the dogs dragged them forth and devoured many bodies throughout the city.[1]

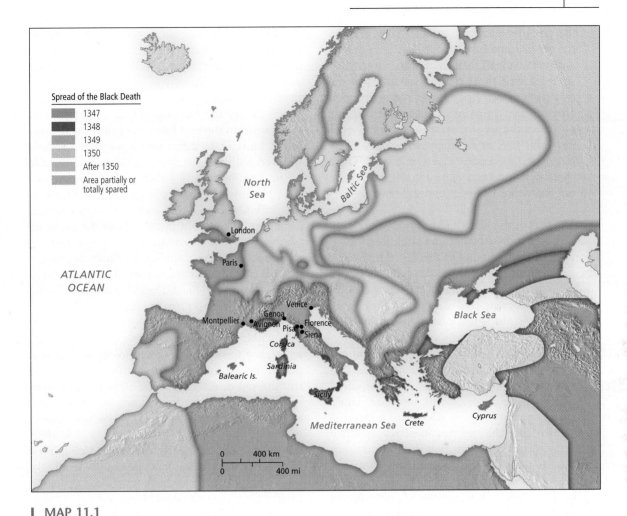

MAP 11.1

Spread of the Black Death

After the Black Death first appeared in the ports of Italy in 1348, it spread relentlessly throughout most of Europe, killing at least 20 million people in Europe alone.

During the summer of 1348 more than half of the Sienese died. The construction of Siena's great cathedral, planned to be the largest in the world, stopped and was never resumed due to a lack of workers. In fact, Siena, once among the most prosperous cities in Europe, never fully recovered and lost its economic preeminence.

No disease left more distinctive and disturbing signs on the body than the Black Death. According to one quite typical contemporary description: "all the matter which exuded from their bodies let off an unbearable stench; sweat, excrement, spittle, breath, so fetid as to be overpowering; urine turbid, thick, black or red...."[2] In the introduction to *The Decameron,* Giovanni Boccaccio described what he had witnessed of the symptoms:

In the year 1348 after the fruitful incarnation of the Son of God, that most beautiful of Italian cities, noble Florence, was attacked by deadly plague....The symptoms...began both in men and women with certain swellings in the groin or under the armpit. They grew to the size of a small apple or an egg, more or less, and were vulgarly called tumors. In a short space of time these tumors spread from the two parts named [to] all over the body. Soon after this the symptoms changed and black or purple spots appeared on the arms or thighs or any other part of the body, sometimes a few large ones, sometimes many little ones. These spots were a certain sign of death, just as the original tumor had been and still remained.[3]

The fear of the Black Death and the inability to discern its causes focused the attention of contemporaries on the bodies of the sick. Almost any discoloration of the skin or glandular swellings could be interpreted as a sign of the Black Death's presence. Physicians and surgeons, of course, were the experts in reading the signs of the body for disease. As victims and their distraught families soon discovered, however, physicians did not really know what the glandular swellings and discolorations of the skin meant. Boccaccio reported that "No doctor's advice, no medicine could overcome or alleviate this disease.... Either the disease was such that no treatment was possible or the doctors were so ignorant that they did not know what caused it, and consequently could not administer the proper remedy."[4]

In the absence of an alternative, government officials resorted to quarantines to stop the spread of the disease. They locked up infected households for 40 days, which was especially hard on the poor who needed to work to eat. To maintain quarantines and bury the dead, city councils created public health bureaucracies, complete with their own staff physicians, grave diggers, and police force. The extraordinary powers granted to the public health authorities helped expand the authority of the state over its citizens in the name of pursuing the common good. The expansion of governmental bureaucracy that distinguished modern from medieval states was partly the result of the need to keep human bodies under surveillance and control—a need that began with the Black Death.

Experts still dispute the cause of the Black Death, but there is growing doubt about the

validity of the traditional theory that the bubonic plague was the most likely culprit. The dispute about the cause of the Black Death is a revealing example of the difficulty of interpreting evidence from the distant past. According to the traditional theory the bubonic plague can appear in two forms. In the first form it is usually transmitted to humans by a flea that has bitten a rodent infected with the *Yersinia pestis* bacillus, usually a rat. The infected flea then bites a human victim. The infection enters the bloodstream, causing inflamed swellings called buboes (hence, "bubonic" plague) in the glands of the groin or armpit, internal bleeding, and discoloration of the skin, symptoms similar to those Boccaccio described, which is why some historians have thought that the "Black Death" was the bubonic plague. The second form of plague was the pneumonic type, which infected the lungs and spread by coughing and sneezing. Either form could be lethal, but the complex epidemiology of bubonic plague meant that the first form could not be transmitted directly from one person to another. According to the traditional theory, after being infected, many victims probably developed pneumonia as a secondary symptom, which then spread quickly to others. As one contemporary physician put it, one person could seemingly infect the entire world. In some cases, the doctor caught the illness and died before the patient did.

The visitations of the bubonic plague in the late nineteenth and twentieth centuries, which have been observed by physicians trained in modern medicine, formed that basis for the traditional theory linking the Black Death to the bubonic plague. Alexandre Yersin discovered the bubonic plague bacillus in Hong Kong in 1894 and traced its spread through rats and fleas. For more than a century, most historians and epidemiologists have thought that something similar to this must have happened in 1348.

However, there are problems with this traditional theory. The Black Death spread much more rapidly from person to person and place to place than the bubonic plague does in modern epidemics. For example, rats do not travel very far very fast, and in modern examples the bubonic plague has rarely spread more than twelve miles per year. In 1348, however, the Black Death traveled as far in a day as rat-borne bubonic plague does in a year. Many of the reported symptoms from the fourteenth century do not match the symptoms observed in modern plague victims. Moreover, the Black Death, unlike the bubonic plague, seems to have had a long incubation period before the first symptoms appeared. Because of the long incubation, those who had the disease transmitted it to others before they knew they were sick, which helps explain why the disease was so lethal despite attempts to quarantine those afflicted with it. The most recent research suggests that the Black Death may have been caused by an unidentified virus that produced bleeding similar to the Ebola virus that has appeared in Africa in recent years.

In Europe about 20 million people died, with the deaths usually clustered in a matter of a few weeks or months after the disease first appeared in a particular locale. The death toll, however, varied erratically from place to place, ranging from about 20 to 90 percent. So great was the toll in southern and western Europe that entire villages were depopulated or abandoned. Paris lost half its population, Florence as much as four-fifths, and Venice two-thirds. In the seaport of Trapani, Italy, everyone apparently died or left. Living in enclosed spaces, monks and nuns were especially hard hit. All the Franciscans of Carcassonne and Marseille in France died. In Montpellier, France, only 7 of the 140 Dominicans survived. In isolated Kilkenny, Ireland, Brother John Clyn found himself left alone among his dead brothers, and he began to write a diary of what he had witnessed because he was afraid he might be the last person left alive in the world. (See *Different Voices* in this chapter.)

THE TRIUMPH OF DEATH

A detail from Francesco Traini's fresco, *The Triumph of Death,* in the Camposanto, Pisa, ca. 1350. Frescoes such as this reflect the horror of the Black Death.

Source: Cemetery, Pisa, Italy/Canali PhotoBank, Milan/SuperStock

DIFFERENT VOICES THE BLACK DEATH FORETELLS THE END OF THE WORLD

Christianity had a long tradition, rooted in the Bible, of prophecies about the end of the world. The most common theology of the end is called millenarianism, the belief that there would be definitive signs in human events of the coming of the end. These prophecies took various forms. One form predicted the reign of Antichrist, who would rule for a 1,000 years before the second coming of Christ. The prophetic tradition encouraged people to look for signs of the Antichrist, and the appearance of the Black Death seemed to be one of those signs. Another form popular in Germany depicted the return from the dead of the Emperor Frederick II, who would cleanse the earth in preparation for Christ's return. The first document reports rumors from Rome in 1349 sent to a friar in England.

There are various prophets in the regions around Rome, whose identity is still secret, who have been making up stories like this for years. They say that this very year, 1349, Antichrist is aged ten, and is a most beautiful child, so well educated in all branches of knowledge that no one now living can equal him. And they also say that there is another boy, now aged twelve and living beyond the land of the Tartars [Mongols], who has been brought up as a Christian and that this is the one who will destroy the Saracens [Muslims] and become the greatest man in Christendom, but his power will be quickly brought to an end by the coming of Antichrist.

These prophets also say, among a great deal else, that the present pope will come to a violent end, and that after his death there will be more revolutions in the world than there have ever been before. But after that another pope will arise, a good and just man, who will appoint God-fearing cardinals, and there will be almost total peace in his time. And after him there will be no other pope, but Antichrist will come and reveal himself.

Source: *The Black Death* trans. and ed. Rosemary Horrox (Manchester and New York: Manchester University Press, 1994), 154. Reprinted by permission.

The second source by Johann von Winterthur, a Franciscan friar, reports events from the time of the Black Death in 1348. Winterthur is decidedly skeptical of the millenarian prophecies.

In these times it was freely spread abroad among men of various races, indeed of every race, that the Emperor Frederick II...would return in the full might of his power to reform the corrupt church completely. The men who believed this also added that it was inevitable that he would return, even if he had been cut into a thousand pieces, or burnt to ashes, because it had been foretold that this would happen and it could not possibly be otherwise....After resuming a power more just and a rule more glorious than before, he will cross the seas with a large army and will resign his power on the Mount of Olives or at the dry tree [that is in Jerusalem].

I do not cease to be amazed by this false belief; that anyone could hope for or believe in the revival of a man dead 80 years, who was emperor for 30 years. The men who hold this false belief have been deceived just like the Jews, who believe that King David will be raised up by the Lord to reign again over Israel as he did in the past. They believe it on the basis that the Lord, speaking through the prophets, said: "I will raise up my

The Black Death kept coming back. In the Mediterranean basin where the many port cities formed a network of contagion, the plague reappeared between 1348 and 1721 in one port or another about every 20 years. Some of the later outbreaks were just as lethal as the initial 1348 catastrophe. Florence lost half its population in 1400; Venice lost a third in 1575–1577 and a third again in 1630–1631.

Less exposed than the Mediterranean, northern Europe suffered less and saw the last of the dread disease in the Great Plague of London of 1665–1666. Most of Poland escaped without any signs of the disease, and east-central Europe in general was far less severely hit than western Europe, probably because the sparse population made the spread of contagion less likely.

FLAGELLANTS

During the Black Death many people believed God was punishing them for their sins. In order to expiate those sins some young men practiced flagellation, a practice once reserved for monks who whipped themselves as a form of penance. In order to control the practice among laymen, confraternities were formed in which collective flagellation was organized. The flagellants depicted here wear the white robes of a confraternity and cover their faces to remain anonymous.

Source: Dagli Orti/Picture Desk, Inc./Kobal Collection

faithful servant David."...But these and other similar authorities are to be understood as referring to Christ or to another of the race of David.

Source: *The Black Death* translated and edited by Rosemary Horrox (Manchester and New York:

Manchester University Press, 1994), 155–156. Reprinted by permission.

For Discussion

1. Why might people want to believe in these prophecies? How does Winterthur go about refuting them?

A COLD WIND FROM THE EAST

■ How did forces outside Europe, in particular the Mongol and Ottoman Empires, influence conditions in the West?

During the same period the West was suffering from deadly microbes, it also faced the mounted warriors of the distant Mongol tribes, whose relentless conquests drove them from Outer Mongolia across central Asia toward Europe. The Mongols and Turks were nomadic peoples from central Asia. Closely related culturally but speaking different languages, these peoples exerted an extraordinary influence on world history despite a rather small population. **Map 11.2** shows the place of origin of the Mongols and Turks and where

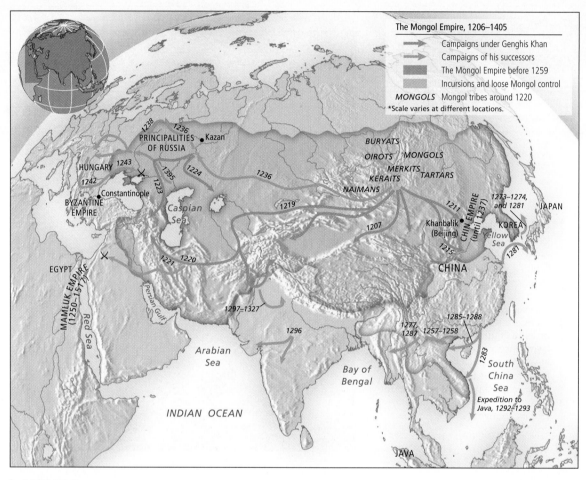

The Mongol Empire, 1206–1405

Campaigns under Genghis Khan
Campaigns of his successors
The Mongol Empire before 1259
Incursions and loose Mongol control
MONGOLS Mongol tribes around 1220
Scale varies at different locations.

PRINCIPALITIES OF RUSSIA
Kazan
1238
1236
HUNGARY 1243
1242
Constantinople
BYZANTINE EMPIRE
1224
1395
1236
Caspian Sea
1219
BURYATS
OIROTS MONGOLS
MERKITS
KERAITS TARTARS
NAIMANS
1211
CHIN EMPIRE (until 1237)
1273–1274, and 1281
JAPAN
Khanbalik (Beijing)
KOREA
Yellow Sea
1207
1215
1281
CHINA
EGYPT
MAMLUK EMPIRE (1250–1517?)
Red Sea
Persian Gulf
1221
1220
1297–1327
1296
Arabian Sea
Bay of Bengal
1277, 1287
1257–1258
1285–1288
1283
South China Sea
Expedition to Java, 1292–1293
INDIAN OCEAN
JAVA

MAP 11.2
The Mongol Empire, 1206–1405

The Mongols and Turks were nomadic peoples who spread out across Asia and Europe from their homeland in the region of Mongolia. The Mongol armies eventually conquered vast territories from Korea to the borders of Hungary and from the Arctic Ocean to the Arabian Sea.

they spread across a wide belt of open, relatively flat steppe land stretching from the Yellow Sea between China and the Korean peninsula to the Baltic Sea and the Danube River basin in Europe. Virtually without forests and interrupted only by a few easily traversed mountain ranges, the broad Eurasian steppes have been the great migration highway of world history from prehistoric times to the medieval caravans and the modern trans-Siberian railway.

As the Mongols and Turks charged westward out of central Asia on their fast ponies, they put pressure on the kingdoms of the West. Mongol armies hobbled Kievan Rus, and Turks destroyed Byzantium. As a consequence, the potential Orthodox allies in the East of the Catholic Christian West were weakened or eliminated. Converts to Islam, the Ottomans pushed into the Balkans. In contrast to the era of the twelfth-century Crusades, Catholic Europe found itself on the defensive against a powerful Muslim foe.

The Mongol Invasions

Whereas the Europeans became successful sailors because of their extensive coastlines and close proximity to the sea, the Mongols became roving horsemen because they needed to migrate several times a year in search of grass and water for their ponies and livestock. They also became highly skilled warriors because they competed persistently with other tribes for access to the grasslands.

Between 1206 and 1258, the Mongols transformed themselves from a collection of disunited tribes with a vague ethnic affinity to create the most extensive empire in the history of the world. The epic rise of the previously obscure Mongols was the work of a Mongol chief named Temujin, who succeeded in uniting the various quarreling tribes and transforming them into a world power. In 1206 Temujin was proclaimed Genghis Khan (ca. 1162–1227)

("Very Mighty King"), the supreme ruler over all the Mongols. Genghis broke through the Great Wall of China, destroyed the Jin (Chin) empire in northern China, and occupied Beijing. His cavalry swept across Asia as far as Azerbaijan, Georgia, northern Persia, and Kievan Rus. Genghis Khan ordered that after his death his empire would be divided into four principalities or khanates for his sons and grandsons. They continued Mongol expansion. Eventually, Mongol armies conquered territories that stretched from Korea to Hungary and from the Arctic Ocean to the Arabian Sea.

The Mongol success was accomplished through a highly disciplined military organization, tactics that relied on extremely mobile cavalry forces, and a sophisticated intelligence network. During the campaign against the Rus in the winter of 1223, the Mongol cavalry moved with lightning speed across frozen rivers. Although the Rus forces

MONGOL HORSEMAN

Unlike the fourteenth-century European representations of the Mongols, this contemporary Chinese illustration accurately depicts the appearance, dress, and equipment of a Mongol Archer on horseback.

ENCOUNTERS AND TRANSFORMATIONS

The Silk Road

Nothing better facilitated encounters between East and West than the Silk Road. The label actually refers to a network of caravan trails connecting China with western Asia and Europe through the Taklimakan, one of the most inhospitable deserts on earth. Travelers had little choice but to pick their way from oasis to oasis across central Asia. On the eastern and western edges of this vast territory the civilizations of China and the West developed, and the Silk Road connected them.

Many highly valuable commodities were transported along these routes besides silk, including ivory, gold, jewels, iron, furs, and ceramics (hence, the term "fine China" for the most precious ceramics). None of these commodities, however, captured the imagination of the West as much as silk, which had been transported from China across the Silk Road since Roman times (see Chapter 6). The importance of the Silk Road required peaceful political conditions to thrive, lest caravans be plundered. Perhaps the greatest era for the Silk Road came under the Chinese T'ang Dynasty (618–907), which provided stability that allowed commerce to flower along the road. After the T'ang dynasty collapsed, the road was unsafe until the Mongol invasions in the thirteenth century.

The Mongol invasions completely altered the composition of Asia and much of eastern Europe—economically, politically, and ethnically. Once the Mongols had conquered new territories, they established the Mongol Peace by reopening the Silk Road across the Asian steppes, making trans-Eurasian trade possible and guaranteeing the safety of merchants. Thanks to the Mongols, European Christians began to traverse the Silk Road to China and to encounter directly the civilizations of the East. The Mongols were tolerant of religious diversity and welcomed the first Christian missionaries into China. A Roman Catholic archbishopric was founded in Beijing in 1307.

The most famous of the many merchants who traversed the Silk Road during the Mongol Peace were the Venetians from the Polo family, including Marco Polo, who arrived at the court of the Great Khan in China in 1275. Marco Polo's book about his travels offers a vivid and often remarkably perceptive account of the Mongol Empire during the Mongol Peace. It also illustrates better than any other source the cultural engagement of the Christian West with the Mongol East during the late thirteenth century. Although Marco Polo was a merchant who traveled to make a profit, his book brought a great store of cultural information, some accurate, some fanciful that stimulated the western imagination about the East. Perhaps most revealing were his discussions of religion. Marco classified peoples according to their religion and evaluated religions with the eye of a western European Catholic. He was harshest about Muslims, but seemed more tolerant of "idolaters," that is Buddhists and Hindus, whose practices he found intriguing. He also reported on magical practices and reports of miracles. Because of the popularity of his book, Marco Polo's views of Asia became the principle source of knowledge in the West about the East until the sixteenth century.

For Discussion

What were the advantages and disadvantages of the Mongol Peace for the West?

CHRONOLOGY: THE MONGOLS

1206–1227	Reign of Genghis Khan
1206–1258	Mongol armies advance undefeated across Eurasia
1260	Defeat in Syria of Mongols by Mamluks of Egypt
1369–1405	Reign of Tamerlane

outnumbered the Mongol armies and had superior armor, they were crushed in every encounter with the Mongols.

The Mongol armies employed clever tactics. First, they unnerved enemy soldiers with a hail of arrows. Then they would appear to retreat, only to draw the enemy into false confidence before the Mongol horsemen delivered a deadly final blow. European chroniclers at the time tried to explain their many defeats at the hands of the Mongols by reporting that the Mongol "hordes" had overwhelming numbers, but evidence clearly shows that their victories were the result not of superior numbers, but of superior discipline and the sophistication of the Mongol intelligence network.

Mongol power climaxed in 1260. In that year the Mongols suffered a crushing defeat in Syria at the hands of the Mamluk rulers of Egypt, an event that ended the Mongol reputation for invincibility. Conflicts and succession disputes among the various Mongol tribes made them vulnerable to rivals and to rebellion from their unhappy subjects. The Mongol Empire did not disappear overnight, but its various successor khanates never recaptured the dynamic unity forged by Genghis Khan. During the fourteenth century the Mongol Peace sputtered to an end.

In the wake of these upheavals, a warrior of Mongol descent known as Tamerlane (r. 1369–1405) created an army composed of Mongols, Turks, and Persians, which challenged the established Mongol khanates. Tamerlane's conquests rivaled those of Genghis Khan, but with very different results. His armies pillaged the rich cities that supplied the caravan routes. Thus, in his attempt to monopolize the lucrative trans-Eurasian trade, Tamerlane largely destroyed it. The collapse of the Mongol Peace broke the thread of commerce across Eurasia and stimulated the European search for alternative routes to China that ultimately resulted in the voyages of Christopher Columbus in 1492. (See *Encounters and Transformations* in this chapter.)

The Rise of the Ottoman Turks

The Mongol armies were never very large, so the Mongols had always augmented their numbers with Turkish tribes. The result was that outside Mongolia, Turks gradually absorbed the Mongols. Turkish replaced Mongolian as the dominant language, and the Turks took over the government of the central Asian empires that had been scraped together by the Mongol conquests. In contrast to the Mongols, many of whom remained Buddhists, the Turks became Muslims and created an exceptionally dynamic, expansionist society of their own (see **Map 11.3**).

Among the Turkish peoples, the most successful state builders were the Ottomans. Named for Osman I (r. 1281–1326), who brought it to prominence, the Ottoman dynasty endured for more than 600 years, until 1924. The nucleus of the Ottoman state was a small principality in Anatolia (a portion of present-day Turkey), which in the early fourteenth century began to expand at the expense of its weaker neighbors, including the Byzantine Empire. The Ottoman state was built not on national, linguistic, or ethnic unity, but on a purely dynastic network of personal and military loyalties to the Ottoman prince, called the sultan. Thus, the vitality of the empire depended on the energy of the individual sultans. The Ottomans thought of themselves as *ghazis*,

MAP 11.3

The Ottoman Empire

The Ottoman state expanded from a small principality in Anatolia, which is south of the Black Sea. From there the Ottomans spread eastward into Kurdistan and Armenia. In the West they captured all of Greece and much of the Balkan peninsula.

warriors for Islam devoted to destroying polytheists, including Christians. (To some Muslims, the Christian belief in the Trinity and veneration of numerous saints demonstrated that Christians were not true monotheists.) During the fourteenth century, incessant Ottoman guerilla actions gradually chipped away at the Byzantine frontier.

The Byzantine Empire in the middle of the thirteenth century was emerging from a period of domination by Frankish knights and Venetian merchants who had conquered Constantinople during the Fourth Crusade in 1204. In 1261, the

Byzantine emperor, Michael VIII Palaeologus (r. 1260–1282), recaptured the great city. The revived Byzantine Empire, however, was a pale vestige of what it once had been, and the Palaeologi emperors desperately sought military assistance from western Europe to defend themselves from the Ottomans. Dependent on mercenary armies and divided by civil wars, the Byzantines offered only pathetic resistance to the all-conquering Ottomans.

From their base in Anatolia, the Ottomans raided far and wide, launching pirate fleets into the Aegean and gradually encircling Constantinople after they crossed over into Europe in 1308. By 1402 Ottoman territory had grown to 40 times its size a century earlier. During that century of conquests, the frontier between Christianity and Islam shifted. The former subjects of the Byzantines in the Balkans fell to the Ottoman Turks. Fragile Serbia, a bastion of Orthodox Christianity in the Balkans, broke under Ottoman pressure. First unified in the late twelfth century, Serbia established political independence from Byzantium and autonomy for the Serbian church. Although the Serbs had taken control over a number of former Byzantine provinces, they fell to the invincible Ottomans at the Battle of Kosovo in 1389. Lamenting the Battle of Kosovo has remained the bedrock of Serbian national identity to this day.

Serbia's western neighbors, the kingdoms of Bosnia and Herzegovina, deflated under Ottoman pressure during the late fifteenth century. Unlike Serbia, where most of the population remained loyal to the Serbian Orthodox Church, in Bosnia and Herzegovina the Serbian-speaking land-holding classes converted to Islam to preserve their property. The subjugated peasants, also Serbian-speaking, remained Orthodox Christians who turned over one-third of everything they raised to their Muslim lords, which created considerable resentment and religious tensions. The Ottomans allowed the Bosnians to keep their territorial identity and name, a unique situation among conquered provinces of the Ottoman Empire.

When Mehmed II, "The Conqueror" (r. 1451–1481), became the Ottoman sultan, he began to obliterate the last remnants of the Byzantine Empire. During the winter of 1451–1452, the sultan ordered the encirclement of Constantinople, a city that had once been the largest in the world but now was reduced from perhaps a million people to fewer than 50,000. The Ottoman siege strategy was to bombard Constantinople into submission with daily rounds from enormous cannons. The largest was a monster cannon, 29 feet long, that could shoot 1,200-pound stones. It required a crew of 200 soldiers and 60 oxen to handle it, and each firing generated so much heat

that it took hours to cool off before it could be fired again. The siege was a gargantuan task because the walls of Constantinople, which had been built, repaired, and improved over a period of a 1,000 years, were formidable. However, the new weapon of gunpowder artillery had rendered city walls a military anachronism. Brought from China by the Mongols, gunpowder had gradually revolutionized warfare. Breaching city walls in sieges was merely a matter of time as long as the heavy metal cannons could be dragged into position. Quarrels among the Christians also hampered the defense of Constantinople's walls. Toward the end, the Byzantine emperor was forced to melt down church treasures so "that from them coins should be struck and given to the soldiers, the sappers and the builders, who selfishly cared so little for the public welfare that they were refusing to go to their work unless they were first paid."[5]

The final assault came in May 1453 and lasted less than a day. When the city fell, the Ottoman army spent the day plundering, raping, and enslaving the populace. The last Byzantine emperor, Constantine XI, was never found amid the multitude of the dead. The fall of Constantinople ended the Christian Byzantine Empire, the continuous remnant of the ancient Roman Empire. But the idea of Rome was not so easily snuffed out. The first Ottoman sultans residing in Constantinople continued to be called "Roman emperors."

Although the western European princes had done little to save Byzantium, its demise shocked them. Now they were also vulnerable to the Ottoman onslaught. For the next 200 years the Ottomans used Constantinople as a base to threaten Christian Europe. Hungary and the eastern Mediterranean empire of Venice remained the last lines of defense for the West, and at various times in succeeding centuries the Ottomans launched expeditions against Europe, including two sieges of Vienna (1529 and 1683) and several invasions of Italy.

Hundreds of years of attacks by the Mongol and Ottoman Empires redrew the map of the West. Events in Europe did not and could not

CHRONOLOGY: THE CONQUESTS OF THE OTTOMAN TURKS

1281–1326	Reign of Osman I
1308	Ottoman Empire advances into Europe
1389	Battle of Kosovo; Serbia becomes vassal state of the Ottomans
1451–1481	Reign of Mehmed II, "The Conqueror"
1453	Fall of Constantinople and death of last Byzantine emperor

take place in isolation from the eastern pressures and influences. The Mongol conquest finished off Kievan Rus. Although Mongols burned down Moscow in the winter of 1238 and pillaged it in 1293, its remote, forested location offered some security from further attacks and occupation. As a result, Moscow and the Republic of Novgorod, which escaped the Mongol attacks entirely, replaced Kiev as the centers of power in what would become Russia. The Ottoman conquests also created a lasting Muslim presence within the borders of Europe, especially in Bosnia and Albania. In succeeding centuries Christian Europe and the Muslim Ottoman Empire would be locked in a deadly competitive embrace, but they also benefited from innumerable cultural exchanges and regular trade. Hostility between the two sides was recurrent but never inevitable and was broken by long periods of peaceful engagement. In fact, the Christian kingdoms of western Europe went to war far more often with one another than with the Turks.

ECONOMIC DEPRESSION AND SOCIAL TURMOIL

■ How did disturbances in the rudimentary global economy of the Middle Ages precipitate almost complete financial collapse and widespread social discontent in Europe?

Adding insult to injury in this time of famine, plague, and conquest, the West began to suffer a major economic depression during the fourteenth century. The economic boom fueled by the agricultural revolution and the revitalization of European cities during the eleventh century and the commercial prosperity of the twelfth and thirteenth centuries petered out in the fourteenth. The causes of this economic catastrophe were complex, but the consequences were obvious. Businesses went bust, banks collapsed, guilds were in turmoil, and workers rebelled.

At the same time, the effects of the depression were unevenly felt. Eastern Europe, which was less fully integrated into the international economy, fared better than western Europe. The economic conditions for many peasants actually improved because there was a labor shortage in the countryside due to the loss of population. Forced to pay their peasants more for their labor and crops, landlords saw their own fortunes decline. Finding it harder to pay the higher prices for food, urban workers probably suffered the most because their wages did not keep up with the cost of living.

The Collapse of International Trade and Banking

After the break up of the Mongol Empire and the conquests of Tamerlane, trade between Europe and Asia dwindled. The entire financial infrastructure of medieval Europe was tied to this international trade in luxury goods. The successful, entrepreneurial Italian merchants who dominated the luxury trade deposited their enormous profits in Italian banks. The Italian bankers lent money to the aristocracy and royalty of northern Europe to finance the purchases of exotic luxuries and to fight wars. The whole system was mutually reinforcing, but it was very fragile. With the disruption of supply sources for luxury goods, the financial networks of Europe collapsed, precipitating a major depression. By 1346, all the banks in Florence, the banking center of Europe, had crashed.

The luxury trade that brought exotic items from Asia to Europe represented only half of the economic equation. The other half was the raw materials and manufactured goods that Europeans sold in exchange, principally woolen cloth. The production of woolen cloth depended on a sophisticated economic system that connected shepherds in England, the Netherlands, and Spain with woolen cloth manufacturers in cities. The manufacture of cloth and other commodities was organized by **guilds,** which were professional associations devoted to protecting the special interests of a particular trade or craft and to monopolizing production and trade in the goods the guild produced.

There were two types of guilds. The first type, merchant guilds, attempted to monopolize the local market for a particular commodity. There were spice guilds, fruit and vegetable guilds, and apothecary guilds. The second type, craft guilds, regulated the manufacturing processes of artisans such as carpenters, bricklayers, woolen-cloth manufacturers, glass blowers, and painters. These guilds were dominated by master craftsmen, who ran their own shops. Working for wages in these shops were the journeymen, who knew the craft but could not yet afford to open their own shops. Under the masters and journeymen were apprentices, who worked usually without pay for a specific number of years to learn the trade.

In many cities the guilds expanded far beyond the economic regulation of trade and manufacturing to become the backbone of urban society and politics. The masters of the guilds constituted part of the urban elite, and guild membership was often a prerequisite for holding public office. One of the obligations of city government was to protect the interests of the guildsmen, who in turn helped stabilize the economy through their influence in city hall. Guilds often organized festivals and sports competitions, endowed chapels, and provided funeral insurance for their members and welfare for the injured and widows of masters.

When the economy declined during the fourteenth century, the urban guilds became lightning rods for mounting social tension. Guild monopolies produced considerable conflict, provoking anger among those who were blocked from joining guilds, young journeymen who earned low wages, and those who found themselves unemployed due to the depression. These tensions exploded into dangerous revolts.

Workers' Rebellions

Economic pressures erupted into rebellion most dramatically among woolen-cloth workers in the urban centers in Italy, the Netherlands, and France. The most famous revolt involved the Ciompi, the laborers in the woolen-cloth industry of Florence, Italy, where guilds were the most powerful force in city government. The Ciompi, who performed the heaviest jobs such as carting and the most noxious tasks such as dyeing, had not been allowed to have their own guild and were therefore deprived of the political and economic rights of guild membership.

Fueling the Ciompi's frustration was the fact that by the middle of the fourteenth century woolen-cloth production in Florence dropped by two-thirds, leaving many workers unemployed. In 1378 the desperate Ciompi rebelled. A crowd chanting, "Long live the people, long live liberty," broke into the houses of prominent citizens, released political prisoners from the city jails, and sacked the rich convents that housed the pampered daughters of the wealthy. Over the course of a few months, the rebels managed to force their way onto the city council, where they demanded tax and economic reforms and the right to form their own guild. The Ciompi revolt is one of the earliest cases of workers demanding political rights. The disenfranchised workers did not want to eliminate the guilds' monopoly on political power. They merely wanted a guild of their own so that they could join the regime. That was not to be, however. After a few weeks of success, the Ciompi were divided and defeated.

Shortly after the Ciompi revolt faded, troubles broke out in the woolen-cloth centers of Ghent and Bruges in Flanders and in Paris and Rouen in France. In these cases, however, the revolt spread beyond woolen-cloth workers to voice the more generalized grievances of urban workers. In Ghent and Bruges the weavers attempted to wrest control of their cities from the local leaders who dominated politics and the economy. In Paris and Rouen in 1380, social unrest erupted in resistance to high taxes and attacks by the poor on the rich.

Like urban workers, many rural peasants also rebelled during the troubled fourteenth century. In France in 1358 a peasant revolt broke out called the *Jacquerie*. Filled with hatred for the aristocracy, the peasants indulged in pillaging, murder, and rape, but they offered no plan for an alternative social system or even for their own participation in the political order, so their movement had no lasting effects. They were quickly defeated by a force of nobles.

Unlike the French Jacquerie, the peasants who revolted in England in 1381 had a clear political vision for an alternative society. The English rebels demanded the abolition of new taxes, lower rents, higher wages, and the end of serfdom, but to these they added a class-based argument against the aristocracy. Influenced by popular preachers, who told them that in the Garden of Eden there had been no aristocracy, the English rebels imagined an egalitarian society without ranks or hierarchy. However, the greatest peasant rebellion in medieval English history ended with broken promises and no tangible achievements.

CHRONOLOGY: ECONOMIC DEPRESSION AND SOCIAL TURMOIL

1310–1320	Famines begin
1348	Arrival of Black Death in Europe
1358	Jacquerie revolt in France
1378	Ciompi revolt in Florence
1379–1385	Urban revolts in Flanders and France
1381	Peasants revolt in England

None of the worker or peasant revolts of the fourteenth century met with lasting success. However, the rebellions revealed for the first time in the West a widespread impulse among the lower classes to question and protest the existing social and economic order. The tradition of worker protest became common and recurrent during subsequent centuries.

AN AGE OF WARFARE

■ How did incessant warfare transform the most powerful medieval states?

Prolonged war between its two largest and previously most stable kingdoms, England and France, further weakened western Europe during the fourteenth century. The **Hundred Years' War** (1337–1453) was a struggle over England's attempts to assert its claims to territories in France. The conflict drained resources from the French and English aristocracies, deepening and lengthening the economic depression.

The Fragility of Monarchies

Medieval monarchies depended on the king to maintain stability. Despite the remarkable legal reforms and bureaucratic centralization of monarchies in England and France during the twelfth and thirteenth centuries (see Chapter 10), weak or incompetent kings were all too common during the fourteenth. Weak kings created a perilous situation made worse by disputed successions. The career of Edward II (r. 1307–1327) of England illustrates the peril. Edward was unable to control the vital judicial and financial mechanisms of royal power. He continued the policy of his father, Edward I, by introducing resident justices of the peace who had replaced the inadequate system of itinerant judges who traveled from village to village to hear cases. In theory, these justices of the peace should have prevented the abuses of justice typical of aristocratic jurisdictions, but even though they were royal officials who answered to the king, most of those appointed were also local landowners who were deeply implicated in many of the disputes that came before them. As a result, justice in England became notoriously corrupt and the cause of discontent. Edward II was so incompetent to deal with the consequences of corrupted justice that he provoked a civil war in which his own queen joined his aristocratic enemies to depose him.

The French monarchy was no better. In fact, the French king was in an even weaker constitutional position than the English monarch. In France the king had effective jurisdiction over only a small part of his realm. Many of the duchies and counties of France were quasi-independent principalities paying only nominal allegiance to the king, whose will was ignored with impunity. In these regions the administration of justice, the collection of taxes, and the recruitment of soldiers all remained in the hands of local lords. To explain why he needed to raise taxes, Philip IV, "The Fair" (r. 1285–1314), created a representative assembly, the Estates General, which met for the first time in 1302, but he still had to negotiate with each region and town individually to collect the taxes. Given the difficulty of raising taxes, the French kings resorted to makeshift solutions that hurt the economy, such as confiscating the property of vulnerable Jewish and Italian merchants and debasing the coinage. Such a system made the finances of the kingdom of France especially shaky because the king lacked a dependable flow of revenue.

The Hundred Years' War

The Hundred Years' War revealed the fragility of the medieval monarchies. The initial cause of the war involved disputes over the duchy of Aquitaine. The king of England inherited the title of duke of Aquitaine, who was a vassal of the French crown, which meant that the English kings technically owed military assistance to the French kings whenever they asked for it. A long succession of English kings had reluctantly paid homage as dukes of Aquitaine to the king of France, but the unusual status of

the duchy held by the king of England was a continuing source of contention.

The second cause of the war derived from a dispute over the succession to the French crown. When King Charles IV died in 1328, his closest surviving relative was none other than the arch-enemy of France, Edward III (r. 1327–1377), king of England. To the barons of France, the possibility of Edward's succession to the throne was unthinkable, and they excluded him because his relation to the French royal family was through his mother. Instead the barons elected to the throne a member of the Valois family, King Philip VI (r. 1328–1350). At first Edward reluctantly accepted the decision. However, when Philip started to hear judicial appeals from the duchy of Aquitaine, Edward changed his mind. He claimed the title of king of France for himself, sparking the beginning of more than a century of warfare (see **Map 11.4**).

The Hundred Years' War (1337–1453) was not a continuous formal war, but a series of occasional pitched battles, punctuated by long truces and periods of general exhaustion. Nineteenth-century historians invented the term *Hundred Years' War* to describe the prolonged time of troubles between the two countries. France, far richer and with three times the population, held the advantage over sparsely populated England, but the English were usually victorious because of superior discipline and the ability of their longbows to break up cavalry charges. As a rule, the English avoided open battle, preferring raids, sieges of isolated castles, and capturing French knights for ransom. For many Englishmen the objective of fighting in France was to get rich by looting. Because all the fighting took place on French soil, France suffered extensive destruction and significant civilian casualties from repeated English raids.

FROM ENGLISH VICTORIES TO FRENCH SALVATION In the early phases of the war, the English enjoyed a stunning series of victories. At the Battle of Sluys in 1340, a small English fleet of 150 ships carrying the English invasion forces ran into a French blockade of more than 200

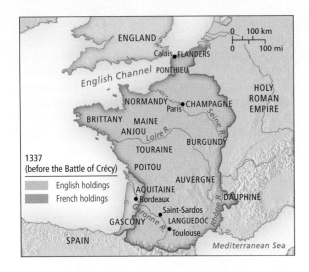

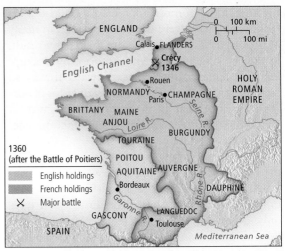

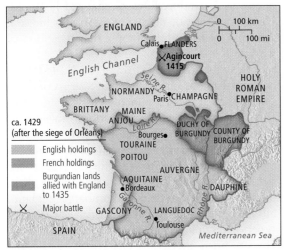

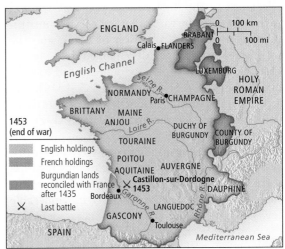

MAP 11.4

The Hundred Years' War

This map illustrates four phases of the Hundred Years' War. In the first phase (1337), England maintained a small foothold in the southwest of France. In the second phase (1360), England considerably expanded the territory around Aquitaine and gained a vital base in the north of France. In the third phase (ca. 1429), England occupied much of the north of France, and England's ally Burgundy established effective independence from French authority. In the fourth phase at the end of the war (1453), England had been driven from French soil except at Calais, and Burgundy maintained control over most of its scattered territories.

ships. In the heavy hand-to-hand combat, the English captured 166 French ships and killed some 20,000 men, so many that it was later said, "If fish could talk, they would speak French." At Agincourt in 1415, King Henry V (r. 1413–1422) and England's disease-racked

army of 6,000 were cut off by a French force of about 20,000, yet in the ensuing battle the English archers repelled a hasty French cavalry charge and the fleeing, terrified horses trampled the French men-at-arms as they advanced. The English lost only a few hundred, but the French

ENGLISH LONGBOW ARCHERS

English archers use the longbow at the Battle of Crecy in 1346. The English longbow archers on the right are massacring the French crossbowmen on the left. Because of the cumbersome process of cranking back the bowstring between shots, the crossbow had a much slower shooting rate than a longbow.

suffered nearly 10,000 casualties. After Agincourt, the French never again dared challenge King Henry in open battle, and were forced to recognize him as the heir to the French throne.

English victory appeared complete, but by 1422 Henry V was dead, leaving two claimants to the French throne. The English asserted the rights of the infant King Henry VI of England, son of King Henry V. Most of the French defended the claim of the Dauphin (the title of the heir to the throne) Charles, the only surviving son of the late King Charles VI of France. The Hundred Years' War entered a new phase with factions of the French aristocracy supporting the two rivals in a bloody series of engagements. The war was now as much a civil war as one between kingdoms.

By 1429 the English were again on the verge of final victory. They occupied Paris and Rheims, and their army was besieging Orleans. The Dauphin Charles was penniless and indecisive. Even his own mother denied his legitimacy as the future king. At this point, a 17-year-old illiterate peasant from Burgundy, Joan of Arc (Jeanne d'Arc, ca. 1412–1431), following "divine voices," went to Orleans to lead the French armies. Under her inspiration Orleans was relieved, French forces began to defeat the English, much of the occupied territory was regained, and the Dauphin was crowned King Charles VII (r. 1429–1461) in the cathedral of Rheims. After Joan failed to recapture Paris, however, her successes ceased. (See *Justice in History* in this chapter.) The final victory of the French came from the leadership of King Charles and the general exhaustion of the English forces.

Charles VII reorganized the French army and gradually chipped away at the English holdings in France, eventually taking away Aquitaine in 1453. The English lost all their possessions in France except Calais, which was finally surrendered in 1558. There was no peace treaty, just a fading away of war in France, especially after England stumbled into civil war—the War of the Roses (1455–1485).

The Trial of Joan of Arc

After only 15 months as the inspiration of the French army, Joan of Arc fell into the hands of the English, who brought her to trial at Rouen in 1431 for witchcraft. The English needed to stage a show trial to demonstrate to their own demoralized forces that Joan's remarkable victories resulted from witchcraft rather than military superiority. In the English trial, Joan testified that she was merely responding to spiritual voices she heard that commanded her to wear men's clothing. On the basis of her cross dressing, the ecclesiastical tribunal declared her a witch and a relapsed heretic. The court sentenced her to be burned at the stake.

From the beginning of her emergence onto the political scene, the voices Joan's heard guided her every move. Joan claimed that she heard the voices of St. Catherine, St. Margaret, and the Archangel Michael. To Joan, these voices carried the authority of divine commands. The problem the English judges faced was to demonstrate that the voices came from the Devil rather than from God. If they could prove that, then they had evidence of witchcraft and sorcery. Following standard inquisitorial guidelines, the judges knew that authentic messages from God would always conform to church dogma. Any deviation from official doctrines would constitute evidence of demonic influence. Thus, during Joan's trial the judges demanded that she make theological distinctions that were alien to her. When they wanted to know if the voices were those of angels or saints, Joan seemed perplexed and responded, "This voice comes from God....I am more afraid of failing the voices by saying what is displeasing to them than answering you."[6] The judges kept pushing, asking if the saints or angels had heads, eyes, and hair. Exasperated, Joan simply replied, "I have told you often enough, believe me if you will."

The judges reformulated Joan's words to reflect their own rigid scholastic categories and concluded that her "veneration of the saints seems to partake of idolatry and to proceed from a pact made with devils. These are less divine revelations than lies invented by Joan, suggested or shown to her by the demon in illusive apparitions, in order to mock at her imagination while she meddled with things that are beyond her and superior to the faculty of her condition."[7] In other words, Joan was just too naive and uneducated to have authentic visions. But the English judges were on dangerous ground because during the previous 50 years there had been a number of notable female mystics, including St. Catherine of Siena and St. Bridget of Sweden, whose visions the pope had accepted as authentic. The English could not take the chance that they were executing a real saint. So they changed tactics.

If they could not convict her for bad theology, the English needed evidence for superstitious practices. In an attempt to do that, they drew up 70 charges against Joan. Many of these consisted of allegations of performing magic, such as chanting spells, visiting a magical tree at night, and invoking demons. They attempted to prove bad behavior by insinuating that a young man had refused to marry her on account of her immoral life. They asserted that her godmother was a notorious witch who had taught her sorcery. None of these ploys worked, however, because Joan consistently denied the charges. She did, however, admit to one allegation: she dressed as a man.

Some of the charges against her and many of the judges' questions concerned how she dressed:

> The said Joan put off and entirely abandoned women's clothes, with her hair cropped short and round in the fashion of young men, she wore shirt, breeches, doublet, with hose joined together, long and fastened to the said doublet by twenty points, long leggings laced on the outside, a short mantle reaching to the knee, or thereabouts, a close-cut cap, tight-fitting boots or buskins, long spurs, sword, dagger, breastplate, lance and other arms in the style of a man-at-arms.[8]

The judges explained to her that "according to canon law and the Holy Scriptures" a woman dressing as a man or a man as a woman is "an abomination before God."[9] She replied simply and consistently that "everything that I have done, I did by command of the voices" and that wearing male dress "would be for the great good of France."[10] When they asked her to put on a woman's dress in order to take the Eucharist on Easter Sunday, she refused, saying the miracle of the Eucharist did not depend on whether she wore a man's or a woman's clothing. On many occasions she had been asked to put on a woman's dress and refused. "And as for womanly duties, she said there were enough other women to do them."[11]

After a long imprisonment and psychological pressure from her inquisitors, Joan confessed to charges of witchcraft, signed a recantation of her heresy, and agreed to put on a dress. She was sentenced to life imprisonment on bread and water. Why did she confess? Some historians have argued that she was tricked into confessing because the inquisitors really wanted to execute her but could not do so unless she was a *relapsed* heretic. To be relapsed she had to confess and then somehow return to her heretical ways. If that were the inquisitors' intention, Joan soon obliged them. After a few days in prison, Joan threw off the women's clothes she had been given and resumed dressing as a man.

Joan was willing to be burned at the stake rather than disobey her voices. Why? Historians will never know for sure, but dressing as a man may have been necessary for her to fulfill her role as a military leader. In her military career, Joan had adopted the masculine qualities of chivalry: bravery, steadfastness, loyalty, *and* a willingness to accept pain and death. She made herself believable by dressing as a knight. Joan's condemnation was much more than another example of men's attempt to control women. Joan's transgressive gender identity threatened the whole system of neat hierarchical distinctions upon which Christian theology rested. To the theologians, everything in God's Creation had its own proper place and anyone who changed his or her divinely ordained position in society presented a direct affront to God.

JOAN OF ARC

There are no contemporary portraits of Joan, and this image is clearly a generalized one of a young woman rather than a portrait taken from the real Joan.

Source: Marc Charmet/Picture Desk, Inc./Kobal Collection

For Discussion

1. In medieval ecclesiastical trials such as this one, what kinds of evidence were presented and what kind of justice was sought?

2. What did Joan's claim that she heard voices reveal about her understanding of what constituted the proper authority over her life?

Taking It Further

Joan of Arc. *In Her Own Words,* Translated by Willard Trask. 1996. The record of what Joan reputedly said at her trials.

Warner, Marina. *Joan of Arc: The Image of Female Heroism.* 1981. A highly readable feminist reading of the Joan of Arc story.

THE HUNDRED YEARS' WAR IN PERSPECTIVE The Hundred Years' War had broad consequences. First, nearly continuous warfare between the two most powerful kingdoms in the West exacerbated other conflicts as well. Scotland, the German princes, Aragon, Castile, and most importantly Burgundy were drawn into the conflict, making the English-French brawl a European-wide war at certain stages. The squabble between France and England also made it much more difficult to settle the Great Schism that split the Church during the same period. Second, the war devastated France, which eventually regained control of most of its territory but still suffered the most from the fighting. During the century of war, the population dropped by half, due to the ravages of combat, pillage, and plague. Third, the deaths of so many nobles and destruction of their fortunes diminished the international luxury trade. Merchants and banks as far away as Italy went broke. In addition, the war disrupted the Flemish woolen industry causing further economic damage. Finally, the war helped make England more English. Before the war the Plantagenet dynasty in England was more French than English. The monarchs possessed extensive territories in France and were embroiled in French affairs. English aristocrats also had business in France, spoke French, and married their French cousins. After 1450 the English abandoned the many French connections that had stretched across the English Channel since William the Conqueror sailed from Normandy to England in 1066. Henceforth, the English upper classes cultivated English rather than French language and culture.

The Military Revolution

The "military revolution" first became evident during the Hundred Years' War but lasted well into the seventeenth century. It refers to changes in warfare that marked the transition from the late medieval to the early modern state. The heavily armored mounted knights, who had dominated European warfare and society since the Carolingian period, were gradually supplanted by foot soldiers as the most effective fighting unit in battle. Infantry units were composed of men who fought on foot in disciplined ranks, which allowed them to break up cavalry charges by concentrating firepower in deadly volleys. Infantry soldiers could fight on a greater variety of terrains than mounted knights, who needed level ground and plenty of space for their horses to maneuver. The effectiveness of infantry units made battles more ferocious but also more decisive, which was why governments favored them. Infantry, however, put new requirements on the governments that recruited them. Armies now demanded large numbers of well-drilled foot soldiers who could move in disciplined

CHRONOLOGY: AN AGE OF WARFARE

1285	Philip IV, "The Fair," succeeds to the throne of France
1307	Edward II succeeds to the throne of England
1327	Edward III succeeds to the throne of England
1328	Philip VI succeeds to the throne of France
1337	Hundred Years' War begins
1340	Battle of Sluys
1413	Henry V succeeds to the throne of England
1415	Battle of Agincourt
1429	Charles VII succeeds to the throne of France
1455–1485	War of the Roses in England

ranks around a battlefield. Recruiting, training, and drilling soldiers made armies much more complex organizations than they had been, and officers needed to possess a wide range of management skills. Governments faced added expenses as they needed to arrange and pay for the logistical support necessary to feed and transport those large numbers. The creation of the highly centralized modern state resulted in part from the necessity to maintain a large army in which infantry played the crucial role.

Infantry used a variety of weapons. The English demonstrated the effectiveness of longbowmen during the Hundred Years' War. Capable of shooting at a much more rapid rate than the French crossbowmen, the English longbowmen at Agincourt protected themselves behind a hurriedly erected stockade of stakes and rained a shower of deadly arrows on the French cavalry to break up charges. In the narrow battlefield, which was wedged between two forests, the French cavalry had insufficient room to maneuver; when some of them dismounted to create more room, their heavy armor made them easy to topple over and spear through the underarm seam in their armor. Some English infantry units deployed ranks of pikemen who created an impenetrable wall of sharp spikes.

The military revolution of the fourteenth and fifteenth centuries also introduced gunpowder to European warfare. Arriving from China with the Mongol invasions, gunpowder was first used in the West in artillery. Beginning in the 1320s besieging armies shot stone or iron against fortifications from huge wrought-iron cannons. By the early sixteenth century bronze muzzle-loading cannons were used in field battles. With the introduction during the late fifteenth century of the handgun and the harquebus (a predecessor to the musket), properly drilled and disciplined infantrymen could deliver destructive firepower. Gunshots pierced plate armor, whereas arrows bounced off. The slow rate of fire of these guns, however, necessitated carefully planned battle tactics. Around 1500 the Spanish introduced mixed infantry formations that pursued "shock" and "shot" tactics. Spanish pikemen provided the shock, which was quickly followed by gunshot or missile fire. This combination of technology and technique enabled Spanish infantry formations to defeat cavalry even in the open field without defensive fortifications, an unprecedented feat. By the end of the fifteenth century, every army included trained infantry.

The military revolution precipitated a major shift in European society. The successful states were those that created the financial base and bureaucratic structures necessary to field a professional army composed of infantry units and artillery. Superior armies required officers capable of drilling infantry or understanding the science of warfare to serve as an artillery officer.

A TROUBLED CHURCH AND THE DEMAND FOR RELIGIOUS COMFORT

■ Why did the Church fail to provide leadership and spiritual guidance during these difficult times?

In reaction to the suffering and widespread death during the fourteenth century, many people turned to religion for spiritual consolation and for explanations of what had gone wrong. But the spiritual authority of the Church was so dangerously weakened during this period that it failed to satisfy the popular craving for solace. The moral leadership that had made the papacy such a powerful force for reform during the eleventh through thirteenth centuries evaporated in the fourteenth. Many laypeople found their own means of religious expression, making the Later Middle Ages one of the most religiously creative epochs in Christian history.

The Babylonian Captivity of the Church and the Great Schism

Faced with anarchy in the streets of Rome as local aristocrats engaged in incessant feuding, seven consecutive popes chose to reside in the relative calm of Avignon, France. This period of voluntary papal exile is known as the **Babylonian Captivity of the Church** (1305–1378), a biblical reference recalling the captivity of the Jews in Babylonia (587–539 B.C.E.). The popes' presumed subservience to the kings of France during this period dangerously politicized the papacy, destroying its ability to rise above the petty squabbles of the European princes and to serve as a spiritual authority to all. Even though these French popes residing in France were never the French kings' lackeys, the enemies of the kings of France did not trust them. The loss of revenues from papal lands in Italy lured several popes into questionable financial schemes, which included accepting kickbacks from appointees to church offices, taking bribes for judicial decisions, and selling **indulgences,** certificates that allowed penitents to atone for their sins and reduce their time in Purgatory.

When Pope Urban VI (r. 1378–1389) announced his intention to reside in Rome, a group of disgruntled French cardinals returned to Avignon and elected a rival French pope. The Church was then divided over allegiance to Italian and French claimants to the papal throne, a period called the **Great Schism** (1378–1417). Toward the end of the schism there were actually four rival popes. During the Great Schism the kings, princes, and cities of Europe divided their allegiances between the rival candidates. Competing political alliances, not doctrinal differences, split the Church.

The **Conciliar Movement** attempted to create a mechanism for ending the Schism. The conciliarists, however, also sought to restrict the theoretical and practical authority of the papacy. They argued that a general meeting or *council* of the bishops of the Church had authority over the pope. A king could call such a council to undertake reforms, pass judgment on a standing pope, or order a conclave to elect a new one. Several general councils convened during the early fifteenth century to resolve the schism and initiate reforms, but the intertwining of political and Church affairs made solutions were difficult to achieve. The Council of Constance (1414–1417) finally succeeded in

restoring unity to the Church and also in formally asserting the principle that a general council was superior to the pope and should be called frequently. The Council of Basel (1431–1449) approved a series of necessary reforms, but Pope Eugene IV (r. 1431–1447), who opposed conciliarism, never implemented them. The failure of even the timid reforms of the Council of Basel opened the way for the more radical rejection of papal authority during the Protestant Reformation of the sixteenth century.

The Search for Religious Alternatives

The popes' loss of moral authority during the Babylonian Captivity and the Great Schism opened the way for a remarkable variety of reformers, mystics, and preachers. Most of these movements were traditional in their doctrines, but some were heretical. The weakened papacy was unable to control them, as it had successfully done during the thirteenth-century crusade against the Albigensians.

PROTESTS AGAINST THE PAPACY: NEW HERESIES For most Catholic Christians during the fourteenth century, religious life consisted of witnessing or participating in the seven sacraments, the formal rituals celebrated by duly consecrated priests usually within the confines of churches. After baptism, which was universally performed on infants, the most common sacraments for lay adults were penance and communion. Both of these sacraments emphasized the authority of the clergy over the laity and therefore were potential sources for resentment. The sacrament of penance required the layperson to confess his or her sins to a priest, who then prescribed certain penalties to satisfy the sin. At communion, it was believed, the priest changed the substance of an unleavened wafer of bread, called the Eucharist, into the body of Christ and a chalice of wine into Christ's blood, a miraculous process of transubstantiation (see Chapter 10). Priests and lay recipients of communion both ate the wafer, but the chalice was reserved for the priest alone. More than anything else, the reservation of the chalice for priests profoundly symbolized the privileges of the clergy. Because medieval Catholicism was primarily a sacramental religion, reformers and heretics tended to concentrate their criticism on sacramental rituals.

The most serious discontent about the authority of the popes, the privileges of the clergy, and the efficacy of the sacraments appeared in England and Bohemia (a region in the modern Czech Republic). An Oxford professor, John Wycliffe (1320–1384), criticized the power and wealth of the clergy, played down the value of the sacraments for encouraging ethical behavior, and exalted the benefits of preaching, which promoted a sense of personal responsibility. During the Great Schism, Wycliffe rejected the authority of the rival popes and asserted instead the absolute authority of the Bible, which he wanted to make available to the laity in English rather than in Latin, which most laypeople could not understand.

Outside England Wycliffe's ideas found their most sympathetic audience among a group of reformist professors at the University of Prague in Bohemia, where Jan Hus (1369–1415) regularly preached to a large popular following. Hus's most revolutionary act was to offer the chalice of consecrated communion wine to the laity, thus symbolically diminishing the special status of the clergy. When Hus also preached against indulgences, which he said converted the sacrament of penance into a cash transaction, Pope John XXIII excommunicated him. Hus attended the Council of Constance to defend his ideas. Despite the promise of a safe-conduct from the Holy Roman emperor (whose jurisdiction included Bohemia and Constance) that should have made him immune from arrest, Hus was imprisoned, his writings were condemned, and he was burned alive as a heretic.

Wycliffe and Hus started movements that survived their own deaths. In England Wycliffe's followers were the Lollards and in Bohemia the Hussites carried on reform ideas. Both groups were eventually absorbed into the Protestant Reformation in the sixteenth century.

IMITATING CHRIST: THE MODERN DEVOTION   In the climate of religious turmoil of the fourteenth and fifteenth centuries, many Christians sought deeper spiritual solace than the institutionalized Church could provide. By stressing individual piety, ethical behavior, and intense religious education, a movement called the **Modern Devotion** built on the existing traditions of spirituality and became highly influential. Promoted by the Brothers of the Common Life, a religious order established in the Netherlands, the Modern Devotion was especially popular throughout northern Europe. In the houses for the Brothers, clerics and laity lived together without monastic vows, shared household tasks, joined in regular prayers, and engaged in religious studies. (A similar structure was devised for women.) The lay brothers continued their occupations in the outside world, thus influencing their neighbors through their pious example. The houses established schools that prepared boys for church careers through constant prayer and rigorous training in Latin. Many of the leading figures behind the Protestant Reformation in the sixteenth century had attended schools run by the Brothers of the Common Life.

The Modern Devotion also spread through the influence of the best-seller of the late fifteenth century, the *Imitation of Christ*, written about 1441 by a Common Life brother, probably Thomas à Kempis. By emphasizing frequent private prayer and moral introspection, the *Imitation* provided a manual to guide laypeople in the path toward spiritual renewal that had traditionally been reserved for monks and nuns. There was nothing especially reformist about the *Imitation of Christ*, which emphasized the need for regular confession and communion. However, its popularity helped prepare the way for a broad-based reform of the Church by turning the walls of the monastery inside out, spilling out a large number of lay believers who were dedicated to becoming living examples of moral purity for their neighbors.

CHRONOLOGY: TROUBLES IN THE CHURCH

1305–1378	Babylonian Captivity of the Church; popes reside in Avignon
1320–1384	John Wycliffe
1369–1415	Jan Hus
1378–1417	Great Schism; more than one pope
1414–1417	Council of Constance
1431–1449	Council of Basel
ca. 1441	*Imitation of Christ*

THE CULTURE OF LOSS

■ How did European culture offer explanations and solace for the otherwise inexplicable calamities of the times?

During the fourteenth and early fifteenth centuries, the omnipresence of violence and death provoked widespread anxiety. This anxiety had many manifestations. Some people went on long penitential pilgrimages to the shrines of saints or to the Holy Land. During the fourteenth century the tribulations of the pilgrim's travels became a metaphor for the journey of life itself, stimulating creative literature. Still others tried to find someone to blame for calamities. The search for scapegoats focused on minority groups, especially Jews and Muslims.

Reminders of Death

In no other period of Western civilization has the idea of death so pervaded popular cultures as during the fourteenth and fifteenth centuries. The Reminders of Death was a theme found in religious books, literary works, and the visual arts. A contemporary book of moral guidance advised the reader that "when he goes to bed, he should imagine not that he is putting himself to bed, but that others are laying him in his grave."[12] Reminders of Death became the everyday theme of preachers, and popular woodcuts represented death in simple but disturbing images. The Reminder of Death tried to encourage ethical behavior in this life by showing that in everyone's future was neither riches, nor fame, nor love, nor pleasure, but only the decay of death.

The most famous Reminder of Death was the Dance of Death. First appearing in a poem of 1376, the Dance of Death evolved into a street play, performed to illustrate sermons that called for repentance. It also appeared in church murals, depicting a procession led by a skeleton that included representatives of the social orders, from children and peasants to pope and emperor. All danced to their inevitable deaths. At the Church of the Innocents in Paris, the inscription that accompanies the mural depicting the Dance of Death reads:

> Advance, see yourselves in us, dead, naked, rotten and stinking. So will you be....To live without thinking of this risks damnation....Power, honor, riches are nothing; at the hour of death only good works count....Everyone should think at least once a day of his loathsome end [in order to escape] the dreadful pain of hell without end which is unspeakable.[13]

In earlier centuries, tombs had depicted death as serene: On top of the tomb rested an effigy of the deceased, dressed in the finest clothes with hands piously folded and eyes open to the promise of eternal life. In contrast, during the fourteenth century, tomb effigies began to depict putrefying bodies or naked skeletons, symbols of the futility of human status and achievements. These tombs were disturbingly graphic Reminders of Death. Likewise, poems spoke of the disgusting smell of rotting flesh, the livid color of plague victims, and the cold touch of the dead.

DANCE OF DEATH
This late-fifteenth century painted engraving illustrates the widespread preoccupation with death during the period. The skeletons dance and play musical instruments. The cadaver on the right holds his own entrails.

Late medieval society was completely frank about the unpleasant process of dying, unlike modern societies that hide the dying in hospitals and segregate mourning to funeral homes. Dying was a public event, almost a theatrical performance. The last rites of the Catholic Church and the Art of Dying served to assist souls in their final test before God and to separate the departed from their kin. According to the Art of Dying, outlined in numerous advice books and illustrations, the sick or injured person should die in bed, surrounded by a room full of people, including children. Christians believed that a dying person watched a supernatural spectacle visible to him or her alone as the heavenly host fought with Satan and his demon minions for the soul. The Art of Dying compared the deathbed contest to a horrific game of chess in which the Devil did all he could to trap the dying person into a checkmate just at the moment of death. In the best of circumstances, a priest arrived in time to hear a confession, offer words of consolation, encourage the dying individual to forgive his or her enemies and redress any wrongs, and perform the last rites.

Pilgrims of the Imagination

During the Middle Ages, a pilgrimage offered a religiously sanctioned form of escape from the omnipresent suffering and peril. Pious Christians could go on a pilgrimage to the Holy

TOMB EFFIGY OF A KNIGHT

This effigy above the tomb of Jean d'Alluy shows the deceased as if he were serenely sleeping, still dressed in the armor of his worldly profession.

Source: Tomb Effigy of Jean d'Alluye. Mid-thirteenth Century. From France, Touraine, Loire Valley. Limestone, 83 1/2 × 34 1/4 in. (212.1 × 87 cm). The Cloisters Collection, 1925 (25.120.201). Image copyright © The Metropolitan Museum of Art/Art Resource, NY

Land, Rome, or the shrine of a saint, such as Santiago de Compostela in Spain, Canterbury in England, or Częstochowa in Poland. The usual motive for a pilgrimage was to fulfill a vow or promise made to God, or to obtain an indulgence, which exempted the pilgrim from some of the time spent in punishment in Purgatory after death. The pilgrimage became the instrument for spiritual liberation and escape from difficulties. As a result, going on a pilgrimage became a compelling model for creative literature, especially during the fourteenth century. Not all of these great works of literature were fictional pilgrimages, but many evoked the pilgrim's impulse to find a refuge from the difficulties of daily life or to find solace in the promise of a better life to come.

DANTE ALIGHIERI AND *THE DIVINE COMEDY* In *The Divine Comedy* an Italian poet from Florence, Dante Alighieri (1265–1321), imagined the most fantastic pilgrimage ever attempted, a journey through Hell, Purgatory,

DECOMPOSING CADAVER

The tomb effigy of Jean de Lagrange.

Source: Musee du Petit Palais, Avignon, France

THE ART OF DYING
In this death scene, the dying man receives extreme unction (last rites) from a priest. A friar holds a crucifixion for him to contemplate. Above his head a devil and angel compete for his soul, while behind him Death lurks waiting for his moment.

and Paradise. A work of astounding originality, *The Divine Comedy* remains the greatest masterpiece of medieval literature. Little is known about Dante's early life except that somehow he acquired expertise in Greek philosophy, scholastic theology (the application of logic to the understanding of Christianity, discussed in Chapter 10), Latin literature, and the newly fashionable poetic forms in Provençal, the language of southern France. Dante's involvement in the dangerous politics of Florence led to his exile under pain of death if he ever returned. During

his exile Dante wandered for years, suffering grievously the loss of his home: "Bitter is the taste of another man's bread and...heavy the way up and down another man's stair" (*Paradiso*, canto 17). He sustained himself by writing his great poetic vision of human destiny and God's plan for redemption.

In the poem Dante himself travels into the Christian version of the afterlife. Dante's trip, initially guided by the Latin poet Virgil, the epitome of ancient wisdom, starts in Hell. As he travels deeper into Hell's harsh depths, a cast of sinful characters who inhabit the world of the damned warn Dante of the harmful values of this world. In Purgatory his guide becomes Beatrice, Dante's deceased beloved, who stands for the Christian virtues. In this section of the poem, he begins the painful process of spiritual rehabilitation in which he comes to accept the Christian image of life as a pilgrimage. In Paradise he achieves spiritual fulfillment by speaking with figures from the past who have defied death. Although the poem is deeply Christian, it displays numerous non-Christian influences. The passage through Hell, for example, derived from a long Muslim poem reconstructing Muhammad's *miraj*, a night journey to Jerusalem and ascent to heaven.

The lasting appeal of this long and difficult poem is a wonder. Underlying the appeal of *The Divine Comedy* is perhaps its optimism, which expresses Dante's own cure to his depressing condition as an exile. The power of Dante's poetry established the form of the modern Italian language. Even in translation the images and stories can intrigue and fascinate.

GEOFFREY CHAUCER AND *THE CANTERBURY TALES* Geoffrey Chaucer (ca. 1342–1400) was the most outstanding English poet prior to William Shakespeare. As a courtier and diplomat, Chaucer was a trusted adviser to three successive English kings. But he is best known for his literary output, including *The Canterbury Tales*.

In *The Canterbury Tales* a group of 30 pilgrims tell stories as they travel on horseback to the shrine at Canterbury. Chaucer's use of the pilgrimage as a framing device for telling the stories allowed him to bring together a collection of people from across the social spectrum, including a wife, indulgence hawker, miller, town magistrate, clerk, landowner, lawyer, merchant, knight, abbess, and monk. The variety of characters who told the tales allowed Chaucer to experiment with many kinds of literary forms, from a chivalric romance to a sermon. The pilgrimage combined the considerations of religious morality with the fun of a spring vacation. Many pilgrims were more concerned with the pleasures of this world than preparing for the next, which was the avowed purpose of going on a pilgrimage. In this intertwining of the worldly and the spiritual, Chaucer brought the abstract principles of Christian morality down to a level of common understanding.

CHRISTINE DE PISAN AND THE DEFENSE OF FEMALE VIRTUE The work of the poet Christine de Pisan (1364–1430) was not a spiritual pilgrimage like Dante's or Chaucer's but a thoughtful and passionate commentary on the tumultuous issues of her day. At age 15 Pisan married a notary of King Charles V of France, but by age 25 she was a widow with three young children. In order to support her family, she turned to writing and relied on the patronage of the royalty and wealthy aristocrats of France, Burgundy, Germany, and England.

Christine de Pisan championed the cause of women in a male-dominated society. Following the fashion of the times, she invented a new chivalric order, the Order of the Rose, whose members took a vow to defend the honor of women. She wrote a defense of women for a male readership and an allegorical autobiography. But she is most famous for the two books she wrote for women readers, *The Book of the City of Ladies* and *The Book of Three Virtues* (both about 1407). In these she recounted tales of the heroism and virtue of women and offered moral instruction for women in different social roles. In 1415 she retired to a convent where in the last year of her life she wrote a masterpiece of ecstatic lyricism that celebrated the early victories of Joan of Arc. Pisan's book turned the martyred Joan into the heroine of France.

Defining Cultural Boundaries

During the Later Middle Ages, systematic discrimination against certain ethnic and religious groups increased markedly in Europe. As European society enforced ever-higher levels of religious uniformity, intolerance spread in the ethnically mixed societies of the European periphery. Intolerance was marked in three areas: Spain with its mixture of Muslim, Jewish, and Christian cultures; the German borderlands in east-central Europe, where Germans mingled with Slavs; and Ireland and Wales, where Celts came under the domination of the English. Within the heartland of Europe were other areas of clashing cultures—Switzerland, for example, where the folk culture of peasants and shepherds living in the isolated mountains collided with the intense Christian religiosity of the cities.

RELIGIOUS COMMUNITIES IN TENSION The Iberian peninsula was home to thriving communities of Muslims, Jews, and Christians. Since the eleventh century the aggressive northern Christian kingdoms of Castile and Aragon had engaged in a protracted program of Reconquest (*Reconquista*) against the Muslim states of the peninsula. By 1248 the Reconquest was largely completed, with only a small Muslim enclave in Granada holding out until 1492. The Spanish Reconquest placed former enemies in close proximity to one another. Hostilities between Christians and Muslims ranged from active warfare to tense stalemate, with Jews working as cultural intermediaries between the two larger communities.

During the twelfth and thirteenth centuries Muslims, called the Mudejars, who capitulated to the conquering Christians, received guarantees that they could continue to practice their own religion and laws. During the fourteenth century, however, Christian kings gradually reneged on these promises. In 1301 the king of Castile decreed that the testimony of any two Christian witnesses could convict a Jew or Muslim, notwithstanding any previously granted privileges that allowed them to be tried in their own courts. The Arabic language began to disappear in Spain as the Mudejars suffered discrimination on many levels. By the sixteenth century, the practice of Islam became illegal, and the Spanish state adopted a systematic policy to destroy Mudejar culture by prohibiting Muslim dress, customs, and marriage practices.

The Jews also began to feel the pain of organized, official discrimination. Christian preachers accused Jews of poisonings, stealing Christian babies, and cannibalism. When the Black Death arrived in 1348, the Jews of Aragon were accused of having poisoned the wells, even though Jews were dying just like Christians. Beginning in 1378, a Catholic prelate in Seville, Ferrant Martínez, commenced an anti-Jewish preaching campaign by calling for the destruction of all 23 of the city's synagogues, the confinement of Jews to a ghetto, the dislodging of all Jews from public positions, and the prohibition of any social contact between Christians and Jews. His campaign led to an attack on the Jews of Seville in 1391. Violence spread to other cities throughout the peninsula and the nearby Balearic Islands. Jews faced a stark choice: conversion or death. After a year of mob violence, about 100,000 Jews had been murdered and an equal number had gone into hiding or fled to more tolerant Muslim countries. The 1391 pogroms led to the first significant forced conversions of Jews in Spain. A century later in 1492, on the heels of the final Christian victory of the Reconquest, all remaining Jews in Spain were compelled to either leave or convert.

Violence against religious minorities occurred in many places, but besides Spain it was most systematic in German-speaking lands. Between November 1348 and August 1350, violence against Jews occurred in more than 80 German towns. Like the allegations in Aragon, the fear that Jews poisoned the wells led to massacres in German lands even *before* plague had arrived in these communities. The frequent occurrence of violence on Sundays or feast days suggests that preachers consciously or unconsciously encouraged the rioting mobs.

Jews had already been expelled from England in 1290 and France in 1306. The situation for Jews was better in Italy where the small population of Jews signed contracts with local towns offering them protection. This pattern of friction among ethnic communities was largely absent in Poland, however, where King Casimir III the Great (1333–137) granted Jews special privileges and welcomed Jewish immigrants, many of them fleeing persecution elsewhere.

ETHNIC COMMUNITIES IN TENSION   Other regions with diverse populations also witnessed discrimination and its brutal consequences. During the population boom of the twelfth and thirteenth centuries, German-speaking immigrants had established colonial towns in the Baltic and penetrated eastward, creating isolated pockets of German culture in Bohemia, Poland, and Hungary. During the fourteenth and fifteenth centuries, hostilities between the native populations and the colonizing Germans arose, particularly in Bohemia. One Czech prince offered 100 silver marks to anyone who brought him 100 German noses. The Teutonic Knights, who had been the vanguard of the German migrations in the Baltic, began to require German ancestry for membership. In German-speaking towns along the colonized borderlands of east-central Europe, city councils and guilds began to use ethnicity as a qualification for holding certain offices or joining a guild. The most famous example was the "German Paragraph" in guild statutes, which required candidates for admission to a guild to prove German descent. As the statutes of a bakers' guild put it, "Whoever wishes to be a member must bring proof to the councilors and the guildsmen that he is born of legitimate, upright German folk." Others required members to be "of German blood and tongue," as if language were a matter of biological inheritance.[14] German guildsmen were also forbidden to marry non-Germans.

In the Celtic fringe of the British Isles, too, discrimination became far more evident in the fourteenth century. In Ireland the ruling English promulgated laws that attempted to protect the cultural identity of the English colonists. The English prohibited native Irish from citizenship in town or guild membership. The Statutes of Kilkenny of 1366 attempted to legislate ethnic purity: They prohibited intermarriage between English and Irish and required English colonists to speak English, use English names, wear English clothes, and ride horses in the English way. They also forbade the English to play Irish games or listen to Irish music. A similar pattern appeared in Wales, where the lines dividing the Welsh and English communities hardened as the English community attempted to prevent its absorption into the majority culture.

CONCLUSION

Looking Inward

Unlike the more dynamic, outward-looking thirteenth century, Europeans during the fourteenth and early fifteenth centuries turned their attention inward to their own communities and their own problems. Europe faced one calamity after another, each crisis compounding the misery. The process of changing Western identities during this period can be seen in two ways.

First, as a result of the Western encounters with the Mongol and Ottoman Empires, the political and religious frontiers of the West shifted. These two empires redrew the map of the West by ending the Christian Byzantine Empire. With the Mongol invasions, the eastward spread of Christianity into Asia ended. The Ottoman conquests left a lasting Muslim influence inside Europe, particularly in Bosnia and Albania. The Ottoman Empire remained hostile to and frequently at war with the Christian West for more than 200 years.

Second, most Europeans reinforced their identity as Christians and became more self-conscious of the country in which they lived. At the same time Christian civilization was becoming eclipsed in parts of the Balkans, it revived in the Iberian peninsula, where the Muslim population, once the most extensive in the West, suffered discrimination and defeat. The northern Spanish kingdoms, for example, began to unify their subjects around a militant form of Christianity that was overtly hostile to Muslims and Jews. In many places in the West, religious and ethnic discrimination against minorities increased. A stronger sense of self-identification by country can be most dramatically seen in France and England as a consequence of the Hundred Years' War.

Except for the very visible military conquests of the Mongols and the Ottomans, the causes of most of the calamities of the fourteenth century were invisible or unknown. No one recognized a climate change or understood the dynamics of the population crisis. No one understood the cause of the epidemics. Only a few merchants grasped the role of the Mongol Empire in the world economy or the causes for the collapse of banking and trade. Unable to distinguish how these forces were changing their lives, Europeans only witnessed their consequences. In the face of these calamities, European culture became obsessed with death and with finding scapegoats to blame for events that could not be otherwise explained. However, calamity also bred creativity. The search for answers to the question, "Why did this happen to us?" produced a new spiritual sensibility and a rich literature. Following the travails of the fourteenth century, moreover, there arose in the fifteenth a new, more optimistic cultural movement—the Renaissance. Gloom and doom were not the only responses to troubles. As we will see in the next chapter, during the Renaissance some people began to search for new answers to human problems in a fashion that would transform the West anew.

KEY TERMS

Black Death
guilds
Hundred Years' War
Babylonian Captivity
   of the Church

indulgences
Great Schism
Conciliar Movement
Modern Devotion

CHAPTER QUESTIONS

1. What caused the deaths of so many Europeans? (page 331)
2. How did forces outside Europe, in particular the Mongol and Ottoman Empires, influence conditions in the West? (page 337)
3. How did disturbances in the rudimentary global economy of the Middle Ages precipitate almost complete financial collapse and widespread social discontent in Europe? (page 344)
4. How did incessant warfare transform the most powerful medieval states? (page 347)
5. Why did the Church fail to provide leadership and spiritual guidance during these difficult times? (page 353)
6. How did European culture offer explanations and solace for the otherwise inexplicable calamities of the times? (page 356)

TAKING IT FURTHER

1. Many of the responses to the calamities of the fourteenth century seem "irrational" to modern eyes. Why might people have reacted in these ways? If one-third of the population of the United States were to die from a mysterious disease in a matter of a few months, how do you think people would react today?
2. Calamities provoked fear. Who were the most likely victims of widespread fear?
3. How could the Church have better helped Christians deal with their suffering during this period?

✓●⎯Practice on MyHistoryLab

12

The Italian Renaissance and Beyond: The Politics of Culture

- The Cradle of the Renaissance: The Italian City-States
- The Influence of Ancient Culture
- The Early Modern European State System

NICCOLÒ MACHIAVELLI (1469–1527) IS BEST KNOWN AS THE FATHER OF MODERN POLITICAL THOUGHT. His little book, *The Prince* (1513), became a classic because it unmasked the realities of political life. For 15 years he worked as a diplomat and political adviser, at the center of the action in his hometown of Florence. But in 1512 the regime there changed. Distrusted by the new rulers and suspected of involvement in an assassination plot, he was imprisoned, tortured, and exiled to his suburban farm. Impoverished, and miserable, Machiavelli survived by selling lumber from his woods to his former colleagues, who cheated him. To help feed his family he snared birds. For entertainment he played cards with the local innkeeper, a butcher, a miller, and two bakers. As he put it, "caught this way among these lice I wipe the mold from my brain (by playing cards) and release my feeling of being ill-treated by Fate."

In the evenings, however, Machiavelli transformed himself. He put on the elegant robes he had worn as a government official. And then, "dressed in a more appropriate manner I enter into the ancient courts of ancient men and am welcomed by them kindly." Machiavelli was reading the works of the ancient Greek and Roman historians, but he described it as a conversation: He asked the ancients

about the reasons for their actions, and he found answers in their books. He recorded their answers in *The Prince*. For four hours, "I feel no boredom, I dismiss every affliction, I no longer fear poverty nor do I tremble at the thought of death: I become completely part of them."

Renaissance means "rebirth," and historians use the word to describe a movement that sought to imitate and understand the culture of antiquity. Machiavelli's evening conversations with the ancients perfectly expressed the sensibility of the Italian Renaissance. This bored, unhappy, disillusioned man found in the ancients the stimulating companions he missed in life. For him, the ancient past was more alive than the present. In this sense Machiavelli was very much a Renaissance man, because feeling part of antiquity is what the Renaissance was all about. Ancient examples of leadership promised to be a cure for the ills of a troubled time.

As we discussed in Chapter 11, during the fourteenth and fifteenth centuries, many Europeans experienced a sense of loss, a preoccupation with death, and pessimism about the human capacity for good. Yet in Florence during this same period, a cultural movement we call the Renaissance began to express a more optimistic view of life. The Renaissance

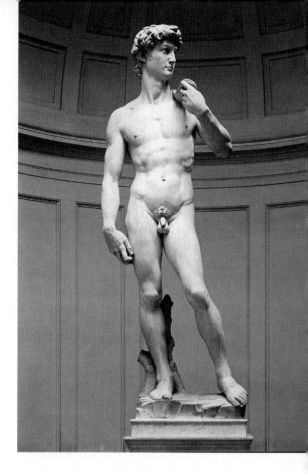

THE IDEALIZED BODY

Michelangelo's statue of the biblical warrior King David transformed the young boy who slew the giant Goliath into a kind of superman whose physical bearing was greater than any normal man. Michelangelo wanted to improve upon nature by altering the proportions of a natural man, making the head and hands significantly larger than normal.

emphasized the responsibilities of humans to improve their communities through social welfare, to beautify their cities, and to devote themselves to the duties of citizenship. Machiavelli—despite the bleak circumstances of his later life—was one of the Renaissance thinkers who thought the world could be set right through concerted political action. Like medieval thinkers he was pessimistic about human nature, but he believed that strong leadership and just laws could counteract human weakness. In this respect he differed from the medieval writers who thought the contemplative life of the monk was the highest calling to which a person could aspire.

The Renaissance came alive in Italy because the political structures of its city-states encouraged cultural experimentation. The idea that society could be reengineered according to the principles that made ancient Greece and Rome

great first appeared in the early 1400s in Italy, but by 1500, the Renaissance had spread to much of western Europe.

The Italian Renaissance was not the first time the West experienced a revival of ancient learning and thought. In the ninth century, members of the Emperor Charlemagne's court had reinvigorated education in Latin (Chapter 9). And in the twelfth century, a European-wide intellectual movement had led to the foundation of the universities, the reintroduction of Roman law, and the spread of scholastic philosophy and theology (Chapter 10). But unlike these earlier rediscoveries of classical learning, the Italian Renaissance helped refashion the concept of Western civilization. From the fifth to the fourteenth centuries, the West identified itself primarily through conformity to Latin Christianity or Roman Catholicism, which meant the celebration of uniform religious rituals in Latin and obedience to the pope. The Renaissance added a new element to this identity. Although by no means anti-Christian, Renaissance thinkers began to think of themselves as the heirs of pre-Christian cultures—Hebrew, Greek, and Roman. They began to imagine Western civilization identified by more than Christianity. Western civilization became the history of a common culture dating back to Antiquity. Through reading the texts and viewing the works of art of the long-dead ancients, people during the Italian Renaissance gained historical and visual perspective on their own world and cultivated a critical attitude about both the past and their own culture. How then did the encounter during the Renaissance with the philosophy, literature, and art of the Ancient world transform the way Europeans thought?

THE CRADLE OF THE RENAISSANCE: THE ITALIAN CITY-STATES

■ How did the political and social climate of the Italian city-states help create Renaissance culture?

Compared with the rest of Europe and other world civilizations, Renaissance Italy had many politically autonomous city-states. The Netherlands and parts of the Rhine valley were as thoroughly urbanized, but only in Italy did cities have so much political power.

The evolution of the Italian city-states went through two distinct phases. The first phase established the institutions of self-government, the procedures for electing officials, and the theory of republicanism. During the eleventh and twelfth centuries, about 100 Italian towns became independent republics, also known as communes because they practiced a "communal" form of government. They developed the laws and institutions of self-government. The male citizens of these tiny republics gathered on a regular basis in the town square to debate important issues. To conduct the day-to-day business of government, they elected city officials from among themselves.

The governmental practices of these city-states produced the political theory of **republicanism,** which described a state in which government officials were elected by the people or a portion of the people. The theory of republicanism was first articulated in the Middle Ages by Marsilius of Padua (1270–1342) in *The Defender of the Peace,* a book that relied on the precedents established by the ancient Roman republic. Marsilius recognized two kinds of government—principalities and republics. Principalities relied upon the idea that political authority came directly from God and trickled down through kings and princes to the rest of humanity. According to this principle, government's job was to enforce God's laws. Marsilius, however, suggested that laws derive not from God, but from the will of the people, who freely choose their own form of government and can change it. In Marsilius's theory, citizens regularly expressed their will through voting.

In the second phase of the evolution, which occurred during the fourteenth century, most city-states abandoned or lost their republican institutions and came to be ruled by princes. This transformation was related to the economic and demographic turmoil created by the international economic collapse and the Black Death (see Chapter 11). Two of the largest republics, however, Florence and Venice survived without losing their liberty to a prince. The Renaissance began in these two city-states (see **Map 12.1**). Their survival as republics helps explain the origins of the Renaissance. Renaissance culture, at least at first, required the freedom of a city-republic.

The Renaissance Republics: Florence and Venice

In an age of despotic princes, Florence and Venice were keenly aware of how different they were from most other cities, and they feared they might suffer the same fate as their neighbors if they did not defend their republican institutions and liberty. In keeping alive the traditions of republican self-government, these

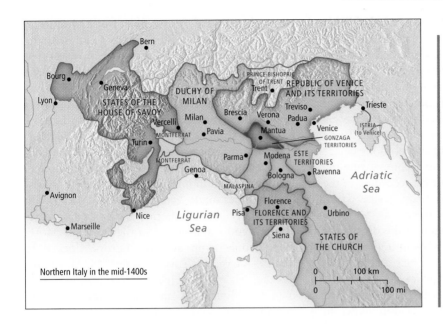

MAP 12.1

Northern Italy in the Mid-Fifteenth Century

During the Renaissance the largest city-states, such as Milan, Venice, and Florence, gained control of the surrounding countryside and smaller cities in the vicinity, establishing regional territorial states. Among the large states, only Venice and Florence remained republics. Milan and Savoy were ruled by dukes. The Gonzaga family ruled Mantua and the Este family Modena and Ferrara. The states of the Church were ruled by the pope in Rome.

two cities created an environment of competition and freedom that stimulated creative ingenuity. Although neither of these cities were democracies or egalitarian, they were certainly more open to new ideas than cities ruled by princes. In both Florence and Venice, citizens prized discussion and debate, the skills necessary for success in business and politics. By contrast, in the principalities all cultural activity tended to revolve around and express the tastes of the ruler, who monopolized much of the wealth. In Florence and Venice a few great families called the *patriciate* controlled most of the property, but these patricians competed among themselves to gain recognition and fame by patronizing great artists and scholars. This patronage by wealthy men and women made the Renaissance possible. Because the tastes of these patricians dictated what writers and artists could do, understanding who these patricians were helps explain Renaissance culture.

FLORENCE UNDER THE MEDICI   The greatest patron during the early Renaissance was the fabulously rich Florentine banker Cosimo de' Medici (1389–1464). Based on his financial power,

Cosimo effectively took control of the Florentine republic in 1434, ushering in a period of unprecedented peace in the city and artistic splendor called the Medicean Age (1434–1494). Cosimo's style of rule was clever. Instead of making himself a prince, which most of the citizens of Florence would have opposed, he managed the policies of the republic from behind the scenes. He seldom held public office, but he made himself the center of Florentine affairs through shrewd negotiating, quiet fixing of elections, and generous distribution of bribes, gifts, and jobs. Cosimo's behind-the-scenes rule illustrated a fundamental value of Renaissance culture—the desire to maintain appearances. In this case, the appearance of a republic was saved, even as the reality of liberty was compromised.

Cosimo's patronage of intellectuals and artists mirrored a similar ambition to maintain appearances. It helped make him appear a great statesman similar to those of the ancient Roman republic, such as the orator and senator Cicero. Cosimo appreciated intelligence and merit wherever he found it. He frequented the discussions of prominent scholars, some of whom became his friends. He financed the acquisition of manuscripts of ancient Latin and Greek literature and philosophy. In return for his financial support, many Florentine scholars dedicated their works to Cosimo. His artistic patronage helped create the image of an open-handed and benevolent godfather for his community. Because he had not been elected to rule Florence, he needed to find a way to create a proper image that would justify his power. To do that, he decorated the private chapel in his palace with frescoes that depicted him accompanying the Magi, the wise men or kings who according to the Bible brought gifts to the baby Jesus. Thus, Cosimo made himself appear similar to those ancient kings who first recognized the divinity of Christ. This image of great wisdom and religious piety helped Cosimo justify the fact that he controlled elections and dictated policies.

Cosimo's grandson Lorenzo the Magnificent (r. 1469–1492) expanded Medici dominance in Florentine politics through "veiled lordship." Although Lorenzo never took the title of prince, he behaved like one by intervening publicly in the affairs of state. Unlike Cosimo's public patronage, Lorenzo's interest in the arts concentrated on building villas, collecting precious gems, and commissioning small bronze statues, things that gave him private pleasure rather than a public reputation. Although a fine poet and an intellectual companion of the most renowned scholars of his age, Lorenzo ignored the republican sensibilities of the Florentines with his princely style of rule and undermined public support for the Medici.

VENICE, THE COSMOPOLITAN REPUBLIC   Venice was more politically stable than Florence. Situated in the midst of a vast lagoon, Venice's main streets consisted of broad channels in which great seagoing merchant ships were moored and canals choked with private boats for local transportation. To protect their fragile city from flooding, the Venetians recognized that they had to cooperate among themselves, and thus the imperative for survival helped create a republic that became a model of stability and ecological awareness. The Venetians, for example, created the world's first environmental regulatory agencies, which were responsible for hydrological projects, such as building dikes and dredging canals, and for forestry management to prevent soil erosion and the consequent silting up of the lagoon.

Venice was among the first European powers to possess overseas colonies. To guarantee its merchant ships access to the eastern Mediterranean and Constantinople, Venice conquered a series of ports along the Adriatic and in Greece. Its involvement in international trade and its distant colonies made Venice unusually cosmopolitan. Many Venetian merchants spent years abroad, and some settled in the colonies. Moreover, people from all over Europe flocked to Venice—Germans, Turks, Armenians, Albanians, Greeks, Slavs, and Jews—each creating their own neighborhoods and institutions. Venetian households owned Russian, Asian, Turkish, and African slaves, all of whom contributed to the diversity of the city.

The most influential foreign group in Venice consisted of the Greeks. Venice had long maintained close commercial and cultural ties with the Greek world. Many of Venice's churches were modeled after the huge basilicas of Constantinople, and many Venetian merchants spoke Greek. After the fall of the Byzantine Empire to the Ottoman Turks in 1453, Greek Christian refugees found a home in Venice and other Italian cities, including scholars who reintroduced Greek philosophy and literature to eager Italian readers. One of these scholars was John Bessarion (1403–1472), a Byzantine archbishop who compiled a library of Greek manuscripts that he left to the republic of Venice. Venice also became the leading center in western Europe for the publication of Greek books.

The defining characteristics of Venetian government were its social stability and liberty, traits that made it the envy of more troubled cities in Italy and republican-minded reformers throughout Europe, especially in England, the Netherlands, and Poland. Whereas the Florentine republic was notoriously unstable and subject to subversion by the Medici, Venice's republican constitution lasted from 1297 to 1797, making it the longest-surviving republic in history. It was, however, an exclusive republic. Out of a total population of nearly 150,000, only the political elite of 2,500 nobles could vote or hold high office. This elite and Venice's many wealthy religious institutions patronized Renaissance thinkers and artists.

At the top of Venetian society was the *doge,* a member of the nobility who was elected to the office for life. The most notable Renaissance doge was Andrea Gritti (r. 1523–1538). Gritti sometimes bent the laws in his favor, but he never manipulated elections or managed Venice's affairs as completely as Cosimo de' Medici did in Florence a century before. Like the Medici, however, Gritti used his own financial resources and his personal influence to transform his city into a major center of Renaissance culture.

Gritti hired some of the most prominent European artists, musicians, and poets to come to Venice. These included the architect and sculptor Jacopo Sansovino (1486–1570). As official architect of the city, Sansovino transformed its appearance with his sculptures, palaces, and churches that imitated the styles of classical Greece and Rome. One of his most notable buildings is the Marciana Library, which was begun in 1537 to house Bessarion's collection of Greek manuscripts.

Princes and Courtiers

Although the Renaissance began in the relative freedom of republics, such as Florence, it soon spread to the Italian principalities. In contrast to the multiple sources of support for the arts and

THE MARCIANA LIBRARY

Built by the architect Jacopo Sansovino, the Marciana Library was built to house the collection of Greek manuscripts given to the Republic of Venice by the exiled Greek archbishop John Bessarion. The Marciana, the oldest public library in the world, is still housed in this building and is open to scholars and university students.

learning in the republics, patronage in the principalities was more constricted, confined to the ruler and members of his court. The term *prince* refers to rulers who possessed formal aristocratic titles, such as the Marquis of Mantua, the Duke of Milan, or the King of Naples. Most Renaissance princes came from local families who seized control of the government by force. Some, however, had been soldiers of fortune who had held on to a city as a spoil of war or had even overthrown a government that had once employed them to defend the city. Regardless of how a prince originally obtained power, his goal was to establish a dynasty, that is, to guarantee the rights of his descendants to continue to rule the city. Some dynasties—such as that of the d'Este family, which ruled Ferrara from 1240 to 1597—were well established and popular.

THE IDEAL PRINCE Federico II da Montefeltro (1422–1482), Duke of Urbino, achieved the glorious reputation that so many princes craved. Although he was illegitimate, his father sent him to study at the most fashionable school in Italy and to apprentice as a soldier under a renowned mercenary captain. In Renaissance Italy, an illegitimate boy could not inherit his father's property. Thus, he usually had two career options: He could become a priest to obtain a living from the church, or he could become a mercenary and take his chances at war. Federico became a mercenary. From among the peasants of Urbino he recruited an army that he hired out to the highest bidder. He soon earned a European-wide reputation for his many victories and enriched the duchy with the income from mercenary contracts and plunder. When his half-brother was assassinated in 1444, Federico became the ruler of Urbino; by 1474 he obtained from the pope the title of duke. Federico epitomized the ideal Renaissance prince—a father figure to his subjects, astute diplomat, brilliant soldier, generous patron, avid collector, and man of learning.

Federico's rule was stern but paternalistic. He personally listened to his subjects' complaints and judged their disputes. His conquests tripled the size of his duchy and financed his building projects and collection of Latin manuscripts. Federico's personal library surpassed that of any contemporary university in Europe, and his wide-ranging reading showed his openness to the latest developments in learning. His greatest achievement, however, was the building of a vast palace, the best example of Renaissance architectural ideals. Because of Federico, the small mountainous duchy of Urbino acquired a cultural importance far greater than its size of 18,000 inhabitants warranted.

THE IDEAL PRINCESS Isabella d'Este (1474–1539), the Marchioness of Mantua, was the ideal Renaissance princess, known during her lifetime as "the first lady of the world." Enjoying an education that was exceptional for a woman in the fifteenth century, she grew up in the court at Ferrara, where she was surrounded by painters and poets and where she cultivated ambassadors and intellectuals. But her influence went far beyond that. When her husband was absent and after his death, she ruled Mantua by herself, earning a reputation as a negotiator and diplomat. An avid reader and collector, she knew virtually all the great artists and writers of her age.

THE IDEAL COURTIER The Renaissance republics developed a code of conduct for the ideal citizen that encouraged citizens to devote their time and energies to public service: to hold public office, pay taxes honestly, and beautify the city through patronage of the arts.

The Renaissance principalities also created a code for the ideal courtier. A courtier was a man or woman who lived in or regularly visited the palace of a prince. Courtiers performed all kinds of services for princes, such as taking care of the family's wardrobe, managing servants, educating children, providing entertainment, keeping accounts, administering estates, going on diplomatic missions, and fighting battles. To best serve the princely family, a courtier needed to cultivate many skills. Men trained in horsemanship, swordplay, and athletics to stay in shape for war. Women learned to draw, dance, play musical

ISABELLA D'ESTE, THE IDEAL PRINCESS
The Marchioness of Mantua, Isabella d'Este, was the most famous woman of the early sixteenth century. She set the fashions for all of Europe, but most important, she was a brilliant negotiator and ruler in her husband's absence.

Source: Titian (c. 1488–1576). Portrait Isabella d'Este (1474–1539), Margravine of Mantua, wife of Francesco Gonzaga, Margrave of Mantua. 1534. Oil on canvas, 102 × 64 cm. Kunsthistorisches Museum, Vienna, Austria. © Erich Lessing/Art Resource, NY

instruments, and engage in witty conversation. Both men and women needed to speak foreign languages to converse with visitors and diplomats. Men, and some of the women, also learned Latin and Greek, which were the foundations of a formal education.

The courtiers performed many of the essential functions in the princely states that elected officials did in the republics. To preserve the peace of the state, princes needed to prevent conflicts among the courtiers. Baldasar Castiglione (1478–1529), who wrote the most influential guide to how a courtier should behave, *The Book of the Courtier*, maintained that two general principles governed all courtly manners—nonchalance and ease:

> I have found quite a universal rule which...seems to me valid above all others, and in all human affairs whether in word or deed: and that is to avoid affectation in every way possible as though it were some very rough and dangerous reef; and...to practice in all things a certain nonchalance, so as to conceal all art and make whatever is done or said appear to be without effort and almost without any thought about it....
>
> Therefore we may call that art true art which does not seem to be art; nor must one be more careful of anything than of concealing it, because if it is discovered, this robs a man of all credit and causes him to be held in slight esteem.[1]

In other words, Castiglione praised the ability to appear to be natural and effortless while doing something that required training and effort. The need to maintain appearances, which we saw in the disguised ruler of Cosimo de' Medici in Florence, became a distinguishing trait of Italian Renaissance culture. *The Book of the Courtier* translated the ideals of civility so admired in Renaissance culture into a plan for human comportment. By using courtly manners, human beings governed the movements of the body according to an almost mathematical ideal of proportion.

By studying *The Book of the Courtier* and its many imitators, which were translated into Latin, English, French, and Spanish, any literate young man or woman of talent and ambition could aspire to act and speak like an aristocrat. Many of its precepts of the courtly ideal were incorporated into the curriculum of schools.

THE PAPAL PRINCE   The Renaissance popes combined the roles of priests and princes. They were

COURTIERS WAITING ON A PRINCELY FAMILY

On the right side of this fresco male courtiers pose while waiting around in the court of the -Gonzaga in Mantua. These elegant gentlemen epitomized the nonchalance and ease idealized in Baldasar Castiglione's *The Book of the Courtier.* On the left, the prince they serve receives a letter from a messenger. Other courtiers surround the prince, princess, and their family.

the heads of the Church. They also had jurisdiction over the Papal States in central Italy. The Papal States were supposed to supply the pope with the income to run the Church, but when the popes had resided in Avignon (France) from 1305 to 1378 and during the Great Schism of 1378–1417, they had lost control of the Papal States. To reassert their control, popes had to force rebellious lords and cities into obedience. Julius II (r. 1503–1513) took his princely role so seriously that he donned armor and personally led troops in battle. The popes also fought with neighboring Italian states that had taken advantage of the weakness of the papacy.

These military adventures undermined the popes' ability to provide moral leadership. In addi-

tion, Pope Alexander VI (r. 1492–1503) ignored his priestly vows of celibacy and fathered four children by his favorite mistress. He financed his son Cesare Borgia's attempts to carve out a principality for himself in Italy. He also married off his daughter, Lucrezia Borgia, in succession to Italian princes who were useful allies in the pope's military ambitions. The enemies of the Borgia family accused them of all kinds of evil deeds, including poisoning one of Lucrezia's husbands, incest, and conducting orgies in the Vatican. Many of these allegations were false or exaggerated, but the papacy's reputation suffered.

Despite their messy engagement with politics, several Renaissance popes gained lasting fame as builders and patrons of the arts. They were embarrassed by the squalor of the city of Rome, which had become a neglected ruin. They sought to create a capital they felt worthy for Christendom. During the reign of Leo X (1513–1521), a son of Lorenzo the Magnificent, Rome became a center of Renaissance culture. Leo's ambition for the city can best be measured in his project to rebuild St. Peter's Basilica as the largest church in the world. He tore down the old basilica, which had been a major pilgrimage destination for more than 1,000 years, and planned the great church that still dominates Rome today.

The Contradictions of the Patriarchal Family

The princes and even the popes justified their authority, in part, on the principle that men should rule. Governments were based on the theory of the patriarchal family in which husbands and fathers dominated women and children. (See *Justice in History* in this chapter.) In advice books on family management, such as Leon Battista Alberti's *Four Books on the Family* (written in the 1430s), patriarchs were the sources of social order and discipline for all society. Although mothers or marriage brokers might arrange marriages, by law fathers or male guardians had to approve the arrangement. They sought beneficial financial and political alliances with other families. This gave older men an advantage in the marriage market because they were usually better off financially than younger ones. As a result, husbands tended to be much older than wives. In Florence in 1427, for example, the typical first marriage was between a 30-year-old man and an 18-year-old woman. Husbands were encouraged to treat their spouses with a kindly but distant paternalism. All women were supposed to be kept under strict male supervision. The only honorable role for an unmarried woman was as a nun.

However, reality often contradicted patriarchal theory. First, death from epidemic diseases, especially the Black Death, and separations due to marital strife, which were common even though divorce was not possible, made family life insecure. Second, the wide age gap meant that husbands were likely to die long before their wives. Thus many women became widows at a relatively young age with children still to raise. Third, many men, especially international merchants and migrant workers, were away from their families for long periods. So regardless of the patriarchal theory that fathers should be in control, in reality they were often absent or dead. Mothers who were supposed to be modest, obedient to their husbands, and invisible to the outside world not only had to raise children alone but often had to manage their dead or absent husbands' business and political affairs. By necessity, many resilient, strong, and active women were involved in worldly affairs, and

CHRONOLOGY: THE CRADLE OF THE RENAISSANCE, THE ITALIAN CITY-STATES

ca. 1070	Founding of first city republics or communes
1324	Marsilius of Padua publishes *The Defender of the Peace*
1434	30-year long rule of Cosimo de' Medici in Florence begins
1444	40-year long rule of Federico II da Montefeltro, Duke of Urbino, begins
1469	Rule of Lorenzo, the Magnificent, de' Medici in Florence begins
1474	Birth of Isabella d'Este, Marchioness of Mantua
1492	Alexander VI becomes pope
1503	Pontificate of Julius II begins
1508	Baldasar Castiglione begins writing *The Book of the Courtier*
1513	Pontificate of Leo X begins
1523	Rule of Andrea Gritti, Doge of Venice, begins

JUSTICE IN HISTORY

Vendetta as Private Justice

During the fourteenth and fifteenth centuries, the official justice the law courts provided competed with the private justice of revenge. Private justice was based on the principle of retaliation. When someone was murdered or assaulted, the victim's closest male relatives were obliged to avenge the injury by harming the perpetrator or one of his relatives to a similar degree. A son was obliged to avenge the death of his father, a brother the injury of his brother. Because governments were weak, the only effective justice was often private justice or, as the Italians called it, *vendetta*. As the most significant source of disorder during the Renaissance, vendetta was a practice that all governments struggled to eradicate.

While criminals tried to cover their tracks, vendetta avengers committed their acts openly and even bragged about them. An act of revenge was carried out in public, so there would be witnesses, and often in a highly symbolic way to humiliate the victim. Private justice always sought to deliver a message.

An episode of revenge from the most sophisticated city in Europe on the eve of the Renaissance illustrates the brutality of private justice, especially the need to make a public example of the victim. After a period of disorder in 1342, the Florentines granted extraordinary judicial powers to a soldier of fortune, Walter of Brienne, known as the Duke of Athens. But Walter offended many Florentines by arresting and executing members of prominent families. In September 1342 a crowd led by these families besieged the government palace in Florence and captured the duke's most hated henchmen, the "conservator" and his son. An eyewitness reported what happened next:

> The son was pushed out in front, and they cut him up and dismembered him. This

done, they shoved out the conservator himself and did the same to him. Some carried a piece of him on a lance or sword throughout the city, and there were those so cruel, so bestial in their anger, and full of such hatred that they ate the raw flesh.[2]

Another account from nearly 200 years later tells of the murder of Antonio Savorgnan, a nobleman who had killed a number of his enemies. Rather than attempting to have Antonio arrested as they could have, the murderers avenged their dead relatives through private justice. One eyewitness recounted that Antonio was attacked while leaving church, and then, "It was by divine miracle that Antonio Savorgnan was wounded: his head opened, he fell down, and he never spoke another word. But before he died, a giant dog came there and ate all his brains, and one cannot possibly deny that his brains were eaten."[3] This time a dog did the avengers' work for them.

In both of these accounts, the writers wanted readers to believe that the victim had been eaten, by humans or by a dog. The eating of a victim signaled that avengers were killing as an act of private justice, a legitimate act of revenge for the murder of close relatives. To convey that message, avengers had to confront their opponent in broad daylight before witnesses. There had to be the appearance, at least, of a fair fight. And to symbolize their revenge, murderers butchered the corpses as if they were the prey of a hunt and fed the remains to hunting dogs or even ate it themselves.

Governments, whether of a tiny city-state or a great monarchy, tried to substitute public justice for private justice, but the violent tradition was strong. Violent crime rates were extremely high during the Renaissance.

By some estimates the murder rate was ten times higher than in the inner cities of the United States today. As governments sought to control violence and the values of moderation spread, a different kind of private justice appeared—the duel. Traditionally, the duel had been a means for knights to resolve disputes, but during the sixteenth century, duels became more common, even among men who had never been soldiers. Duelists had to conform to elaborate rules: There had to be legitimate causes for a challenge to a duel, the combatants had to recognize each other as honorable men, the fight took place only after extensive preparations, judges who were experts on honor had to serve as witnesses, and the combatants had to swear to accept the outcome and not to fight one another again.

Dueling, in effect, civilized private justice. The complexity of the rules of dueling limited the violence and meant that fewer fights took place. Although dueling was always against the law, princes tended to wink at duels because they kept conflicts among their own courtiers under control. But governments became far less tolerant of other forms of private justice, especially among the lower classes. They attempted to abolish feuds and vendettas and insisted that all disputes be submitted to the courts.

For Discussion

1. Why was private justice a challenge to the emerging states of the Renaissance?
2. How did private justice reflect Renaissance values, such as the value of keeping up appearances?

Taking it Further

Muir, Edward. *Mad Blood Stirring: Vendetta in Renaissance Italy.* 1998. A study of the most

PRIVATE JUSTICE

In Titian's painting *The Bravo* (ca. 1515/1520), a man wearing a breastplate and hiding a drawn sword behind his back grabs the collar of his enemy before assaulting him. To enact honorable revenge the attacker could not stab his enemy in the back, but had to give him a chance in a fair fight.

extensive and long-lasting vendetta in Renaissance Italy. It traces the evolution of vendetta violence into dueling.

Weinstein, Donald. *The Captain's Concubine: Love, Honor, and Violence in Renaissance Tuscany.* 2000. An engaging account of an ambush and fight between two nobles over a woman who was the concubine of the father of one of the fighters and the lover of the other. It reveals the relationship between love and violence in Renaissance society.

mothers had much more direct influence on children than fathers. Despite the theory of patriarchy, the families of Renaissance Italy were matriarchies in which mothers ruled.

The contradictions of family life and the tenuous hold many families had on survival encouraged examinations of family life in the culture of Renaissance Italy. Making fun of impotent old husbands married to unfulfilled young wives became a major theme in comic drama. Given the demographic ravages of the Black Death, preachers showed particular concern for the care of children; the chubby little cherubs that seem to fall from the sky in many Renaissance paintings show the universal craving for healthy children.

THE INFLUENCE OF ANCIENT CULTURE

■ How did ancient culture influence the Renaissance?

The need in Renaissance Italy to provide effective models for how citizens, courtiers, and families should behave stimulated a reexamination of ancient culture. The civilizations of ancient Greece and Rome had long fascinated the educated classes in the West. In Italy, where most cities were built among the ruins of the ancient past, antiquity was particularly seductive. During the fourteenth and fifteenth centuries Italian thinkers and artists attempted to foster a rebirth of ancient cultures. At first they merely tried to imitate the Latin of the best Roman writers. Then contact with Greek-speaking refugees from Byzantium led scholars to do the same thing with Greek. Artists trekked to Rome to sketch ancient ruins, sculptures, and medallions. Wealthy collectors hoarded manuscripts of ancient philosophy, built libraries to house them, bought every ancient sculpture they could find, and dug up ruins to find more antiquities to adorn their palaces. Patrons demanded that artists imitate the styles of the ancients and display similar concern for rendering natural forms. They especially prized lifelike representations of the human body.

Patrons, artists, and scholars during the Renaissance also began to understand the enormous cultural distance between themselves and the ancients, which gave them a sense of their place in history The leaders in the reexamination of ancient cultures were the **humanists**, scholars who studied ancient Greek and Latin texts. The humanists developed techniques of literary analysis to determine when a text had been written and to differentiate authentic texts from ones that copyists' mistakes had corrupted. Humanists devoted themselves to grammar, rhetoric, history, poetry, and ethics. The modern university disciplines in the Humanities are the descendants of the Renaissance humanists.

The Humanists

The first humanist was Francesco Petrarca (1304–1374), known in English as Petrarch. Petrarch and his follower Lorenzo Valla (1407–1457) developed critical methods by editing classical texts to establish the original words, a method different from the medieval scribe's temptation to alter or improve a text as he saw fit. Petrarch's method was called **philology,** the study of the meaning of words in a specific historical context. The meaning of many Latin words had changed since the fall of Ancient Rome, and Petrarch attempted to trace the changes in meaning. He strived to get the words right because he wanted to understand exactly what an ancient author had meant. This concern with finding original texts and the meaning of words gave Petrarch and his followers insight into the individuality of writers who lived and wrote many centuries before.

An interest in the meaning of words led Petrarch to study **rhetoric,** the art of persuasive or emotive speaking and writing. He came to think that rhetoric was superior to philosophy because he preferred a good man over a wise one, and rhetoric offered examples worthy of imitation rather than abstract principles subject to debate. Petrarch wanted people to behave morally. And he believed that the most efficient way to inspire his readers to do the right thing was to write moving rhetoric. (See *Encounters and Transformations* in this chapter.)

ENCOUNTERS AND TRANSFORMATIONS

Encounters with the Ancient World: Petrarch Writes a Letter to Cicero's Ghost

Petrarch was famous for his poetry, in both his native Italian and Latin. To improve his Latin style, he was always watching for anything by the Roman orator Cicero (106–43 B.C.E.). In 1345 Petrarch discovered a previously unknown collection of letters Cicero had written to his friend Atticus.

As Petrarch read the letters, however, he suffered a shock. Cicero had a reputation as the greatest Roman sage, a model of Latin style, philosophical sophistication, and ethical standards. But in the letters Petrarch found not sage moral advice, but gossip, rumors, and crude political calculations. Cicero looked like a scheming politician, a man of crass ambition rather than grand philosophical wisdom. Although Petrarch could never forgive Cicero for failing to live up to his philosophical ideals, he had discovered a man so human he could imagine having a conversation with him.

And a conversation was precisely what Petrarch set out to have. Cicero, however, had been dead for 1,388 years. So Petrarch wrote a letter to his ghost. Adopting Cicero's own elegant Latin, Petrarch attacked the Roman for going against the moral advice he had given others. Petrarch quoted Cicero back to Cicero, asking how he could be such a hypocrite: "I long had known how excellent a guide you have proved for others; at last I was to learn what sort of guidance you gave yourself.... Now it is your turn to be the listener."[4]

Petrarch lectured Cicero for his corruption and moral failures. The point of the exercise of writing a letter to a dead man was in part to practice good Latin style, but also to compare the ideals Cicero had avowed in his philosophical work and the way he really lived. Making comparisons is an elementary critical technique, and it became the hallmark of Petrarch's analysis. His letter made the ancients seem like other men who made mistakes and told lies. No longer a repository of timeless truths, the ancient world became a specific time and place. After his letter to Cicero, Petrarch wrote letters to other illustrious ancients in which he revealed their human qualities and shortcomings.

Petrarch's encounter with the ancients changed how he understood the past and humanity. The ancients were history in the most literal sense. They were long dead. But they were also human, capable of brave deeds and vulnerable to temptations, just the way Petrarch and his contemporaries were.

For Discussion

How did Petrarch's encounter with Cicero transform his view of his own culture? How can an encounter with another culture change how you view your own?

Renaissance humanists sought to resurrect a form of Latin that had been dead for more than 1,000 years and was distinct from the living Latin used by the Church, law courts, and universities—which they thought inferior to ancient Latin. In this effort, humanists acquired a difficult but functional skill that opened many employment opportunities to them and gave them public influence. They worked as schoolmasters, secretaries, bureaucrats, official historians, and ambassadors. Many other humanists were wealthy men who did not need a job but were fascinated with the way the new learning could be used to persuade other people to do what they wanted them to do.

Because humanists could be found on different sides of almost all important questions, the significance of their work lies less in what they said than in how they said it. They wrote about practically everything: painting pictures, designing buildings, planting crops, draining swamps, raising children, managing a household, and educating women. They debated the nature of human liberty, the virtues of famous men, the vices of wicked ones, the meaning of Egyptian hieroglyphics, and the cosmology of the universe.

How did the humanists' use of Latin words and grammar influence the understanding of this vast range of subjects? Each language organizes experience according to the needs of the people who speak it, and all languages make arbitrary distinctions, dividing up the world into different categories. People who study a foreign language run across these arbitrary distinctions when they learn that some expressions can never be translated exactly. When humanists read classical Latin texts, they encountered unfamiliar words, sentence patterns, and rhetorical models—the linguistic leftovers of ancient experience and culture. Humanists' recovery of what can be called the *Latin point of view* often altered their own perceptions and shaped their own cultural experiences in subtle ways.

For example, when a fifteenth-century humanist examined what the ancient Romans had written about painting, he found the phrase *ars et ingenium*. *Ars* referred to skills that could be learned by following established rules and adhering to models provided by the best painters. Thus, the ability of a painter to draw a straight line, to mix colors properly, and to identify a saint with the correct symbol were examples of *ars* or what we would call craftsmanship. The meaning of *ingenium* was more difficult to pin down, however. It referred to the inventive capacity of the painter, to his or her ingenuity. The humanists discovered that the ancients had made a distinction between the craftsmanship and the ingenuity of a painter. As a result, when humanists and their pupils looked at paintings, they began to make the same distinction and began to admire the genius of artists whose work showed ingenuity as well as craftsmanship. Ingenuity came to refer to the

ability of the painter to arrange figures in a novel way, to employ unusual colors, or to create emotionally exciting effects that conveyed piety, sorrow, or joy as the subject demanded. So widespread was the influence of the humanists that the most ingenious artists demanded higher prices and became the most sought after. In this way, creative innovation was encouraged in the arts, but it all started very simply with the introduction of new words into the Latin vocabulary of the people who paid for paintings. A similar process of establishing new categories altered every subject the humanists touched.

The humanist movement spread rapidly during the fifteenth century. Leonardo Bruni (ca. 1370–1444), who became the chancellor of Florence (the head of the government's bureaucracy), created **civic humanism** to defend the republican institutions and values of the city. By reading the ancient writers, Bruni rediscovered the ethics of public service. Civic humanists argued that the ethical man should devote himself to active service to his city rather than to passive contemplation in scholarly retreat or monastic seclusion.

Lorenzo Valla employed humanist scholarship to undermine papal claims to authority over secular rulers. The pope's theoretical authority depended on the so-called Donation of Constantine, according to which the Emperor Constantine had transferred his imperial authority in Italy to the pope in the fourth century. By using philology, Valla demonstrated that many of the Latin words found in the Donation could not have been written before the eighth century. For example, the document used the word *satrap*, which Valla was confident a Roman at the time of Constantine would not have known. Thus, he proved that this famous document was a forgery. Valla's analysis of the Donation was one of the first uses of philology and historical analysis of documents to serve a political cause. As a result, many rulers and especially the popes saw the need to hire a humanist to defend their own interests.

The intellectual curiosity of the humanists led them to master many topics. This breadth of accomplishment contributed to the ideal of the "Renaissance Man (or "Renaissance Woman"), a person who sought excellence in everything he or she did. No one came closer to this ideal than Leon Battista Alberti (1404–1472). As a young man, Alberti wrote Latin comedies and satirical works that drew on Greek and Roman models, but as he matured he tackled more serious subjects. Although he was a bachelor and thus knew nothing firsthand about marriage, he drew upon the ancient writers to create the most influential Renaissance book on the family, which included sections on relations between husbands and wives, raising children, and estate management. He composed the first grammar of the Italian language. He dabbled in mathematics and wrote on painting, law, the duties of bishops, love, horsemanship, dogs, agriculture, and flies. He mapped the city of Rome and wrote the most important fifteenth-century work on the theory and practice of architecture. His interest in architecture, moreover, was not just theoretical. In the last decades of his life, Alberti dedicated much of his spare time to building projects that included restoring an ancient church in Rome, designing Renaissance façades for medieval churches, and erecting a palace for his most important patron. One of his last projects was the first significant work for making and deciphering secret codes in the West.

The humanists guaranteed their lasting influence through their innovations in education. Humanist education did not seek to train specialists or professionals, such as the theologians, lawyers, and physicians. Instead, humanists aimed to create well-rounded men (women were not usually accepted in humanist schools), critical thinkers who could tackle any problem that life presented. The curriculum emphasized the study of Greek and Latin and the best authors in those ancient languages. Command of good grammar, the ability to write and speak effectively, knowledge of history, and an appreciation for virtuous behavior were the goals of humanist education. It was a curriculum well suited for the active life of civic leaders, courtiers, princes, and churchmen. The influence of the humanist curriculum persists in the general education requirements of modern American universities, which require students, now of both sexes, to obtain intellectual breadth before they specialize in narrow professional training.

Historians have identified a few female humanists from the Renaissance. Because they were so unusual, learned humanist women were often ridiculed. Jealous men accused the humanist Isotta Nogarola (1418–1466) of promiscuity and incest, and other women insulted her in public. A famous male schoolmaster said that Isotta was too feminine in her writings and should learn how to find "a man within the woman."[5] Laura Cereta (1475–1506), who knew Greek as well as Latin and was adept at mathematics, answered the scorn of a male critic with rhetorical insult:

> I would have been silent, believe me, if that savage old enmity of yours had attacked me alone....But I cannot tolerate your having attacked my entire sex. For this reason my thirsty soul seeks revenge, my sleeping pen is aroused to literary struggle, raging anger stirs mental passions long chained by silence. With just cause I am moved to demonstrate how great a reputation for learning and virtue women have won by their inborn excellence, manifested in every age as knowledge, the [purveyor] of honor. Certain, indeed, and legitimate is our possession of this inheritance, come to us from a long eternity of ages past.[6]

These few humanist women were among the first feminists. They advocated female equality and female education but also urged women to take control of their lives. Cereta maintained that if women paid as much attention to learning as they did to their appearances, they would achieve equality. But despite the efforts of female humanists, progress in women's education was slow. The universities remained closed to women until late in the nineteenth century. The first woman to earn a degree from a university only did so in 1678. It took another 200 years before many others could follow her example. (See *Different Voices* in this chapter.)

The humanists educated generations of wealthy young gentlemen whose appreciation of Antiquity led them to collect manuscripts of

DIFFERENT VOICES THE BATTLE OF THE SEXES

Abusive writing about women was pervasive in Western literature. However, during the Renaissance the "women's question" raised the issue of whether education could improve women's lot in life. What distinguished this debate during the Renaissance was the active role women took in defending their own interests.

Although they wrote in the seventeenth century, Ferrante Pallavicino (1618–1644) and Arcangela Tarabotti (1604–1652) represented the culmination of the Italian Renaissance debate about women. Pallavicino pulled out the usual litany of the anti-woman argument. Tarabotti answered Pallavicino on every point.

Ferrante Pallavicino, Letter addressed to "Ungrateful Woman"

I know how you mock my scorn: a woman never grieves unless she weeps tears of blood, and her normal tears are pure deceit in liquid form, the holding back of pretense....

Your ingratitude has reached the limit in bad manners; it has taught me that there is nothing human in a woman but her face, with which she lies even when silent and warns how there is nothing to expect but falsity from a being who deceives at first sight. She shares the same genus of animal with man, appropriating for herself, however, all the bestial qualities that ensure, while differing from man in that she simply has no reason whatsoever: as a consequence, she acts like a brute animal....

Unfortunate women are those without men to provide the support that remedies their own weakness! Without men they could not avoid being flung down at every moment, like the blind and the mad, into a thousand chasms. The women of Tartary (Mongolia and Turkey) understood this well: it was their custom never to allow their head to be covered by a more precious headdress than the form of a human foot, to signify that woman, brainless and witless, finds her greatest glory in her subjection to man. Representing themselves in the act of being trodden underfoot, they paid homage to their noblest part; they were not foolish like other women, adorning their heads with treasures from robbed tombs or weighed down with braided chains dotted with gems.

---

ancient literature, philosophy, and science. These patrons also encouraged artists to imitate the ancients. What began as a narrow literary movement became the stimulus to see human society and nature through entirely new eyes. Some humanists, especially in northern Europe, applied the techniques of humanist scholarship with revolutionary results to the study of the Bible and the sources of Christianity.

Understanding Nature: Moving Beyond the Science of the Ancients

The humanists' initial concern was to imitate the language of the ancients. Most of them preferred to spend time reading rather than observing the world. In fact, their methods were ill-suited to understanding nature: When they wanted to explain some natural phenomenon such as the movement of blood through the body or the apparent movements of the planets and stars, they looked to ancient authorities for answers rather than to nature itself. Renaissance scientists searched for ancient texts about nature, and then debated about which ancient author had been correct. The humanists' most prominent contributions to science consisted of recovering classical texts and translating the work of ancient Greek scientists into the more widely understood Latin. The Renaissance approach contrasted to the scientific method of today, in which scientists form a hypothesis and then determine whether it is correct by experimenting and observing the natural world as directly as possible.

Arcangela Tarabotti, "Misognynists Named and Unnamed Are Condemned" from *Paternal Tyranny*

(Divine Omnipotence) wills (women) supreme authority over the male sex to be made manifest, as he is unworthy of any other treatment but prison and stripes (scars from whipping). So it is simply not true that man, like staves to the vine, supports the woman who otherwise would fall spineless; rather he approaches her to induce her to fall by countless ploys and be supported by him.

A clever mind wishing to operate in a sinister fashion easily manages to invent chimeras (an absurd creation of the imagination) that distort the true nature of things and force the strangest meanings from bits of arcane learning. And thus our most astute author wrongly interprets the custom of women of Tartary, who bore on their heads as their most precious ornament a human foot. The correct meaning is that woman, as quick and ready for noble deeds, runs with many feet along the path of virtue, keeping one united with her mind so she can walk securely on her way, without stumbling. She needs the extra assistance so as not to fall into the snares and traps set for her innocent nature without end by the cursed "genius" of the male sex, who is always opposed to doing good.

His interpretation, therefore, that there is no greater glory for a woman, a mindless creature with no sense, than to be subject to the male is obviously false. The contrary is true: that her greatest torment and suffering is to find herself subjected to the tyranny and inhumane whims of men.

Source: Arcangela Tarabotti, *Paternal Tyranny*, edited and translated by Letizia Panizza. (Copyright © 2004 by The University of Chicago. Reprinted by permission of the University of Chicago Press.) 146–149, 158–162.

For Discussion

1. Do Pallavicino and Tarabotti argue through rhetoric or logic? What is the difference between the two ways of arguing?

2. How would you refute Pallavicino? How would you refute Tarabotti?

The texts rediscovered and translated during the Renaissance, nevertheless, broadened the discussion of two subjects crucial to the scientific revolution of the late sixteenth and seventeenth centuries—astronomy and anatomy. In 1543 the Polish humanist Nicolaus Copernicus (1473–1543) resolved the complications in the system of the second-century astronomer Ptolemy. Whereas Ptolemy's writings had placed Earth at the center of the universe, Copernicus cited other ancient writers who put the sun in the center. Thus, the first breakthrough in theoretical astronomy was achieved not by making new observations, but by comparing ancient texts. Nothing was proven, however, until Galileo Galilei (1564–1642) turned his newly invented telescope to the heavens in 1610 to observe the stars through his own eyes rather than through an ancient text (see Chapter 17).

Andreas Vesalius (1514–1564) built upon recently published studies in anatomy from ancient Greece to write a survey of human anatomy, *On the Fabric of the Human Body* (1543), a book that encouraged dissection of corpses and anatomical observations. With Vesalius, anatomy moved away from relying exclusively on the authority of ancient books to encouraging medical students and physicians to examine the human body with their own eyes. Building upon Vesalius's work, Gabriele Falloppio (ca. 1523–1562) made many original observations of muscles, nerves, kidneys, bones, and most famously the "fallopian tubes," which lead from the ovaries to the uterus in the female reproductive system, which he described for the first time.

Besides recovering ancient scientific texts, the most important Renaissance contributions to science came secondhand from developments in the visual arts and technology. Florentine artists during the early fifteenth century applied mathematics to paintings. The goal was to make paintings more accurately represent reality by creating the visual illusion of the third dimension of depth on a two-dimensional rectangular surface, a technique known as linear perspective (see the next section, "Antiquity and Nature in the Arts"). These artists contributed to a more refined understanding of how the eye perceives objects, which led to experiments with glass lenses. A more thorough knowledge of optics made possible the invention of the telescope and microscope.

Invented in the 1450s the printing press combined with the availability of cheap paper led to the printing revolution, which rapidly expanded the availability of books. Scientific books accounted for only about 10 percent of the titles of the first printed books, but the significance of printing for science was greater than the sales figures would indicate. Print meant that new discoveries and ideas reached a wider audience, duplication of scientific investigation could be avoided, illustrations were standardized, and scientists built upon each other's work. With the invention of the printing press, scientific work became closely intertwined with publishing, so that published scientific work advanced science, and scientific work that was not published went largely unnoticed. Leonardo da Vinci (1452–1519), the greatest Renaissance observer of nature, contributed nothing to science because he failed to publish his findings. Because he hid the drawing he made of an airplane in a secret notebook, he had no influence on the development of air travel. The fundamental principle of modern science and, in fact, of all modern scholarship is that research must be made available to everyone through publication.

Antiquity and Nature in the Arts

More than any other age in Western history, the Italian Renaissance is identified with the visual

LEONARDO INVENTS A FLYING MACHINE AND PARACHUTE

Leonardo da Vinci's notebooks are filled with numerous examples of his unprecedented inventions. In his drawings on the top he designed a flying machine similar to a modern helicopter and a parachute. On the bottom are modern models based on his drawings. Leonardo kept his inventions in his secret notebooks, which meant no one could follow up on his ideas.

arts. The unprecedented numbers of brilliant artists active in a handful of Italian cities during the fifteenth and sixteenth centuries overshadow any other contribution of Renaissance culture.

Under the influence of the humanists, Renaissance artists began to imitate the sculpture, architecture, and painting of the artists from classical Greece and Rome. At first they merely tried to copy ancient styles and poses. Just as humanists recaptured antiquity by collecting, translating, and analyzing the writings of classical authors, so Renaissance artists made drawings of classical medals, sculpture, and

CHRONOLOGY: INFLUENCE OF ANCIENT CULTURE

1345	Francesco Petrarca (Petrarch), first humanist, discovers Cicero's letters to Atticus
1402	Leonardo Bruni, chancellor of Florence, begins to write about civic humanism
1404–1472	Leon Battista Alberti, humanist and architect
1418–1466	Isotta Nogarola, first female humanist
1440	Lorenzo Valla begins circulating his critique of the Donation of Constantine
ca. 1454	Johannes Gutenberg begins printing books
1475–1506	Laura Cereta, humanist
1543	Nicolaus Copernicus publishes new cosmological theory
	Andreas Vesalius publishes on human anatomy
1561	Gabriele Falloppio publishes his *Anatomy*
1610	Galileo Galilei, astronomer, publishes discoveries made possible by the telescope

architecture. Because artists believed that classical art was superior to their own, these sketches became valuable models from which other artists could learn. Two of the most influential Florentine artists, the architect Filippo Brunelleschi (1377–1446) and the sculptor Donatello (1386–1466), probably went to Rome together as young men to sketch the ancient monuments.

Renaissance artists, however, wanted not only to copy ancient styles, they also wanted to understand how the ancients had made their figures so lifelike. That led them to observe nature itself more directly, especially the anatomy of the human body. Renaissance art, then, was driven by the passionate desire of artists and their patrons to imitate both ancient works and nature. These twin desires produced a creative tension in their work because the ancients, whose works of art often depicted gods and goddesses, had idealized and improved on what they observed in nature. Renaissance artists sought to depict simultaneously the ideal and the real—an impossible goal, but one that sparked remarkable creativity.

The work of the most important painter of the early Renaissance in Florence, Masaccio (1401–ca. 1428) exemplified this blending of the idealized and the natural. In the Brancacci chapel, Masaccio depicted street scenes from Florence complete with portraits of actual people, including himself. These

were examples of naturalism. On other figures in the scene called *The Tribute Money* (shown on the next page)—Jesus, St. Peter, and St. John—he placed heads copied from ancient sculptures of gods. These were examples of idealized beauty, which were especially suitable for saints. The realistic figures helped viewers identify with the subject of the picture by allowing them to recognize people they actually knew. The idealized figures represented the saintly, whose superior moral qualities made them appear different from average people.

The Renaissance style evolved in Masaccio's hometown of Florence early in the fifteenth century. In 1401 the 24-year-old Brunelleschi entered a competition to design bronze panels depicting the biblical account of Abraham's willingness to sacrifice his son Isaac for the north doors of the Baptistery of Florence's cathedral. He lost to Lorenzo Ghiberti (1378–1455). Look at the illustrations on page 385. Ghiberti's panel shown on the right reveals the two characteristic elements of the early Renaissance style: idealization and naturalism. The head of Isaac is modeled after a classical Roman sculpture, and the figures and horse on the left of his panel are depicted as realistically as possible. In these elements, Ghiberti was imitating both antiquity and nature.

Ghiberti worked on the north doors for 21 years. He won such fame that when he finished he was immediately offered a new commission to

THE TRIBUTE MONEY: COMBINING NATURAL AND IDEALIZED REPRESENTATIONS

In this detail of a fresco of Christ and his apostles, Masaccio mixed naturalism and idealized beauty. The figure on the right with his back turned to the viewer is a tax collector, who is depicted as a normal human being. The head of the fourth figure to the left of him, who represents one of the apostles, was copied from an ancient statue that represents ancient ideals of beauty.

Source: Dagli Orti/Picture Desk, Inc./Kobal Collection

complete panels for the east doorway. These doors, begun in 1425, took 27 years to finish. In the east doors, Ghiberti substituted a simple square frame for the Gothic frame of the north doors, thereby liberating his composition. In the illustration on page 386, which depicts the biblical story of the brothers Jacob and Esau, the background architecture of rounded arches and classical columns creates the illusion of depth. This illusion is achieved through **linear perspective**, that is, the use of geometrical principles to depict a three-dimensional space on a flat, two-dimensional surface. Linear perspective, a method for imitating the way nature appears to

the human eye, was an achievement of the Renaissance, something never perfected before. In the panels of the east doors, Ghiberti created the definitive Renaissance interpretation of the ancient principles of the harmony produced by geometry. Michelangelo said that the doors were fit to serve as the "gates of paradise."

Most humanist theorists of painting linked artistic creativity with masculinity. By the sixteenth century, however, these theorists were proved wrong, as female painters rose to prominence. The most notable was Sofonisba Anguissola (ca. 1532–1625). Born into an aristocratic family, she received a humanist education along

THE COMPETITION PANELS OF THE SACRIFICE OF ISAAC

These two panels were the finalists in a competition to design the cast bronze doors on the north side of the Baptistery in Florence. Each demonstrates a bold new design that attempted to capture the emotional trauma of the exact moment when an angel arrests Abraham's arm from sacrificing his son Isaac (Genesis 22:1–12). Both artists went on to be closely associated with the new style of the Renaissance. The panel on the left, by Filippo Brunelleschi, lost to the one on the right, by Lorenzo Ghiberti. Notice how the Ghiberti relief better conveys the drama of the scene by projecting the elbow of Abraham's upraised arm outward toward the viewer. As a result, the viewer's line of sight follows the line of the arm and knife directly toward Isaac's throat.

with her five sisters and brother. As a woman, she was prohibited from studying anatomy or drawing male models. So she specialized in portraits, often of members of her family, and self-portraits. She developed a distinctive style of depicting animated faces as in the portrait of her sisters playing chess shown on page 387. Her fame was so great that King Philip II of Spain hired her as his official court painter. Her example inspired other aristocratic women to take up painting.

The Renaissance Patron

All the Renaissance arts displayed the influence of patrons, the wealthy people who controlled the city-states and had been educated in humanist schools. Until the end of the sixteenth century, all painters, sculptors, and even poets worked for a patron. A patron, who could be an individual or a group, such as a religious order or a government, commissioned a work of art, such as an altar painting, portrait bust, statue, or palace. Patron and artist would agree on a contract, which might specify exactly what the artist was to do, what kinds of materials he was to use (almost all Renaissance artists were men), how much they could cost, how much he could rely on assistants, how much he had to do himself, and even how he was to arrange figures in the work. Michelangelo Buonarroti (1475–1564) sculpted *David*, which has become the most famous work of Renaissance art, to fulfill a contract that had been debated in a

LINEAR PERSPECTIVE
In these square panels Ghiberti explored the full potential of the newly discovered principles of linear perspective.

committee meeting of the government of Florence. Regardless of their talent, artists could never do whatever they wanted.

Some patrons supported the career of an artist for an extended time. Princes, in particular, liked to take on an artist—give him a regular salary and perhaps even an official title—in exchange for having him do whatever the prince wanted. Thus, Duke Lodovico Sforza (1451–1508) brought Leonardo da Vinci to Milan, where Leonardo painted a portrait of the duke's mistress, devised plans for a giant equestrian statue of the duke's father, designed stage sets and carnival pageants, painted the interior decorations of the castle, and did engineering work.

Most patrons supported the arts to enhance their own prestige and power. Some, such as Pope Julius II, had exceptional influence on artists. He persuaded Michelangelo, who saw himself as a sculptor, to paint the ceiling of the Sistine Chapel.

The Spread of the Renaissance

The Renaissance spread as other Europeans encountered the culture of Italy. Princes and aristocrats who studied or fought in Italy were the

PORTRAITS IN RENAISSANCE ART
Sofonisba Anguissola excelled at portrait painting. In this collective portrait of her three sisters and their nurse, she rejected the traditional props associated with women, such as pets or needlework, to show them engaged in the challenging intellectual game of chess. In this way Anguissola subverted female stereotypes.

first to export Italian art and artists abroad. King Philip of Spain was just one of many sixteenth-century monarchs who lured Italian artists to his court. Leonardo da Vinci spent his last years living in a great chateau given him by the king of France. Perhaps no country was more enthralled with the Italian Renaissance than Poland where many aristocrats who had studied in Italy built

CHRONOLOGY: ANTIQUITY AND NATURE IN THE ARTS

1401	Lorenzo Ghiberti and Filippo Brunelleschi compete for commission to make the door panels on the Florentine baptistery
1404–1407	Donatello, Florentine sculptor, and Filippo Brunelleschi go to Rome to investigate Antiquities
ca. 1425	Filippo Brunelleschi, Florentine sculptor and architect, demonstrates the use of linear perspective
1452–1519	Leonardo da Vinci, Florentine painter and inventor
1504	Michelangelo Buonarroti, Florentine sculptor, painter, architect, poet, completes his statue of David
ca. 1532–1625	Sofonisba Anguissola, painter

palaces and whole planned towns in imitation of Renaissance ideals. Even the Kremlin in Moscow was designed by Italian architects.

After the collapse of the Italian city-states during the Italian Wars (1494–1530), the growing power of the western European monarchies facilitated the spread of Renaissance culture outside of Italy. As we discuss next, the French invaded the Italian peninsula at the end of the fifteenth century and sparked years of warfare in Italy; however, King Francis I (r. 1515–1547) was impressed by what he saw. He had the first Renaissance-style chateau built in France and hired Italian artists, including Leonardo da Vinci, to bring Renaissance culture to his kingdom.

THE EARLY MODERN EUROPEAN STATE SYSTEM

■ How did the monarchies of western Europe become more assertive and effective during the late fifteenth and early sixteenth centuries?

The civic independence that had made the Italian Renaissance possible was challenged during the Italian Wars when France, Spain, and the Holy Roman Empire attempted to carve up the peninsula for themselves. The wars started in 1494 when the French king attempted to seize the kingdom of Naples. His invasion of Italy drew in rival monarchs from Spain and the Holy Roman Empire who could not tolerate French control of wealthy Italy and pitted the Italian city-states against one another as they attempted to save themselves from foreign conquest. These wars were a disaster for Italy. For nearly 40 years wave after wave of foreign armies crossed the Alps and turned Italy into a battle ground. The low point was the sack of Rome in 1527 when German mercenaries plundered the city, destroyed works of art, and imprisoned the Medici pope. By 1530 the king of Spain had defeated his rival in France for control of Italy. All of the large cities except Venice came under Spanish domination.

The surrender of the rich city-states of Italy was the first sign of a transformation in the European system of states. Only the large monarchies of the West, such as France, Spain, and England, could muster the materiel and manpower necessary to put and keep a large army in the field. The Italian Wars revealed the outlines of the early modern European state system, which was built on the power of large countries ruled by kings. These kings amassed unprecedented resources that not only crushed Italy, but also enabled Europe to dominate much of the globe through colonies in the Americas, Asia, and Africa (see Chapter 13).

The Origins of Modern Historical and Political Thought

The revival of the monarchies of western Europe and the loss of the independence of the Italian city-states forced a rethinking of politics. As in so many other fields, the Florentines led the way. To understand their own troubled city-state, they analyzed politics by comparing one kind of government with another and observing current events.

The shock of the Italian Wars that began in 1494 stimulated a quest for understanding the causes of Italy's fall and prompted a new kind of history writing that went beyond the medieval chronicles. There had been critical histories during the Middle Ages, such as Jean Froissart's account of France during the Hundred Years' War and Jan Dlugosz's history of the kings of Poland. The new Renaissance history, however, set new standards for criticizing evidence and borrowed from the rhetorical precepts of the humanists to make arguments. The first person to write a successful history in the new vein was Francesco Guicciardini (1483–1540). Born to a well-placed Florentine family, educated in a humanist school and experienced as a diplomat, governor, and adviser to the Medici, Guicciardini combined literary skill and practical political experience. Besides collecting information about contemporary events, he kept a record of how his own thoughts and values evolved in response to what he observed. One of the hallmarks of his work was that as he analyzed the motives of others, he engaged in self-scrutiny and self-criticism. His masterpiece, *The History of Italy* (1536–1540), was the first account of events that occurred across the entire Italian peninsula. Guicciardini saw human causes for historical events rather than the hidden hand of God. He suggested, for example, that emotions mattered more than rational calculation and noted that nothing ever turns out as anticipated.

Just as Guicciardini examined the causes of historical change, Niccolo Macchiavelli explored the dynamics of effective rule. In *The Prince* Machiavelli encouraged rulers to understand the underlying principles of political power, which differed from the personal morality expected of those who were not rulers. A prince had to appear to be a moral person, but Machiavelli pointed out that the successful prince might sometimes have to be immoral to protect the state. How would the prince know when this might be the case?

Machiavelli's answer was that "necessity" forced political decisions to override normal morality. The prince "must consider the end result," which meant that his highest obligation was preserving the existence of the state that had been entrusted to him and providing security for all its citizens. This obligation took precedence even over his religious duty.

Through Guicciardini's analysis of human motivations and Machiavelli's attempt to discover what made certain actions necessary, historical and political thought moved in a new direction. The key to understanding history and politics was in the details of human events. To Guicciardini, these details provided clues to the psychology of leaders. To Machiavelli, they revealed the hidden mechanisms of chance and planning that governed not just political decisions, but all human events.

Monarchies: The Foundation of the State System

The European state system was one of the most lasting achievements of the Renaissance. By the state system, historians referred to a complex of interrelated changes. First, governments established standing armies. As a result of the military revolution that brought large numbers of infantry to the field of battle and gunpowder cannons to besiege cities and castles, governments had to modernize their armies or face defeat. Since the ninth century, kings had relied on feudal levies in which soldiers were recruited to fulfill their personal obligation to a lord, but by the late fifteenth century, governments began to organize standing professional armies. These armies, however, were expensive because the soldiers had to be regularly paid and the new artillery was costly. Moreover, fortifications had to be improved to withstand the artillery. As a result, kings were desperate for new revenues.

The need for revenues led to the second development, the growth of taxation. Every European state struggled with the problem of taxation. The need to tax efficiently produced the beginnings of a bureaucracy of tax assessors and collectors. People resisted the new taxes, creating tension with the monarch.

This tension led to the third development. Monarchs attempted to weaken the resistance by abolishing the tax exemptions of local communities and ignoring regional assemblies and parliaments that were supposed to approve new taxes. During the twelfth and thirteenth centuries, effective government was local government, and kings could seldom interfere in the affairs of towns and regions. During the fifteenth century, however, to raise taxes and impose their will throughout the realm, kings everywhere tried to eliminate or erode the independence of towns and parliaments.

Fourth, monarchs tried to reduce the independence of the aristocracy and the Church. In the kingdoms of western Europe, the most significant threats to the power of the king were the aristocrats. Kings struggled to co-opt these aristocrats or force them to submit. Most monarchs also sought to oblige churchmen to become agents of government policy. Monarchs were most successful in reducing the power of the aristocrats and the Church in France, England, and Spain. In eastern Europe, despite the attempts by kings to accomplish what their western cousins had done, the aristocracy remained in control. In Poland, Bohemia, and Hungary, the aristocrats elected the kings and kept royal power in check.

The fifth development in the evolution of the Renaissance Europe state system was the institution of resident ambassadors. During the Italian Wars, the kings of Europe began to exchange ambassadors who resided at foreign capitals and were responsible for informing their sovereign about conditions in the host country and representing their rulers' interests abroad. Resident ambassadors became the linchpins in a sophisticated information network that provided intelligence about the intentions and capabilities of other kings, princes, and cities. These ambassadors typically enjoyed a humanist education, which helped them adapt to strange and unpredictable situations, understand foreign languages, negotiate effectively, and speak persuasively. Ambassadors cultivated courtly manners, which smoothed over personal conflicts. For the new state system, gathering reliable information became as important as maintaining armies and collecting taxes. Although the Italian city states were the first in many of these developments, they were soon outstripped by the larger monarchies of the West.

France, with the largest territory and population (more than 16 million) in western Europe, had the potential to become the most powerful state in Europe. Under King Charles VII (r. 1422–1461), France created its first professional army. Equally important, the **Pragmatic Sanction of Bourges** (1438) guaranteed the virtual autonomy of the French Church from papal control, enabling the French king to interfere in religious affairs and exploit Church revenues for government purposes. A third important weapon in the development of the French national monarchy was the *taille*, an annual direct tax. During the final years of the Hundred Years' War, which ended in 1453, the Estates General (France's parliament) granted the king the right to collect the *taille*. After the war, Louis XI (r. 1461–1483) turned it into a permanent source of revenue for himself and his successors. Armed with the financial resources of

the *taille*, Louis and his successors expanded the reach of the French monarchy.

In contrast to France, the kingdoms of Spain had never been major players in European affairs during the Middle Ages. The Iberian peninsula was home to several small kingdoms—Portugal, Castile, Navarre, and Aragon, which were all Christian, and Granada, which was Muslim. Each kingdom had its own laws, political institutions, customs, and language. Unlike France, these Christian kingdoms were poor, underpopulated, and preoccupied with the reconquest, the attempt to drive the richer Muslims from the peninsula. There was little reason to assume that this region would become one of the greatest powers in Europe, the rival of France. The Renaissance made that possible.

That rise to power began with a wedding. In 1469 Isabella, who later would become queen of Castile (r. 1474–1504), married Ferdinand, who later would be king of Aragon (r. 1479–1516). The objective of this arranged marriage was to solidify an alliance between the two kingdoms, not to unify them, but in 1479 Castile and Aragon were combined into the kingdom of Spain. Of the two, Castile was the larger, with a population of perhaps six million, and wealthier. Together Isabella and Ferdinand, each still ruling their own kingdoms, at least partially subdued the rebellious aristocracy and built up a bureaucracy of well-educated middle-ranking lawyers and priests to manage the government.

The Christian kings of Iberia had long wanted to make the entire peninsula Christian. In 1492 the armies of Isabella and Ferdinand defeated the last remaining Iberian Muslim kingdom of Granada. While celebrating the victory over Islam, the monarchs made two momentous decisions. The first was to rid Spain of Jews as well as Muslims. Isabella and Ferdinand decreed that within six months all Jews had to either convert to Christianity or leave. To enforce conformity to Christianity among the converted Jews who did not leave, the king and queen authorized an ecclesiastical tribunal, the Spanish Inquisition, to investigate the sincerity of conversions. The second decision was Isabella's alone. She financed a voyage by a Genoese sea captain, Christopher Columbus, to sail west into the Atlantic in an attempt to reach India and China. Isabella seemed to have wanted to outflank the Muslim kingdoms of the Middle East and find allies in Asia. As we shall see in the next chapter, Columbus's voyage had consequences more far-reaching than Isabella's intentions, adding to the crown of Castile immense lands in the Americas.

Despite the diversity of their kingdoms, Isabella and Ferdinand made Spain a great power and established the framework for the

diplomatic relations among European states for the next century and a half (see **Map 12.2**). They married their children into the royal houses of England, Portugal, Burgundy, and the Holy Roman Empire, creating a network of alliances that isolated France. As a result of these marriage alliances, their grandson, Charles V, succeeded to the Habsburg lands of Burgundy, inherited the crown of Spain, was elected Holy Roman Emperor, which included all of Germany, ruled over the Spanish conquests in Italy, and was the Emperor of the Indies, which included all of Spanish Central and South America and the Philippines. This was the greatest accumulation

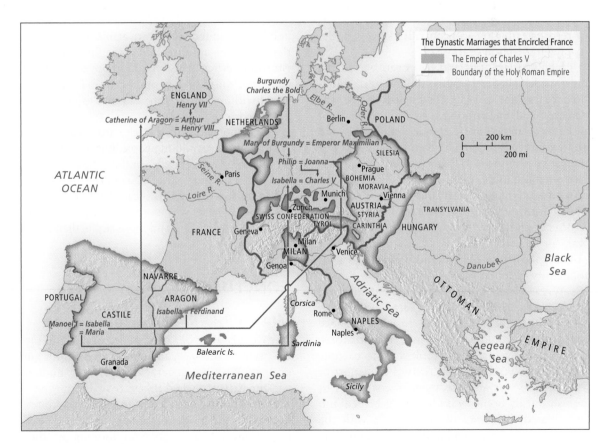

MAP 12.2

The Dynastic Marriages That Encircled France

Through skillfully arranging the marriages of their sons and daughters, Ferdinand of Aragon and Isabella of Castile managed to completely surround the rival kingdom of France with a network of alliances.

CHRONOLOGY: THE EARLY MODERN EUROPEAN STATE SYSTEM

1422	Charles VII succeeds to the throne of France
1455	Wars of the Roses in England underway
1461	Louis XI succeeds to the throne of France
1474	Isabella succeeds to the throne of Castile
1479	Ferdinand succeeds to the throne of Aragon
1479	Unification of Castile and Aragon
1485	Henry VII succeeds to the throne of England; Wars of Roses ends
1492	Conquest of Granada; expulsion of the Jews from Spain; voyage of Christopher Columbus
1494	The Italian Wars begin with the French invasion of Naples
1515	Francis I succeeds to the throne of France
1516	Charles V succeeds to the throne of Spain

of territories by a European ruler since Charlemagne in the ninth century.

Unlike Spain, England had been one of the great medieval powers, but at the end of the Hundred Years' War in 1453, the English crown was defeated and England exhausted. Thousands of disbanded mercenaries flooded England and enlisted in feuds among aristocratic families. The mercenaries brought to England the violence they had practiced in the wars with France. Under the tensions caused by defeat and revolt, the royal family fractured into the two rival branches of Lancaster and York, which fought a vicious civil war, now known as the Wars of the Roses (1455–1485) from the red and white roses used to identify members of the opposing sides.

When Henry Tudor finally ended the civil wars and became King Henry VII (r. 1485–1509), there was little reason to believe that England could again become a major force in European events. Henry took years to become safe on his own throne. He revived the Court of Star Chamber as an instrument of royal will to punish unruly nobles who had long bribed and intimidated their way out of trouble with the courts. Because his own hand-picked councilors served as judges, Henry could guarantee that the court system became fairer and more obedient to his wishes. He confiscated the lands of rebellious lords, thereby increasing his own income,

and he prohibited all private armies except those that served his interests. By managing his administration efficiently, eliminating unnecessary expenses, and staying out of war, Henry governed without the need to call on Parliament for increased revenues.

England was still a backward country with fewer than three million people. But by nourishing an alliance with newly unified Spain, Henry brought England back into European affairs. When his son Henry VIII succeeded to the throne, the Tudor dynasty was more secure than any of its predecessors and England more stable than it had ever been.

CONCLUSION

The Politics of Culture

The Renaissance began as an attempt to imitate the style of the best ancient Latin authors and orators. Within a generation, however, humanists and artists pushed this narrow literary project into a full-scale attempt to refashion human society on the model of ancient cultures. Reading about the ancients and looking at their works of art provoked comparisons with contemporary Renaissance society. The result was the development of a critical approach to the past and present. The critical approach fostered an enhanced historical sensibility, which transformed the idea of the West from one defined primarily by religious identification with Christianity to one forged by a common historical experience.

During the sixteenth century, western Europeans absorbed the critical-historical methods of the Renaissance and turned them in new directions. In northern Europe scholars used the critical historical methods of the humanists to better understand the historical sources of Christianity, especially the Bible. With that development, Christianity began to take on new shades of meaning, and many Christians attempted to make the practices of the Church conform more closely to the Bible. The humanist approach to religion led down a path that permanently divided Christian camps over the interpretation of Scripture. As we will see in Chapter 14, the sixteenth-century Reformation shattered the hard-won unity of the Catholic West.

As the next chapter shows, however, in the century before the Reformation Spanish and Portuguese sailors encountered previously unknown cultures in the Americas and only vaguely known ones in Africa and Asia. Because of the Renaissance, those who thought and wrote about these strange new cultures did so with the perspective of antiquity in mind.

KEY TERMS

Renaissance
republicanism
humanists
philology
rhetoric

civic humanism
linear perspective
Pragmatic Sanction of
   Bourges

CHAPTER QUESTIONS

1. How did the political and social climate peculiar to the Italian city-states help create Renaissance culture? (page 366)
2. How did ancient culture influence the Renaissance? (page 376)
3. How did the monarchies of western Europe become more assertive and effective during the last half of the fifteenth and early sixteenth centuries? (page 388)

TAKING IT FURTHER

1. How did rhetoric influence different kinds of Renaissance activities, such as humanism, visual arts, and political theory?
2. How did the political turmoil of the Italian Wars stimulate new thinking about history and politics?
3. How was the Italian Renaissance encounter with the culture of the ancient world similar to other encounters discussed in this book? How was it different?

✓●─Practice on **MyHistoryLab**

13

The West and the World: The Significance of Global Encounters, 1450–1650

■ Europeans in Africa ■ Europeans in the Americas ■ Europeans in Asia
■ The Beginnings of the Global System

ON A HOT OCTOBER DAY IN 1492, CHRISTOPHER COLUMBUS AND HIS MEN, dressed in heavy armor, clanked onto the beach of an island in the Bahamas. The captain and his crew had been at sea sailing west from the Canary Islands for five weeks, propelled by winds they thought would take them straight to Asia. As the ships under Columbus's command vainly searched among the islands of the Caribbean for the rich ports of Asia, Columbus thought he must be in India and thus called the natives he met "Indians." At another point he thought he might be among the Mongols of central Asia, which he described in his journal as the "people of the Great Khan." Both of Columbus's guesses about his location were incorrect, but they have left a revealing linguistic legacy: "Indians" for native Americans, and both "cannibals" and "Caribbean" from Columbus's inconsistent spellings of Khan. Columbus believed that the people he called the Cannibals or Caribs ate human flesh. But he got that information—also incorrect—from their enemies. Thus began one of the most lasting misunderstandings from Columbus's first voyage. Historians know very little about the natives' first thoughts of the arrival of their foreign visitors, largely because within a few generations the Caribs almost completely died out. By the

time someone was interested in hearing it, no one was left to pass down their story.

Western civilization at the end of the fifteenth century hardly seemed on the verge of encircling the globe with outposts and colonies. Its kingdoms had barely been able to reorganize themselves sufficiently for self-defense, let alone world exploration and foreign conquest. The Ottoman threat was so great that all of southern and eastern Europe was on the defensive. The hostilities between Turks and Christians blocked the traditional trade routes to Asia, which had stimulated the great medieval economic expansion of Europe. In comparison with the Ottoman Empire or Ming China, Europe's puny, impoverished states seemed more prone to quarreling among themselves than to seeking expanded horizons.

Nevertheless, by 1500 Europeans could be found fighting and trading in Africa, the Americas, and Asia. A mere 50 years later, Europeans had destroyed the two greatest civilizations in the Americas, begun the forced migration of Africans to the Americas through the slave trade, and opened trading posts throughout South and East Asia.

Before 1492 the West, identified by its languages, religions, agricultural technology, literature, folklore, music, art, and common intellectual tradition that

CHRISTOPHER COLUMBUS
This near contemporary portrait of the mariner depicts him as a well-dressed Renaissance gentleman.

stretched back to pre-Christian antiquity, was largely confined to Europe and the Middle East. Barely a century after Columbus's voyages, Western culture could be found in many distant lands, and western European languages and forms of Christianity were adopted by or forced upon other peoples. The West was now more of an idea than a place, a certain kind of culture that thrived in many different environments. As western Europeans came under the influence of the far-flung peoples they visited, they were themselves transformed as they began to discover the principle of cultural relativity and tolerate human differences. The European voyages integrated the globe biologically and economically. Microbes, animals, and plants that had once been isolated were now transported throughout the world. Because the Europeans possessed the ships for transport and the guns for coercion, they became the dominant players in international trade, even in places thousands of miles from the European homeland. The question raised by this first phase of the European global encounters is, how were both the West and the rest of the world transformed?

EUROPEANS IN AFRICA

■ Why did the European incursions into sub-Saharan Africa lead to the vast migration of Africans to the Americas as slaves?

Medieval Europeans had accumulated a substantial knowledge about North Africa, but except for Ethiopia they were almost completely ignorant of the region south of the Sahara desert. By the fifteenth century, Muslim contacts with sub-Saharan Africa made it clear that the region was a source of gold and slaves. In search of these, Europeans, especially the Portuguese, began to journey down the west coast of Africa.

Sub-Saharan Africa Before the Europeans Arrived

For centuries highly developed, prosperous kingdoms had governed the interior of sub-Saharan Africa. During the fifteenth and sixteenth centuries when European contacts with the sub-Sahara dramatically expanded, however, the once-strong kingdoms were either in decline or engaged in protracted struggles with regional rivals. The Europeans arrived at precisely the moment when they could take advantage of the weaknesses produced by internal African conflicts.

The Muslim kingdom of Mali, a landlocked empire between the Upper Senegal and Niger Rivers, had long had a monopoly of the gold caravans that carried the coveted metal from the fabled city of Timbuktu across the Sahara to the gold-greedy Mediterranean. During the European Middle Ages Mali was the greatest empire in sub-Saharan Africa, but by 1400 it was in decline. Internal power struggles had split apart the once-vast empire. In 1482, when the Portuguese founded a gold-trading post at Elmina, they found the rulers of Mali much weaker than they had been 100 years before (see the trade routes and towns on **Map 13.1**).

Influenced by Mali, the forest kingdoms of Guinea were built on a prosperous urban society and extensive trading networks. European travelers compared the great city of Benin favorably with the principal European cities of the time. The towns of Guinea held regular markets, similar to the periodic fairs of Europe, and carefully scheduled them so they would not compete with each other. The staples of the long-distance trade routes in this region were high-value luxury goods, especially imported cloth, kola nuts (a mild stimulant popular in Muslim countries), metalwork such as cutlasses, ivory, and of course gold. However, civil wars weakened these kingdoms during the sixteenth century, opening the way for greater European influence.

Unlike the kingdoms of the western sub-Sahara, which tended to be Muslim, mountainous Ethiopia was predominantly Christian. In fact, Europeans saw Ethiopians as potential allies against Islam. Diplomatic contacts between Rome and Ethiopia intensified at the time of the Council of Florence in 1439, which attempted to unify all Christians in defense against Ottoman Turks. Learned Ethiopian churchmen became known in western Europe and created the impression that Ethiopia was an abundant land peopled by pious Christians. Portuguese visitors were duly impressed by the splendor of the emperor of Ethiopia, the Negus, who traveled with 2,000 attendants and 50,000 mules to carry provisions and tents. By the early sixteenth century, however, the Ethiopian kingdom had become overextended. In the 1520s and 1530s Muslims attacked deep into the Ethiopian heartland, raiding and burning the wealthy Ethiopian monasteries. The raids severely weakened the power of the Negus. Ethiopia survived, but competing Christian warlords weakened the central authority.

European Voyages Along the African Coast

Gold brought Europeans to sub-Saharan Africa. European merchants traded European silver for African gold in the Maghreb, the collective name for the present-day regions of Morocco, Algeria, and Tunisia. The Maghreb was the northern terminus of the gold caravans from Mali. European merchants made handsome profits from the gold trade, but they recognized they could make even greater profits if they could cut out the middlemen of the Maghreb. The Europeans had little hope, however, of using the camel caravan routes across the Sahara because of the hostility of Muslim inhabitants who were wary about foreign interlopers, especially Christian ones.

The alternative for Europeans was to outflank the Muslims by a sea route. As early as the thirteenth century, European voyagers ventured down the west coast of Africa into uncharted waters, but such voyages soon ran into trouble. Adapted to the calm waters of the Mediterranean,

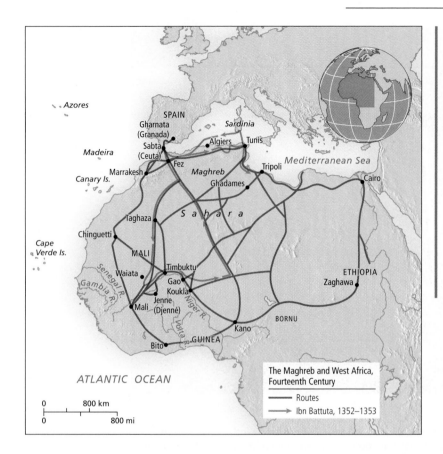

MAP 13.1

The Maghreb and West Africa, Fourteenth Century

Long before the arrival of the Portuguese via sea routes, caravans of camels criss-crossed the Sahara desert during the fourteenth century, linking the sources of gold in Mali with the Maghreb (the coast of north-west Africa) and the seaports of the Mediterranean. The greatest medieval Arabic traveler, Ibn Battuta (1304–1368/69), crossed the Sahara and spent more than a year in Mali. He left the most extensive account of medieval West Africa.

European galleys were ill-suited for voyaging on the heavy seas of the Atlantic. Such ships were not only easily swamped, they also required the feeding of large crews of oarsmen. In addition, the long coastline of West Africa lacked protective harbors for refuge from storms. For Europeans to gain direct access to the gold of Mali, they needed to develop new kinds of ships.

New Maritime Technology During the fifteenth century changes in the technology of ocean sailing surmounted the disadvantages of Mediterranean galleys. The location of the Iberian peninsula (the land of present-day Portugal and Spain) made possible the building of a hybrid ship that combined features of Mediterranean and Atlantic designs.

The new ship was the **caravel**. Iberians modified the older cog design, the dominant ship in the Atlantic, by adding extra masts and creating a new kind of rigging that combined the square sails of Atlantic ships, suitable for sailing in the same direction as the wind was blowing, with the triangular "lateen" sails of Mediterranean galleys, which permitted sailing into the wind. The result was a ship that could sail in a variety of winds, carry large cargoes, be managed by a small crew, and be defended by guns mounted in the castle superstructure. These hybrid three-mast caravels first appeared about 1450; for the next 200 years Europeans sailed ships of this same basic design on long ocean voyages to the very ends of the Earth.

Other late-medieval innovations also assisted European navigators. The compass, originally from China, provided an approximate indicator of direction. The astrolabe, borrowed from Muslim mariners, and naked-eye celestial

FIFTEENTH-CENTURY CARAVEL
The caravel was typical of the hybrid ship developed during the fifteenth century on the Iberian peninsula. The two sails toward the bow are square rigged, the two at the stern are lateen. This ship is an exact replica of the Niña, one of the ships on Columbus's first voyage.

navigation made it possible to estimate latitudes. Books of sailing directions, called portolanos, many of which were adapted from Islamic sources, included charts of ports and recorded the location of dangerous shoals and safe harbors for future voyages.

Technology alone, however, does not explain why Europeans set sail around the globe in this era. There had been great ocean navigating efforts before. For centuries, Polynesians successfully navigated their way across the Pacific Ocean in open canoes. The Vikings regularly crossed the North Atlantic from the tenth to fourteenth centuries, and the Chinese engaged in extensive exploratory voyages throughout the Indian Ocean earlier in the fifteenth century. The desire to profit from an expanded trade network

and to outflank the Muslims who blocked the eastern trade routes motivated European voyages in the fifteenth and sixteenth centuries.

NEW COLONIALISM   The search for greater profits created new kinds of colonies. Mediterranean colonies established during the Crusades of the twelfth and thirteenth centuries had relied on native inhabitants to produce commodities that the colonizers expropriated. These were either aristocratic colonies in which a few warriors occupied castles to dominate the native population or mercantile colonies built around a trading post for foreign merchants.

During the fifteenth century, Castile and Portugal founded colonies in the Canary Islands, the Madeira archipelago, the Azores, and the

Cape Verde Islands. The climate of these islands was similar to that of the Mediterranean and invited the cultivation of typical Mediterranean crops, such as grains and sugar cane, but the islands lacked a native labor force for either an aristocratic or a mercantile colony. When Europeans arrived, the Canaries had few inhabitants and the other islands were uninhabited. In response to the labor shortage, two new types of colonies emerged, both of which were later introduced into the Americas.

The first new type of colony was the **settler colony.** The settler colony derived from the medieval, feudal model of government, in which a private person obtained a license from a king to seize an island or some part of an island. The king supplied financial support and legal authority for the expedition. In return, the settler promised to recognize the king as his lord and occasionally to pay a fee after the settlement was successful. The kings of Castile and Portugal issued such licenses for the exploitation of the Atlantic islands. The actual expeditions to colonize these islands were private enterprises, and adventurers from various parts of Europe vied for a license from any king who would grant them one. For example, the first European settlement in the Canary Islands was led by a Norman-French knight, who could not obtain sufficient support from the king of France and thus switched loyalties to the king of Castile.

After the arrival of the Europeans, all the natives of the Canaries, called the Guanches, were killed or died off from European diseases, creating the need for settler families from Europe to till the land and maintain the Castilian claim on the islands. These European peasants and artisans imported their own culture. They brought with them their traditional family structures, customs, language, religion, seeds, livestock, and patterns of cultivation. Wherever settler colonies were found, whether in the Atlantic islands or the New World, they remade the lands in the image of the Old World.

The second new type of colony was the **plantation colony.** Until the occupation of the Cape Verde Islands in the 1460s, the Atlantic island colonies had relied on European settlers for labor. However, the Cape Verdes attracted few immigrants, and yet the islands seemed especially well-suited for growing the lucrative sugar cane crop. The few permanent European colonists there tended to be exiled criminals who were disinclined to work. Because there was no indigenous population to exploit on the Cape Verdes, the Europeans began to look elsewhere for laborers. They voyaged to the African coast, where they bought slaves who had been captured by African slavers from inland villages. These slaves worked as agricultural laborers in the Cape Verdes sugar cane fields.

Thus, in the Cape Verdes began the tragic conjunction between African slavery and the European demand for sugar. When sugar began to replace honey as the sweetener of choice for Europeans, sugar cultivated by slaves in plantation colonies, first in the Atlantic islands and later in the West Indies and American mainland, met the almost insatiable demand. Over the next 300 years, this pattern for plantation colonies was repeated for other valuable agricultural commodities, such as indigo for dyes, coffee, and cotton, which were grown to sell in European markets. The first loop of what would eventually become a global trading circuit was now completed.

THE PORTUGUESE IN AFRICA The Portuguese launched the first European voyages along the African coast during the fifteenth century. The sponsor of these voyages was Prince Henry the Navigator (1394–1460). As governor of Algarve, the southernmost province of Portugal, Henry financed numerous exploratory voyages. Although the many voyages of Henry's sailors did not fulfill his dreams of conquest and enormous riches, his sailors discovered bases near the Senegal and Gambia Rivers for the Malinese gold trade. He and other members of his family also helped colonize Madeira and the Azores. As a source of sugar, Madeira became a valuable colony (see Maps 13.1 and **13.2**).

After Henry's death, Portuguese exploration of the African coast accelerated. In only six years, a private merchant of Lisbon commissioned voyages

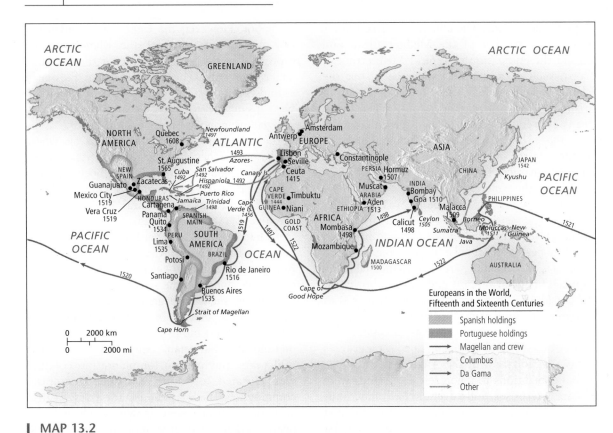

MAP 13.2

Europeans in the World, Fifteenth and Sixteenth Centuries

During the fifteenth and sixteenth centuries European sailors opened sea lanes for commerce across the Atlantic, Pacific, and Indian Oceans. Dates indicate first arrival of Europeans.

that added 2,000 miles of coastline to what was known to the Portuguese. In 1482 the Portuguese royal family took control of trade with Africa and transformed what had been a loose and haphazard enterprise under private contractors into a lucrative source of revenue for the monarchy. The monarchy required that all sailings be authorized and all cargoes inventoried. To protect the trade, the Por-

CHRONOLOGY: EUROPEANS IN AFRICA	
1270	Beginnings of the Ethiopian kingdom
1316	Papal delegation sent to Ethiopia
1394–1460	Life of Prince Henry the Navigator of Portugal
1450s	Appearance of new European ship design, the caravel
ca. 1450	European slave trade in Africa begins
1460s	Occupation of Cape Verde Islands
1482	Portuguese gold-trading post founded at Elmina
1520–1530s	Muslim attacks against Ethiopian kingdom

tuguese built a permanent fortress at Elmina near the mouth of the Volta River in modern Ghana in West Africa. Rather than establishing new settler or plantation colonies, the Portuguese on the African coast relied on **trading posts** that supplied gold, ivory, pepper, and slaves.

EUROPEANS IN THE AMERICAS

■ How did the arrival of Europeans in the Americas transform native cultures and life?

The first European voyagers to the Americas also coveted gold and sought an alternative route to India and China. Europeans relied on Asian sources for medicines, spices, and all kinds of luxury goods that were unavailable elsewhere. The desire to profit from this trade impelled men to take great risks to find an alternative route around the Ottoman Empire to East Asia. In the short run, the Americas proved to be an impediment because the two continents stood in the way of getting to Asia. But in the long run, the European voyages to the Americas brought consequences unimaginable to those who first began to sail west from Europe.

The Americas Before the Conquistadores

Prior to their contact with Europeans, the peoples of the Americas displayed remarkable cultural variety. Nomadic hunters spread across the sub-Arctic regions, western North America, and the Amazon jungles, while farming settlements prevailed in much of South America and eastern North America. Some of these North American cultures, such as the Anasazi and Iroquois, developed highly sophisticated forms of political organization, but none matched the advanced civilizations of Mesoamerica and the central Andes to the south. On the eve of the arrival of Europeans, two great civilizations, the Aztecs of central Mexico and the Incas of highland Peru, had built extensive empires that dominated their neighbors.

THE AZTEC EMPIRE OF MEXICO   Mesoamerica (the region known today as Mexico and Central America) had been the home of a series of highly urbanized, politically centralized cultures: the Mayas (300–900), the Toltecs (900–1325), and finally the Aztecs (1325 to the Spanish conquest in 1522). The Aztecs found safety from incessant warfare with neighboring tribes on an island in Lake Texcoco, where they established the city of Tenochtitlán, now Mexico City. From their base at Tenochtitlán the Aztecs followed a brilliantly successful policy of divide and conquer, first allying with powerful neighbors to attack weaker groups, then turning against former allies. With the riches gained from conquest, the Aztecs transformed Tenochtitlán from a dusty town of mud houses to a great imperial capital built of stone with a grand botanical garden that displayed plants taken from various climates.

The Aztecs excelled in the perpetual state of war that had long been the dominant fact of life in Mexico, and as a result, they attributed great religious value to war. They practiced the "flowery war," a staged occurrence during which states agreed to a predetermined time and place for a battle, the only objective of which was to take prisoners for temple sacrifice. Sustaining the gods' hunger for human sacrifices became the most notorious feature of Aztec religion. The Aztecs attributed their military successes to their tribal god, Huitzilpochti, the giver of light and all things necessary for life, but Huitzilpochti could be nourished only with human blood, creating the need among the Aztec faithful to acquire human captives.

The rituals of sacrifice permeated Aztec society. An estimated 10,000 victims were sacrificed each year, with the number rising to 50,000 on the eve of the Spanish conquest. From the very first encounters, the paradox of Aztec culture baffled Europeans. Despite their practice of human sacrifice, the Aztecs displayed refined

THE AZTEC RITE OF HUMAN SACRIFICE

An Aztec priest in a cape prepares to cut the heart out of a sacrificial victim as assistants hold him down.

manners, a sensitivity to beauty, and a highly developed religion. Whatever biases the Europeans brought with them about the "savages" of the New World, it was obvious that the Aztecs had created a great civilization.

THE INCAN EMPIRE OF THE ANDES   At about the same time the Aztecs were thriving in Mexico, the Incas expanded their empire in Peru. Whereas the Aztecs created a loosely linked empire based on tribute payments, the Incas employed a more direct form of rulership. Around 1438 the first Incan emperor spread his

rule beyond the valley of Cuzco. By the end of the fifteenth century, the Incas had begun to integrate by force the distinctive cultures of the various conquered regions. In this way, they created a mountain empire 200 miles wide and 2,000 miles long, stretching from modern Chile to Ecuador and comprising a population of about ten million. From his capital at Cuzco, the Incan emperor lived in luxury and established an elaborately hierarchic political structure. His authority was carried through layers of aristocrats down to officials who were responsible for every ten families in every village. These families supplied food and tribute for the empire, worked on roads and bridges, and served in the army. State-owned warehouses of food guaranteed the peasants freedom from starvation and provided for the sick and elderly. A superb network of roads and bridges covered more than 18,000 miles and made it possible to communicate with relays of runners who could cover as much as 140 miles a day. Troops could also be quickly dispatched to trouble spots via these roads.

Despite this well-organized imperial system, the Incan Empire became overly centralized because decisions could only be made by the emperor himself. Emperor Huayna Capac (r. 1493–1525) founded a second capital further south at Quito in an attempt to decentralize the overextended empire, but at his death a bitter civil war broke out between the northern and southern halves of the empire, led respectively by his rival sons. This war weakened Incan unity on the eve of the Spanish conquest.

The Mission of the European Voyagers

The European arrival in the Americas was the result of Christopher Columbus's (1451–1506) epic miscalculation. Born in Genoa to an artisan family, Columbus followed the destiny of so many of his compatriots by becoming a sailor. "From a very small age," he reported late in life, "I went sailing upon the sea."[1] He spent more than 40 years sailing everywhere sailors went. Columbus certainly had extensive experience as a seaman, but more crucial to understanding his mistake was his religious devotion. Columbus believed that he had been predestined to fulfill biblical prophecies. If he could reach China, he could outflank the Ottoman Turks and recapture Jerusalem from the Muslims who had held it since 1187. Columbus believed that the recapture of the Holy City would usher in the Second Coming of Christ. To persuade Queen Isabella of Castile to finance his voyage to China by sailing west, Columbus later admitted that he ignored navigational data and, instead, relied "entirely on holy, sacred Scripture and certain prophetic texts by certain saintly persons, who by divine revelation have had something to say on this matter."[2]

Europeans had long recognized that it was theoretically possible to reach China by sailing west. Most educated people, and certainly all those influenced by the Renaissance humanists, agreed the world was round. Sailors knew the world was round because they could see that the hull of a ship disappeared on the horizon before its masts did. The problem was not a theoretical one about the shape of the Earth but a practical one about getting around it. During Columbus's life the most widely accepted authority on the circumference of the Earth was the ancient Greek geographer Ptolemy, who had estimated that the distance across the Atlantic Ocean from Europe to Asia was more than 10,000 miles. No ship in Columbus's day could hope to sail that far without landfalls along the way for finding provisions and making repairs. In fact, Ptolemy had underestimated the size of the Earth by 25 percent.

Columbus, however, decided that Ptolemy had overestimated the distance. He also claimed that the wealthy islands of Japan lay farther east of the Asian continent than they actually do, thus further minimizing the distance of the voyage. When Columbus first proposed sailing west to Asia, King John II of Portugal consulted a committee of experts who quite correctly pointed out Columbus's miscalculations, which seem to have been more the result of wishful thinking and religious fervor than geographical expertise.

King John's rejection led Columbus to seek patronage elsewhere. Columbus applied to Queen Isabella of newly unified Spain, whose own advisers at first recommended against the voyage for the same reasons the Portuguese experts had rejected the plan. When the Spanish defeated the Muslim kingdom of Granada in 1492, which completed the Christian reconquest of the Iberian peninsula, Isabella succumbed to the religious enthusiasm of the moment and relented. She offered Columbus a commission for the voyage in the hope that it would ensure a final Christian victory over Islam.

On August 3, 1492, Columbus set sail with three small ships—the Niña, Pinta, and Santa Maria—and a crew of 90 men and boys. After refitting in the Canary Islands, the modest convoy entered unknown waters guided only by Columbus's faith in finding China, which was, in fact, thousands of miles farther west than he thought it would be. At two in the morning on the moonlit night of October 12, a lookout spied land, probably Watling Island in the Bahamas.

In all, Columbus made four voyages across the Atlantic (1492, 1493, 1498, 1502), exploring the Caribbean Islands, the coast of Central America, and part of the coast of South America. He never abandoned the belief that he had arrived in Asia. His four voyages were filled with adventures. On the third voyage, he was arrested by the newly appointed Spanish governor of Hispaniola on false charges and sent home in chains for trial; on the fourth he was marooned for nearly a year on Jamaica after worms weakened the timbers of his ships. He garnered considerable wealth in gold found on his voyages, but he never received the titles and offices that Queen Isabella had promised him before his first voyage. (See *Justice in History* in this chapter.)

Soon after Columbus returned to Spain from his first voyage, the Spanish monarchs who had sponsored him tried to obtain a monopoly to explore the western Atlantic. They appealed to Pope Alexander VI, who was himself a Spaniard and sympathetic to their request. The pope ordered a line of demarcation drawn along a north-south line 100 leagues (about 300 miles)

JUSTICE IN HISTORY

The Trial of Christopher Columbus

On October 12, 1998, a court put Christopher Columbus on trial in Tegucigalpa, Honduras. The Honduran jury, which included two Catholic priests, found Columbus guilty on ten charges, including kidnapping, rape, enslavement, invasion of peaceful lands, murder, torture, and genocide against the natives of the Americas. A life-size painting of the handcuffed explorer stood in for the defendant, who had been dead for nearly 500 years. The trial took place before a crowd of about 2,000 people, many from the indigenous Lenca people. According to the two priests on the jury, the original plan for the show trial had been to find Columbus guilty and then hold him prisoner until the Spanish government made reparation payments. However, as the jury began to deliberate, the crowd started chanting, demanding he receive capital punishment. Complying with the demands of the people, two Lenca warriors executed Columbus by firing a dozen arrows into the painting.

The Honduran trial was not the only one that has questioned Columbus's reputation in recent years. In the United States elementary school teachers have organized their classes for mock trials of the famous explorer. In New York City a fourth grade class charged Columus with land theft, enslavement, torture, and murder. After a lively mock trial the class unanimously sentenced Columbus to jail time and ordered he undergo psychotherapy. In response, several Italian-American associations launched a campaign to preserve the Italian explorer's image as a hero. The figure of Columbus remains a powerful symbol of the encounters, so often violent and deadly, between the the Europeans and the native peoples of the Americas.

A controversial figure even in his own time, Columbus was, in fact, arrested and put on trial by a royal judge on the island of Hispaniola in 1500. Columbus was an intrepid explorer, but even he admitted he was a poor administrator. He had established a Spanish colony on the island of Hispaniola (Haiti and Domican Republic today), but after six years of his governorship, the island suffered recurrent rebellions, not only from the Indians but from the colonists as well. Part of the problem was that Columbus promised the colonists far more than he could deliver. He depicted the island as offering abundant gold that could be virtually picked off the ground and compliant Indians who would do the setters' work for them. As a result, the colony attracted idlers and former convicts who quickly discovered that the island had a difficult environment and was inhabited by self-reliant Indians who were quite unwilling to become slaves of the Spaniards. When Columbus returned to Hispaniola on his third voyage in 1498, he discovered widespread abuse of the Indians and open rebellion against his governorship by the settlers on the southern part of the island. The arbitrary rule of Columbus and his brothers, who had been in charge during his absence, enraged the rebels. The rebels demanded the right to appeal to the Crown, a demand that raised a fundamental issue about how a colony so far from Spain could be ruled with respect to the law. Columbus himself recognized he was neither suited to be an administrator nor properly educated to act as a judge. He requested one be sent from Spain to help quell the rebellion and bring justice to the island.

Ferdinand and Isabella responded by appointing Francisco de Bobadilla, an aristocratic lawyer, to put down the rebellion and to investigate the numerous charges against Columbus. Bobadilla arrived in Hispaniola with a poor opinion of Columbus based on conversations in Spain with numerous men who had returned from the New World. Bobadilla arrived with the authority to take over the government of Hispaniola if he thought there was a legitimate case against

Ex Ferdinandus intellectis difcordijs quæ oborta inter Columbum & Rola...

THE ARREST OF CHRISTOPHER COLUMBUS BY BOBADILLA

This image represents what was one of the most famous incidents in the Columbus saga. The engraving shows Bobadilla, the figure in the center-left, wielding a baton, which symbolized his royal authority. In the center right is Columbus gesturing his dismay as irons are fitted to his ankles. Behind Bobadilla the rebels are shown welcoming Bobadilla as he crosses a gang plank. In the far right soldiers load Columbus onto a small boat to be towed out to the caravel anchored at sea ready to transport him back to Spain.

Columbus. Columbus's son Ferdinand reported what happened next:

On his arrival, Bobadilla, who was most anxious to remain in office, neither held a hearing nor took any evidence. Instead, early in October, 1500, he put the Admiral [Columbus] and his brother Diego in chains aboard ship under a strong guard; he forbade anyone publicly to mention them, on pain of very severe penalties.

He then held a farcical inquest, taking testimony from their open enemies, the rebels, and showing public favor to and even egging on all who wished to speak ill of the prisoners. From the wicked and shameless things these people said, one had to be blind not to see that they were guided by prejudice rather than truth.[3]

Columbus considered himself a martyr. On board ship the captain offered to remove the chains, but Columbus refused, wanting to keep them on so that he could embarrass the king and queen when he arrived in their presence. Aboard ship he wrote a series of letters in which he reflected on his humiliation and its causes. He admitted he had exceeded his authority by arbitrarily hanging colonists accused of rebellion, but he justified himself by arguing that he was attempting to bring order to a frontier inhabited by savages. Whereas after his first voyage he had depicted the Indians as peace loving and naturally good, he now changed his mind. The Indians, he said, were warlike and wild, incapable of conforming to civilized society. They were people of the Devil. He blamed them even more than the Spanish rebels who had actually caused his downfall. Ferdinand and Isabella freed Columbus from his shackles and the charges against him, but he never fully regained his authority as the governor of Hispaniola.

The trial of Columbus marked a moment of transformation in the European experience in the New World. Even Columbus had to admit he had not discovered a paradise, but an impoverished land whose inhabitants could barely feed themselves, let alone support invaders unwilling to work. His own attitudes toward the native inhabitants switched to match the bigotry of the other settlers who treated the Indians with contempt. The creaky Spanish legal system showed how ill equipped it was for bringing justice to a distant colony. The experience of 1499–1500 on Hispaniola would be repeated time and again in the Spanish conquests in America. The most brutal men in Spanish society found ways to disregard authority, to abuse the natives, and to subvert justice largely because there was no one capable of stopping them. The fantasy world of a terrestrial paradise Columbus had created in his mind began to collapse around him.

For Discussion

1. What issues were at stake in the trial of Columbus on Hispaniola?

2. What do Columbus's troubles reveal about the strengths and weaknesses of the Spanish colonial system?

3. What do mock trials of historical figures such as Columbus seek to accomplish? Are they successful?

Taking It Further

Felipe Fernández-Armesto, *Columbus*. 1991. Among the many studies of Columbus this may be the most trustworthy and balanced.

The Life of the Admiral Christopher Columbus by his Son Ferdinand. Translated and Annotated by Benjamin Keen. 1959. A fascinating account of events from Columbus's point of view.

west of the Azores and Cape Verde Islands. Spain received all lands to the west of the line; Portugal obtained the lands to the east. This line of demarcation seemed to limit the Portuguese to Africa, which alarmed them and led to direct negotiations between the Portuguese and the Spaniards. The result of the negotiations was the Treaty of Tordesillas in 1494, which moved the line of demarcation to 370 leagues (about 1,110 miles) west of the Cape Verde Islands, a decision that granted to Portugal all of Africa, India, and Brazil.

Despite Columbus's persistent faith that he had found a route to the East Indies, other voyagers began to suspect, even before Columbus's death, that he had not found Asia at all and that other routes had to be explored. Another Italian, the Florentine Amerigo Vespucci (1454–1512), met Columbus, helped him prepare for the third voyage, and later made at least two voyages of his

SPANISH CONQUISTADORES LAND ON AN ISLAND IN THE NEW WORLD

The armored Spaniards are met by the naked inhabitants who offer them jewels and gold. As one of their first acts, the Spaniards erect a cross, symbolizing the Christian conquest of the New World.

own across the Atlantic. From his voyages, Vespucci recognized something of the immensity of the South American continent and was the first to use the term *New World*. Because he coined the term and because the account of his voyages got into print before Columbus's, Vespucci's given name, Amerigo (America), came to be attached to the New World rather than Columbus's. By the 1520s, Europeans had explored the Americas extensively enough to recognize that the New World was nowhere near India or China.

Explorers followed two distinct strategies for finding a sea route to East Asia. The first strategy was the Portuguese pursuit of routes to the south and east around Africa. Between 1487

and 1488, Bartholomew Dias (ca. 1450–1500) reached the Cape of Good Hope at the southern tip of the African continent. This discovery made it evident that passage to India could be achieved by sailing south, rounding the tip of Africa, and crossing the Indian Ocean. Political and financial problems in Portugal, however, prevented a follow-up to Dias's voyage for ten years. Between 1497 and 1499, Vasco da Gama (ca. 1460–1524) finally succeeded in sailing from Lisbon to India around the Cape of Good Hope. As a consequence of the route opened by da Gama, the Portuguese were the first Europeans to establish trading posts in Asia. They reached the Malabar Coast of India in 1498 and soon found their way to the Spice Islands and China. By the middle of the sixteenth century, the Portuguese had assembled a string of more than 50 trading posts and forts from Sofala on the east coast of Africa to Nagasaki in Japan.

The second strategy for reaching Asia consisted of Spanish attempts to pursue Columbus's proposed route west. The problem faced by those sailing under the Spanish flag was to find a way around the barrier presented by the American continents. A Portuguese sailor named Ferdinand Magellan (ca. 1480–1521) persuaded the king of Spain to sponsor a voyage to Asia sailing west around South America. That venture (1519–1522), which began under Magellan's command, passed through the strait named after him at the tip of South America and crossed the Pacific in a voyage of extreme hardship. His men suffered from thirst and hunger and died of scurvy. Magellan himself was killed by natives in the Philippines. After three years at sea, 18 survivors from the original 240 in Magellan's fleet reached Seville, Spain, having sailed around the world for the first time. Contemporaries immediately recognized the epic significance of the voyage, but the route opened by Magellan was too long and arduous for the Spanish to employ as a reliable alternative to the Portuguese route around Africa.

In the course of three centuries (about 1480–1780), European navigators linked the previously isolated routes of seaborne commerce, opened all the seas of the world to trade, and encountered many of the cultures and peoples of the world. Within the Indian Ocean and the western Pacific, the Europeans faced stiff competition from Arab and Chinese merchant sailors. But for the first 100 years or so, the Portuguese and Spanish effectively maintained a monopoly over the global trade routes back to Europe. Gradually English, Dutch, and French sailors also made their way around the globe. In the Americas, inadvertently made known to Europeans by Christopher Columbus, the Spanish immediately

began settlements and attempted to subdue the indigenous populations.

The Fall of the Aztec and Incan Empires

Following the seafaring captains, such as Columbus and Magellan, came the **conquistadores,** who actually conquered the new-found land. They were Spanish adventurers, usually from impoverished minor noble families, who sought fortune and royal recognition through exploration and conquest. Spain was a poor land with few opportunities for advancement, a bleak situation that made the lands of the New World a powerful lure to many men seeking a fortune. Embroiled in almost continuous warfare in Europe, the Spanish crown was also perennially strapped for cash, which meant the king of Spain was highly motivated to encourage profitable foreign conquests. Many of the conquistadores launched their own expeditions with little or no legal authority, hoping to acquire sufficient riches to impress the king to give them official sanction for additional conquests. Those who did acquire legal authority from the crown received the privilege to conquer new lands in the name of the king of Spain and to keep a portion of those territories for themselves. In return they were obliged to turn over to the king one-fifth— the "royal fifth"—of everything of value they acquired, an obligation enforced by a notary sent along with the conquistadores to keep a record of valuables that were found. The conquistadores also extended Spanish sovereignty over new lands and opened the way for missionaries to bring millions, at least nominally, into the Christian fold.

The king required all conquistadores to read a document, called the **requerimiento,** to the natives before making war on them. Derived from the Muslim declaration of *jihad* or holy war, this Spanish Christian document briefly explained the principles of Christianity and commanded the natives to accept them immediately along with the authority of the pope and the sovereignty of the king of Spain. If the natives refused, the conquistador warned that they would be forced through war to subject themselves "to the yoke and obedience of the Church and of Their Highnesses. We shall take you and your wives and your children, and shall make slaves of them, and as such shall sell and dispose of them as Their Highnesses may command. And we shall take your goods, and shall do you all the mischief and damage that we can."[4] The *requerimiento* revealed the conflicting motives behind the Spanish conquest. On the one hand, the Spanish were sincerely interested in converting the natives to Christianity. On the other, the conquistadores tried to justify their actions by suggesting that the natives had brought the attack on themselves by refusing to obey the Spanish king.

Hernán Cortés and the Conquest of Mexico

Among the first and most successful of the conquistadores was Hernán Cortés (1485–1547). Cortés arrived on the Yucatán peninsula of present-day Mexico in February 1519, beginning a conquest that culminated in the collapse of the Aztec Empire and the Spanish colonization of Mexico. Cortés followed a policy with the natives of divide and conquer, making alliances with peoples who resented Aztec domination and then using their warriors on the front lines of his battles where they absorbed most of the losses. If after a reading of the *requerimiento* the native chieftains did not immediately surrender, Cortés's men attacked them, breaking through their lines on horses, which the natives had never seen before.

Cortés's greatest achievement was the conquest of the Aztec capital. After a number of bloody battles, he set off with only 450 Spanish troops, 15 horses, and 4,000 native allies to seize Tenochtitlán, a city of at least 300,000 and defended by thousands of warriors. As Cortés approached, Montezuma II was slow to set up a strong defense, because he suspected Cortés might be the white god, Quetzalcóatl, who according to prophecies would arrive one day from the east. The result was disastrous for the Aztecs. Montezuma knew his reign was doomed

unless he could gain the assistance of other gods to drive Quetzalcóatl away. Thus, rather than an ardent military campaign, the king's defense primarily took the form of human sacrifices to please the gods. By the time Tenochtitlán finally surrendered, the shiny jewel that had so impressed the Spanish when they first glimpsed it from the surrounding mountains lay in smoldering ruins.

By 1522 Cortés controlled a territory in New Spain—as Mexico was renamed—larger than Old Spain itself. Aztec culture and its religion of human sacrifice disappeared as Franciscan friars arrived to evangelize the surviving population.

Francisco Pizarro and the Conquest of Peru

A small contingent of Spanish conquistadores also managed to conquer the vast Incan Empire in Peru. In 1531 Francisco Pizarro (ca. 1478–1541) left Panama with a small expedition of 180 men and 30 horses. He sailed to northern Peru and sent out spies who discovered that the Incan emperor, Atahuallpa, could be found in the highland city of Cajamarca. When Pizarro and his forces arrived there, the central square was empty, but Atahuallpa was encamped nearby with a large army. Pizarro invited Atahuallpa to come for a parlay, but instead treacherously took him captive. The news of the capture plunged the overly centralized Incan Empire into a crisis because no one dared take action without the emperor's orders. In an attempt to satisfy the Spaniards' hunger for riches and to win his freedom, Atahuallpa had a room filled with gold and silver for the conquistadores, but the treasure merely stimulated their appetite for more. In July 1533 Pizarro executed the emperor, and by the following November he had captured the demoralized Incan capital of Cuzco.

The conquest of Peru gave the Spanish access to untold wealth. Through the collection of the royal fifth, gold and silver flowed into the royal coffers in Spain. The discovery in 1545 of the fabulous Peruvian silver mine of Potosí (in what is now southern Bolivia) coincided with the introduction of the mercury amalgamation process that separated silver from ore. Mercury

CORTÉS ARRIVES IN MEXICO

The figure on the right is the native woman La Malinche, who served as Cortés's mistress and translator, a position often occupied by native women who served as mediators between the indigenous and Spanish cultures. She is interpreting for the bearded Hernando Cortés at his meeting with Montezuma II (seated on left) at Tenochtitlan in November 1519.

amalgamation enabled the Spaniards to replace surface gathering of silver ore with tunneling for ore, a procedure that led to greatly elevated yields of precious metals. For a century the silver of Peru helped otherwise impoverished Spain become the most powerful kingdom in Europe.

Spanish America: The Transplanting of a European Culture

With the defeat of the Aztec and Incan Empires, the process of transplanting Spanish society to the Americas began in earnest. The arrival of Europeans was a catastrophe for most native peoples, some of whom—in the Caribbean, northern Argentina, and central Chile—completely disappeared through the ravages of conquest and diseases. Spanish became the language of government and education, and Latin the language of religion. Nevertheless, many native languages and cultural traditions survived. Spanish America became not only the first outpost of Western civilization outside of Europe, but also the home of new hybrid cultures and ethnicities.

The basic form of economic and social organization in Spanish America was the **encomienda** system, created as an instrument to exploit native labor. An encomienda was a royal grant awarded

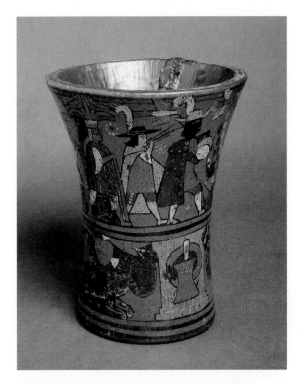

THE ENCOUNTER OF THREE CULTURES

On this wooden bottle painted in the Incan style about 1650, an African drummer leads a procession, followed by a Spanish trumpeter and an Incan official. The mixing of cultures that occurred after the arrival of the Spanish and Portuguese distinguished the Americas from other civilizations.

rose from rags to riches in the New World were so compelling that during the sixteenth century alone more than 200,000 Spaniards migrated there. They came from every part of the Iberian peninsula, from every class except the peasantry, and they practiced a wide variety of trades. There were nobles, notaries, lawyers, priests, physicians, merchants, artisans, and sailors, as well as vagabonds prone to crime and rebellion. In effect, these immigrants duplicated the Spanish Catholic society in the New World, complete with its class divisions and tensions, except that the native population or African slaves substituted for the peasants. Included among the immigrants were an unknown number of Jews who hid their faith and who escaped the rigors of the Spanish Inquisition by fleeing to the Americas, where they were less likely to suffer persecution.

Only one in ten of Spanish immigrants was a woman, and for a long time the colonies suffered from a shortage of Spanish women. Although native Americans were usually excluded from Spanish society, many native women who were the mistresses or wives of Spaniards became partially assimilated to European culture and helped pass it on to their offspring. These women knew both languages, which made them valuable interpreters, and were familiar with both cultures, which enabled them to explain native customs to the Spanish. The progeny of European men and Indian women constituted the *mestizo*, or genetically mixed, population.

The king of Spain was represented in the Americas by two viceroys, the highest colonial officials. One in Mexico City governed the West Indies, the mainland north of Panama, Venezuela, and the Philippines. The other in Lima, Peru, had authority over all of Spanish South America, excluding Venezuela. However, the vast territory of Spanish America and the enormous cultural diversity within it precluded any rigorous centralized control either from Spain or from the viceroys' capitals.

In Spanish America the church was a more effective presence than the state. Driven by the same religious fervor as Columbus, Catholic missionaries trekked into the farthest reaches of Spanish America, converting the native populations to

for military or other services that gave the conquistadores and their successors the right to gather tribute from the Indians in a defined area. In return, the encomendero (the receiver of the royal grant and native tribute) was theoretically obliged to protect the natives and teach them the rudiments of the Christian faith. Because the encomiendas were very large, only a small number of Spanish settlers were actually encomenderos. In greater Peru, which included modern Peru, Ecuador, and Bolivia, there were never more than 500 encomenderos. By the seventeenth century these encomiendas had evolved to become great landed estates called **haciendas.**

There were only a few prosperous encomenderos, but the stories about those who

ENCOUNTERS AND TRANSFORMATIONS

Between Indian and Christian: Creating Hybrid Religion in Mexico

As conquest passed into colonialism during the sixteenth century, Christian missionaries began to exert a profound influence on Indian moral and religious practices. However, as the Indians accepted Christianity they adapted it to meet their needs and to fit into their culture. As a result, native Americans created a new hybrid religion that combined both Christian and Indian elements, as Indian uses of the cross and adoption of flagellation illustrate.

As his army marched across Mexico, Cortés replaced native idols with Christian crosses. Missionaries later placed crosses in churches, encouraged making the sign of the cross a ritual practice, and introduced the wearing of miniature crosses as a kind of personal talisman that offered protection from illness and evil influences. Mayas readily adopted the Christian cross because they already had a symbol similar to it. However, the Maya at first misunderstood what the missionaries meant about the cross and took the example of Christ too literally. Some Maya actually performed crucifixions, usually of children, whose hands were nailed or tied to the cross and whose hearts were torn out in a vestige of pre-Christian practices. There are also reports of pigs and dogs sacrificed on crosses. Even though the Maya had missed the point of Christ's singular sacrifice, they had understood the power behind the Christian symbol, which the Spaniards had used in their conquest of the Maya, and they wanted some of that power for themselves.

When the Franciscan friars arrived in Mexico City in 1524, they introduced the practice of flagellation, which imitated Christ's whipping at the hands of Roman soldiers and served as a means of penance for sins. The friars employed self-flagellation as a tool for impressing the natives. Fray Antonio de Roa encouraged conversions through dramatic flagellations, called "a general discipline." After a collective flagellation in which

HYBRID RELIGION

Here a priest flagellates a naked Incan in Peru. Introduced by Christian missionaries, flagellation became one of the more extreme forms of religious practice among the newly converted Indians.

the Indians who had converted to Christianity imitated Fray Roa, he proceeded out of the church, naked from the waist up, with a cord around his neck, and shoeless. He walked over hot coals, and then delivered a sermon about how much greater the pains of Hell would be than those from the burning coals. After the sermon he doused his whole body with boiling water.

During the sixteenth century the Indians themselves began to practice flagellation, especially during processions conducted during Holy Week (the week before Easter). The natives flogged themselves with such evident enthusiasm that the friars had to intervene to prevent the Indians from seriously harming themselves. On many occasions during the colonial period, the Indians used self-flagellation as a means of rousing their fellows in protest against Spanish domination. Flagellation became not just a form of penance, but a means for arousing the passions of spectators, which could be turned toward rallying Mexicans against the Spanish. Even now flagellation remains the most distinctive feature of the Mexican passion plays. By adapting European Christian rituals for purposes other than those intended by the Christian missionaries, the natives created a new hybrid religious culture that was distinctively Mexican.

For Discussion

How did the native Mexican adaptations of Christianity compare to the popular medieval religious practices discussed in Chapter 11? Had the Mexicans become part of the West by accepting Christianity?

Christianity with much more success than in Africa or Asia. Greed had enticed the conquistadores, but an ardent desire to spread the gospel of Christianity spurred the missionaries. The most zealous missionaries were members of religious orders—Franciscans, Dominicans, and Jesuits—who were distinguished from the parish priests by their autonomy and special training for missionary work.

Church officials generally assumed that it took ten years for the transition to a settled Christian society, a policy that meant that Christianity arrived in two stages. First, members of a religious order evangelized the population by learning the native language, then preaching and teaching in it. They also introduced the celebration of the Catholic sacraments. Once churches were built and Christianity was accepted by the local elite, the missionaries moved on to be replaced, in the second stage, by parish priests who expected to stay in one place for their entire lives. In the border regions, evangelizing never ceased and members of the missionary orders stayed on until the end of colonial times. (See *Encounters and Transformations* in this chapter.)

Portuguese Brazil: The Tenuous Colony

In 1500 Pedro Cabral sighted the Brazilian coast, claiming it for Portugal under the Treaty of Tordesillas. While the Spaniards busied themselves with the conquest of Mexico and Peru, the Portuguese largely ignored Brazil, which lacked any obvious source of gold or temptingly rich civilizations to conquer. Instead, the Portuguese concentrated on developing their lucrative empire in Asia.

The impetus for the further colonization of Brazil was the growing European demand for sugar. The Brazilian climate was perfectly suited for cultivating sugar cane. Between 1575 and 1600, Brazil became the Western world's leading producer of sugar, luring thousands of poor young men from Portugal and the Azores who took native women as wives, thereby producing a distinctive *mestizo* population. Sugar cane production required backbreaking, dangerous labor to clear the land, to weed, and especially to cut the cane. To help work the vast coastal plantations the Portuguese attempted to enslave the Tupí-Guaraní natives, but European diseases soon killed them off.

The Portuguese increasingly looked to Africans to perform the hard labor they were unwilling to do themselves. As a result, the Brazilian demand for slaves intensified the Portuguese presence in West Africa and the African presence in Brazil. In the search for even more slaves, Portuguese slave buyers enlarged their area of operations in Africa south to Angola, where in 1575 they founded a trading post. This post became the embarkation point for slave traders who sailed directly to Brazil and sold slaves in exchange for low-grade Brazilian tobacco, which they exchanged for more slaves when they returned to Angola.

As in Spanish America, Portuguese authorities felt responsible for converting the natives to Christianity. In Brazil, the Jesuits took the lead during the last half of the sixteenth century by establishing a school for the training of missionaries on the site of the present city of São Paulo. Once converted, natives were resettled into villages called **aldeias,** which were similar to Spanish missions. The Jesuits attempted to protect the natives against the white colonists who wanted to enslave them, creating a lasting conflict between the Jesuit fathers and local landowners. Both Jesuits and colonists appealed to the king to settle their dispute. Finally, the king gave the Jesuits complete responsibility for all Indians in aldeias, but he allowed colonists to enslave Indians who had not been converted or who were captured in war. The Portuguese connected Christian conversion with settlement in aldeias, which meant that any unsettled native was, by definition, a heathen. Nevertheless, these restrictions on enslaving Indians created a perceived labor shortage and further stimulated the demand for African slaves.

More rural and more African than Spanish America, Brazil during its colonial history remained a plantation economy in which the few dominant white European landowners were vastly outnumbered by their African slaves. In certain areas a racially mixed population created its own vibrantly hybrid culture that combined native, African, and European elements, especially in the eclectic religious life that fused Catholicism with polytheistic forms of worship. Although Brazil occupied nearly half of the South American continent, until the twentieth century most of the vast interior was unexplored by Europeans and unsettled except by the small native population.

North America: The Land of Lesser Interest

Compared with Central and South America, North America outside Mexico held little attraction for Europeans during the sixteenth century. During the reign of Queen Elizabeth I (r. 1558–1603), English efforts finally turned to establishing colonies in the Americas. Two prominent courtiers, Humphrey Gilbert and his stepbrother, Walter Raleigh, sponsored a series of voyages intended to establish an English colony called Virginia in honor of Elizabeth, "The Virgin Queen." The English interest in colonization was made possible by Elizabeth's success in strengthening the monarchy, building up the fleet, and encouraging investments in New World colonies. In 1585 the first English colonists in the Americas landed on Roanoke Island off the coast of North Carolina, but they were so poorly prepared that this attempt and a second one in 1587 failed. The inexperienced and naive English settlers did not even make provisions for planting crops.

The successful English colonies came a generation later. Learning from past mistakes, the colonists of Jamestown in Virginia, who landed in 1607, brought seeds for planting, built fortifications for protection, and established a successful form of self-government. From these modest beginnings, the English gradually established vast plantations along the rivers of Virginia. There they raised tobacco to supply the new European habit of smoking, which had been picked up from native Americans. In 1620 religious refugees from England settled in Massachusetts Bay, but in contrast to Central and South America, North America by 1650 remained only marginally touched by Europeans and played a very minor role in European economic interests.

EUROPEANS IN ASIA

■ Why was the European encounter with Asian civilizations far less disruptive than those in Africa and the Americas?

India, the Malay peninsula, Indonesia, the Spice Islands, and China were the ultimate goal of the European voyagers during the fifteenth and sixteenth centuries. They were eventually reached by many routes—by the Portuguese sailing around Africa, by the Spanish sailing around

CHRONOLOGY: EUROPEANS IN THE AMERICAS

1438	Founding of Incan Empire in Peru
1492–1493	First two voyages of Christopher Columbus
1498	Third voyage of Columbus
1500	Cabral sights Brazil
1502	Fourth voyage of Columbus
1519–1522	Spanish conquer Mexico
1533	Spanish conquer Peru
1545	Discovery of silver at Potosí
1585	English establish colony on Roanoke Island, North Carolina
1607	English establish colony at Jamestown, Virginia
1620	English establish colony at Massachusetts Bay

South America, and by the Russians trekking across the vastness of Siberia.

Asia Before the European Empires

The greatest potential rival to the Europeans who sought access to Asian trade was Ming China (1368–1644), a highly advanced civilization with maritime technology and organizational capability to launch exploratory voyages far superior to Europe's. Even before the Portuguese began their slow progress down the west coast of Africa, the Chinese organized a series of huge maritime expeditions into the Indian Ocean that reached far down the east coast of Africa. Between 1405 and 1433 the Chinese established diplomatic contacts and demanded tribute in dozens of kingdoms in India and Africa. The size and ambition of these fleets far surpassed anything that sailed from Europe at this time, and the massive crews of as many as 27,500 men (compared to Columbus's crew of 90) included a complement of scholars to communicate with foreign kings and highly skilled technicians to make repairs to the fleet. The Chinese fleets took

trade goods, such as silk, tea, and porcelains, and brought back to China strange animals, hostage kings, and possible trade items. After nearly 30 years of searching the Indian Ocean ports, the Ming emperors concluded that China already possessed all the goods that were available abroad, that China was indeed the center of civilization, and that further investments in oceangoing expeditions were unwarranted.

The European and Chinese voyages of the fifteenth century differed in their objectives and in the motives of the governments that sponsored them. The Europeans were mostly privateers seeking personal profit or captains who enjoyed official government backing in return for a portion of the profits. The economic motive behind the European voyages made them self-sustaining because the Europeans sailed only to places where they could make money. In contrast, the imperial Chinese expeditions were only partially motivated by the desire for economic gain. The official purpose of the Chinese voyages was to learn about the world, and once the Chinese found out what they wanted, they ceased the official voyages. Chinese merchant traders continued to ply the seas on their own, however, and when the Europeans arrived in East Asia, they simply inserted themselves into this already developed Chinese-dominated trade network.

In contrast to the trade in Africa and America, Europeans failed to monopolize trade in Asia. The Europeans were just one among many trading groups, some working under government sponsorship, such as the Portuguese, and others working alone, such as the Chinese.

The Trading Post Empires

For 300 years after establishing the first trading posts in Asia, Europeans had little influence there in comparison to the Americas. In 1497–1499 Vasco da Gama opened the most promising route for the Portuguese around Africa to South and East Asia. But the sailing distances were long, limiting the number of people who could be transported to Asia. In contrast to the Americas, the Asian empires were well equipped to defend themselves against European conquest. Because Europeans lacked the support system, which in the Americas the colonial system provided, few Europeans settled in Asia, and even missionary work proved much more difficult than in the Americas.

Unlike Brazil, where the Portuguese established colonial plantations, in Asia they established trading posts along the coasts of India, China, and the Spice Islands. When the Portuguese first arrived at a location with a safe harbor and easy access to the hinterland, they built a fort and forced, bribed, or tricked the local political authority, usually a chieftain, to cede the land around the post to Portugal. The agents sent to trade in Asia were called *factors* and their trading posts were called **factories.** But they were not factories in the modern sense of sites for manufacturing. They were safe places where merchants could trade and store their merchandise. The factors lived in the factories with a few other Portuguese traders, a small detachment of troops, and servants recruited from the local population. Nowhere did Portuguese authority extend very far into the hinterland. The traditional political structures of local chieftains remained, and the local elites usually went along with the arrangement because they profited by reselling European wares, such as cloth, guns, knives, and many kinds of cheap gadgets. The factors acquired silks, gold, silver, raw cotton, pepper, spices, and medicines. Some of these outposts of the Portuguese Empire survived until late in the twentieth century, but their roots remained exceedingly shallow. Even in places such as East Timor, an island in Indonesia, and Macao on the south China coast, which were Portuguese outposts for more than four centuries, only a small native elite ever learned the Portuguese language or adapted to European culture.

The European trading posts in Asia proved very lucrative. Consider the search for the spice nutmeg. In an account published in 1510, an Italian traveler, Ludovico di Varthema, described the previously unknown nutmeg trees, which he found growing in the Banda Islands, a small archipelago some 1,000 miles east of Java. These were the only places in the world where nutmeg grew. Besides adding flavor to foods, nutmeg was believed to possess powers to cure all kinds of diseases and to induce a hallucinatory euphoria. The demand for nutmeg was so great and the supply so limited that exporting it yielded enormous profits. At one time, nutmeg was the most valuable commodity in the world after gold and silver. In the early seventeenth century the markup on a pound of nutmeg transported from the Banda Islands to Europe was 60,000 percent. It is no wonder European traders were willing to risk their lives on long, dangerous sea voyages to obtain nutmeg and other spices.

In return for raw materials such as nutmeg, European merchants typically traded manufactured goods, and they made every effort to ensure that other European powers were excluded from competing in this trade in Asia. Crucial to enforcing the system was a network of factories and a strong navy, which was primarily used against other European and occasionally Muslim interlopers. Through the trading post empires, commercial rivalries among European states extended abroad to Asia. Competition over these trading posts foreshadowed the beginnings of a global economy dominated by Europeans. It also demonstrated the Europeans' propensity to transform European wars into world wars.

In addition to trade, the Portuguese and other European powers sought to spread Christianity. To accomplish conversions, missionaries resorted to persuasion, because without the backing of a full-scale conquest as in the Americas, resorting to force was usually not an option. The missionaries frequently drew the ire of local rulers, who viewed the converts as traitors—a situation that led to the persecution of some of the new Christians. To accomplish their task of conversion, Christian missionaries had to learn the native languages and something of the native culture and religion. In this effort, the Jesuits were particularly dedicated. They sent members of their order to the Chinese imperial court, where they lived incognito for decades, although they made few converts. Jesuits also traveled to Japan, where they established an outpost of Christianity at Nagasaki. With the exception of the Spanish Philippines, which was nominally converted to Catholicism by 1600, Christian missionaries in Asia were far less successful than in the Americas. Perhaps one million Asians outside the Philippines had been converted during this period, but many of these conversions did not last. Christians were most successful in converting Buddhists and least effective among Muslims, who almost never abandoned their faith.

By the end of the sixteenth century, Portuguese and Spanish shipping in Asian waters faced recurrent harassment from the English, French, and Dutch. The Dutch drove the Portuguese from their possessions in Ceylon, India, and the Spice Islands, except for East Timor. But none of these sixteenth-century European empires was particularly effective at imposing European culture on Asia in a way comparable with the Americas. In the Spanish Philippines, for example, few natives spoke Spanish, and there were fewer than 5,000 Spanish inhabitants as late as 1850. European states competed among themselves for trade and tried to enforce monopolies, but the Europeans remained peripheral to Asian culture until the late eighteenth and early nineteenth centuries, when the British expanded their power in India and colonized Australia and New Zealand.

The expansion of the Russian Empire into Asia depended not on naval power but on cross-country expeditions. The heartland of the Russian Empire was Muscovy, the area around Moscow, but the empire would eventually spread from the Baltic Sea to the Pacific Ocean. After 1552 Russians began to push across the Ural mountains into Siberia, lured by the trade in exotic furs, which were in great demand among the upper classes of northern Europe, both to keep warm and as fashion statements. The Russians' search for furs was equivalent to the Spanish search for gold; like gold, fur attracted adventurous and desperate men. Following the navigable rivers and building strategic forts along the way, expeditions collected furs locally

CHRONOLOGY: EUROPEANS IN ASIA	
1487–1488	Bartholomew Dias reaches Cape of Good Hope
1497–1499	Vasco da Gama reaches India via Cape of Good Hope
1498	Portuguese reach Malabar coast of India
1514	Portuguese reach China
1519–1522	Ferdinand Magellan's crew circumnavigate the globe

and then advanced deeper into the frozen wilds of Siberia. Several of the great aristocratic families of Russia acquired enormous wealth from the Siberian fur trade, which was so lucrative that Russian trappers kept pushing farther and farther east. In this quest for furs, expeditions reached the Pacific coast in 1649, by which time Russia had established a network of trading posts over all of northern Asia.

The significance of the European trading post empires lies less in the influence of Europe on Asia than in the influence of Asia on Europe. Asian products from spices and opium to silk cloth and oriental rugs became commonplace items in middle- and upper-class European households. European collectors became fascinated with Chinese porcelains, lacquered boxes, and screen paintings. At the same time, Asian tourists began to visit Europe, a tradition begun when four Japanese converts to Christianity arrived in Lisbon in 1586 and made a celebrated tour of Europe.

THE BEGINNINGS OF THE GLOBAL SYSTEM

■ How was the world tied together in a global biological and economic system?

As a result of the European voyages of the fifteenth and sixteenth centuries, a network of cultural, biological, and economic connections formed along intercontinental trading routes. For many thousands of years, Europe, northern Africa, and Asia had been in contact with one another, but the system that formed during the sixteenth century encompassed most of the globe, including sub-Saharan Africa and the Americas. Unlike earlier international trading systems that linked Europe and Asia, the new global system was dominated by Europeans. Today's global economy, based on cellular telephones, the internet, air transportation, and free trade, is merely an extension and elaboration of the system that first appeared on a global scale during the sixteenth century. This system transformed human society by bringing into contact what had previously been separate and isolated—regional cultures, biological systems, and local economies.

The Columbian Exchange

The most dramatic changes were at first produced by the trade of peoples, plants, animals, microbes, and ideas between the Old and New Worlds—a process known as the **Columbian Exchange.** For the native Americans, the importation of Europeans, Africans, and microbes had devastating consequences—threatening indigenous religions, making native technology irrelevant, disrupting social life, and destroying millions of lives. For Europeans, the discovery of previously unknown civilizations profoundly shook their own understanding of human geography and history. Neither the ancient philosophers nor the Bible, which was understood to be an accurate history of humankind since the creation of the world, had provided a hint about the peoples of the Americas.

THE SLAVE TRADE   Slavery and the slave trade had existed long before the Europeans expanded the practice. All of the ancient civilizations had been slave societies with as many as one-third of the population in bondage. During the Middle Ages a small number of slaves were employed as domestic servants and concubines in the Christian cities of the Mediterranean, and in Muslim countries large

numbers of slaves were found in harems, used as laborers, and even trained as soldiers. During the wars between Christians and Muslims, victors habitually enslaved captives. In the sixteenth and seventeenth centuries Barbary pirates in the Mediterranean captured approximately 850,000 white Europeans during sea raids and forced them into slavery in Muslim North Africa. Large-scale transportation of black Africans began during the ninth and tenth centuries, when Muslim traders took tens of thousands from the island of Zanzibar off the east coast of Africa to lower Iraq, where they performed the heavy labor of draining swamps and cutting sugar cane. Slavery was also widespread in Islamic West Africa. Mali depended heavily on slave labor, and in Muslim Ghana slaves constituted about one-third of the population. Thus, the enslavement of Africans by Africans was well established when the Europeans arrived.

The slave trade flourished only when and where it was profitable. The necessary conditions for profitability were a strong demand for labor-intensive agricultural commodities, a perceived shortage of local labor, a supply of people who could be captured elsewhere, and a moral and legal climate that permitted slavery. These conditions were all present in the late fifteenth and sixteenth centuries. The population of Europe developed a taste for exotic products such as sugar, tobacco, coffee, and indigo dye. The European colonizers who sought to supply the demand for these goods needed agricultural workers, first for the colonies in the Atlantic islands and then for plantations in the Americas where European diseases decimated the indigenous population, creating a labor shortage. Europeans also found it difficult to enslave the native peoples, who knew the territory and could easily escape.

The flourishing demand for labor was supplied by the population of Africa. Once Europeans started to buy up slaves in the coastal trading posts, enterprising African chieftains sent out slave-hunting expeditions. As a consequence, the slave-trading states of the Guinea coast gained power at the expense of their neighbors and spread the web of the slave trade deep into the African interior. The slave hunters sold captives to the Europeans for transportation across the Atlantic. Following the Portuguese in the trade came the Dutch, English, French, and Danes, who eventually established their own trading posts to obtain slaves.

In addition to the economic incentive for slavery, both Christianity and Islam provided a moral justification and legal protection for it. Enslaving others was considered legitimate punishment for unbelievers. Of all the Western religions, only Judaism demonstrated a consistent moral resistance to the slave trade because Jewish identity depended heavily on remembering the biblical account of the enslavement of the ancient Hebrews in Egypt. Notable exceptions were the few Jewish plantation owners in Surinam, who did use slave labor. The problem for Christian and Muslim slavers was that when a slave converted to Christianity or Islam, the pretext for enslavement disappeared. To solve this problem, Christians created a new rationalization by connecting slavery to race. As the African slave trade expanded during the seventeenth and eighteenth centuries, Europeans began to associate slavery with "blackness," which was considered inferior to "whiteness." Among Muslims, the justification for enslavement remained a religious one, and when a slave converted to Islam he or she was, at least theoretically, supposed to be freed.

Due to slavery large parts of the Americas were transformed into outposts of sub-Saharan African cultures. Blacks came to outnumber native Americans and constituted the majority of the colonial population in most of the Caribbean and broad parts of coastal Central America, Venezuela, Guyana, and Brazil. Much of the male population of Angola was transported directly to Brazil, a forced migration that resulted in a dramatic excess of females over males in the most heavily depopulated areas of Angola. During the nearly 400 years of the European slave trade (ca. 1519–1867),

about eleven million Africans were shipped to the Americas.

The slave ships that sailed the infamous Middle Passage across the Atlantic were so unhealthy, with Africans "stacked like books on a shelf," that a significant portion of the human cargo died en route. The physical and psychological burdens that slavery placed on its victims can scarcely be imagined, in large part because few slaves were ever allowed to learn to read and write, and thus direct records of their experiences are rare. Documents from ship surgeons, overseers, and slave masters, however, indicate that slaves were subjected to unhealthy living conditions, backbreaking work, and demoralization. Despite these crushing hardships and even within the harsh confines of white-owned plantations, black slaves created their own institutions, family structures, and cultures.

BIOLOGICAL EXCHANGES How did a few thousand Europeans so easily conquer the civilizations of the Americas, populated by millions of people? After all, the Aztecs, Incas, and others put up a stubborn resistance to the conquistadores, and yet the Europeans triumphed time after time. The answer: epidemics. Along with their gunpowder weapons, the conquistadores' most effective allies were the invisible microbes of Old World diseases, such as smallpox. A native of the Yucatán peninsula recalled the better days before the conquest:

> There was then no sickness; they had no aching bones; they had then no high fever; they had then no smallpox; they had then no burning chest; they had then no abdominal pain; they had then no consumption; they had then no headache. At that time the course of humanity was orderly. The foreigners made it otherwise when they arrived here.[5]

The toll that epidemic disease had on the natives soon after their initial contact with Europeans stunned nearly every chronicler of the New World conquests. Between 1520 and 1600, Mexico suffered 14 major epidemics, and Peru 17. By the 1580s the populations of the

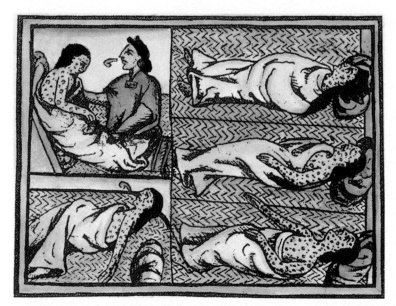

BIOLOGICAL EXCHANGES

A medicine man treats dying Aztecs during a smallpox epidemic in Mexico.

Caribbean islands, the Antilles, and the lowlands of Mexico and Peru had almost completely died off. Historians estimate the deaths in the tens of millions. The pre-conquest population of Mexico, which has been estimated at about 19 million, dropped in 80 years to 2.5 million. Even the infrequent contacts between European fishermen and fur traders with natives on the coast of what is now Canada led to rapid depopulation.

The most deadly culprit was smallpox, but measles, typhus, scarlet fever, and chicken pox also contributed to the devastation. All of these were dangerous and even life-threatening to Europeans and Africans alike, but from exposure, people of the Old World had either died young or survived the illness with a resistance to infection from the disease. However, native Americans had never been exposed to these diseases and as a population completely lacked immunities to them. As a result, all it took was for one infected person to arrive from the Old World to kill off many millions in the New World. After Cortés's men were first driven from Tenochtitlán, a Dominican friar reported that a new ally appeared: "When the Christians were

exhausted from war, God saw fit to send the Indians smallpox, and there was a great pestilence in the city...."[6] The Spaniards' immunity to the very diseases that killed off so many Indians reinforced the impression that the Europeans were favored agents of the gods or gods themselves.

In exchange, the New World gave the Old World syphilis, or at least contemporary Europeans thought so. Historians and epidemiologists have long debated what they call the **Columbian question** about the origins of syphilis. Some argue that syphilis or a venereal disease that might be classified as its ancestor came back from the New World with Columbus's sailors, but others assert that syphilis was widespread in the Old World long before 1492. Scholars still do not know the answer to the Columbian question, but it is true that after 1492 there were epidemic outbreaks of sexually transmitted diseases, leading many to assume an American origin.

The exchange of other forms of life was less obviously disastrous. Following the European settlers came a flood of European animals and plants. With the conquistadores came pigs, cattle, goats, sheep, donkeys, and horses—all previously unknown in the New World. Pigs that escaped from the first Spanish ships to land in Florida were the ancestors of the ubiquitous wild razorback pigs of the southern United States. Vast areas of Mexico and Peru depopulated of humans were repopulated with enormous herds of sheep. The cattle herded by the present-day gauchos of Argentina derive from Iberian stock. The characteristic Latin American burro came from Europe as did the horse, which came to be so prized by the plains Indians of North America. Sheep, cattle, and horses, in particular, completely changed the way of life of the native American peoples.

From Europe came the lucrative plantation crops of sugar, cotton, rice, and indigo, crops that required a large supply of field hands. European varieties of wheat, grapes, and olives soon appeared as major crops in Mexico and elsewhere. In exchange, the Americas offered new crops to the Old World such as tobacco, cocoa, paprika, American cotton, pumpkins, beans, tomatoes, maize (corn), and potatoes. European peasant farmers discovered that maize and the potato provided an attractive substitute for wheat. In many places, the potato replaced wheat as the staple in the diet of the poor. By yielding more calories per acre than wheat or virtually any other traditional grain, the potato made it possible to support more people on a given amount of land. With the spread of the potato as a food source, European populations began to increase rapidly, a trend that created population pressures, which in turn stimulated additional European migrations to the Americas.

THE PROBLEM OF CULTURAL DIVERSITY Before Columbus sailed west, Europeans possessed two systems of thought that seemed to explain everything to them—the Aristotelian and the Christian. The ancient Greek philosopher Aristotle and his commentators provided a systematic explanation of geography and cosmology based on what they knew of the world. They had named the continents, described their peoples, and estimated the size of the globe. Particularly in the European universities, Aristotle was still considered practically infallible, the primary source of all human knowledge. But Aristotle had not even imagined the Americas, and that fact raised the possibility that he was wrong on other matters as well. He knew nothing of the llama, the potato, or syphilis—common knowledge to even the most ignorant conquistador. Aristotle had assumed that the heat of the equatorial zone was so great that no one could live there, but the Spanish had found great civilizations thriving astride the equator. In 1570, when Joseph de Acosta felt a chill in the tropics on his way to America, he

observed, "what could I else do then but laugh at Aristotle's Meteors and his Philosophy."[7] Travelers to the New World began to realize that the ancients had not known half the truth about the world.

For Jews and Christians, the Bible remained the unchallenged authority on the origins of the whole world, but the New World created numerous problems for biblical interpretation. The book of Genesis told of the Creation and the great flood, which had destroyed all people and all animals except those saved in Noah's ark. The New World brought into question that vision of a single creation and cleansing flood simply because it could not explain why the plants and animals of the Americas were so different. If the only animals on Earth were those Noah preserved, then why were they different on the two sides of the Earth? About the New World a French writer asked, "How falls it out that the nations of the world, coming all of one father, Noah, do vary so much from one another, both in body and mind?"[8] Thinkers argued either that there must have been more than one creation or that the great flood must not have covered the entire Earth. However, these solutions tacitly recognized that a literal reading of the words of Scripture could not produce a satisfactory account of the history of the world.

The greatest conceptual challenges to Christian Europe were the New World peoples themselves. If these people were not the children of God's Creation, then how did they get there? If they were God's children, then why were they so different from Europeans? In the terms available to sixteenth-century thinkers, there were three possible ways to answer these questions. One was to assume that the native Americans were subhumans, demons, or some strange form of animal life. This answer was the most convenient one to those who sought to exploit the natives. Often with little or no foundation, these Europeans believed that the natives practiced devil worship, incest, sexual promiscuity, polygamy, sodomy, and cannibalism—all signs of their demonic nature.

DIFFERENT VOICES DEBATE OVER THE TREATMENT OF INDIANS

Bartolomé de las Casas and Juan Ginés de Sepúlveda engaged in a famous debate in Valladolid, Spain, in 1550 over the legitimacy of the Spanish conquest of the Americas. Emperor Charles V organized the debate to determine whether the Indians were capable of self-government. Las Casas had actual experience in the New World, having served as a bishop in Mexico. Lacking any personal experience in the Americas, Sepúlveda relied on the reports of others. Las Casas was shocked by the brutal treatment of the natives and argued the Indians needed protection. Instead of enslaving Indians, Las Casas advocated enslaving Africans, an argument he later regretted. In contrast, Sepúlveda argued the Indians were "natural slaves."

Bartolomé de las Casas, *A Short Account of the Destruction of the Indies* (1542)

God made all the peoples of this area, many and varied as they are, as open and as innocent as can be imagined. The simplest people in the world—unassuming, long-suffering, unassertive, and submissive—they are without malice or guile, and are utterly faithful and obedient both to their own native lords and to the Spaniards in whose service they now find themselves. Never quarrelsome or belligerent or boisterous, they harbour no grudges and do not seek to settle old scores; indeed, the notions of revenge, rancour, and hatred are quite foreign to them....

They are innocent and pure in mind and have a lively intelligence, all of which makes them particularly receptive to learning and understanding the truths of our Catholic faith and to being instructed in virtue; indeed, God has invested them with fewer impediments in this regard than any other people on earth. Once they begin to learn of the Christian faith they become so keen to know more, to receive the Sacraments, and to worship God, that the missionaries who instruct them do truly have to be men of exceptional patience and forbearance; and over the years I have time and again met Spanish laymen who have been so struck by the natural goodness that shines through these people that they frequently can be heard to explain: "These would be the most blessed people on earth if only they were given the chance to convert to Christianity."

Source: Bartolomé de las Casas, *A Short Account of the Destruction of the Indies,* edited and Translated by Nigel Griffin, copyright 1991 by Nigel Griffin, introduction by Anthony Pagden (Penguin Classics 1992). Trans. and notes copyright © 1992 by Nigel Griffin. Introduction copyright © 1992 by Anthony Pagden. Reproduced by permission of Penguin Books Ltd.

Juan Ginés de Sepúlveda, *The Second Democrates* (1547)

The man rules over the woman, the adult over the child, the father over his children. That is to say, the most powerful and most perfect rule over the weakest and most imperfect. This same relationship exists among men, there being some who by nature are masters and others who by nature are slaves. Those who surpass the rest in prudence and intelligence, although not in

In this extreme form of European belief, the natives did not even possess a human soul and were neither capable of converting to Christianity nor worthy of human rights.

A second answer to why the peoples of the New World were so different sprung from a belief that the natives were complete innocents. The native peoples lived in a kind of earthly Paradise, unspoiled by the corruption of European society. Some of the early English explorers of Virginia found the natives "most gentle, loving and faithful, void of any guile or treason," and one missionary found them "all the more children of God owing to their very lack of capacity and skill."[9] A tiny number of unconventional theological thinkers hypothesized that the native Americans had been created before the Hebrews as reported in the

physical strength, are by nature the masters. On the other hand, those who are dim-witted and mentally lazy, although they may be physically strong enough to fulfill all the necessary tasks, are by nature slaves. It is just and useful that it be this way. We even see it sanctioned in divine law itself, for it is written in the Book of Proverbs: "He who is stupid will serve the wise man." And so it is with the barbarous and inhumane peoples (the Indians) who have no civil life and peaceful customs. It will always be just and in conformity with natural law that such people submit to the rule of more cultured and humane princes and nations. Thanks to their virtues and the practical wisdom of their laws, the latter can destroy barbarism and educate these (inferior) people to a more humane and virtuous life. And if the latter reject such rule, it can be imposed upon them by force of arms. Such a war will be just according to natural law....

And you must realize that prior to the arrival of the Christians, they did not live in that peaceful kingdom of Saturn (the Golden Age) that the poets imagine, but on the contrary they made war against one another continually and fiercely, with such fury that victory was of no meaning if they did not satiate their monstrous hunger with the flesh of their enemies.... These Indians are so cowardly and timid that they could scarcely resist the mere presence of our soldiers. Many times thousands upon thousands of them scattered, fleeing like women before a very few Spaniards, who amounted to fewer than a hundred....

Until now we have not mentioned their impious religion and their abominable sacrifices, in which they worship the Devil as God, to whom they thought of offering no better tribute than human hearts.... Interpreting their religion in an ignorant and barbarous manner, they sacrificed human victims by removing the hearts from the chests. They placed these hearts on their abominable altars. With this ritual they believed that they had appeased their gods. They also ate the flesh of the sacrificed men....

War against these barbarians can be justified not only on the basis of their paganism but even more so because of their abominable licentiousness, their prodigious sacrifice of human victims, the extreme harm that they inflicted on innocent persons, their horrible banquets of human flesh, and the impious cult of their idols.

Source: From Pike, Frederick B. *Latin American History: Select Problems*, 1/e. Copyright © 1969 Wadsworth, a part of Cengage Learning, Inc. Reproduced by permission. www.cengage.com/permissions.

For Discussion

1. How did las Casas and Sepúlveda differ in their understanding of the basic nature of the Indians? How did these differing understandings shape their opposing arguments?
2. How reliable are these accounts of the native peoples of the Americas?
3. What was at stake for the definition of the West in these debates?

Bible, and, therefore, had not been subject to the Fall of Man and still lived in the earthly Paradise.

The most influential spokesman during the sixteenth century for this idea of native innocence was the powerful advocate of human rights Bartolomé de Las Casas (1474–1566). Throughout his career, Las Casas forcefully argued against the enslavement and ill treatment of the native Americans, which he chronicled in his most important published work, *A Short Account of the Destruction of the Indies* (1542). He saw the natives as innocents who needed to be guided rather than forced to accept Christianity and should not be enslaved. (See *Different Voices* in this chapter.)

The third response to the question of how to explain the New World peoples neither

MUTILATION OF NATIVE AMERICANS

In this illustration for one of Bartholomew de Las Casas's books condemning Spanish policy in America, a conquistador is shown terrorizing the natives with vicious dogs, a frequently employed technique. The conquistador dangles two infants while the dogs bite them. To the left a priest baptizes a young child whose mother has been hanged.

who tried to make sense of the new discoveries. Perplexed by the cultural diversity he had observed in the New World, Peter Martyr D'Anghiera (1457–1526), a pious priest and astute historian of Spanish explorations, noted that different peoples made judgments on the basis of different criteria: "The Ethiopian thinks the black color to be fairer than the white, and the white man thinks otherwise. The bearded man supposes he is more comely than he that wants a beard. As appetite therefore moves, not as reason persuades, men run into these vanities, and every province is ruled by its own sense...."[10] What others thought fundamental moral truths, Martyr considered manifestations of superficial cultural differences. The discovery in the New World that non-Christians could

dehumanized them nor assumed them innocent but simply recognized their differences as the natural consequence of human diversity. Advocates of this position proposed toleration. Deciding whether a particular people were bad or good raised questions about the criteria for making such judgments, and these questions introduced the principle of cultural relativism. **Cultural relativism** recognized that many (but not necessarily all) standards of judgment are specific to particular cultures rather than fixed truths established by natural or divine law. Cultural relativists attempt to understand why other people think and act the way they do. Such an approach can be traced to a small group of sixteenth-century European thinkers

lead moral lives, love their families, practice humility and charity, and benefit from highly developed religious institutions shook the complacent sense of European superiority.

CONCLUSION

The Significance of the Global Encounters

The world was forever changed by the European voyages from about 1450 to 1650. The significance of these encounters lay not so much in the Europeans' geographical discoveries as in the scale of permanent contact these voyages made possible among previously isolated peoples of the world. The European voyages of the fifteenth and sixteenth centuries created the global capitalist system.

As a result of the European slaving enterprises on the coast of West and Central Africa, millions of Africans were uprooted, transported in chains to a strange land, and forced to toil in subhuman conditions on plantations. There they grew crops for the increasingly affluent European consumers and generated profits often used to buy more slaves in Africa, parts of which became depopulated in the process. Until well into the nineteenth century, every cup of coffee, every puff of tobacco, every sugar candy, and every cotton dress of indigo blue came from the sweat of a black slave.

Many of the native Americans lost their lives, their land, and their way of life as a result of European encounters. In the Americas, native peoples suffered from the invasion of Old World microbes even more than from the invasion of Old World conquerors. The destruction of the Aztec and Incan Empires were certainly the most dramatic, but everywhere native peoples struggled to adapt to an invasion of foreign beings from a foreign world.

Asia was far less altered by contact with Europeans. The most thorough European conquest in Asia—the Russians in Siberia—was of the least populated region of the entire continent. European civilization remained on the cultural periphery of Asia. But European access to Asian luxury goods remained a crucial component in the expanding global economy that became one of the first fruits of European capitalism.

Coming to terms with the variety of world cultures became a persistent and absorbing problem in Western civilization. Most Europeans retained confidence in the inherent superiority of their civilization, but the realities of the world began to chip away at that confidence, and economic globalization profoundly altered Western civilization itself. Westerners began to confront the problem of understanding "other" cultures and in so doing changed themselves. The West came to mean less a place in Europe than a certain kind of culture that was exported throughout the world through conversion to Christianity, the acquisition of Western languages, and the spread of Western technology.

KEY TERMS

caravel	haciendas
settler colony	aldeias
plantation colony	factories
trading posts	Columbian Exchange
conquistadores	Columbian question
requerimiento	Cultural relativism
encomienda	

CHAPTER QUESTIONS

1. Why did the European incursions into sub-Saharan Africa lead to the vast migration of Africans to the Americas as slaves? (page 395)
2. How did the arrival of Europeans in the Americas transform native cultures and life? (page 401)
3. Why was the European encounter with Asian civilizations far less disruptive than those in Africa and the Americas? (page 414)
4. How was the world tied together in a global biological and economic system? (page 417)

TAKING IT FURTHER

1. What motivated the European voyagers and conquistadores to take such great risks?
2. Compare and contrast the European treatment of Africans with that of the natives of the New World.
3. The European global encounters of the fifteenth and sixteenth centuries produced one of the greatest disasters in human history. Agree or disagree. What are your reasons?

✓•—Practice on MyHistoryLab

14

The Reformations of Religion

- Causes of the Reformation
- The Diversity of Protestantism
- The Lutheran Reformation
- The Catholic Reformation

ACCORDING TO A POWERFULLY EVOCATIVE STORY THAT MAY OR MAY NOT BE TRUE, THE REFORMATION BEGAN ON HALLOWEEN, OCTOBER 31, 1517. An obscure monk-turned-university-professor nailed to the door of the cathedral in Wittenberg, Germany, an announcement containing 95 theses or debating propositions. Martin Luther had no hint of the ramifications of this simple act—as common then as posting an announcement for a lecture or concert on a university bulletin board now. But Luther's seemingly harmless deed sparked a revolution. Whether or not he ever posted the theses on the cathedral door, he certainly did have copies printed. Within weeks, all Germany was ablaze over Luther's daring attack on the pope. Within a few short years Wittenberg became the European center for a movement to reform the Church. As the pope and high churchmen resisted Martin Luther's call for reform, much of Germany and eventually most of northern Europe and Britain broke away from the Catholic Church. The **Protestant Reformation** dominated European affairs from 1517 until 1560.

Martin Luther succeeded because he expressed in print what many felt in their hearts—that the Church was failing in its most fundamental obligation to help Christians achieve salvation. In contrast, many Catholics considered the Protestants dangerous heretics whose errors made salvation

impossible. Moreover, for the many Catholics who had long recognized the need for reforms in the Church and been diligently working to achieve them, the intemperate Martin Luther only made matters worse.

The division between Protestants and Catholics split the West into two distinctive religious cultures. The result was that the hard-won unity of the West, which had been achieved during the Middle Ages through the expansion of Christianity to the most distant corners of the European continent and through the leadership of the papacy, was lost. Catholics and Protestants continued to share a great deal of the Christian tradition, but fateful issues divided them: their understanding of salvation, the function of the sacraments in promoting pious behavior, the celebration of the liturgy in Latin, and obedience to the pope.

The fundamental conflict during the Reformation was about religion, but religion can never be entirely separated from politics or society. The competition among the kingdoms and the social tensions within the cities of central and northern Europe magnified religious controversies. The Reformation raised this question: How did encounters between Catholics and Protestants permanently transform religious unity into religious division in the West?

426

THE IMITATION OF CHRIST

In Albrecht Dürer's self-portrait at age 28, he literally shows himself imitating Christ's appearance. The initials AD are prominently displayed in the upper left-hand corner. They stand for Albrecht Dürer, but also for *anno domini*, "the year of our Lord."

Source: Albrecht Duerer, "Self-Portrait". 1500. Oil on Panel. 26 1/4" × 19 1/4" (66.7 × 49 cm). Alte Pinakothek, Munich. SCALA/ Art Resource, NY

CAUSES OF THE REFORMATION

■ What caused the religious rebellion that began in German-speaking lands and spread to much of northern Europe?

The Protestant Reformation was the culmination of nearly 200 years of turmoil within the Church. During the fourteenth and fifteenth centuries the contradiction between the Church's divine mission and its obligations in this world hampered its moral influence. On the one hand, the Church taught that its mission was otherworldly, the source of spiritual solace and the guide to eternal salvation. On the other hand, the Church was thoroughly of

427

this world. It owned vast amounts of property, maintained a far-reaching judicial bureaucracy to enforce canon (Church) law, and was headed by the pope, who was also the territorial prince of the Papal State in central Italy. Whereas from the eleventh to the thirteenth centuries the popes had been the source of moral reform and spiritual renewal in the Church, by the fifteenth century the popes had become part of the problem. The problem was not so much that they had become corrupt, but they were unable to respond effectively to the demands of ordinary people who were increasingly concerned with their own salvation and the effective government of their communities.

Three developments, in particular, contributed to the demand for religious reform: the search for the freedom of private religious expression; the print revolution; and the northern Renaissance interest in the Bible and other sources of Christian knowledge.

The Search for Freedom

As we saw in Chapter 11, a series of events during the fourteenth century weakened the authority of the popes and led believers to look elsewhere for spiritual leadership and consolation. Between 1305 and 1378 seven popes in a row abandoned Rome and chose to reside in the relative calm of Avignon, France. The period came to be called the Babylonian Captivity of the Church, a pejorative term that reflected the widespread opinion outside France that the popes had become subservient to the kings of France and were financially corrupt. During the Great Schism (1378–1417), rival Italian and French popes divided the Church and eroded papal authority even further.

While the papacy's moral authority declined, lay Christians were drawn to new forms of worship. Particularly influential was the Modern Devotion, encouraged by the *Imitation of Christ* written about 1441. The Modern Devotion channeled believers' desire to transcend this world of evil and pain by emphasizing frequent private prayer and moral introspection. The *Imitation*

provided a kind of spiritual manual that helped laypeople follow the same path toward spiritual renewal that traditionally had been reserved for monks and nuns. The goal was to imitate Christ so thoroughly that Christ entered the believer's soul. In a self-portrait influenced by the Modern Devotion (shown on page 427), Albrecht Dürer (1471–1528) resembles Christ himself.

The religious fervor that drew many Christians to such profound forms of religious expression further alienated many from the papacy. They began to see the pope as a thieving foreigner who extorted money that could be better spent locally. German communities, in particular, protested against the financial demands and the questionable practices of the pope and higher clergy. Some bishops neglected their duties regarding the spiritual guidance of their flock. Some never resided in their dioceses (the district under the bishop's care), knew nothing of the problems of their people, and were concerned only with retaining their incomes and lavish living standards. Living amid the pleasures of Rome, these high clergymen were in no position to discipline parish priests, some of whom also ignored their moral responsibilities by living openly with concubines and even selling the sacraments. Although immorality of this sort was probably not widespread, a few notorious examples bred enormous resentment among the laity.

In an effort to assert control over the church in their own communities, city officials known as magistrates attempted to stem the financial drain and end clerical abuses. They restricted the amount of property ecclesiastical institutions could own, tried to tax the clergy, made priests subject to the town's courts of law, and eliminated the churchmen's exemption from burdensome duties, such as serving in the town militia or providing labor for public works. On the eve of the Reformation—especially in the cities of Germany and the Netherlands—magistrates had already begun to assert local control over the Church, a tendency that prepared the way for the Protestants' efforts. For many laypeople, the overriding desire was to obtain greater spiritual and fiscal freedom from the Church hierarchy.

The Print Revolution

Until the mid-fifteenth century, the only way in the West to reproduce any kind of text—a short business record or a long philosophical book—was to copy it laboriously by hand. As medieval scribes made copies on parchment, however, they often introduced errors or "improved" the original text as they saw fit. Thus, two different copies of the same text could read differently. Parchment books were also very expensive; a book as long as the Bible might require the skins of 300 sheep to make the parchment sheets and hundreds of hours of labor to copy the text. The high cost meant that books were limited to churchmen and to the very rich. Few Christians ever actually read the Bible simply because Bibles—like all books—were so rare.

Two fifteenth-century inventions revolutionized the availability of books. First, movable metal type was introduced around 1450, and after that time printed books first began to appear. Perhaps the very first was a Bible printed by Johannes Gutenberg (ca. 1398–1468) in Mainz, Germany. Equally important, cheap manufactured paper replaced expensive sheepskins. These two developments reduced the cost of books to a level that made them available even to artisans of modest incomes.

The demand for inexpensive printed books was astounding. During the first 40 years of print, more books were produced than had been copied by scribes during the previous 1,000 years. By 1500, presses in more than 200 cities and towns had printed six million books. Half of the titles were on religious subjects, and because the publishing industry (then as now) produced only what people wanted to buy, the predominance of religion reveals what was on the minds of the reading public.

The buyers of printed books included, of course, the traditionally literate classes of university students, churchmen, professionals, and aristocratic intellectuals. Remarkably, however, there was also an enormous demand among people for whom books had previously been an unimaginable luxury. During the fourteenth and fifteenth centuries literacy rates had steadily risen, although they varied a great deal across Europe. The knowledge of what was in books, however, spread widely beyond the literate few because reading for most people in the fifteenth and sixteenth centuries was an oral, public activity. In parish churches, taverns, and private houses the literate read books out loud to others for their entertainment and edification.

The expansion of the university system during this period also created more demand for books. Between 1300 and 1500 the number of European universities grew from 20 to 70. The universities also developed a new way of reading. During the fifteenth century the Sorbonne in Paris and Oxford University decreed that libraries were to be quiet places, an indication of the spread of silent reading among the most highly educated classes. Compared with the tradition of reading aloud, silent reading was faster and more private. The silent reader learned more quickly and also decided independently the meaning of what had been read. Once many cheap books were available to the silent readers among the best educated, the interpretation of texts, especially the notoriously difficult text of the Bible, could no longer be easily regulated.

It is difficult to imagine that the Reformation could have succeeded without the print revolution. Print culture radically changed how information was disseminated and gave people new ways to interpret their experiences. Between 1517 and 1520, Martin Luther wrote some 30 tracts, mostly in a riveting colloquial German. Three hundred thousand copies were printed and distributed throughout Europe. No other author's ideas had ever spread so fast to so many.

The Northern Renaissance and the Christian Humanists

As discussed in Chapter 12, the humanists were devoted to rediscovering the lost works of antiquity and imitating the style of the best Greek and Latin authors of the ancient world. As the humanists examined these ancient texts, they developed the study of philology, of how the meanings of words change over time. These endeavors stimulated a new kind of approach to the sources of Christianity. The humanist Lorenzo Valla (ca. 1407–1457), for example, questioned the accuracy of the Vulgate, the Latin translation of the Bible accepted by the Church.

The humanists who specialized in subjecting the Bible to philological study were called the **Christian humanists.** In examining the sources of Christianity, their goal was not to criticize Christianity or the Church but to understand the precise meaning of its founding texts, especially the Bible and the writings of the Church fathers, who wrote in Greek and Latin and commented on the Bible during the early centuries of Christianity. The Christian humanists first sought to correct what they saw as mistakes in interpreting Christian doctrine. Their second goal was to improve morals. They believed that the path to personal morality and to Church reform lay in imitating "the primitive church," which meant the practices of Christianity at the time of Jesus and the apostles. Most of the Christian humanists came from northern Europe. They constituted the most influential wing of the **northern Renaissance,** a movement that built on the foundations of the Italian Renaissance. Through their efforts, the Christian humanists brought the foundations of Christianity under intense scrutiny during the early sixteenth century.

Exploiting the potential of the relatively new printing industry, the Dutchman, Desiderius Erasmus (ca. 1469–1536), became the most influential and inspiring of the Christian humanists. During times of war, Erasmus eloquently called for peace. He also published a practical manual for helping children develop a sense of morality, and he laid out easy-to-follow guidelines for spiritual renewal in the *Handbook for the Militant Christian.* The artist Albrecht Dürer transformed the theme of that book into a visual allegory shown on page 431. Erasmus's penchant for moral criticism reached the level of high satire in his masterpiece, *The Praise of Folly* (1514). In it he attacked theologians preoccupied by silly questions, such as whether the Resurrection could take place at night; he lampooned corrupt priests who took money from dying men to read the last rites; he ridiculed gullible pilgrims who bought phony relics as tourist souvenirs; and he parodied the vanity of monks who thought the color of their robes more important than helping the poor. Erasmus also translated the Greek New Testament into a new Latin version. His critical studies were the basis of many new translations of the Hebrew and Greek Bible into vernacular languages, including the popular English translation, the King James Bible.

Erasmus's friend, the Englishman Thomas More (1478–1535), is best known for his book *Utopia* (1516). More's little book established the genre of utopian fiction, which described imaginary, idealized worlds. It depicted an imaginary island found in the New World, "Utopia," a double entendre in Greek meaning both "nowhere" and "good place." The Utopians were monotheists who, although not Christians, intuitively understood pure religion and lived a highly regulated life. Utopia represented More's understanding of how a society that imitated the primitive church might appear. In particular he promoted communism based on the passage in Scripture that states believers in Christ "were of one heart and soul, and no one claimed private ownership of any possessions, but everything they owned was held in common" (Acts 4:32). More shared some of Erasmus's ideas about the critical study of Scripture and a purer Church, but unlike Erasmus he was no pacifist.

Erasmus and More remained loyal Catholics, but as a chancellor of the English government, More ruthlessly persecuted Protestants. Nevertheless, the work of these two men helped popularize some of the ideas that came to be associated with the Protestant reformers. To them, the test for the legitimacy of any religious practice was twofold. First, could it be found in the Bible? Second, did it promote moral behavior? By focusing attention on the sources of Christianity, the Christian humanists emphasized the deep disparity they perceived between the Christianity of the New Testament and the state of the Church in their own time.

ALBRECHT DÜRER, *THE KNIGHT, DEATH, AND THE DEVIL*

This engraving of 1513 illustrates Erasmus's *Handbook for the Militant Christian* by depicting a knight steadfastly advancing through a frightening landscape. A figure of death holds an hourglass, indicating that the knight's time on Earth is limited. A devil follows behind him threateningly. His valiant horse and loyal dog represent the virtues that a pious Christian must acquire.

Source: Albrecht Dürer, "Knight, Death and the Devil". Engraving. (MM14997 B). The Metropolitan Museum of Art, Harris Brisbane Dick Fund, 1943. (43.106.2)

THE LUTHERAN REFORMATION

■ How did the Lutheran Reformation create a new kind of religious culture?

The Protestant Reformation began with the protests of Martin Luther against the pope and certain Church practices. Like Erasmus and

More, Luther used the Bible as the litmus test of what the Church should do. If a practice could not be found in the Bible, Luther thought, then it should not be considered Christian. But unlike Erasmus and More, he also introduced theological innovations that made compromise with the papacy impossible.

Luther and his followers, however, would not have succeeded without the support of local political authorities who had their own grievances against the pope and the Holy Roman Emperor, a devout defender of the Catholic faith. The Lutheran Reformation first spread in Germany with the assistance and encouragement of those local authorities—the town magistrates and the territorial princes. Under the sponsorship of princes and kings, Lutheranism spread from Germany into Scandinavia.

Martin Luther and the Break with Rome

Martin Luther (1483–1546) suffered a grim childhood and uneasy relationship with his father, a miner who wanted his son to become a lawyer. During a break from the University of Erfurt, where he was studying law, Luther was thrown from his horse in a storm and nearly died. That frightening experience impelled him to become a monk, a decision that infuriated his father because it meant young Luther abandoned a promising professional career. By becoming a monk, Luther replaced the control of his father with obedience to his superiors in the Augustinian Order. They sent him back to the University of Erfurt for advanced study in theology and then transferred him from the lovely garden city of Erfurt to Wittenberg in Saxony, a scruffy town "on the edge of beyond," as Luther described it. At Wittenberg Luther began to teach at an undistinguished university, far from the intellectual action. Instead of lamenting his isolation, Luther brought the world to his university by making it the center of the religious reform movement.

As a monk, Luther had been haunted by a deep lack of self-worth:

> In the monastery, I did not think about women, or gold, or goods, but my heart trembled, and doubted how God could be gracious to me. Then I fell away from faith, and let myself think nothing less than that I had come under the Wrath of God, whom I must reconcile with my good works.[1]

Obsessed by the fear that no amount of charitable good works, prayers, or religious ceremonies would compensate for God's contempt of him, Luther suffered from anxiety attacks and prolonged periods of depression. He understood his psychic turmoil and shaky faith as any monk would—the temptations of the Devil, who was a very powerful figure for Luther.

Over several years, while preparing and revising his university lectures on St. Paul, Luther gradually worked out a solution to his own spiritual crisis by reexamining the theology of penance. The sacrament of penance provided a way to confess sins and receive absolution for them. If a penitent had lied, for example, he could seek forgiveness for the sin by feeling sorry about it, confessing it to a priest, and receiving a penalty, usually a specified number of prayers. Penance took care of only those penalties the Church could inflict on sinners. God's punishment for sins would take place in Purgatory (a place of temporary suffering for dead souls) and at the Last Judgment. But Catholic theology taught that penance in this world would reduce punishment in the next. In wrestling with the concept of penance, Luther long meditated on the meaning of a difficult passage in St. Paul's epistle to the Romans (1:17): "The just shall live by faith." Luther came to understand this passage to mean that eternal salvation came not from performing the religious good works of penance, but from faith, which was a gift from God. That gift was called "grace" and was completely unmerited. Luther called this process of receiving God's grace **justification by faith** alone, because the ability to

have faith in Christ was a sign that one had received God's grace.

Luther's emphasis on justification by faith alone left no room for human free will in obtaining salvation, because Luther believed that faith could come only from God's grace. This did not mean that God controlled every human action, but it did mean that humans could not will to do good. They needed God's help. Those blessed with God's grace would naturally perform good works. This way of thinking about God's grace had a long tradition going back to St. Augustine, the Church father whose work profoundly influenced Luther's own thought. In fact, many Catholic thinkers embraced a similar position, but they did not draw the same conclusions about free will that Luther did. Luther's interpretation of St. Augustine on free will separated Lutheran from Catholic theology. Based on his rejection of free will, Luther condemned all but two of the Church sacraments as vain works that deluded people into thinking they could earn salvation by performing them. He retained communion and baptism because they were clearly authorized by the Bible, but disputes over the meaning of these two sacraments created divisions within the Protestant Reformation movement itself. Luther and other Protestants, moreover, changed the ceremonies of communion, allowing the laity to partake of the wine, which the Catholics had reserved for priests alone. The woodcut on page 433 by Lucas Cranach illustrates the Lutheran ritual of communion.

For Luther this seemingly bleak doctrine of denying the human will to do good was liberating. It freed him from his persistent fears of damnation. He no longer had to worry whether he was doing enough to please God or could muster enough energy to fight the Devil. All he had to do was trust in God's grace. After this breakthrough, Luther reported that "I felt myself to be born anew, and to enter through open gates into paradise itself. From here, the whole face of the Scriptures was altered."[2]

THE 95 THESES In 1517 Luther became embroiled in a controversy that led to his and his followers' separation from the Roman Catholic

COMMUNION IN BOTH KINDS

In this woodcut by Lucas Cranach the Elder, Lutheran ministers offer both the communion wine and bread to the laity. Catholics reserved the wine for the priests, which set them apart from the laity. Changes in the rituals of the Eucharist or communion were among the most divisive issues separating Catholic from Protestant.

Church. In order to finance the building of a new St. Peter's Basilica in Rome, Pope Leo X had issued a special new "indulgence," a particular form of penance whereby a sinner could remove years of punishment in Purgatory after death by performing a good work here on Earth. For example, pilgrims to Rome or Jerusalem often received indulgences, concrete measures of the value of their penances. Indulgences formed one of the most intimate bonds between the Church and the laity because they offered a means for the forgiveness of specific sins.

During the fourteenth century popes in need of ready cash had begun to sell indulgences. But Pope Leo's new indulgence went far beyond the promise of earlier indulgences by offering a one-time-only opportunity to escape penalties in Purgatory for all sins. Moreover, the special indulgence could apply not only to the purchaser, but to the dead already in Purgatory. The new indulgence immediately made all other indulgences worthless because it removed all penalties for sin whereas others removed only some.

Frederick the Wise, the Elector of Saxony (a princely title indicating that he was one of those who elected the emperors of the Holy Roman Empire) and the patron of Martin Luther's university, prohibited the sale of Pope Leo's special indulgence in Electoral Saxony, but it was sold just a few miles away from Wittenberg, across the border in the domain of Archbishop Albrecht of Mainz. Albrecht needed the revenues that the sale of indulgences would bring because he was in debt. He had borrowed enormous sums to bribe Pope Leo to allow him to hold simultaneously three ecclesiastical offices—a practice that was against Church law. To help Albrecht repay his debts, the pope allowed Albrecht to keep half of the revenue from the indulgence sale in his territories. Wittenbergers began to trek over the border to Albrecht's lands to listen to the sales pitch of a shameless indulgence hawker, the Dominican John Tetzel (1470–1519). Tetzel staged an ecclesiastical version of a carnival barker's act in which he harangued the crowd about their dead parents who could be immediately released from the flames of Purgatory for the sacrifice of a few coins. He allegedly ended his sermons with the notorious jingle,

As soon as the coin in the coffer rings,
Right then the soul to heaven springs.[3]

A group of the Wittenbergers who heard Tetzel asked Martin Luther for his advice about buying the indulgence. Luther responded less as a pastor offering comforting advice to his flock than as a university professor keen for debate. He prepared in Latin 95 theses—arguments or talking points—about indulgences that he announced he was willing to defend in an academic disputation. Luther had a few copies printed and, as we saw at the beginning of this chapter, probably posted one on the door of Wittenberg Cathedral. The **95 theses** were hardly revolutionary in themselves. They argued a simple point that salvation could not be bought and sold, a proposition that was sound, Catholic theology, and they explicitly accepted the authority of the pope even as they set limits on that authority. On that point, Luther followed what the Church councils of the fifteenth century had decreed. Luther's tone was moderate. He simply suggested that Pope Leo may have been misled in issuing the new indulgence. No one showed up to debate Luther, but someone translated the 95 theses into German and printed them. Within a few weeks, the previously unknown professor from an obscure university was the talk of the German-speaking lands.

The Dominicans counterattacked. Tetzel himself drew up opposing theses, which provoked a public clamor that Luther had tried to avoid. In 1519 at Leipzig before a raucous crowd of university students, Luther finally debated the theses and other issues with Johann Eck, a professor from the University of Ingolstadt. When Eck cleverly backed him into a logical corner, Luther refused to retreat. He insisted that the Bible was the sole guide to human conscience, and he questioned the authority of both popes and councils when they departed from the Bible. This was the very teaching for which earlier heretics had been burned at the stake. At this point Luther had no choice but to abandon his allegiance to the Church to which he had dedicated his life. By this time, Luther also had a large following in Wittenberg and beyond. The core of this group, who called themselves "evangelicals," consisted of university students, younger humanists, and well-educated, reform-minded priests and monks.

THE PATH TO THE DIET OF WORMS   In the wake of the Leipzig debate, Luther abandoned his moderate tone and launched an inflammatory pamphlet campaign. All were available in Luther's acerbic German prose, which delighted readers.

Freedom of a Christian (1520) argued that the Church's emphasis on good works had distracted Christians from the only source of salvation—God's grace, which was manifest in the faith of the Christian. It proclaimed the revolutionary doctrine of the **priesthood of all believers,** which reasoned that those of pure faith did not need a priest to stand between them and God, a doctrine that undermined the authority of the

33. Ego sum Papa! (Ich bin der Papst!)
Anonyme, zeitgenössische Karikatur des lasterhaften Papstes Alexander VI.
Nach einem französischen Holzschnitt.

ANTI-CATHOLIC PROPAGANDA

This woodcut, titled *I Am the Pope,* satirizes the papacy by depicting Pope Alexander VI as a monster. Alexander was infamous for allegedly conducting orgies in the Vatican. This kind of visual propaganda was an effective way to undermine support for the papacy.

Catholic clergy over the laity. The most inspirational pamphlet, *To the Christian Nobility of the German Nation* (1520), called upon the German princes to reform the Church and to defend Germany from exploitation by the corrupt Italians who ran the Church in Rome. When Pope Leo ordered Luther's books burned and demanded Luther retract his writings, Luther responded with a defiant demonstration in which he and his students burned the pope's decree and all of the university library's books of Church law. The die was cast.

The pope demanded that Luther be arrested, but Luther's patron, the Elector Frederick, answered by defending the professor. Frederick refused to make the arrest without first giving Luther a hearing at the Imperial Diet (parliament), which was set to meet at the town of Worms in 1521. Assembled at the Diet of Worms were haughty princes, grave bishops, and the resplendent young emperor Charles V (r. 1519–1558), who was presiding over his first Imperial Diet. The emperor ordered Luther to disavow his writings, but Luther refused to do so. For several days the Diet was in an uproar, divided by friends and foes of Luther's doctrines. Just before he was to be condemned by the emperor, Luther disappeared, and rumors flew that he had been assassinated. For days no one knew the truth. The truth was that Frederick the Wise had kidnapped Luther for his own safety and hid him in the castle at Wartburg, where for nearly a year he labored in quiet seclusion translating Erasmus's version of the New Testament into German (See *Justice in History* in this chapter).

The Appeal of Luther's Message

In its early phases the Reformation spread most rapidly among the educated urban classes. During the sixteenth century, 50 of the 65 German imperial cities, at one time or another, officially accepted the Protestant Reformation. Most of the 200 smaller German towns with a population of more than 1,000 also experienced some form of the Protestant movement. During the 1520 and 1530s, the magistrates (mayors and other officeholders) of these towns took command of the Reformation movement by seizing control of the local churches. The magistrates implemented Luther's reform of worship, disciplined the clergy, and stopped the drain of revenues to irresponsible bishops and the distant pope.

The German princes of the Holy Roman Empire had their own reasons to resent the power of the Church. They wanted to appoint their own nominees to ecclesiastical offices and to diminish the legal privileges of the clergy. Despite his steadfast Catholicism, Emperor Charles V was in no position to resist their demands. During most of his reign, Charles faced a two-front war—against France and against the Ottoman Turks. Charles desperately needed the German princes' military assistance. At the first Imperial Diet of Speyer in 1526, Charles allowed the princes to decide whether they would enforce the edict of the Diet of Worms against Luther and his followers. To preserve the empire from external enemies, the emperor was forced to allow its internal division along religious lines.

Luther's message especially appealed to women. In the early days of the movement, many women felt that Luther's description of "the priesthood of all believers" included them. Women understood Luther's phrase "the freedom of a Christian" as freeing them from the restrictive roles that had traditionally kept them silent and at home. Moreover, Luther and the other major reformers saw positive religious value in the role of wife and mother. Abandoning the Catholic Church's view that celibate monks and nuns were morally superior to married people, Luther declared marriage holy and set an example by taking a wife, the ex-nun Katherina von Bora. In countless popular images of them, Martin and Luther became the model married couple as shown on page 438. The wives of the reformers often became partners in the Reformation, taking particular responsibility for organizing charities and ministering to the poor.

In the early phases of the Reformation, women preached and published on religious

JUSTICE IN HISTORY

Here I Stand: Luther at the Diet of Worms

The Elector Frederick the Wise chose to defend Martin Luther, saving him from arrest and possible execution. Nevertheless, Frederick probably did not fully agree with Luther's positions. He claimed to have never exchanged more than 20 words with Luther. For Frederick, the issue was a matter of law and his own personal authority not of religion, even though he was a pious man. As Luther's lord and the patron of the University of Wittenberg, Frederick felt the obligation to protect his own subject from outside interference, especially from distant Rome.

Luther's case had already been lost in the papal court of Rome with the issuing of a formal ban against him, but Frederick saw some hope by appealing to the new emperor, Charles V, who would be presiding over the Imperial Diet when it met at the city of Worms. The oath the emperor had taken at his coronation obligated him to follow the letter of the law. Two clauses in the imperial constitution, which was revised for Charles's coronation, applied to the Luther case. One guaranteed that no German could be tried outside of Germany. The other stated that no one could be condemned without just cause and a formal hearing. No matter what the emperor's personal views, as a constitutional monarch he could neither pack Luther off to Rome in chains nor refuse to grant a review of the charges against him.

In addition, the old jurisdictional conflicts between the emperor and the pope, which went back to the Investiture Controversy of the eleventh century (see Chapter 10), prevented Charles from accepting too readily the pope's authority in the case. For the same reason the papal party, led by Rome's representative to the Diet of Worms, Aleander, rejected the very idea that Luther should receive a judicial hearing before the Diet. Aleander argued that Emperor Charles should simply implement the Church's decision to condemn the wayward professor. The inexperienced young emperor faced violently conflicting advice from those for and against Luther, but after considerable deliberation he accepted Frederick's position. Luther deserved a hearing. Martin Luther set off for Worms with the full expectation that he was going to his own execution.

When Luther arrived in Worms in a two-wheeled cart with a few companions, he was met by a huge crowd of 2,000 partisans who accompanied him through the streets. The city of Worms was tense. Posters defending Luther were plastered everywhere, and rough-looking Spanish soldiers swaggered about intimidating Luther's followers. The day after his arrival the imperial marshal brought Luther before the electors, members of the Diet, and the emperor, who declared, "That fellow will never make a heretic of me." Piled on a table in front of the emperor were Luther's books. An official named Eck (but not the same Johann Eck of the Leipzig debate) conducted the interrogation. He asked the monk if the books were his. Luther said they were and that he had written even more. "Do you defend them all, or do you care to reject a part?" To everyone's surprise the combative theology professor asked for more time to think things over.

Late the following afternoon Luther returned and Eck put the question to him again. This time he had an answer: "Most serene emperor, most illustrious princes, most clement lords, if I have not given some of you your proper titles I beg you to forgive me. I am not a courtier, but a monk. You asked me yesterday whether the books were mine and whether I would repudiate them. They are all mine, but as for the second question, they are not all of one sort."

Luther had made a clever distinction, one that gave him the opportunity to make a speech rather than answer simply yes or no. First, he pointed out that some of the books quoted Scripture and dealt with fundamental Christian truths. He could hardly damn himself by reputiating what all Christians held true. A second group of books complained about "the desolation of the Christian world by the evil lives and teaching of the papists." To this provocative statement, the emperor blurted out, "No." Luther went on to decry the "incredibile tyranny" to which the papacy had subjected Germany. This appeal to German nationalist sentiment awakened many in the Diet to his cause even if they disagreed with him on doctrinal matters. The third group of books attacked individuals, and although Luther admitted his attacks may have crossed a line for a university professor, he insisted that he could not repudiate these writings either without encouraging future tyrants. Finally, he declared that if he could be convinced of his errors on the grounds of Scripture he would be the first to throw his books into the flames. Eck, however, was not satisfied and demanded a plain answer, "Do you or do you not repudiate your books and the errors which they contain?"

Luther's recorded reply became one of the great moments in the history of religious liberty: "Since then Your Majesty and your lordships desire a simple reply, I will answer.... Unless I am convicted by Scripture and plain reason—I do not accept the authority of popes and councils, for they have contradicted each other—my conscience is captive to the Word of God. I cannot and I will not recant anything, for to go against conscience is neither right nor safe. God help me. Amen."The first printed account of Luther's speech added a final phrase, "Here I stand, I can do no other." Whether he ever spoke it or not, "Here I stand," became the motto of the Lutheran defiance of papal and imperial authority.[4]

The Diet of Worms issued an edict condemning Luther and his writings, making future compromises impossible. Luther himself, however, had managed to ignite the national fervor of the Germans, and it was they who kept Luther and the movement he started alive.

For Discussion

1. What were the legal issues involved in Luther's hearing before the Diet of Worms?

LUTHER BEFORE THE EMPEROR AT THE DIET OF WORMS IN 1521

Luther's courageous stand at the Imperial Diet became one of the most dramatic moments in the Luther story. The young Emperor Charles V is seated on a throne at the left, flanked by the Electors and cardinals. In front of him is a table containing Luther's books. The image captures the episode when Luther was asked whether he would repudiate his books or not.

2. Did the law of the empire serve justice in the case of Luther?
3. What did the ruling imply for the future relationship between church and state on religious questions?

Taking It Further

Roland H. Bainton, *Here I Stand: A Life of Martin Luther*. 1950. Although dated the book is still useful for an account of the legal issues involved in Luther's trial.

Hieko A. Oberman, *Luther: Man between God and the Devil*. Translated by Eileen Walliser-Schwarzbart. 1989. Less detailed on the trial than Bainton, it is the best overall biography of the reformer.

KATHERINA VON BORA AND MARTIN LUTHER

For many pious Lutherans the images of Luther and his wife, herself a former nun, replaced the images of the Virgin Mary and the saints favored by the Catholics.

matters. These women demanded to be heard in churches and delivered inspiring sermons. Marie Dentière, a former abbess of a French convent who joined the Reformation cause, asked, "Do we have two Gospels, one for men and the other for women?... For we [women] ought not, any more than men, hide and bury within the earth that which God has...revealed to us women?"[5] Most women were soon disappointed because their preaching and writing threatened the male authorities. In some places laws were passed that prohibited women from discussing religious questions. In England, women were even prevented from reading the Bible aloud to others. The few women who were able to speak and act openly in public were either queens or the wives of prominent reformers. Most women confined their participation in the Reformation to the domestic sphere, where they instructed children, quietly read the Bible, and led prayer circles.

One of the attractions of Protestantism was that it allowed divorce, which was prohibited by Catholic Church law. However, the reform leaders were quite reluctant to grant women the same rights as their husbands in obtaining a divorce.

During the early years of the Reformation, there were many marriages in which one spouse followed the old faith and the other the new. But if the woman converted and her husband did not, the Protestant reformers counseled that she should obey her husband even if he forced her to act contrary to God's will. She could pray for his conversion but could not leave or divorce him. Most women were forced to remain married regardless of their feelings. A few exceptional women left their husbands anyway and continued to proclaim their religious convictions to the world. One such woman, Anne Askew from England, was tortured and executed for her beliefs.

THE GERMAN PEASANTS' REVOLT   The Reformation also appealed to many peasants because it offered them a simplified religion and, most important, local control of their churches. The peasants of Wendelstein, a typical South German village, had been complaining about the conduct of its priests for some time. In 1523, they hired a "Christian teacher" and told him in no uncertain terms: "We will not recognize you as a lord, but only as a servant of the community. We will command you, not you us, and we order you to preach the gospel and the word of God purely, clearly, and truthfully—without any human teachings—faithfully and conscientiously."[6] These villagers understood the Reformation to mean that they could take control of their local church and demand responsible conduct from the minister they hired. However, other peasants understood the Reformation in more radical terms as licensing social reforms that Luther himself never supported.

In June 1524 a seemingly minor event sparked a revolt of peasants in many parts of Germany. When an aristocratic lady demanded that the peasants in her village abandon their grain harvest to gather snails for her, they rebelled and set her castle on fire. Over the next two years, the rebellion spread as peasants rose up against their feudal lords to demand the adoption of Lutheran reforms in the Church, a reduction of feudal privileges, the abolition of serfdom, and the self-government of their communities. Their rebellion was unprecedented. It was the largest and best-organized peasant movement ever in Germany, a measure of the powerful effect of the Protestant reform message. Like the Reformation, the revolt was the culmination of a long period of discontent, but unlike the Reformation, it was a tragic failure.

These peasants were doing exactly what they thought Luther had advocated when he wrote about the "freedom of the Christian." They interpreted his words to mean complete social as well as religious freedom. However, Luther had not meant anything of the sort. To him, the freedom of the Christian referred to inner, spiritual freedom, not liberation from economic or political bondage. Instead of supporting the rebellion begun in his name, Luther and nearly all the other reformers backed the feudal lords and condemned in uncompromising terms the violence of the peasant armies. In *Against the Thieving, Murderous Hordes of Peasants* (1525), Luther expressed his own fear of the lower classes and revealed that despite his acid-tongued attacks on the pope, he was fundamentally a conservative thinker who was committed to law and order. He urged that the peasants be hunted down and killed like rabid dogs. And so they were. Between 70,000 and 100,000 peasants died, a slaughter far greater than the Roman persecutions of the early Christians. To the peasants, Luther's conservative position on social and economic issues felt like betrayal, but it enabled the Lutheran Reformation to retain the support of the princes, which was essential for its survival.

LUTHERAN SUCCESS   Soon after the crushing of the Peasants' Revolt, the Lutheran Reformation faced a renewed threat from its Catholic opponents. In 1530 Emperor Charles V bluntly commanded all Lutherans to return to the Catholic fold or face arrest. Enraged, the Lutherans refused to comply. The following year the Protestant princes formed a military alliance, the Schmalkaldic League, against the emperor. Renewed trouble with France and the Turks prevented a military confrontation between the league and the emperor for 15 years, giving the Lutherans enough breathing space to put the Reformation on a firmer basis in Germany by training ministers and educating the laity in the new religion. In the meantime Lutheranism spread beyond Germany into Scandinavia, where it received support from the kings of Denmark and Sweden as it had among the princes of northern Germany.

After freeing himself from foreign wars, Charles V turned his armies against the Protestants. However, in 1552 the Protestant armies defeated him, and Charles was forced to relent. In 1555 the **Religious Peace of Augsburg** established the principle of *cuius regio, eius religio*, which means "he who rules determines the religion of the land." Protestant princes were permitted to retain all church lands seized before 1552 and to enforce Protestant worship, but Catholic princes were also allowed to enforce Catholic worship in their territories. Those who disagreed with their ruler's religion would not be tolerated. Their options were to change religion or to emigrate elsewhere. With the Peace of Augsburg the religious division of the Holy Roman Empire became permanent.

The following year, Emperor Charles, worn out from ceaseless warfare, the anxieties of holding his vast territories together, and nearly 40 years of trying to stamp out Protestantism, abdicated his throne and retired to a monastery, where he died in 1558.

THE DIVERSITY OF PROTESTANTISM

■ How and why did Protestant denominations multiply to such an extent in northern Europe and Britain?

The term *Protestant* originally applied only to the followers of Luther who *protested* the decisions of the second Imperial Diet of Speyer in 1529, which attempted to force them back into the Catholic fold, but the term came to describe much more than that small group. Protestantism encompassed innumerable churches and sects, all of which refused to accept the authority of the pope. Many of these have survived since the Reformation, some disappeared in the violence of the sixteenth century, and others have sprung up since, especially in North America, where Protestantism has thrived.

The varieties of Protestantism can be divided into two types. The first was the product of the **Magisterial Reformation,** which refers to the churches that received official government sanction. These included the Lutheran churches (Germany and Scandinavia); the Reformed and Calvinist churches (Switzerland, Scotland, the Netherlands, and a few places in Germany); and the Anglican Church (England, Wales, parts of Ireland, and later in England's colonies). The second was the product of the **Radical Reformation** and included the movements that failed to gain official recognition and were at best tolerated, at worst persecuted. This strict division into Magisterial and Radical Protestantism broke down in eastern Europe, where the states did not enforce religious conformity (see **Map 14.1**).

The Reformation in Switzerland

The independence of Switzerland from the Holy Roman Empire meant that from the beginning of the Reformation local authorities could cooperate

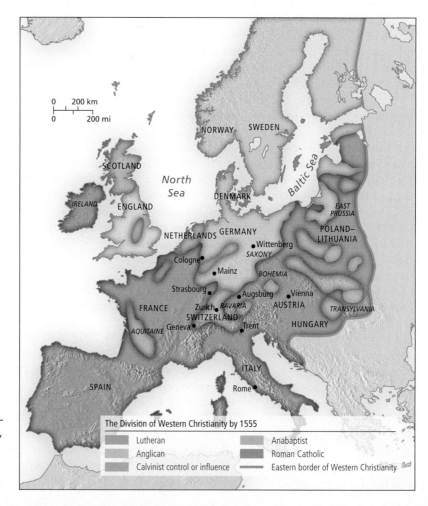

MAP 14.1

The Division of Western Christianity by 1555

The West, which had been culturally unified by Christianity for more than 1,000 years, split apart during the sixteenth century. These religious divisions persist to this day.

The Division of Western Christianity by 1555

- Lutheran
- Anglican
- Calvinist control or influence
- Anabaptist
- Roman Catholic
- ——— Eastern border of Western Christianity

with the reformers without opposition from the emperor. The Swiss Confederation bound together 13 fiercely proud regions, called cantons. Except for the leading cities of Zürich, Basel, and Geneva, Switzerland remained an impoverished land of peasants who could not fully support themselves from the barren mountainous land. To supplement their meager incomes, young Swiss men fought as mercenaries in foreign armies, often those of the pope. Each spring, mercenary captains recruited able-bodied Swiss men from the mountain villages. The Swiss men left the women behind to tend the animals and farms. By summer, the villages were emptied of all men except the old and invalid. Each fall at the end of the fighting season, the survivors of that season's campaign trudged home, always bringing bad news to a fresh group of widows. The strain created by the mercenary's life stimulated the desire for sweeping reforms in Switzerland.

ZWINGLI'S ZÜRICH   Ulrich Zwingli (1484–1531) had served as a chaplain with the Swiss mercenaries under the pope in Italy. In 1520, after being named the People's Priest of Zürich, Zwingli criticized his superior bishop for recruiting local young men to die in the papal armies. That same year he began to call for reform of the Church, advocating the abolition of the Roman Catholic mass, the marriage of priests, and the closing of monasteries. One of the novel features of Zwingli's reform was the strict emphasis on preaching the Word of Scripture during Church services, in contrast with the emphasis on ritual in the traditional Catholic liturgy. Zwingli ordered the removal of all paintings and statues

from churches because they distracted parishioners from concentrating on the preaching. The Zwinglian Reformation began independently of the Lutheran Reformation and created a separate reform center from which reform ideas spread throughout Switzerland, southern Germany, and England.

Two features distinguished the Zwinglian from the Lutheran Reformation. One was Zwingli's desire to have reformed ministers participate in governmental decisions. In Lutheran Germany, church and state supported each other, but they remained legally separate, and the prince alone had the authority to determine the religion of the land. In Zürich, the moral Christian and the good citizen were one and the same, and Zwingli worked with the magistrates of the city council, who step-by-step legalized the Reformation and enforced conformity through its police powers.

Luther and Zwingli also differed in their understanding of the nature of the Eucharist, the communion sacrament that reenacted Christ's Last Supper with his apostles. Luther believed that Christ's body was spiritually present in the communion bread. "You will receive," as he put it, "as much as you believe you receive."[7] This emphasis on the inner, spiritual state of the believer was very characteristic of Luther's introspective piety. In contrast to Luther, Zwingli could not accept the idea of the presence of Almighty God in a humble piece of bread. To Zwingli, the Eucharistic bread was just a symbol that stood for the body of Christ. The problem with the symbolic interpretation of the Eucharist was that the various reformers could not agree with Zwingli

CHRONOLOGY: THE LUTHERAN REFORMATION

1517	Luther posts the 95 theses
1519	Luther debates Johann Eck at Leipzig; election of Charles V as Holy Roman Emperor
1521	Diet of Worms
1524–1525	German peasants revolt
1531	Formation of the Schmalkaldic League
1555	The Religious Peace of Augsburg

on exactly what the Eucharist symbolized. As early as 1524, it became evident that each reformer was committed to a different interpretation, and these different interpretations became the basis for different Protestant churches.

CALVIN'S GENEVA In the next generation the momentum of the Reformation shifted to Geneva, Switzerland, under the leadership of John Calvin (1509–1564). Trained as a lawyer and exiled from his home in France in 1533 for his reformist views, Calvin spent several years wandering, searching for a quiet retreat, and collaborating with other reformers. After he settled in Geneva in 1536, Calvin spent the rest of his life transforming the town into the City of God. The linchpin of the Genevan reform was the close cooperation between the magistrates of the city council and the clergy in enforcing the moral discipline of the citizens.

Calvin's theology extended the insights of Luther and Zwingli to their logical conclusions. This pattern is most obvious in Calvin's understanding of justification by faith. Luther had argued that the Christian could not earn salvation through good works and that faith came only from God. Calvin reasoned that if an all-knowing, all-powerful God knew everything in advance and caused everything to happen, then the salvation of any individual was predetermined or, as Calvin put it, "predestined." Calvin's doctrine of **predestination** was not new. In fact, it had long been discussed among Christian theologians. But for Calvin two considerations made it crucial. First was Calvin's certainty that God was above any influence from humanity. The "majesty of God," as Calvin put it, was the principle from which everything else followed. Second, Calvin and other preachers had noticed that in a congregation attending a sermon, only a few paid attention to what was preached, while the vast majority seemed unable or unwilling to understand. The reason for this disparity seemed to be that only the Elect, as the Bible decreed, could truly follow God's Word. The Elect were those who had received God's grace and would be saved. The Elect were known only to God, but Calvin's theology encouraged the

converted to feel the assurance of salvation and to accept a "calling" from God to perform his will on Earth. God's **calling** gave Calvinists a powerful sense of personal direction, which committed them to a life of moral activity, whether as preacher, wife, or shoemaker.

Calvin composed an elegant theological treatise, the *Institutes of the Christian Religion*, first published in six chapters in 1535 but constantly revised and expanded until it reached 80 chapters in the definitive 1559 edition. Calvin the lawyer wrote a tightly argued and reasoned work, like a trial attorney preparing a case. In Calvin's theology the parts fit neatly together like a vast, intricate puzzle. Calvin's work aspired to be a comprehensive reformed theology that would convince through reasoned deliberation, and it became the first systematic presentation of Protestant doctrine. Whereas Luther spun out his sometimes contradictory ideas in a series of often polemical pamphlets, Calvin devoted himself to perfecting his comprehensive theology of Protestantism. (See *Different Voices* in this chapter.)

Given its emphasis on building a holy community, Calvinism helped transform the nuclear family into a social unit for training and disciplining children. Because women were responsible for educating children, they had to be literate. Calvinist women and men were both disciplined and liberated—disciplined to avoid physical and material pleasures, liberated from the necessity to do good works but guided by God's grace to do them anyway. Calvinism spread far beyond its Swiss home, becoming the dominant form of Protestantism in France, the Netherlands, Scotland, and New England.

The Reformation in Britain

Great Britain, as the island kingdom is known today, did not exist in the sixteenth century. The Tudor dynasty, which began in 1485 with Henry VII (see Chapter 12), ruled over England, Wales, and Ireland, but Scotland was still a separate kingdom with its own monarch and church institutions. These countries had distinctive political traditions, cultures, and languages, and as a

ICONOCLASM IN THE NETHERLANDS

Protestants sometimes initiated reform by vandalizing churches through acts of iconoclasm—the removing, breaking, or defacing of religious statues, paintings, and symbols such as crucifixes. In this engraving the men on the left of the church haul down statues. Note that one statue is already lying on the ground. On the right side of the church, men are breaking the stained glass windows with clubs. Reformers justified iconoclasm because the money for images could be better spent feeding the poor and because they thought paintings and sculptures distracted parishioners from listening to preaching.

result their Reformation experiences differed considerably. The Tudors imposed the Reformation as a matter of royal policy, and they were mostly successful in England and Wales. But they hardly made a dent in the religious culture of Ireland, which was a remarkable exception to the European pattern of conformity to the religion of the ruler. There the vast majority of the population remained Catholic. Scotland, also an exception to the rule, wholeheartedly accepted the Protestant Reformation against the will of its Catholic queen and most of the clergy.

THE TUDORS AND THE ENGLISH REFORMATION In 1527 the rotund, self-absorbed, but crafty King Henry VIII (r. 1509–1547) announced that he had come to the pious conclusion that he had gravely

sinned by marrying his brother's widow, Catherine of Aragon. By this time the couple had been married for 18 years, their only living child was the princess Mary, and at age 42 Catherine was unlikely to give birth to more children. Henry let it be known that he wanted a son to secure the English throne for the Tudor dynasty. He also had his eye on the most engaging woman of the court, Anne Boleyn, who was less than half Catherine's age. In the past, popes had usually been cooperative when a powerful king needed an annulment, but Pope Clement VII (r. 1523–1534) was in no position to oblige Henry. At the time of the marriage, the papal curia had issued a dispensation for Henry to marry his brother's widow, a practice that is prohibited in the Bible. In effect, Henry was asking the papacy to admit it had made a mistake.

DIFFERENT VOICES A CATHOLIC CARDINAL CHALLENGES JOHN CALVIN

In 1539 Cardinal Jacopo Sadoleto wrote a letter to the magistrates and citizens of Geneva inviting them to return to the Catholic Church. A few months later the reformer John Calvin replied to Sadoleto. Although both letters are polemical in tone, they isolate the significant differences between the two faiths. In these excerpts from the two letters, Sadoleto and Calvin show how Catholics and Protestants had a very different understanding of what constituted "the Church."

Sadoleto's Letter to the Genevans, March 18, 1539

The point in dispute is whether is it more expedient for your salvation, and whether you think you will do what is more pleasing to God, by believing and following what the Catholic Church throughout the whole world, now for more than 1,500 years, or (if we require clear and certain recorded notice of the facts) for more than 1,300 years approves with general consent; or innovations introduced within these 25 years, by crafty or, as they think themselves, acute men; but men certainly who are not themselves the Catholic Church? For, to define it briefly, the Catholic Church is that which in all parts, as well as at the present time in every region of the world, united and consenting in Christ, has been always and everywhere directed by the one Spirit of Christ; in which Church no dissension can

exist; for all its parts are connected with each other, and breathe together. But should any dissension and strife arise, the great body of the Church indeed remains the same, but an abscess is formed by which some corrupted flesh, being torn off, is separated from the spirit which animates the body, and no longer belongs in substance to the body ecclesiastic. I will not here descend to the discussion of single points, or load your ears with a multitude of words and arguments.... [Then he proceeds to do just that] I will say nothing of the Eucharist, in which we worship the most true body of Christ.... Nor will I speak of confession of sins to a priest, in which confession that which forms the strongest foundation of our safety, viz., true Christian humility, has both been demonstrated by Scripture, and established and enjoined by the Church; this humility these men have studied calumniously to evade, and presumptuously to cast away. Nor will I say anything either of the prayers of the saints to God for us, or of ours for the dead, though I would fain know what these same men would be at when they despise and deride them. Can they possibly imagine that the soul perishes along with its body? This they certainly seem to insinuate, and they do it still more openly when they strive to procure for themselves a liberty of conduct set loose from all ecclesiastical laws, and a license for their lusts.

In addition, at the moment when Henry's petition for divorce arrived, Clement was under the control of Catherine's nephew, the Emperor Charles V, whose armies had recently captured and sacked the city of Rome. In 1531 Henry gave up trying to obtain papal approval and divorced Catherine anyway. Eighteen months later he secretly married Anne. England's compliant Archbishop Thomas Cranmer (1489–1556) pronounced the marriage to Catherine void and the one to Anne valid. But the marriage to Anne did not last. When she failed to produce a male heir, Henry had her arrested,

charged with incest with her brother and adultery with other men. She was convicted and beheaded.

The English separation from the Roman Catholic Church took place in 1534 through the Acts of Supremacy and Succession. The separation has often been understood as a by-product of Henry's capricious lust and the plots of his brilliant minister, Thomas Cromwell (ca. 1485–1540). It is certainly true that Henry's desire to rid himself of Catherine led him to reject papal authority and to establish himself as the head of the Church of England. It is also certainly true that Henry was an

Calvin's Reply to Sadoleto, September 1, 1539

You are mistaken in supposing that we desire to lead away the people from that method of worshipping God which the Catholic Church always observed. You either labor under a delusion as to the term *church,* or, at least, knowingly and willingly give it a gloss. I will immediately show the latter to be the case, though it may also be that you are somewhat in error. First, in defining the term, you omit what would have helped you in no small degree to the right understanding of it. When you describe it as that which in all parts, as well as at the present time in every region of the earth, being united and consenting in Christ, has been always and everywhere directed by the one Spirit of Christ, what comes of the Word of the Lord [i.e., the Bible], that clearest of all marks, and which the Lord himself, in pointing out the Church, so often recommends to us? For seeing how dangerous it would be to boast of the Spirit without the Word, He declared that the Church is indeed governed by the Holy Spirit, but in order that that government might not be vague and unstable, He annexed it to the Word. For this reason Christ exclaims that those who are of God hear the Word of God—that His sheep are those which recognize His voice as that of their Shepherd, and any other voice as that of a stranger (John X. 27). For this reason the Spirit, by the mouth of Paul declares (Eph. ii. 20) that the Church is built upon the foundation of the Apostles and Prophets. Also, that the Church is made holy to the Lord, by the washing of water in the Word of life. In short, why is the preaching of the gospel so often styled the kingdom of God, but because it is the scepter by which the heavenly King rules His people?

Source: From *A Reformation Debate:* John Calvin and Jacopo Sadoleto. Ed. by John C. Olin (NY: Fordham University Press, 2000), copyright © 2000, Fordham University Press.

For Discussion

1. How do the definitions of the Church in these two writers differ?

2. What is at stake in the differences between these definitions? In other words, who gains and who loses from the Catholic versus the Calvinist definition?

3. Notice how Sadoleto suggests the Calvinists "imagine the soul perishes along with its body." What does this mean? If true what would it mean for the Christian notion of eternal salvation?

4. Notice how often Calvin refers to the Word, that is Scripture. What does he achieve by emphasizing Scripture over all other sources of authority?

---

inconstant husband: Of his six wives, two were divorced and two beheaded. However, historians do not explain the English Reformation simply as the consequence of royal whim or the machinations of a single minister.

The English Reformation began as a declaration of royal independence from papal supervision rather than an attempt to reform the practices of the Church. Under Henry VIII the English Reformation could be described as Catholicism without the pope. Protestant doctrine, at first, had little role in the English Reformation, and Henry himself had sharply criticized Martin Luther in a treatise probably ghost-written by Thomas More. Royal supremacy established control over the Church by granting to the king supervising authority over liturgical rituals and religious doctrines. Thomas Cromwell, who worked out the practical details for parliamentary legislation, was himself a Protestant, and no doubt his religious views emboldened him to reject papal authority. But the principal theorist of royal supremacy was a Catholic, Thomas

Starkey (ca. 1499–1538). A sojourn in Italy had acquainted Starkey with Italian Renaissance political theory, which emphasized concepts of civic liberty. In fact, many English Catholics found royal supremacy acceptable as long as it meant only abandoning submission to the pope in distant Rome. Those who opposed cutting the connection to Rome suffered for their opposition, however. Bishop John Fisher (ca. 1469–1535) and Sir Thomas More, the humanist author of *Utopia* and former chancellor of England, were executed for their refusal to go along with the king's decision.

With this display of despotic power, Henry seized personal control of the English church and then closed and confiscated the lands of the monasteries. He redistributed the monastic lands to the nobility in an effort to purchase their support and to make money for the crown. Henry's officials briefly flirted with some Protestant reform but largely avoided theological innovations. On the local level many people embraced the Reformation for their own reasons, often because it gave them a sense of control over the affairs of their community. Others went along simply because the power of the king was too strong to resist.

Henry's six wives bore three surviving children. As each succeeded to the throne, the official religion of England gyrated wildly. Because his youngest child, Edward, was male, Henry designated him successor to the throne. His two daughters, Mary and Elizabeth, were to succeed only if Edward died without an heir, which he did. Only ten years old when he followed his father to the throne, King Edward VI (r. 1547–1553) was the pawn of his Protestant guardians, some of whom pushed for a more thorough Protestant Reformation in England than Henry had espoused. After Edward's premature death, his half-sister, Queen Mary I (r. 1553–1558), daughter of Henry and Catherine of Aragon, attempted to bring England back to obedience to the pope. Her unpopular marriage to Philip II of Spain and her failure to retain the support of the nobles, who were the foundation of Tudor government, damaged the Catholic cause in England.

Mary's successor and half-sister, Elizabeth Tudor, the daughter of Henry and Anne Boleyn, was an entirely different sort. Queen Elizabeth I (r. 1558–1603), raised as a Protestant, kept her enemies off balance and her quarrelsome subjects firmly in hand with her charisma and shrewd political judgments. Elizabeth became one of the most successful monarchs ever to reign anywhere. Without the considerable talents of Elizabeth, England could easily have fallen into civil war over religion—as the Holy Roman Empire and France did and as England itself did some 40 years after her death.

Between 1559 and 1563, Elizabeth repealed the Catholic legislation of Mary and promulgated her own Protestant laws, collectively known as the Elizabethan Settlement, which established the Church of England, known as the Anglican Church (Episcopalian in the United States). Her principal adviser, William Cecil (1520–1598), implemented the details of the reform through reasonable debate and compromise rather than by insisting on doctrinal purity and rigid conformity. The touchstone of the Elizabethan Settlement was the 39 Articles (finally approved by Parliament in 1571), which articulated a moderate version of Protestantism. It retained the ecclesiastical hierarchy of bishops as well as an essentially Catholic liturgy translated into English.

The Church of England under Elizabeth permitted a wide latitude of beliefs, but it did not tolerate "recusants," those who as a matter of principle refused to attend Church of England services. These were mostly Catholics who set up a secret network of priests to serve their sacramental needs and whom the government considered dangerous agents of foreign powers. Many others were militant Protestants who thought the Elizabethan Settlement did not go far enough in reforming religion. The most vocal and influential of the Protestant dissenters were the Puritans, Calvinists who demanded a church purified of what they thought were remnants of Roman Catholicism.

SCOTLAND: THE CITADEL OF CALVINISM   While England groped its way toward moderate Protestantism, neighboring Scotland became one of the most thoroughly Calvinist countries in Europe. In 1560 the parliament of Scotland overthrew Roman

Catholicism against the will of Mary Stuart, Queen of Scots (1542–1587). The wife of the French king, Mary was absent in France during the crucial early phases of the Reformation and returned to Scotland only after her husband's death in 1561. Despite her Catholicism, Mary proved remarkably conciliatory toward the Protestants by putting royal funds at the disposal of the new Reformed Kirk (Church) of Scotland. But the Scottish Calvinists never trusted her, and their mistrust would bring about her doom when they rebelled against her and drove her into exile in England. There Queen Elizabeth had her imprisoned and eventually executed because she remained a dangerous symbol for Catholics in England and Scotland.

The Scots Confession of 1560, written by a panel of six reformers, established the new church. John Knox (ca. 1514–1572) breathed a strongly Calvinist air into the church through his many polemical writings and the official liturgy he composed in 1564, the *Book of Common Order*. Knox emphasized faith and individual Christian conscience over ecclesiastical authority. Instead of the episcopal structure in England, which granted bishops the authority over doctrine and discipline, the Scots Kirk established a Presbyterian form of organization, which gave organizational authority to the pastors and elders of the congregations, all of whom had equal rank. As a result the Presbyterian congregations were independent from any central authority.

The Radical Reformation

The magisterial reformers in Germany, Switzerland, England, and Scotland managed to obtain official sanction for their religious reforms, often at the cost of some compromise with governmental authorities. As a result of those compromises, radicals from among their own followers challenged the magisterial reformers and demanded faster, more thorough reform. In most places the radicals represented a small minority, perhaps never more than two percent of all Protestants. But their significance outstripped their small numbers, in part because they forced the magisterial reformers to respond to their arguments

and because their enemies attempted to eradicate them through extreme violence.

The radicals divided into three categories: Anabaptists, who attempted to construct a holy community on the basis of literal readings of the Bible; Spiritualists, who abandoned all forms of organized religion to allow individuals to follow the inner voice of the Holy Spirit; and Unitarians, who advocated a rational religion that emphasized ethical behavior over ceremonies.

ANABAPTISTS: THE HOLY COMMUNITY For Anabaptists, the Bible was a blueprint for reforming not just the church, but all of society. Because the Bible reported that Jesus was an adult when he was baptized, the Anabaptists rejected infant baptism and adopted adult baptism. (**Anabaptism** means to rebaptize.) An adult, they believed, could accept baptism as an act of faith, unlike an oblivious infant. Anabaptists saw the sacraments of baptism and communion as symbols of faith, which had no purpose or meaning unless the recipient was already a person of faith. Adult baptism reserved for the Elect allowed the creation of a pure church, isolated from the sinfulness of the world.

Because they did not want the Elect to have to compromise with the sinful, Anabaptists advocated the complete separation of Church and state. Anabaptists sought to obey only God and completely rejected all established religious and political authorities. They required adherents to refuse to serve in government offices, swear oaths, pay taxes, or serve as soldiers. Anabaptists sought to live in highly disciplined "holy communities," which excommunicated errant members and practiced simple services based on scriptural readings. Because the Anabaptist communities consisted largely of uneducated peasants, artisans, and miners, a dimension of economic radicalism colored the early Anabaptist movement. For example, some Anabaptist radicals advocated the elimination of all private property and the sharing of wealth. On the position of women, however, Anabaptists were staunchly conservative, denying women any public role in religious affairs and insisting that they remain under the strict control of their fathers and husbands. By subordinating women, they thought they were following the Bible, but so did their more egalitarian opponents. Literal readings of the Bible proved slippery.

Because the Anabaptists promoted a radical reorganization of society along biblical lines, they provoked a violent reaction. In Zürich the city council decreed that the appropriate punishment for all Anabaptists was to be drowned in the local river where they had been rebaptizing themselves. By 1529 it became a capital offense in the Holy Roman Empire to be rebaptized; during the sixteenth century perhaps as many as 5,000 Anabaptists were executed for the offense, a persecution that tended to fragment the Anabaptists into isolated, secretive rural communities.

During a brief period in 1534 and 1535, an extremely radical group of Anabaptists managed to seize control of the northern German city of Münster. An immigrant Dutch tailor, John of Leiden, set up a despotic regime in Münster that punished with death any sin, even gossiping or complaining. John of Leiden introduced polygamy and collective ownership of property. He set an example by taking 16 wives, one of whom he beheaded for talking back, stomping on her body in front of the other frightened wives. As the besieging armies closed in, John forced his followers to crown him king and worship him. After his capture, John was subjected to an excruciating torture, and as a warning to others, his corpse was displayed for many years hanging in an iron cage.

The surviving Anabaptists abandoned the radicalism of the Münster community and embraced pacifism and nonviolent resistance. However, even these peaceful souls suffered persecution. "God opened the eyes of the governments by the revolt at Münster," as the Protestant reformer Heinrich Bullinger put it, "and thereafter no one would trust even those Anabaptists who claimed to be innocent."[8] A Dutchman, Menno Simons (1496–1561), tirelessly traveled about the Netherlands and Germany, providing solace and guidance to the isolated survivors of the Münster disaster. His followers, the Mennonites, preserved the noblest features of the Anabaptist tradition of quiet resistance to persecution. Both the Mennonites and the Amish in North America are direct descendants of sixteenth- and seventeenth-century Anabaptist groups. Under Mennonite influence, Thomas Helwys founded the first Baptist church in England in 1612. As the leader of the English Baptists, Helwys wrote an unprecedented appeal for the absolute freedom of religion. In it he defended the religious rights of Jews, Muslims, and even atheists as well as all varieties of Christians. For his views he was imprisoned, where he died.

SPIRITUALISTS: THE HOLY INDIVIDUAL Whereas the Anabaptists radicalized the Swiss Reformation's emphasis on building a godly community, the **Spiritualists** radicalized Luther's commitment to personal introspection. Perhaps the greatest Spiritualist was the aristocratic Caspar Schwenckfeld (1490–1561), who was a friend of Luther's until he broke with the reformer over what he considered the weak spirituality of established Lutheranism. Schwenckfeld believed that depraved humanity was incapable of casting off the bonds of sin, which only a supernatural act of God could achieve. An intense conversion experience revealed this separation from sinfulness and granted spiritual illumination to the believer. Schwenckfeld called this illumination the "inner Word," which he understood as a living form of the Scriptures that the hand of God wrote directly on the believer's soul. Schwenckfeld also prized the "outer Word," that is, the Scriptures, but he found the emotional experience of the inner Word more powerful than the intellectual experience that came from reading the Bible. Spiritualists reflected an inner peace evident in their calm physical appearance, lack of anxiety, and mastery of bodily appetites—a state Schwenckfeld called the "castle of peace."

The most prominent example of the Spiritualist tendency in the English-speaking world is the Quakers, who first appeared in England a century after the Lutheran Reformation. The Quakers, or Society of Friends, interpreted the priesthood of all believers to mean that God's spirit, which they called the Light of Christ, was given equally to all men and women. This belief led them to abandon a separately ordained ministry and to replace organized worship with meetings in which any man, woman, or child could speak, read Scripture, pray, or sing, as the spirit moved them. The Quakers' belief in the sacredness of all human beings also inclined them toward pacifism and egalitarianism. In no other religious tradition have women played such a prominent role for so long. From the very beginning of the movement, female Friends were prominent in preaching the Quaker gospel. In Quaker marriages, wives were completely equal to their husbands—at least in religious matters.

UNITARIANS: A RATIONALIST APPROACH In the middle of the sixteenth century numerous sects that rejected the divinity of Christ emerged as part of the Radical Reformation. They were called Arians, Socinians, Anti-Trinitarians, or **Unitarians** because of their opposition to the Christian doctrine of the Trinity. Since 325, when the Council of Nicaea established the Trinity as official Christian dogma, Christians had accepted that the one God has three identities: God the Father, God the Son, and God the Holy Spirit. The doctrine of the Trinity made it possible for Christians to believe that at a particular moment in history, God the Son became the human being Jesus Christ. The Church Fathers at Nicaea embraced Trinitarian doctrine in response to Arians who accepted Jesus as a religious leader, but denied that he was fully divine and "co-eternal" with God the Father. During the intellectual tumult of the Reformation, radicals revived various forms of the Arian doctrine. The Italian Faustus Socinus (1539–1604) taught a rationalist interpretation of the Scriptures and argued that Jesus was a divinely inspired man, not God-become-man. Born in Siena, Italy, Socinus's rejection of the doctrine of the Trinity made life dangerous for him in Italy, and he escaped to Poland where he found the freedom to proclaim his views. Socinus's ideas remain central to Unitarianism and form the core theology of the Polish Brethren.

Catholics and magisterial Protestants alike were extremely hostile to Unitarians, who tended to be well-educated humanists and men of letters. Unitarian views thrived in advanced intellectual circles in northern Italy and eastern Europe, but the most famous critic of the Trinity was the brilliant, if eccentric, Spaniard Michael Servetus (1511–1553). Trained as a physician and widely read in the literature of the occult, Servetus published influential anti-Trinitarian works and daringly sent his provocative works to the major Protestant reformers. Based on a tip from the Calvinists in Geneva, the Catholic inquisitor-general in Lyons, France, arrested Servetus, but he escaped from prison during his trial. While passing through Geneva on his way to refuge in Italy, he was recognized while attending a church service and again imprisoned. Although no law in Geneva allowed capital punishment, Servetus was convicted of heresy and burned alive.

The Free World of Eastern Europe

Because eastern Europe offered a measure of religious freedom and toleration unknown elsewhere in sixteenth-century Europe, it attracted refugees from the oppressive princes of western Europe, none of whom tolerated more than one religion in their territories if they could help it. Religious toleration was made possible by the relative weakness of the monarchs in Bohemia, Hungary, Transylvania, and Poland-Lithuania, where the great landowning aristocrats exercised nearly complete freedom on their estates. The Reformation radicalized many aristocrats who dominated the parliaments, enabling Protestantism to take hold even against the wishes of the monarch.

In Bohemia (now in the Czech Republic), the Hussite movement in the fourteenth century had rejected papal authority and some of the sacramental authority of the priesthood long before the Protestant Reformation. After the Lutherans and Calvinists attracted adherents in Bohemia, the few surviving Hussites and the new Protestants formed an alliance in 1575, which made common cause against the Catholics. In addition to this formal alliance, substantial numbers of Anabaptists found refuge from persecution in Bohemia and lived in complete freedom on the estates of tolerant landlords who were desperate for settlers to farm their lands.

The religious diversity of Hungary was also remarkable by the standards of the time. By the end of the sixteenth century, much of Hungary's population had accepted some form of Protestantism. Among the German-speaking city dwellers and the Hungarian peasants in western Hungary, Lutheranism prevailed, whereas in eastern Hungary Calvinism was dominant.

No other country was as tolerant of religious variety as Transylvania (now in Romania), largely because of the weak monarchy, which could not have enforced religious uniformity even if the king had wanted to do so. In Transylvania, Unitarianism took hold more firmly than anywhere else. In 1572 the tolerant ruler Prince István Báthory (r. 1571–1586) granted the Unitarians complete legal equality to establish their own churches along with Catholics, Lutherans, and Calvinists—the only place in Europe where equality of religions was achieved. Transylvania was also home to significant communities of Jews, Armenian Christians, and Orthodox Christians.

The sixteenth century was the golden age of the Polish-Lithuanian Commonwealth, the largest territorial unit in Europe. From the Lutheran cities in the German-speaking north to the vast open plains of Great Poland, religious lines often paralleled ethnic or class divisions: Calvinism took hold among the independent-minded nobility while the vast majority of peasants remained loyal to Orthodoxy or Catholicism. Nevertheless, the Commonwealth escaped the religious wars that plagued the Holy Roman Empire. King Sigismund August (r. 1548–1572) declared to the deputies in the Polish parliament, "I am not king of your consciences," and inaugurated extensive toleration of Protestant churches. Fleeing persecution in other countries, various Anabaptist groups and Unitarians found refuge in Poland. Jews also began to flock to Poland in the sixteenth century where they would eventually create the largest gathering of Jews in Europe.

THE CATHOLIC REFORMATION

■ How did the Catholic Church respond to the unprecedented threat to its dominance of religious authority in the West?

The Catholic Reformation, also known as the Counter Reformation, profoundly revitalized the Catholic Church. The **Catholic Reformation** was a series of efforts to purify the Church. These were not just a reaction to the Protestant Reformation but evolved out of late medieval spirituality, driven by many of the same impulses that stimulated the Protestants.

The Religious Orders in the Catholic Reformation

The new Catholic religious orders of the sixteenth century exhibited a religious vitality that had little to do with the Protestant threat. In fact, none of the new orders began near the centers of Protestantism, such as Germany. Italy, which remained strongly Catholic, produced the largest number of new orders, followed by Spain and France.

CHRONOLOGY: THE DIVERSITY OF PROTESTANTISM

1520	Zwingli declared the People's Priest in Zürich
1534	Parliament in England passes the Acts of Supremacy and Succession
1534–1535	Anabaptist control of Münster, Germany
1535	Execution of John Fisher and Thomas More; first edition of John Calvin's *Institutes of the Christian Religion*
1559–1563	The Elizabethan Settlement of the Anglican Church
1560	Scots Confession

JESUITS: THE SOLDIERS OF GOD Officially organized in 1540, the Society of Jesus elected Ignatius Loyola (1491–1556) the first General of the Society. Loyola's dynamic personality and intense spirituality gave the new order its distinctive commitment to moral action in the world. Loyola began his career as a courtier to King Ferdinand of Aragon and a soldier. The Society of Jesus preserved some of the values Loyola had acquired as a courtier-soldier—social refinement, loyalty to authority, sense of duty, and high-minded chivalry.

Loyola's personal contribution to religious literature was the *Spiritual Exercises* (1548), which became the foundation of Jesuit practice. Republished in more than 5,000 editions in hundreds of languages, the *Exercises* prescribe a month-long retreat devoted to a series of meditations in which the participant mentally experiences the spiritual life, physical death, and miraculous resurrection of Christ. Much of the power of the *Exercises* derives from the systematic employment of each of the five senses to produce a defined emotional, spiritual, and even physical response. Participants in the *Exercises* seem to hear the blasphemous cries of the soldiers at Christ's crucifixion, feel the terrible agony of his suffering on the cross, and experience the blinding illumination of his resurrection from the dead. Those who participated in the *Exercises* considered the experience life-transforming and usually made a steadfast commitment to serve the Church. As a result, the Jesuit order grew rapidly. At Loyola's death in 1556 there were about 1,000 Jesuits, but by 1700 there were nearly 20,000, and many young men who wished to join had to be turned away because there were insufficient funds to train them.

The Jesuits, like Franciscans and Dominicans, distinguished themselves from other religious orders by ministering to others. They did not wear clerical clothing, and on foreign missions they devoted themselves to learning the language and culture of the peoples they hoped to convert. Jesuits became famous for their loyalty to the pope, and some took a special fourth vow (in addition to the three traditional vows of poverty, chastity, and obedience) to go on a mission if the pope requested it. Many traveled as missionaries to distant parts of the globe, such as China and Japan. In Europe and the Americas the Jesuits established a vast network of colleges. These colleges offered free tuition, which made them open to the poor, and combined a thorough training in languages, humanities, and sciences with religious instruction and moral guidance. They became especially popular because the Jesuit fathers were much more likely to pay personal attention to their students than professors in the established universities. In Europe the Jesuit college system transformed the culture of the Catholic elite. These colleges attracted the sons of the aristocrats and the wealthy who absorbed from the Jesuit instructors the values of Renaissance humanism and the Catholic Reformation.

WOMEN'S ORDERS: "AS IF THEY WERE DEAD" Creating a ministry that was active in the world was much more difficult for the female orders than for the Jesuits and the other male orders. Women who sought to reinvigorate old orders or found new ones faced hostility from ecclesiastical and civic authorities, who thought women had to be protected by either a husband or the cloister wall. Women in convents were supposed to be entirely separated from the world, "as if they were dead."

The most famous model for convent reform was provided by Teresa of Avila (1515–1582), who wrote a strict new rule for the Carmelites. The new rule required mortifications of the flesh and complete withdrawal from the world. Teresa described her own mystical experiences in her *Autobiography* (1611) and in the *Interior Castle* (1588), a compelling masterpiece in the literature of mysticism. Teresa advocated a very cautious brand of mysticism, which was checked by regular confession and skepticism about extreme acts of self-deprivation. For example, she recognized that a nun who fell into an apparent rapture after extensive fasting was probably just having hallucinations from the hunger.

Many women who willingly chose the religious life thrived in a community of women where they were liberated from the rigors of childbearing and freed from direct male supervision. These women could devote themselves to

THE ECSTASY OF ST. TERESA

Teresa of Avila eloquently expressed the intimate connection between physical and spiritual experiences that was a common feature of Catholic mysticism. Often afflicted by an intense pain in her side, Teresa reported a vision of an angel who thrust a lance tipped with fire into her heart. This "seraphic vision," which became the subject of Gianlorenzo Bernini's famous sculpture in Santa Maria della Vittoria in Rome (1645–1652), epitomized the Catholic Reformation sensibility of understanding spiritual states through physical feelings. In Teresa's case, her extreme bodily deprivations, paralysis, and intense pain conditioned how she experienced the spiritual side of her nature. Many have seen an erotic character to the vision, which may be true, but the vision best demonstrates a profound psychological awareness that bodily and spiritual sensations cannot be precisely distinguished.

cultivating musical or literary talents to a degree that would have been impossible in the outside world. Nuns created their own distinctly female culture, producing a number of learned women and social reformers who had considerable influence in the arts, education, and charitable work such as nursing.

Paul III, The First Catholic Reformation Pope

Despite the many earlier attempts at reform and the Protestant threat, the Catholic Church was slow to initiate its own reforms because of resistance among bishops and cardinals of the Church hierarchy. More than 20 years after Luther's defiant stand at the Diet of Worms in 1521, Pope Paul III (r. 1534–1549) finally launched a systematic counterattack. As a member of the powerful Farnese family, who had long treated church offices as their private property, Paul seemed an unlikely reformer. But more than any other pope, Paul understood the necessity to respond to Protestantism. It was Pope Paul, for example, who formally approved the Jesuits and began to employ them as missionary soldiers for the Church. To counter Protestantism, Pope Paul III also used three other tools: the Roman Inquisition, the *Index of Forbidden Books*, and, most importantly, the Council of Trent.

In 1542, on the advice of an archconservative faction of cardinals, Paul III reorganized the Roman Inquisition, called the Holy Office. The function of the Inquisition was to inquire into the beliefs of all Catholics primarily to discover indications of heresies, such as those of the Protestants. Jews, for example, were exempt from its authority, although Jews who had converted or been forced to convert to Christianity did fall under the jurisdiction of the Inquisition. There had been other inquisitions, but most had been local or national. The Spanish Inquisition was controlled by the Spanish monarchs, for example. In contrast, the Holy Office came under the direct control of the pope and cardinals and termed itself the Universal Roman Inquisition. Its effective authority did not reach beyond northern and central Italy, but it set the tone for the entire Catholic Reformation Church. The Inquisition subjected defendants to lengthy interrogations and stiff penalties, including prison sentences and even execution in exceptional cases.

A second effort to stop the spread of Protestant ideas led to the *Index of Forbidden Books*, first drawn up in 1549 in Venice, the capital of the publishing industry in Italy. The *Index* censored or banned many books that the Church considered detrimental to the faith and the authority of the Church. Most affected by the strictures were books about theology and philosophy, but the censors also prohibited or butchered books of moral guidance, such as the works of Erasmus, and classics of literature, such as Giovanni Boccaccio's *The Decameron*. The official papal *Index* of 1559 prohibited translations of the Bible into vernacular languages such as Italian because laypeople required a trained intermediary in the person of a priest to interpret and explain the Bible. The Church's protective attitude about biblical interpretation clearly distinguished the Catholic from the Protestant attitude of encouraging widespread Bible reading. It remained possible to buy certain heretical theological books "under the counter," but possessing such books could be dangerous if agents of the Inquisition conducted a raid.

The Council of Trent

By far the most significant of Pope Paul III's contributions to the Catholic Reformation was his call for a general council of the Church, which began to meet in 1545 in Trent on the border between Italy and Germany. The Council of Trent established principles that guided the Catholic Church for the next 400 years.

Between 1545 and 1563 the council met under the auspices of three different popes in three separate sessions, with long intervals of as much as ten years between sessions. The objective of these sessions was to find a way to respond to the Protestant criticisms of the Church, to reassert the authority of the pope, and to launch reforms to guarantee a well-educated and honest clergy.

THE INQUISITION CRITICIZES A WORK OF ART

This painting, now called the *Supper in the House of Levi*, originally depicted the Last Supper when Christ introduced the mass to his apostles. Because there are many figures in it who are not mentioned in the biblical account and the supper appears as if it were a Renaissance banquet, the Inquisitors asked the artist, Paolo Veronese, to answer questions about his intended meaning. Ordered to remove the offending figures, Veronese instead changed the name of the painting to depict the less theologically controversial supper in the house of Levi.

Source: Paolo Verones, "The Feast in the House of Levi". 1573. Oil on Canvas. 18'2" × 41' (5.54 × 12.8 m). Galleria dell' Accademia, Venice. SCALA/Art Resource, NY

THE DEATH OF THE VIRGIN

The Council of Trent enjoined artists to use their art to teach correct doctrine and to move believers to true piety. Religious art had to convey a message simply, directly, and in terms that unlettered viewers could understand. The best Catholic art employed dramatic theatrical effects in lighting and the arrangement of figures to represent deep emotional and spiritual experiences. The Italian painter Caravaggio (1573–1610) most thoroughly expressed the ideal of dramatic spirituality envisioned by the Council. In this image of the death of Virgin Mary, the overhanging drapery evokes a stage curtain as do the lighting effects. The gestures of the apostles and Mary Magdalen imitate those of actors. However, the realism of the scene went too far and got Caravaggio into trouble. The dead Virgin is dressed in red, the color of prostitutes, not her usual blue, and, in fact, Caravaggio used as his model a dead prostitute who had drowned in the Tiber River. In addition, the realism of the corpse offended many.

The decrees of the Council of Trent, which had the force of legislation for the entire Church, defied the Protestants by refusing to yield any ground on the traditional doctrines of the Church. The decrees confirmed the efficacy of all seven of the traditional sacraments, the reality of Purgatory, and the spiritual value of indulgences. In order to provide better supervision of the Church, bishops were ordered to reside in their dioceses. Trent decreed that every diocese should have a seminary to train priests, providing a practical solution to the problem of clerical ignorance.

CHRONOLOGY: THE CATHOLIC REFORMATION

1534	Pontificate of Pope Paul III begins
1540	Founding of the Society of Jesus
1542	Reorganization of the Roman Inquisition or Holy Office
1545	Council of Trent opens
1548	*Spiritual Exercises* of Ignatius Loyola
1549	*Index of Forbidden Books*
1563	Council of Trent concludes

The Council of Trent represented a dramatic reassertion of the authority of the papacy, the bishops, and the priesthood. Yet it had no effect whatsoever in luring Protestants back into the Catholic fold.

CONCLUSION

Competing Understandings

The Reformation permanently divided the West into two discordant religious cultures of Protestant and Catholic. The religious unity of the West achieved during the Middle Ages had been fruit of many centuries of diligent effort by missionaries, monks, popes, and crusading knights. That unity was lost through the conflicts between, on the one hand, reformers, city magistrates, princes, and kings who wanted to control their own affairs and, on the other, popes who continued to cling to the medieval concept of the papal monarchy. In the West, Christians no longer saw themselves as dedicated to serving God in the same way as all other Christians. Instead, Catholics and Protestants emphasized their differences.

The differences between these two cultures had lasting implications for how people understood and accepted the authority of the Church and the state, how they conducted their family life, and how they formed their own identities as individuals and as members of a larger community. The next Chapter 15 will explore all of these themes.

The division also had tragic consequences. From the late sixteenth century to the late seventeenth century, European states tended to create diplomatic alliances along this ideological and religious divide, allowed disputes about doctrine to prevent peaceful reconciliation, and conducted wars as if they were a fulfillment of God's plan. Even after the era of religious warfare ended, Protestant and Catholic cultures remained ingrained in all aspects of life, influencing not just government policy but painting, music, literature, and education. This division reshaped the West into a place of intense religious and ideological conflict, which by the eighteenth century drove many thoughtful people to reject the traditional forms of Christianity altogether and to advocate religious toleration and the separation of Church and state, ideas that were barely conceivable in the sixteenth century.

KEY TERMS

Protestant Reformation	Magisterial Reformation
Christian humanists	Radical Reformation
northern Renaissance	predestination
justification by faith	calling
95 theses	Anabaptism
priesthood of all believers	Spiritualists
Religious Peace of	Unitarians
Augsburg	Catholic Reformation

CHAPTER QUESTIONS

1. What caused the religious rebellion that began in German-speaking lands and spread to much of northern Europe? (page 427)
2. How did the Lutheran Reformation create a new kind of religious culture? (page 431)
3. How and why did Protestant denominations multiply to such an extent in northern Europe and Britain? (page 439)
4. How did the Catholic Church respond to the unprecedented threat to its dominance of religious authority in the West? (page 450)

TAKING IT FURTHER

1. How did the critical and historical approach of the humanists alter thinking about religion?
2. Compare Catholic and Protestant religious cultures as they were formulated in the sixteenth century.
3. Why did the Protestant Reformation cause so much opposition and even violence?

✓•⌐Practice on **MyHistoryLab**

15

The Age of Confessional Division

■ The Peoples of Early Modern Europe ■ Disciplining the People ■ Hunting Witches
■ The Confessional States ■ States and Confessions in Eastern Europe

ON JULY 10, 1584, CATHOLIC EXTREMIST FRANÇOIS GUION, WITH A brace of pistols hidden under his cloak, surprised William the Silent, the Prince of Orange, as he was leaving the dining hall of his palace and shot him at point-blank range. William led the Protestant nobility in the Netherlands, which was in revolt against the Catholic king of Spain. Guion masqueraded as a Protestant for seven years in order to ingratiate himself with William's party, and before the assassination he consulted three Catholic priests who confirmed the religious merit of his plan. Spain's representative in the Netherlands, the Duke of Parma, had offered a reward of 25,000 crowns to anyone who killed William; at the moment of the assassination four other potential assassins were in Delft trying to gain access to the Prince of Orange.

The murder of William the Silent exemplified an ominous figure in Western civilization—the religiously motivated assassin. There had been many assassinations before the late sixteenth century, but those assassins tended to be motivated by the desire to gain political power or to avenge a personal or family injury. Religion hardly ever supplied a motive. In the wake of the Reformation, killing a political leader of the opposing faith to serve God's plan became all too common. The assassination of William illustrated patterns of violence that have since become the *modus operandi* of the political

assassin—the use of deception to gain access to the victim, the vulnerability of leaders who wish to mingle with the public, the lethal potential of easily concealed pistols (a new weapon at that time), the corruption of politics through vast sums of money, and the obsessive hostility of zealots against their perceived enemies. The widespread acrimony among the varieties of Christian faith created a climate of religious extremism during the late sixteenth and early seventeenth centuries.

Religious extremism was just one manifestation of an anxiety that pervaded European society at the time—a fear of hidden forces controlling human events. In an attempt to curb that anxiety, the European monarchs formulated their politics based on the **confessions** of faith, or statements of religious doctrine, peculiar to Catholics or the various forms of Protestantism. During this age of confessional division, European countries polarized along confessional lines, and governments persecuted followers of minority religions, whom they saw as threats to public security. Anxious believers everywhere were consumed with pleasing an angry God, but when they tried to find God within themselves, many Christians seemed only to find the Devil in others.

The religious controversies of the age of confessional division redefined the West. During the Middle Ages, the West came to be identified with

PROCESSION OF THE CATHOLIC LEAGUE

During the last half of the sixteenth century, Catholics and Protestants in France formed armed militias or leagues. Bloody confrontations between these militias led to prolonged civil wars. In this 1590 procession of the French Catholic League, armed monks joined soldiers and common citizens in a demonstration of force.

the practice of Roman Catholic Christianity. The Renaissance added to that identity an appreciation of pre-Christian history going back to Greek and Roman Antiquity. The Reformation of the early sixteenth century eroded the unity of Christian Europe by dividing the West into Catholic and Protestant camps. This division was especially pronounced in western Europe, but less so in eastern Europe because it did not create confessional states. During the late sixteenth and seventeenth centuries, governments reinforced religious divisions and attempted to unify their peoples around a common set of beliefs. How did the encounter between the confessions and the state transform Europe into religiously driven camps?

THE PEOPLES OF EARLY MODERN EUROPE

■ How did the expanding population and price revolution exacerbate religious and political tensions?

During the tenth century if a Rus had wanted to see the sights of Paris—assuming he had even heard of Paris—he could have left Kiev and walked under the shade of trees all the way to France, so extensive were the forests and so sparse the human settlements of northern Europe. By the end of the thirteenth century, the wanderer from Kiev would have needed a hat to protect him on the shadeless journey. Instead of human settlements forming little islands in a sea of forests, the forests were by then islands in a sea of villages and farms, and from almost any church tower the sharp-eyed traveler could have seen other church towers, each marking a nearby village or town. At the end of the thirteenth century, the European continent had become completely settled by a dynamic, growing population, which had cleared the forests for farms.

During the fourteenth century all of that changed. A series of crises—periodic famines, the catastrophic Black Death, and a general economic collapse—left the villages and towns of Europe intact, but a third or more of the population was gone. In that period of desolation, many villages looked like abandoned movie sets, and the cities did not have enough people to fill in the empty spaces between the central market square and the city walls. Fields that had once been put to the plow to feed the hungry children of the thirteenth century were neglected and overrun with bristles and brambles. During the fifteenth century a general European depression and recurrent epidemics kept the population stagnant.

In the sixteenth century the population began to rebound as European agriculture shifted from subsistence to commercial farming.

The sudden swell in human numbers brought dramatic and destabilizing consequences that contributed to pervasive anxiety.

The Population Recovery

During a period historical demographers call the "long sixteenth century" (ca. 1480–1640), the population of Europe began to grow consistently again for the first time since the late thirteenth century. As shown in Figure 15.1, *European Population,* in 1340 on the brink of the Black Death, Europe had about 74 million inhabitants, or 17 percent of the world's total. By 1400 the population of all of Europe had dropped to 52 million or 14 percent of the world's total. Over the course of the long sixteenth century, Europe's population grew to 77.9 million, just barely surpassing the pre–Black Death level.

Figure 15.2, *European Population, 1500–1600,* depicts some representative population figures for the larger European countries during the sixteenth century. Two important facts emerge from these data. The first is the much greater rate of growth in northern Europe compared with southern Europe. England grew by 83 percent, Poland grew by 76 percent, and even the tiny, war-torn Netherlands gained 58 percent. During the same period Italy grew

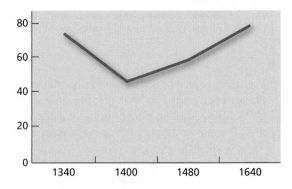

I **FIGURE 15.1** European Population in Millions

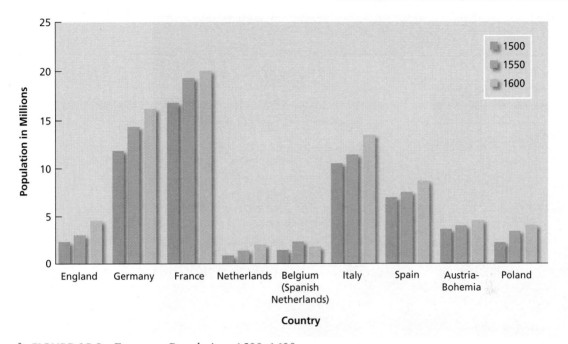

FIGURE 15.2 European Population, 1500–1600

Source: Jan de Vries, "Population," In *Handbook of European History 1400–1600: Late Middle Ages, Renaissance and Reformation,* Vol. 1: *Structures and Assertions,* (eds.) Thomas A. Brady, Jr., Heiko A. Oberman, and James D. Tracy (1994), Table 1, 13. Copyright © 1994 by Brill Academic Publishers. Reproduced with permission of Brill Academic Publishers via Copyright Clearance Center.

by only 25 percent and Spain by 19 percent. These trends signal a massive, permanent shift of demographic and economic power from the Mediterranean countries of Italy and Spain to northern, especially northwestern, Europe. The second fact to note from these data is the overwhelming size of France, which was home to about a quarter of Europe's population. Once France recovered from its long wars of religion, its demographic superiority overwhelmed competing countries and made it the dominant power in Europe, permanently eclipsing its chief rival, Spain.

What explains the growth in the population? To a large extent, the transformation from subsistence to commercial agriculture in certain regions of Europe made it possible. Peasants who practiced subsistence farming consumed about 80 percent of everything they raised, and what little was left over went almost entirely to the landlord as feudal dues and to the church as tithing—the obligation to give to God one-tenth of everything earned or produced. Peasant families lived on the edge of existence. During the sixteenth century, subsistence agriculture gave way to commercial crops, especially wheat, which was sold in town markets and the great cities such as London, Antwerp, Amsterdam, Paris, Milan, Venice, and Barcelona. As commercial agriculture spread, the population grew because the rural population was better fed and more prosperous.

The amount of land available, however, could not provide enough work for the growing farm population. As a result, the landless were forced to take to the road to find their fortunes. These vagabonds, as they were called, exemplified the social problems that emerged from the uneven distribution of

THE RISE OF COMMERCIAL AGRICULTURE
During the sixteenth century commercial agriculture began to produce significant surpluses for the expanding population of the cities. This scene depicts a
windmill for grinding grain and a train of wagons hauling produce from the
country to be marketed in a city.

wealth created by the new commerce. Because large-scale migrations to the Americas had not yet begun, except from Spain, the landless had few options other than to seek opportunities in a city.

The Thriving Cities

By the 1480s cities began to grow, but the growth was uneven with the most dramatic growth occurring in the cities of the North, especially London, Antwerp, and Amsterdam. The surpluses of the countryside, both human and agricultural, flowed into the cities during the sixteenth century. Compared with even the prosperous rural villages, the cities seemed incomparably rich. Half-starved vagabonds marveled at shops piled high with food (white bread, fancy pies, fruit, casks of wine, roasting meats); they wistfully passed taverns full of drunken,

laughing citizens; and they begged for alms in front of magnificent, marble-faced churches.

Every aspect of the cities exhibited dramatic contrasts between the rich and poor, who lived on the same streets and often in different parts of the same houses. Around 1580 Christian missionaries brought a Native American chief to the French city of Rouen. Through an interpreter he was asked what impressed him the most about European cities, so unlike the villages of North America. He replied that he was astonished that the rag-clad, emaciated men and women who crowded the streets did not grab the plump, well-dressed rich people by the throat.

City officials recognized the social problems caused by the disparities in wealth. Every city maintained storehouses of grain and regulated the price of bread and the size of a loaf so that the poor could be fed. The impulse to feed the poor was less the result of humanitarian motives than fear of a hungry mob. Cities guarded carefully against revolts and crime. Even for petty crime, punishment was swift, sure, and gruesome. The beggar who stole a loaf of bread from a baker's cart had his hand amputated on a chopping block in the market square. A shabbily dressed girl who grabbed a lady's glittering trinket had her nose cut off so that she could never attract a man. A burglar was tortured, drawn, and quartered, with his severed head impaled on an iron spike at the town gate as a warning to others.

However talented or enterprising, new arrivals to the city had very limited opportunities. They could hardly start up their own business because all production was strictly controlled by the guilds, which were associations of merchants or artisans organized to protect their interests. Guilds rigidly regulated their membership and required an apprenticeship of many years. Guilds also prohibited technological innovations, guaranteed certain standards of workmanship, and did not allow branching out into new lines. Given the limited opportunities for new arrivals, immigrant men and women begged on the streets or took charity from the public dole. The men picked up any heavy-labor jobs they could find. Both men and women became servants, a job that paid poorly but at least guaranteed regular meals.

Among the important social achievements of both Protestant and Catholic Reformations were efforts to address the problems of the destitute urban poor, who constituted at least a quarter of the population, even in the best of times. In Catholic countries such as Italy, Spain, southern Germany, and France, there was an enormous expansion of credit banks, which were financed by charitable contributions in order to provide small loans to the poor. Catholic cities established convents for poor young women who were at risk of falling into prostitution and for women who had retired from the sex trade. Catholic and Protestant cities established orphanages, hospitals for the sick, hospices for the dying, and public

housing. Both Catholic and Protestant cities attempted to distinguish between the "honest" poor—those who were disabled and truly deserving—and the "dishonest" poor who were thought to be malingerers. Protestant cities established poorhouses, which segregated the poor, subjected them to prisonlike discipline, and forced the able-bodied to work.

The more comfortable classes of the cities enjoyed large palaces and luxurious lifestyles. They hired extensive staffs of servants, feasted on meat and fine wines, and purchased exotic imports such as silk cloth, spices from the East, and, in the Mediterranean cities, slaves from eastern Europe, the Middle East, or Africa. Rich merchants maintained their status by marrying within their own class, monopolizing municipal offices, and educating their children in the newly fashionable humanist schools. The wealthy of the cities were the bastions of social stability. They possessed the financial resources and economic skills to protect themselves from the worst consequences of economic instability, especially the corrosive wave of price inflation that struck the West after about 1540.

The Price Revolution

Price inflation became so pervasive during the last half of the sixteenth century that it contributed to the widespread fear that hidden forces controlled events. After a long period of falling or stable prices that stretched back to the fourteenth century, Europe experienced sustained price increases, beginning around 1540, in what historians called the **Price Revolution**. The inflation lasted a century, forcing major economic and social changes that permanently altered the face of Western society. During this period overall prices across Europe multiplied five- or sixfold.

What caused the inflation? The basic principle is simple. The price paid for goods and services is fundamentally the result of the relationship between *supply* and *demand*. If the number of children who need to be fed grows faster than the supply of grain, the price of bread goes up. This happens simply because mothers who can afford it will be willing to pay a higher price to save their children from hunger. If good harvests allow the supply of grain to increase at a greater rate than the demand for bread, then prices go down. Two other factors influence price. One is the *amount of money in circulation.* If the amount of gold or silver available to make coins increases, there is more money in circulation. When more money is circulating, people can buy more things, which creates the same effect as an increase in demand—prices go up. The other factor is called the *velocity of money in circulation,* which refers to the number of times money changes hands to buy things. When people buy commodities with greater frequency, it has the same effect as increasing the amount of money in circulation or of increasing demand—again, prices go up.

The precise combination of these factors in causing the great Price Revolution of the sixteenth century has long been a matter of considerable debate. Most historians would now agree that the primary cause of inflation was population growth, which increased demand for all kinds of basic commodities, such as bread and woolen cloth for clothing. As Europe's population finally began to recover, it meant that more people needed and desired to buy more things. This explanation is most obvious for commodities that people need to survive, such as grain to make bread. These commodities have what economists call *inelastic demand,* that is, consumers do not have a great deal of discretion in purchasing them. Everybody has to eat. The commodities that people could survive without if the price is too high are said to have *elastic demand,* such as dancing shoes and lace collars. In England between 1540 and 1640 overall prices rose by 490 percent. More telling, however, is that the price of grain (inelastic demand) rose by a stunning 670 percent, whereas the price of luxury goods (elastic demand) rose much less, by 204

percent. Thus, inflation hurt the poor, who needed to feed their children, more than the rich, whose desires were more elastic.

Monetary factors also contributed to inflation. The Portuguese brought in significant amounts of gold from Africa, and newly opened mines in central Europe increased the amount of silver by fivefold as early as the 1520s. The discovery in 1545 of the fabulous silver mine of Potosí (in present-day Bolivia) brought to Europe a flood of silver, which Spain used to finance its costly wars. As inflation began to eat away at royal incomes, financially strapped monarchs all across western Europe debased their currency because they believed, mistakenly, that producing more coins containing less silver would buy more. In fact, the minting of more coins meant each coin was worth less and would buy less. In England, for example, debasement was a major source of inflation during the 1540s and 1550s.

The Price Revolution severely weakened governments. Most monarchs derived their incomes from their own private lands and taxes on property. As inflation took hold, property taxes proved dangerously inadequate to cover royal expenses. Even frugal monarchs such as England's Elizabeth I (r. 1558–1603) were forced to take extraordinary measures, in her case to sell off royal lands. Spendthrift monarchs faced disaster. Spain was involved in the costly enterprise of nearly continuous war during the sixteenth century. To pay for the wars, Charles V resorted to a form of deficit financing in which he borrowed money by issuing *juros,* which provided lenders an annuity yielding between three and seven percent on the amount of the principal. By the 1550s, however, the annuity payments of the *juros* consumed half of the royal revenues. Charles's son, Philip II, inherited such an alarming situation that in 1557, the year after he assumed the throne, he was forced to declare bankruptcy. Philip continued to fight expensive wars and borrow wildly, and thus failed to get his financial house in order. He declared bankruptcy again in 1575 and 1596. Philip squandered

Spain's wealth, impoverishing his own subjects through burdensome taxes and contributing to inflation by borrowing at high rates of interest and debasing the coinage. Although the greatest military power of the sixteenth century, Spain sowed the seeds of its own decline by fighting on borrowed money.

Probably the most serious consequence of the Price Revolution was that the hidden force of inflation caused widespread human suffering. During the late sixteenth and early seventeenth centuries, people felt their lives threatened, but they did not know the source and so they imagined all kinds of secret powers at work, especially supernatural ones. The suspicion of religious differences created by the Reformation provided handy, if utterly false, explanations for what had gone wrong. Catholics suspected Protestants, Protestants suspected Catholics, both suspected Jews, and they all worried about witches. Authorities sought to relieve this widespread anxiety by looking in all the wrong places—disciplining the populace, hunting for witches, and battling against enemies from the opposite side of the confessional divide.

DISCIPLINING THE PEOPLE

■ How did religious and political authorities attempt to discipline the people?

The first generation of the Protestant and Catholic Reformations had been devoted to doctrinal disputes and to either rejecting or defending papal authority. Subsequent generations of reformers faced the formidable task of building the institutions that would firmly establish a Protestant or Catholic religious culture. Leaders of all religious confessions, whether Lutheran, Calvinist, Catholic, or Anglican, attempted to revitalize the Christian community by disciplining nonconformists, enforcing moral rigor, and attacking popular culture. Discipline required cooperation between church and secular authorities, but it was not entirely imposed from above. Many people wholeheartedly cooperated with moral correction and even encouraged reformers to go further. Others actively or resentfully resisted it.

Establishing Confessional Identities

Between 1560 and 1650 religious confessions reshaped European culture. A confession consisted of the adherents to a particular statement of religious doctrine—the Confession of Augsburg for Lutherans, the Helvetic Confessions for Calvinists, the Thirty-Nine Articles for Anglicans, and the decrees of the Council of Trent for Catholics.

The process of establishing confessional identities did not happen overnight. During the second half of the sixteenth century, Lutherans turned from the struggle to survive within the hostile Holy Roman Empire to building Lutheranism wherever it was the chosen religion of the local prince. They had to recruit clergy and provide each clergyman with a university education, which was made possible by scholarship endowments from the Lutheran princes of the empire. Once established, the Lutheran clergy became a branch of the civil bureaucracy, received a government stipend, and enforced the will of the prince. Calvinist states followed a similar process, but where they were in a minority, as in France, Calvinists had to go it alone, and the state often discriminated against them. In those places confessional identities were established in opposition to the state and the dominant confession. Catholics responded with their own aggressive plan of training new clergymen, educating the laity, and reinforcing the bond between church and state. Just as with the Lutheran princes, Catholic princes in the Holy Roman Empire associated conformity to Catholicism with loyalty to themselves, making religion a pillar of the state.

Everywhere in western Europe (except for Ireland, the Netherlands, a few places in the Holy Roman Empire, and for a time France) the only openly practiced religion was the religion of the state. The eastern European states of Poland, Bohemia, Hungary, and Transylvania offered greater religious freedom.

Regulating the Family

One matter on which Calvinists, Lutherans, and Catholics agreed was that the foundation of society should be the authority fathers had over their families. This principle of patriarchy, as discussed in Chapter 12, was a traditional *ideal*. The *reality* of high mortality from disease, however, destabilized family life during the fifteenth and sixteenth centuries. Unstable families often lacked fathers and senior males, making it difficult if not impossible to sustain patriarchy in daily life. The confessions that emerged from the Reformation attempted to combat this trend by reinforcing patriarchy. According to an anonymous treatise published in 1586 in Calvinist Nassau, the three pillars of Christian society were the church, the state, and the household. This proposition made the father's authority parallel to the authority of the clergy and king. To enforce patriarchy, ecclesiastical and secular authorities regulated sexuality and the behavior of children. The authorities' goal seems to have been to encourage self-discipline as well as respect for elders. Self-discipline reached into all aspects of life from sexual behavior to table manners. (See *Encounters and Transformations* in this chapter.)

Despite the near universal acceptance of the theory of patriarchy, the reality of the father's and husband's authority varied a great deal. Since the early Middle Ages in northwestern Europe—in Britain, Scandinavia, the Netherlands, northern France, and western Germany—couples tended to wait to marry until their mid- or late twenties, well beyond the age of sexual maturity. The couple had to be economically independent before they married, which meant both had to accumulate savings or the husband needed to inherit from his deceased father before he could marry. When they did finally marry, they established their own household separate from either of their parents. Husbands were usually only two or three years older than their wives, and that proximity of age tended to make those relationships more cooperative and less authoritarian than the theory of patriarchy might suggest. By contrast, in southern Europe, men in their late twenties or thirties married teenaged women over whom they exercised authority by virtue of the age difference. In eastern Europe, both spouses married in their teens and resided in one of the parental households for many years, which placed both spouses for extended periods under the authority of one of their fathers.

The marriage pattern in northwestern Europe required prolonged sexual restraint by young men and women until they were economically self-sufficient. In addition to individual self-control, sexual restraint required social control by church and secular authorities. Their efforts seem to have been generally successful. For example, in sixteenth-century Geneva, where the elders were especially wary about sexual sins, the rates of illegitimate births were extremely low. The elders were particularly concerned to discipline women and keep them subservient. In 1584 in another Swiss town, Calvinist elders excommunicated Charlotte Arbaleste and her entire household because she wore her hair in curls, which the elders thought were too alluring.

Northwestern European families also tended to be smaller, as married couples began to space their children through birth control and family planning. These self-restrained couples practiced withdrawal, the rhythm method, or abstinence. When mothers no longer relied on wet nurses and nursed their own infants, often for long periods, they also reduced their chances of becoming pregnant. Thus, limiting family size became the social norm in northwestern Europe, especially among the educated and urban middle classes. Protestant families tended to have fewer children than Catholic families, but Catholics in this region also practiced some form of birth control, even though Church law prohibited all forms except abstinence.

The moral status of marriage also demonstrated regional variations during the early modern period. Protestants no longer considered husbands and wives morally inferior to celibate monks and nuns, and the wives of preachers in Protestant communities certainly had a respected social role never granted to the concubines of priests. But the favorable Protestant attitude toward marriage did not necessarily translate into a positive attitude toward women. In Germany the numerous books of advice, called the Father of the House literature, encouraged families to subordinate the individual interests of servants, children, and the mother to the dictates of the father, who was advised to be fair but who always had to be obeyed. Even if a wife was brutally treated by her husband, she could neither find help from authorities nor expect a divorce.

Discipline also played a large role in raising children. The *Disquisition on the Spiritual Condition of Infants* (1618) pointed out that because of original sin, babies were naturally evil. The godly responsibility of the father was to break the will of his evil offspring, taming them so that they could be turned away from sin toward virtue. The very title of a 1591 Calvinist treatise revealed the strength of the evil-child argument: *On Disciplining Children: How the Disobedient, Evil, and Corrupted Youth of These Anxious Last Days Can Be Bettered.* The treatise advised that the mother's role should be limited to her biological function of giving birth. In order to break the will of their infants, mothers were encouraged to wean them early and turn them over for a strict upbringing by their fathers. It directed fathers to be vigilant so that their wives did not corrupt the children, because women "love to accept strange, false beliefs, and go about with benedictions and witches' handiwork."[1]

THE DOMESTIC IDEAL

During the late sixteenth and seventeenth centuries, idealized depictions of harmonious family life became very popular, especially in the Netherlands. This painting by Pieter De Hooch is a prime example of the simple pleasures of domesticity. A young child opens the door to a bedroom while her mother is making a bed.

Source: Pieter de Hooch (Dutch 1629–1684), "The Bedroom" ca. 1658/1660. Oil on canvas. 20" × 23 1/2" (51.0 × 60.0 cm). Widener Collection. 1942.9.33. Photograph © Board of Trustees, National Gallery of Art, Washington, D.C.

JUSTICE IN HISTORY

The *Auto-da-Fé:* The Power of Penance

Performed in Spain and Portugal from the sixteenth to eighteenth centuries, the *auto-da-fé* merged the judicial processes of the state with the sacramental rituals of the Catholic Church. An *auto* took place at the end of a judicial investigation conducted by the inquisitors of the Church after the defendants had been found guilty of a sin or crime. The term **auto-da-fé** means "act of faith," and the goal was to persuade or force a person who had been judged guilty to repent and confess. Organized through the cooperation of ecclesiastical and secular authorities, autos-da-fé brought together an assortment of sinners, criminals, and heretics for a vast public rite that dramatized the essential elements of the sacrament of penance: *contrition,* by which the sinner recognized and felt sorry for the sin; *confession,* which required the sinner to admit the sin to a priest; and *satisfaction* or *punishment,* by which the priest absolved the sinner and enacted some kind of penalty. The auto-da-fé transformed penance, especially confession and satisfaction, into a spectacular affirmation of the faith and a manifestation of divine justice.

The *auto* symbolically anticipated the Last Judgment. By suffering bodily pain in this life the soul might be relieved from worse punishments in the next. Officers of the Inquisition forced the sinners, convicts, and heretics, now considered penitents, to march in a procession that went through the streets of the city from the cathedral to the town hall or place of punishment. These processions would typically include some 30 or 40 penitents, but in moments of crisis they could be far larger. In Toledo in 1486 there were three *autos*—one parading 750 penitents and two displaying some 900 each.

A 1655 *auto* in Córdoba illustrates the symbolic character of the rites. Soldiers carried torches to light the pyre for those to be burnt. Following them in a procession came three bigamists who wore on their heads conical miters or hats painted with representations of their sin, four witches whose miters depicted devils, and three criminals with harnesses around their necks to demonstrate their status as captives. The sinners carried unlit candles to represent their lack of faith. Criminals who had escaped arrest were represented in the procession by effigies made in their likeness; for those who had died before punishment, effigies were carried in their coffins. The marching sinners appeared before their neighbors and fellow citizens stripped of the normal indicators of status, dressed only in the emblems of their sins. Among them walked a few who wore the infamous *sanbenitos,* a kind of tunic or vest with a yellow strip down the back, and a conical hat painted with flames. These were the *relajados,* the unrepentant or relapsed sinners.

The procession ended in the town square at a platform on which the sinners performed their public penances as on the stage of a theater. Forced to their knees, priests asked the penitents to confess and to plead for readmission into the bosom of the church. For those who did confess, a herald announced the sentence that would rescue them from the pains of Purgatory and the flames of the *auto.* The sentence required them to join a penitential procession for a certain number of Fridays, perform self-flagellation in public, or wear a badge of shame for a prescribed period of time. Those who failed to confess faced a more immediate sentence.

The most horrendous scenes of suffering awaited the *relajados.* If holdouts confessed prior to the reading of the sentence, then the *auto* was a success, a triumph of the Christian faith over its enemies. Therefore, priests attempted everything that they could to elicit confessions, including haranguing, humiliating, and torturing the accused until their stubborn will broke. If the accused finally confessed after the herald read the sentence, then the executioner would strangle them before burning, but if they held out to the very end, the executioner lit the flames while

❙ *AUTO-DA-FÉ* IN LISBON

they were still living. From the ecclesiastics' point of view, the refusal to confess was a disaster for the entire Church because the flames of the pyre opened a window into Hell. They would certainly prefer to see the Church's authority acknowledged through confession than to see the power of Satan manifest in such a public fashion.

Eyewitnesses reported that crowds watched the violence of the autos-da-fé with silent attention in a mood of deep dread, not so much of the inquisitors, it seems, as for the inevitability of the final day of divine judgment that would arrive for them all. The core assumption of the auto-da-fé was that bodily pain could save a soul from damnation. As one contemporary witness put it, the inquisitors removed "through external ritual [the sinners'] internal crimes." Church authorities assumed that the public ritual framework for the sacrament of penance would have a salutary effect on those who witnessed the *auto* by encouraging them to repent before they too faced divine judgment.

For Discussion

1. How did the auto-da-fé contribute to the formation of an individual and collective sense of being a Catholic?

2. In the auto-da-fé, inflicting physical pain was more than punishment. How was pain understood to have been socially and religiously useful?

Taking It Further

Flynn, Maureen. "Mimesis of the Last Judgment: The Spanish *Auto da fé*," *Sixteenth Century Journal* 22 (1991): 281–297. The best analysis of the religious significance of the auto-da-fé.

Flynn, Maureen. "The Spectacle of Suffering in Spanish Streets," In Barbara A. Hanawalt and Kathryn L. Reyerson (eds.), *City and Spectacle in Medieval Europe* (1994). In this fascinating article Flynn analyzes the spiritual value of physical pain.

ENCOUNTERS AND TRANSFORMATIONS

The Introduction of the Table Fork: The New Sign of Western Civilization

Sometime in the sixteenth century, western Europeans encountered a new tool that initiated a profound and lasting transformation in Western society: the table fork. Before the table fork, people dined in a way that, to our modern sensibilities, seems disgusting. Members of the upper classes indulged themselves by devouring meat in enormous quantities. Whole rabbits, lambs, and pigs roasted on a spit were placed before diners. A quarter of veal or venison or even an entire roast beef, complete with its head, might be heaved onto the table. Diners used knives to cut off a piece of meat that they then ate with their hands, allowing the juices to drip down their arms. They used the long sleeves of their shirts to wipe meat juices, sweat, and spittle from their mouths and faces. These banquets celebrated the direct physical contact between the body of the dead animal and the bodies of the diners themselves who touched, handled, chewed, and swallowed it.

During the sixteenth century, puritanical reformers who were trying to abolish the cruder aspects of popular culture also promoted new table manners.

THE INTRODUCTION OF THE TABLE FORK
During the late sixteenth century the refinement of manners among the upper classes focused on dining. No innovation was more revolutionary than the spread of the use of the table fork. Pictured here is the travel cutlery, including two table forks, of Queen Elizabeth I.

New implements made certain that diners did not come into direct physical contact with their food before they placed it in their mouths. In addition to napkins—which came into widespread use to replace shirt sleeves for wiping the mouth—table forks appeared on upper-class tables. It became impolite to transfer food directly from the common serving plate to the mouth. Food first had to go onto each individual's plate and then be cut into small portions and raised to the mouth. A French treatise of 1672 warned that "meat must never be touched…by hand, not even while eating."[2]

This prohibition had nothing to do with cleanliness because bacteria were not discovered until the end of the nineteenth century. The use of the table fork had more to do with civility than hygiene. Certain foods, such as bread or many fruits such as cherries, were and still are always eaten with the hands. In determining when to use a fork it was not cleanliness that mattered, but the kind of food consumed. Forks enabled sixteenth-century diners to avoid their growing sense of discomfort with the textures and juices of meats that reminded them of an animal's flesh and blood.

Forks, then, enabled cultured people to distance themselves from the dead animal that they were eating. More generally, the spreading use of the fork was part of a set of changes linked to growing revulsion with the more physical aspects of human nature, such as reproduction—or the killing and consumption of animals. Just as sixteenth-century church authorities sought to regulate sexuality, so table manners regulated meat eating.

Paradoxically, the civility that resulted from the use of the table fork both created and eroded social divisions. Eating meat with a fork became one more way for those in the upper social ranks to distinguish themselves from the "uncivilized" masses below. Yet everyone—regardless of their social origins—could learn how to use a fork. A clerk or governess could disguise a humble background simply by learning how to eat properly. Gradually—very gradually—behavior replaced birth as a marker of "good breeding." In the end, the transformations that occurred in Western society because of its encounter with the table fork—the blurring of class distinctions and creation of a universal code of manners—were so gradual and subtle that few of us who use a table fork daily are even aware of its profound significance.

For Discussion

How do manners, both good and bad, communicate messages to other people? Why is it important to have good manners?

HUNTING WITCHES

- Why did people in the sixteenth century think witches were a threat?

The most catastrophic manifestation of the widespread anxiety of the late sixteenth and seventeenth centuries was the great **witch-hunt**. The judicial prosecution of alleged witches in either church or secular courts dramatically increased about the middle of the sixteenth century and lasted until the late seventeenth, when the number of witchcraft trials rapidly diminished and stopped entirely in most of Europe.

Throughout this period, people accepted the reality of two kinds of **magic**. The first kind was natural magic, such as the practice of alchemy or astrology, which involved the manipulation of occult forces believed to exist in nature. The fundamental assumption of natural magic was that everything in nature is alive. The trained magician could coerce the occult forces in nature to do his bidding. During the Renaissance many humanists and scientific thinkers were drawn to natural magic because of its promise of power over nature. Natural magic, in fact, had some practical uses. Alchemists, for example, devoted themselves to discovering what they called the "philosopher's stone," the secret of transmuting base metals into gold. In practice this meant that they learned how to imitate the appearance of gold, a very useful skill for counterfeiting coins or reducing the content of precious metals in legal coins. Natural magic did not imply any kind of contact with devils. Most practitioners of natural magic desired to achieve good, and many considered it the highest form of curative medicine.

Many people of the sixteenth and seventeenth centuries also believed in a second kind of magic—demonic magic. The practitioner of this kind of magic—usually but not always a female witch—called upon evil spirits to gain access to power. Demonic magic was generally understood as a way to work harm by ritual means. Belief in the reality of harmful magic can be found in the Bible and had been widespread for centuries, but only in the fifteenth century did ecclesiastical and secular authorities, convinced that large groups of people were engaging in such heretical practices, prosecute them in large numbers. By the sixteenth century the Protestants' literal readings of the Bible and the disorienting conflicts of the Reformation contributed to fears about witches.

People in many different places—from shepherds in the mountains of Switzerland to Calvinist ministers in the lowlands of Scotland—thought they perceived the work of witches in human and natural events. The alleged practice of witchcraft took two forms: *maleficia* (doing harm by magical means) and *diabolism* (worshiping the devil). There were many kinds of *maleficia,* including coercing an unwilling lover by sprinkling dried menstrual blood in his food, sickening a pig by cursing it, burning a barn after marking it with a hex sign, bringing wasting diarrhea to a child by reciting a spell, and killing an enemy by stabbing a wax statue of him.

Midwives and women who specialized in healing were especially vulnerable to accusations of witchcraft. The intention behind a particular action they might have performed was often obscure, making it difficult to distinguish between magic designed to bring beneficial results, such as the cure of a child, and *maleficia* designed to bring harmful ones. With the high

infant mortality rates of the sixteenth and seventeenth centuries, performing magical rituals for a sick baby could be very risky. The logic of witchcraft beliefs implied that a bad ending must have been caused by bad intentions.

While some people certainly attempted to practice *maleficia,* the second and far more serious kind of ritual practice associated with demonic magic, diabolism, certainly never took place. The theory behind diabolism was that the alleged witch made a pact with the Devil, by which she received her magical power, and worshiped him as her god.

The most influential witchcraft treatise, *The Hammer of Witches* (1486), had an extensive discussion of the ceremony of the pact. After the prospective witch had declared her intention to enter his service, Satan appeared to her, often in the alluring form of a handsome young man who offered her rewards, including a demonic lover, called an *incubus.* To obtain these inducements, the witch was obligated to renounce her allegiance to Christ, usually signified by stomping on the cross. The Devil then rebaptized the witch, guaranteeing that her soul belonged to him. To signify that she was one of his own, the Devil marked her body in a hidden place, creating a sign, which could easily be confused with a birthmark or blemish. To an inquisitor or judge, a mark on the skin that did not bleed and was insensitive to pain when pierced with a long pin often confirmed the suspicion that she was a witch.

After making the pact witches allegedly gathered in large numbers to worship the devil at nocturnal assemblies known as sabbaths. The devil was believed to have given them the power to fly to these gatherings. At these assemblies, so it was claimed, witches killed and ate babies, danced naked, and had promiscuous sexual relations with other witches and demons. The belief that witches attended sabbaths, which judicial authorities confirmed by forcing them to confess under severe torture, explains why witch-hunting took a high toll in human life. Between 1450 and 1750, approximately 100,000 people in Europe

BURNING OF A WITCH
Authorities burned a young woman accused of witchcraft, Anne Hendricks, in Amsterdam in 1571.

were tried for witchcraft, and about 50,000 were executed. Approximately half of the trials took place in the German-speaking lands of the Holy Roman Empire, where the central judicial authorities exercised little control over the determination of local judges to secure convictions. Prosecutions were also extensive in Switzerland, France, Scotland, Poland, Hungary, and Transylvania. Relatively few witches were executed in Spain, Portugal, Italy, Scandinavia, the Netherlands, England, and Ireland.

The determination of both Catholics and Protestants to discipline deviants of all sorts and to wage war against the Devil intensified the hunt for witches. The great majority of trials occurred between 1560 and 1650, when religious tensions were strong and economic conditions severe. The

trials rarely occurred in a steady flow, as one would find for other crimes. In many cases the torture of a single witch would lead to her naming many alleged accomplices, who would then also be tried. This would lead to a witch panic in which scores and sometimes hundreds of witches would be tried and executed. Eighty percent of accused witches were women, especially those who were unmarried or widowed, but men and even young children could be accused of witchcraft as well. The hunts came to an end when judicial authorities recognized that no one was safe, especially during witch panics, and when they realized that legal evidence against witches was insufficient for conviction. The Dutch Republic was the first to ban witch trials in 1608. (See *Different Voices* in this chapter.)

DIFFERENT VOICES WERE THERE REALLY WITCHES?

Even during the height of the witch-hunt the existence of witches was controversial. Most authorities assumed that the devil worked evil on earth and that hunting witches, therefore, was an effective means of defending Christians. These authorities used the church and secular courts to interrogate alleged witches, sometimes supplemented by torture, to obtain confessions and the identities of other confederate witches. These authorities considered the hunting of witches part of their duty to protect the public from harm. Others accepted the reality of witchcraft but doubted the capacity of judges to determine who was a witch. A few doubted the reality of witchcraft altogether.

Johann Weyer (1515?–1588) was a physician who argued that most witches were deluded old women who suffered from depression and need medical help rather than legal punishment. The devil deceived them into thinking they had magical powers, but because Weyer had a strong belief that only God had power over nature, he did not credit the devil or witches with any special powers. No one else during the sixteenth century disputed the reality of the powers of witches as systematically as he. Jean Bodin (1529?–1596) was one of the greatest legal philosophers of the sixteenth century. Although he was once skeptical of the reality of witchcraft, he changed his mind after witnessing several cases in which women voluntarily confessed to performing evil acts under the guidance of Satan. He considered witchcraft a threat to society and condemned Weyer's soft-hearted view.

Johan Weyer's letter to Johann Brenz (1565)

Witches have no power to make hail, storms, and other evil things, but they are deceived by the devil. For when the devil, with the permission and decree of God, can make hail and storms, he goes to his witches and urges them to use their magic and charms, so that when the trouble and punishment come, the witches are convinced that they and the devil have caused it. Thus, the witches cannot make hail and other things, but they are deluded and blinded by the devil himself to whom they have given themselves. In this way they think that they have made hail and storms. Not on that account but for their godless lives should they be punished severely....

Our witches have been corrupted in their phantasy by the devil and imagine often that they have done evil things that didn't even happen or caused natural occurrences that actually did not take place. In their confessions, especially under torture, they admit to doing and causing many things which are impossible for them and for anyone. One should not believe them when they confess that they have bound themselves to the devil, given themselves to his will, promised to follow his evil goals, just as we do not believe their confession that they make hail and storms, disturb and poison the air, and other impossible deeds....

Even if an old woman, in deep depression, gives herself to the devil, one should not immediately condemn her to the fire but instead have regard for her confused, burdened, and depressed spirits and use all possible energy to convert her that she may avoid evil, and give herself to Christ. In this way we may bring her to her senses again, win her soul, and save her from death....

THE CONFESSIONAL STATES

■ How did religious differences provoke violence and start wars?

The Religious Peace of Augsburg of 1555 provided the model for a solution to the religious divisions produced by the Reformation. According to the principle of *cuius regio, eius religio* (he who rules determines the religion of the land), each prince in the Holy Roman Empire determined the religion to be followed by his subjects; those who disagreed were obliged to convert or emigrate. Certainly, forced exile was economically

Jean Bodin, On the Demonic Madness of Witches (1580)

The judgment which was passed against a witch in a case to which I was called on the last day of April, 1578, gave me occasion to take up my pen in order to clarify the subject of witches—persons who seem strange and wondrous to everyone and incredible to many. The witch whom I refer to was named Jeanne Harvillier, a native of Verbery near Compiegne. She was accused of having murdered many men and beasts, as she herself confessed without questioning or torture, although she at first stubbornly denied the charges and changed her story often. She also confessed that her mother presented her at the age of twelve years to the devil, disguised as a tall black man, larger than most men and clothed in black. The mother told him that as soon as her daughter was born she had promised her to him, whom she called the devil. He in turn promised to treat her well and to make her happy. And from then on she had renounced God and promised to serve the devil. And at that instant she had had carnal copulation with the devil, which she had continued to the age of 50, or thereabouts, when she was captured. She said also that [the] devil presented himself to her when she wished, always dressed as he had been the first time, booted and spurred, with a sword at his side and his horse at the door. And no one saw him but her. He even fornicated with her often without her husband noticing although he lay at her side. . . .

Now we have shown that ordinarily women are possessed by demons more often than men and that witches are often transported bodily but also often ravished in an ecstasy, the soul having separated itself from the body, by diabolical means, leaving the body insensible and stupid. Thus, it is completely ridiculous to say that the illness of the witches originates in melancholy, especially because the diseases coming from melancholy are always dangerous. . . . Thus, Weyer must admit that there is a remarkable incongruity for one who is a doctor, and a gross example of ignorance (but it is not ignorance) to attribute to women melancholy diseases which are as little appropriate for them as are the praiseworthy effects of a tempered melancholy humor. This humor makes a man wise, sober, and contemplative (as all of the ancient philosophers and physicians remark), which are qualities as incompatible with women as fire with water. And even Solomon, who as a man of the world knew well the humor of women, said that he had seen a wise man for every 1,000 men, but that he had never seen a wise woman. Let us therefore abandon the fanatic error of those who make women into melancholics.

Source: Robert M. Kingdon (ed.), *Transition and Revolution: Problems and Issues of European Renaissance and Reformation History* (Minneapolis: Burgess Publishing Company, 1974), 221–232. Reprinted by permission.

For Discussion

1. How can the uncoerced confessions of women to witchcraft be explained?

2. Why would an otherwise intelligent observer such as Jean Bodin be so willing to believe in the reality of the power of witches?

and personally traumatic for those who emigrated, but it preserved what was almost universally believed to be the fundamental principle of successful rulership—one king, one faith, one law. In other words, each state should have only one church. Except in the states of eastern Europe and a few small troubled principalities in the Holy Roman Empire, few thought it desirable to allow more than one confession in the same state.

The problem with this political theory of religious unity was the reality of religious divisions created by the Reformation. In some places there were as many as three active confessions—Catholic, Lutheran, and Calvinist—in addition to the minority sects, such as the Anabaptists and the Jewish communities. The alternative to religious unity would have been religious toleration, but hardly anyone in a position of authority was willing to advocate that. John Calvin expelled advocates of religious toleration, and Martin Luther was aggressively hostile to those who disagreed with him on seemingly minor theological points. After 1542 with the establishment of the Universal Inquisition, the Catholic Church was committed to exposing and punishing anyone who professed a different faith, with the exception of Jews in Italy, who were under papal protection. Geneva and Rome became competing missionary centers, each flooding the world with polemical tracts and specially trained missionaries willing to risk their lives by going behind the enemy lines to console their co-religionists and evangelize for converts.

Religious passions ran so high that during the late sixteenth century a new word appeared to describe a personality type that may not have been entirely new but was certainly much more common—the **fanatic**. Originally referring to someone possessed by a demon, *fanatic* came to mean a person who expressed immoderate enthusiasm in religious matters, a person who pursued a supposedly divine mission, often to violent ends. Fanatics from all sides of the religious divide initiated waves of political assassinations and massacred their opponents. François Guion, the assassin of William the Silent, whose story began this chapter, was in many ways typical of fanatics in his steadfast pursuit of his victim and his willingness to masquerade for years under a false identity. During the sixteenth and seventeenth centuries, no religious community had a monopoly on fanatics. They served the pope as well as the Protestant churches.

Wherever there were significant religious minorities within a state, the best that could be hoped for was a condition of anxious tension, omnipresent suspicion, and periodic hysteria (see **Map 15.1**). The worst possibility was civil war in which religious affiliations and political rivalries intertwined in such complicated ways that finding peaceful solutions was especially difficult. Between 1560 and 1648 several religious civil wars broke out, including the French Wars of Religion, the Dutch revolt against Spain, the Thirty Years' War in Germany, and the English Civil War. (The latter two will be discussed in Chapter 16.)

The French Wars of Religion

When King Henry II (r. 1547–1559) of France died unexpectedly from a jousting accident, he left behind his widow, the formidable Catherine de' Medici (1519–1589), and a brood of young children—including his heir, Francis II (r. 1559–1560), who was only 15. Henry II had been a peacemaker. In contrast, Catherine and her children, including three sons who successively ascended to the throne, utterly failed to keep the peace, and for some 40 years France was torn apart by a series of desperate civil wars.

THE HUGUENOTS: THE FRENCH CALVINIST COMMUNITY By 1560 Calvinism had made significant inroads into predominantly Catholic France. Pastors sent from Geneva had been especially successful in the larger provincial towns, where their evangelical message appealed to enterprising merchants, professionals, and skilled artisans. One in ten of the French had become Calvinists, or **Huguenots** as French Protestants were called. The political strength of the Huguenots was greater than their numbers might indicate, because between one-third and one-half of the lower nobility professed Calvinism. Calvinism was popular among the French nobility for two reasons. One involved the imitation of social superiors. The financial well-being of any noble depended on his patron, an aristocrat of higher rank who had access to the king and who could distribute jobs and lands to his clients. When a high aristocrat converted to Protestantism, he tended to bring into the new faith his noble clientele, who converted through loyalty to their patron or through the patron's ability to persuade those who were financially dependent on him. As a result of a few aristocratic conversions in southwest France, Calvinism spread through "a veritable religious spider's web,"[3] as one contemporary put it.

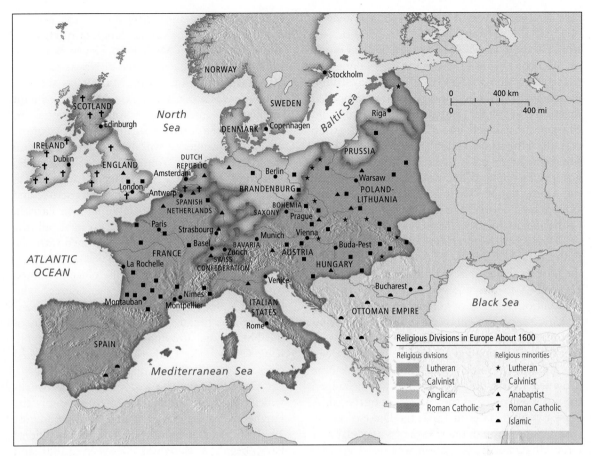

MAP 15.1

Religious Divisions in Europe About 1600

After 1555 the religious borders of Europe became relatively fixed, with only minor changes in confessional affiliations to this day.

A second reason for the spread of Calvinism was the influence of aristocratic women. The sister of King Francis I of France (r. 1515–1547), Marguerite of Angoulême (1492–1549), married the King of Navarre (an independent kingdom situated between France and Spain) and created a haven in Navarre for Huguenot preachers and theologians. Her example drew other aristocratic ladies to the Huguenot cause, and many of the Huguenot leaders during the French Wars of Religion were the sons and grandsons of these early female converts. Marguerite's daughter, Jeanne d'Albret, sponsored Calvinist preachers

for several years before she publicly announced her own conversion in 1560. Her son, Henry Bourbon (Henry of Navarre), became the principal leader of the Huguenot cause during the **French Wars of Religion** and the person responsible for eventually bringing the wars to an end.

THE ORIGINS OF THE RELIGIOUS WARS Like all civil wars, the French Wars of Religion exhibited a bewildering pattern of intrigue, betrayal, and treachery. Three distinct groups constituted the principal players. The first group was the royal family, consisting of Queen Catherine de' Medici and her four sons by Henry II—King Francis II (r. 1559–1560), King Charles IX (r. 1560–1574), King Henry III (r. 1574–1589), and Duke Francis of Alençon (1554–1584)—and her daughter, Marguerite Valois (1553–1615). The royal family remained Catholic but on occasion reconciled themselves with the Huguenot opposition, and Marguerite married into it. The second group was the Huguenot faction of nobles led by the Bourbon family who ruled Navarre. The third group was the hard-line Catholic faction led by the Guise family. These three groups vied for supremacy during the successive reigns of Catherine de' Medici's three sons.

During the reign of the sickly and immature Francis II, the Catholic Guise family dominated the government and raised the persecution of the Huguenots to a new level. In response to that persecution, a group of Huguenot nobles plotted in 1560 to kill the Guises. The Guises got wind of the conspiracy and surprised the plotters as they arrived in small groups at the royal chateau of Amboise. Some were ambushed, some drowned in the Loire River, and some hanged from the balconies of the chateau's courtyard. A tense two years later in 1562, the Duke of Guise was passing through the village of Vassy just as a large Huguenot congregation was holding services in a barn. The duke's men attacked the worshipers, killing some 740 of them and wounding hundreds of others.

Following the massacre at Vassy, civil war broke out in earnest. For nearly 40 years religious wars sapped the strength of France. Most of the battles were indecisive, which meant neither side sustained military superiority for long. Both sides relied for support on their regional bases: The Huguenots' strength was in the southwest; the Catholics', in Paris and the north. Besides military engagements, the French Wars of Religion spawned political assassinations and massacres.

MASSACRE OF ST. BARTHOLOMEW'S DAY   After a decade of bloody yet inconclusive combat, the royal family tried to resolve the conflict by making peace with the Protestants, a shift of policy

signified by the announcement of the engagement of Marguerite Valois, daughter of Henry II and Catherine de' Medici, to Henry Bourbon, the son of the Huguenot King of Navarre. At age 19, Marguerite—or Queen Margot, as she was known—was already renowned for her brilliant intelligence—and for her wanton morals. To complicate the situation further, on the eve of the wedding Marguerite was having an affair with another Henry, the young Duke of Guise who was the leader of the intransigent Catholic faction. The marriage between Marguerite and Henry of Navarre was to take place in Paris in August 1572, an event that brought all the Huguenot leaders to the heavily armed Catholic capital for the first time in many years. The gathering of all their enemies in one place presented too great a temptation for the Guises, who hatched a plot to assassinate the Huguenot leaders. Perhaps because she had become jealous of the Huguenots' growing influence on her son, King Charles IX, Catherine suddenly switched sides and became implicated in the plot.

Catherine somehow convinced the weak-willed king to order the massacre of the Huguenot nobles gathered in Paris. On August 14, 1572, St. Bartholomew's Day, the people of Paris began a slaughter. Between 3,000 and 4,000 Huguenots were butchered in Paris and more than 20,000 were put to death throughout the rest of France. Henry of Navarre saved his life by pretending to convert to Catholicism, while most of his companions were murdered.

Catherine's attempted solution for the Huguenot problem failed to solve anything. Henry of Navarre escaped his virtual imprisonment in the royal household, set Marguerite up in an isolated castle, returned to Navarre and his faith, and reinvigorated Huguenot resistance.

The wars of religion continued until the assassination of King Henry III, brother of the late Charles IX. Both Charles IX and Henry III had been childless, a situation that made Henry Bourbon of Navarre the rightful heir to the throne, even though he was a Huguenot. Henry Bourbon became King Henry IV (r. 1589–1610). He recognized that predominantly Catholic

ST. BARTHOLOMEW'S DAY MASSACRE
A Protestant painter, François Dubois, depicted the merciless slaughter of Protestant men, women, and children in the streets of Paris in 1572. The massacre was the most bloody and infamous in the French Wars of Religion and created a lasting memory of atrocity.

France would never accept a Huguenot king, and so in 1593 with his famous quip, "Paris is worth a mass," Henry converted to Catholicism. Most Catholic opposition to him collapsed. Once Henry became a Catholic he managed to have the pope annul his childless marriage to Marguerite so that he could marry Marie de' Medici

and obtain her huge dowry. Affable, witty, generous, and exceedingly tolerant, "Henry the Great" became the most popular king in French history, reuniting the war-torn country by ruling with a very firm hand. With the **Edict of Nantes** of 1598, he allowed the Huguenots to build a quasi-state within the state, giving them the right to have their own troops, church organization, and political autonomy within their walled towns, but banning them from the royal court and the city of Paris.

Despite his enormous popularity, Henry too fell victim to fanaticism. After surviving 18 attempts on his life, in 1610 the king was fatally stabbed by a Catholic fanatic, who took advantage of the opportunity presented when the royal coach unexpectedly stopped behind a cart loading hay. Catholics and Protestants alike mourned Henry's death and considered the assassin mad. Henry's brilliant conciliatory nature and the horrors of the religious wars had tempered public opinion.

Philip II, His Most Catholic Majesty

France's greatest rivals were the Habsburgs, who possessed vast territories in the Holy Roman Empire, controlled the elections for emperor, and had dynastic rights to the throne of Spain. During the late sixteenth century, Habsburg Spain took advantage of French weakness to establish itself as the dominant power in Europe. When Emperor Charles V (who had been both Holy Roman Emperor and king of Spain) abdicated his thrones in 1556, the Habsburg possessions in the Holy Roman Empire and the emperorship went to his brother, Ferdinand I, and the balance of his vast domain to his son, Philip II (r. 1556–1598). Philip's inheritance included Spain,

CHRONOLOGY: THE FRENCH WARS OF RELIGION, 1560–1598

1560	Huguenot conspiracy of Amboise against Catholic Guise family
1572	Massacre of St. Bartholomew's Day, Catholics murder Huguenots
1598	Edict of Nantes granting Huguenots religious toleration

Milan, Naples, Sicily, the Netherlands, scattered outposts on the north coast of Africa, colonies in the Caribbean, Central America, Mexico, Peru, and the Philippines. In 1580 Philip also inherited Portugal and its far-flung overseas empire, which included a line of trading posts from West Africa to the Spice Islands and the vast colony of unexplored Brazil.

This grave, distrustful, rigid man saw himself as the great protector of the Catholic cause and committed Spain to perpetual hostility toward Muslims and Protestants. On the Muslim front he first bullied the Moriscos, the descendants of the Spanish Muslims. The Moriscos had received Christian baptism but were suspected of secretly practicing Islam. In 1568 Philip issued an edict that banned all manifestations of Muslim culture and ordered the Moriscos to turn over their children to Christian priests to educate. The remaining Moriscos were eventually expelled from the country in 1609.

Philip once said he would rather lose all his possessions and die a hundred times than be the king of heretics. (See *Justice in History* in this chapter.) His attitude toward Protestants showed that he meant what he said. Through his marriage to Queen Mary I of England (r. 1553–1558), Philip encouraged her persecutions of Protestants, but they got their revenge. After Mary's death her half-sister, Queen Elizabeth I, refused Philip's marriage proposal and in 1577 signed a treaty to assist the Protestant provinces of the Netherlands, which were in rebellion against Spain. To add insult to injury, the English privateer Sir Francis Drake (ca. 1540–1596) conducted a personal war against Catholic Spain by raiding the Spanish convoys bringing silver from the New World. In 1587 Drake's embarrassing successes culminated with a daring raid on the great Spanish port city of Cadiz, where, "singeing the king of Spain's beard," he destroyed the anchored Spanish fleet and many thousands of tons of vital supplies.

Philip retaliated by building a huge fleet of 132 ships armed with 3,165 cannons, which in 1588 sailed from Portugal to rendezvous with the Spanish army stationed in the Netherlands and launch an invasion of England. As the Invincible Armada, as it was called, passed through the English Channel, it was met by a much smaller English fleet, assembled out of merchant ships refit for battle. Unable to maneuver as effectively as the English in the fluky winds of the channel and mauled by the rapid-firing English guns, the **Spanish Armada** suffered heavy losses and was forced to retreat to the north, where it sustained further losses in storms off the coast of Scotland and Ireland. Barely more than half of the fleet finally straggled home. The defeat severely shook Philip's sense of invincibility.

The reign of Philip II illustrated better than any other the contradictions and tensions of the era. No monarch had at his grasp as many resources and territories as Philip, and yet defending them proved extremely costly. The creaky governmental machinery of Spain put a tremendous burden on a conscientious king such as Philip, but even his unflagging energy and dedication to his duties could not prevent military defeat and financial disaster. Historians remember Philip's reign for its series of state bankruptcies and for the loss of the Dutch provinces in the Netherlands, the most precious jewel in the crown of Spain.

The Dutch Revolt

The Netherlands boasted some of Europe's richest cities, situated amid a vast network of lakes, rivers, channels, estuaries, and tidal basins that periodically replenished the exceptionally productive soil through flooding. The Netherlands consisted of 17 provinces, each with its own distinctive identity, traditions, and even language. The southern provinces were primarily French-speaking; those in the north spoke a bewildering variety of Flemish and Dutch dialects. When Philip II became king of Spain he also inherited all of the Netherlands. With his characteristic bureaucratic mentality, Philip treated Dutch affairs as a management problem rather than a political sore spot, an attitude that subordinated the Netherlands to Spanish interests. Foreign rule irritated the Dutch, who had long enjoyed ancient privileges including the right to raise their own taxes and muster their own troops.

Philip's harsh attitude toward Protestants upset the Netherlands' delicate balance among Catholic, Lutheran, Calvinist, and Anabaptist communities, as did the arrival of Huguenot refugees from the French Wars of Religion. In 1566 Calvinist fanatics occupied many Catholic churches and destroyed paintings and statues.

In response Philip issued edicts against the heretics and strengthened the Spanish Inquisition. The Inquisition in Spain was an arm of the monarchy charged with ensuring religious conformity, but when introduced in the Netherlands, it became an investigating agency devoted to finding, interrogating, and, if necessary, punishing Protestants.

Philip also dispatched 20,000 Spanish troops under the command of the Duke of Alba (1508–1582), a veteran of the Turkish campaigns in North Africa and victories over the Lutheran princes in the Holy Roman Empire. Alba directly attacked the Protestants. He personally presided over the military court, the Council of Troubles, which became so notoriously tyrannical that the people called it the Council of Blood. As an example to others, he systematically razed several small villages where there had been incidents of desecrating Catholic images and slaughtered every inhabitant. Alba himself boasted that during the campaign against the rebels, he had 18,000 people executed, in addition to those who died in battle or were massacred by soldiers. Sixty thousand refugees, about two percent of the population, went into exile.

The Prince of Orange, William the Silent (1533–1584), organized the **Dutch Revolt** to resist to Alba. Within a few short years, William the Silent seized permanent control of the provinces of Holland and Zealand, which were then flooded by Calvinist refugees from the southern provinces.

His policies a failure, Alba was recalled to Spain in 1573. After Alba's departure, no one kept control of the unpaid Spanish soldiers, who in mutinous rage turned against cities loyal to Spain, including Brussels, Ghent, and most savagely Antwerp, the rich center of trade. Antwerp lost 7,000 citizens and one-third of its houses to the "Spanish fury," which permanently destroyed its prosperity.

Alba's replacement, the shrewd statesman and general the Duke of Parma (r. 1578–1592), ultimately subdued the southern provinces, which remained a Spanish colony. The seven northern provinces, however, united in 1579, declared independence from Spain in 1581, and formally organized as a republic in 1588 (see **Map 15.2**). William the Silent became the *stadholder* (governor) of the new United Provinces, and after his assassination in 1584 his 17-year-old son, Maurice of Nassau, inherited the same title.

The Netherlands' struggle for independence transformed the population of the United

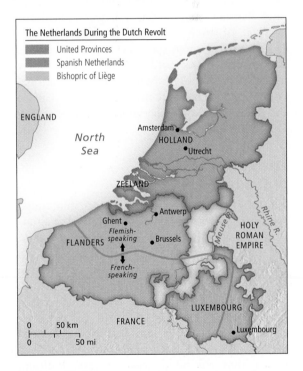

MAP 15.2

The Netherlands During the Dutch Revolt, ca. 1580

During the late sixteenth century the northern United Provinces separated from the Spanish Netherlands. The independence of the United Provinces was not recognized by the other European powers until 1648.

CHRONOLOGY: SPAIN AND THE NETHERLANDS, 1568–1648

1568	Edict against Morisco culture
1580	King Philip II inherits Portugal and the Portuguese Empire
1584	Assassination of William the Silent
1588	Defeat of the Spanish Armada, failed Spanish invasion of England; the seven northern provinces of the Netherlands becomes a republic
1609	Expulsion of the Moriscos from Spain
1648	Treaty of Westphalia recognizes independence of the Netherlands

Provinces from mixed religions to staunch Calvinism. The alliance with England, which provided much-needed financial and moral support, reinforced the Protestant identity of the Dutch, and the failure of the Spanish Armada to land Parma's men in England guaranteed the survival of an independent Netherlands. The Dutch carried on a sporadic and inconclusive war against Spain until the end of the Thirty Years' War in 1648, when the international community recognized the independent United Provinces of the Netherlands, known as the Dutch Republic.

Literature in the Age of Confessional Division

Churches and monarchs everywhere demanded religious conformity in word and deed, a situation that would seem to stifle creativity, and yet the late sixteenth and early seventeenth centuries were one of the most remarkable periods in the history of creative literature. Some literary figures did find their works banned and some had political or personal troubles with their monarch. But the controversies of the day seemed to have stimulated rather than inhibited great writers. Political and religious turmoil led them to rise above the petty religious squabbles that preoccupied so many of their contemporaries and to ask penetrating questions about the meaning of life. And importantly, they did so in their native languages. During this period the native or **vernacular languages** of western Europe

became literary languages, replacing Latin as the dominant form of expression, even for the educated elite.

FRENCH LITERATURE DURING THE RELIGIOUS TURMOIL In France royal decrees in 1520 and 1539 substituted French for Latin in official legal and government documents. A century later, with the founding of the Académie Française, it became government policy to promote, protect, and refine the French language. The greatest masters of French prose during this crucial period were François Rabelais (ca. 1483–1553) and Michel de Montaigne (1533–1592).

Trained as a lawyer, Rabelais became a friar and priest but left the Church under a cloud of heresy to become a physician. Rabelais's satirical masterpiece, a series of novels recounting the fantastic and grotesque adventures of the giants Gargantua and Pantagruel, combined an encyclopedic command of humanist thought with stunning verbal invention that has had a lasting influence on humorous writers to this day. Rabelais's optimistic vision of human nature represented a startling contrast to the growing anxiety provoked by the religious controversies of his time. Rabelais's controversial work was banned, and he was briefly forced into exile.

It is ironic that Montaigne became a master of French prose. His mother was a Catholic of Spanish-Jewish origin, and the young Michel spoke only Latin for the first six years of his life because his German tutor knew no French. After a modestly successful legal career, Montaigne retired to the family chateau to discover himself by writing essays, a literary form well suited to reflective introspection. In his essays, Montaigne struggled with his lasting grief over the premature death from dysentery of a close friend, reflected on his own experience of the intense physical pain of illness, and diagnosed the absurd causes of the French Wars of Religion. Montaigne's essays were a profound series of meditations on the meaning of life and death, presented in a calm voice of reason to an age of violent fanaticism. In one essay, for example, he exposed the presumption of human beings: "The most vulnerable and frail of all creatures is man, and at the same time the most arrogant." Montaigne thought it presumptuous that human beings picked themselves out as God's favorite creatures. How did they know they were superior to other animals? "When I play with my cat, who knows if I am not a pastime to her more than she is to me?"[4] His own skepticism about religion insulated him from the sometimes violent passions of his era. His essay "On Cannibals" pointed to the hypocrisy of Christians who condemned the alleged cannibalism of the native Americans but justified the torture and murder of other Christians over some minor theological dispute. Montaigne argued that the capacity to understand and tolerate cultural and religious differences, not rigid adherence to biblical laws, defined a truly ethical, truly Christian person.

STIRRINGS OF THE GOLDEN AGE IN IBERIA   The literary tradition in the Iberian peninsula thrived in several languages: Basque, Galician, Portuguese, Castilian, and Catalan. The greatest lyric poet of the peninsula, Luís Vaz de Camões (1524–1580), lost an eye in battle and was sent to the Portuguese East Indies after he killed a royal official in a street brawl. When he returned years later, he completed his epic poem *The Lusiads* (1572), a celebration of Vasco da Gama's discovery of the sea route to India, which became the national poem of Portugal. Camoes modeled this work on the

ancient epics, especially the *Aeneid*, the greatest Latin epic of ancient Rome, and even included the gods of Olympus as commentators on the human events of Camões's time. By connecting Portugal directly to the glories of the ancient empires, Camões elevated the adventures of his fellow Portuguese in Asia to an important moment in the history of the world.

The period when Spain was the dominant power in Europe coincided with the Golden Age of Spanish literature. Because Spain was unified around the crown of Castile, the Castilian language became the language we now call Spanish. The greatest literary figure was Miguel de Cervantes Saavedra (1547–1616), an impoverished son of an unsuccessful doctor with little formal education. Like Camões, Cervantes survived many adventures. He lost the use of his left hand at the naval Battle of Lepanto and spent five years languishing in a Turkish prison after his capture by Algerian pirates. The disabled veteran wrote plays for the Madrid theater and worked as a tax collector, but was still imprisoned several times for debts. Desperate to make money, Cervantes published a serial novel in installments between 1605 and 1615. It became the greatest masterpiece in Spanish literature, *Don Quixote*.

The prototype of the modern novel form, *Don Quixote* satirizes chivalric romances. Cervantes presented reality on two levels, the "poetic truth" of the master and dreamer Don Quixote and the "historic truth" of his squire and realist Sancho Panza. Don Quixote's imagination persistently ran away with him as he tilted at windmills, believing they were fierce dragons. It remained to Sancho Panza to point out the unheroic truth. Cervantes pursued the interaction between these two incongruous views of truth as a philosophical commentary on existence. For Cervantes there was no single, objective truth, only psychological truths revealed through the interaction of the characters, an idea that contrasted with the notion of dogmatic religious truth that dominated the time.

THE ELIZABETHAN RENAISSANCE During the reign of Elizabeth I (r. 1558–1603), the Renaissance arrived in England. The daughter of Henry VIII and Anne Boleyn, Elizabeth faced terrible insecurity as a girl. Her father had her mother beheaded, she was declared illegitimate, and her half-sister Mary imprisoned her in the Tower of London for treason. After she ascended to the throne in 1558, however, she proved to be a brilliant leader. Elizabeth prevented the kind of religious civil wars that broke out in France by establishing a moderate form of Protestantism as the official religion. She presided over the beginnings of England's rise as a major European power. Perhaps most remarkably, she became a patron and inspiration for England's greatest age of literature.

The principal figure of the Elizabethan Renaissance was a professional dramatist, William Shakespeare (1564–1616). In a series of theaters, including the famous Globe on the south side of the Thames in London, Shakespeare wrote, produced, and acted in comedies, tragedies, and history plays. Shakespeare's enormous output of plays, some of which made veiled allusions to the politics of Elizabeth's court, established him not only as the most popular dramatist of his time, but the greatest literary figure in the English language. The power of his plays derives from the subtle understanding of human psychology found in his characters and the stunning force of his language. For Shakespeare, as for Montaigne, the source of true knowledge was self-knowledge, which most people lacked. Pride and human authority prevented people from knowing themselves:

> But man, proud man,
> Drest [dressed] in a little brief authority,

QUEEN ELIZABETH I OF ENGLAND
Carried by her courtiers Elizabeth presided over the greatest age of English literature.

Most ignorant of what he's most assured,
His glassy [dull] essence, like an angry ape,
Plays such fantastic tricks before high
    heaven
As make the angels weep.
(*Measure for Measure* II, ii, 117)

Unlike most contemporary authors, Shakespeare wrote for a broad audience of paying theater goers that included common workers as well as highly educated members of Elizabeth's court. This need to appeal to a large audience who gave instant feedback helped him hone his skills as a dramatist.

STATES AND CONFESSIONS IN EASTERN EUROPE

■ How did the countries of eastern Europe during the late sixteenth century become enmeshed in the religious controversies that began in western Europe during the early part of the century?

The religious diversity of eastern Europe contrasted with the religious conformity of western Europe's confessional states. Whereas in western Europe the religious controversies stimulated writers to investigate deeply the human condition but made them cautious about expressing nonconforming religious opinions, writers and creative people in eastern Europe during this period were able to explore a wide range of ideas in a relatively tolerant atmosphere. Bohemia and Poland, in particular, allowed levels of religious diversity unheard of elsewhere. During the last decades of the sixteenth century and early decades of the seventeenth, however, dynastic troubles compromised the relative openness of the eastern states, enmeshing them in conflicts among themselves that had an increasingly strong religious dimension. In the Holy Roman Empire, the weakness of the mad Emperor Rudolf permitted religious conflicts to fester, setting the

stage for the disastrous Thirty Years' War (1618–1648) that pitted Catholic and Protestant princes against one another.

Around the Baltic Sea, rivalries among Lutheran Sweden, Catholic Poland-Lithuania, and Orthodox Russia created a state of almost permanent war in a tense standoff among three very different political and religious states. The enormous confederation of Poland-Lithuania sustained the most decentralized, religiously diverse state anywhere in Europe. By the end of the century, it remained politically decentralized but had become an active theater of the Catholic Reformation where dynastic policy firmly supported the Roman Church. Russia began to strengthen itself under the authoritarian rule of the tsars, who began to transform it into a major European power.

The Dream World of Emperor Rudolf

In Goethe's *Faust*, set in sixteenth-century Germany, drinkers in a tavern sing:

The dear old Holy Roman Empire,
How does it hang together?

Good question. How did this peculiarly decentralized state—neither holy, nor Roman, nor an empire, as Voltaire would later put it—hang together? In the late sixteenth century the empire consisted of one emperor; seven electors; 50 bishops and archbishops, 21 dukes, margraves, and landgraves; 88 independent abbots and assorted prelates of the Church; 178 counts and other sovereign lords; about 80 free imperial cities; and hundreds of free imperial knights. The emperor presided over all, and the Imperial Diet served as a parliament, but the Holy Roman Empire was, in fact, a very loose confederation of semi-independent, mostly German-speaking states, many of which ignored imperial decrees that did not suit them. During the first half of the sixteenth century the empire faced a number of challenges—the turmoil within the empire created by Lutheranism, endless French enmity on the western borders, and the tenacious Ottoman threat on the eastern frontier. Only the universal vision and firm hand of Emperor Charles V kept the empire together. The universal vision and firm hand disappeared in the succeeding generations of emperors to be replaced by petty dynastic squabbles and infirm minds.

The crippling weakness of the imperial system became most evident during the reign of Rudolf II (r. 1576–1612). The Habsburg line had a strain of insanity going back to Joanna "The Mad," the mother of Emperors Charles V (r. 1519–1558) and Ferdinand I (r. 1558–1564), who happened to be Rudolf's two grandfathers, giving him a double dose of Habsburg genes. Soon after his election to the imperial throne, Rudolf moved his court from bustling Vienna to the lovely quiet of Prague in Bohemia. Fearful of noisy crowds and impatient courtiers, stand-offish toward foreign ambassadors who presented him with difficult decisions, paranoid about scheming relatives, and prone to wild emotional gyrations from deep depression to manic grandiosity, Rudolf was hardly suited for the imperial throne. In fact, many contemporaries, who had their own reasons to underrate him, described him as hopelessly insane. Rudolf certainly suffered from moments of profound melancholy and irrational fears that may have had genetic or organic causes, but he was probably unhinged by the conundrum of being the emperor, a position that trapped him between the glorious universal imperial ideal and the ignoble reality of unscrupulous relatives and petty rivalries.

Incapable of governing, Rudolf transmuted the imperial ideal of universality into a strange dream world. In Prague he gathered around him a brilliant court of humanists, musicians, painters, physicians, astronomers, astrologers, alchemists, and magicians. These included an eclectic assortment of significant thinkers—the great astronomers Tycho Brahe and Johannes Kepler, the notorious occult philosopher Giordano Bruno, the theoretical mathematician and astrologer John Dee, and the remarkable inventor of surrealist painting

Giuseppe Arcimboldo. Many of these figures became central figures in the Scientific Revolution, but Rudolf also fell prey to fast-talking charlatans. These included Cornelius Drebber who claimed to have invented a perpetual-motion machine. This weird court, however, was less the strange fruit of the emperor's hopeless dementia than the manifestation of a striving for universal empire. Rudolf sought to preserve the cultural and political unity of the empire, to eradicate religious divisions, and to achieve peace at home. Rudolf's court in Prague was perhaps the only place left during the late sixteenth century where Protestants, Catholics, Jews, and even radical heretics such

EMPEROR RUDOLF II

Among the many creative people in the Emperor Rudolf's court was the Italian surrealist painter Giuseppe Arcimboldo, who specialized in creating images out of fruits, vegetables, flowers, and animals. This is a portrait of the Emperor Rudolf.

as Bruno could gather together in a common intellectual enterprise. The goal of such gatherings was to discover the universal principles that governed nature, principles that would provide the foundations for a single unifying religion and a cure for all human maladies. It was a noble, if utterly improbable, dream.

While Rudolf and his favorite courtiers isolated themselves in their dream world, the religious conflicts within the empire reached a boiling point. Without a strong emperor, confessional squabbles paralyzed the Imperial Diets. In 1607, the Catholic Duke of Bavaria annexed Donauworth—a city with a Lutheran majority—to his own territories. Despite the illegality of the duke's action, Rudolf passively acquiesced, causing fear among German Protestants that the principles of the Religious Peace of Augsburg of 1555 might be ignored. The Religious Peace had allowed princes and imperial free cities, such as Donauworth, to determine their own religion. The Duke of Bavaria's violation of Donauworth's status as a free city jeopardized not only civic liberty but religious liberty. In the following decade, more than 200 religious revolts or riots took place. In 1609 the insane Duke John William of Jülich-Cleves died without a direct heir, and the most suitable claimants to the Catholic duchy were two Lutheran princes. The succession of a Lutheran prince to this Catholic dukedom would have seriously disrupted the balance between Catholics and Protestants in Germany. Religious tensions boiled over. As Chapter 16 will describe, in less than a decade the empire began to dissolve in what became the Thirty Years' War.

The Renaissance of Poland-Lithuania

As the major power in eastern Europe, Poland-Lithuania engaged in a tug-of-war with Sweden over control of the eastern Baltic and almost constant warfare against the expansionist ambitions of Russia (see **Map 15.3**). Nevertheless, during the late sixteenth and early seventeenth centuries, Poland-Lithuania experienced a remarkable cultural and political renaissance inspired by influences from Renaissance Italy linked to strong commercial and diplomatic ties to the Republic of Venice and intellectual connections with the University of Padua. But perhaps the most remarkable achievement of Poland-Lithuania during this contentious time was its unparalleled level of religious toleration and parliamentary rule.

Very loosely joined since 1385, the Kingdom of Poland and the Grand Duchy of Lithuania formally united as the Polish-Lithuanian Commonwealth in 1569. The republican thought from Renaissance Italy directly influenced the political structure and values of the Commonwealth. Polish jurists studied law at the universities of Padua and Bologna where they learned to apply the civic values of Italy to the Polish context. Under these influences, the Polish constitution guaranteed that there would be no changes of the law, no new taxes, and no limitations on freedoms without the consent of the parliament, known as the Sejm. The novel feature of the Commonwealth was how the nobles (*szlachta*) reserved power for themselves through their control of regional assemblies, which in turn dominated the Sejm. The *szlachta* consisted of between 6.6 and 8 percent of the population and nearly 25 percent of ethnic Poles. Elsewhere in Europe, except for Spain, the nobility accounted for no more than 1 to 3 percent of the population. Thus, a much higher percentage of the population of Poland-Lithuania enjoyed political rights than in any other country in Europe. In 1573 the Sejm introduced a highly limited monarchy for Poland. The Sejm elected the king and treated him, at best, as a hired manager. While the rest of Europe moved toward ever more authoritarian monarchies, Poland moved in the opposite direction toward broader political participation.

The Warsaw Confederation of 1573 prohibited religious persecution, making the Commonwealth the safest and most tolerant place in Europe. Poland-Lithuania contained an incomparable religious mixture of Roman

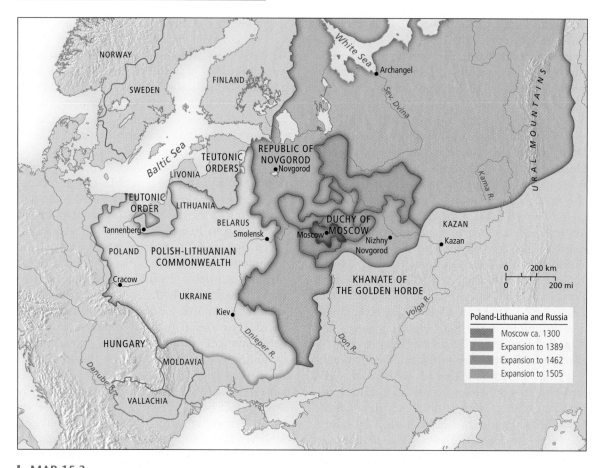

MAP 15.3

Poland-Lithuania and Russia

These countries were the largest in Europe in the size of their territories but were relatively under populated compared to the western European states.

Catholics, Lutherans, Calvinists, Russian Orthodox, Anabaptists, Unitarians, Armenians, and Jews. These communities, however, were strongly divided along geographic and social lines. Lutheranism was a phenomenon of the German-speaking towns, the peasants of Poland remained Catholic, those in Lithuania were Orthodox, and many of the nobles were attracted to Calvinism.

During the late sixteenth century, however, many Protestants in Poland returned or converted

to the Roman Catholic faith. The key to the transformation was the changing attitude of the Polish *szlachta,* who had promoted religious diversity because they believed that religious liberty was the cornerstone of political liberty. The revival of Catholicism owed a great deal to Stanislas Hosius (1504–1579), who had studied in Italy before he returned to Poland to become successively a diplomat, bishop, and cardinal. Imbued with the zeal of the Italian Catholic Reformation, Hosius invited the Society of Jesus (Jesuits) into Poland

and worked closely with the papal *nuncios* (the diplomatic representatives of the pope), who organized a campaign to combat all forms of Protestantism. Between 1565 and 1586, 44 Polish nobles studied at the Jesuit college in Rome. When they returned, they took up the most influential church and government offices in Poland. Jesuit colleges sprouted up in many Polish towns, attracting the brightest sons of the nobility and urban bourgeoisie. A close alliance between the kings of Poland and the Jesuits enhanced the social prestige of Catholicism.

The cultural appeal of all things Italian also helped lure many members of the Polish nobility back to Catholicism. Through the spread of elite education, Catholicism returned to Poland largely through persuasion rather than coercion. But the transformation did not occur without violent repercussions. Lutheran, Calvinist, and Bohemian Brethren churches were burned. In Cracow armed confrontations between Protestant and Catholic militants led to casualties. In 1596 the Polish king and Catholic fanatics imposed Catholicism on the Orthodox in the eastern parts of the Commonwealth. Although allowed to retain their rites, Orthodox believers had to accept the authority of the pope. Despite the growing religious hostility, Poland did not degenerate into civil war, as did France or the Netherlands over much the same issues.

Not all Poles and Lithuanians interpreted the Italian influence as affirming the Catholic Reformation. In 1580 Count Jan Zamoyski (1542–1605) founded the city of Zamość, designed as an ideal Renaissance city on the Italian model. Zamoyski had studied at Padua and returned to Poland determined to build his own Padua. He invited Armenians and Jews to inhabit the new town as citizens. A forceful advocate of civic freedom against royal authority and religious toleration, he built a Roman Catholic Church, a Calvinist chapel, an Armenian Orthodox church, and two synagogues. In Zamoyski's planned town the religions of the West encountered one another on a daily basis

ZAMOŚĆ

One of the finest examples of a Renaissance planned-town, Zamość in eastern Poland imitated the arcaded streets of Padua, Italy.

and exemplified one of the most attractive features of the Polish Renaissance.

Perhaps most remarkable was the position of Jews in Poland. During the early modern period Poland-Lithuania became the center of European Jewish culture. Jews described Vilnius as the "new Jerusalem." Jews had their own parliament and sent nonvoting representatives to the Sejm, a form of unequal citizenship but a guarantee of certain rights without parallel elsewhere in Europe. Unlike other parts of Europe, in Poland-Lithuania Jews were not forced to assimilate or hide and were allowed to develop their own distinctive communities.

The Troubled Legacy of Ivan the Terrible

While Poland experimented with a decentralized confederation dominated by nobles that severely restricted the king's initiative, Russia did the opposite. During the late fifteenth and sixteenth centuries, the grand dukes of Moscow who became the tsars of Russia gradually expanded their power over the **boyars** (the upper-level nobles who dominated Russian society) and challenged Moscow's neighbors—Poland-Lithuania and the Republic of Novgorod.

Although well integrated into the European diplomatic community and engaged in trade with its western neighbors, Russia for more than 300 years had been under the "Tartar Yoke," a term describing the Mongolian tribes that overran the country, pillaging and depopulating it. Ivan III, "The Great" (1462–1505), succeeded in gradually throwing off the Tartar Yoke by refusing to continue to pay tribute to the Mongols.

Ivan's marriage to Zoë, the niece of the last Greek emperor of Constantinople, gave him the basis for claiming that the Russian rulers were the heirs of Byzantium and the exclusive protectors of Orthodox Christianity, the state religion of Russia. Following the Byzantine tradition of imperial pomp, Ivan practiced Byzantine court ceremonies, and his advisers developed the theory of the Three Romes. According to this theory, the authority of the

THE MOSCOW KREMLIN

The Kremlin in Moscow was the seat of government for the Russian tsars until 1712. Originally built in 1156, the present enclosure of the Kremlin dates from the sixteenth century and reflects the influence of Italian architects brought to Moscow as well as traditional Byzantine styles. This view shows the Cathedral of St. Michael the Archangel and Bell Tower of Ivan the Great.

ancient Roman Empire had passed first to the Byzantine Empire, which God had punished with the Turkish conquest, and then to Moscow as the third and last "Rome." Ivan celebrated this theory by assuming the title of tsar (or "Caesar"). With his wife's assistance, he hired Italian architects to rebuild the grand ducal palace, the Kremlin.

With his capture of the vast northern territories of the Republic of Novgorod, Ivan expanded the Russian state north to the White Sea and east to the Urals. In 1478 Ivan sent his army to Novgorod, massacred the population, abolished the parliament, and burned the archive, ending the rich republican tradition of northern Russia. Ivan's invasion of parts of Lithuania embroiled Russia in a protracted conflict with Poland that lasted more than a century. Like his fellow monarchs in western Europe, Ivan began to bring the aristocrats under control by incorporating them into the bureaucracy of the state.

Ivan III's grandson, Ivan IV, "The Terrible" (1533–1584), succeeded his father at age three and became the object of innumerable plots, attempted coups, and power struggles among his mother, uncles, and the boyars. The trauma of his childhood years and a painful disease of the spine made him inordinately suspicious and prone to acts of impulsive violence. When at age 17 Ivan was crowned, he reduced the power of the dukes and the boyars. He obliged them to give up their hereditary estates. In return he redistributed lands to them with the legal obligation to serve the tsar in war. In weakening the boyars, Ivan gained considerable support among the common people and was even remembered in popular songs as the people's tsar. At first, he was a great reformer who introduced a code of laws and a church council. By setting aside half of the realm as his personal domain, he created a strong financial base for the army, which led to military successes in the prolonged wars against Poland-Lithuania and Sweden.

Nevertheless, Ivan distrusted everyone, and his struggle with the boyars led him to subvert his own reforms. He often arrested people on charges of treason, just for taking trips abroad. In a cruel revenge to his enemies among the boyars, he began a reign of terror in which he personally committed horrendous atrocities. His massacre in 1570 of the surviving inhabitants of Novgorod, whom he suspected of harboring Polish sympathies, contributed to his reputation as a bloody tyrant. During his reign, the Polish threat and boyar opposition to his rule revealed signs of the fragility of Russian unity.

Then, during the **"Time of Troubles"** (1604–1613), Russia fell into chaos. Boyar families struggled among themselves for supremacy, the Cossacks from the south led a popular revolt, and Poles and Swedes openly interfered in Russian affairs. Finally, the Time of Troubles ended when in 1613 the national assembly elected Tsar Michael Romanov, whose descendants ruled Russia until 1917. During the seventeenth century the Romanovs gradually restored order to Russia, eroded the independence of local governments, and introduced serfdom to keep the peasants on the land. By the

CHRONOLOGY: STATES AND CONFESSIONS IN EASTERN EUROPE

1480	Grand Duke and later Tsar Ivan III, "The Great," of Russia refuses to pay tribute to Tartars
1569	Constitutional Union established Polish-Lithuanian Commonwealth
1604–1613	Time of Troubles in Russia
1613	Michael Romanov elected Tsar of Russia

end of the seventeenth century Russia was strong enough to reenter European affairs as a major power.

CONCLUSION

The Divisions of the West

During the late sixteenth and early seventeenth centuries, hidden demographic and economic pressures eroded the confidence and security of many Europeans, creating a widespread sense of unease. Most people retreated like confused soldiers behind the barricades of a rigid confessional faith, which provided reassurance that was unavailable elsewhere. To compensate for the absence of predictability in daily life, societies everywhere imposed strict discipline—discipline of women, children, the poor, criminals, and alleged witches. The frenzy for social discipline displaced the fear of those things that could not be controlled (such as price inflation) onto the most easily controllable people, especially the weak, the subordinate, and those perceived to be different in some way.

The union between religion and political authority in the confessional states bolstered official religious faith with the threat of legal or military coercion. Where different religious confessions persisted within one state—most notably France and the Netherlands—the result was riots, assassinations, and civil war. The West had become divided along religious lines in two ways. The first kind of division was within countries with religiously mixed populations, where distinctive religious communities competed for political power and influence. In these countries religion became the cornerstone to justify patriotism or rebellion, loyalty or disloyalty to the monarch. The second kind of division was international. The confessional states formed alliances, crafted foreign policies, and went to war, with religion determining friend and foe. Over the subsequent centuries, religious differences mutated into ideological differences, but the sense that alliances among states should be linked together by a common set of beliefs has persisted to this day as a legacy from the sixteenth century.

During the period of the middle seventeenth to eighteenth centuries, confessional identity and the fear of religious turmoil led monarchs throughout Europe to build absolutist regimes, which attempted to enforce stability through a strengthened, centralized state. The principles of religious toleration and the separation of church and state were still far in the future. They were made possible only as a consequence of the hard lessons learned from the historical turmoil of the late sixteenth and seventeenth centuries.

KEY TERMS

confessions	French Wars of Religion
Price Revolution	Edict of Nantes
auto-da-fé	Spanish Armada
witch-hunt	Dutch Revolt
magic	vernacular languages
fanatic	boyars
Huguenots	Time of Troubles

CHAPTER QUESTIONS

1. How did the expanding population and price revolution exacerbate religious and political tensions? (page 458)
2. How did religious and political authorities attempt to discipline the people? (page 463)
3. Why did people in the sixteenth century think witches were a threat? (page 469)

4. How did religious differences provoke violence and start wars? (page 472)

5. How did the countries of eastern Europe during the late sixteenth century become enmeshed in the religious controversies that began in western Europe during the early part of the century? (page 483)

TAKING IT FURTHER

1. Why was it so difficult to establish religious toleration in the sixteenth century?

2. A common emotion during the age of confessional division was fear. How do you explain the spread of collective fears?

3. How did religious fanatics perceive the world during this period?

✓•—Practice on MyHistoryLab

16

Absolutism and State Building, 1618–1715

■ The Nature of Absolutism   ■ The Absolutist State in France and Spain
■ Absolutism and State Building in Central and Eastern Europe
■ Resistance to Absolutism in England and the Dutch Republic

IN 1651 THOMAS HOBBES, AN ENGLISH PHILOSOPHER LIVING IN EXILE IN France, was convinced that the West had descended into chaos. As he looked around him, Hobbes saw nothing but political instability, rebellion, and civil war. The turmoil had begun in the late sixteenth century, when the Reformation sparked the religious warfare described in the last chapter. In 1618 the situation deteriorated when another cycle of political strife and warfare erupted. The Thirty Years' War (1618–1648) began as a religious and political dispute in the Holy Roman Empire but soon became an international conflict involving the armies of Spain, France, Sweden, England, and many German states. The war wreaked economic and social havoc in Germany, decimated its population, and forced governments throughout Europe to raise large armies and tax their subjects to pay for them. The entire European economy suffered as a result.

During the 1640s, partly as a result of that devastating conflict, the political order of Europe collapsed. In England a series of bloody civil wars led to the destruction of the monarchy and the establishment of a republic. In France a civil war over constitutional issues drove the royal family from Paris. In Spain the king faced rebellions in four of his territories, while in Ukraine Cossacks staged a military uprising against the Polish-Lithuanian Commonwealth, killing more than one million people.

Hobbes proposed a solution to this multifaceted crisis. In *Leviathan* (1651), a theoretical treatise on the origin of political power, he argued that in the absence of a strong government society would degenerate into a constant state of war. In this dangerous world life would soon become, in Hobbes's famous words, "solitary, poor, nasty, brutish, and short."[1] The only way for people to find political stability would be to agree with their neighbors to form a political society by surrendering their independent power to a ruler who would make laws, administer justice, and maintain order. In this society the ruler would not share power with others. His subjects, having agreed to endow him with such extensive power, could not resist or depose him. The term used to designate the type of government Hobbes was recommending is **absolutism.** In the most general terms, absolutism means a political arrangement in which one ruler possesses unrivaled power.

During the seventeenth and early eighteenth centuries many European monarchs tried to introduce absolutism and increase the wealth and power of the states they ruled. These efforts always met with resistance. In most cases the rulers and their ministers prevailed, and Europe entered the "age of absolutism," which did not end until the outbreak of the French Revolution in 1789. This chapter addresses this question: Why did some European rulers achieve greater success than others in realizing these political objectives?

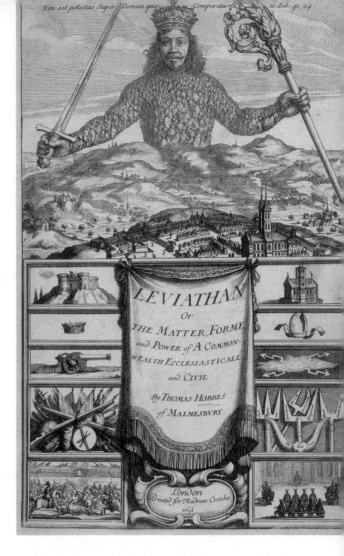

THE FRONTISPIECE OF THOMAS HOBBES'S TREATISE *LEVIATHAN*, PUBLISHED IN LONDON IN 1651

The ruler is depicted as incorporating the bodies of all his subjects, as they collectively authorized him to govern.

THE NATURE OF ABSOLUTISM

- What did absolutism mean, both as a political theory and as a practical program, and how was absolutism related to the growth of the power of the state?

Seventeenth-century absolutism had both a theoretical and a practical dimension. Theoretical absolutists included writers such as Hobbes who described the nature of power in the state and explained the conditions for its acquisition and continuation. Practical absolutists were the rulers who took concrete political steps to gain control over all other political authorities within the state.

The Theory of Absolutism

When seventeenth-century political writers referred to the monarch's absolute power, they usually meant that he did not share the power to make law with representative assemblies. Hobbes, for example, referred to the absolute ruler as "sole legislator," while the French magistrate Jean Bodin (1530–1596), one of the earliest proponents of absolutist theory, argued in *Six*

Books of a Commonwealth (1576) that the most important power of an absolute ruler was the right to make law by himself.

Absolute rulers also claimed that they were above the law. This meant that when monarchs acted for reason of state, that is, for the benefit of the entire kingdom, they did not have to obey the law of their kingdoms. Nor could they be held legally accountable for their actions because they had no legal superior to judge them. Being above the law, however, did not mean monarchs could act arbitrarily, illegally, or despotically, even though some of them did so from time to time. Absolutist theorists claimed monarchs were obliged to respect the property rights of their subjects whenever they were not acting for reason of state. Under all circumstances monarchs were expected to follow the law of God.

Some absolutist theorists, although not Hobbes, claimed that rulers received their power directly from God. This theory of **divine right** supported royal absolutism, so the theorists claimed, because God would only invest the ruler he appointed with powers that resembled his own. The theory of divine right also supported the absolutist argument that subjects could not resist their monarch under any circumstances.

The Practice of Absolutism

In their quest for absolute power European monarchs employed three strategies. First, they sought to eliminate or weaken national legislative assemblies. In France, which historians consider the most absolutist state in seventeenth-century Europe, the monarchy stopped summoning its national legislature, the **Estates General,** in 1614. In Spain monarchs sought to reduce the powers of the legislative assemblies, the **Cortes,** of their various kingdoms, while in Germany many princes stopped consulting the **diets** of their territorial states.

The second strategy of absolutist rulers was to subordinate the nobility to the king and make them dependent on his favor. Monarchs who aspired to a position of unrivaled power in their kingdoms took steps to keep the nobility in line by suppressing aristocratic challenges to their authority and by appointing men from different social groups as their chief ministers. Yet the king could not afford to alienate these wealthy and high-ranking men, upon whom he still relied for running his government and maintaining order in the localities. Absolute monarchs, therefore, offered nobles special privileges, such as exemption from taxation, positions in the king's government, and freedom to exploit their peasants in exchange for their recognition of the king's absolute authority. In this way, nobles became junior partners in the management of the absolutist state.

The third strategy of absolute monarchs was to control the administrative machinery of the state and use it to enforce royal policy throughout their kingdoms. Absolute monarchs were by nature state builders. They established centralized bureaucracies that extended the reach of their governments down into the smallest towns and villages and out into the most remote regions of their kingdoms. The business conducted by these centrally controlled bureaucracies included the collection of taxes, the recruitment of soldiers, and the operation of the judicial system. Some absolute monarchs used the power of the state to impose and maintain religious conformity. As the seventeenth century advanced, they also used the same power to regulate the price of grain, stimulate the growth of industry, and relieve the plight of the poor. In these ways, absolutist policies had an impact on the lives of all royal subjects, not just noblemen and royal councilors.

Warfare and the Absolutist State

The growth of European states in the seventeenth century was closely related to the conduct of war. During the period from 1600 to 1721, European powers were almost constantly at war. To meet the demands of war, rulers began keeping men under arms at all times. By the middle of the seventeenth century, after the Thirty Years' War had come to an end, most European states had acquired such **standing armies.** These military forces not only served their rulers in foreign wars, but also helped to maintain order and enforce royal policy at home. Standing armies became one of the main props of royal absolutism.

European armies also became larger, in many cases tripling in size. In the 1590s Philip II of Spain had mastered Europe with an army of 40,000 men. By contrast, in the late seventeenth century Louis XIV of France needed an army of 400,000 men to become the dominant power on the continent. The increasing size of these forces partly stemmed from the introduction and extensive use of gunpowder in the fifteenth and sixteenth centuries. Gunpowder led to the widespread use of the musket, a heavy shoulder firearm carried by a foot soldier. The use of the musket demanded the recruitment and equipment of large armies of infantry, who marched in square columns with men holding long pikes (long wooden shafts with pointed metal heads) to protect the musketeers from enemy attacks. As the size of these armies of foot soldiers grew, the role of mounted soldiers, who had dominated medieval warfare, shrank.

Changes in military technology and tactics also necessitated more intensive military training. In the Middle Ages mounted knights had acquired great individual skill, but they did not need to work in precise unison with other men under arms (see "The Military Revolution" in Chapter 11). Seventeenth-century foot soldiers, however, had to learn to march in formation, to coordinate their maneuvers, and to fire without harming their comrades in arms. Therefore, they needed to be drilled. Drilling took place in peacetime as well as during war. The wearing of uniforms, which began when the state assumed the function of clothing its thousands of soldiers, gave further unity and cohesion to the trained fighting force.

The cost of recruiting, training, and equipping these mammoth armies was staggering. In the Middle Ages individual lords often had sufficient financial resources to assemble their own private armies. By the beginning of the seventeenth century the only institution capable of putting the new armies in the field was the state itself. The same was true for navies, which now consisted of heavily armed sailing ships, each of which carried as many as 400 sailors. To build these large armies and navies, as well as to pay the increasing cost of waging war itself (which rose 500 percent between 1530 and 1630), governments had to identify new methods of raising and collecting taxes. In times of war as much as 80 percent of state revenue went for military purposes.

The equipment and training of military forces and the collection and allocation of the revenue necessary to subsidize these efforts stimulated the expansion and refinement of the state bureaucracy. Governments employed thousands of new officials to supervise the collection of new taxes. To make the system of tax collection more efficient governments often introduced entirely new administrative systems. Some states completely reorganized their bureaucracies to meet the demands of war. They created new departments to supervise the recruitment of soldiers, the manufacture of equipment and uniforms, the building of fleets, and the provisioning of troops in time of war.

THE ABSOLUTIST STATE IN FRANCE AND SPAIN

■ How did France and Spain implement absolutism in the seventeenth century and how powerful did those states become?

The first two European monarchies to become absolutist states were France and Spain. The political development of these two countries, however, followed very different courses. The kingdom of France became a model of state building and gradually emerged as the most powerful country in Europe. The Spanish monarchy, on the other hand, struggled to introduce absolutism at a time when the overall economic condition of the country was deteriorating and its military forces were suffering a series of defeats.

The Foundations of French Absolutism

The first serious efforts to establish absolutism in France took place during the reign of Louis XIII (r. 1610–1643). When Louis was only eight years old, a Catholic assassin killed his father, Henry IV (1589–1610). Louis's mother, Marie de' Medici, assumed the leadership of the government during his youth. This period of **regency**, in which aristocratic factions vied for supremacy at court, exposed the main weakness of the monarchy, which was the rival power of the great noble families of the realm. The statesman who addressed this problem most directly was Louis's main councilor, Cardinal Armand Jean du Plessis de Richelieu (1585–1642), who became the king's chief minister in 1628. Richelieu directed all his energies toward centralizing the power of the French state in the person of the king.

Richelieu's most immediate concern was to bring the independent nobility to heel and subordinate their local power to that of the state. He suppressed several conspiracies and rebellions led by noblemen and restricted the independent power of the provincial assemblies and the eight regional **parlements**, which were the highest courts in the country. Richelieu's great administrative achievement was the strengthening of the system of the **intendants**. These paid crown officials, who were recruited from the professional classes and the lower ranks of the nobility, became the main agents of French local administration. Responsible only to the royal council, they collected taxes, supervised local administration, and recruited soldiers for the army.

Richelieu's most challenging task was increasing the government's yield from taxation, a task

CARDINAL RICHELIEU
Triple portrait of Cardinal Richelieu, who laid the foundations of French absolutism.

that became more demanding during times of war. Levying taxes on the French population was always a delicate process; the needs of the state conflicted with the privileges of various social groups, such as the nobles, who were exempt from taxation, and the estates of individual provinces, such as Brittany, that claimed the right to tax the people themselves. Using a variety of tactics, Richelieu managed to increase the yield from the *taille,* the direct tax on land, as much as threefold during the period from 1635 to 1648. He supplemented the taille with taxes on office-holding. Even then, the revenue was insufficient to meet the extraordinary demands of war.

Richelieu's protégé and successor, Jules Mazarin (1602–1661), continued his policies but was unable to prevent civil war from breaking out in 1648. This challenge to the French state, known as the *Fronde* (a pejorative reference to a Parisian game in which children flung mud at passing carriages), had two phases. The first, the Fronde of the Parlement (1648–1649), began when the members of the Parlement of Paris, the most important of all the provincial parlements, refused to register a royal edict that required them to surrender four years' salary. This act of resistance led to demands that the king sign a document limiting royal authority. The rebels put up barricades in the streets of Paris and forced the royal family to flee the city. The second and more violent phase was the Fronde of the Princes (1650–1653), during which the Prince de Condé and his noble allies waged war on the government and even formed an alliance with France's enemy, Spain. Only after Condé's military defeat did the entire rebellion collapse.

The Fronde stands as the great crisis of the seventeenth-century French state. It revealed the strength of the local, aristocratic, and legal forces with which the king and his ministers had to contend. In the long run, however, these forces could not destroy the achievement of Richelieu and Mazarin. By the late 1650s the damage had been repaired and the state had resumed its growth.

Absolutism in the Reign of Louis XIV

The man who presided over the development of the French state for the next 50 years was the king himself, Louis XIV (r. 1643–1715), who assumed direct control of his government after the death of Mazarin in 1661. In an age of absolute monarchs, Louis towered over his contemporaries. His reputation as the most powerful ruler of the seventeenth century derives as much from the image he conveyed as from the policies he pursued. Artists, architects, dramatists, and members of his immediate entourage helped the king project an image of incomparable majesty and authority. Paintings and sculptures of the king depicted him in sartorial splendor, holding the symbols of power and displaying expressions of regal superiority that bordered on arrogance. At Versailles, about ten miles from Paris, Louis

CHRONOLOGY: FRANCE IN THE AGE OF ABSOLUTISM	
1598	The Edict of Nantes grants toleration to French Calvinists, known as Huguenots
1610	Assassination of Henry IV of France, who was succeeded by Louis XIII (r. 1610–1643)
1628	Cardinal Richelieu becomes chief minister of Louis XIII of France
1643	Death of Louis XIII of France and accession of Louis XIV; Louis's mother, Anne of Austria, becomes queen regent with Cardinal Mazarin as his minister
1648–1653	The Fronde
1661	Death of Cardinal Mazarin; Louis XIV assumes personal rule
1685	Revocation of the Edict of Nantes
1715	Death of Louis XIV of France; succeeded by his grandson, Louis XV

constructed a lavishly furnished palace that became his main residence and the center of his court. The palace was built in the **baroque** style, which emphasized the size and grandeur of the structure while also conveying a sense of unity and balance among its diverse parts. The sweeping façades of baroque buildings gave them a dynamic quality that evoked an emotional response from the viewer. The baroque style, criticized by contemporaries for its exuberance and pomposity, appealed to absolute monarchs who wished to emphasize their unrivaled position within society and their determination to impose order and stability on their kingdoms.

Court life at Versailles revolved entirely around the king. Court dramas depicted Louis, who styled himself "the sun king," as Apollo, the god of light. The paintings in the grand Hall of Mirrors at Versailles, which recorded the king's military victories, served as reminders of his unrivaled accomplishments. Louis's formal routine in receiving visitors created appropriate distance between him and his courtiers while keeping his subjects in a state of subservient anticipation of royal favor.

Louis's greatest political achievement was securing the complete loyalty and dependence of the old nobility. This he achieved first by requiring the members of these ancient families to come to Versailles for a portion of every year, where they stayed in apartments within the royal palace itself. At Versailles Louis involved them in the elaborate cultural activities of court life and in ceremonial rituals that emphasized their subservience to the king. He also excluded these nobles from holding important offices in the government of the realm, a strategy designed to prevent them from building an independent power

VERSAILLES PALACE, CENTER OF THE COURT OF LOUIS XIV AFTER 1682
The palace was constructed between 1669 and 1686. Its massiveness and grandeur and the order it imposed on the landscape made it a symbol of royal absolutism.

base within the bureaucracy. Instead he recruited men from the mercantile and professional classes to run his government. This policy of taming the nobility and depriving them of central administrative power could work only if they received something in return. Like all the absolute monarchs of western Europe, Louis used the patronage at his disposal to grant members of the nobility wealth and privileges in exchange for their loyalty to the crown. In this way the monarchy and the nobility served each other's interests.

In running the actual machinery of government Louis built upon and perfected the centralizing policies of Richelieu and Mazarin. After the death of Mazarin in 1661, the king, then 23 years old, became his own chief minister, presiding over a council of state that supervised the work of government. An elaborate set of councils at the highest levels of government set policy that department ministers then implemented. The provincial intendants became even more important than they had been under Richelieu and Mazarin, especially in providing food, arms, and equipment for royal troops. The intendants secured the cooperation of local judges, city councils, and parish priests as well as the compliance of the local population. If necessary they could call upon royal troops to enforce the king's policies, but for the most part they preferred to rely on the more effective tactics of negotiation and compromise with local officials. The system, when it worked properly, allowed the king to make decisions that directly affected the lives and beliefs of his 20 million subjects.

In the late seventeenth century the French state also became involved in the economic and financial life of the country. The minister most responsible for this increase in state power was Jean Baptiste Colbert (1619–1683), a protégé of Mazarin who in 1661 became controller general of the realm. Born into a family of merchants, and despised by the old nobility, Colbert epitomized the type of government official Louis recruited into his service. Entrusted with the supervision of the entire system of royal taxation, Colbert increased royal revenues by reducing the cut taken by tax collectors.

Even more important, Colbert exploited the country's economic resources for the benefit of the state. The theory underlying this set of policies was **mercantilism,** which held that the wealth of the state depended on its ability to import fewer commodities than it exported. Its goal was to secure the largest possible share of the world's monetary supply. Colbert increased the size of France's merchant fleet, founded overseas trading companies, and levied high tariffs on France's commercial rivals. To make France economically self-sufficient, he encouraged the growth of the French textile industry, improved the condition of the roads, built canals throughout the kingdom, and reduced some of the burdensome tolls that impeded internal trade.

The most intrusive exercise of the power of the state during Louis XIV's reign was his decision to enforce religious uniformity. In 1598 the Edict of Nantes had given French Calvinists, known as Huguenots, the freedom to practice their religion. Louis considered the existence of this large Huguenot minority within his kingdom an affront to his sense of order. In 1685 therefore Louis revoked the Edict, thereby denying freedom of religious worship to about one million of his subjects. The army enforced public conversions to Catholicism and closed Protestant churches. Large numbers of Huguenots emigrated to the Netherlands, England, Germany, and North America. Few exercises of absolute power in the seventeenth century caused more disruption in the lives of ordinary people than this attempt to realize Louis's ideal of "one king, one law, one faith."

Louis XIV and the Culture of Absolutism

A further manifestation of the power of the French absolutist state was Louis's success in influencing and transforming French culture. Kings had often served as patrons of the arts by providing income for artists, writers, and musicians and endowing cultural and educational institutions. Louis took this type of royal patronage to a new level, making it possible for him to control the dissemination of ideas and the very production of culture itself. During Louis's reign royal patronage, emanating from the court, extended the king's influence over the entire cultural landscape. The architects of the palace at Versailles, the painters of historical scenes that hung in its hallways and galleries, the composers of the plays and operas performed in its theaters, the sculptors who created busts of the king to decorate its chambers, and the historians and pamphlet writers who celebrated the king's achievements in print all benefited from Louis's direct financial support.

Much of Louis's patronage went to cultural institutions. He took over the Academy of Fine Arts in 1661, founded the Academy of Music in 1669, and chartered a theater company, the *Comédie Française*, in 1680. Two great French dramatists of the late seventeenth century, Jean Baptiste Molière (1622–1673), the creator of French high comedy, and Jean Racine (1639–1699), who wrote tragedies in the classical style, benefited from the king's patronage. Louis even subsidized the publication of a new journal, the *Journal des savants*, in which writers advanced their ideas. In 1666 Louis extended his patronage to the sciences with the founding of the *Académie des Sciences*, which had the twofold objective of advancing scientific knowledge and glorifying the king. It also benefited the state by devising improvements in ship design and navigation.

Of all the cultural institutions that benefited from Louis XIV's patronage, the *Académie Française* had the most enduring impact on French culture. This society of literary scholars founded in 1635, sought to standardize the French language and preserve its integrity. In 1694, 22 years after Louis became the academy's patron, the first official French dictionary appeared in print. This achievement of linguistic uniformity, in which words received authorized spellings and definitions, reflected the pervasiveness of Louis's cultural influence as well as the search for order that became the defining characteristic of his reign.

The Wars of Louis XIV, 1667–1714

Colbert's financial and economic policies, coupled with the military reforms of the Marquis de Louvois, laid the foundation for the creation of a formidable military machine. In 1667 Louis XIV began unleashing its full potential. With an army 20 times larger than the French force that had invaded Italy in 1494, Louis fought four separate wars against an array of European powers between 1667 and 1714. His goal in all these wars was territorial acquisition (see **Map 16.1**). In this case Louis set his sights mainly on the German and Spanish territories in the Rhineland along the eastern borders of his kingdom. Contemporaries

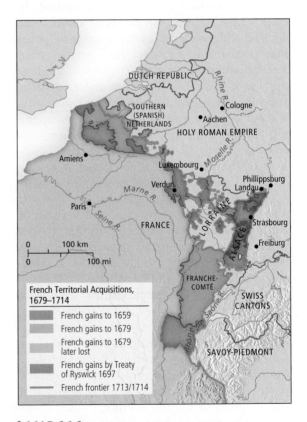

MAP 16.1

French Territorial Acquisitions, 1679–1714

Louis XIV thought of the Rhine River as France's natural eastern boundary, and territories acquired in 1659 and 1697 allowed it to reach that limit.

suggested, however, that he was thinking in grander terms than traditional French dynastic ambition. Propagandists for the king in the late 1660s claimed that Louis harbored visions of establishing a "universal monarchy" or an "absolute empire," reminiscent of the empires of ancient Rome, Charlemagne in the ninth century, and Charles V in the sixteenth century.

Louis never attained the empire of his dreams. After he launched an offensive against German towns along the Rhine River in 1688, Great Britain, the Dutch Republic, Spain, and Austria formed a coalition against him. Finally matched by the combined military strength of these allies, forced to wage war on many different fronts (including North America), and unable to collect enough taxes to pay for the war, France felt compelled to conclude peace in 1697. The Treaty of Ryswick marked the turning point in the expansion of the French state and laid the groundwork for the establishment of a **balance of power** in the next century, an arrangement whereby various countries form alliances to prevent any one state from dominating the others.

The Treaty of Ryswick, however, did not mark the end of French territorial ambition. In 1701 Louis went to war once again, this time as part of an effort to place a French Bourbon candidate, his grandson Duke Philip of Anjou, on the Spanish throne. The impending death of the mentally weak, sexually impotent, and chronically ill King Charles II of Spain (r. 1665–1700) without heirs had created a succession crisis. In 1698 the major European powers had agreed to a treaty that would divide Spanish lands between Louis and the Holy Roman Emperor, both of whom were Charles's brothers-in-law. By his will, however, Charles left the Spanish crown and all its overseas possessions to Philip. This bequest offered France more than it would have received on the basis of the treaty. If the will had been upheld, the Pyrenees Mountains would have disappeared as a political barrier between France and Spain, and France, as the stronger of the two kingdoms, would have controlled unprecedented expanses of European and American territory.

Dreaming once again of universal monarchy, Louis rejected the treaty in favor of King Charles's will. The British, Dutch, and Austrians responded by forming a Grand Alliance against France and Spain. After a long and costly conflict, known as the War of the Spanish Succession (1701–1713), the members of this coalition were able to dictate the terms of the Treaty of Utrecht (1713). Philip, who suffered from fits of manic depression and went days without dressing or leaving his room, remained on the Spanish throne as Philip V (r. 1700–1746), but only on the condition that the French and Spanish crowns would never be united. Spain ceded its territories in the Netherlands and in Italy to the Austrian Habsburg Monarchy and its strategic port of Gibraltar at the entrance to the Mediterranean to the British. Britain also acquired large parts of French Canada, including Newfoundland and Nova Scotia, The treaty thus dashed Louis's hopes of universal monarchy and confirmed the new balance of power in Europe.

The loss of French territory in North America, the strains placed on the taxation system by the financial demands of war, and the weakening of France's commercial power as a result of this conflict made France a less potent state at the time of Louis's death in 1715 than it had been in the 1680s. Nevertheless, the main effects of a century of French state building remained, including a large, well-integrated bureaucratic edifice that allowed the government to exercise unprecedented control over the population and a military establishment that remained the largest and best equipped in Europe.

Absolutism and State Building in Spain

The history of Spain in the seventeenth century is almost always written in terms of failure, as the country endured a long period of economic decline that began in the late sixteenth century. With a precipitate drop in the size of the population, the monarchy became progressively weaker under a series of ineffective kings, To make matters worse,

LOUIS XIV

Portrait of Louis XIV in military armor, with his plumed helmet and his crown on the table to the right. The portrait was painted during the period of French warfare. In the background is a French ship.

Spain, like France, underwent a period of state building during the seventeenth century, and that its government, like that of France, gravitated toward absolutism.

The Spanish monarchy in 1600 ruled more territory than did France, but its many principalities and small kingdoms possessed far more independence than even the most remote and peripheral French provinces. The center of the monarchy was the kingdom of Castile, with its capital at Madrid. This kingdom, the largest and wealthiest territory within the Iberian Peninsula, had been united with the kingdom of Aragon in 1479 when King Ferdinand II of Aragon (r. 1479–1516), the husband of Queen Isabella of Castile (r. 1474–1504), ascended the throne. These two kingdoms, however, continued to exist as separate states after the union, each having its own representative institutions and administrative systems. Each of them, moreover, contained smaller, semiautonomous kingdoms and provinces that retained their own distinctive political institutions. Outside the Iberian Peninsula the Spanish monarchy ruled territories in the Netherlands, Italy, and the New World.

the country suffered a series of military defeats, most of them at the hands of the French. As a result, Spain lost its position as the major European power (see **Map 16.2**). By the early eighteenth century Spain was a shadow of its former self, and its culture reflected uncertainty, pessimism, and nostalgia for its former imperial greatness. None of this failure, however, should obscure the fact that

The only institution besides the monarchy itself that provided any kind of administrative unity to all these Spanish territories in the seventeenth century was the Spanish Inquisition, a centralized ecclesiastical court with a supreme council in Madrid and 21 regional tribunals in different parts of Spain, Italy, and America.

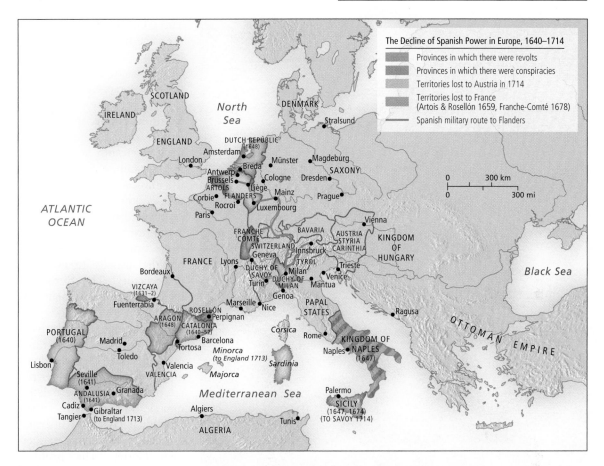

MAP 16.2

The Decline of Spanish Power in Europe, 1640–1714

Revolts in the United Provinces of the Netherlands and Portugal account for two of the most significant losses of Spanish territory. Military defeat at the hands of the French in 1659 and Austria in 1714 account for the loss of most of the other territories.

The great challenge for the Spanish monarchy in the seventeenth century was to integrate the various kingdoms and principalities of Spain into a more highly centralized state and make the machinery of that state more efficient and profitable. The statesman who made the most sustained efforts at realizing these goals was the energetic and authoritarian Count-Duke of Olivares (1587–1645), the contemporary of Richelieu during the reign of the Spanish king Philip IV (1621–1665). Olivares faced a daunting task. As a result of decades of warfare, the Spanish

monarchy in the 1620s was penniless, the kingdom of Castile had gone bankrupt, and the entire country had entered a period of protracted economic decline.

To deal with these deep structural problems Olivares proposed a reform of the entire financial system, the establishment of national banks, and the replacement of the tax on consumption, the *millones*, with proportional contributions from towns and villages in Castile. He also tried to make all the Spanish kingdoms and principalities contribute to the national

DIEGO DE VELÁZQUEZ, PORTRAIT OF THE PRINCE BALTASAR CARLOS, HEIR TO THE SPANISH THRONE

The depiction of the six-year-old prince on a rearing horse was intended to suggest military and political power at a time when the monarchy was losing both. The prince died in 1646, before he could succeed to the throne.

Three factors explain his failure. The first was the opposition he confronted within Castile itself, especially from the cities represented in the Cortes, over the question of taxation. The second, a problem facing Spain throughout the seventeenth century, was military failure. Spanish losses to France during the final phase of the Thirty Years' War aggravated the financial crisis and prevented the monarchy from capitalizing on the prestige that usually attends military victory. The third and most serious impediment was opposition to the policy of subordinating the outlying Spanish regions to the kingdom of Castile. The kingdoms and provinces on the periphery of the country were determined to maintain their individual laws and liberties, especially the powers of their own Cortes. The problem became more serious when Olivares, in the wake of military defeat by the French and Dutch, put more pressure on these outlying kingdoms and provinces to contribute to the war effort. During the tenure of Olivares, Spain faced separatist revolts in Portugal, Catalonia, Sicily, and Naples. With the exception of Portugal, which recovered its sovereignty in 1640, the monarchy managed to retain its provincial and Italian territories, but it failed to bring these areas under central government control.

The relative weakness of the Spanish monarchy became most apparent in the late seventeenth century, the age of Louis XIV. In two important respects the Spanish government failed to match

defense on a proportionate basis. His goal was to unify the entire peninsula in a cohesive Spanish national state, similar to that of France. This policy involved suppression of the historic privileges of the various kingdoms and principalities and the direct subordination of each area to the king. It was, in other words, a policy based on the principles of royal absolutism.

Olivares was unable to match the state-building achievement of Richelieu in France.

CHRONOLOGY: INTERNATIONAL CONFLICT IN THE SEVENTEENTH CENTURY

1609	Truce between the seven Dutch provinces and Spain
1618	Bohemian revolt against Habsburg rule; beginning of the Thirty Years' War
1620	Imperial forces defeat Bohemians at Battle of White Mountain
1648	Treaty of Westphalia, ending the Thirty Years' War; Treaty of Münster, ending the Dutch War of Independence
1667	Beginning of the wars of Louis XIV
1672	William III of Orange-Nassau becomes captain-general of Dutch; beginning of the war against France (1672–1678)
1688–1697	War of the League of Augsburg (Nine Years' War); England and Scotland join forces with Prussia, Austria, the Dutch Republic, and many German states against France
1697	Treaty of Ryswick
1700–1721	Great Northern War in which Russia eventually defeated Sweden; emergence of Russia as a major power
1701–1713	War of the Spanish Succession
1713	Treaty of Utrecht

the achievement of the French. First, Spain could never escape the grip that the old noble families had on the central administration. The unwillingness of the nobility to recruit ministers and officials from the mercantile and professional groups in society (which were small to begin with in Spain) worked against the achievement of bureaucratic efficiency and made innovation almost impossible. Second, unlike the French government during Colbert's ministry, the Spanish government failed to encourage economic growth. The hostility of the aristocratic ruling class to mercantile affairs, coupled with a traditional Spanish unwillingness to follow the example of foreigners (especially when they were Protestants) prevented the country from stemming its own economic decline and the government from solving the formidable financial problems facing it. To make matters worse, the Spanish government failed to make its system of tax collection more efficient.

The mood that prevailed within the upper levels of Castilian society in the seventeenth century reflected the failure of the government and the entire nation. The contrast between the glorious achievements of the monarchy during the reign of Philip II (r. 1555–1598) and the somber realities of the late seventeenth century led most members of the ruling class to retreat into the past, a nostalgia that only encouraged further economic and political stagnation. The work of Miguel de Cervantes (1547–1616), the greatest Spanish writer of the seventeenth century, reflected this change in the Spanish national mood. In 1605 and 1615 Cervantes published (in two parts) *Don Quixote*, the story of an idealistic wandering nobleman who pursued dreams of an elusive military glory. This work, which as we have seen in Chapter 15, explored the relationship between illusion and reality, served as a commentary on a nobility that had lost confidence in itself.

Paradoxically Spanish painting entered its Golden Age at the time the country began to lose its economic, political, and military vitality. Little in the paintings of the great Spanish artist Diego de Velázquez (1599–1660) would suggest the malaise that was affecting Spain and its nobility at the time. Velázquez painted in the baroque style that was in favor in European courts. He depicted his subjects in heroic poses and imbued them with a sense of royal or aristocratic dignity. One of his historical paintings, *The Surrender of Breda* (1634), commemorated a rare Spanish military victory over the Dutch in 1625 and the magnanimity of the Spanish victors toward their captives. All this was intended to reinforce the prestige of the monarchy, the royal family, and Spain itself at a time when the imperial grandeur of the past had faded. Velázquez's painting reflected the ideals of absolutism but ignored the realities of Spanish political and military life.

ABSOLUTISM AND STATE BUILDING IN CENTRAL AND EASTERN EUROPE

■ What was the nature of royal absolutism in central and eastern Europe, and how did the policies of the Ottoman Empire and Russia help to establish the boundaries of the West during this period?

The forces that led to the establishment of absolutism and state building in France and Spain also made an impact on central and eastern Europe. In Germany the Thirty Years' War led to the establishment of two absolutist states, Prussia and the Austrian Habsburg Monarchy. Farther to the east, the Ottoman and Russian Empires developed political systems that shared many of the same characteristics as states in western and central Europe. These policies challenged the traditional European perception that both empires belonged entirely to an Eastern, Asian world.

Germany and the Thirty Years' War, 1618–1648

Before 1648 the main political power within the geographical area known as Germany was the Holy Roman Empire. This large political formation was a loose confederation of kingdoms, principalities, duchies, ecclesiastical territories,

and cities, each of which had its own laws and political institutions. The emperor, who was elected by a body of German princes, exercised immediate jurisdiction only in his own dynastic possessions and in the imperial cities. He also convened a legislative assembly known as the *Reichstag*, over which he exercised limited influence. The emperor did not have a large administrative or judicial bureaucracy through which he could enforce imperial law in the localities. The empire was not in any sense a sovereign state, even though it had long been a major force in European diplomacy. It had acquired and maintained that international position by relying on the military and financial contributions of its imperial cities and the lands controlled directly by the Habsburg emperors.

The Thirty Years' War permanently altered the nature of this intricate political structure. That war began as a conflict between Protestant German princes and the Catholic emperor over religious and constitutional issues. The incident that triggered it in 1618 was the so-called Defenestration of Prague, when members of the predominantly Protestant Bohemian legislature, known as the Diet, threw two imperial officials out a castle window as a protest against the religious policies of their recently elected king, the future emperor Ferdinand II. The Diet proceeded to depose Ferdinand, a Catholic, and elect a Protestant prince, Frederick V of the Palatinate, to replace him. The war soon broadened into a European-wide struggle over the control of German and Spanish territory, as the Danes, Swedes, and French successively entered the conflict against the emperor and his Spanish Habsburg relatives. For a brief period in the late 1620s England also entered the conflict against Spain. The war, which was fought mainly on German soil, had a devastating effect on the country. More than one million soldiers marched across German lands, sacking towns and exploiting the resources of local communities. Germany lost up to one-third of its population, while the destruction of property retarded the economic development of the country for more than 50 years.

DEFENESTRATION OF PRAGUE, MAY 23, 1618
The Thirty Years' War was touched off when Protestant nobles in the Bohemian legislature threw two Catholic imperial governors out the window of a castle in Prague.

The political effects of the war were no less traumatic. By virtue of the Treaty of Westphalia, which ended the war in 1648, the empire was permanently weakened, although it continued to function until 1806 (see **Map 16.3**). The individual German territories within the empire developed more institutional autonomy than they had before the war. They became sovereign states, with their own armies, foreign policies, and central bureaucracies. Two of these German states became major European powers and developed their own forms of absolutism. The first was Brandenburg-Prussia, a collection of various territories in northern Germany that was transformed into the kingdom of Prussia at the beginning of the eighteenth century. The second state was the Austrian Habsburg Monarchy, which in the eighteenth century was usually identified simply as Austria. The Habsburgs had long dominated the Holy Roman Empire and continued to secure election as emperors after the Treaty of Westphalia. In the late seventeenth century, however, the Austrian Habsburg Monarchy acquired its own institutional identity, distinct from that of the Holy Roman Empire. It consisted of the lands that the Habsburgs controlled directly in the southeastern part of the empire and other territories, including the kingdom of Hungary, which lay outside the territorial boundaries of the empire.

The Growth of the Prussian State

In 1648, at the end of the Thirty Years' War, Prussia could barely claim the status of an independent state, much less an absolute monarchy. The core of the Prussian state was Brandenburg,

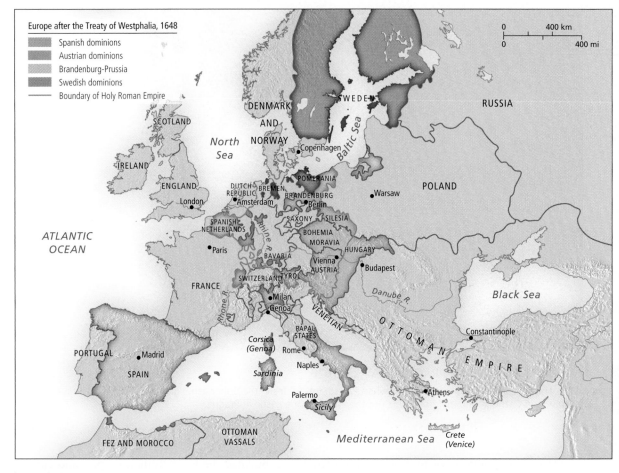

MAP 16.3

Europe after the Treaty of Westphalia, 1648

The Holy Roman Empire no longer included the Dutch Republic, which was now independent of Spain. Some of the lands of the Austrian Habsburg Monarchy and Brandenburg-Prussia lay outside the boundaries of the Holy Roman Empire. Italy was divided into a number of small states in the north, while Spain ruled Naples, Sicily, and Sardinia.

which was an electorate because its ruler cast one of the ballots to elect the Holy Roman Emperor. The Hohenzollern family, which controlled the electorate, held lands that lay scattered throughout northern Germany and stretched into eastern Europe. The largest was Prussia, a Baltic territory lying outside the boundaries of the Holy Roman Empire. As ruler of these disparate and noncontiguous lands, the Elector of Brandenburg had virtually no state

bureaucracy, collected few taxes, and commanded only a small army. Most of his territories, moreover, lay in ruins in 1648, having been devastated by Swedish and imperial troops at various times during the war.

The Great Elector Frederick William (r. 1640–1688) began the long process of turning this ramshackle structure into a powerful and cohesive German state (see **Map 16.4**). His son and grandson, King Frederick I (r. 1688–1713)

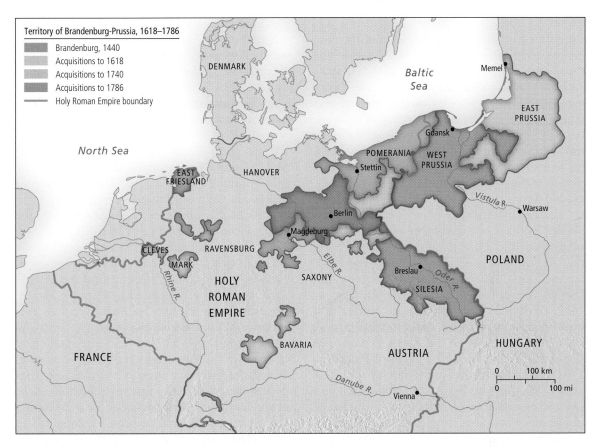

MAP 16.4

The Growth of Brandenburg-Prussia, 1618–1786

By acquiring lands throughout northern Germany, Prussia became a major European power. The process began during the early seventeenth century, but it continued well into the eighteenth century. The Prussian army, which was the best trained fighting force in Europe in the eighteenth century, greatly facilitated Prussia's growth.

and Frederick William I (r. 1713–1740), completed the transformation. The key to their success, as it was for all aspiring absolute monarchs in eastern Europe, was to secure the compliance of the traditional nobility, who in Prussia were known as **Junkers**. The Great Elector Frederick William achieved this end by granting the Junkers a variety of privileges, including exemption from import duties and the excise tax. The most valuable concession was the legal confirmation of their rights over their serfs. During the previous 150 years Prussian peasants had lost their freedom, becoming permanently bound to

the estates of their lords and completely subject to the Junkers' arbitrary brand of local justice. The Junkers had a deeply vested interest in perpetuating this oppressive system of serfdom, and the lawgiver Frederick was able to provide them with the legal guarantees they required.

With the loyalty of the Junkers secure, Frederick William began building a powerful Prussian state with a standing army and a large bureaucracy that superintended military and financial affairs. The army grew rapidly, rising to 30,000 men in 1690 and 80,000 by 1740. It consisted of a combination of carefully recruited volunteers, foreign mercenaries, and, after 1713, conscripts from the general population. Its most famous regiment, known as the Blue Prussians or the Giants of Potsdam, consisted of 1,200 men, each of whom was at least six feet tall. Commanded by officers drawn from the nobility and reinforced by Europe's first system of military reserves, this army quickly became the best trained fighting force in Europe. Prussia became a model military state, symbolized by the transformation of the royal gardens into an army training ground during the reign of Frederick William I.

As this military state grew in size and complexity, its rulers acquired many of the attributes of absolute rule. Most significantly, they became the sole legislators within the state. The main representative assembly in the electorate, the Diet of Brandenburg, met for the last time in 1652. Frederick William and his successors, however, continued to consult with smaller local assemblies, especially in the matter of taxation. The naming of Frederick I as king of Prussia in 1701 marked a further consolidation of royal power. His son's style of rule, which included physical punishment of judges whose decisions displeased him, suggested that the Prussian monarchy not only had attained absolute power, but could occasionally abuse it.

The Austrian Habsburg Monarchy

The Austrian Habsburgs were much less successful than the Hohenzollerns in building a centralized, consolidated state along absolutist lines. The various territories that made up the Austrian Habsburg Monarchy in the late seventeenth century were larger and more diverse than those that belonged to Prussia. **Map 16.3** shows that in addition to the cluster of duchies that form present-day Austria, the Austrian Habsburg monarchy embraced two subordinate kingdoms. The kingdom of Bohemia, lying to the north, had struggled against Habsburg control for nearly a century and included the provinces of Moravia and Silesia. The kingdom of Hungary, lying to the southeast, included the large semiautonomous principality of Transylvania. The Habsburgs

regained Hungary from the Ottoman Empire in stages between 1664 and 1718. In 1713 the monarchy also acquired the former Spanish Netherlands and the Italian territories of Milan and Naples.

The Austrian Habsburg monarchs of the seventeenth and early eighteenth centuries never succeeded in integrating these ethnically, religiously, and politically diverse lands into a unified, cohesive state similar to that of France. The main obstacle was a lack of a unified bureaucracy. The only centralized administrative institutions in this amalgam of kingdoms were the Court Chamber, which superintended the collection of taxes throughout the monarchy, and the Austrian army, which included troops from all Habsburg lands. Even these centralized institutions had difficulty operating smoothly. For all practical purposes, the Habsburgs had to rule their various kingdoms separately.

In governing its Austrian and Bohemian lands, this decentralized Habsburg monarchy nonetheless acquired some of the characteristics of absolutist rule. After defeating the Bohemians at the Battle of White Mountain in 1620 during the Thirty Years' War, Emperor Ferdinand II (r. 1618–1637) strengthened his authority not only in Bohemia, but over all the territories under his direct control. After punishing the rebels and exiling many of the Protestant nobility, he undertook a deliberate expansion of his legislative and judicial powers, and he secured direct control over all his administrative officials.

A policy of severe religious repression accompanied this increase in the emperor's authority. Ferdinand assumed that Protestantism served as a justification for rebellion, and he therefore decided that its practice could not be tolerated. He required that Protestants in all the emperor's territories take a Catholic loyalty oath, and he banned Protestant education.

Habsburgs were not so successful in trying to impose absolutism on Hungary in the late seventeenth and eighteenth centuries. Hungarians had a long tradition of limited, constitutional rule in which the national Diet exercised powers of legislation and taxation, just as Parliament did in England. Habsburg emperors made some limited inroads on these traditions but they were never able to break them. They also were unable to achieve the same degree of religious uniformity that they had imposed on their other territories. In Hungary the Habsburgs encountered the limits of royal absolutism.

The Ottoman Empire: Between East and West

In the seventeenth and early eighteenth centuries the southeastern border of the Habsburg monarchy separated the kingdom of Hungary from the Ottoman Empire. This militarized frontier marked not only the political boundary between two empires, but a deeper cultural boundary between East and West.

As we have seen in previous chapters, the West is not just a geographical area. It is also a cultural area; the people who inhabit this territory share many of the same religious, political, legal, and philosophical traditions. In the eyes of most Europeans, the Ottoman Turks, who posed a recurrent military threat to the Habsburg monarchy, did not belong to this Western world. Because the Ottoman Turks were Muslims, Europeans considered them enemies of Christianity, infidels who were bent on the destruction of Christendom. Ottoman emperors, known as sultans, were reputedly despots who ruled over their subjects as slaves. Western literature also depicted the sultans as cruel and brutal tyrants, the opposite of the ideal Christian prince. One French play of 1612 showed the mother of the sultan Mehmed the Conquerer (r. 1451–1481) drinking the blood of a victim.

These stereotypes of the Turks gave Europeans a sense of their own Western identity. Turks became a negative reference group with whom Europeans could compare themselves. The realities of Ottoman politics and culture, however, were quite different from their representations in European literature. Turkish despotism, the name Europeans gave to the Ottoman system of government, existed only in theory. Ever since the fourteenth century Ottoman writers had claimed for

the sultan extraordinary powers, including the right to seize the landed property of his subjects at will. In practice, however, the sultan never exercised unlimited power. The spirit of Muslim law limited his prerogatives, and he shared power with the grand vizier, his chief executive officer. By the 1660s, when most European states had entered the age of absolutism, the sultan's power had become largely titular. Moreover, the Ottoman practice of tolerating non-Muslim religions within the empire made the sultans less absolutist than most of their seventeenth-century European counterparts. (See *Different Voices* in this chapter.)

Even the Ottoman Empire's high degree of administrative centralization did not extend to all the territories it ruled. Many of its provinces, especially those in the Balkans, enjoyed a considerable measure of autonomy, especially in the seventeenth century. The Balkans, which were geographically part of Europe, never experienced the full force of direct Turkish rule. As in most monarchies of western and central Europe, a complex pattern of negotiation between the central imperial administration and local officials characterized Ottoman rule. In Europe the Ottoman Empire bore the closest resemblance to the Spanish monarchy, which also ruled many far-flung territories. Like Spain, the Ottoman Empire declined in power during the seventeenth century and lost effective control of some of its outlying provinces.

Ottoman Turks and Europeans frequently went to war against each other, but their interactions with the West were not always hostile. The Turks had been involved in European warfare since the fifteenth century, and they had formed diplomatic alliances with the French against the Austrian Habsburgs on a number of occasions. Europeans and Ottomans often acquired military technology and administrative techniques from each other. Trade between European countries and the Ottoman Empire remained brisk throughout this period. Europe supplied hardware and textiles to the Turks while they in turn shipped coffee, tobacco, and tulips to European ports. Communities of Turks and other Muslims lived in European cities, while

DIFFERENT VOICES WESTERN WRITERS EVALUATE THE OTTOMAN TURKS

Western commentators displayed ambivalent feelings toward the Ottoman Turks in the seventeenth century. On the one hand, Westerners were impressed with the power of the Sultan, the size of the Ottoman Empire, the discipline of their soldiers, and the political obedience of their subjects to their sovereign. On the other hand, Westerners considered the Turks barbarous. Richard Knolles (1550–1610) reflected this ambivalence in the preface to his history of the Turks with an analysis of their greatness. He then condemned the ways in which this barbarous people violated international and natural law. Thomas Smith, a clergyman at Oxford University, agreed with Knolles that the Turks were a barbarous nation, but he attributed this trait to their lack of interest in education and their intolerance of other religions.

An English Writer Criticizes the Turks for Violating the Law

But to come nearer unto the causes of the Turks greatness, ... first in them is to be noted an ardent and infinite desire of sovereignty, wherewith they have long since promised unto themselves the monarchy of the whole world, a quick motive unto their so haughty designs. Then, such a rare unity and agreement amongst them, as well in the manner of their religion (if it be so to be called) as in matters concerning their state (especially in all their enterprises to be taken in hand for the augmenting of their Empire) as that thereof they call themselves *Islami*, that is to say, men of one mind, or at peace among themselves; so as it is not to be marveled, if thereby they grow strong themselves, and dreadful to others. Join unto this their courage, conceived by the wonderful success of their perpetual fortune, their notable vigilance in taking the advantage of

every occasion for the enlarging of their monarchy, their frugality and temperateness in their diet and other manner of living, their straight observing of their ancient military discipline, their cheerful and almost incredible obedience unto their princes and Sultans; such, as in that point no nation in the world was to be worthily compared unto them—all great causes why their empire hath so mightily increased and so long continued....

And yet these great ones not contented by such commendable and lawful means still to extend or establish their far spreading empire, if that point once come in question, they stick not in their devilish policy to break and infringe the laws both of nations and nature. Their leagues grounded upon the law of nations, be they with never so strong capitulations concluded, or solemnity of oath confirmed, have with them no longer force than stands with their own profit, serving indeed but as snares to entangle other princes in, until they have singled out him whom they purpose to devour; the rest fast bound still looking on as if their own turn should never come, yet with no more assurance of their safety by their leagues than had the other whom they see perish before their faces. As for the kind law of nature, what can be thereunto more contrary than for the father most unnaturally to embrue his hands in the blood of his own children and the brother to become the bloody executioner of his own brethren, a common matter among the Ottoman emperors? All which most execrable and inhumane murders they cover with the pretended safety of their state, as thereby freed from the fear of all aspiring competitors (the greatest torment of the mighty) and by the preservation of the integrity of their Empire, which they thereby keep whole and entire unto themselves, and so

numerous European merchants resided in territories under Ottoman control.

These encounters between Turks and Europeans suggest that the militarized boundary

between the Habsburgs and the Ottoman Empire was more porous than its fortifications suggested. Military conflict and Western contempt for Turks disguised a complex process of political and

deliver it as it were by hand from one to another, in no part dismembered or impaired. By these and such like means is this barbarous empire (of almost nothing) grown to that height of majesty and power, as that it hath in contempt all the rest, being it self not inferior in greatness and strength unto the greatest monarchies that ever yet were upon the face of the earth, the Roman Empire only excepted.

Source: Richard Knolles, *The General History of the Turks from the First Beginnings of That Nation to the Rising of the Ottoman Family*, 1603.

An English Clergyman Comments on the Learning and Religious Intolerance of the Turks

The Turks are justly branded with the character of a barbarous nation, which censure does not relate either to the cruelty and severity of their punishments...or to want of discipline...or to want of civil behavior among themselves...but to the intolerable pride and scorn wherewith they treat all the world besides.

Their temper and genius, the constitution of their government, and the principles of their education incline them to war, where valor and merit are sure to be encouraged, and have their due reward. They have neither leisure nor inclination to entertain the studies of learning or the civil arts, which take off the roughness and wildness of nature, and render men more agreeable in their conversation. And though they are forced to commend and admire the ingenuity of the Western Christians, when they see any mathematical instrument, curious pictures, map, or sea-charts, or open the leaves of any printed book, or the like; yet they look upon all this as a curiosity, that not only may be spared, but what ought to be

carefully avoided, and kept out of their empire, as tending to soften men's minds, and render them less fit for arms, which they look upon as the best and truest end of life, to enlarge their greatness and their conquests.

But it is not so much their want of true and ingenuous learning which makes them thus intractable and rude to strangers as a rooted and inveterate prejudice against and hatred of all others who are of a different religion. It is not to be expected that where this principle prevails, and is looked upon as a piece of religion and duty, they who embrace it should be guilty of any act of kindness and humanity; except when they are bribed to it with hope of reward and gain, or forced to it by the necessities of state, or wrought upon more powerfully, as it were against their wills by the resentments of some favors and kindnesses received, which may happen now and then in some of better natures and more generous tempers.

Source: Thomas Smith, *Remarks upon the Manners, Religion and Government of the Turks*, 1678.

For Discussion

1. Which characteristics of the Turks given in the two documents did the authors view as positive and which did they view as negative?

2. To what extent do these two descriptions of the Turks support the Western view that the Ottoman Empire was an "oriental despotism"?

3. These two writers based their assessments of the Turks upon reports from travelers. What value do such reports have as historical evidence?

cultural interaction between the two civilizations. Europeans tended to think of the Ottoman Empire as "oriental," but it is more accurate to view it as a region lying between the East and the West.

Russia and the West

The other power that marked the boundary between East and West was the vast Russian Empire, which stretched from its boundary with

Poland-Lithuania in the west to the Pacific Ocean in the east. Until the end of the seventeenth century, the kingdom of Muscovy and the lands attached to it seemed, at least to Europeans, part of the Asiatic world. Dominated by an Eastern Orthodox branch of Christianity, Russia drew very little upon the cultural traditions associated with western Europe. Unlike its Slavic neighbor Poland, Russia had not absorbed large doses of German culture. It also appeared to Europeans to be another example of "oriental despotism," a state in which the ruler, known as the tsar (the Russian word for Caesar), could rule his subjects at will, "not bound up by any law or custom."

During the reign of Tsar Peter I, known as Peter the Great (r. 1682–1725), Russia underwent a process of Westernization, bringing it more into line with the culture of European countries and becoming a major European power. This policy began after Peter visited England, the Dutch Republic, northern Germany, and Austria in 1697 and 1698. Upon his return he directed his officials and members of the upper levels of Russian society to adopt Western styles of dress and appearance, including the removal of men's beards. (Scissors were kept in the customs house for this purpose alone.) Beards symbolized the backward, Eastern Orthodox culture from whose grip Peter hoped to extricate his country. Young Russian boys were sent abroad for their education. Women began to participate openly in the social and cultural life of the cities, in violation of Orthodox custom. Smoking was permitted despite the Church's insistence that Scripture condemned it. The calendar was reformed and books were printed in modern Russian type. Peter's importation of Western art and the imitation of Western architecture complemented this policy of enforced cultural change.

Westernization also involved military and political reforms that changed the character of the Russian state. During the first 25 years of his reign Peter had found himself unable to achieve sustained military success against his two great enemies, the Ottoman Turks to the south and the Swedes to the west. During the Great Northern War with Sweden (1700–1721), Peter introduced

a number of military reforms that eventually turned the tide against his enemy. Having learned about naval technology from the British and Dutch, he built a large navy. He introduced a policy of conscription, giving him a standing army of more than 200,000 men. A central council, established in 1711, not only directed financial administration but also levied and supplied troops.

This new military state also acquired many of the centralizing and absolutist features of western European monarchies. Efforts to introduce absolutism in Russia had begun during the reigns of Alexis (r. 1645–1676) and Fedor (r. 1676–1682), who had strengthened the central administration and brutally suppressed peasant rebellions. Peter built upon his predecessors' achievement. He created a new structure for managing the empire, appointing twelve governors to superintend Russia's 43 separate provinces. He brought the Church under state control. By establishing a finely graded hierarchy of official ranks in the armed forces, the civil administration, and the court, Peter not only improved administrative efficiency, but he also made it possible for men of nonaristocratic birth to attain the same privileged status as the old landowning nobility. He won the support of all landowners by introducing **primogeniture** (inheritance of the entire estate by the eldest son), which prevented the subdivision of their estates, and supporting the enserfment of the peasants. In dealing with his subjects Peter claimed more power than any other absolute monarch in Europe. Muscovites often told foreign visitors that the tsar treated them like slaves, punishing them at will and executing them without due process.[2] During the trial of his own son, Alexis, for treason in 1718, Peter told the clergy that "we have a sufficient and absolute power to judge our son for his crimes according to our own pleasure."[3]

The most visible sign of Peter's policy of westernization was the construction of the port city of St. Petersburg on the Gulf of Finland, which became the new capital of the Russian Empire. One of the main objectives of Russian foreign policy during Peter's reign was to secure access to the Baltic Sea, allowing Russia to open

ENCOUNTERS AND TRANSFORMATIONS

St. Petersburg and the West

The building of a new capital city, St. Petersburg, symbolized the encounter between Russia and the West during the reign of Peter the Great. Peter had seized the land on which the city was located, the marshy delta of the Neva River, from Sweden during the Northern War. The construction of the city, which first served as a fortress and then a naval base, occurred at a tremendous cost in treasure and human life. Using the royal powers he had significantly augmented earlier in his reign, Peter ordered more than 10,000 workers (and possibly twice that number) from throughout his kingdom to realize this ambitious and risky project. The harsh weather conditions, the ravages of malaria and other diseases, and the chronic shortages of provisions in a distant location resulted in the death of thousands of workers. Beginning in 1710 Peter ordered the transfer of central governmental, commercial, and military functions to the new city. The city became the site for Peter's Winter Palace, the residences of Russia's foreign ambassadors, and the headquarters of the Russian Orthodox Church. The Academy of Fine Arts and the Academy of Sciences were built shortly thereafter. During the 1730s Russia's first bourse, or exchange, fulfilled the prophecy of a British observer in 1710 that the city, with its network of canals, "might one day prove a second Amsterdam or Venice." Thus, St. Petersburg came to embody all the modernizing and westernizing achievements of Peter the Great.

The location of the new city and its architecture reflected Russia's encounter with the West. With access to the Baltic Sea, the new city, often described as "a window on the West," looked toward the European ports with which Russia increased its commerce and the European powers that Russia engaged in battle and diplomacy. The architects, stonemasons, and interior decorators that Peter commissioned came from France, Italy, Germany, and the Dutch Republic, and they constructed the buildings in contemporary European styles. The general plan of the city, drawn up by a French architect, featured straight, paved streets with stone paths that are now called sidewalks. St. Petersburg thus became a port through which Western influences entered Russia. The contrast with the old capital, Moscow, which was situated in the center of the country and embodied the spirit of the old Russia that Peter strove to modernize, could not have been clearer.

The construction of St. Petersburg played a central role in transforming Russia from a medieval kingdom on the fringes of Europe into a modern, Western power. It did not, however, eliminate the conflict in Russia between those who held the West up as the cultural standard that Russia should emulate and those who celebrated Russia's cultural superiority over the West. This conflict, which began in the eighteenth century, has continued to the present day. During the period of communism in the twentieth century, when St. Petersburg was renamed Leningrad and Moscow once again became the political capital of the country, the tradition that emphasized Russia's Eastern orientation tended to prevail. It was no coincidence that the collapse of communism and the disintegration of the Union of Soviet Socialist Republics in 1989 led to a renewed emphasis on Russia's ties with the West. The restoration of St. Petersburg's original name in 1991 and the celebration of its 300th anniversary in 2003 were further attempts to integrate Russia more fully into the West.

For Discussion

1. How did the founding of St. Petersburg contribute to the growth of the Russian state?

2. How did Peter the Great's absolute power facilitate the growth of the city?

PICTURE OF ST. PETERSBURG (1815)
This view of St. Petersburg from the quay in front of the Winter Palace reveals the city's Western character. The buildings lying across the Neva River, including the bourse, were designed by European architects. The gondolas, seen in the foreground docking at the quay, enhanced St. Petersburg's reputation as "Venice of the North."

Taking It Further

Russell Bova (ed.), *Russia and Western Civilization: Cultural and Historical Encounters.* (2003).

Lindsey Hughes, *Russia in the Age of Peter the Great.* (1998).

maritime trade with Europe and become a Western naval power. By draining a swamp on the estuary of the Neva River, Peter laid the foundations of a city that became the new capital of his empire. Construction began in 1703, and within 20 years St. Petersburg had a population of 40,000 people. With his new capital city now looking westward, and an army and central administration reformed on the basis of Prussian and French example, Peter could enter the world of European diplomacy and warfare as both a Western and an absolute monarch. (See *Encounters and Transformations* in this chapter.)

RESISTANCE TO ABSOLUTISM IN ENGLAND AND THE DUTCH REPUBLIC

■ Why did absolutism fail to take root in England and the Dutch Republic during the seventeenth century?

Royal absolutism did not succeed in all European states. In Poland-Lithuania and Hungary, for example, where the nobility exercised considerable political power, legislative assemblies continued to meet throughout the seventeenth and eighteenth centuries. Both countries had long traditions of constitutional government, and the Poles elected their kings. In western Europe the kingdom of England and the northern provinces of the Netherlands also resisted efforts to implement royal absolutism. In England this resistance to absolutism resulted in the temporary destruction of the monarchy in the middle of the seventeenth century and the permanent limitation of royal power after 1688. In the northern Netherlands, an even more resounding rejection of absolutism occurred. After winning their independence from absolutist Spain, the Dutch established a republic with a decentralized form of government that lasted the entire seventeenth and eighteenth centuries.

The English Monarchy

At different times in the seventeenth century English monarchs tried to introduce royal absolutism, but the political traditions of the country stood as major obstacles to their designs. The most important of these traditions was that the king could not make law or tax his subjects without the consent of Parliament, which consisted of the House of Lords (the nobility and the bishops) and the House of Commons, an elected assembly that included the lesser aristocracy, lawyers, and townsmen.

In the early seventeenth century some members of the House of Commons feared that this tradition of parliamentary government might come to an end. The first Stuart king, James I (r. 1603–1625), aroused some of these fears as early as 1604 when he called his first parliament. James thought of himself as an absolute monarch, and in a number of speeches and published works he emphasized the height of his independent royal power, which was known in England as the **prerogative.** James's son, Charles I (r. 1625–1649), gave substance to these fears of absolutism by forcing his subjects to lend money to the government during a war with Spain (1625–1629), imprisoning men who refused to make these loans, and collecting duties on exports without parliamentary approval. When

members of the House of Commons protested against these policies, Charles dismissed Parliament in 1629 and decided to rule without summoning it again.

This period of nonparliamentary government, known as the **personal rule,** lasted until 1640. During these years Charles, unable to collect taxes by the authority of Parliament, used his prerogative to bring in new revenues, especially by asking all subjects to pay "ship-money" to support the outfitting of ships to defend the country against attack. During the personal rule the king's religious policy fell under the control of William Laud, who was named archbishop of Canterbury in 1633. Laud's determination to restore many of the rituals associated with Roman Catholicism alienated large numbers of the more zealous Protestants, known as Puritans, and led to a growing perception that members of the king's government were engaged in a conspiracy to destroy both England's ancient constitution and the Protestant religion.

The personal rule might have continued indefinitely if Charles had not once again faced the financial demands of war. In 1636 the king tried to introduce a new religious liturgy in his northern kingdom of Scotland. The liturgy included a number of rituals that the firmly Calvinist Scottish population considered Roman Catholic. The new liturgy so angered a group of women in Edinburgh that they threw their chairs at the bishop when he introduced it. In response to this affront to their religion, the infuriated Scots signed a National Covenant (1638) pledging to defend the integrity of their Church, abolished episcopacy (government of the church by bishops) in favor of a Presbyterian system of church government, and mobilized a large army. To secure the funds to fight the Scots, Charles was forced to summon his English Parliament, thereby ending the period of personal rule.

The English Civil Wars and Revolution

Tensions between the reconvened English Parliament and Charles led to the first revolution of modern times. The Long Parliament, which met in November 1640, impeached many of the king's ministers and judges and dismantled the judicial apparatus of the eleven years of personal rule, including the courts that had been active in the prosecution of Puritans. Parliament declared the king's nonparliamentary taxes illegal and enacted a law limiting the time between the meetings of Parliament to three years.

This legislation did not satisfy the king's critics in Parliament. Their suspicion that the king was conspiring against them and their demand to approve all royal appointments created a poisoned political atmosphere in which neither side trusted the other. In August 1642 civil war began between the Parliamentarians, known as Roundheads because many of the artisans who supported them had close-cropped hair styles, and the Royalists or Cavaliers, who often wore their hair in long flowing locks. Parliament, with the military support of the Scots and a well-trained, efficient fighting force, the New Model Army, won this war in 1646 and took Charles prisoner. The king's subsequent negotiations with the Scots and the English Presbyterians, who had originally fought against him, led to a second civil war in 1648. In this war, which lasted only a few months, the New Model Army once again defeated Royalist forces.

This defeat of the king's forces led to a revolution. Following the wishes of the army, Parliament set up a court that tried and executed the king in January 1649. (See *Justice in History* in this chapter.) Shortly thereafter the House of Commons abolished the monarchy itself, thus making England a republic. This revolutionary change in the form of English government, however, did not lead to the establishment of a democratic regime. Democracy, in which a large percentage of the adult male population could vote, was the goal of the Levellers, a political party that originated in the New Model Army and attracted considerable support in London. The Levellers called for annual parliaments, the separation of powers between the executive and legislative branches of government, and the introduction of universal suffrage for men. The army officers, however, resisted these demands, and after an unsuccessful mutiny in the army, the Leveller party collapsed. The defeat of the Levellers guaranteed that political power in the new English republic would remain in the hands of men who occupied the upper levels of English society, especially those who owned property in land.

The republican government established in 1649 did not last. Tensions between the army and Parliament, fueled by the belief that the

CHRONOLOGY: A CENTURY OF REVOLUTION IN ENGLAND AND SCOTLAND

1603	James VI of Scotland (r. 1567–1625) becomes James I of England (r. 1603–1625)
1625	Death of James I and accession of Charles I (r. 1625–1649)
1629–1640	Personal rule of Charles I
1640	Opening of the Long Parliament
1642–1646	Civil War in England, ending with the capture of King Charles I
1648	Second Civil War
1649	Execution of Charles I of England and the beginning of the Republic
1653	End of the Long Parliament; Oliver Cromwell becomes Protector of England, Scotland, and Ireland
1660	Restoration of the monarchy in the person of Charles II
1685	Death of Charles II and accession of his brother, James II (r. 1685–1688)
1688–1689	Glorious Revolution in England and Scotland
1707	England and Scotland politically joined to form the United Kingdom of Great Britain

JUSTICE IN HISTORY

The Trial of Charles I

In January 1649, after the New Model Army had defeated Royalist forces in England's second civil war and purged Parliament of its Presbyterian members, the few remaining members of the House of Commons voted by a narrow margin to erect a High Court of Justice to try King Charles I. This trial, which resulted in Charles's execution, marked the only time in European history that a monarch was tried and executed while still holding the office of king.

The decision to try the king formed part of a deliberate political strategy. The men who arranged the proceeding knew that they were embarking upon a revolutionary course by declaring that the House of Commons, as the elected representative of the people, was the highest power in the realm. They also knew that the republican regime they were establishing did not command a large body of popular support. By trying the king publicly in a court of law and by ensuring that the trial was reported in daily newspapers (the first such trial in history), they hoped to prove the legitimacy of their cause and win support for the new regime.

The decision to bring the king to justice created two legal problems. The first was to identify a crime upon which the trial would be based. For many years members of Parliament had insisted that the king had violated the ancient laws of the kingdom. The charge read that he had "wickedly designed to erect an unlimited and tyrannical power" and had waged war against his people in two civil wars. His prosecutors claimed that those activities amounted to the crime of treason. The problem was that treason in England was a crime a subject committed against the king, not the king against his subjects. In order to try the king for this crime, his accusers had to construct a new theory of treason, according to which he had attacked his own political body, which they identified with the kingdom or the state.

The second problem was to make the court itself a legitimate tribunal. According to English constitutional law, the king possessed the highest legal authority in the land. He appointed his judges, and the courts represented his authority. Parliament could vote to erect a special court, but the bill authorizing it would become law only if the king agreed to it. In this case the House of Commons had set up the court by its own authority, and it had named 135 men, most of whom were army officers, to serve as its judges. The revolutionary nature of this tribunal was difficult to disguise, and Charles made its illegality the basis of his defense. When asked how he would plead, he refused, demanding to be told by what authority he had been brought into court.

The arguments presented by King Charles and John Bradshawe, the president of the court, regarding the legitimacy of the court reflected the main constitutional conflict in seventeenth-century England. On the one hand was the doctrine of divine-right absolutism, according to which the king received his authority from God. He was therefore responsible to God alone, not the people. His subjects could neither try him in a court of law nor fight him on the battlefield. "A king," said Charles, "cannot be tried by any superior jurisdiction on earth." On the other hand was the doctrine of popular sovereignty, which held that political power came from the people. As Bradshawe said in response to Charles's objection, "Sir, as the law is your superior, so truly Sir, there is something that is superior to the law, and that is indeed the parent or author of law, and that is the people of England." This trial, therefore, involved not only a confrontation between Charles and his revolutionary judges but an encounter between two incompatible political ideologies.

In 1649 the advocates of popular sovereignty triumphed over those of divine right. Charles was convicted as a "tyrant, traitor, murderer, and public enemy of the good people of this nation." The verdict was never in doubt, although only 67 of

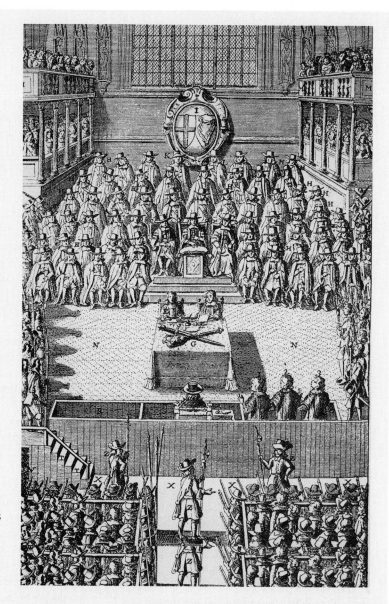

TRIAL OF CHARLES I AT WESTMINSTER HALL, JANUARY 1649

The king is sitting in the prisoner's box in the foreground, facing the commissioners of the High Court of Justice. His refusal to plead meant that a full trial could not take place.

the 135 men originally appointed as judges voted to convict the king, and a mere 59 signed the death warrant. The trial succeeded only to the extent that it facilitated the establishment of the new regime. With Charles gone, the revolutionaries move ahead with the abolition of the monarchy and the establishment of a republic. But in dramatic terms the trial was a complete failure. Charles, a small shy man with a nervous stammer, was expected to make a poor impression, but he spoke eloquently when he refused to plead, and he won support from spectators in the gallery. In the greatest show trial of the seventeenth century, the royal defendant stole the show.

When Charles's son, Charles II, was restored to the throne in 1660, Royalists finally had their revenge against the judges of this court. Those who could be found alive were hanged, disemboweled, and quartered. For those who were already dead, there was to be another type of justice. In 1661 Royalists exhumed the badly decomposed corpses of Bradshawe, Henry Ireton, and Oliver Cromwell, the three men who bore the largest responsibility for the execution of the king. The three cadavers were hanged and their skulls were placed on pikes on top of Westminster Hall. This macabre ritual served as the Royalists' way of vilifying the memory of the judges of this illegal and revolutionary trial, and their unpardonable sin of executing an anointed king.

For Discussion

1. The men who brought King Charles to trial often spoke about bringing him to "justice." How is justice best understood in this context?

2. How does this trial reveal the limitations of divine-right absolutism in England?

Taking It Further

Peacey, Jason (ed). *The Regicides and the Execution of Charles I.* 2001. A collection of essays on various aspects of this episode and the men who signed the death warrant.

Wedgewood, C. V. *The Trial of Charles I.* 1964. Presents a full account and analysis of the trial.

---

government was not creating a godly society, resulted in the army's dissolution of the Long Parliament in 1653 and the selection of a small legislative assembly consisting of zealous Puritans who were nominated by the army. When this "Parliament of the Saints" broke down later that year, Oliver Cromwell (1599–1658), the commander in chief of the army and the most prominent member of the republican government after 1649, assumed the title of Lord Protector. The protectorate, in which Cromwell shared legislative power with Parliament, represented an effort to return to a more traditional form of government. Cromwell however, relied primarily on the army to maintain power, thereby alienating many of the members of the landed class. After Cromwell's death in 1658, renewed tension between the army and Parliament led to a period of political chaos. In 1660 the army and Parliament decided to restore the monarchy by inviting Charles, the son of Charles I, to return from exile. When he returned, not only the monarchy but also the House of Lords and the Church of England were restored. The revolution had officially come to an end.

Later Stuart Absolutism and the Glorious Revolution

Charles II (r. 1660–1685) and his brother James II (r. 1685–1688) were both absolutists who admired the political achievement of their cousin, Louis XIV of France. They realized, however that they could never return to the policies of their father, much less adopt those of Louis. Neither of them attempted to rule indefinitely without Parliament, as Charles I had. Instead they sought to destroy the independence of Parliament by packing it with their own supporters and using the prerogative to weaken the force of the parliamentary statutes to which they objected.

The main political crisis of Charles II's reign was the attempt by a group of members of Parliament, headed by the Earl of Shaftesbury (1621–1683) and known by their opponents as Whigs, to exclude the king's brother, James, from the throne on the grounds that he was a Catholic. Charles opposed this strategy because it violated the theory of hereditary divine right, according to which God sanctioned the right of the king's closest heir to succeed him. Those members of Parliament who supported Charles on this issue, called Tories, thwarted the designs of the Whigs in three successive parliaments between 1679 and 1681.

An even more serious political crisis occurred after James II succeeded to the throne in 1685. James began to exempt his fellow Catholics from the penal laws, which prevented them from worshiping freely, and from the Test Act of 1673, which denied them the right to hold political office. James began appointing Catholics to positions in the army, the central administration, and local government. These efforts to grant toleration and political power to Catholics revived the traditional English fears of absolutism and "popery." Not only the Whigs but also the predominantly Anglican Tories became alarmed at the king's policies. The birth of a Catholic son to James by his second wife, the Italian princess Mary of Modena, in June 1688 created the fear that the king's religious policy might continue indefinitely. A group of seven Whigs and Tories, including the Bishop of London, invited William III of Orange, the captain-general of the military forces of the Dutch Republic and James's nephew, to come to England to defend their Protestant religion and their constitution. William was married to James's eldest daughter, the Protestant Princess Mary, and as the king's nephew he also had a claim to the throne himself.

Invading with an international force of 12,000 men, William gathered substantial support from the English population. When James's army defected, the king was forced to flee to France without engaging William's forces in battle. The Convention, a special parliament convened by William in 1689, offered the crown to William and Mary while at the same time securing their assent to the Declaration of Rights, a document that later became the parliamentary statute known as the Bill of Rights. This bill, which the English consider the cornerstone of their constitution, corrected many of the abuses of royal power at the hands of James and

Charles, especially the practice of exempting individuals from the penalties of the laws made by Parliament. By proclaiming William king and by excluding Catholics from the throne, the Bill of Rights also destroyed the theory of hereditary divine right.

The events of 1688–1689 were decisive in defeating once and for all the absolutist designs of the Stuart kings and in guaranteeing that Parliament would form a permanent and regular place in English government. The Glorious Revolution also prompted the publication of a political manifesto, John Locke's *Two Treatises of Government* (1690). Locke, a radical Whig, had written the *Treatises* in the early 1680s as a protest against the absolutist policies of Charles II, but only after the abdication and flight of James II could he safely publish his manuscript. Like Hobbes, Locke argued that people left the state of nature and agreed to form a political society mainly to protect their property Unlike Hobbes, however, Locke asserted that the people never relinquished their sovereignty and could replace a government that had violated the trust placed in it. Locke's treatises constituted an uncompromising attack on the system of royal absolutism, which he equated with slavery.

We have seen that the success of absolutism in continental European countries led to the expansion of state power. Paradoxically, the defeat of absolutism in England fostered the growth of the English state. As long as Parliament had remained suspicious of the Stuart kings, it had been reluctant to facilitate the growth of the state, which until 1688 was under direct royal control. Once the Glorious Revolution permanently restricted king's power, and Parliament emerged as the highest power within the country, Members of Parliament (MPs) had less to fear from the executive branch of government. The inauguration of a long period of warfare against France in 1689 required the development of a large army and navy, the expansion of the bureaucracy, government borrowing on an unprecedented scale, and an increase in taxes. By

1720 the kingdom of Great Britain, which had been created by the parliamentary union of England and Scotland in 1707, could rival the French state in military power, wealth, and diplomatic prestige.

The Dutch Republic

In many respects the United Provinces of the Netherlands, known as the Dutch Republic, forms the most striking exception to the pattern of state building in seventeenth-century Europe. Formally established in 1588 during its revolt against Spanish rule, the Dutch Republic was the only major European power to maintain a republican form of government throughout the seventeenth century. As a state it also failed to conform to the pattern of centralization and consolidation that became evident in virtually all European monarchies. Having successfully resisted the centralizing policies of a large multinational Spanish monarchy, the Dutch Republic never acquired much of a centralized bureaucracy of its own. The provinces formed little more than a loose confederation of sovereign republican states. Each of the provinces sent deputies to the States General, where unanimity was required on all important issues, such as the levying of taxes, the declaration of war, and the ratification of treaties.

Political power in the Dutch Republic lay mainly with the wealthy merchants and bankers who served as regents in the councils of the towns. The members of this bourgeois elite did not tend to seek admission to landed society in the way that successful English merchants often did. Nor were they lured into becoming part of an ostentatious court in the manner of the French nobility. Immersed in the world of commerce, they remained part of mercantile society and used their political power to guarantee that the Dutch state would serve the interests of trade.

The political prominence of Dutch merchants reflected the commercial character of the Dutch economy. Shortly after its truce with Spain in 1609, the Dutch cities, especially the port city of Amsterdam in Holland, began to dominate European and world trade. The Dutch served as middlemen and shippers for all the other powers of Europe, transporting grain from the Baltic, textiles from England, timber from Scandinavia, wine from Germany, sugar from Brazil and Ceylon, silk from Persia and China, and porcelain from Japan to markets throughout the world. The Dutch even served as middlemen for their archenemy Spain, providing food and manufactured goods to the Spanish colonies in the New World in exchange for silver from the mines of Peru and Mexico. As part of this process Dutch trading companies, such as the Dutch East India Company, began to establish permanent outposts in India, Indonesia, North America, the Caribbean, South America, and South Africa. Thus, a relatively small country with one-tenth the population of France became a colonial power.

To support their dynamic mercantile economy, Dutch cities developed financial institutions and techniques favorable to trade. An Exchange Bank in Amsterdam, which had a monopoly on the exchange of foreign currencies, eased international transactions. A stock market, also situated in Amsterdam, facilitated the buying and selling of shares in commercial ventures. Dutch merchants developed rational and efficient methods of bookkeeping. Even lawyers contributed to the success of Dutch commerce. In *The Freedom of the Sea* (1609), the great legal and political philosopher Hugo Grotius (1583–1645) defended the freedom of merchants to use the open seas for trade and fishing, thereby challenging the claims of European monarchs who wished to exclude foreigners from the waters surrounding their countries. Grotius, who also wrote *The Law of War and Peace* (1625), gained a reputation as the founder of modern international law.

One of the most striking contrasts between the Dutch Republic and the kingdom of France

THE AMSTERDAM STOCK EXCHANGE IN 1668
Known as the Bourse, this multipurpose building served as a gathering point for merchants trading in different parts of the world. The main activity was the buying and selling of shares of stock in trading companies during trading sessions that lasted for two hours each day.

in the seventeenth century lay in the area of religious policy. Whereas in France the revocation of the Edict of Nantes represented the culmination of a policy enforcing religious uniformity and the suppression of Protestant dissent, the predominantly Calvinist Dutch Republic gained a reputation for religious toleration. The Dutch Reformed Church did not always deserve this reputation, but secular authorities, especially in the cities, proved remarkably tolerant of different religious groups. Amsterdam, which attracted a diverse immigrant population during its period of rapid growth, contained a large community of Jews, including the philosopher Baruch Spinoza (1632–1677). The country became the center for religious exiles and political dissidents,

accommodating French Huguenots who fled their country after the repeal of the Edict of Nantes in 1685 as well as English Whigs (including the Earl of Shaftesbury and John Locke) who were being pursued by the Tory government in the 1680s.

This tolerant bourgeois republic also made a distinct contribution to European culture during the seventeenth century, known as its Golden Age. The Dutch cultural achievement was greatest in the area of the visual arts, where Rembrandt van Rijn (1606–1669), Franz Hals (ca. 1580–1666), and Jan Steen (1626–1679) belonged to an astonishing concentration of artistic genius in the cities of Amsterdam, Haarlem, and Leiden. Dutch painting reflected the

REMBRANDT, *SYNDICS OF THE CLOTHMAKERS OF AMSTERDAM* (1662)
Rembrandt's realistic portrait depicted wealthy Dutch bourgeoisie, who had great political as well as economic power in the Dutch Republic.

religious, social, and political climate of this era. The Protestant Reformation had ended the tradition of devotional religious painting that had flourished during the Middle Ages, and the absence of a baroque court culture reduced the demand for royal and aristocratic portraiture and for paintings of heroic classical, mythological, and historical scenes. Instead the Dutch artists of the Golden Age produced intensely realistic portraits of merchants and financiers, such as Rembrandt's famous *Syndics of the Clothmakers of Amsterdam* (1662). Realism became one of the defining features of Dutch painting, evident in the numerous street scenes, still lifes, and landscapes that Dutch artists painted and sold to a largely bourgeois clientele.

In the early eighteenth century the Dutch Republic lost its position of economic superiority to Great Britain and France, which developed even larger mercantile empires of their own and began to dominate world commerce. The long period of war against France, which ended in 1713, took its toll on Dutch manpower and wealth, and the relatively small size of the country and its decentralized institutions made it more difficult for it to recover its position in European diplomacy and warfare. As a state it could no longer fight above its weight, and it became vulnerable to attacks by the French in the nineteenth century and the Germans in the twentieth. But in the seventeenth century this highly urbanized and commercial country showed that a small, decentralized republic could hold its own with the absolutist states of France and Spain as well as with the parliamentary monarchy of England.

CONCLUSION

The Western State in the Age of Absolutism

Between 1600 and 1715 three fundamental political changes helped redefine the West. The first was the dramatic and unprecedented growth of the state. During these years all Western states grew in size and strength. They became more cohesive as they brought the outlying provinces of kingdoms more firmly under central governmental control. The administrative machinery of the state became more complex and efficient. The armies of the state could be called upon at any time to take action against internal rebels and foreign enemies. The income of the state increased as royal officials collected higher taxes, and governments became involved in the promotion of trade and industry and in the regulation of the economy. By the beginning of the eighteenth century one of the most distinctive features of Western civilization was the prevalence of these large, powerful, bureaucratic states. There was nothing like them in the non-Western world.

The second change was the introduction of absolutism into these Western states. With the notable exception of Poland and Hungary, rulers aspired to complete and unrivaled power. These efforts achieved varying degrees of success, and in two states, England and the Dutch Republic, they ended in failure. Nevertheless, during the seventeenth and eighteenth centuries the absolutist state became the main form of government in the West. For this reason historians refer to the period of Western history beginning in the seventeenth century as the age of absolutism.

The third change was the conduct of a new style of warfare by Western absolutist states. The West became the arena where large armies, funded, equipped, and trained by the state, engaged in long, costly, and bloody military campaigns. The conduct of war on this scale threatened to drain the state of its financial resources, destroy its economy, and decimate its civilian and military population. Western powers were not unaware of the dangers of this type of warfare. The development of international law and the attempt to achieve a balance of power among European powers represented efforts to place restrictions on seventeenth-century warfare. These efforts, however, were not completely successful, and in the eighteenth and nineteenth centuries warfare in the West entered a new and even more dangerous phase, aided by the technological innovations that the Scientific and Industrial Revolutions made possible. To the first of those great transformations, the revolution in science, we now turn.

KEY TERMS

absolutism	baroque
divine right	balance of power
Estates General	mercantilism
Cortes	Junkers
diets	balance of power
standing armies	primogeniture
regency	prerogative
parlements	personal rule
intendants	

CHAPTER QUESTIONS

1. What did absolutism mean, both as a political theory and as a practical program, and how was absolutism related to the growth of the power of the state? (page 493)
2. How did France and Spain implement absolutism in the seventeenth century and how powerful did those states become? (page 495)
3. What was the nature of royal absolutism in central and eastern Europe, and how did the policies of the Ottoman Empire and Russia help to establish the boundaries of the West during this period? (page 506)

4. Why did absolutism fail to take root in England and the Dutch Republic during the seventeenth century? (page 516)

TAKING IT FURTHER

1. Absolutist rulers sought unrivalled power, but they frequently encountered resistance. Why were they often unable to achieve the power they desired?
2. The Thirty years' War was a major turning point in German and European history. What impact did it have on the development of absolutist theory and the development of modern states?
3. Many American notions of liberty originated in seventeenth-century England. How did developments in the two English Revolutions of the seventeenth century contribute to the ideology of religious liberty?
4. How would you define the political and cultural boundaries of the West by the beginning of the eighteenth century.

✔•⎯Practice on MyHistoryLab

The Scientific Revolution

■ The Discoveries and Achievements of the Scientific Revolution
■ The Search for Scientific Knowledge   ■ The Causes of the Scientific Revolution
■ The Intellectual Consequences of the Scientific Revolution
■ Humans and the Natural World

IN 1609 GALILEO GALILEI, AN ITALIAN MATHEMATICIAN AT THE UNIVERSITY OF Padua, directed a new scientific instrument, the telescope, toward the heavens. Having heard that a Dutch artisan had put together two lenses in a way that magnified distant objects, Galileo built his own such device. Anyone who has looked through a telescope can appreciate his excitement. Objects that appeared one way to the naked eye looked entirely different when magnified by his new "spyglass," as he called it. The surface of the moon, long believed to be smooth, uniform, and perfectly spherical, now appeared full of mountains and craters. Galileo's spyglass showed that the sun, too, was imperfect, marred by spots that appeared to move across its surface. Such sights challenged traditional science, which assumed that "the heavens," the throne of God, were perfect and thus never changed. Traditional science was shaken even further, when Galileo showed that Venus, viewed over many months, appeared to change its shape, much as the moon did in its phases. This discovery provided evidence for the relatively new theory that the planets, including Earth, revolved around the sun rather than the sun and the planets around the Earth.

Galileo shared the discoveries he made not only with fellow scientists, but also with other educated members of society. He also staged a number of public demonstrations of his new astronomical instrument, the first of which took place on top of one of the city gates of Rome in 1611. To convince those who doubted the reality of the images they saw, Galileo turned the telescope toward familiar landmarks in the city. Interest in the new scientific instrument ran so high that a number of amateur astronomers acquired telescopes of their own.

Galileo's discoveries were part of what historians call the Scientific Revolution. This development changed the way Europeans viewed the natural world, the supernatural realm, and themselves. It led to controversies in religion, philosophy, and politics and changes in military technology, navigation, and business. It also set the West apart from the civilizations of the Middle East, Asia, and Africa and provided a basis for claims of Western superiority over the people in those lands.

The scientific culture that emerged in the West by the end of the seventeenth century was the product of a series of cultural encounters. It resulted from a complex interaction among scholars proposing different ideas of how nature operated. Some of these ideas originated in Greek philosophy. Others came from Christian sources. Still other ideas came from a tradition of late medieval science that had been influenced by the scholarship of the Islamic Middle East.

The main question this chapter seeks to answer is this: How did European scientists in the sixteenth and seventeenth centuries change the way in which people in the West viewed the natural world?

THE TELESCOPE

The telescope was the most important of the new scientific instruments that facilitated discovery. This engraving depicts an astronomer using the telescope in 1647.

THE DISCOVERIES AND ACHIEVEMENTS OF THE SCIENTIFIC REVOLUTION

■ What were the achievements and discoveries of the Scientific Revolution?

Unlike political revolutions, such as the English Revolution of the 1640s discussed in the last chapter, the Scientific Revolution developed gradually over a long period of time. It began in the mid-sixteenth century and continued into the eighteenth century. Even though it took a relatively long time to unfold, it was revolutionary in the sense that it transformed human thought, just as political revolutions have fundamentally changed systems of government. The most important changes in seventeenth-century science took place in astronomy, physics, chemistry, and biology.

Astronomy: A New Model of the Universe

The most significant change in astronomy was the acceptance of the view that the sun, not the Earth, was the center of the universe. Until the mid-sixteenth century, most natural philosophers—as scientists were known at the time—accepted the views of the ancient Greek astronomer Claudius Ptolemy (100–170 C.E.). Ptolemy's observations and calculations supported the cosmology of the Greek philosopher Aristotle (384–322 B.C.E.). According to Ptolemy and Aristotle, the center of the universe was a stationary Earth, around which the moon, the sun, and the other planets revolved in circular orbits. Beyond the planets a large sphere carried the stars, which stood in a fixed relationship to each other, around the Earth from east to west once every 24 hours, thus accounting for the rising and setting of the stars. Each of the four known elements—earth, water, air, and fire—had a natural place within this universe, with the heavy elements, earth and water, being pulled down toward the center of the Earth and the light ones, air and fire, hovering above it. All heavenly

a

b

TWO VIEWS OF THE PTOLEMAIC OR PRE-COPERNICAN UNIVERSE

(a) In this sixteenth-century engraving the Earth lies at the center of the universe and the elements of water, air, and fire are arranged in ascending order above the Earth. The orbit that is shaded in black is the firmament or stellar sphere. The presence of Christ and the saints at the top reflects the view that Heaven lay beyond the stellar sphere. (b) A medieval king representing Atlas holds a Ptolemaic cosmos. The Ptolemaic universe is often referred to as a two-sphere universe: The inner sphere of the Earth lies at the center and the outer sphere encompassing the entire universe rotates around the Earth.

bodies, including the sun and the planets, were composed of a fifth element, called ether, which unlike matter on Earth was thought to be eternal and could not be altered, corrupted, or destroyed.

This traditional view of the cosmos had much to recommend it, and some educated people continued to accept it well into the eighteenth century. The Bible, which in a few passages referred to the motion of the sun, reinforced the authority of Aristotle. And human observation seemed to confirm the motion of the sun. We do, after all, see the sun "rise" and "set" every day, so the idea that the Earth rotates at high speed and revolves around the sun contradicts the experience of our senses. Nevertheless, the Earth-centered model of the universe failed to explain many patterns that astronomers observed in the sky, most notably the paths followed by planets. Whenever ancient or medieval astronomers confronted a new problem as a result of their observations, they tried to accommodate the results to the Ptolemaic model. By the sixteenth century this model had been

modified or adjusted so many times that it had gradually become a confused collection of planets and stars following different motions.

Faced with this situation, a Polish cleric, Nicolaus Copernicus (1473–1543), looked for a simpler and more plausible model of the universe. In *The Revolutions of the Heavenly Spheres*, which was published shortly after his death, Copernicus proposed that the center of the universe was not the Earth but the sun. The book was widely circulated, but it did not win much support for the sun-centered theory of the universe. Only the most learned astronomers could understand Copernicus' mathematical arguments, and even they were not prepared to adopt his central thesis. In the late sixteenth century the great Danish astronomer Tycho Brahe (1546–1601) accepted the argument of Copernicus that the planets revolved around the sun but still insisted that the sun revolved around the Earth.

Significant support for the Copernican model of the universe among scientists began to

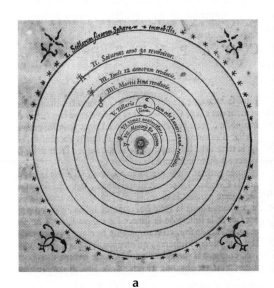

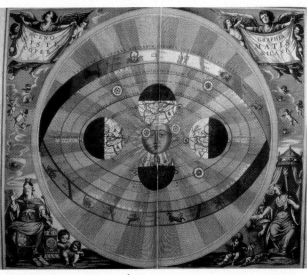

a   b

TWO EARLY MODERN VIEWS OF THE SUN-CENTERED UNIVERSE

(a) The depiction by Copernicus. Note that all the orbits are circular, rather than elliptical, as Kepler was to show they were. The outermost sphere is that of the fixed stars. (b) A late-seventeenth-century depiction of the cosmos by Andreas Cellarius in which the planets follow elliptical orbits. It illustrates four different positions of the Earth as it orbits the sun.

materialize only in the seventeenth century. In 1609 a German astronomer, Johannes Kepler (1571–1630), using data that Brahe had collected, confirmed the central position of the sun in the universe. In *New Astronomy* (1609) Kepler also demonstrated that the planets, including the Earth, followed elliptical rather than circular orbits and that physical laws governed their movements. Not many people read Kepler's book, however, and his achievement was not fully appreciated until many decades later.

Galileo Galilei (1564–1642) was far more successful in gaining support for the sun-centered model of the universe. Galileo had the literary skill, which Kepler lacked, of being able to write for a broad audience. Using the evidence gained from his observations with the telescope, and presenting his views in the form of a dialogue between the advocates of the two competing worldviews, Galileo demonstrated the plausibility and superiority of Copernicus's theory.

The publication of Galileo's *Dialogue Concerning the Two Chief World Systems— Ptolemaic and Copernican* in 1632 won many converts to the sun-centered theory of the universe, but it lost him the support of Pope Urban VIII, who had been one of his patrons. The character in *Dialogue* who defends the Ptolemaic system is named Simplicio (that is, a simple—or stupid—person). Urban wrongly concluded that Galileo was mocking him. In 1633 Galileo was tried before the Roman Inquisition, an ecclesiastical court whose purpose was to maintain theological orthodoxy. The charge against him was that he had challenged the authority of Scripture and was therefore guilty of heresy, the denial of the theological truths of the Roman Catholic Church. (See *Justice in History* in this chapter.)

As a result of this trial, Galileo was forced to abandon his support for the Copernican model of the universe, and *Dialogue* was placed on the Index of Prohibited Books, a list compiled by the papacy of all printed works containing heretical ideas. Despite this setback, by 1700 Copernicanism commanded widespread support among scientists and the educated public. *Dialogue*, however, was not removed from the Index until 1822.

Physics: The Laws of Motion and Gravitation

Galileo made his most significant contributions to the Scientific Revolution in physics. In the seventeenth century the main branches of physics were mechanics (the study of motion and its causes) and optics (the study of light). Galileo formulated a set of laws governing the motion of material objects that challenged the accepted theories of Aristotle regarding motion and laid the foundation of modern physics.

According to Aristotle, whose views dominated science in the late Middle Ages, the motion of every object—except the natural motion of falling toward the center of the Earth—required another object to move it. If the mover stopped, the object fell to the ground or simply stopped moving. But this theory could not explain why a projectile, such as a discus or a spear, continued to move after a person threw it. Galileo's answer to that question was a theory of inertia, which became the basis of a new theory of motion. According to Galileo, an object continues to move or lie at rest until something external to it intervenes to change its motion. Thus, motion is neither a quality inherent in an object nor a force that it acquires from another object. It is simply a state in which the object finds itself.

Galileo also discovered that the motion of an object occurs only in relation to things that do not move. A ship moves through the water, for example, but the goods that the ship carries do not move in relationship to the moving ship. This insight explained to the critics of Copernicus how the Earth can move even though we do not experience its motion. Galileo's most significant contribution to mechanics was his formulation of a mathematical law of motion that explained how the speed and acceleration of a falling object are determined by the distance it travels during equal intervals of time.

The greatest achievements of the Scientific Revolution in physics belong to English scientist Sir Isaac Newton (1642–1727). His research changed the way future generations viewed the world. As a boy Newton felt out of place in his small village, where he worked on his mother's farm and attended school. Fascinated by mechanical devices, he spent much of his time building wooden models of windmills and other machines. When playing with his friends he always found ways to exercise his mind, calculating, for example, how he could use the wind to win jumping contests. It became obvious to all who knew him that Newton belonged at a university. In 1661 he entered Cambridge University, where, at age 27, he became a chaired professor of mathematics.

Newton formulated a set of mathematical laws to explain the operation of the entire physical world. In 1687 he published his theories in *Mathematical Principles of Natural Philosophy*. The centerpiece of this monumental work was the **universal law of gravitation,** which demonstrated that the same force holding an object to the Earth also holds the planets in their orbits. This law represented a synthesis of the work of other scientists, including Kepler on planetary motion and Galileo on inertia. Newton paid tribute to the work of these men when he said, "If I have seen farther, it is by standing on the shoulders of giants." But Newton went further than any of them by establishing the existence of a single gravitational force and by giving

SIR ISAAC NEWTON

This portrait was painted by Sir Godfrey Kneller in 1689, two years after the publication of *Mathematical Principles of Natural Philosophy.*

it precise mathematical expression. His book revealed the unity and order of the entire physical world and thus offered a scientific model to replace that of Aristotle.

CHRONOLOGY: DISCOVERIES OF THE SCIENTIFIC REVOLUTION

1543	Copernicus publishes *The Revolutions of the Heavenly Spheres*
1609	Johannes Kepler publishes *New Astronomy*
1628	William Harvey publishes *On the Motion of the Heart and Blood in Animals*
1632	Galileo publishes *Dialogue Concerning the Two Chief World Systems*
1638	Galileo publishes *Discourses on the Two New Sciences of Motion and Mechanics*
1659	Robert Boyle invents the air pump and conducts experiments on the elasticity and compressibility of air
1687	Newton publishes *Mathematical Principles of Natural Philosophy*

Chemistry: Discovering the Elements of Nature

At the beginning of the seventeenth century, the science today called chemistry was considered part of either medicine or **alchemy,** the magical art of attempting to turn base metals into gold or silver. The most famous chemist of the sixteenth century was the Swiss physician Paracelsus (1493–1541), who rejected the theory advanced by the ancient Greek physician Galen (129–200 C.E.) that an imbalance of the four "humors" or fluids in the body—blood, phlegm, black bile, and yellow bile—caused diseases. The medical practice of drawing blood from sick patients to cure them by correcting this alleged imbalance was based on Galen's theory. Instead, to cure certain diseases, Paracelsus began to treat his patients with chemicals, such as mercury and sulfur. Paracelsus is often dismissed for his belief in alchemy, but his prescription of chemicals helped give chemistry a respectable place within medical science.

During the seventeenth century chemistry became a legitimate field of scientific research, largely as the result of the work of Robert Boyle (1627–1691). Boyle destroyed the prevailing idea that all basic constituents of matter share the same structure. He contended that the arrangement of their components, which he identified as corpuscles or atoms, determined their characteristics. He also conducted experiments on the volume, pressure, and density of gas and the elasticity of air. Boyle's most famous experiments, undertaken with an air pump, proved the existence of a vacuum. Largely as a result of Boyle's discoveries, chemists won acceptance as legitimate members of the company of scientists.

Biology: The Circulation of the Blood

The English physician William Harvey (1578–1657) made one of the great medical discoveries of the seventeenth century by demonstrating in 1628 that blood circulates throughout the human body. Traditional science had maintained that blood originated in the liver and then flowed outward through the veins. A certain amount of blood

PORTRAIT OF ROBERT BOYLE WITH HIS AIR PUMP IN THE BACKGROUND (1664)

Boyle's pump became the center of a series of experiments carried on at the Royal Society in London.

flowed from the liver into the heart, where it passed from one ventricle to the other and then traveled through the arteries to different parts of the body. During its journey this arterial blood was enriched by a special *pneuma* or "vital spirit" that was necessary to sustain life. When this enriched blood reached the brain, it became the body's "psychic spirits," which influenced human behavior.

Through experiments on human cadavers and live animals in which he weighed the blood that the heart pumped every hour, Harvey demonstrated that rather than sucking in blood, the heart pumped it through the arteries by means of contraction and constriction. The only gap in his theory was the question of how blood went from the ends of the arteries to the ends of the veins. This question was answered in 1661, when scientists, using a new instrument known as a microscope, could see the capillaries connecting the veins and arteries. Harvey, however, had set the standard for future biological research.

THE SEARCH FOR SCIENTIFIC KNOWLEDGE

- What methods did scientists use during this period to investigate nature, and how did they think nature operated?

The natural philosophers who made these scientific discoveries worked in different disciplines, and each followed his own procedures for discovering scientific truth. In the sixteenth and seventeenth centuries there was no "scientific method." Many natural philosophers, however, shared similar views about how nature operated and the means by which humans could acquire knowledge of it. In searching for scientific knowledge, these scientists observed and experimented, used deductive reasoning, expressed their theories in mathematical terms, and argued that nature operated like a machine. These features of scientific research ultimately defined a distinctly Western approach to solving scientific problems.

Observation and Experimentation

The most prominent feature of scientific research in sixteenth- and seventeenth-century Europe was the observation of nature, combined with the testing of hypotheses by rigorous experimentation. This was primarily a process of **induction,** in which theories emerged only after the accumulation and analysis of data. It assumed a willingness to abandon preconceived ideas and base scientific conclusions on experience and observation. This approach is also described as empirical: **empiricism** demands that all scientific theories be tested by experiments based on observation of the natural world.

In *New Organon* (1620), the English philosopher Francis Bacon (1561–1626) promoted this

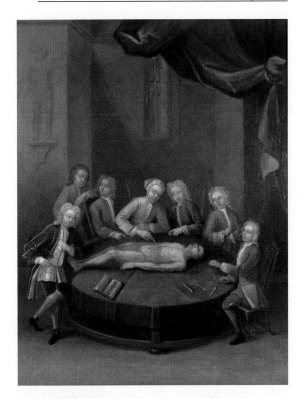

DISSECTION

The English surgeon William Cheselden giving an anatomical demonstration to spectators in London around 1735. As medical science developed in the sixteenth and seventeenth centuries, the dissection of human corpses became a standard practice in European universities and medical schools. Knowledge of the structure and composition of the human body, which was central to the advancement of physiology, could best be acquired by cutting open a corpse to reveal the organs, muscles, and bones of human beings. The practice reflected the emphasis scientists placed on observation and experimentation in conducting scientific research.

empirical approach to scientific research. Bacon complained that all previous scientific endeavors, especially those of ancient Greek philosophers, relied too little on experimentation. In contrast, his approach involved the thorough and systematic investigation of nature, a process that Bacon, who was a lawyer and judge, compared to the interrogation of a person suspected of committing a crime. For Bacon, scientific experimentation was "putting nature to the question," a phrase that referred to questioning a prisoner under torture to determine the facts of a case.

Deductive Reasoning

The second feature of sixteenth- and seventeenth-century scientific research was the use of **deductive reasoning** to establish basic scientific truths or principles. From these principles other ideas or laws could be deduced logically. Just as induction is linked to empiricism, so deduction is connected to **rationalism.** Unlike empiricism—the idea that we know truth through what the senses can experience—rationalism insists that the mind contains rational categories independent of sensory observation.

Unlike the inductive experimental approach, which found its most enthusiastic practitioners in England, the deductive approach had its most zealous advocates on the European continent. The French philosopher and mathematician René Descartes (1596–1650) became the foremost champion of this methodology. In his *Discourse on the Method* (1637), Descartes recommended that to solve any intellectual problem, a person should first establish fundamental principles or truths and then proceed from those ideas to specific conclusions.

Mathematics, in which one also moves logically from certain premises to conclusions by means of equations, provided the model for deductive reasoning. Although rational deduction proved to be an essential feature of scientific methodology, the limitations of an exclusively deductive approach became apparent when Descartes and his followers deduced a theory of gravitation from the principle that objects could influence each other only if they actually touched. This theory, as well as the principle upon which it was based, lacked an empirical foundation and eventually had to be abandoned.

Mathematics and Nature

The third feature of scientific research in the sixteenth and seventeenth centuries was the application of mathematics to the study of the physical world. Scientists working in both the inductive and the deductive traditions used mathematics. Descartes shared with Galileo the conviction that nature had a geometrical structure and could therefore be understood in mathematical terms. The physical dimensions of matter, which Descartes claimed were its only properties, could of course be expressed mathematically. Galileo claimed that mathematics was the language in which philosophy was written in "the book of the universe."

Isaac Newton's work provided the best illustration of the application of mathematics to scientific problems. Newton used observation and experimentation to confirm his theory of universal gravitation, but he wrote his *Mathematical Principles of Natural Philosophy* in the language of mathematics. His approach to scientific problems, which became a model for future research, used examples derived from experiments and deductive, mathematical reasoning to discover the laws of nature.

The Mechanical Philosophy

Much of seventeenth-century scientific experimentation and deduction assumed that the natural world operated as if it were a machine made by a human being. This **mechanical philosophy** of nature appeared most clearly in the work of Descartes. Medieval philosophers had argued that natural bodies had an innate tendency to change, whereas artificial objects, that is, those constructed by humans, did not. Descartes, as well as Kepler, Galileo, and Bacon, denied that assumption. Mechanists argued that nature operated in a mechanical way, just like a piece of machinery. The only difference was that the operating structures of natural mechanisms could not be observed as readily as the structures of a machine.

Mechanists perceived the human body itself as a machine. Harvey, for example, described the heart as "a piece of machinery in which, though one wheel gives motion to another, yet all the wheels seem to move simultaneously." The only difference between the body and other machines was that the mind could move the body, although how it did so was controversial. According to Descartes, the mind was completely different from the body and the rest of the material world. Unlike the body, the mind was an immaterial substance that could be not be extended in space, divided, or measured mathematically, the way one could record the dimensions of the body. Because Descartes made this sharp distinction between the mind and the body, we describe his philosophy as **dualistic.**

Descartes and other mechanists argued that matter was completely inert or dead. It did not possess a soul or any innate purpose. Its only property was "extension," or the physical dimensions of length, width, and depth. Without a spirit or any other internal force directing its action, matter simply responded to the power of the other bodies with which it came in contact. According to Descartes, all physical phenomena could be explained by reference to the dimensions and the movement of particles of matter. He once claimed, "Give me extension and motion and I will construct the universe."[1]

The view of nature as a machine implied that it operated in a regular, predictable way in accordance with unchanging laws of nature. Scientists could use reason to discover what those laws were and thus learn how nature performed under any circumstances. The scientific investigations of Galileo and Kepler were based on those assumptions, and Descartes made them explicit. The immutability of the laws of nature implied that the entire universe was uniform in structure, an assumption that underlay Newton's formulation of the laws of motion and universal gravitation.

THE CAUSES OF THE SCIENTIFIC REVOLUTION

■ Why did the Scientific Revolution take place in western Europe at this time?

Why did the Scientific Revolution take place at this particular time, and why did it originate in western European countries? There is no simple

answer to this question. We can, however, identify developments that inspired these scientific discoveries. Some of these developments arose out of earlier investigations conducted by natural philosophers in the late Middle Ages, the Renaissance, and the sixteenth century. Others emerged from the religious, political, social, and economic life of early modern Europe.

Developments Within Science

The three internal causes of the Scientific Revolution were the research into motion conducted by natural philosophers in the fourteenth century, the scientific investigations conducted by Renaissance humanists, and the collapse of the dominant conceptual frameworks, or paradigms, that had governed scientific inquiry and research for centuries.

LATE MEDIEVAL SCIENCE Modern science can trace some of its origins to the fourteenth century, when the first significant modifications of Aristotle's scientific theories began to emerge. The most significant of these refinements was the theory of impetus. Aristotle had argued that an object would stop as soon as it lost contact with the object that moved it. Late medieval scientists claimed that objects in motion acquire a force that stays with them after they lose contact with the mover. This theory of impetus questioned Aristotle's authority, and it influenced some of Galileo's early thought on motion.

Natural philosophers of the fourteenth century also began to recommend direct, empirical observation in place of the traditional tendency to accept preconceived notions regarding the operation of nature. This approach to answering scientific questions did not result in the type of rigorous experimentation that Bacon demanded three centuries later, but it did encourage scientists to base their theories on the facts that emerged from an empirical study of nature.

The contribution of late medieval science to the Scientific Revolution should not be exaggerated. Philosophers of the fourteenth century continued to accept Ptolemy's cosmology and Galen's anatomical theories. The unchallenged position of theology as the dominant subject in late medieval universities also guaranteed that new scientific ideas would receive little favor if they challenged Christian doctrine.

RENAISSANCE SCIENCE Natural philosophers during the Renaissance contributed more than their late medieval predecessors to the rise of modern science. Many of the scientific discoveries of the late sixteenth and seventeenth centuries drew their inspiration from Greek scientific works that had been rediscovered during the Renaissance. Copernicus, for example, found the idea of his sun-centered universe in the writings of Aristarchus of Samos, a Greek astronomer of the third century B.C.E. whose work had been unknown during the Middle Ages. Similarly, the works of the ancient Greek philosopher Democritus in the late fifth century B.C.E. introduced the idea, developed by Boyle and others in the seventeenth century, that matter was divisible into small particles known as atoms. The works of Archimedes (287–212 B.C.E.), which had been virtually unknown in the Middle Ages, stimulated interest in the science of mechanics. The recovery and translation of previously unknown texts also made scientists aware that Greek scientists did not always agree with each other and thus provided a stimulus to independent observation and experimentation as a means of resolving their differences.

Renaissance revival of the philosophy of **Neoplatonism** (see Chapter 7) made an even more direct contribution to the birth of modern science. While most medieval natural philosophers relied on the ideas of Aristotle, Neoplatonists drew on the work of Plotinus (205–270 C.E.), the last great philosopher of antiquity who synthesized the work of Plato, other ancient Greek philosophers, and Persian religious traditions. Neoplatonists stressed the unity of the natural and spiritual worlds. Matter is alive, linked to the divine soul that governs the entire universe. To unlock the mysteries of this living world, Neoplatonists turned to mathematics, because they believed the divine expressed itself in geometrical harmony, and to alchemy, because they sought to

uncover the shared essence that linked all creation. They also believed that the sun, as a symbol of the divine soul, logically stood at the center of the universe.

Neoplatonic ideas influenced seventeenth-century scientists. Copernicus, for example, took from Neoplatonism his idea of the sun sitting at the center of the universe, as "on a royal throne ruling his children, the planets which circle around him." From his reading in Neoplatonic sources Kepler acquired his belief that the universe was constructed according to geometric principles. Newton was fascinated by the subject of alchemy, and the original inspiration of his theory of gravitation probably came from his Neoplatonist professor at Cambridge, who insisted on the presence of spiritual forces in the physical world. Modern science resulted from an encounter between the mechanical philosophy, which held that matter was inert, and Neoplatonism, which claimed that the natural world was alive.

THE COLLAPSE OF PARADIGMS The third internal cause of the Scientific Revolution was the collapse of the intellectual frameworks that had governed scientific research since antiquity. In all historical periods scientists prefer to work within an established conceptual framework, or what the scholar Thomas Kuhn has referred to as a **paradigm,** rather than introduce new theories. Every so often, however, the paradigm that has governed scientific research for an extended period of time can no longer account for many different observable phenomena. A scientific revolution occurs when the old paradigm collapses and a new paradigm replaces it.[2]

The revolutionary developments we have discussed in astronomy and biology were partly the result of the collapse of old paradigms. In astronomy the paradigm that had governed scientific inquiry in antiquity and the Middle Ages was the Ptolemaic model, in which the sun and the planets revolved around the Earth. By the sixteenth century, however, new observations had so confused and complicated this model that, to men like Copernicus, it no longer provided a satisfactory explanation for the material universe. Copernicus looked for a simpler and more plausible model of the universe. His sun-centered theory became the new paradigm within which Kepler, Galileo, and Newton all worked.

In biology a parallel development occurred when the old paradigm constructed by Galen, in which the blood originated in the liver and traveled from the heart through the arteries, also collapsed because it could not explain the findings of medical scholars. Harvey introduced a new paradigm, in which the blood circulated through the body. As in astronomy, Harvey's new paradigm served as a framework for subsequent biological research and helped shape the Scientific Revolution.

Developments Outside Science

Nonscientific developments also encouraged the development and acceptance of new scientific ideas. These developments include the spread of Protestantism, the patronage of scientific research, the invention of the printing press, and military and economic change.

PROTESTANTISM Protestantism played a limited role in causing the Scientific Revolution. In the early years of the Reformation, Protestants were just as hostile as Catholics to the new science. Reflecting the Protestant belief in the literal truth of the Bible, Luther referred to Copernicus as "a fool who went against Holy Writ." Throughout the sixteenth and seventeenth centuries, moreover, Catholics as well as Protestants engaged in scientific research. Indeed, some of the most prominent European natural philosophers, including Galileo and Descartes, were devout Catholics. Nonetheless, Protestantism encouraged the emergence of modern science in three ways.

First, as the scientific revolution gained steam in the seventeenth century, Protestant governments were more willing than Catholic authorities to allow the publication and dissemination of new scientific ideas. Protestant governments, for example, did not prohibit the publication of books that promoted novel scientific ideas on the grounds

that they were heretical, as the papacy did in compiling the Index of Prohibited Books. The greater willingness of Protestant governments, especially those of England and the Dutch Republic, to tolerate the expression of new scientific ideas helps to explain why the main geographical arena of scientific investigation shifted from the Catholic Mediterranean to the Protestant North Atlantic in the second half of the seventeenth century. (See *Different Voices* in this chapter.)

Second, seventeenth-century Protestant writers emphasized the idea that God revealed his intentions not only in the Bible, but also in nature itself. They claimed that individuals therefore had a duty to study nature, just as it was their duty to read Scripture to gain knowledge of God's will. Kepler's claim that the astronomer was "as a priest of God to the book of nature" reflected this Protestant outlook.

Third, many seventeenth-century Protestant scientists believed that the millennium, a period of one thousand years when Christ would come again and rule the world, was about to begin. Millenarians believed that during this period knowledge would increase, society would improve, and humans would gain control over nature. Protestant scientists, including Boyle and Newton, conducted their research and experiments believing that their work would contribute to this improvement of human life after the Second Coming of Christ.

PATRONAGE Scientists could not have succeeded without financial and institutional support. Only an organizational structure could give science a permanent status, let it develop as a discipline, and give its members a professional identity. The universities, which today support scientific research, were not the main source of that support in the seventeenth century. They remained predominantly clerical institutions with a vested interest in defending the medieval fusion of Christian theology and Aristotelian science. Instead of the universities, scientists depended on the patronage of wealthy and influential individuals, especially the kings, princes, and great nobles who ruled European states.

DIFFERENT VOICES COPERNICUS AND THE PAPACY

In dedicating his book, On the Revolution of the Heavenly Spheres *(1543), to Pope Paul II (r. 1464–1471), Copernicus explained that he drew inspiration from ancient philosophers who had imagined that the Earth moved. Anticipating condemnation from those who based their astronomical theories on the Bible, he appealed to the pope for protection while showing contempt for the theories of his opponents. Paul II neither endorsed nor condemned Copernicus's work, but in 1616, the papacy suspended the book's publication because it contradicted Scripture.*

Copernicus on Heliocentrism and the Bible

...I began to chafe that philosophers could by no means agree on any one certain theory of the mechanism of the Universe, wrought for us by a supremely good and orderly Creator...I therefore took pains to read again the works of all the philosophers on whom I could lay my hand to seek out whether any of them had ever supposed that the motions of the spheres were other than those demanded by the mathematical schools. I found first in Cicero that Hicetas had realized that the Earth moved. Afterwards I found in Plutarch that certain others had held the like opinion....

Taking advantage of this I too began to think of the mobility of the Earth; and though the opinion seemed absurd, yet knowing now that others before me had been granted freedom to imagine such circles as they chose to explain the phenomena of the stars, I considered that I also might easily be allowed to try whether, by assuming some motion of the Earth, sounder explanations than theirs for the revolution of the celestial spheres might so be discovered.

Thus assuming motions, which in my work I ascribe to the Earth, by long and frequent observations I have at last discovered that, if the motions of the rest of the planets be brought into relation with the circulation of the Earth and be reckoned in proportion to the circles of each planet...the orders and magnitudes of all stars and spheres, nay the heavens themselves, become so bound together that nothing in any part thereof could be moved from its place without producing confusion of all the other parts and of the Universe as a whole....

It may fall out, too, that idle babblers, ignorant of mathematics, may claim a right to pronounce a judgment on my work, by reason of a certain passage of Scripture basely twisted to serve their purpose. Should any such venture to criticize and carp at my project, I make no account of them; I consider their judgment rash, and utterly despise it.

This group included Pope Urban VIII, ruler of the Papal States.

Patronage, however, could easily be withdrawn. Scientists had to conduct themselves and their research to maintain the favor of their patrons. Galileo referred to the new moons of Jupiter that he observed through his telescope as the Medicean stars to flatter the Medici family that ruled

CHRONOLOGY: THE FORMATION OF SCIENTIFIC SOCIETIES

1603	Prince Cesi founds the Academy of the Lynx-Eyed in Rome
1657	Cosimo II de' Medici founds the Academy of Experiment in Florence
1662	Founding of the Royal Society of London under the auspices of Charles II
1666	Founding of the Academy of Sciences in Paris

Source: From Nicolaus Copernicus, *De Revolutionibus Orbium Coelestium* (1543), trans. by John F. Dobson and Selig Brodetsky in *Occasional Notes of the Royal Astronomical Society*, 2(10), 1947. Reprinted by permission of Blackwell Publishing.

Papal Decree against Heliocentrism, 1616

Decree of the Holy Congregation of his Most Illustrious Lord Cardinals especially charged by His Holiness Pope Paul V and by the Holy Apostolic See with the index of books and their licensing, prohibition, correction and printing in all of Christendom....

This Holy Congregation has also learned about the spreading and acceptance by many of the false Pythagorean doctrine, altogether contrary to the Holy Scripture, that the earth moves and the sun is motionless, which is also taught by Nicholaus Copernicus's *On the Revolutions of the Heavenly Spheres* and by Diego de Zuñiga's *On Job*. This may be seen from a certain letter published by a certain Carmelite Father, whose title is *Letter of the Reverend Father Paolo Antonio Foscarini on the Pythagorean and Copernican Opinion of the Earth's Motion and Sun's Rest and on the New Pythagorean World System*...in which the said Father tries to show that the above mentioned doctrine of the sun's rest at the center of the world and the earth's motion is consonant with the truth and does not contradict Holy Scripture. Therefore, in order that this opinion may

not creep any further to the prejudice of Catholic truth, the Congregation has decided that the books by Nicholaus Copernicus (*On the Revolution of Spheres*) and Diego de Zuniga (*On Job*) be suspended until corrected; but that the book of the Carmelite Father Paolo Antonini Foscarini be completely prohibited and condemned; and that all other books which teach the same be likewise prohibited, according to whether with the present decree it prohibits condemns and suspends them respectively. In witness thereof this decree has been signed by the hand and stamped with the seal of the Most Illustrious and reverend Lord cardinal of St. Cecilia. Bishop of Albano, on March 5, 1616.

Source: From *The Galileo Affair: A Documentary History*, ed. and trans. by Maurice A. Finocchairo, copyright © 1989 by The Regents of the University of California, is reprinted by permission of the University of Calfornia Press.

For Discussion

1. Why did the papal authorities prohibit and condemn the work by Antonini Foscarini but only suspend those of Copernicus and Diego de Zuñia?
2. How did Copernicus and the papal authorities differ about classical antiquity and the truth of Holy Scripture?

Florence. His publications were inspired as much by his obligation to glorify Grand Duke Cosimo II as by his belief in the sun-centered theory.

Academies in which groups of scientists could share ideas and work served as a second important source of patronage. One of the earliest of these institutions was the Academy of the Lynx-Eyed in Rome, named after the animal whose sharp vision symbolized the power of observation required by the new science. Founded in 1603 by Prince Cesi, the Academy published many of Galileo's works. In 1657 Cosimo II founded a similar institution in

Florence, the Academy of Experiment. These academies offered a more regular source of patronage than scientists could acquire from individual positions at court, but they still served the function of glorifying their founders, and they depended on patrons for their continued existence. The royal academies established in the 1660s, however, especially the Royal Academy of Sciences in France and the Royal Society in England (1662), became in effect public institutions that operated with a minimum of royal intervention and made possible a continuous program of work.

THE FOUNDING OF THE FRENCH ACADÈMIE DES SCIENCES

Like the Royal Society in England, the French Academy of Sciences was dependent upon royal patronage. Louis XIV, seen sitting in the middle of the painting, used the occasion to glorify himself as a patron of the sciences as well as the arts. The painting also commemorates the building of the Royal Observatory in Paris, which is shown in the background.

the authors supplied. Illustrations, diagrams, tables, and other schematic drawings that helped to convey the author's findings could also be printed. The entire body of scientific knowledge thus became cumulative. Printing also made members of the nonscientific community aware of the latest advances in physics and astronomy and so helped to make science an integral part of the culture of educated Europeans.

The mission of the Royal Society in England was the promotion of scientific knowledge through experimentation. It also placed the results of scientific research at the service of the state. Members of the Royal Society, for example, did research on ship construction and military technology. These attempts to use scientific technology to strengthen the power of the state show how the growth of the modern state and the emergence of modern science were related.

THE PRINTING PRESS   Printing made it much easier for scientists to share their discoveries with others. During the Middle Ages, books were handwritten. Errors could creep into the text as it was being copied, and the number of copies that could be made of a manuscript limited the spread of scientific knowledge. The spread of printing ensured that scientific achievements could be preserved more accurately and presented to a broader audience. The availability of printed copies also made it much easier for other scientists to correct or supplement the data that

MILITARY AND ECONOMIC CHANGE
The Scientific Revolution occurred at roughly the same time that both the conduct of warfare and the European economy were undergoing dramatic changes. As territorial states increased the size of their armies and arsenals, they demanded more accurate weapons with longer range. Some of the work that physicists did during the seventeenth century was deliberately meant to improve weaponry. Members of the Royal Society in England, for example, conducted extensive scientific research on the trajectory and velocity of missiles, and so followed Francis Bacon's recommendation that scientists place their research at the service of the state.

The needs of the emerging capitalist economy also influenced scientific research. The study of mechanics, for example, led to new techniques to ventilate mines and raise coal or ore from them, thus making mining more profitable. Some of the questions discussed at the meetings of the Royal Society suggest that its members undertook research to make capitalist ventures more productive and profitable. The research did not always produce immediate results, but ultimately it increased economic profitability and contributed to the English economy in the eighteenth century.

THE INTELLECTUAL CONSEQUENCES OF THE SCIENTIFIC REVOLUTION

■ How did the Scientific Revolution influence philosophical and religious thought in the seventeenth and early eighteenth centuries?

The Scientific Revolution profoundly affected the intellectual life of educated Europeans. The discoveries of Copernicus, Kepler, Galileo, and Newton, as well as the assumptions on which their work was based, influenced what educated people in the West studied, how they approached intellectual problems, and what they thought about the supernatural realm.

Education

During the seventeenth and early eighteenth centuries, especially between 1680 and 1720, science and the new philosophy that was associated with it became an important part of university education. Outside academia, learned societies, public lectures, discussions in coffeehouses, and popular scientific publications spread the knowledge of science among the educated members of society. In this way science secured a permanent foothold in Western culture.

The spread of science did not go unchallenged. It encountered academic rivals committed not only to traditional Aristotelianism but also to Renaissance humanism. In the late seventeenth century, a conflict arose between "the ancients," who revered the wisdom of classical authors, and "the moderns," who emphasized the superiority of the new scientific culture. The most concrete expression of this conflict was the Battle of the Books, an intellectual debate that raged over the question of which group of thinkers had contributed more to human knowledge. No clear winner in this battle emerged, and the conflict between the ancients and the moderns was never completely resolved. The humanities and the sciences, while included within the same curriculum at many universities, are still often regarded as representing separate cultural traditions.

Skepticism and Independent Reasoning

The Scientific Revolution encouraged the habit of **skepticism,** the tendency to doubt what we have been taught and are expected to believe. This skepticism formed part of the method that seventeenth-century scientists adopted to solve philosophical problems. As we have seen, Descartes, Bacon, Galileo, and Kepler all refused to acknowledge the authority of classical or medieval texts. They preferred to rely upon the knowledge they acquired from observing nature and using their own rational faculties.

In *Discourse on the Method,* Descartes showed the extremes to which this skepticism could be taken. Descartes doubted the reality of his own sense perceptions and even his own existence until he realized that the very act of doubting proved his existence as a thinking being. As he wrote in words that have become famous, "I think, therefore I am."[3] Upon this foundation Descartes went on to prove the existence of God and the material world, thereby conquering the skepticism with which he began his inquiry. In the

CHRONOLOGY: THE IMPACT OF THE SCIENTIFIC REVOLUTION

1620	Francis Bacon argues for the necessity of rigorous experimentation
1633	Galileo tried by the Roman Inquisition
1637	René Descartes publishes *Discourse on the Method*
1670	Baruch Spinoza publishes *Treatise on Religion and Political Philosophy,* challenging the distinction between spirit and matter
1686	Bernard de Fontenelle publishes *Treatises on the Plurality of Worlds*

process, however, he developed an approach to solving intellectual problems that asked people to question authority and think clearly and systematically for themselves. The effects of this method became apparent in the late seventeenth century, when skeptics invoked Descartes' methodology to challenge both orthodox Judaism and Christianity. Some of the most radical of those opinions came from Baruch Spinoza (1632–1677), who grew up in Amsterdam in a community of Spanish and Portuguese Jews who had fled the Inquisition. Although educated as an Orthodox Jew, Spinoza also studied Latin and read Descartes and other Christian writers. From Descartes, Spinoza learned "that nothing ought to be admitted as true but what has been proved by good and solid

BARUCH SPINOZA

Spinoza was one of the most radical thinkers of the seventeenth century. His identification of God with nature made him vulnerable to charges of atheism. His followers in the Dutch Republic, who were known as freethinkers, laid the foundations for the Enlightenment in the eighteenth century.

reason." This skepticism and independence of thought led to his excommunication from the Jewish community at age 24.

Spinoza used Descartes' skepticism to challenge Descartes himself. He rejected Descartes' separation of the mind and the body and his radical distinction between the spiritual and the material. For Spinoza there was only one substance in the universe, which he identified with both God and nature. The claim that God and nature were two names for the same reality challenged not only the ideas of Descartes, but also the fundamental tenets of Christianity, including the belief in a personal God who had created the natural world by design and continued to govern it. In *A Treatise on Religion and Political Philosophy* (1670), Spinoza described "a universe ruled only by the cause and effect of natural laws, without purpose or design."

Spinoza's skeptical approach to solving philosophical and scientific problems revealed the radical intellectual potential of the new science. The freedom of thought that Spinoza advocated, as well as the belief that nature followed unchangeable laws and could be understood in mathematical terms, served as important links between the Scientific Revolution and the Enlightenment of the eighteenth century. We will discuss those connections more fully in Chapter 19.

Science and Religion

The new science presented two challenges to traditional Christian belief. The first involved the apparent contradiction between the sun-centered theory of the universe and biblical references to the sun's mobility. Because the Bible was considered the inspired word of God, the Church took everything it said, including any passages regarding the operation of the physical world, as literally true. The Bible's reference to the sun moving across the sky served as the basis of the papal condemnation of sun-centered theories in 1616 and the prosecution of Galileo in 1633.

The second challenge to traditional Christian belief was the implication that if the universe functioned as a machine, on the basis of unchanging natural laws, then God played little part in its operation. God was akin to an engineer, who had designed the perfect machine, and therefore had no need to interfere with its workings. This position, which thinkers known as **deists** adopted in the late seventeenth and eighteenth centuries, denied the Christian belief that God was constantly active in the operation of the world. More directly, it rejected the possibility of miracles. None of the great scientists of the seventeenth century were themselves deists, but their acceptance of the mechanical philosophy made them vulnerable to the charge that they denied Christian doctrine.

Although the new science and seventeenth-century Christianity appeared to be on a collision course, some scientists and theologians insisted that there was no conflict between them. They argued that religion and science had different concerns. Religion dealt with the relationship between humanity and God. Science explained how nature operated. As Galileo wrote in 1615, "The intention of the Holy Ghost is to teach us how one goes to heaven, not how heaven goes."[4] Scripture was not intended to explain natural phenomena, but to convey religious truths that human reason could not grasp.

Another argument for the compatibility of science and religion was the claim that the mechanical philosophy, rather than relegating God to the role of a retired engineer, actually manifested God's unlimited power. In a mechanistic universe God was still the creator of the physical world and the maker of the laws by which nature operated. He was still all-powerful and present everywhere. According to Boyle and Newton, moreover, God played a supremely active role in governing the universe. Not only had he created the universe, but as Boyle argued, he also continued to keep all matter constantly in motion. This theory served the purpose of redefining God's power without diminishing it in any way. Newton arrived at a similar position in his search for an immaterial agent who would cause gravity to operate. He proposed that God himself, who he believed "endures always and is present everywhere," made bodies move according to gravitational laws. Throughout the early eighteenth century this feature of Newtonian natural philosophy served as a powerful argument for the active involvement of God in the universe.

As the new science became more widely accepted, many theologians, especially Protestants, accommodated scientific knowledge to their religious beliefs. Some Protestants welcomed the discoveries of science as an opportunity to purify the Christian religion by combating the superstition, magic, and ignorance that they claimed the Catholic Church had been promoting. Clergymen argued that because God worked through the processes of nature, scientific inquiry could lead to knowledge of God. Religion and science could illuminate each other.

Theologians and philosophers also began to expand the role that reason played in religion. The English philosopher John Locke (1632–1704) argued that reason should be the final judge of the existence of the supernatural and the true meaning of the Bible. This new emphasis on the role of reason in religion coincided with a rejection of the religious zeal that had prevailed during the Reformation and the wars of religion. Increasingly, political and ecclesiastical authorities condemned religious enthusiasm as dangerous and irrational.

The new emphasis on the reasonableness of religion and the decline of religious enthusiasm are often viewed as evidence of a trend toward the **secularization** of European life, a process in which religion gave way to more worldly concerns. In one sense this secular trend was undeniable. By 1700, theology had lost its dominant position at the universities and religion had lost much of its influence on politics, diplomacy, and economic activity.

Religion, however, had not lost its relevance. It remained a vital force in the lives of most Europeans. Many of those who accepted the new science continued to believe in a providential God and the divinity of Christ. Moreover, a small but influential group of educated people, following the lead of the French scientist and philosopher Blaise Pascal (1623–1662), argued that religious faith occupied a higher sphere of knowledge that reason and science could not penetrate. Pascal, the inventor of a calculating machine and the promoter of a system of public coach service in Paris, was an

JUSTICE IN HISTORY

The Trial of Galileo

The events leading to the trial of Galileo for heresy in 1633 began in 1616, when a committee of theologians reported to the Roman Inquisition that the sun-centered theory of Copernicus was heretical. Those who accepted this theory were declared to be heretics not only because they questioned the Bible itself, but because they denied the exclusive authority of the Catholic Church to interpret the Bible. The day after this report was submitted, Pope Paul V (r. 1605–1621) instructed Cardinal Robert Bellarmine (1542–16210, a theologian who was on good terms with Galileo, to warn him to abandon his Copernican views. Galileo had written extensively in support of the sun-centered thesis, especially in his *Letters on Sunspots* (1613) and his *Letter to the Grand Duchess Christina* (1615), although he had never admitted that the theory was proved conclusively. Then he was told not to hold, teach, or defend in any way the opinion that the sun was stable or the Earth moved. If he ignored that warning, he would be prosecuted as a heretic.

During the next 16 years Galileo published two books. The first, *The Assayer* (1623), attacked the views of an Italian philosopher regarding comets. The book won Galileo support, especially from the new pope, Urban VIII (r. 1623–1644), who was eager to be associated with the most fashionable intellectual trends. Urban took Galileo under his wing and made him the intellectual star of his court. Urban even declared that support for Copernicanism was rash but not heretical.

The pope's patronage may have emboldened Galileo to exercise less caution in writing his second book of this period, *Dialogue Concerning the Two Chief World Systems* (1632). Ostensibly an impartial presentation of the rival Ptolemaic and Copernican cosmologies, this book promoted Copernicanism in its own quiet way. Galileo sought proper authorization from ecclesiastical authorities to put the book in print, but he allowed it to be published in Florence before it received official approval from Rome.

The publication of *Dialogue* precipitated Galileo's fall from the pope's favor. Urban, accused of leniency with heretics, ordered the book taken out of circulation in the summer of 1632 and appointed a commission to investigate Galileo's activities. After receiving their report, he turned the matter over to the Roman Inquisition, which charged Galileo with heresy.

The Roman Inquisition had been established in 1542 to preserve the Catholic faith and prosecute heresy. Like the Spanish Inquisition, this Roman ecclesiastical court has acquired a reputation for being harsh and arbitrary, for administering torture, for proceeding in secrecy, and for denying the accused the right to know the charges before the trial. There is some validity to these criticisms, although the Inquisition did not torture Galileo or deny him the opportunity to defend himself. The most unfair aspect of the proceeding, and of inquisitorial justice in general, was that the same judges who had brought the charges against the accused and conducted the interrogation also decided the case. This meant that in a politically motivated trial such as Galileo's, the verdict was a foregone conclusion. To accept Galileo's defense would have been a sign of weakness and a repudiation of the pope.

Although the underlying issue in the trial was whether Galileo was guilty of heresy for denying the sun's motion and the Earth's immobility, the more technical question was whether by publishing *Dialogue* he had violated the prohibition of 1616. In his defense Galileo claimed he had only written *Dialogue* to present "the physical and astronomical reasons that can be advanced for one side or the other." He denied holding Copernicus's opinion to be true.

In the end the court determined that by publishing *Dialogue*, Galileo had violated the injunction of 1616. He had disseminated "the false opinion of

THE TRIAL OF GALILEO, 1633

Galileo is shown here presenting one of his four defenses to the Inquisition. He claimed that his book *Dialogue Concerning the Two Chief World Systems* did not endorse the Copernican model of the universe.

Source: Gérard Blot/Art Resource/ Reunion des Musees Nationaux

the Earth's motion and the sun's stability," and he had "defended the said opinion already condemned." Even Galileo's efforts "to give the impression of leaving it undecided and labeled as probable" was still a serious error, because there was no way that "an opinion declared and defined contrary to divine Scripture may be probable." The court also declared that Galileo had obtained permission to publish the book in Florence without telling the authorities there that he was under the injunction of 1616.

Throughout the trial every effort was made to distance the pope from his former protégé. The papal court feared that because the pope had been Galileo's patron and had allowed him to develop his ideas, he himself would be implicated in Galileo's heresy. Information regarding the pope's earlier support for Galileo would not be allowed to surface during the trial. The court made sure, for example, that no one from the court of the Grand Duke of Tuscany in Florence, who had secured Galileo's appointment at the University of Padua and had defended him throughout this crisis, would testify for him. The trial tells us as much about Urban VIII's efforts to save face as about the Catholic Church's hostility to the new science.

The Inquisition required Galileo to renounce his views and avoid further defense of Copernicanism.

After making this humiliating submission to the court, he was sent to Siena and later that year was allowed to return to his villa near Florence, where he remained under house arrest until his death in 1642.

For Discussion

1. Galileo was silenced because of what he had printed. Why had he published these works, and why did the Church consider his publications a threat?

2. Should disputes between science and religion be resolved in a court of law? Why or why not?

Taking It Further

Finocchiaro, Maurice (ed). *The Galileo Affair: A Documentary History.* 1989. A collection of original documents regarding the controversy between Galileo and the Roman Catholic Church.

Sharratt, Michael. *Galileo: Decisive Innovator.* 1994. A study of Galileo's place in the history of science that provides full coverage of his trial and papal reconsiderations of it in the late twentieth century.

advocate of the new science. He endorsed the Copernican model of the universe and opposed the condemnation of Galileo. He introduced a new scientific theory regarding fluids that later became known as Pascal's law of pressure. But by claiming that knowledge of God comes from the heart rather than the mind, Pascal challenged the contention of Locke and Spinoza that reason was the ultimate arbiter of religious truth.

HUMANS AND THE NATURAL WORLD

■ How did the Scientific Revolution change the way in which seventeenth- and eighteenth-century Europeans thought of the place of human beings in nature?

The spread of scientific knowledge not only redefined the views of educated people regarding the supernatural, but also led them to reconsider their relationship to nature. This process involved three separate but related inquiries: to determine the place of human beings in a sun-centered universe, to investigate how science and technology had given human beings greater control over nature, and to reconsider the relationship between men and women in light of new scientific knowledge about the human mind and body.

The Place of Human Beings in the Universe

The astronomical discoveries of Copernicus, Kepler, and Galileo offered a new outlook about the position of human beings in the universe. The Earth-centered Ptolemaic cosmos that dominated scientific thought during the Middle Ages was also human-centered. Human beings inhabited the planet at the very center of the universe, and on that planet they enjoyed a privileged position. They were, after all, created in the image of God, according to Christian belief.

The acceptance of a sun-centered model of the universe began to change these views of

humankind. Once it became apparent that the Earth was not the center of the universe, human beings began to lose their privileged position in nature. The Copernican universe was neither Earth-centered nor human-centered. Scientists such as Descartes continued to claim that human beings were the greatest of nature's creatures, but their habitation of a tiny planet circling the sun inevitably reduced the sense of their own importance. Moreover, as astronomers began to recognize the incomprehensible size of the cosmos, the possibility emerged that there were other habitable worlds in the universe, calling into further question the unique status of humankind.

In the late sixteenth and seventeenth centuries a number of literary works explored the possibility of other inhabited worlds and forms of life. Kepler's *Somnium*, or *Lunar Astronomy* (1634), a book that combined science and fiction, described various species of moon dwellers, some of whom were rational and superior to humans. The most ambitious of these books on extraterrestrial life was Bernard de Fontenelle's *Conversations on the Plurality of Worlds* (1686). This fictional work by a dramatist and poet who was also well versed in scientific knowledge became immensely popular throughout Europe and was more responsible than any purely scientific achievement for leading the general reading public to call into question the centrality of human beings in Creation.

The Control of Nature

The Scientific Revolution strengthened the confidence human beings had in their ability to control nature. By disclosing the laws governing the operation of the universe, the new science gave humans the tools they needed to make nature serve them more effectively than it had in the past. Francis Bacon, for example, believed that knowledge of the laws of nature could restore the dominion over nature that humans had lost in the biblical Garden of Eden. Bacon thought that nature existed for human beings to control and exploit for their own benefit. His famous saying, "knowledge is power," conveyed his confidence that science would give human beings this type of control. This optimism regarding human control of nature found support in the belief that God permitted such mastery, first by creating a regular and uniform universe and then by giving humans the rational faculties by which they could understand nature's laws.

Many seventeenth-century scientists emphasized the practical applications of their research, just as scientists often do today. Descartes, who used his knowledge of optics to improve the grinding of lenses, considered how scientific knowledge could drain marshes, increase the velocity of bullets, and use bells to make clouds give rain. In his celebration of the French Academy of Sciences in 1699, Fontenelle wrote that "the application of science to nature will constantly grow in scope and intensity and we shall go on from one marvel to the next; the day will come when man will be able to fly by fitting on wings to keep him in the air...till one day we shall be able to fly to the moon."[5]

The hopes of seventeenth-century scientists for the improvement of human life by means of technology remained in large part unfulfilled until the eighteenth century. Only then did the technological promise of the Scientific Revolution begin to be realized, most notably with the innovations that preceded or accompanied the Industrial Revolution (see Chapter 21). By the middle of the eighteenth century, the belief that science would improve human life became an integral part of Western culture. Faith in human progress also became one of the main themes of the Enlightenment, which will be discussed in Chapter 19.

Women, Men, and Nature

The new scientific and philosophical ideas challenged ancient and medieval notions about women's physical and mental inferiority to men but not other traditional ideas about gender roles.

Until the seventeenth century, a woman's sexual organs were thought to be imperfect versions of a man's, an idea that made woman an inferior version of man and, in some respects,

a freak of nature. During the sixteenth and seventeenth centuries, scientific literature advanced the new idea that women's sexual organs were perfect in their own right and served distinct functions in reproduction. Aristotle's view that men made a more important contribution to reproduction than women also came under attack. Semen was long believed to contain the form of both the body and the soul, while a woman only contributed the formless matter on which the semen acted. By 1700, however, most scholars agreed that both sexes contributed equally to the process of reproduction.

Some seventeenth-century natural philosophers also questioned ancient and medieval ideas about women's mental inferiority to men. In making a radical separation between the mind and the human body, Descartes, for example, found no difference between the minds of men and women. As one of his followers wrote in 1673, "The mind has no sex."[6] A few upper-class women provided evidence to support this revolutionary claim of female intellectual equality. Princess Elisabeth of Bohemia, for example, carried on a long correspondence with Descartes during the 1640s and challenged many of his ideas on the relationship between the body and the soul. The English noblewoman Margaret Cavendish (1623–1673) wrote scientific and philosophical works and conversed with leading philosophers. In early eighteenth-century France, small groups of women and men gathered in the salons or private sitting rooms of the nobility to discuss philosophical and scientific ideas. In Germany women helped their husbands run astronomical observatories.

Although seventeenth-century science laid the foundations for a theory of sexual equality, it did not challenge other traditional ideas that compared women unfavorably with men. Most educated people continued to ground female behavior in the humors, claiming that because women were cold and wet, as opposed to hot and dry, they were naturally more deceptive, unstable, and melancholic than men. They also continued to identify women with nature itself, which had always been depicted as female.

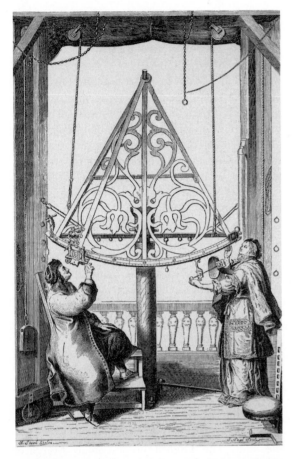

ASTRONOMERS IN SEVENTEENTH-CENTURY GERMANY

Elisabetha and Johannes Hevelius working together with a sextant in a German astronomical observatory. More than 14 percent of all German astronomers were female. Most of them cooperated with their husbands in their work.

Bacon's use of masculine metaphors to describe science and his references to "man's mastery over nature" therefore seemed to reinforce traditional ideas of male dominance over women. His language also reinforced traditional notions of men's superior rationality.[7] In 1664 the secretary of the Royal Society, which excluded women from membership, proclaimed that the mission of that institution was to develop a "masculine philosophy."[8]

The new science thus strengthened the theoretical foundations for the male control of women at a time when many men expressed concern over women's "disorderly" and "irrational" conduct. In a world populated with witches, rebels, and other women who refused to adhere to conventional standards of proper feminine behavior, the adoption of a masculine philosophy was associated with the reassertion of patriarchy.

CONCLUSION

Science and Western Culture

Unlike many of the cultural developments in the history of the West, the Scientific Revolution owes very little to Eastern influences. During the Middle Ages the Islamic civilizations of the Middle East produced a rich body of scientific knowledge that influenced the development of medieval science in Europe, but by the time of the Scientific Revolution, Middle Eastern science no longer occupied the frontlines of scientific research. Middle Eastern natural philosophers had little to offer their European counterparts as they made their contributions to the Scientific Revolution.

China and India had also accumulated a large body of scientific knowledge in ancient and medieval times. When Jesuit missionaries began teaching Western science and mathematics to the Chinese in the sixteenth and seventeenth centuries, they learned about earlier Chinese technological advances, including the invention of the compass, gunpowder, and printing. They also learned that ancient Chinese astronomers had been the first to observe solar eclipses and comets. By the time the Jesuits arrived, however, Chinese science had entered a period of decline. When those missionaries returned home, they introduced Europeans to many aspects of Chinese culture but very few scientific ideas that Europeans natural philosophers found useful.

None of these Eastern civilizations had a scientific revolution comparable to the one that occurred in the West in the late sixteenth and seventeenth centuries. For China the explanation probably lies in the absence of military and political incentives to promote scientific research at a time when the vast Chinese empire was relatively stable. In the Middle East the explanation is more likely that Islam during these years failed to give priority to the study of the natural world. In Islam nature was either entirely secular (that is, not religious) and hence not worthy of study on its own terms or so heavily infused with spiritual value that it could not be subjected to rational analysis. In Europe, however, religious and cultural traditions allowed scientists to view nature as both a product of supernatural forces and something that was separate from the supernatural. Nature could therefore be studied objectively without losing its religious significance. Only when nature was viewed as both the creation of God and at the same time as independent of God, could it be subjected to mathematical analysis and brought under human control.

Scientific and technological knowledge became a significant component of Western culture, and in the eighteenth century Western science gave many educated Europeans a new source of identity. These people believed that their knowledge of science, in conjunction with their Christian religion, their classical culture, and their political institutions made them different from, if not superior to, people living in the East.

The rise of Western science and technology played a role in the growth of European dominance over Africa, Asia, and the Americas. Science gave Western states the military and navigational technology that helped them gain control of foreign lands. Knowledge of botany and agriculture allowed Western powers to develop the resources of the areas they colonized and use these resources to improve their own societies. Some Europeans even appealed to science to justify their dominance of the people in the lands they settled and ruled. To this process of Western imperial expansion we now turn.

KEY TERMS

universal law of gravitation
alchemy
induction
empiricism
deductive reasoning
rationalism

mechanical philosophy
dualistic
Neoplatonism
paradigm
skepticism
deists
secularization

CHAPTER QUESTIONS

1. What were the achievements and discoveries of the Scientific Revolution? (page 529)
2. What methods did scientists use during this period to investigate nature, and how did they think nature operated? (page 535)
3. Why did the Scientific Revolution occur in Western Europe at this particular time? (page 537)
4. How did the Scientific Revolution influence philosophical and religious thought in the seventeenth and early eighteenth centuries? (page 543)
5. How did the Scientific Revolution change how Europeans thought about the place of human beings in nature? (page 548)

TAKING IT FURTHER

1. Were the changes in astronomy, physics, chemistry, and biology in the sixteenth and seventeenth centuries revolutionary? In which field were the changes most significant?
2. Scientists today often refer to the scientific method. Was there a scientific method in the seventeenth century or did scientists employ various methods?
3. Why did the scientific revolution occur at this time? Did it owe its development more to internal or external developments? Scientists today often refer to the scientific method. Was there a scientific method in the seventeenth century or did scientists employ various methods?
4. What does the conflict between the supporter of a sun-centered theory and the Catholic Church suggest about the compatibility of science and religion in the seventeenth century?

✓ Practice on MyHistoryLab

GLOSSARY

absolutism (p. 492)   A form of government in the seventeenth and eighteenth centuries in which a ruler possessed unrivalled power.

acropolis (p. 79)   The defensible hilltop around which a polis grew. In classical Athens, the Acropolis was the site of the Parthenon (Temple of Athena).

Aeneid (p. 182)   Written by Virgil (70–19 B.C.E.), this magnificent epic poem celebrates the emperor Augustus by linking him to his mythical ancestor, Aeneas, the Trojan refugee who founded the Roman people. Considered by many to be the greatest work of Latin literature, the poem has had enormous influence in the West.

agora (p. 79)   An open area in the town center of a Greek polis that served as a market and a place for informal discussion.

agricultural revolution (p. 300)   Refers to technological innovations that began to appear during the eleventh century, making possible a dramatic growth in population. The agricultural revolution came about through harnessing new sources of power with water and wind mills, improving the pulling power of animals with better collars, using heavy plows to better exploit the soils of northern Europe, and employing a three-field crop rotation system that increased the amount and quality of food available.

agricultural societies (p. 65)   Settled communities in which people depend on farming and raising livestock as their sources of food.

alchemy (p. 534)   A form of learned magic that was intended to turn base metals into precious ones.

aldeias (p. 414)   Settlements for natives who had converted to Christianity in Brazil. In these settlements the Jesuit fathers protected the natives from enslavement.

Alexandrianism (p. 130)   A style of Hellenistic poetry that demonstrated a command of meter and language and appealed more to the intellect than the emotions.

Allies (p. 785)   During World War I, the states allied against the Central Powers of Germany and Austria-Hungary. During World War II, the states allied against the regimes of Nazi Germany, fascist Italy and imperial Japan.

Amarna Letters (p. 44)   A collection of over 370 cuneiform tablets discovered at Tell El-Amarna in 1887 that contains the diplomatic and imperial correspondence of the pharaohs from the mid-fourteenth century B.C.E.

Amarna Period (p. 39)   Time of religious ferment during the reign of Amenhotep IV (1351–1334 B.C.E.) in New Kingdom Egypt.

Anabaptism (p. 447)   Meaning "to rebaptize;" refers to those Protestant radicals of the sixteenth century who rejected infant baptism and adopted adult baptism. Anabaptists treated the Bible as a blueprint for reforming not just the church but all of society, a tendency that led them to reject the authority of the state, to live in self-governing "holy communities," and in some cases to practice a primitive form of communism.

anarchism (p. 737)   Ideology that views the state as unnecessary and repressive and rejects participation in parliamentary politics in favor of direct, usually violent, action.

anticlericalism (p. 765)   Opposition to the political influence of the Roman Catholic Church.

Antonine Decree (p. 180)   In 212 C.E. the emperor Aurelius Antoninus, called Caracalla, issued a decree that granted citizenship to all the free inhabitants of the Roman Empire. The decree enabled Roman law to embrace the entire population of the empire.

apartheid (p. 904)   System of racial segregation and discrimination put into place in South Africa in 1948.

appeasement (p. 860)   British diplomatic and financial efforts to stabilize Germany in the 1920s and 1930s and so avoid a second world war.

Arians (p. 213)   Christians who believe that God the Father is superior to Jesus Christ his Son. Most of the Germanic settlers in western Europe in the fifth century were Arians.

aristocracy (p. 587)   A term that originally applied to those who were considered the most fit to rule and later identified the wealthiest members of society, especially those who owned land.

asceticism (p. 215)   The Christian practice of severely suppressing physical needs and daily desires in an effort to achieve a spiritual union with God. Asceticism is the practice that underlies the monastic movement.

Auschwitz (p. 880)   Technically Auschwitz-Birkenau; death camp in Poland that has become the symbol of the Holocaust.

auto-da-fé (p. 466)   Meaning literally a "theater of faith," an *auto* was practiced by the Catholic Church in early modern Spain and Portugal as an extended public ritual of penance designed to cause physical pain among the sinful and promote fear of God's judgment among those who witnessed it.

Babylonian Captivity of the Church (p. 354) Between 1305 and 1378 seven consecutive popes voluntarily chose to reside in Avignon, France, in order to escape anarchy in the streets of Rome. During this period the popes became subservient to the kings of France.

Babylonian Exile (p. 67)   The period of Jewish history between the destruction of Solomon's temple in Jerusalem by Babylonian armies in 587 B.C.E., and 538 B.C.E, when Cyrus of Persia permitted Jews to return to Palestine and rebuild the temple.

balance of power (p. 501)   An arrangement in which various countries form alliances to prevent any one state from dominating the others.

Balfour Declaration (p. 817)   Declaration of 1917 that affirmed British support of a Jewish state in Palestine.

barbarians (p. 108)   A term used by Greeks to describe people who did not speak Greek and who were therefore considered uncivilized.

baroque (pp. 126, 498)   A dynamic style in art, architecture, and music that was intended to elicit an emotional response. Baroque buildings were massive, imposing structures with sweeping façades. The baroque style represented a development of Greek classicism in the Hellenistic period. In the seventeenth century the baroque style was closely associated with royal absolutism.

Berlin Wall (p. 908)   Constructed by the East German government, the wall physically cut the city of Berlin in two and prevented East German citizens from access to West Germany; stood from 1961 to 1989.

Big Three (p. 892)   Term applied to the British, Soviet, and U.S. leaders during World War II: until 1945, Winston Churchill, Joseph Stalin, and Franklin Roosevelt; by the summer of 1945, Clement Atlee, Joseph Stalin, and Harry Truman.

Black Death (p. 332)   An epidemic disease, possibly Bubonic plague, that struck Europe between 1348

and the 1350s killing at least one-third of the total population.

blitzkrieg (p. 861)   "Lightning war;" offensive military tactic making use of airplanes, tanks, and motorized infantry to punch through enemy defenses and secure key territory. First demonstrated by the German army in World War II.

Bolsheviks (p. 809)   Minority group of Russian socialists, headed by Vladimir Lenin, who espoused an immediate transition to a socialist state. It became the Communist Party in the Soviet Union.

boule (p. 83)   A council of 400 male citizens established by Solon in Greece in the sixth century B.C.E. It served as an advisory body for the general assembly of all male citizens.

Bourbon reforms (p. 560)   Measures introduced by the Bourbon Kings of Spain in the eighteenth century to make the Spanish empire more manageable and profitable.

bourgeoisie (p. 594)   A social group, technically consisting of those who were burghers in the towns, that included prosperous merchants and financiers, members of the professions, and some skilled craftsmen known as "petty bourgeoisie."

boyars (p. 488)   Upper-level nobles who dominated Russian society until the tsars began to supplant them in the fifteenth and sixteenth centuries.

Bretton Woods Agreement (p. 894)   Agreement signed in 1944 that established the post-World War II economic framework in which the U.S. dollar served as the world's reserve currency.

brinkmanship (p. 905)   Style of Cold War confrontation in which each superpower endeavored to convince the other that it was willing to wage nuclear war.

bronze (p. 36)   An alloy of tin and copper that produces a hard metal suitable for weapons, tools, ornaments, and household objects. Bronze production began about 3200 B.C.E.

Byzantine Empire (p. 225)   The eastern half of the Roman Empire, which lasted from the founding of Constantinople in 324 to its conquest by the Ottoman Turks in 1453.

caliphate (p. 250)   The Islamic imperial government that evolved under the leadership of Abu Bakr (r. 632–634), the successor of the prophet Muhammad. The sectarian division within Islam between the Shi'ites and Sunni derived from a disagreement over how to determine the hereditary succession from Muhammad to the caliphate, which combined governmental and some religious responsibilities.

calling (p. 442) The Calvinist doctrine that God calls the Elect to perform his will on earth. God's calling gave Calvinists a powerful sense of personal direction.

canon law (p. 276) The collected laws of the Roman Catholic Church. Canon law applied to cases involving the clergy, disputes about church property, and donations to the Church. It also applied to the laity for annulling marriages, legitimating bastards, prosecuting bigamy, protecting widows and orphans, and resolving inheritance disputes.

capital (p. 663) All the physical assets used in production, including fixed capital, such as machinery, and circulating capital, such as raw materials; more generally the cost of these physical assets.

caravels (p. 397) Hybrid three-masted ships developed about 1450 in the Iberian peninsula by combining the rigging of square with triangular lateen sails. These ships could be sailed in a variety of winds, carry large cargoes, be managed by a small crew, and be defended by guns mounted in the castle superstructure.

Carolingian Renaissance (p. 275) The "rebirth" of interest in ancient Greek and Latin literature and language during the reign of the Frankish emperor Charlemagne (r. 768–814). Charlemagne promoted the intensive study of Latin to promote governmental efficiency and to propagate the Christian faith.

Catholic Reformation (p. 450) A series of efforts during the sixteenth century to purify the Church that evolved out of late medieval spirituality and that included the creation of new religious orders, especially the Society of Jesus.

Central Powers (p. 785) Germany and Austria-Hungary in World War I.

Chalcedonians (p. 213) Christians who followed the doctrinal decisions and definitions of the Council of Chalcedon in 451 C.E. stating that Christ's human and divine natures were equal, but entirely distinct and united in one person "without confusion, division, separation, or change." Chalcedonian Christianity came to be associated with the Byzantine Empire and is called Greek Orthodoxy. In western Europe it is known as Roman Catholicism.

Chartists (p. 702) A British group of workers and middle-class radicals who drafted a People's Charter in 1837 demanding universal male suffrage and other political reforms.

chinoiserie (p. 578) A French word for an eighteenth-century decorative art that combined Chinese and European motifs.

Christian Democracy, Christian Democratic parties (p. 916) Conservative and confessionally based (Roman Catholic) political parties that dominated much of western European politics after World War II.

Christian humanists (p. 430) During the fifteenth and sixteenth centuries these experts in Greek, Latin, and Hebrew subjected the Bible to philological study in an attempt to understand the precise meaning of the founding text of Christianity.

Church Fathers (p. 220) Writers in Late Antiquity from both the Greek and Latin-speaking worlds who sought to reconcile Christianity with classical learning.

circuit court (p. 321) Established by King Henry II (r. 1154–1189) to make royal justice available to virtually anyone in England. Circuit court judges visited every shire in England four times a year.

civic humanism (p. 378) A branch of humanism introduced by the Florentine chancellor Leonardo Bruni who defended the republican institutions and values of the city. Civic humanism promoted the ethic of responsible citizenship.

civilization (p. 12) The term used by archaeologists to describe a society differentiated by levels of wealth and power, and in which religious, economic, and political control are based in cities.

civil society (p. 935) Public organizations and activities separate from the state, commerce, or the family that help to create community life.

clans or kin groups (p. 267) The basic social and political unit of Germanic society consisting of blood relatives obliged to defend one another and take vengeance for crimes against the group and its members.

class consciousness (p. 674) The awareness of people from different occupations that they belonged to a class.

classicism (p. 591) A style in art, architecture, music, and literature that emphasizes proportion, adherence to traditional forms, and a rejection of emotion and enthusiasm.

Cluny (p. 306) A monastery founded in Burgundy in 910 that became the center of a far-reaching movement to reform the Church that was sustained in more than 1,500 Cluniac monasteries, modeled after the original in Cluny.

Cold War (p. 892)   Struggle for global supremacy between the United States and the Soviet Union, waged from the end of World War II until 1990.

collectivization (p. 840)   The replacement of private and village farms with large cooperative agricultural enterprises run by state-employed managers. Collectivization was a key part of Joseph Stalin's plans for modernizing the Soviet economy and destroying peasant opposition to communist rule.

colons (p. 581)   White planters in the French Caribbean colony of Saint Domingue (Haiti).

Columbian exchange (p. 418)   The trade of peoples, plants, animals, microbes, and ideas between the Old and New Worlds that began with Columbus.

Columbian question (p. 420)   The debate among historians and epidemiologists about whether syphilis or its ancestor disease originated in the Americas and was brought to the Old World after Columbus's voyages.

Common Market (p. 917)   Originally comprising West Germany, France, Italy, Belgium, Luxembourg, and the Netherlands, the Common Market was formed in 1957 to integrate its members' economic structures and so foster both economic prosperity and international peace. Also called the European Economic Community (EEC). Evolved into the European Union (EU).

communes (p. 303)   Sworn defensive associations of merchants and workers that appeared in north-central Italy after 1070 and that became the effective government of more than a hundred cities. The communes evolved into city-states by seizing control of the surrounding countryside.

communism (p. 690)   The revolutionary form of socialism developed by Karl Marx and Friedrich Engels that promoted the overthrow of bourgeois or capitalist institutions and the establishment of a dictatorship of the proletariat.

Companions (p. 110)   Elite regiments of cavalrymen armed with heavy lances formed by Philip of Macedon.

Concert of Europe (p. 696)   The joint efforts made by Austria, Prussia, Russia, Britain, and France during the years following the Congress of Vienna to suppress liberal and nationalist movements throughout Europe.

Conciliar Movement (p. 354)   A fifteenth-century movement that advocated ending the Great Schism and reforming church government by calling a general meeting or council of the bishops, who would exercise authority over the rival popes.

confessions (p. 456)   The formal sixteenth-century statements of religious doctrine: the Confession of Augsburg for Lutherans, the Helvetic Confessions for Calvinists, the Thirty-Nine Articles for Anglicans, and the decrees of the Council of Trent for Catholics.

Congress of Vienna (p. 649)   A conference of the major powers of Europe in 1814–1815 to establish a new balance of power at the end of the Napoleonic Wars.

conquistadores (p. 408)   Spanish adventurers in the Americas who explored and conquered the lands of indigenous peoples, sometimes without legal authority but usually with a legal privilege granted by the king of Spain who required that one-fifth of all things of value be turned over to the crown. The conquistadores extended Spanish sovereignty over new lands.

conservatism (p. 686)   A nineteenth-century ideology intended to prevent a recurrence of the revolutionary changes of the 1790s and the implementation of liberal policies.

containment (p. 896)   Cold War policy of blocking communist expansion; inaugurated by the Truman Doctrine in 1947.

corporatism (p. 834)   The practice by which committees (or "corporations") made up of representatives of workers, employers, and the state direct the economy.

Corpus Juris Civilis (pp. 143, 226)   The body of Roman law compiled by the emperor Justinian in Constantinople in 534. The Corpus became a pillar of Latin-speaking European civilization.

Cortes (p. 494)   Legislative assemblies in the Spanish kingdoms.

cosmology (p. 134)   A theory concerning the structure and nature of the universe such as those proposed by Aristotle in the fourth century B.C.E. and Copernicus in the sixteenth century.

counties (p. 275)   Territorial units devised by the Carolingian dynasty during the eighth and ninth centuries for the administration of the empire. Each county was administered by a count who was rewarded with lands and sent to areas where he had no family ties to serve as a combined provincial governor, judge, military commander, and representative of the king.

courtly love (p. 326)   An ethic first found in the poems of the late twelfth- and thirteenth-century troubadours that portrayed the ennobling possibilities of the love between a man and a woman. Courtly love formed the basis for the modern idea of romantic love.

creoles (p. 560) People of Spanish descent who had been born in Spanish America.

Crusades (p. 288) Between 1095 and 1291, Latin Christians heeding the call of the pope launched eight major expeditions and many smaller ones against Muslim armies in an attempt to gain control of and hold Jerusalem.

Cubism (p. 763) Modernist artistic movement of the early twentieth century that emphasized the fragmentation of human perception through visual experiments with geometric forms.

cultural relativism (p. 422) A mode of thought first explored during the sixteenth century to explain why the peoples of the New World did not appear in the Bible. Cultural relativism recognized that many (but not necessarily all) standards of judgment are specific to particular cultures rather than the fixed truths established by natural or divine law.

culture (p. 12) The knowledge and adaptive behavior created by communities that helps them to mediate between themselves and the natural world through time.

cuneiform (p. 24) A kind of writing in which wedge-shaped symbols are pressed into clay tablets to indicate words and ideas. Cuneiform writing originated in ancient Sumer.

curia (p. 309) The administrative bureaucracy of the Roman Catholic Church.

Cynics (p. 132) Followers of the teachings of Antisthenes (ca. 445–360 B.C.E.) who rejected pleasures, possessions, and social conventions to find peace of mind.

Darwinian theory of evolution (p. 753) Scientific theory associated with nineteenth-century scientist Charles Darwin that highlights the role of variation and natural selection in the evolution of species.

Decembrists (p. 697) Russian liberals who staged a revolt against Tsar Nicholas I on the first day of his reign in December 1825.

de-Christianization (p. 636) A program inaugurated in France in 1793 by the radical Jacobin and former priest Joseph Fouché that closed churches, eliminated religious symbols, and attempted to establish a purely civic religion.

decolonization (p. 904) The retreat of Western powers from their imperial territories.

deduction, deductive reasoning (pp. 24, 536) The logical process by which ideas and laws are derived from basic truths or principles.

Defenders (p. 582) Irish Catholic peasants who joined the United Irishmen in the rebellion against Britain in 1798.

deists (p. 545) Seventeenth- and eighteenth-century thinkers who believed that God created the universe and established immutable laws of nature but did not subsequently intervene in the operation of nature or in human affairs.

Delian League (p. 92) The alliance among many Greek cities organized by Athens in 478 B.C.E. in order to fight Persian forces in the eastern Aegean Sea. The Athenians gradually turned the Delian League into the Athenian Empire.

demand (p. 664) The desire of consumers to acquire goods and the need of producers to acquire raw materials and machinery.

democracy (p. 82) A form of government in which citizens devise their own governing institutions and choose their leaders; began in Athens, Greece, in the fifth century B.C.E.

de-Stalinization (p. 912) Nikita Khrushchev's effort to decentralize political and economic control in the Soviet Union after 1956.

détente (p. 930) During the 1970s, a period of lessened Cold War hostilities and greater reliance on negotiation and compromise.

dialectic (p. 688) The theory that history advanced in stages as the result of the conflict between different ideas or social groups.

dialectical materialism (p. 689) The socialist philosophy of Karl Marx according to which history advanced as the result of material or economic forces and would lead to the creation of a classless society.

Diaspora (p. 195) Literally "dispersion of population;" usually used to refer to the dispersion of the Jewish population after the Roman destruction of the Temple in Jerusalem in 70 C.E.

diets (p. 494) Legislative assemblies in German territories.

divination (p. 24) The practice of discerning the future by looking for messages imprinted in nature.

divine right (p. 494) The theory that rulers received their power directly from God.

division of labor (p. 660) The assignment of one stage of production to a single worker or group of workers to increase efficiency and productive output.

domestication (p. 13)   Manipulating the breeding of animals over many generations in order to make them more useful to humans as sources of food, wool, and other byproducts. Domestication of animals began about 10,000 years ago.

domestic system (p. 660)   An economic arrangement developed in the sixteenth century in which capitalist entrepreneurs employed families in rural areas to spin and weave cloth and make nails and cutlery.

Dreyfus Affair (p. 730)   The trials of Captain Alfred Dreyfus on treason charges dominated French political life in the decade after 1894 and revealed fundamental divisions in French society.

dualistic (pp. 88, 537)   A term used to describe a philosophy or a religion in which a rigid distinction is made between body and mind, good and evil, or the material and the immaterial world.

Dutch Revolt (p. 479)   The rebellion against Spanish rule of the seven northern provinces of the Netherlands between 1579 and 1648, which resulted in the independence of the Republic of the United Provinces.

Edict of Nantes (p. 477)   Promulgated by King Henry IV in 1598, the edict allowed the Huguenots to build a quasi-independent state within the kingdom of France, giving them the right to have their own troops, church organization, and political autonomy within their walled towns, but banning them from the royal court and the city of Paris. King Louis XIV revoked the edict in 1685.

Einsatzgruppen (p. 879)   Loosely translated as strike force or task force; SS units given the task of murdering Jews and Communist Party members in the areas of the Soviet Union occupied by Germany during World War II.

empires (pp. 20, 554)   Large political formations consisting of different kingdoms or territories outside the boundaries of the states that control them.

empiricism (p. 535)   The practice of testing scientific theories by observation and experiment.

enclosure (p. 663)   The consolidation of scattered agricultural holdings into large, compact fields which were then closed off by hedges, bushes, or walls, giving farmers complete control over the uses of their land.

encomienda (p. 410)   The basic form of economic and social organization in early Spanish America, based on a royal grant awarded to a Spaniard for military or other services that gave the grantee and

his successors the right to gather tribute from the Indians in a defined area.

English Parliament (p. 321)   King Edward I (r. 1272–1307) began to call the English Parliament in order to raise sums of money for his foreign wars. The English Parliament differed from similar assemblies on the Continent. It usually included representatives of the "commons," which consisted of townsmen and prosperous farmers who lacked titles of nobility, but whom the king summoned because he needed their money. As a result, a broader spectrum of the population joined Parliament than in most other medieval kingdoms.

enlightened despots (p. 613)   The term assigned to absolute monarchs who initiated a series of legal and political reforms in an effort to realize the goals of the Enlightenment.

Enlightenment (p. 596)   An international intellectual movement of the eighteenth century that emphasized the use of reason and the application of the laws of nature to human society.

Epicureans (p. 131)   Followers of the teachings of the philosopher Epicurus (341–271 B.C.E.). Epicureans tried to gain peace of mind by choosing pleasures rationally.

Estates General (p. 494)   The legislative assembly of France in the Old Regime.

ethnic cleansing (p. 948)   A term introduced during the wars in Yugoslavia in the 1990s; the systematic use of murder, rape, and violence by one ethnic group against members of other ethnic groups in order to establish control over a territory.

Etruscans (p. 139)   A people of unknown origin who maintained a loose confederation of independent cities in central Italy and who strongly influenced the culture of ancient Rome.

Eucharist (p. 318)   Also known as Holy Communion or the Lord's Supper, the Eucharistic rite of the Mass celebrates Jesus' last meal with his apostles when the priest-celebrant consecrates wafers of bread and a chalice of wine as the body and blood of Christ. In the Middle Ages the wafers of bread were distributed for the congregation to eat, but drinking from the chalice was a special privilege of the priesthood. Protestants in the sixteenth century and Catholics in the late twentieth century began to allow the laity to drink from the chalice.

eugenics (p. 832)   The effort to improve the physical and intellectual capacities of the population by encouraging individuals with "desirable" traits to reproduce and/or by discouraging those individuals designated as "undesirable" from reproducing.

Euro-Islam (p. 956)   The identity and belief system being forged by European Muslims who argue that Islam does not contradict or reject European values.

European Economic Community (EEC) (p. 917)   Originally comprising West Germany, France, Italy, Belgium, Luxembourg, and the Netherlands, the EEC was formed in 1957 to integrate its members' economic structures and so foster both economic prosperity and international peace. Also called the Common Market.

European Union (EU) (p. 949)   A successor organization to the EEC; the effort to integrate European political, economic, cultural, and military structures and policies.

excommunication (p. 309)   A decree by the pope or a bishop prohibiting a sinner from participating in the sacraments of the Church and forbidding any social contact whatsoever with the surrounding community.

existentialism (p. 822)   Twentieth-century philosophy that emerged in the interwar era and influenced many thinkers and artists after World War II. Existentialism emphasizes individual freedom in a world devoid of meaning or coherence.

Expressionism (p. 763)   Modernist artistic movement of the early twentieth century that used bold colors and experimental forms to express emotional realities.

factories (p. 416)   Trading posts established by European powers in foreign lands.

fanatic (p. 474)   Originally referring to someone possessed by a demon, during the sixteenth century a fanatic came to mean a person who expressed immoderate enthusiasm in religious matters or who pursued a supposedly divine mission, often to violent ends.

fascism (p. 833)   Twentieth-century political ideology that rejected the existing alternatives of conservatism, communism, socialism, and liberalism. Fascists stressed the authoritarian power of the state, the efficacy of violent action, the need to build a national community, and the use of new technologies of influence and control.

federalists (p. 628)   The name assigned by radical Jacobins to provincial rebels who opposed the centralization of the state during the French Revolution.

feminism, feminist movement (p. 741)   International movement that emerged in the second half of the nineteenth century and demanded broader political, legal, and economic rights for women.

Fertile Crescent (p. 13)   Also known as the Levantine Corridor, this twenty-five mile wide arc of land stretching from the Jordan River to the Euphrates River was the place where food production and settled communities first appeared in Southwest Asia (the Middle East).

feudalism (p. 281)   A term historians use to describe a social system common during the Middle Ages in which lords granted fiefs (tracts of land or some other form of income) to dependents, known as vassals, who owed their lords personal services in exchange. Feudalism refers to a society governed through personal ties of dependency rather than public political institutions.

fief (p. 281)   During the Middle Ages a fief was a grant of land or some other form of income that a lord gave to a vassal in exchange for loyalty and certain services (usually military assistance).

Final Solution (p. 879)   Nazi term for the effort to murder every Jew in Europe during World War II.

fin-de-siecle (p. 757)   French term for the "turn of the century;" used to refer to the cultural crisis of the late nineteenth century.

First Triumvirate (p. 163)   The informal political alliance made by Julius Caesar, Pompey, and Crassus in 60 B.C.E. to share power in the Roman Republic. It led directly to the collapse of the Republic.

Forms (p. 103)   In the philosophical teachings of Plato, these are eternal, unchanging absolutes such as Truth, Justice, and Beauty that represent true reality, as opposed to the approximations of reality that humans encounter in everyday life.

Forum (p. 138)   The political and religious center of the city of Rome throughout antiquity. All cities in the empire had a forum in imitation of the capital city.

Fourteen Points (p. 814)   The principles outlined by U.S. President Woodrow Wilson as the basis for a new world order after World War I.

franchise (p. 602)   The right to vote; also called suffrage.

freemasons (p. 611)   Members of secret societies of men and women that flourished during the Enlightenment, dedicated to the creation of a society based on reason and virtue and committed to the principles of liberty and equality.

French Wars of Religion (p. 475)   A series of political assassinations, massacres, and military engagements between French Catholics and Calvinists from 1560 to 1598.

friars (p. 315) "Brothers" who wandered from city to city and throughout the countryside begging for alms. Unlike monks who remained in a cloister, friars tried to help ordinary laypeople with their problems by preaching and administering to the sick and poor.

Gaullism (p. 923) The political ideology associated with twentieth-century French political leader Charles DeGaulle. Gaullism combined the advocacy of a strong, centralized state with social conservatism.

genocide (p. 807) The murder of an entire people.

German-Soviet Non-Aggression Pact (p. 859) Signed by Joseph Stalin and Adolf Hitler in 1939, the agreement publicly pledged Germany and the Soviet Union not to attack each other and secretly divided up Poland and the Baltic states between the two powers.

Girondins (p. 627) The more conservative members of the Jacobin party who favored greater economic freedom and opposed further centralization of state power during the French Revolution.

glasnost (p. 937) Loosely translated as openness or honesty; Gorbachev's effort after 1985 to break with the secrecy that had characterized Soviet political life.

globalization (p. 964) The process by which global systems of production, distribution, and communication link together the peoples of the world.

Gnostic, Gnosticism (p. 197) Religious doctrine that emphasizes the importance of *gnosis*, or hidden truth, as a way of releasing spiritual reality from the prison of the essentially unreal or evil material world.

Gothic (p. 327) A style in architecture in western Europe from the late twelfth and thirteenth centuries, characterized by ribbed vaults and pointed arches, which drew the eyes of worshipers upward toward God. Flying buttresses, which redistributed the weight of the roof, made possible thin walls pierced by large expanses of stained glass.

grand jury (p. 321) In medieval England after the judicial reforms of King Henry II (r. 1154–1189), grand juries were called when the circuit court judge arrived in a shire. The sheriff assembled a group of men familiar with local affairs who constituted the grand jury and who reported to the judge the major crimes that had been committed since the judge's last visit.

Great Depression (p. 834) Calamitous drop in prices, reduction in trade, and rise in unemployment that devastated the global economy in 1929.

Great Persecution (p. 207) An attack on Christians in the Roman empire begun by the emperor Galerius in 303 C.E. on the grounds that their worship was endangering the empire. Several thousand Christians were executed.

Great Purge (p. 842) Period of mass arrests and executions particularly aimed at Communist Party members. Lasting from 1934 to 1939, the Great Purge enabled Joseph Stalin to consolidate his one-man rule over the Soviet Union.

Great Schism (p. 354) The division of the Catholic Church (1378–1417) between rival Italian and French claimants to the papal throne.

Green movement, Green politics (p. 932) A new style of politics and set of political ideas resulting from the confluence of environmentalism, feminism, and anti-nuclear protests of the 1970s.

guilds (p. 345) Professional associations devoted to protecting the special interests of a particular trade or craft and to monopolizing production and trade in the goods the guild produced.

haciendas (p. 411) Large landed estates that began to be established in the seventeenth century replaced encomiendas throughout much of Spanish America.

habiru (p. 55) Peasants who existed outside the palace system of the Late Bronze Age; often seen as bandits.

Hallstatt (p. 122) The first Celtic civilization in central Europe is called Halstatt. From about 750 to about 450 B.C.E., Hallstatt Celts spread throughout Europe.

Hellenistic (p. 108) The word used to describe the civilization, based on that of Greece, that developed in the wake of the conquests of Alexander the Great.

helots (p. 82) The brutally oppressed subject peoples of the Spartans. Tied to the land they farmed for Spartan masters, they were treated little better than beasts of burden.

hetairai (p. 97) Elite courtesans in ancient Greece who provided intellectual as well as sexual companionship.

hieroglyphs (p. 32) Ancient Egyptian system of writing that represented both sounds and objects.

Holocaust (p. 877) Adolf Hitler's effort to murder all the Jews in Europe during World War II.

Homo sapiens sapiens (p. 13) Scientific term meaning "most intelligent people" applied to physically and intellectually modern human beings that first appeared between 200,000 and 100,000 years ago in Africa.

hoplites (p. 81)   Greek soldiers in the Archaic Age who could afford their own weapons. Hoplite tactics made soldiers fighting as a group dependent on one another. This contributed to the internal cohesion of the polis and eventually to the rise of democracy.

Huguenots (p. 474)   The term for French Calvinists, who constituted some 10 percent of the population by 1560.

humanists (p. 376)   During the Renaissance humanists were writers and orators who studied Latin and sometimes Greek texts on grammar, rhetoric, poetry, history, and ethics.

Hundred Years' War (p. 346)   Refers to a series of engagements (1337–1453) between England and France over England's attempts to assert its claims to territories in France.

hyperinflation (p. 827)   Catastrophic price increases and currency devaluation, such as that which occurred in Germany in 1923.

iconoclasm (p. 241)   The destruction of religious images in the Byzantine empire in the eighth century.

icons (p. 240)   The Christian images of God and saints found in Byzantine art.

ideologies (p. 684)   Theories of society and government that form the basis of political programs.

induction (p. 535)   The mental process by which theories are established only after the systematic accumulation of large amounts of data.

indulgences (p. 354)   Certificates that allowed penitents to atone for their sins and reduce their time in purgatory. Usually these were issued for going on a pilgrimage or performing a pious act, but during the Babylonian Captivity of the Church (1305–1378) popes began to sell them, a practice Martin Luther protested in 1517 in an act that brought on the Protestant Reformation.

industrial capitalism (p. 671)   A form of capitalism characterized by the ownership of factories by private individuals and the employment of wage labor.

intendants (p. 496)   French royal officials who became the main agents of French provincial administration in the seventeenth century.

interdict (p. 309)   A papal decree prohibiting the celebration of the sacraments in an entire city or kingdom.

Investiture Controversy (p. 308)   A dispute that began in 1076 between the popes and the German emperors over the right to invest bishops with their offices. The most famous episode was the conflict between Pope Gregory VII and Emperor Henry IV.

The controversy was resolved by the Concordat of Worms in 1122.

"Iron Curtain" (p. 892)   Metaphor for the Cold War division of Europe after World War II.

Islamism (p. 952)   Islamic radicalism or *jihadism*. The ideology that insists that Islam demands a rejection of Western values and that violence in this struggle against the West is justified.

Jacobins (p. 623)   A French political party supporting a democratic republic that found support in political clubs throughout the country and dominated the National Convention from 1792 until 1794.

Jim Crow (p. 777)   Series of laws mandating racial segregation throughout the American South.

Junkers (pp. 509, 705)   The traditional nobility of Prussia.

justification by faith (p. 432)   Refers to Martin Luther's insight that humanity is incapable of performing enough religious good works to earn eternal salvation. Salvation is an unmerited gift from God called grace. Those who receive grace are called the Elect.

Keynesian economics (p. 846)   Economic theories associated with the British economist John Maynard Keynes that advocate using the power of the democratic state to ensure economic prosperity.

knight (p. 281)   During the Middle Ages a knight was a soldier who fought on horseback. A knight was a vassal or dependent of a lord, who usually financed the knight's expenses of armor and weapons and of raising and feeding horses with a grant of land known as a fief.

Koine (p. 124)   The standard version of the Greek language spoken throughout the Hellenistic world.

La Tène (p. 122)   A phase of Celtic civilization that lasted from about 450 to 200 B.C.E. La Tène culture became strong especially in the regions of the Rhine and Danube Rivers.

laissez-faire (p. 686)   The principle that governments should not regulate or otherwise intervene in the economy unless it is necessary to protect property rights and public order.

late antiquity (p. 202)   The period between about 250 and 600, which bridged the classical world and the Middle Ages.

Latin Christendom (p. 214)   The parts of medieval Europe, including all of western Europe, united by Christianity and the use of Latin in worship and intellectual life. Latin served as an international language among the ruling elites in western Europe, even though they spoke different languages in their daily lives.

Latin War (p. 144)   A war that the Latin peoples of Italy waged against the Roman Republic between 340 and 338. B.C.E.

Law Code of Hammurabi (p. 25)   The world's oldest complete surviving compendium of laws, promulgated during the reign of Hammurabi (1792–1750 B.C.E.) of Babylon.

lay investiture (p. 307)   The practice of nobles, kings, or emperors installing churchmen and giving them the symbols of office.

League of Nations (p. 814)   Association of states set up after World War I to resolve international conflicts through open and peaceful negotiation.

Lend-Lease Act (p. 869)   Passed in March 1941, the act gave Britain access to U.S. industrial products during World War II, with payment postponed for the duration of the war.

Levantine Corridor (p. 13)   Also known as the Fertile Crescent, this arc of land stretching from the Jordan River to the Euphrates River was the place where food production and settled communities first appeared in Southwest Asia (the Middle East).

liberalism (p. 686)   An ideology based on the conviction that individual freedom is of supreme importance and the main responsibility of government is to protect that freedom.

"Linear B" (p. 47)   The earliest written form of Greek, used by the Mycenaeans.

linear perspective (p. 384)   In the arts the use of geometrical principles to depict a three-dimensional space on a flat, two-dimensional surface.

liturgy (p. 262)   The forms of Christian worship, including the prayers, chants, and rituals to be said, sung, or performed throughout the year.

lord (p. 276)   During the Middle Ages a lord was someone who offered protection to dependents, known as vassals, who took an oath of loyalty to him. Most lords demanded military services from their vassals and sometimes granted them tracts of land known as fiefs.

ma'at (p. 30)   Ancient Egyptian concept of the fundamental order established by the gods.

Macedonian Renaissance (p. 242)   During the Macedonian dynasty's rule of Byzantium (867–1056), aristocratic families, the Church, and monasteries devoted their immense riches to embellishing Constantinople with new buildings, mosaics, and icons.

The emperors sponsored historical, philosophical, and religious writing.

Mafia (p. 711)   Organizations of armed men who took control of local politics and the economy in late nineteenth-century Sicily.

magic (p. 469)   Learned opinion described two kinds of magic: natural magic, which involved the manipulation of occult forces believed to exist in nature, and demonic magic, which called upon evil spirits to gain access to power. Widely accepted as a reality until the middle of the seventeenth century.

Magisterial Reformation (p. 440)   Refers to Protestant churches that received official government sanction.

Magna Carta (p. 321)   In 1215 some English barons forced King John to sign the "great charter," in which the king pledged to respect the traditional feudal privileges of the nobility, towns, and clergy. Subsequent kings swore to uphold it, thereby accepting the fundamental principle that even the king was obliged to respect the law.

Malthusian population trap (p. 670)   The theory of Thomas Malthus (1766–1834) that the natural tendency of population to grow faster than the food supply would eventually drive the size of populations back to sustainable levels and end periods of economic expansion that usually accompany the growth of population.

Manhattan Project (p. 875)   Code name given to the secret Anglo-American project that resulted in the construction of the atom bomb during World War II.

manor (p. 301)   A medieval unit of agricultural management in which a lord managed and served as the presiding judge over peasants who worked the land.

marches (p. 275)   Territorial units of the Carolingian empire for the administration of frontier regions. Each march was ruled by a margrave who had special powers necessary to defend vulnerable borders.

Marshall Plan (p. 896)   The use of U.S. economic aid to restore stability to Europe after World War II and so undercut the appeal of communist ideology.

mass politics (p. 725)   A political culture characterized by the participation of non-elites.

matriarchy (p. 47)   A social or cultural system in which family lineage is traced through the mother and/or in which women hold significant power.

metropolis (p. 553).   The "mother state" that controlled an empire.

mechanical philosophy (p. 536)   The seventeenth-century philosophy of nature, championed by René

Descartes, holding that nature operated in a mechanical way, just like a machine made by a human being.

megalith (p. 000)   A very large stone used in prehistoric European monuments in the second millennium B.C.E.

mercantilism (p. 499)   The theory that the wealth of a state depended on its ability to import fewer commodities than it exported and thus acquire the largest possible share of the world's monetary supply. The theory encouraged state intervention in the economy and the regulation of trade.

meritocracy (p. 642)   The practice of appointing people to office solely on the basis of ability and performance rather than social or economic status.

mesmerism (p. 612)   A pseudoscience developed by Franz Anton Mesmer in the eighteenth century that treated sickness by massaging or hypnotizing the patient to produce a crisis that restored health.

mestizos (p. 574)   People of mixed white and Indian ancestry.

metropolis (p. 553)   The parent country of a colony or imperial possession.

Middle Passage (p. 571)   The journey taken by European ships bringing slaves from Africa to the Americas.

Modern Devotion (p. 355)   A fifteenth-century religious movement that stressed individual piety, ethical behavior, and intense religious education. The Modern Devotion was promoted by the Brothers of the Common Life, a religious order whose influence was broadly felt through its extensive network of schools.

modernism (p. 757)   Term applied to artistic and literary movements from the late nineteenth century through the 1950s. Modernists sought to create new aesthetic forms and values.

monastic movement (p. 215)   In Late Antiquity, Christian ascetics organized communities where men and women could pursue a life of spirituality through work, prayer, and asceticism. Called the monastic movement, this spiritual quest spread quickly throughout Christian lands.

Monophysites (p. 214)   Christians who do not accept the Council of Chalcedon (see Chalcedonians). Monophysites believe that Jesus Christ has only one nature, equally divine and human.

monotheism (p. 39)   The belief in only one god, first attributed to the ancient Hebrews. Monotheism is the foundation of Judaism, Christianity, Islam, and Zoroastrianism.

Montagnards (p. 627)   Members of the radical faction within the Jacobin party who advocated the centralization of state power during the French Revolution and instituted the Reign of Terror.

mosque (p. 247)   A place of Muslim worship.

Mountain, the (p. 627)   The radical faction of Jacobins in the National Convention during the French Revolution.

mulattos (p. 565)   People of mixed white and black race.

Munich Agreement (p. 859)   The agreement in 1939 between the governments of Nazi Germany, Britain, and France that granted Germany sovereignty over the Sudetenland; part of the effort to appease the Nazi government and avoid a second total war in Europe.

nabobs (p. 578)   Members of the British East India Company who made fortunes in India and returned to Britain, flaunting their wealth.

Napoleonic Code (p. 642)   The name given to the Civil Code of 1804, promulgated by Napoleon, which gave France a uniform and authoritative code of law.

nation (p. 690)   A large community of people who possess a sense of unity based on a belief that they have a common homeland and share a similar culture.

national consciousness (p. 691)   The awareness or belief of people that they belong to a nation.

nationalism (p. 690)   The belief that the people who form a nation should have their own political institutions and that the interests of the nation should be defended and promoted at all costs.

national self-determination (p. 690)   The doctrine advanced by nationalists that any group that considers itself a nation has the right to be ruled only by the members of their own nation and to have all members of the nation included in that state.

nation-state (p. 690)   A political structure sought by nationalists in which the boundaries of the state and the nation are identical, so that all the members of a nation are governed by the same political authorities.

natural law (p. 143)   A law that is believed to be inherent in nature rather than established by human beings.

nawabs (p. 575)   Native provincial governors in eighteenth-century India.

Nazism (p. 835)   Twentieth-century political ideology associated with Adolf Hitler that adopted many fascist ideas but with a central focus on racism and particularly anti-Semitism.

neoclassicism (p. 591)   The revival of the classical art and architecture of ancient Greece and Rome in the eighteenth century.

Neolithic Age (p. 10)   The New Stone Age, characterized by the development of agriculture and the use of stone tools.

Neoplatonism (pp. 221, 538)   A philosophy based on the teachings of Plato and his successors that flourished in Late Antiquity, especially in the teachings of Plotinus. Neoplatonism influenced Christianity in Late Antiquity. During the Renaissance Neoplatonism was linked to the belief that the natural world was charged with occult forces that could be used in the practice of magic.

New Conservatism (p. 932)   Political ideology that emerged at the end of the 1970s combining the free market approach of nineteenth-century liberalism with social conservatism.

New Economic Policy (NEP) (p. 824)   Vladimir Lenin's economic turnaround in 1921 that allowed and even encouraged small private businesses and farms in the Soviet Union.

new feminism (p. 931)   Reemergence of the feminist movement in the 1970s.

new imperialism (p. 766)   The third phase of modern European imperialism, that occurred in the late nineteenth and early twentieth centuries and extended Western control over almost all of Africa and much of Asia.

New Left (p. 926)   Leftwing political and cultural movement that emerged in the late 1950s and early 1960s; sought to develop a form of socialism that rejected the over-centralization, authoritarianism, and inhumanity of Stalinism.

New Testament (p. 197)   The collection of texts that together with the Hebrew Bible, or Old Testament, comprise the Christian Bible. New Testament texts include the Epistles (letters of Paul of Tarsus to early Christians), the Gospels (stories of Jesus Christ's life, death, and resurrection), and other early Christian documents.

95 theses (p. 434)   Propositions about indulgences Martin Luther announced he was willing to defend in debate. The publication of the 95 theses in 1517 started the Protestant Reformation.

nobility (p. 588)   Members of the aristocracy who received official recognition of their hereditary status, including their titles of honor and legal privileges.

nobility of the robe (p. 588)   French noblemen whose families acquired their status by appointment to office.

no-man's-land (p. 793)   The area between the combatants' trenches on the Western Front during World War I.

North Atlantic Treaty Organization (NATO) (p. 897)   Defensive anti-Soviet alliance of the United States, Canada, and the nations of western Europe established in 1949.

northern Renaissance (p. 430)   A movement in northern Europe that built on the foundations of the Italian Renaissance, especially to subject the Bible and the sources of Christianity to critical scrutiny.

Nuremberg trials (p. 874)   Post-World War II trials of members of the Nazi Party and German military; conducted by an international tribunal.

Old Regime (p. 613)   The political order of eighteenth-century France, dominated by an absolute monarch and a privileged nobility and clergy.

oligarchy (p. 82)   A government consisting of only a few people rather than the entire community.

Olympic Games (p. 79)   Greek athletic contests held in Olympia every four years between 776 B.C.E and 217. C.E.

Oppian Law (p. 147)   A law of the Roman Republic passed in 217 B.C.E. to help pay the cost of war. The law restricted the amount of gold or silver a single woman or widow could hold and restricted the articles of clothing they could wear.

Ottonian Renaissance (p. 285)   Under the patronage of the Saxon Emperor Otto I (936–973) and his brother Bruno, learned monks, Greek philosophers from Byzantium, and Italian scholars gathered at the imperial court, stimulating a cultural revival in literature and the arts. The writers and artists enhanced the reputation of Otto.

pagan (p. 211)   The Christian term for polytheist worship (worshiping more than one god). In the course of Late Antiquity, the Christian church suppressed paganism, the traditional religions of the Roman empire.

palace system (p. 52)   Late Bronze Age social system that concentrated religious, economic, political, and military power in the hands of an elite, who lived apart from most people in monumental fortified compounds.

pan-Arabism (p. 849)   Nationalist ideology that called for the political unification of all Arabs, regardless of religious affiliation.

panhellenic (p. 79)   This word means covering all Greek communities. It applies, for example, to the Olympic Games, in which competitors came from all over the Greek world.

papacy (p. 209)   The bishop of the city of Rome is called the Pope, or Father. The papacy refers to the administrative and political institutions controlled by the Pope. The papacy began to gain strength in the sixth century in the absence of Roman imperial government in Italy.

papal infallibility (p. 765)   The doctrine of the Roman Catholic Church proclaimed at the First Vatican Council in 1870 that the pope could not err when making solemn declarations regarding faith or morals.

paradigm (p. 538)   A conceptual model or intellectual framework within which scientists conduct their research and experimentation.

parlements (p. 496)   The highest provincial courts in France, the most important of which was the Parlement of Paris.

patriarchy (p. 28)   A social or cultural system in which men occupy the positions of power; in a family system, a father-centered household.

patricians (p. 140)   In ancient Rome, patricians were aristocratic clans with the highest status and the most political influence.

patrons and clients (p. 156)   In ancient Roman society, a powerful man (the patron) would exercise influence on behalf of a social subordinate (the client) in anticipation of future support or assistance.

Pax Romana (p. 168)   Latin for "Roman Peace," this term refers to the Roman Empire established by Augustus that lasted until the early third century C.E.

Pentateuch (p. 72)   The first five books of the Hebrew Bible.

perestroika (p. 939)   Loosely translated as "restructuring;" Gorbachev's effort to decentralize, reform, and thereby strengthen Soviet economic and political structures.

personal rule (p. 517)   The period from 1629 to 1640 in England when King Charles I ruled without Parliament.

phalanx (p. 81)   The military formation favored by hoplite soldiers. Standing shoulder to shoulder in ranks often eight men deep, hoplites moved in unison and depended on one another for protection.

pharaoh (p. 36)   Title for the Egyptian king, used during the New Kingdom period.

philology (p. 376)   A method reintroduced by the humanists during the Italian Renaissance devoted to the comparative study of language, especially to understanding the meaning of a word in a particular historical context.

philosophes (p. 596)   The writers and thinkers of the Enlightenment, especially in France.

pilgrimages (p. 219)   Religious journeys made to holy sites in order to encounter relics.

Pillars of Islam (p. 248)   The five basic principles of Islam as taught by Muhammad.

plantation colony (p. 399)   First appearing in the Cape Verde Islands and later in the tropical parts of the Americas, these colonies were established by Europeans who used African slave labor to cultivate cash crops such as sugar, indigo, cotton, coffee, and tobacco.

plebeians (p. 140)   The general body of Roman citizens.

plebiscite (p. 634)   A popular vote for or against a form of government or rule by a particular person.

pogroms (p. 740)   An organized and often officially encouraged riot or attack to persecute a particular ethnic or religious group, especially associated with eastern European attacks against Jews.

polis (p. 79)   A self-governing Greek city-state

polytheistic (p. 23)   Refers to polytheism, the belief in many gods.

pop art (p. 920)   Effort by artists in the 1950s and 1960s both to utilize and to critique the material plenty of post-World War II popular culture.

Popular Front (p. 846)   A political coalition of liberals, socialists, and communists to defeat fascist and racist-nationalist political rivals.

popular sovereignty (p. 636)   The claim that political power came from the people and that the people constituted the highest political power in the state.

positivism (p. 692)   The philosophy developed by August Comte in the nineteenth century according to which human society passed through a series of stages, leading to the final positive stage in which the accumulation of scientific data would enable thinkers to discover the laws of human behavior and bring about the improvement of society.

positivist (p. 756) The emphasis on the use of the scientific method to reach truth; a stress on observable fact.

postindustrialism, postindustrial society (p. 962) A service rather than manufacturing-based economy characterized by an emphasis on marketing and information and by a proliferation of communications technologies.

postmodernism (p. 957) Umbrella term covering a variety of artistic styles and intellectual theories and practices; in general, a rejection of a single, universal, Western style of modernity.

Potsdam Conference (p. 895) The meeting in July 1945 of the Allied leaders of Britain, the Soviet Union, and the United States in the German city of Potsdam.

Pragmatic Sanction of Bourges (p. 390) An agreement in 1438 that guaranteed the virtual autonomy of the French Church from papal control, enabling the French king to interfere in religious affairs and exploit Church revenues for government purposes.

Prague Spring (p. 915) Short-lived popular effort in 1968 to reform Czechoslovakia's political structures; associated with the phrase "socialism with a human face."

predestination (p. 442) The doctrine promoted by John Calvin that since God, the all-knowing and all-powerful being, knew everything in advance and caused everything to happen, then the salvation of any individual was predetermined.

prerogative (p. 517) The set of powers exercised by the English monarch alone, rather than in conjunction with Parliament.

Price Revolution (p. 462) After a long period of falling or stable prices that stretched back to the fourteenth century, Europe experienced sustained price increases between about 1540 and 1640, causing widespread social and economic turmoil.

priesthood of all believers (p. 434) Martin Luther's doctrine that all those of pure faith were themselves priests, a doctrine that undermined the authority of the Catholic clergy over the laity.

primogeniture (p. 514) The legal arrangement by which the eldest son inherits the entire estate upon the death of the father.

proletariat (p. 690) The word used by Karl Marx and Friedrich Engels to identify the class of workers who received their income from wages.

prophetic movement (p. 70) An important phase in the development of what became Judaism. In the ninth century B.C.E., Hebrew religious reformers, or prophets, demanded the transformation of religious and economic practices to reflect ideals of social justice and religious purity.

protectionism (p. 562) The policy of shielding domestic industries from foreign competition through a policy of levying tariffs on imported goods.

Protestant Reformation (p. 426) Dominated European affairs between 1517 and 1560 when the movement for religious reform begun by Martin Luther led Germany, Britain, and most of northern Europe to break away from the Catholic Church.

Radical Reformation (p. 440) Refers to Protestant movements that failed to gain official government recognition and were at best tolerated, at worst persecuted, during the sixteenth century.

rationalism (p. 536) The theory that the mind contains rational categories independent of sensory observation; more generally that reason is the primary source of truth.

Realpolitik (p. 712) The adoption of political tactics based solely on their realistic chances of success.

redistributive economies (p. 18) Type of economic system characteristic of ancient Mesopotamian societies. The central political authority controls all agricultural resources and their redistribution.

regency (p. 496) Rule by relative of a monarch during a period when the monarch was too young to rule or otherwise incapacitated.

Reign of Terror (p. 628) A purging of alleged enemies of the French state between 1793 and 1794, superintended by the Committee of Public Safety, that resulted in the execution of 17,000 people.

Reinsurance Treaty (p. 787) Treaty of 1887 in which the governments of Germany and Russia agreed to remain neutral if either was attacked.

relics (p. 219) In Christian belief, relics are sacred objects that have miraculous powers. They are associated with saints, biblical figures, or some object associated with them. They served as contacts between Earth and Heaven and were verified by miracles.

Religious Peace of Augsburg (p. 439) In 1555 this peace between Lutherans and Catholics within the Holy Roman Empire established the principle of *cuius regio, eius religio*, which means "he who rules determines the religion of the land." Protestant princes in the Empire were permitted to retain all church lands seized before 1552 and to enforce Protestant worship, but Catholic princes were also allowed to enforce Catholic worship in their territories.

Renaissance (p. 364) A term meaning "rebirth" used by historians to describe a movement that sought to imitate and understand the culture of antiquity. The Renaissance generally refers to a movement that began in Italy and then spread throughout Europe from about 1350 to 1550.

reparations (p. 814) Payments imposed upon Germany after World War I by the Versailles Treaty to cover the costs of the war.

republic (p. 139) A state in which political power resides in the people or their representatives rather than in a monarch.

republicanism (p. 366) A political theory first developed by the ancient Greeks, especially the philosopher Plato, but elaborated by the ancient Romans and rediscovered during the Italian Renaissance. The fundamental principle of republicanism as developed during the Italian Renaissance was that government officials should be elected by the people or a portion of the people.

Republic of Virtue (p. 628) The ideal form of government proposed by Maximilien Robespierre and other Jacobins during the French Revolution. Its proponents wished to make the republic established in 1792 more egalitarian and secular and inspire civic pride and patriotism in the people.

requerimiento (p. 408) A document read by conquistadores to the natives of the Americas before making war on them. The document briefly explained the principles of Christianity and commanded the natives to accept them immediately along with the authority of the pope and the sovereignty of the king of Spain. If the natives refused, they were warned they would be forced to accept Christian conversion and subjected to Spain anyway.

Resistance, the (p. 883) Label given to the many different underground political and partisan movements directed against Nazi rule in German-occupied Europe during World War II.

revisionism, socialist revisionism (p. 736) The belief that an equal society can be built through participation in parliamentary politics rather than through violent revolution.

rhetoric (p. 376) The art of persuasive or emotive speaking and writing, which was especially valued by the Renaissance humanists.

Roman Forum (p. 136) The central area in the city of Rome between the Palatine hill and the Capitoline hill.

Roman Republic (p. 137) The name given to the Roman state from about 500 B.C.E., when the last king of Rome was expelled, to 31 B.C.E., when Augustus established the Roman Empire.

Romanesque (p. 327) A style in architecture that spread throughout western Europe during the eleventh and the first half of the twelfth centuries and characterized by arched stone roofs supported by rounded arches, massive stone pillars, and thick walls.

Romanization (p. 177) The process by which conquered peoples absorbed aspects of Roman culture, especially the Latin language, city life, and religion.

romanticism (p. 693) An artistic and literary movement of the late eighteenth and nineteenth centuries that involved a protest against classicism, appealed to the passions rather than the intellect, and emphasized the beauty and power of nature.

Rome-Berlin Axis (p. 859) Alliance between Benito Mussolini's Italy and Adolf Hitler's Germany formed in 1936.

salons (p. 611) Private sitting rooms or parlors of aristocratic French women where discussions of philosophy, science, littérature, and politics took place in the eighteenth century.

sans-culottes (p. 623) The militant citizens of Paris who refused to wear the pants worn by noblemen and provided support for the Jacobins during the French Revolution; literally, those without breeches.

satraps (p. 115) Persian provincial governors who collected taxes and oversaw the bureaucracy.

Schlieffen Plan (p. 788) German military plan devised in 1905 that called for a sweeping attack on France through Belgium and the Netherlands.

scholasticism (p. 324) A term referring to a broad philosophical and theological movement that dominated medieval thought and university training. Scholasticism used logic learned from Aristotle to interpret the meaning of the Bible and the writings of the Church Fathers, who created Christian theology in its first centuries.

Scramble for Africa (p. 773) The frenzied imposition of European control over most of Africa that occurred between 1870 and 1914.

scriptorium (p. 271) The room in a monastery where monks copied books and manuscripts.

Sea Peoples (p. 54) Name given by the Egyptians to the diverse groups of migrants whose attacks helped bring the International Bronze Age to an end.

Second Industrial Revolution (p. 723)   A new phase in the industrialization of the processes of production and consumption, underway in Europe in the 1870s.

Second Triumvirate (p. 165)   In 43 B.C.E. Octavian (later called Augustus), Mark Antony, and Lepidus made an informal alliance to share power in Rome while they jockeyed for control. Octavian emerged as the sole ruler of Rome in 31 B.C.E.

secularization (p. 545)   The reduction of the importance of religion in society and culture.

seigneur (p. 593)   The lord of a French estate who received payments from the peasants who lived on his land.

separate spheres (p. 609)   The theory that men and women should conduct their lives in different social and political environments, confining women to the domestic sphere and excluding them from the public sphere of political involvement.

sepoys (p. 576)   Indian troops serving in the armed forces of the British East India Company.

Septuagint (p. 125)   The Greek translation of the Hebrew Bible (Old Testament).

serfs (p. 301)   During the Middle Ages serfs were agricultural laborers who worked and lived on a plot of land granted them by a lord to whom they owed a certain portion of their crops. They could not leave the land, but they had certain legal rights that were denied to slaves.

settler colony (p. 399)   A colony authorized when a private person obtained a license from a king to seize an island or parcel of land and occupied it with settlers from Europe who exported their own culture to the new lands. Settler colonies first appeared among the islands of the eastern Atlantic and portions of the Americas.

simony (p. 307)   The practice of buying and selling church offices.

skepticism (p. 543)   A tendency to doubt what one has been taught or is expected to believe.

Social Darwinism (p. 755)   The later-nineteenth-century application of the theory of evolution to entire human societies.

social democracy (pp. 843, 887) Political system in which a democratically elected parliamentary government endeavors to ensure a decent standard of living for its citizens through both economic regulation and the maintenance of a welfare state.

socialism (p. 687)   An ideology calling for the ownership of the means of production by the community with the purpose of reducing inequalities of income, wealth, opportunity and economic power.

socialist revisionism (p. 736)   The belief that an equal society can be built through participation in parliamentary politics rather than through violent revolution.

Social War (p. 159)   The revolt of Rome's allies against the Republic in 90 B.C.E. demanding full Roman citizenship

Solidarity (p. 935)   Trade union and political party in Poland that led an unsuccessful effort to reform the Polish communist state in 1981; survived to lead Poland's first non-communist government since World War II in 1989.

Sophists (p. 102)   Professional educators who traveled throughout the ancient Greek world, teaching many subjects. Their goal was to teach people the best ways to lead better lives.

soviets (p. 808)   Workers' and soldiers' councils formed in Russia during the Revolution of 1917.

Spanish Armada (p. 478)   A fleet of 132 ships, which sailed from Portugal to rendezvous with the Spanish army stationed in the Netherlands and launch an invasion of England in 1588. The English defeated the Armada as it passed through the English Channel. The defeat marked a shift in the power balance from Spain to England.

Spanish Reconquest (p. 260)   Refers to the numerous military campaigns by the Christian kingdoms of northern Spain to capture the Muslim-controlled cities and kingdoms of southern Spain. This long, intermittent struggle began with the capture of Toledo in 1085 and lasted until Granada fell to Christian armies in 1492.

spiritualists (p. 448)   A tendency within Protestantism, especially Lutheranism, to emphasize the power of personal spiritual illumination, called the "inner Word," a living form of the Scriptures written directly on the believer's soul by the hand of God.

stagflation (p. 930)   Term coined in the 1970s to describe an economy troubled by both high inflation and high unemployment rates.

standing armies (p. 495)   Trained and equipped military forces that were not disbanded after the conclusion of war. Standing armies often helped maintain order and enforce governmental policy at home.

states (p. 554)   Consolidated territorial areas that have their own political institutions and recognize no higher political authority.

Stoics (p. 132)   Followers of the philosophy developed by Zeno of Citium (ca. 335–ca. 263 B.C.E.) that urged acceptance of fate while participating fully in everyday life.

structuralism (p. 920)   Influential post-World War II social theory that explored the common structures of language and thought.

Struggle of the Orders (p. 140)   The political strife between patrician and plebeian Romans beginning in the fifth century B.C.E. The plebeians gradually won political rights and influence as a result of the struggle.

suffragettes (p. 746)   Feminist movement that emerged in Britain in the early twentieth century. Unlike the suffragists, who sought to achieve the national vote for women through rational persuasion, the suffragettes adopted the tactics of violent protest.

suffragists (p. 745)   Feminists who sought to achieve the national vote for women through rational persuasion and parliamentary politics.

supply (p. 664)   The amounts of capital, labor, and food that are needed to produce goods for the market as well as the quantities of those goods themselves.

syncretism (p. 69) The practice of equating two gods and fusing their cults was common throughout the Roman Empire and helped to unify the diverse peoples and religions under Roman rule.

syndicalism (p. 737)   Ideology of the late nineteenth and early twentieth century that sought to achieve a working-class revolution through economic action, particularly through mass labor strikes.

Talmud's (p. 217)   Commentaries on Jewish law. Rabbis completed the Babylonian Talmud and the Jerusalem Talmud by the end of the fifth century C.E.

tetrarchy (p. 205)   The government by four rulers established by the Roman emperor Diocletian in 293 C.E. that lasted until 312. During the tetrarchy many administrative and military reforms altered the fabric of Roman society.

Third Estate (p. 621)   The component of the Estates General in Old Regime France that technically represented all the commoners in the kingdom.

Third Reich (p. 864)   Term for Adolf Hitler's Germany; articulates the Nazi aim of extending German rule across Europe.

Third World (p. 909)   Term coined in 1955 to describe nations that did not align with either the Soviet Union or the United States; commonly used to describe the industrially underdeveloped nations.

Thomism (p. 325)   A branch of medieval philosophy associated with the work of the Dominican thinker,

Thomas Aquinas (1225–1274), who wrote encyclopedic summaries of human knowledge that confirmed Christian faith.

Time of Troubles (p. 489)   The period from 1604 to 1613 when Russia fell into chaos, which ended when the national assembly elected Tsar Michael Romanov, whose descendants ruled Russia until they were deposed in 1917.

Torah (p. 72)   Most commonly, the first five books of the Hebrew Bible; also used to refer to the whole body of Jewish sacred writings and tradition.

total war (p. 784)   A war that demands extensive state regulation of economic production, distribution, and consumption; and that blurs (or erases entirely) the distinction between civilian and soldier.

trading posts (p. 401)   Built by European traders along the coasts of Africa and Asia as a base for trade with the interior. Trading posts or factories were islands of European law and sovereignty, but European authority seldom extended very far beyond the fortified post.

transubstantiation (p. 318)   A doctrine promulgated at the Fourth Lateran Council in 1215 that explained by distinguishing between the outward appearances and the inner substance how the Eucharistic bread and wine changed into the body and blood of Christ.

Treaty of Brest-Litovsk (p. 797)   Treaty between Germany and Bolshevik-controlled Russia, signed in March, 1918, that ceded to Germany all of Russia's western territories.

trial by jury (p. 321)   When disputes about the possession of land arose after the late twelfth century in England, sheriffs assembled a group of twelve local men who testified under oath about the claims of the plaintiffs, and the circuit court judge made his decision on the basis of their testimony. The system was later extended to criminal cases.

Triple Alliance (p. 787)   Defensive alliance of Germany, Austria-Hungary, and Italy, signed in 1882.

Triple Entente (p. 787)   Informal defensive agreement linking France, Great Britain, and Russia before World War I.

triremes (p. 90)   Greek warships with three banks of oars. Triremes manned by the poorest people of Athenian society became the backbone of the Athenian empire.

troubadours (p. 326)   Poets from the late twelfth and thirteenth centuries who wrote love poems, meant to be sung to music, which reflected a new sensibility, called courtly love, about the ennobling possibilities of the love between a man and a woman.

Truman Doctrine (p. 896)   Named after U.S. president Harry Truman, the doctrine that in 1947 inaugurated the Cold War policy of resisting the expansion of communist control.

Twelfth-Century Renaissance (p. 325)   An intellectual revival of interest in ancient Greek philosophy and science and in Roman law in western Europe during the twelfth and early thirteenth centuries. The term also refers to a flowering of vernacular literature and the Romanesque and Gothic styles in architecture.

tyrants (p. 81)   Rulers in Greek city-states, usually members of the aristocracy, who seized power illegitimately rather than acquiring it by heredity or election. Tyrants often gained political support from the hoplites and the poor.

Unitarians (p. 449)   A religious reform movement that began in the sixteenth century and rejected the Christian doctrine of the Trinity. Unitarians (also called Arians, Socinians, and Anti-Trinitarians) taught a rationalist interpretation of the Scriptures and argued that Jesus was a divinely inspired man, not God who became a man as did other Christians.

universal law of gravitation (p. 533)   A law of nature established by Isaac Newton in 1687 holding that any two bodies attract each other with a force that is directly proportional to the product of their masses and indirectly proportional to the square of the distance between them. The law was presented in mathematical terms.

universal male suffrage (p. 627)   The granting of the right to vote to all adult males.

vassals (p. 281)   During the Middle Ages men voluntarily submitted themselves to a lord by taking an oath of loyalty. Vassals owed the lord certain services—usually military assistance—and sometimes received in exchange a grant of land known as a fief.

Vatican II (p. 922)   Popular term for the Second Vatican Council that convened in 1963 and introduced a series of changes within the Roman Catholic Church.

vernacular languages (p. 480)   The native spoken languages of Europe, which became literary languages and began to replace Latin as the dominant form of learned expression during the sixteenth century.

Versailles Treaty (p. 814)   Treaty between Germany and the victorious Allies after World War I.

Vichy, Vichy regime, Vichy government (p. 864)   Authoritarian state established in France after defeat by the German army in 1940.

Vulgate (p. 214)   The Latin translation of the Bible produced about 410 by the monk Jerome. It was the standard Bible in western Christian churches until the sixteenth century.

Wahhabism (p. 850)   A religious reform and revival movement founded by Muhammad Abd al-Wahhab (1703–1787) in the eighteenth century to purify Islam by returning to a strict interpretation of the *Sharia,* or Islamic law. Revived during the 1920s in Saudi Arabia.

Warsaw Pact (p. 897)   Military alliance of the Soviet Union and its eastern European satellite states in the Cold War era.

Weimar Republic (p. 825)   The democratic German state constructed after defeat in World War I and destroyed by the Nazis in 1933.

wergild (p. 267)   In Germanic societies the term referred to what an individual was worth in case he or she suffered an injury. It was the amount of compensation in gold that the wrongdoer's family had to pay to the victim's family.

witch-hunt (p. 469)   Refers to the dramatic increase in the judicial prosecution of alleged witches in either church or secular courts from the middle of the sixteenth to the middle of the seventeenth centuries.

Yalta Conference (p. 894)   Meeting in 1945 of the leaders of the Allied states of Britain, the Soviet Union, and the United States to devise plans for postwar Europe.

ziggurat (p. 23)   Monumental tiered or terraced temple characteristic of ancient Mesopotamia.

Zionism (p. 741)   Nationalist movement that emerged in the late nineteenth century and sought to establish a Jewish political state in Palestine (the Biblical Zion).

Zoroastrianism (p. 88)   The monotheistic religion of Persia founded by Zoroaster that became the official religion of the Persian Empire.

SUGGESTIONS FOR FURTHER READING

CHAPTER 1. THE BEGINNINGS OF CIVILIZATION, 10,000–1150 BCE.

Andrews, Anthony P. *First Cities.* 1995. An excellent introduction to the development of urbanism in Southwest Asia, Egypt, India, China, and the Americas.

Crawford, Harriet. *Sumer and the Sumerians.* 2004. A comprehensive study of the interplay between the physical environment, emerging political structures, and technological change. Clearly illustrated.

Dalley, Stephanie. *Mari and Karana: Two Old Babylonian Cities.* 1984. Despite the rather forbidding title, a delightful exploration of daily life in the eighteenth century B.C.E., using excavations of two small kingdoms in northwest Mesopotamia.

Fagan, Brian. *People of the Earth: An Introduction to World Prehistory.* 1998. A comprehensive textbook that introduces basic issues with a wealth of illustrations and explanatory materials.

Hornung, Erik. *History of Ancient Egypt: An Introduction,* trans. David Lorton. 1999. A concise and lucid overview of Egyptian history and life.

Kuhrt, Amélie. *The Ancient Near East, ca. 3000–330 B.C.,* 2 vols. 1995. A magisterial overview, with an excellent bibliography. The place to start for a continuous historical narrative of the region.

Redford, Donald B. *Egypt, Canaan, and Israel in Ancient Times.* 1993. A distinguished Egyptologist discusses 3,000 years of uninterrupted contact between Egypt and southwestern Asia.

Sasson, Jack M, ed. *Civilizations of the Ancient Near East,* Vol. 2. 1995. Contains a number of very helpful essays, particularly on Egypt.

Schmandt-Besserat, Denise. *How Writing Came About.* 1996. A highly readable and groundbreaking argument that cuneiform writing developed from a method of counting with tokens.

Schulz, Regine, and Matthias Seidel, eds. *Egypt: The World of the Pharaohs.* 1999. A sumptuously illustrated collection of essays on all aspects of Egyptian society and life by leading experts.

Snell, Daniel C. *Life in the Ancient Near East.* 1997. A concise account of the major developments over 5,000 years.

Spindler, Konrad. *The Man in the Ice: The Discovery of a 5,000-Year-Old Body Reveals the Secrets of the Stone Age.* 1994. A leader of the international team of experts interprets the corpse of a Neolithic hunter found in the Austrian Alps.

Stiebing, William H. *Ancient Near Eastern History and Culture.* 2008. Clear and comprehensive survey of important political and cultural events.

Trigger, Bruce G. *Early Civilizations: Ancient Egypt in Context.* 1995. A leading cultural anthropologist examines Old and Middle Kingdom Egypt through comparison with the early civilizations of China, Peru, Mexico, Mesopotamia, and Africa.

Van De Mieroop, Marc. *A History of the Ancient Near East ca. 3000–323 B.C.* 2007. Authoritative and up to date.

Wenke, Robert J. *Patterns in Prehistory: Humankind's First Three Million Years.* 4th ed. 1999. An often witty, highly readable account.

CHAPTER 2. THE AGE OF EMPIRES: THE INTERNATIONAL BRONZE AGE AND ITS AFTERMATH, CA. 1500–550 BCE.

Bryce, Trevor. *Life and Society in the Hittite World.* 2002. A lively look at Hittite customs, laws, and social structures.

Bryce, Trevor. *The Letters of the Great Kings of the Ancient Near East: The Royal Correspondence of the Late Bronze Age.* 2003. Bryce explores the Club of the Great Powers through their surviving correspondence.

Bryce, Trevor. *The Trojans and Their Neighbors.* 2005. An up-to-date examination of the historical Troy.

Cohen, Raymond, and Raymond Westbrook, eds. *Amarna Diplomacy: The Beginnings of International Relations.* 2000. An intriguing collaboration of archaeologists, linguists, and specialists in international diplomacy, this book looks at the Amarna Letters from the context of modern international relations.

Dever, William G. *What Did the Biblical Writers Know and When Did They Know It?: What Archaeology Can Tell Us about the Reality of Ancient Israel.* 2001. A clear and often entertaining account of the writing of the Hebrew Bible.

Dever, William G. *Who Were the Early Israelites and Where Did They Come From?* 2003. A clear and lively account that takes the reader step-by-step through the various historical, archaeological, and political controversies that bedevil the study of ancient Israel.

Dickinson, Oliver. *The Aegean Bronze Age.* 1994. Now the standard treatment of the complex archaeological data.

Dothan, Trude, and Moshe Dothan. *People of the Sea: The Search for the Philistines.* 1992. A survey of the archaeological material, written for non-specialists.

Finkelstein, Israel, and Neil Asher Silberman. *David and Solomon: In Search of the Bible's Sacred Kings and the Roots of the Western Tradition.* 2006. An important, if controversial archaeological interpretation that views David and Solomon as tribal chieftains and the "United Monarchy" as a fiction, this elegantly written study also explores the impact of the biblical story on Western identity.

Fitton, J. Lesley. *Minoans: Peoples of the Past.* 2002. Accessible account of recent research and conclusions.

Fitton, J. Lesley. *The Discovery of the Greek Bronze Age.* 1996. A lucid and well-illustrated study of the archaeologists who brought the Greek Bronze Age to light in the nineteenth and early twentieth centuries.

Kuhrt, Amélie. *The Ancient Near East, ca. 3000–330 B.C.*, 2 vols. 1995. A magisterial overview, with an excellent bibliography. The place to start for a continuous historical narrative of the region.

Latacz, Joachim. *Troy and Homer: Towards a Solution of an Old Mystery.* 2004. One of the most recent efforts to solve the puzzle of the historicity of Homer's account of the Trojan War.

Markoe, Glenn. *Phoenicians.* 2000. An important treatment of Phoenician society by a noted expert.

Miller, Patrick D. *Chieftains of the Highland Clans: A History of Israel in the 12th and 11th Centuries B.C.* 2003. Uses not only archaeological and textual evidence but also anthropological methodology to explore the history of the early Israelites.

Redford, Donald B. *Egypt, Canaan and Israel in Ancient Times.* 1992. An excellent, detailed synthesis of textual and archaeological evidence that emphasizes interconnections among cultures.

Stiebing, William H. *Ancient Near Eastern History and Culture.* 2008. A comprehensive survey that also pays close attention to historiographical and archaeological controversies. The chapter on the end of the International Bronze Age is particularly well done.

Van De Mieroop, Marc. *A History of the Ancient Near East ca. 3000–323 BC.* 2007. An excellent survey, with clear maps and useful time lines.

Walker, Christopher, ed. *Astronomy Before the Telescope.* 1996. A fascinating collection of essays about astronomy in the premodern period, which makes clear Western civilization's enormous debt to the Babylonians.

CHAPTER 3. GREEK CIVILIZATION

Boardman, John. *Persia and the West: An Archaeological Investigation of the Genesis of Achaemenid Art.* 2000. A brilliantly illustrated study that stresses intercultural influences in every aspect of Persian art.

Boyce, Mary. *A History of Zoroastrianism*, Vol. 2. 1975. This authoritative examination provides a masterful overview of the religion of the Persian Empire.

Burkert, Walter. *The Orientalizing Revolution: Near Eastern Influence on Greek Culture in the Early Archaic Age*, trans. Margaret Pinder and Walter Burkert. 1993. Explains how the Semitic East influenced the development of Greek society in the Archaic Age.

Cohn, Norman. *Cosmos, Chaos, and the World to Come: The Ancient Roots of Apocalyptic Faith.* 1993. Expert critical analysis of apocalyptic religions in the West, including Zoroastrianism, ancient Judaism, Christianity, and other faiths.

Finkelstein, Israel, and Neil Asher Silberman. *The Bible Unearthed: Archaeology's New Vision of Ancient Israel and the Origin of the Sacred Texts.* 2001. An important archaeological interpretation that challenges the narrative of the Hebrew Bible and offers a reconsideration of biblical history.

Gottwald, Norman K. *The Hebrew Bible: A Socio-Literary Introduction.* 1985. Combines a close reading of the Hebrew Bible with the latest archaeological and historical evidence.

Just, Roger. *Women in Athenian Law and Life.* 1989. Provides an overview of the social context of women in Athens.

Kuhrt, Amélie. *The Ancient Near East, ca. 3000–330 B.C.,* Vol. 2. 1995. This rich and comprehensive bibliography is a remarkably concise and readable account of Persian history with excellent discussion of ancient textual evidence. Many important passages appear in fluent translation.

Lindberg, David C. *The Beginnings of Western Science: The European Scientific Tradition in Philosophical, Religious, and Institutional Context, 600 B.C. to A.D. 1450.* 1992. This highly readable study provides an exciting survey of the main developments in Western science.

Markoe, Glenn. *Phoenicians.* 2000. The best and most up-to-date treatment of Phoenician society by a noted expert.

Murray, Oswyn. *Early Greece.* 1983. A brilliant study of all aspects of the emergence of Greek society between the Dark Age and the end of the Persian Wars.

Osborne, Robin. *Greece in the Making, 1200–479 B.C.* 1996. An excellent narrative of the development of Greek society with special regard to the archaeological evidence.

Stewart, Andrew. *Art, Desire, and the Body in Ancient Greece.* 1997. A provocative study that examines Greek attitudes toward sexuality and art.

Walker, Christopher, ed. *Astronomy Before the Telescope.* 1996. A fascinating collection of essays about astronomy in the premodern period, which makes clear our enormous debt to the Babylonians.

Wieshöfer, Josef. *Ancient Persia from 550 B.C. to A.D. 650,* trans. Azizeh Azodi. 1996. A fresh and comprehensive overview of Persian cultural, social, and political history that relies on Persian evidence more heavily than on biased Greek and Roman sources.

CHAPTER 4. HELLENISTIC CIVILIZATION

Auatin, Michel. *The Hellenistic World from Alexander to the Roman Conquest: A Selection of Ancient Sources in Translation,* 2nd ed. 2006. A major collection of more than 325 documents from this period.

Boardman, John, Jasper Griffin, and Oswyn Murray, eds. *Greece and the Hellenistic World. The Oxford History of the Classical World.* 1988.

A synthesis of all aspects of Hellenistic life, with excellent illustrations and bibliography.

Bosworth, A. B. *Alexander and the East: The Tragedy of Triumph.* 1997. A negative interpretation of Alexander as a totalitarian ruler.

Bugh, Glenn R., *The Cambridge Companion to the Hellenistic World.* 2006. A collection of essays on 15 different aspects of Hellenistic politics and culture.

Cartledge, Paul, Peter Garnsey, and Erich Gruen, eds. *Hellenistic Constructs: Essays in culture, history and historiography.* 1997.

Cohen, Getzel M. *The Hellenistic Settlements in Europe, the Islands, and Asia Minor.* 1996. The standard reference work on the cities founded in these areas during the Hellenistic period.

Cohn, Norman. *Cosmos, Chaos, and the World to Come: The Ancient Roots of Apocalyptic Faith.* 1993. This brilliant study explains the development of ideas about the end of the world in the cultures of the ancient world.

Cunliffe, Barry. *The Ancient Celts.* 1997. This source analyzes the archaeological evidence for the Celtic Iron Age, with many illustrations and maps.

Cunliffe, Barry, ed. *The Oxford Illustrated Prehistory of Europe.* 1996. A collection of well-illustrated essays on the development of European cultures from the end of the Ice Age to the Classical period.

Fox, Robin Lane. *Alexander the Great.* 1994. Shows that the myth Alexander created is as influential today as it was in the ancient world.

Green, Peter. *Alexander to Actium: The Historical Evolution of the Hellenistic Age.* 1990. A vivid interpretation of the world created by Alexander until the victory of Augustus.

Gruen, Erich S. *The Hellenistic World and the Coming of Rome.* 1984. An important study of how Rome entered the eastern Mediterranean world.

Kuhrt, Amélie, and Susan Sherwin-White, eds. *Hellenism in the East: The Interaction of Greek and Non-Greek Civilizations from Syria to Central Asia After Alexander.* 1987. These studies help us understand the complexities of the interaction of Greeks and non-Greeks in the Hellenistic world.

Momigliano, Arnaldo. *Alien Wisdom: The Limits of Hellenization.* 1975. A study of Greek attitudes toward the contemporary civilizations of the Romans, Celts, Jews, and Persians.

Onians, John. *Art and Thought in the Hellenistic Age: The Greek World View, 350–50 BC.* 1979.

Pollitt, J. J. *Art in the Hellenistic Age.* 1986. A brilliant interpretation of the development of Hellenistic art. Discusses the freedom of aristocratic Greek women in Egypt during this period.

Pomeroy, Sarah B. *Women in Hellenistic Egypt: From Alexander to Cleopatra.* 1984.

Steele, James. *Hellenistic Architecture in Asia Minor.* 1992. Challenges the belief that Hellenistic architecture represented a degradation of the Greek classical style.

CHAPTER 5. THE ROMAN REPUBLIC

Bringmann, Klaus. *A History of the Roman Republic.* 2007. A useful survey that not only provides a detailed narrative but also challenges some of the traditional interpretations.

Cornell, T. J. *The Beginnings of Rome: Italy and Rome from the Bronze Age to the Punic Wars (ca. 1000–264 B.C.).* 1996. A synthesis of the latest evidence with many important new interpretations.

Crawford, Michael, *The Roman Republic*, 2nd ed. 1992. An overview by a leading scholar.

Flower, Harriet I., ed. *The Cambridge Companion to the Roman Republic.* 2004. Includes essays on political and military history, Roman society, republican territorial expansion, culture, and the influence of the Republic on the French and American revolutions.

Gardner, Jane F. *Women in Roman Law and Society.* 1986. Explains the legal position of women in the Roman world.

Goldsworthy, Adrian. *The Fall of Carthage: The Punic Wars, 265–146 B.C.* 2003.

Gruen, Erich S. *The Last Generation of the Roman Republic.* 1995. An exhaustive study of a crucial period of the republic.

Lintott, Andrew. 2003. *The Constitution of the Roman Republic.* An authoritative and well-written treatment of the subject.

Orlin, Eric. *Temples, Religion and Politics in the Roman Republic.* 2002.

Pocock, J. G. A. *The Machiavellian Moment.* 1975. An immense scholarly discussion of the use of republican thought in Renaissance Europe, late seventeenth century England and eighteenth-century British America.

Pomeroy, Sarah B. *Goddesses, Whores, Wives, and Slaves: Women in Classical Antiquity.* 1995.

Sherwin-White, A. N. *Roman Citizenship.* 1980. A comprehensive treatment of the subject. A general study of women in the ancient world.

Stein, Peter. *Roman Law in European History.* A superb overview, beginning with the Law of the Twelve Tables.

CHAPTER 6. ENCLOSING THE WEST: THE EARLY ROMAN EMPIRE AND ITS NEIGHBORS: 31 BCE-235 CE.

Barrett, Anthony A. *Livia: First Lady of Imperial Rome.* 2002. Recent biography of one of the most intriguing figures in the Roman Empire.

Beard, Mary, John North, and Simon Price. *Religions of Rome.* 1995. The first volume contains essays on polytheist religions, and the second contains translated ancient sources.

Chancey, Mark. *Greco-Roman Culture and the Galilee of Jesus.* 2005. A concise but broad-ranging survey of the title topic.

Crossan, J. D. *The Birth of Christianity.* 1998. Lively account of the Roman context of this new religious force.

Futrell, Alison. *Blood in the Arena: The Spectacle of Roman Power.* 1997. Explores the role of violent spectacle in creating and sustaining Roman rule.

Gardner, Jane F. *Women in Roman Law and Society.* 1987. Discusses issues pertaining to women in Rome.

Garnsey, Peter, and Richard Saller. *The Roman Empire: Economy, Society, and Culture.* 1987. Stresses the economic and social foundations of the Roman Empire.

Isaac, Benjamin. *The Creation of Racism in Classical Antiquity.* 2004. A highly readable discussion of ancient social prejudices and discriminatory stereotypes that influenced the development of modern racism.

Nickelsburg, George W. E. *Ancient Judaism and Christian Origins. Diversity, Continuity, and Transformation.* 2003. Innovative study of the emergence of Christianity from Judaism.

Ramage, Nancy H., and Andrew Ramage. *Roman Art,* 4th ed. 2005. An excellent, beautifully illustrated introduction to Roman art and architecture.

Romm, James. *The Edges of the Earth in Ancient Thought: Geography, Exploration, and Fiction.* 1992. An exciting introduction to the Roman understanding of real and imaginary peoples.

Scott, Sarah, and Jane Webster, eds. *Roman Imperialism and Provincial Art.* 2003. A collection of essays that explores new approaches to the cultural interconnections between the Romans and the peoples they ruled.

Talbert, Richard, ed. *The Barrington Atlas of the Classical World.* 2000. This atlas contains the best maps available.

Webster, Graham. *The Roman Imperial Army,* 3rd ed. 1985. Discusses military organization and life in the empire.

Wells, Peter S. *The Battle That Stopped Rome.* 2003. A lively account of the Battle of Teutoberg Forest that provides a clear and comprehensive demonstration of the way archaeological evidence helps shape our understanding of the past.

Wolfram, Herwig. *The Roman Empire and Its Germanic Peoples.* 1997. Examines the interrelation of Romans and Germans over several centuries.

Woolf, G., ed. *The Cambridge Illustrated History of the Roman World.* 2003. Richly illustrated and comprehensive.

Woolf, Greg. *Becoming Roman: The Origins of Provincial Civilization in Gaul.* 1998. The best recent study of Romanization.

CHAPTER 7. LATE ANTIQUITY: THE AGE OF NEW BOUNDARIES, 250-600

Bowersock, G. W. *Hellenism in Late Antiquity.* 1990. Explains the important role of traditional Greek culture in shaping late antiquity.

Bowersock, G. W., Peter Brown, and Oleg Grabar, eds. *Late Antiquity: A Guide to the Postclassical World.* 1999. An indispensable handbook containing synthetic essays and shorter encyclopedia entries.

Brown, Peter. *The Cult of the Saints: Its Rise and Function in Late Antiquity.* 1981. A brilliant and highly influential study.

Brown, Peter. *The Rise of Western Christendom: Triumph and Diversity.* 1997. An influential and highly accessible survey.

Brown, Peter. *The World of Late Antiquity.* 1971. A classic treatment of the period.

Cameron, Averil. *The Later Roman Empire.* 1993. *The Mediterranean World in Late Antiquity.* 1997. Excellent textbooks with bibliography and maps.

Clark, Gillian. *Women in Late Antiquity: Pagan and Christian Life-Styles.* 1993. The starting point of modern discussion; lucid and reliable.

Harries, Jill. *Law and Empire in Late Antiquity.* 1999. Explores the presence and practice of law in Roman society.

Lee, A. D. *Information and Frontiers: Roman Foreign Relations in Late Antiquity.* 1993. An exciting and original investigation.

Maas, Michael. *The Cambridge Companion to the Age of Justinian.* 2005. A collection of 20 chapters by different experts on all aspects of the Mediterranean world in the sixth century.

Maas, Michael. *Readings in Late Antiquity: A Sourcebook.* 2000. Hundreds of ancient sources in translation illustrating all aspects of late antiquity.

Markus, Robert. *The End of Ancient Christianity.* 1995. Excellent introduction to the transformation of Christianity in late antiquity.

Rich, John, ed. *The City in Late Antiquity.* 1992. Important studies of changes in late antique urbanism.

Thompson, E. A. *The Huns,* rev. Peter Heather. 1997. The best introduction to major issues.

CHAPTER 8. MEDIEVAL EMPIRES AND BORDERLANDS: BYZANTIUM AND ISLAM

Bowersock, Glen, Peter Brown, and Oleg Grabar, eds. *Late Antiquity: A Guide to the Post-Classical World.* 1999. Interpretive essays combined with encyclopedia entries make this a starting point for discussion.

Brown, Thomas S. *Gentlemen and Officers: Imperial Administration and Aristocratic Power in Byzantine Italy,* A.D. *554–800.* 1984. The basic study of Byzantine rule in Italy between Justinian and Charlemagne.

Bulliet, Richard W. *The Camel and the Wheel.* 1990. A fascinating investigation of the importance of the camel in history.

Cook, Michael. *Muhammad.* 1996. A short, incisive account of Muhammad's life that questions the traditional picture.

Cormack, Robin. *Writing in Gold: Byzantine Society and Its Icons.* 1985. An expert discussion of icons in the Byzantine world.

Donner, Fred M. *The Early Islamic Conquests.* 1981. Discusses the first phases of Islamic expansion.

Fletcher, Richard. *Moorish Spain.* 1992. Highly readable.

Franklin, Simon, and Jonathan Shepard. *The Emergence of Rus: 750–1200.* 1996. The standard text for this period.

Hawting, G. R. *The first dynasty of Islam: the Umayyad caliphate, AD 661–750.* 2000. The most up-to-date study of the Umayyads.

Herrin, Judith. *The Formation of Christendom.* 2001. An exceptionally learned and lucid book; Herrin sees Byzantium as crucial both for the development of Christianity and Islam.

Hourani, George. *Arab Seafaring in the Indian Ocean in Ancient and Early Medieval Times.* 1995. The standard discussion of Arab maritime activity.

King, Charles. *The Black Sea: A History.* 2004. A comprehensive history of the Black Sea region from antiquity to the present. It is especially useful for anyone interested in this borderland among cultures.

Moorhead, John. *The Roman Empire Divided, 400–700.* 2001. A reliable and up-to-date survey of the period.

Robinson, Francis, ed. *The Cambridge Illustrated History of the Islamic World.* 1978. Many excellent and well-illustrated articles that will be useful for beginners.

Treadgold, Warren. *A History of the Byzantine State and Society.* 1998. A reliable narrative of Byzantine history.

Treadgold, Warren T. *A Concise History of Byzantium.* 2001. A reliable and insightful short survey.

CHAPTER 9. MEDIEVAL EMPIRES AND BORDERLANDS: THE LATIN WEST

Bachrach, Bernard S. *Early Medieval Jewish Policy in Western Europe.* 1977. A significant revisionist view of the history of the Jews in Latin Christian Europe.

Bartlett, Robert. *The Making of Europe: Conquest, Colonization and Cultural Change: 950–1350.* 1993. The best, and often greatly stimulating, analysis of how Latin Christianity spread in post-Carolingian Europe.

Brown, Peter. *The Rise of Western Christendom: Triumph and Diversity A.D. 200–1000.* 2001. A brilliant interpretation of the development of Christianity in its social context.

Cohen, Jeremy. *Living Letters of the Law: Ideas of the Jew in Medieval Christianity.* 1999. A masterful investigation of early medieval Judaism.

Geary, Patrick J. *The Peoples of Europe in the Early Middle Ages.* 2002. Discusses the emergence of the new kingdoms of Europe, stressing the incorporation of Roman elements.

Hollister, C. Warren. *Medieval Europe: A Short History.* 1997. This concise, crisply written text presents the development of Europe during the Middle Ages by charting its progression from a primitive rural society, sparsely settled and impoverished, to a powerful and distinctive civilization.

Jones, Gwyn. *A History of the Vikings.* 2001. A comprehensive, highly readable analysis.

Keen, Maurice, ed. *Medieval Warfare: A History.* 1999. Lucid specialist studies of aspects of medieval warfare.

Lawrence, C. H. *Medieval Monasticism.* 2001. A fine introduction to the phenomenon of Christian monasticism.

Maalouf, Amin. *The Crusades through Arab Eyes.* 1984. Based on the works of Arab chroniclers, this book depicts a culture nearly destroyed both by internal conflicts and the military threat of the alien Christian culture.

Mayr-Harting, Henry. *The Coming of Christianity to Anglo-Saxon England.* 1991. How a Germanic people were converted to Christianity.

McKitterick, Rosamond. *The Early Middle Ages.* 2001. The best up-to-date survey for the period 400–1000. It is composed of separate essays by leading specialists.

Moorhead, John. *The Roman Empire Divided, 400–700.* 2001. The best recent survey of the period.

Reuter, Timothy. *Germany in the Early Middle Ages, c. 800–1056.* 1991. A lucid explanation of the complexities of German history in this period.

Reynolds, Susan. *Fiefs and Vassals: The Medieval Evidence Reinterpreted.* 1994. The most important reexamination of the feudalism problem.

Riché, Pierre. *Education and Culture in the Barbarian West, Sixth Through Eighth Centuries,* translated from the third French edition. by John J. Contreni. 1975. Demonstrates the rich complexity of learning during this period, once thought to be the Dark Ages of education.

Riché, Pierre. *The Carolingians: A Family Who Forged Europe.* 1993. Translated from the 1983 French edition, this book traces the rise, fall, and revival of the Carolingian dynasty, and shows how it molded the shape of a post-Roman Europe that still prevails today. This is basically a family history, but the family dominated Europe for more than two centuries.

Riley-Smith, Jonathan Simon Christopher. *The Crusades: A Short History.* 1987. Exactly what the title says.

Riley-Smith, Jonathan Simon Christopher. *The Oxford Illustrated History of the Crusades.* 2001. An utterly engaging, comprehensive study.

Stenton, Frank M. *Anglo-Saxon England.* 2001. This classic history covers the period ca. 550–1087 and traces the development of English society from the oldest Anglo-Saxon laws and kings to the extension of private lordship.

Strayer, Joseph B., ed. *Dictionary of the Middle Ages.* 1986. An indispensable reference work.

Webster, Leslie, and Michelle Brown, eds. *The Transformation of the Roman World*, A.D. 400–900. 1997. A well-illustrated synthesis with maps and bibliography.

Wickham, Chris. *Early Medieval Italy: Central Government and Local Society, 400–1000.* 1981. Examines the economic and social transformation of Italy.

CHAPTER 10. MEDIEVAL CIVILIZATION: THE RISE OF WESTERN EUROPE

Bony, Jean. *French Gothic Architecture of the Twelfth and Thirteenth Centuries.* 1983. With many beautiful illustrations, this is a good way to begin an investigation of these magnificent buildings.

Colish, Marcia L. *Medieval Foundations of the Western Intellectual Tradition, 400–1400.* 1997. The best general study.

Gimpel, Jean. *The Medieval Machine: The Industrial Revolution of the Middle Ages.* 1976. A short, lucid account of the power and agricultural revolutions.

Keen, Maurice. *Chivalry.* 1984. Readable and balanced in its coverage of this sometimes misunderstood phenomenon.

Lambert, Malcolm. *Medieval Heresy: Popular Movements from the Gregorian Reform to the Reformation,* 2nd ed. 1992. The best general study of heresy.

Lawrence, C. H. *The Friars: The Impact of the Early Mendicant Movement on Western Society.* 1994. The best general study of the influence of Dominicans and Franciscans.

Moore, R. I. *The Formation of a Persecuting Society: Power and Deviance in Western Europe, 950–1250.* 1987. A brilliant analysis of how Europe became a persecuting society.

Morris, Colin. *The Papal Monarchy: The Western Church from 1050 to 1250.* 1989. A thorough study that should be the beginning point for further investigation of the many fascinating figures in the medieval Church.

Mundy, John H. *Europe in the High Middle Ages, 1150–1309,* 3rd ed. 1999. A comprehensive introduction to the period.

Peters, Edward. *Europe and the Middle Ages.* 1989. An excellent general survey.

Strayer, Joseph R. *On the Medieval Origins of the Modern State.* 1970. Still the best short analysis.

CHAPTER 11. THE MEDIEVAL WEST IN CRISIS

Carmichael, Ann G. *Plague and the Poor in Renaissance Florence.* 1986. An innovative study that both questions the traditional theory of the bubonic plague as the cause of the Black Death and examines how fear of the disease led to regulation of the poor.

Cohn, Samuel. *The Black Death Transformed: Disease and Culture in Early Renaissance Europe.* 2003. A well-argued case that the Black Death was not caused by the bubonic plague.

Duby, Georges. *France in the Middle Ages, 987–1460: From Hugh Capet to Joan of Arc.* 1991. Traces the emergence of the French state.

Gordon, Bruce, and Peter Marshall, eds. *The Place of the Dead: Death and Remembrance in Late Medieval and Early Modern Europe.* 2000. A collection of essays that shows how the placing of the dead in society was an important activity that engendered considerable conflict and negotiation.

Herlihy, David. *The Black Death and the Transformation of the West.* 1997. A pithy, readable analysis of the epidemiological and historical issues surrounding the Black Death.

Holmes, George. *Europe: Hierarchy and Revolt, 1320–1450.* 1975. Excellent examination of rebellions.

Huizinga, Johan. *The Autumn of the Middle Ages,* trans. Rodney J. Payton and Urlich Mammitzsch. 1996. A new translation of the classic study of France and the Low Countries during the fourteenth and fifteenth centuries. Dated and perhaps too pessimistic, Huizinga's lucid prose and broad vision still make this an engaging reading experience.

Imber, Colin. *The Ottoman Empire, 1300–1481.* 1990. The basic work that establishes a chronology for the early Ottomans.

Jordan, William C. *The Great Famine: Northern Europe in the Early Fourteenth Century.* 1996. The most comprehensive book on the famine.

Lambert, Malcolm. *Medieval Heresy: Popular Movements from the Gregorian Reform to the Reformation.* 1992. Excellent general study of the Hussite and Lollard movements.

Le Roy Ladurie, Emmanuel. *Times of Feast, Times of Famine: A History of Climate Since the Year 1000,* trans. Barbara Bray. 1971. The book that introduced the idea of the Little Ice Age and promoted the study of the influence of climate on history.

Lynch, Joseph H. *The Medieval Church: A Brief History*. 1992. A pithy, elegant survey of ecclesiastical institutions and developments.

Morgan, David O. *The Mongols*. 1986. Best introduction to Mongol history.

Nirenberg, David. *Communities of Violence: Persecution of Minorities in the Middle Ages*. 1996. An important analysis of the persecution of minorities that is deeply rooted in Spanish evidence.

Scott, Susan, and Christopher Duncan. *Biology of Plagues: Evidence from Historical Populations*. 2001. An analysis by two epidemiologists who argue that the Black Death was not the bubonic plague but probably a virus similar to Ebola.

Sumption, Jonathan. *The Hundred Years' War: Trial by Battle*. 1991. First volume goes only to 1347. When it is completed, it will be the best comprehensive study.

Swanson, R. N. *Religion and Devotion in Europe, c. 1215–c. 1515*. 1995. The best up-to-date textbook account of late medieval religious practice.

CHAPTER 12. THE ITALIAN RENAISSANCE AND BEYOND: THE POLITICS OF CULTURE

Baxandall, Michael. *Painting and Experience in Fifteenth Century Italy: A Primer in the Social History of Pictorial Style*. 1988. A fascinating study of how the daily social experiences of Florentine bankers and churchgoers influenced how these individuals saw Renaissance paintings and how painters responded to the viewers' experience. One of the best books on Italian painting.

Brown, Howard M. *Music in the Renaissance*. 1976. Dated but still the best general study of Renaissance music.

Brown, Patricia Fortini. *Art and Life in Renaissance Venice*. 1997. A delightful study about how art fit into the daily lives and homes of the Venetian upper classes.

Brucker, Gene. *Florence: The Golden Age, 1138–1737*. 1998. A brilliant, beautifully illustrated history by the most prominent American historian of Florence.

Burke, Peter. *The Italian Renaissance*. 1999. A concise and readable synthesis of the most recent research.

Hale, J. R. *Renaissance Europe, 1480–1520*. 2000. A witty, engaging, and enlightening study of Europe during the formation of the early modern state system. Strong on establishing the material and social limitations of Renaissance society.

King, Margaret L. *Women of the Renaissance*. 1991. The best general study of women in Renaissance Europe. It is especially strong on female intellectuals and women's education.

Kohl, Benjamin G., and Alison Andrews Smith, eds. *Major Problems in the History of the Italian Renaissance*. 1995. A useful collection of articles and short studies of major historical problems in the study of the Renaissance.

Martines, Lauro. *Power and Imagination: City-States in Renaissance Italy*. 1988. An excellent general survey that is strong on class conflicts and patronage.

Najemy, John M. *A History of Florence, 1200–1575*. 2006. The best and most up-to-date history of the home of the Renaissance.

Nauert, Charles G., Jr. *Humanism and the Culture of Renaissance Europe*. 1995. The best survey of humanism for students new to the subject. It is clear and comprehensive.

Skinner, Quentin. *Machiavelli: A Very Short Introduction*. 2000. This is the place to begin in the study of Machiavelli. Always clear and precise, this is a beautiful little book.

Stephens, John. *The Italian Renaissance: The Origins of Intellectual and Artistic Change Before the Reformation*. 1990. A stimulating analysis of how cultural change took place.

Vasari, Giorgio. *The Lives of the Artists*. 1998. Written by a sixteenth-century Florentine who was himself a prominent artist, this series of artistic biographies captures the spirit of Renaissance society.

CHAPTER 13. THE WEST AND THE WORLD: THE SIGNIFICANCE OF GLOBAL ENCOUNTERS, 1450–1650

Chaudhuri, K. N. *Trade and Civilization in the Indian Ocean: An Economic History from the Rise of Islam to 1750*. 1985. Arguing for the long-term unity of trade routes, the book lays out the importance of Asian merchants to maritime trade networks from the South China Sea to the Mediterranean.

Clendinnen, Inga. *Aztecs: An Interpretation*. 1991. A provocative, sometimes disturbing book that directly confronts the implications of human sacrifice and cannibalism among the Aztecs and offers an explanation for it by analyzing Aztec religion.

Crosby, Alfred W., Jr. *The Columbian Exchange: Biological and Cultural Consequences of 1492*. 1973. The most significant study on the implications of the biological exchanges for the cultural history of both the Old and New Worlds. It has the benefit of being an exciting book to read.

Curtin, Philip D. *African History: From Earliest Times to Independence.* 1995. An excellent survey by one of the most distinguished comparative historians.

Elvin, Mark. *The Pattern of the Chinese Past: A Social and Economic Interpretation.* 1973. An excellent overview of Chinese history that covers Chinese responses to Western encounters.

Fernández-Armesto, Felipe. *Before Columbus: Exploration and Colonization from the Mediterranean to the Atlantic, 1229–1492.* 1987. Engagingly written and original in scope, this is the best single account of early European colonization efforts.

Fernández-Armesto, Felipe. *Columbus.* 1991. The 500th anniversary of Columbus's voyage in 1492 provoked a wide-ranging reappraisal of his motives and career. This pithy, engaging book is by far the most convincing in revising Columbus's image, but it deflated much of the Columbus myth and caused considerable controversy.

Oliver, Roland. *The African Experience from Olduvai Gorge to the 21st Century.* 2000. A highly readable general survey.

Pagden, Anthony. *European Encounters with the New World: From Renaissance to Romanticism.* 1993. A fascinating examination of how Europeans interpreted their encounters with America.

Parry, J. H. *The Age of Reconnaissance.* 1982. An analysis of European shipping technology and the causes behind European explorations. It covers all the major voyages.

Parry, J. H. *The Spanish Seaborne Empire.* 1990. The standard study on the subject. It brings together an enormous range of material and presents it clearly and cogently.

Phillips, William D., Jr., and Carla Rahn Phillips. *The Worlds of Christopher Columbus.* 1992. A balanced analysis of Columbus's attempts to find financing for his voyage that pays equal attention to his personal ambition, Christian zeal, and navigational skills.

CHAPTER 14. THE REFORMATIONS OF RELIGION

Bireley, Robert. *The Refashioning of Catholicism, 1450–1700: A Reassessment of the Counter Reformation.* 1999. A fair reappraisal of the major events by one of the most prominent historians of Catholicism in this period.

Bossy, John. *Christianity in the West, 1400–1700.* 1985. A short study not of the institutions of the Church but of Christianity itself, this book explores the Christian people, their beliefs, and their way of life. The book demonstrates considerable continuities before and after the Reformation and is especially useful in understanding the attitudes of common lay believers as opposed to the major reformers and Church officials.

Cameron, Euan. *The European Reformation.* 1995. The most comprehensive general survey, this bulky book covers all the major topics in considerable detail. It is excellent in explaining theological issues.

Hsia, R. Po-chia. *The World of Catholic Renewal, 1540–1770.* 1998. An excellent survey of the most recent research.

Koenigsberger, H. G., George L. Mosse, and G. Q. Bowler. *Europe in the Sixteenth Century,* 2nd ed. 1989. A good beginner's survey. Strong on political events.

McGrath, Alister E. *Reformation Thought: An Introduction,* 3rd rev. ed. 1999. Indispensable introduction for anyone seeking to understand the ideas of the European Reformation. Drawing on the most up-to-date scholarship, McGrath offers a clear explanation of these ideas, set firmly in their historical contexts.

Muir, Edward. *Ritual in Early Modern Europe,* 2nd ed. 2005. A broad survey of the debates about ritual during the Reformation and the implementation of ritual reforms.

Oberman, Heiko A. *Luther: Man Between God and the Devil,* trans. Eileen Walliser-Schwarzbart. 1992. First published to great acclaim in Germany, this book argues that Luther was more the medieval monk than history has usually regarded him. Oberman claims that Luther was haunted by the Devil and saw the world as a cosmic battleground between God and Satan. A brilliant, intellectual biography that is sometimes challenging but always clear and precise.

O'Malley, John. *Trent and All That: Renaming Catholicism in the Early Modern Era.* 2000. O'Malley works out a remarkable guide to the intellectual and historical developments behind the concepts of Catholic reform and, in his useful term, Early Modern Catholicism. The result is the single best overview of scholarship on Catholicism in early modern Europe, delivered in a pithy, lucid, and entertaining style.

Ozment, Steven. *The Age of Reform, 1250–1550: An Intellectual and Religious History of Late Medieval and Reformation Europe.* 1986. Firmly places the Protestant Reformation in the context of late medieval spirituality and theology; particularly strong on pre-Reformation developments.

Reardon, Bernard M. G. *Religious Thought in the Reformation,* 2nd ed. 1995. A good beginner's survey of the intellectual dimensions of the Reformation.

Scribner, R. W. *For the Sake of the Simple Folk: Popular Propaganda for the German Reformation.* 1994. An innovative and fascinating study of the Lutheran use of visual images.

Scribner, R. W. *The German Reformation.* 1996. A short and very clear analysis of the appeal of the Reformation by the leading social historian of the period. Pays attention to what people actually did rather than just what reformers said they should do.

CHAPTER 15. THE AGE OF CONFESSIONAL DIVISION

Anderson, M. S. *The Origins of the Modern European State System, 1494–1618.* 1998. The best short study for students new to the subject of the evolution of the confessional states in Europe. This book is very good at establishing common patterns among the various states.

Burke, Peter. *Popular Culture in Early Modern Europe.* 1994. This wide-ranging book includes considerable material from eastern Europe and Scandinavia, as well as the more extensively studied western European countries. Extraordinarily influential, it practically invented the subject of popular culture by showing how much could be learned from studying festivals and games.

Davies, Norman. *God's Playground: A History of Poland.* Rev. ed., 2 vols. 1982. By far the most comprehensive study of Polish history, this is particularly strong for the sixteenth and seventeenth centuries. Davies offers a Polish-centered view of European history that is marvelously stimulating even if he sometimes overstates his case for the importance of Poland.

Dukes, Paul. *A History of Russia: Medieval, Modern, Contemporary, ca. 882–1996,* 3rd ed. 1998. A comprehensive survey that synthesizes the most recent research.

Dunn, Richard S. *The Age of Religious Wars, 1559–1715,* 2nd ed. 1980. An excellent survey for students new to the subject.

Evans, R. J. W. *Rudolf II and His World: A Study in Intellectual History, 1576–1612.* 1973. A sympathetic examination of the intellectual world Rudolf created. Evans recognizes Rudolf's mental problems but lessens their significance for understanding the period.

Holt, Mack P. *The French Wars of Religion, 1562–1629.* 1996. A lucid short synthesis of the events and complex issues raised by these wars.

Hsia, R. Po-chia. *Social Discipline in the Reformation: Central Europe, 1550–1750.* 1989. An excellent, lucid, and short overview of the attempts to discipline the people in Germany.

Huppert, George. *After the Black Death: A Social History of Early Modern Europe.* 1986. Engaging, entertaining, and elegantly written, this is the best single study of European social life during the Early Modern period.

Levack, Brian P. *The Witch-Hunt in Early Modern Europe,* 2nd ed. 1995. The best and most up-to-date short examination of the complex problem of the witch-hunt. This is the place to begin for students new to the subject.

Ozment, Steven E. *Ancestors: The Loving Family in Old Europe.* 2001. This comprehensive study of family life demonstrates that families were actually far more loving than the theory of patriarchy would suggest.

Parker, Geoffrey. *The Dutch Revolt,* rev. ed. 1990. The classic study of the revolt by one of the most masterful historians of the period. This study is especially adept at pointing to the larger European context of the revolt.

Parker, Geoffrey. *The Grand Strategy of Philip II.* 1998. Rehabilitates Philip as a significant strategic thinker.

Wiesner, Merry E. *Women and Gender in Early Modern Europe.* 1993. The best short study of the subject. This is the best book for students new to the subject.

CHAPTER 16. ABSOLUTISM AND STATE BUILDING, 1618–1715.

Aylmer, G. E. *Rebellion or Revolution.* 1986. A study of the nature of the political disturbances of the 1640s and 1650s.

Beik, William. *Louis XIV and Absolutism: A Brief Study with Documents.* 2000. An excellent collection of documents.

Collins, James B. *The State in Early Modern France.* 1995. The best general study of the French state.

Elliott, J. H. *Richelieu and Olivares.* 1984. A comparison of the two contemporary absolutist ministers and state builders in France and Spain.

Goffman, Daniel. *The Ottoman Empire and Early Modern Europe.* 2002. A broad survey that challenges many of the Western stereotypes of Ottoman politics and culture, including the belief that Ottoman government was tyrannical.

Harris, Tim. *Politics Under the Later Stuarts.* 1993. The best study of Restoration politics, including the Glorious Revolution.

Hughes, Lindsey. *Russia in the Age of Peter the Great.* 1998. A comprehensive study of politics, diplomacy, society, and culture during the reign of the "Tsar Reformer."

Israel, Jonathan. *The Dutch Republic: Its Rise, Greatness and Fall, 1477–1806.* 1996. A massive and authoritative study of the Dutch Republic during the period of its greatest global influence.

Lincoln, W. Bruce. *Sunlight at Midnight: St. Petersburg and the Rise of Modern Russia.* 2000. The best study of the building of Peter the Great's new capital city.

Parker, David. *The Making of French Absolutism.* 1983. A particularly good treatment of the early seventeenth century.

Parker, Geoffrey. *The Military Revolution.* 1988. Deals with the impact of the military revolution on the world as well as European history.

Rabb, Theodore K. *The Struggle for Stability in Early Modern Europe.* 1975. Employs visual as well as political sources to illustrate the way in which Europeans responded to the general crisis of the seventeenth century.

Schama, Simon. *The Embarrassment of Riches: An Interpretation of Dutch Culture in the Golden Age.* 1987. Contains a wealth of commentary on Dutch art and culture during its most influential period.

Wilson, Peter H. *Absolutism in Central Europe.* 2000. Analyzes both the theory and the practice of absolutism in Prussia and Austria.

CHAPTER 17. THE SCIENTIFIC REVOLUTION

Biagioli, Mario. *Galileo, Courtier: The Practice of Science in the Culture of Absolutism.* 1993. Argues that Galileo's desire for patronage determined the type of research he engaged in and the scientific questions he asked.

Campbell, Mary Blaine. *Wonder and Science, Imagining Worlds in Early Modern Europe.* 1999. Explores the conceptual and celestial worlds opened by science as well as the geographical worlds found in voyages of discovery.

Cohen, H. Floris. *The Scientific Revolution: A Historiographical Inquiry.* 1995. A thorough account of all the different interpretations of the causes and significance of the Scientific Revolution.

Dear, Peter. *Discipline and Experience: The Mathematical Way in the Scientific Revolution.* 1995. Explains the importance of mathematics in the development of seventeenth-century science.

Debus, Allen G. *Man and Nature in the Renaissance.* 1978. Deals with the early history of the Scientific Revolution and develops many of its connections with the Renaissance.

Drake, Stillman, ed. *Discoveries and Opinions of Galileo.* 1957. Includes four of Galileo's most important writings, together with a detailed commentary.

Feingold, Mordechai. *The Newtonian Moment: Isaac Newton and the Making of Modern Culture.* 2004. A richly illustrated volume that contains valuable material on the reception of Newtonian ideas in the eighteenth century as well as a chapter on Newtonian women.

Grayling, A. C. *Descartes: The Life and Times of a Genius.* 2006. A biography that places Descartes in his proper historical context and suggests that he may have served as a spy.

Huff, Toby. *The Rise of Early Modern Science: Islam, China and the West,* 2003. Adresses the question why modern science arose only in the West despite the fact that non-Western science was more advanced in the Middle Ages.

Kuhn, Thomas S. *The Copernican Revolution.* 1957. The most comprehensive and authoritative study of the shift from an Earth-centered to a sun-centered model of the universe.

Needham, Joseph. *The Grand Titration: Science and Society in East and West.* 1979. Discusses the weaknesses and strengths of Chinese science.

Popkin, Richard. *The History of Scepticism from Erasmus to Spinoza.* 1979. Discusses skepticism as a cause as well as an effect of the Scientific Revolution.

Schiebinger, Londa. *The Mind Has No Sex? Women in the Origins of Modern Science.* 1989. Explores the role of women in all aspects of scientific endeavor.

Shapin, Steven. *The Scientific Revolution.* 1996. A study of the origins of the modern scientific worldview that emphasizes the social influences on the production of knowledge and the social purposes for which scientific knowledge was intended.

Shapin, Steven, and Simon Schaffer. *Leviathan and the Air Pump.* 1989. Discusses the difference between Robert Boyle and Thomas Hobbes regarding the value of experimentation.

Shea, William R., and Mariano Artigas. *Galileo in Rome: The Rise and Fall of a Troublesome Genius.* 2004. Attributes some of Galileo's troubles to his tactlessness and headstrong behavior.

Stewart, Matthew. *The Courtier and the Heretic: Leibniz, Spinoza, and the Fate of God in the Modern World.* 2006. Illuminates the conflicting philosophical ideas of Wilhelm Leibniz and Baruch Spinoza, arguing that Spinoza anticipated later philosophical and scientific developments by two and sometimes three centuries.

Thomas, Keith. *Man and the Natural World: A History of the Modern Sensibility.* 1983. A study of the shifting attitudes of human beings toward nature during the period from 1500 to 1800.

Webster, Charles. *The Great Instauration: Science, Medicine and Reform, 1626–1660.* 1975. Explores the relationship between Puritanism and the Scientific Revolution in England.

Westfall, Richard S. *Never at Rest: A Biography of Isaac Newton.* 1980. A superb biography of the most influential scientist in the history of the West.

NOTES

CHAPTER 1

1. Robert J. Wenke, *Patterns in Prehistory: Humankind's First Three Million Years* (1999), 404.
2. Ibid.
3. Marc van de Mieroop, *A History of the Ancient Near East, ca 3000–323 B.C.E.* (2007), 23.
4. Wenke, *Patterns in Prehistory,* 404.
5. Quoted in Stephen Bertman, *Handbook to Life in Ancient Mesopotamia* (2003), 65.
6. Ibid., 179.
7. Quoted in van de Mieroop, *A History of the Ancient Near East,* 113.
8. Ibid.
9. Quoted in Bertman, *Handbook to Life in Ancient Mesopotamia,* 172–173.
10. Jean Bottero, *Mesopotamia: Writing, Reasoning, and the Gods.* Translated by Zainab Bahrani and Mac Van De Mieroop (1992), 33, 127, 129.
11. *Code of Hammurabi,* trans. J. N. Postgate, 55–56. Cited in Postgate, *Early Mesopotamia: Society and Economy at the Dawn of History* (1992), 160.
12. Samuel Greengus, "Legal and Social Institutions of Ancient Near Mesopotamia," in *Civilizations of the Ancient Near East,* ed. Jack M. Sasson, vol. 1 (1995), 471.
13. Ibid., 474.
14. *A Dispute of a Man with His Ba,* probably composed ca. 2180–2040 B.C.E. Quoted in W. Stiebing, *Ancient Near Eastern History and Culture* (2008), 153.
15. *The Admonitions of Ipuwer,* quoted in Stiebing, *Ancient Near Eastern History and Culture,* 164.

CHAPTER 2

1. Quoted in Carlo Zaccagnini, "The Interdependence of the Great Powers," in *Amarna Diplomacy: The Beginnings of International Relations,* eds. Raymond Cohen and Raymond Westbrook (2000), 149.
2. Quoted in Michael Roaf, *Cultural Atlas of Mesopotamia and the Ancient Near East* (2004), 136.

3. Quoted in Trevor Bryce, *Life and Society in the Hittite World* (2002), 113.
4. Quoted in William H. Stiebing, Jr., *Ancient Near Eastern History and Culture* (2008), 229.
5. Quoted in Marc Van De Mieroop, *A History of the Ancient Near East ca. 3000–323 B.C.* (2007), 194.
6. Ibid., 195.
7. A. Kirk Grayson, in *Assyrian and Babylonian Chronicles* (1975).
8. Quoted in Stiebing, *Ancient Near Eastern History and Culture,* 281.
9. Micah 6: 6–8, Revised Standard Version.
10. Ezekiel 34: 15–20. Revised Standard Version.

CHAPTER 3

1. Demosthenes, *Orations,* 59.122.
2. From Euripides, *The Trojan Women.* Translated by Peter Levi, in John Boardman, Jasper Griffith, and Oswyn Murray, eds., *The Oxford History of the Classical World* (1986), 169.
3. Plato, *Phaedo,* 1.118.

CHAPTER 4

1. Athenaios, 253 D; cited and translated in J. J. Pollitt, *Art in the Hellenistic Age* (1986), 271.

CHAPTER 5

1. From *Selected Works* by Cicero, translated by Michael Grant (Penguin Classics 1960, second revised edition 1971). Copyright © Michael Grant 1960, 1965, 1971. Reproduced by permission of Penguin Books Ltd.

CHAPTER 7

1. John Helgeland, *Christians in the Military: The Early Experience* (1985), 64–65.

CHAPTER 8

1. Al-Tabari, *The History of Al-Tabari,* Vol. 17: *The First Civil War,* trans. and annotated by G. R. Hawting (1985), 50.
2. Quoted in Jane S. Gerber, *The Jews of Spain: A History of the Sephardic Experience* (1992), 28.

CHAPTER 9

1. Willibald, *The Life of Boniface,* in Clinton Albertson, trans., *Anglo-Saxon Saints and Heroes* (1967), 308–310.
2. Quoted in Edward Peters, *Europe and the Middle Ages* (1989), 159.

CHAPTER 10

1. Cited in Emmanuel Le Roy Ladurie, *Montaillou: Promised Land of Error.* Translated by Barbara Bray (1978), 130.
2. Ibid., 56.
3. Ibid., 63.

CHAPTER 11

1. Quoted in William Bowsky, "The Impact of the Black Death." In Anthony Molho (ed.), *Social and Economic Foundations of the Italian Renaissance* (1969), 92.
2. Cited in Philip Ziegler, *The Black Death* (1969), 20.
3. Giovanni Boccaccio, *The Decameron.* Translated by Richard Aldington (1962), 30.
4. Ibid.
5. Quoted in Mark C. Bartusis, *The Late Byzantine Army: Arms and Society, 1204–1453* (1992), 133.
6. Trial record as quoted in Marina Warner, *Joan of Arc* (1981), 122.
7. Ibid., 127.
8. Ibid., 143.
9. *The Trial of Joan of Arc.* Translated W. S. Scott (1956), 134.
10. Ibid., 106.
11. Ibid., 135.
12. Johan Huizinga, *The Autumn of the Middle Ages.* Translated Rodney J. Payton and Ulrich Mammitzsch (1996), 156.
13. Quoted in Barbara W. Tuchman, *A Distant Mirror: The Calamitous 14th Century* (1978), 505–506. Translation has been slightly modified by the authors.
14. Cited in Bartlett, *The Making of Europe,* 238.

CHAPTER 12

1. Baldesar Castiglione, *The Book of the Courtier.* Translated by Charles S. Singleton (1959), 43.
2. Giovanni Villani, *Cronica* vol. 7, (1823), 52. Translation by the authors.
3. Agostino di Colloredo, "Chroniche friulane, 1508–18," *Pagine friulane* 2 (1889), 6. Translation by the authors.

4. Francesco Petrarca, "Letter to the Shade of Cicero." In Kenneth R. Bartlett (ed.), *The Civilization of the Italian Renaissance: A Sourcebook* (1992), 31.
5. Quoted in Margaret L. King, *Women of the Renaissance* (1991), 197.
6. "Laura Cereta, "Bibulus Sempronius: Defense of the Liberal Instruction of Women." In Margaret King and Alfred Rabil (eds.), *Her Immaculate Hand: Selected Words by and About the Women Humanists of Quattrocento Italy* (1983), 82.

CHAPTER 13

1. Christopher Columbus, quoted in Felipe Fernández-Armesto, *Columbus* (1991), 6.
2. Ibid., 154.
3. *The Life of The Admiral Christopher Columbus by his Son Ferdinand.* Translated and Annotated by Benjamin Keen (1959), 222.
4. Sir Arthur Helps, *The Spanish Conquest in America,* vol. 1 (1900), 1, 264–267.
5. *The Book of Chilam Balam of Chumayel,* edited and translated Ralph L. Roy (1933), 83.
6. *The Conquistadores: First-Person Accounts of the Conquest of Mexico,* edited and translated Patricia de Fuentes (1963), 159.
7. Quoted in Margaret T. Hodgen, *Early Anthropology in the Sixteenth and Seventeenth Centuries* (1964), 9.
8. Quoted in Ibid., 207. Spelling has been modernized.
9. Quoted in Ibid., 369.
10. Quoted in Ibid., 373–374. Spelling and syntax have been modernized.

CHAPTER 14

1. Quoted in Gordon Rupp, *Luther's Progress to the Diet of Worms* (1964), 29.
2. Ibid., 33.
3. Quote from an anonymous caricature reproduced in A. G. Dickens, *Reformation and Society in Sixteenth-Century Europe* (1966), Figure 46, 61.
4. Quoted in Roland H. Bainton, *Here I Stand: A Life of Martin Luther,* (1950), 166, 181–185.
5. Translated and quoted in Thomas Head, "Marie Dentière: A Propagandist for the Reform." In Katharina M. Wilson (ed.), *Women Writers of the Renaissance and Reformation* (1987), 260.

6. Quoted in Peter Blickle, "The Popular Reformation." In *Handbook of European History 1400–1600: Late Middle Ages, Renaissance and Reformation*, Vol. 2: *Visions, Programs and Outcomes*, Thomas A. Brady, Jr., Heiko A. Oberman, and James D. Tracy (eds.), (1995), 171.
7. Quoted in Heiko A. Oberman, *Luther: Man Between God and the Devil*. Translated by Eileen Walliser-Schwarzbart (1989), 240.
8. Quoted in Dickens, *Reformation and Society*, 134

CHAPTER 15

1. Quoted in R. Po-Chia Hsia, *Social Discipline in the Reformation: Central Europe, 1550–1750* (1989), 147–148.
2. Quoted in Norbert Elias, *The Civilizing Process*, vol. 1: *The History of Manners*. Translated by Edmund Jephcott (1978), 119.
3. Quoted in R. J. Knecht, *The French Wars of Religion, 1559–1598*, 2nd ed. (1996), 13.
4. Michel de Montaigne, *Essays and Selected Writings*. Translated and edited by Donald M. Frame (1963), 219–221.

CHAPTER 16

1. Thomas Hobbes, *Leviathan*, C. B. Macpherson (ed.) (1968), 186.

2. Marshall Poe, "The Truth about Muscovy," *Kritika* 3 (2002), 483.
3. Quoted in Lindsey Hughes, *Russia in the Age of Peter the Great* (1998), 92.

CHAPTER 17

1. René Descartes, *Le Monde*, Book VI.
2. Thomas S. Kuhn, *The Structure of Scientific Revolutions* (1970).
3. René Descartes, *Discourse on the Method and Meditations on First Philosophy*, edited by David Weissmann (1996), 21.
4. Galileo, "Letter to the Grand Duchess Christina." In Stilman Drake (ed.), *Discoveries and Opinions of Galileo* (1957), 186.
5. Quoted in W. Hazard, *The European Mind, 1680–1715* (1964), 362.
6. François Poullain, *De l'égalite des deux sexes* (1673), 85.
7. Francis Bacon, *The Works of Francis Bacon*, vol. 3, J. Spedding (ed.) (1857–1874), 524–539.
8. Henry Oldenburg, "To the Reader." In Robert Boyle (ed.), *Experiments and Considerations in Touching Colours* (1664).

PHOTO CREDITS

INDEX